SOCIOLOGY IN ACTION
A CANADIAN PERSPECTIVE

SOCIOLOGY IN ACTION
A CANADIAN PERSPECTIVE

Diane G. Symbaluk, PhD
Sociology Department
Grant MacEwan University

Tami M. Bereska, PhD
Sociology Department
Grant MacEwan University

NELSON / EDUCATION

NELSON / EDUCATION

Sociology in Action: A Canadian Perspective
by Diane G. Symbaluk and Tami M. Bereska

Vice President, Editorial Higher Education:
Anne Williams

Acquisitions Editor:
Maya Castle

Marketing Manager:
Terry Fedorkiw

Developmental Editor:
Karina Hope

Photo Researcher:
Daniela Glass

Permissions Coordinator:
Daniela Glass

Content Production Manager:
Christine Gilbert

Production Service:
MPS Limited, a Macmillan Company

Copy Editor:
Karen Rolfe

Proofreader:
Jennifer McIntyre

Indexer:
David Luljak

Manufacturing Coordinator:
Ferial Suleman

Design Director:
Ken Phipps

Managing Designer:
Franca Amore

Interior Design:
Greg Devitt

Interior Box Images:
iStockphoto

Cover Design:
Greg Devitt

Cover Image:
Group of people: Andresr/ Shutterstock; Hand holding smartphone: Debbie Yea/ Nelson Education, Ltd.

Compositor:
MPS Limited, a Macmillan Company

Printer:
RR Donnelley

Library and Archives Canada Cataloguing in Publication Data

Symbaluk, Diane, 1967–
    Sociology in action: a Canadian perspective / Diane G. Symbaluk, Tami M. Bereska.

Includes bibliographical references and index.
ISBN 978-0-17-664881-7

    1. Sociology—Canada—Textbooks. 2. Sociology—Textbooks. I. Bereska, Tami M. (Tami Marie), 1968– II. Title.

HM586.S95 2012   301.0971
C2011-907928-3

PKG ISBN-13: 978-0-17-664881-7
PKG ISBN-10: 0-17-664881-X

*For those who have yet to discover sociology
and those who have already come to appreciate it.*

Brief Table of Contents

Detailed Table of Contents

PART 3

Our Changing World   259

List of Figures, Boxes, and Tables

LIST OF FIGURES

LIST OF BOXES

LIST OF TABLES

A Unique Learning System

Four distinctive, yet complementary ways of "doing sociology." Unique to this textbook, we introduce social issues as applied to four distinct perspectives: in theory, in practice, in my community, and in my life.

Sociology in Theory sections highlight theoretical and empirical research by formally trained academics.

SOCIOLOGY IN THEORY

LO³ FUNCTIONALIST FRAMEWORK

The different sociological frameworks, which you were introduced to in Chapter 1, can be used to help us better understand how the mass media influences us and how we, in turn, influence the mass media. Since the main concern of a macro-level functionalist

SOCIOLOGY IN PRACTICE

PARENTAL LEAVE BENEFITS

As women began entering the workforce en masse in the latter half of the 20th century, social policy had to change in order to accommodate the different day-to-day realities of Canadian families. In 1971, women who met eligibility requirements (in terms of the number of paid work hours they had in the past year) were able to claim up to 15 weeks of maternity leave through Unemployment Insurance (now known as Employment Insurance) upon the birth of a child. In recognition of the greater prevalence of shared parenting in families, as well as to further encourage such sharing, in 1990 the federal Parental Benefits Program included an additional 10 weeks of parental leave that could be utilized by either parent (or shared). In 2000, there were further changes to the Parental Benefits Program. Fifteen weeks of maternity leave are now followed by 35 weeks of parental leave that can be shared between parents (Marshall, 2008).

Sociology in Practice boxes consist of applications of sociological concepts for policy development.

Sociology in My Community boxes demonstrate how sociological principles can be transmitted to nonacademic audiences.

SOCIOLOGY IN MY COMMUNITY

HELPING NEW PARENTS

Although the transition to parenthood is associated with declines in relationship quality, people in the midst of this transition are amenable to prevention and intervention efforts intended to improve their intimate relationships. A review of research on couples in this stage of family development finds that those who have attended prenatal classes are less likely to experience significant declines in relationship quality (Mitnick, Heyman, & Smith Slep, 2009). Parenting programs can be found in communities across Canada. For example, the Etobicoke Brighter Futures Coalition offers an array of free programs for parents who are transitioning to parenthood—ranging from prenatal and postnatal nutrition classes to a Parent–Child Mother Goose program, to a Nobody's Perfect Parenting Education program.

SOCIOLOGY IN MY LIFE

HOW DO YOU VIEW POPULAR CULTURE?

Do you think we live in the materialistic culture depicted by proponents of the Frankfurt school and the propaganda model? As a consumer of popular culture, think about what led you to acquire the many things you possess that are indicative of popular culture. Do you believe you are working to acquire things that will render your life and that of future generations more comfortable or is your paycheque mainly supporting the interests of the dominant class? Would you consider posts on YouTube to be one of the ways that the masses might be viewed as resisting capitalist dominance? Why or why not?

Sociology in My Life boxes are applications of sociological knowledge to one's own personal life experiences.

A variety of other features are included to help students and instructors see the interconnections between individuals and society and the overall applicability of the discipline of sociology as a means for facilitating social change:

Learning Objectives and Outcomes are bulleted statements about the intended knowledge and/or skills students should be able to demonstrate following a thorough reading of the chapter. The Learning Objectives and Outcomes run throughout the body of the chapter to encourage critical, focused reading.

LEARNING OBJECTIVES AND OUTCOMES

After completing this chapter, students should be able to do the following:

LO¹ Compare varying definitions of family, and explain why the way family is defined is important.

LO² Identify the key trends that indicate changes in Canadian families.

LO³ Distinguish between the main assumptions of the family decline and family pluralism perspectives.

LO⁴ Describe what comprises sociological knowledge about families.

LO⁵ Describe how colonization affected Aboriginal families, both in the short and long term.

LO⁶ Explain how each of the following theories contributes to knowledge about families: social exchange, family life course development, functionalist, conflict, feminist, and interactionist.

SOCIOLOGY ON SCREEN

ACRES OF SKIN: MEDICAL ABUSE BEHIND BARS

The documentary *Acres of Skin: Medical Abuse behind Bars* (available from Films for the Humanities and Sciences) describes decades of medical experiments conducted by dermatologist Dr. Albert Kligman on inmates of Philadelphia's Holmesburg Prison, and draws comparisons to another well-known syphilis study that took place in Tuskegee, Alabama. This documentary provides firsthand insight into the implications of unethical research and underscores the importance of respecting the dignity and protecting the welfare of research participants.

Sociology on Screen discusses documentaries and/or fictional films that illustrate key concepts and processes.

Sociology in Music includes lyrics from songs that illustrate the importance of sociological concepts in everyday practices.

VIOLENCE IN RAP MUSIC

Violence is prevalent in the music industry as evident in the lyrics of songs that top the billboard charts. At the time of writing this chapter, Eminem's "Love the Way You Lie" featuring Rihanna was number one on the HOT 100 and it contains the confession "I laid hands on her." Much of Eminem's rap music contains references to violence between males and some songs include references to acts of violence committed by males toward their girlfriends. In the now-notorious suicide song "Stan" by Eminem and featuring Dido, we hear the line "Hey Slim, that's my girlfriend screamin in the trunk" shortly before Stan drives his car off a bridge. In a study by Burgess, Dill and Wright (2009) college students reported that the most common representations of women within rap songs they listened to were "ho" or "whore," "bitch," and "slut" and that rappers were most likely to rap about "sex," "drugs," "money," "women," and "violence."

SOCIOLOGY ONLINE

SEEING THE FAMILY DECLINE DEBATE IN ACTION

The Internet has become a valuable tool for organizations that participate in the debate over family decline. Those listed below are some of the best known, and are often referred to in the media, such as when offering their "expert" commentary on the evening news.

Family Decline Perspective

• **The Institute of Marriage and Family Canada** (www.imfcanada.org)
"The IMF exists to present credible, research based evidence—to governments, media, and all Canadians—that supports mom-and-dad marriage and family life."

• **Canada Family Action** (www.familyaction.org)
"For over ten years, CFAC has defended the family by: ... defending traditional marriage with 1.2 million brochures in five languages, 500,000 postcards, 5,000 lawn signs, billboards, and newspaper ads."

Family Pluralism Perspective

• **Council on Contemporary Families** (www.contemporaryfamilies.org)
"The Council on Contemporary Families was formed in response to the misleading representations of family research that have flooded the media in recent years and influenced the debate over such important issues as welfare reform. ... Our organization is particularly interested in ensuring that families that do not fit within conventional norms are included in the national conversation. We believe that the public will benefit from the actual diversity of ... family life."

Source: Adapted from The Institute of Marriage and Family Canada (www.imfcanada.org) and Canada Family Action Coalition (www.familyaction.org) and Council on Contemporary Families (www.contemporaryfamilies.org)

Sociology Online details various sources of information at particular websites that demonstrate key concepts and provide in-depth examples of topics discussed in the chapters.

Sociology in the News contains media coverage illustrating how sociological concepts and processes are presented in statements made to the public.

WEB APPS

Scott McKeen's opinion column is a funny illustration of the growing popularity of web apps. The author, a self-proclaimed "appaholic," notes that soon after he purchased his first iPhone and discovered web applications, he downloaded apps "like a madman." McKeen goes on to describe various apps he'd like to create including one called SIMCITY, SOCIAL LIFE that "converts the real world into streaming video … [and]

connects directly with nearby smartphones, converting speech to text …, concealing your voice and face so you can remain anonymous … [thereby allowing you to] be just as snotty as you are on web forums, without personal consequence." (McKeen, 2010).

Source: Scott McKeen (2010). An app for everything, and everything in an app. *Edmonton Journal*, August 23, p. A 5. © Postmedia Network.

SOCIOLOGY IN WORDS

THE VOICES OF RESIDENTIAL SCHOOL STUDENTS

- "I was literally thrown into St. Mary's Residential School at four years of age.…My very first memory of my entry into the school is a painful flashback. For whatever reason, I am thrown into a kneeling position. My head is bashed against a wooden cupboard by the boys' supervisor" (Kelly, 2008, p. 14).

- "A nun shaved my head and stripped me bare in front of all the other boys, followed by months of repeated beatings, whippings, sexual abuse and solitary confinement in a dark, locked closet. Why? Because I was bad and deserved it. That's what they said" (Kakfwi, 2008, para. 4).

- "I was hungry from the day I went into the school until they took me to the hospital two and a half years later. Not just me. Every Indian pupil smelled of hunger" (cited in Barman, 2003, p. 222).

- "…the constant message [was] that because you are Native, you are part of a weak and defective race, unworthy of a distinguished place in society.… That to me is not training for success, it is training for self-destruction" (cited in Barman, 2003, p. 229).

Sociology in Words includes either the testimony of people who experience sociological concepts first-hand or in-depth explanations by theorists who study sociological issues.

Sociology in Deeds highlights actions of others that demonstrate sociological principles.

INSIGHT INTO PARTICIPANT OBSERVATION

Daniel R. Wolfe (1991), a researcher who joined the Rebels (a motorcycle gang) in order to study them, best explains participant observation like this:

At the time of beginning my fieldwork I had been riding British-made motorcycles for three years and talked briefly to members of the King's Crew MC in Calgary. But this was not enough to comprehend the outlaw biker

community or to study it. My impression of outlaw bikers was narrow and incomplete, and, in that sense, almost as misleading as the stereotype held by most "citizens." I was physically close to the scene but far removed from a balanced understanding; that understanding would only come from "being there" (p.10).

CHAPTER SUMMARY

LO1 **Compare varying definitions of family, and explain why the way family is defined is important.**

Varying definitions of family include structural, functional, and emotional definitions. Structural definitions emphasize the statuses that make up families, while functional definitions focus on the everyday "doing" of family life, and emotional definitions draw attention to love and affection. The definition used has implications at the macro level and the micro level.

LO2 **Identify the key trends that indicate changes in Canadian families.**

Over the past half century, marriage rates have declined, cohabitation has increased, divorce has increased, same-sex relationships have increased, and people may have had fewer children.

LO3 **Distinguish between the main assumptions of the family decline and family pluralism perspectives.**

The family decline perspective claims that recent changes in families are indicative of the institution of the family being "in crisis." In contrast, the family pluralism perspective suggests that changes in families are indicative of fewer constraints and greater freedom than in the past.

LO4 **Describe what comprises sociological knowledge about families.**

Sociological knowledge about families consists of historical, empirical, and theoretical knowledge.

LO5 **Describe how colonization affected Aboriginal families, both in the short and long term.**

Colonization brought with it the reserve system, changes in legislation that made all Aboriginal

people wards of the federal government, and residential schooling, all of which irrevocably changed the way Aboriginal families carried out their daily lives. Several generations of Aboriginal children grew up in residential schools rather than in family environments, and experienced abuse, neglect, and ethnocide. Psychological and social implications continue to the present day.

LO6 **Explain how each of the following theories contributes to knowledge about families: social exchange, family life course development, functionalist, conflict, feminist, and interactionist.**

Social exchange theory claims that all relationships are based on an exchange of resources, and are associated with costs and benefits. Family life course development theory suggests that families progress through a series of qualitatively different stages that are associated with changes in family structures, roles, and interactions. Functionalist theories explore how families are best able to fulfill their functions, such as effective child socialization. Conflict theories state that even within families, there is competition over scarce resources that can be associated with power differentials and family violence. Feminist theories are of a wide range, but the interrelationship between families and gender is central to all of them. Interactionist theories draw attention to the fact that families shape our understandings of the world and ourselves, and that our understandings of the world come into play within our everyday lives as family members.

Chapter Summaries are succinct examples of the kinds of responses students are expected to provide in relation to the learning objectives and outcomes.

Time to Review questions at the end of each major section highlight key points and provide students with a built-in test of their mastery of the material before they proceed to the next section.

Norms: Society's expectations for how we are supposed to act, think, and look.

Normative: Behaviours, appearances, and thoughts that correspond to society's norms.

Margin Definitions provide definitions conveniently located in the text margin beside the section where the term is first introduced. Students can practice their understanding by accessing the interactive flashcards online.

Opening quotations begin each chapter; they are well-known quotes that spark the reader's interest and set the tone for the chapter by highlighting a central concept, issue, or paradox that is pertinent to the topic covered in that chapter.

Other things may change, but we start and end with families.

(Anthony Brandt)[1]

Recommended Readings provide references for additional resources on specified aspects of the issues pertinent to a given chapter.

RECOMMENDED READINGS

1. For a broad introduction to the sociology of families, see: Ward, M., & Belanger, M. (2011). *The Family Dynamic: A Canadian Perspective*. Toronto, ON: Nelson.
2. For more detail on the demographic characteristics of Canadian families revealed by the 2006 Census, refer to: Milan, A., Vézina, M., & Wells, C. (2007). *Family Portrait: Continuity and Change in Canadian*

Families and Households in 2006, 2006 Census. Statistics Canada Catalogue No. 97-553-XIE.
3. To learn more about residential schooling, refer to: Chansonneuve, D. (2005). *Reclaiming Connections: Understanding Residential School Trauma Among Aboriginal People*. Ottawa, ON: Aboriginal Healing Foundation.

For Further Reflection questions present opportunities to examine chapter content in more detail and to demonstrate a personal understanding of the key concepts and processes discussed in the chapter.

FOR FURTHER REFLECTION

1. Where would you situate yourself in the family decline debate?
2. Consider an issue that you consider to be central in your own family. Which of the theories addressed in this chapter do you think could best address that issue? Which of the theories do you think would be the least useful in exploring that issue?

Glossary

A Glossary of all key terms is included at the end of the text.

A

Abolitionism: A movement calling for the dismantling of the criminal justice system. p. 223

Achieved status: A social position obtained through personal effort. p. 108

Acid rain: The dilute sulphuric and nitric acids created when fossil fuels are burned. p. 291

for rule breaking, and unidirectional communication. p. 173

Authoritarian personality: A personality type that values authority and obedience, is low in tolerance, and high in insecurity. p. 182

Auxiliary traits: Characteristics that are presumed to accompany a specific master status. p. 141

Preface

INTRODUCTION

Sociology is about the real world. It is the discipline that can be thought of as the most comprehensive social science (Delanty, 2005*; 2007**), providing a systematic means for understanding the interconnectedness among people, among institutions, and between individuals and the larger society in which they live. A major objective of our textbook is to help you appreciate the importance of developing your sociological imagination (Mills, 1959/2000)†, so you can see how you influence and are influenced by society. In addition, we endeavour to help you hone your critical thinking skills and view issues from different perspectives; we want you to question and evaluate your own position and the position of others on the topics presented in this book and the issues that you encounter every day. By teaching you how sociology is related to every aspect of your daily life, we hope to inspire you to promote social change in your personal life, in your community, in society more generally, and in the world at large.

OVERALL GOAL OF THIS BOOK: HELPING STUDENTS ACQUIRE THE FUNDAMENTALS OF SOCIOLOGY

Persell, Pfeiffer, and Syed (2007)‡ surveyed 44 preeminent leaders in sociology (e.g., ASA presidents, regional presidents, and national grant recipients in sociology), asking them what students need to know by the time they finish a course in introductory sociology. The following nine themes emerged as overall directives for what students should learn about in an introductory sociology course:

1. The "social" part of sociology, or learning to think sociologically
2. The scientific nature of sociology
3. Complex and critical thinking
4. The centrality of inequality
5. A sense of sociology as a field
6. The social construction of ideas
7. The difference between sociology and other social sciences
8. The importance of trying to improve the world
9. The important social institutions in society

Our goal as authors of this textbook was to write an introductory sociology book that creates a foundation upon which those objectives can be met by those teaching introductory sociology, whether in classrooms, online, or in other types of distance learning environments. The feedback of our reviewers was invaluable in enabling us to create this foundation.

ORGANIZATION

Part 1: Thinking Sociologically provides students with a framework for how to think critically about social life. Beginning in Chapter 1, you will start to see the fundamental connection between individual choices and larger social forces, a connection that lies at the heart of the sociological imagination. The sociological imagination is central to understanding the range of topics presented in this textbook, including the mass media, families, culture, social inequality, gender, ethnicity, health and illness, and more. Chapter 1 also describes the role of theory and the role of critical thinking in "doing" sociology. The social scientific research methods discussed in Chapter 2 help us move beyond common-sense ideas to appreciate the scientific nature of sociology as a discipline that provides answers to important questions. In the 21st century, the mass media serves as a central source of information, and have also come to play a central role in connecting members of society to one another. Consequently, a discussion of the mass media, including a critical look at the ways in which the media shape our perceptions, comprises Chapter 3 and concludes the foundations section of this textbook.

---

*Delanty, G. (2005). *Social Science: Philosophical and Methodological Foundations* (2nd ed.). Buckingham, UK: Open University Press.

**Delanty, G. (2007). Sociology. In G. Ritzer (Ed.) *Blackwell Encyclopedia of Sociology*. Blackwell Publishing. Retrieved March 1, 2011, from www.blackwellreference.com.

†Mills, C. W. (1959/2000). The promise. In C. W. Mills *The Sociological Imagination* (40th anniversary ed.), pp. 3–24. New York: Oxford University Press.

‡Persell, C. H., Pfeiffer, K. M. & Syed, A. (2007). What should students understand after taking Introduction to Sociology? *Teaching Sociology, 35* (4), pp. 300–314.

Part 2: Interconnections between Individuals and Society includes eight chapters that focus on the primary components of students' individual and social identities. Chapter 4 helps us appreciate the influence, diversity, and changing nature of Canadian families. Chapter 5 outlines the basic components of culture and social structure. Chapter 6 discusses social inequality as a challenge for many families and as a stable feature of Canadian society. Chapters 7 and 8 consider the implications of gender and ethnicity for who we are, who others say we are, and for larger consequences including socioeconomic status, discrimination, and family life. Chapter 9 focuses on the various ways we come to know what is "true"—through religion, science, and the modern education system—and the ways in which all three are socially constructed. Chapter 10 explores the social construction of deviance and crime, critically examines the criminal justice system, and offers a range of explanations provided by deviance specialists and criminologists. Chapter 11 describes patterns of health and illness with an emphasis on both personal and social determinants of health, as well as the prevention and treatment of illness within the broader context of health-care systems.

Part 3: Our Changing World, identifies the importance of collective action, social movements, and globalization for effecting widespread change. Chapter 12 discusses social change as brought about by various forms of collective behaviour and social movements. Chapter 13 focuses on environmental sociology as part of a global call to action on ecological issues. Chapter 14 describes historical precursors to globalization; outlines technological, economic, political, cultural, and social characteristics of globalization; and assesses the relative merits and drawbacks of globalization.

SPECIAL FEATURES

- *Opening quotes.* Each chapter begins with a well-known quotation that sparks the reader's interest and sets the tone for the chapter by highlighting a central concept, issue, or paradox that is pertinent to the topic covered in that chapter.
- *Four distinctive, yet complementary ways of "doing sociology."* Unique to this textbook, we introduce social issues as applied to four distinct perspectives: in theory, in practice, in my community, and in my life. This approach is especially effective for helping students understand how sociology relates to their everyday lives and how academic sociology (i.e., based in theoretical and empirical research) applies to real life. For example, students can more readily evaluate theoretical assumptions when they can see how they translate into actual policy recommendations on particular issues, or how they are communicated to the public in various forms. Students are especially able to understand the contributions of a sociological perspective when issues are discussed using personal examples they can consider within the context of their own lives.

  - **Sociology in Theory** sections include highlighted theoretical and empirical research by formally trained academics.

  - **Sociology in Practice** boxes consist of applications of sociological concepts for policy development.

  - **Sociology in My Community** boxes demonstrate how sociological principles can be transmitted to nonacademic audiences.

  - **Sociology in My Life** boxes are applications of sociological knowledge to one's own personal life experiences.

- *An emphasis on critical thinking.* Throughout the text, critical thinking is emphasized as each topic is presented and discussed. For example, rather than ask whether the media are biased, we show students the relevance of mass media ownership and control for agenda setting, describe various ways in which the media shape our perceptions, teach students about media literacy, and then ask students to consider if they perceive themselves to be media literate.
- *The impetus for social change.* All introductory sociology textbooks mention C. Wright Mills' concept of the *sociological imagination.* However, they tend to treat the sociological imagination as an end in itself, rather than as a means to an end; when Mills spoke of the sociological imagination, he emphasized

its centrality in creating informed and active citizens. By focusing on the sociological imagination and social action, this textbook provides the impetus for students to become more socially aware and more active as citizens in their communities, in society, and in the world. Whether they become parents, teachers, community-league soccer coaches, entrepreneurs, or social activists trying to create meaningful social change, students will see the value in utilizing their own sociological imaginations.

- *The prevalence of social inequality.* From the stratification of Canadian society into distinct social classes where those who earn more control a disproportionate amount of wealth, to the differential treatment of men and women based on socially constructed gender differences, this book teaches students about the centrality of social inequality. Throughout various chapters, we emphasize how social inequality is built into Canadian society and how various processes and structures lead to its reproduction in subsequent generations.

- *The socially constructed nature of society.* Whether we are debating how to define the family, how to describe deviance, how to measure poverty, what should be considered healthy, or the relevance of gender in our society, this book highlights ways in which key sociological concepts we tend to take for granted are actually social constructions contingent upon specific historical contexts and the needs or interests of particular groups.

- *Ways to engage students and instructors.* Students need to see the relevance of sociology in their everyday lives as well as how this translates into related careers. Similarly, instructors need to find ways to embed sociological concepts in students' interests and course curriculum paths. We include particular pedagogical features to help bring sociology alive and then we translate social issues from theory to practice, and finally into the public and personal domains. A variety of boxes are included to help students and instructors see the interconnections between individuals and society and the overall applicability of the discipline

of sociology as a means for facilitating social change:

- **Sociology on Screen** discusses documentaries and/or fictional films that illustrate key concepts and processes.
- **Sociology in Music** includes lyrics from songs that illustrate the importance of sociological concepts in everyday practices.
- **Sociology Online** pertains to various sources of information at particular websites that demonstrate key concepts and provide in-depth examples of topics discussed in the chapters.
- **Sociology in the News** contains media coverage illustrating how sociological concepts and processes are presented in statements made to the public.
- **Sociology in Words** includes either the testimony of people who experience sociological concepts first-hand or in-depth explanations by theorists who study sociological issues.
- **Sociology in Deeds** highlights actions of others that demonstrate sociological principles.

- *Built-in skill development tools for students.* In each chapter we begin with a set of **learning objectives and outcomes** and end with a **chapter summary** that refers back to those objectives and outcomes. Throughout the chapter, indicators draw students' attention to which learning objective is being addressed in any given section. In addition, we include **Time to Review** questions throughout each chapter so students can see if they understand the main points before moving on to a new section. We also end each chapter with a set of **recommended readings** and **critical reflection** questions.

- **Learning objectives and outcomes** are statements about the intended knowledge and/or skills students should be able to demonstrate following a thorough reading of the chapter.
- **Chapter summaries** are succinct examples of the kinds of responses students

are expected to provide in relation to the learning objectives and outcomes.

– **Time to review** questions at the end of each major section highlight key points and provide students with a built-in test of their mastery of the material before they proceed to the next section.

– **Recommended readings** provide references for additional resources on specified aspects of the issues pertinent to a given chapter.

– **Critical reflection questions** present opportunities to examine chapter content in more detail and to demonstrate a personal understanding of the key concepts and processes discussed in the chapter.

CHAPTER HIGHLIGHTS

Listed below is a sample of the topics and issues covered in specific chapters along with an evaluative comment provided by instructors who reviewed an earlier draft of this manuscript.

Chapter 1 Looking and Acting through the Lens of Sociology

- What can I do with a degree in sociology?
- Comparing sociology and other disciplines
- Using the sociological imagination
- The beginner's guide to critical thinking

OUR REVIEWERS WRITE . . .

The role of a first chapter is not only to provide an introduction to the discipline of sociology but, more importantly in my opinion, to provide an attractive picture of what sociology is and to show why having a sociological perspective is beneficial. This text's chapter one is one of the best that I have seen for accomplishing that goal. Not only are the foundational theories of sociology presented in a language that is student centred, but I also appreciate how the currency of the material and the examples and references "wake up" subject matter that is usually very dry and difficult for students new to sociology.

Chapter 2 Sociological Research Methods

- Goals of sociological research
- Steps for conducting sociological research
- Ethical conduct for research involving humans
- Distinguishing between qualitative and quantitative methods

OUR REVIEWERS WRITE . . .

Chapter 2 does a stellar job on tackling the issue of the scientific nature of sociology: the complexities in scientific research and the value of knowing what a good question is and what needs to be asked; and, how sociology differs from other social sciences.

This chapter is obviously dedicated to showcasing sociology as a science. It also details the sociological research process very well and provides students with an excellent discussion of research methods employed by sociologists.

Chapter 3 Mass Media: Living in the Electronic Age

- YouTube: A media disruptor or force to be reckoned with?
- Agenda setting: The media is not neutral
- Violence is the norm in the mass media
- Media literacy: Thinking critically about the media

OUR REVIEWERS WRITE . . .

Where this chapter leads in excellence is in three main sections:

- *The social part of learning to think sociologically*
- *Complex and critical thinking*
- *The importance of social action.*

Chapter 4 Our Families

- Changing families
- Seeing the family decline debate in action
- The voices of residential school students

OUR REVIEWERS WRITE . . .

Where this chapter is exceptional is in the presentation of the interconnection of the micro and macro contexts (through the review of the history of colonization and impacts on First Nations people). The chapter is also strong in its encouragement of critical thinking, its overview of origins and effects of inequality, and the emphasis on the importance of social action. Certainly the importance and interconnection of social institutions were central in the chapter.

Chapter 5 Culture and Social Structure

- Language as a precursor to shared understandings
- Norms as regulators of shared behaviours
- Values as shared ideas
- The basic components of social structure.

OUR REVIEWERS WRITE . . .

I think the strength of the chapter lies in its encouragement of critical thinking.

Chapter 6 Social Inequality in Canadian Society

- Sociology Online: The growing gap project
- Sociology in My Life: Are you above LICO?
- Sociology in My Community: Make Poverty History Campaign
- Sociology on Screen: *Poor No More*

OUR REVIEWERS WRITE . . .

The highlighting of [Sociology Online, Sociology in Words, and Sociology on Screen boxes] as a way to remind students of the applicability of the contents in different settings is what makes this manuscript essentially profound. I think it is going to be a trailblazer in the way textbooks of this kind will be written going forward.

Chapter 7 Who We Are and Who Others Say We Are: Gender and Sexuality

- Identifying ourselves and identifying others
- Elite discourses
- Gender: The consequences of having been born female or male

OUR REVIEWERS WRITE . . .

This chapter was effective in explaining how gender influences our experiences in the social world (i.e., education, occupation, and family). It was also effective in illustrating how gender is socially constructed and an elite discourse.

Chapter 8 Race and Ethnicity

- Ethnicity, race, and visible minorities
- Contemporary ethnic patterns
- Consequences of ethnic identification
- Prejudice and discrimination

OUR REVIEWERS WRITE . . .

. . . The example discussed at the beginning of the chapter was effective in demonstrating the complexity of ethnicity and illustrating how race and ethnicity intersect with one another. The discussion of economic experiences of Aboriginals and immigrants identified the inequalities that exist among different groups, provided evidence of these inequalities and offered a number of possible explanations. The chapter well illustrated how race and ethnicity are socially constructed (i.e., by indicating that there is minimal genetic difference among different racial groups and that racial categories are social products) and how these social constructions have very "real" consequences for individuals and groups.

Chapter 9 Learning What is "True": Religion, Science, and Education

- Implications of religions
- The transition to scientific truth
- Scientific knowledge as constructed
- The role of education in modern society

OUR REVIEWERS WRITE . . .

The organization of the chapter allows the diversity and depth of the exploration of the topic to flow naturally. By beginning with questions and considerations of the meaning and origin of truth, and then following with an explanation of how truth and beliefs are explained in religion and then in science and then compared, makes logical sense. The topic, by moving to the social institution of education completes the coverage by bringing the student readers from self, to socially accepted ideas, and finally to how the ideas impact on diverse sectors of society . . .

Chapter 10 The World of Deviance and Crime

- Are you deviant?
- Crime classification and statistics
- Harper's "get tough on crime" approach
- Theorizing about the social construction of deviance

OUR REVIEWERS WRITE . . .

The chapter immediately captures interest and leads students into a sociological perspective by first having students think about experiences of social control, and then by leading the students through examples that describe how justice and deviance are socially constructed. This approach, rather than the conventional one of presenting a concept, defining it and then illustrating it, is very successful.

Chapter 11 Health and Illness

- Patterns of health and illness
- Personal determinants of health
- Social determinants of health
- Health-care systems

OUR REVIEWERS WRITE . . .

I think that this chapter achieves the right balance of theory and application. I noticed that the explanation of Foucault theories and post modernism is one of the best for its clarity.

Chapter 12 Social Change: Collective Behaviour and Social Movements

- Sociology in My Life: Debunking urban legends
- Sociology in Practice: Chiropractic delisting
- Sociology in My Community: G20 Summit protests

OUR REVIEWERS WRITE . . .

. . . When a student sees how an issue applies to him/her personally . . ., and then a connection of that issue to policy and public perspectives is made, this is considered an understanding of the sociological imagination. This chapter provides . . . [a foundation] for this kind of thinking and understanding to occur.

Chapter 13 "Going Green": Environmental Sociology

- Social factors posing environmental challenges
- Growing awareness of environmental issues
- Strategies for better environmental choices

OUR REVIEWERS WRITE . . .

In short, I would characterize this chapter as leading edge. For example, the assessment of consumption versus sustainability is current in the study of the environment. The introduction of the concept of disposable societies, the examples and meaning of greenwashing and of current environmental logos are all elements that contribute to the currency of the chapter.

Chapter 14 Globalization

- The International Monetary Fund, World Bank, and World Trade Organization
- The vision of globalization and its reality: the good, the bad, and the ugly
- Global justice movements

OUR REVIEWERS WRITE . . .

This chapter exemplifies our roles as sociologists; the capacity of our discipline to link the micro to the macro . . .

ANCILLARIES

Our textbook has several supplements for instructors and students.

About NETA

The **Nelson Education Teaching Advantage (NETA)** program delivers research-based instructor resources that promote student engagement and higher-order thinking to enable the success of Canadian students and educators.

Instructors today face many challenges. Resources are limited, time is scarce, and a new kind of student has emerged: one who is juggling school with work, has gaps in his or her basic knowledge, and is immersed in technology in a way that has led to a completely new style of learning. In response, Nelson Education has gathered a group of dedicated instructors to advise us on the creation of richer and more flexible ancillaries that respond to the needs of today's teaching environments.

The members of our editorial advisory board have experience across a variety of disciplines and are recognized for their commitment to teaching. They include:

Norman Althouse, Haskayne School of Business, University of Calgary

Brenda Chant-Smith, Department of Psychology, Trent University

Scott Follows, Manning School of Business Administration, Acadia University

Jon Houseman, Department of Biology, University of Ottawa

Glen Loppnow, Department of Chemistry, University of Alberta

Tanya Noel, Department of Biology, York University

Gary Poole, Director, Centre for Teaching and Academic Growth and School of Population and Public Health, University of British Columbia

Dan Pratt, Department of Educational Studies, University of British Columbia

Mercedes Rowinsky-Geurts, Department of Languages and Literatures, Wilfrid Laurier University

David DiBattista, Department of Psychology, Brock University

Dr. Roger Fisher, PhD.

In consultation with the editorial advisory board, Nelson Education has completely rethought the structure, approaches, and formats of our key textbook ancillaries. We've also increased our investment in editorial support for our ancillary authors. The result is the Nelson Education Teaching Advantage and its key components: *NETA Engagement, NETA Assessment,* and *NETA Presentation.* Each component includes one or more ancillaries prepared according to our best practices, and a document explaining the theory behind the practices.

NETA Engagement presents materials that help instructors deliver engaging content and activities to their classes. Instead of instructor's manuals that regurgitate chapter outlines and key terms from the text, NETA Enriched Instructor's Manuals (EIMs) provide genuine assistance to teachers. The EIMs answer questions such as *What should students learn?, Why should students care?,* and *What are some common student misconceptions and stumbling blocks?* EIMs not only identify the topics that cause students the most difficulty, but also describe techniques and resources to help students master these concepts.

Dr. Roger Fisher's *Instructor's Guide to Classroom Engagement* (IGCE) accompanies every Enriched Instructor's Manual.

NETA Assessment relates to testing materials—not only Nelson's test banks and computerized test banks, but also in-text self-tests, study guides and web quizzes, and homework programs such as CourseMate. Under *NETA Assessment*, Nelson's authors create multiple-choice questions that reflect research-based best practices for constructing effective questions and testing not only recall but also higher-order thinking. Our guidelines were developed by David DiBattista, a 3M National Teaching Fellow whose recent research as a professor of psychology at Brock University has focused on multiple-choice testing. All test bank authors receive training at workshops conducted by Professor DiBattista, as do the copyeditors assigned to each test bank. A copy of *Multiple Choice Tests: Getting Beyond Remembering*, Professor DiBattista's guide to writing effective tests, is included with every Nelson Test Bank/Computerized Test Bank package.

NETA Presentation has been developed to help instructors make the best use of PowerPoint® in their classrooms. With a clean and uncluttered design developed by Maureen Stone of StoneSoup Consulting, NETA Presentation features slides with improved readability, more multimedia and graphic materials, activities to use in class, and tips for instructors. A copy of *NETA Guidelines for Classroom Presentations* by Maureen Stone is included with each set of PowerPoint® slides.

INSTRUCTOR ANCILLARIES

Key instructor ancillaries are provided on the *Instructor's Resource CD* (ISBN 0-17-662890-8), giving instructors the ultimate tool for customizing lectures and presentations. The IRCD includes:

NETA Engagement. The Enriched Instructor's Manual was written by Alissa Overend, Grant MacEwan University. The Enriched Instructor's Manual provides strategies for engaging students actively and deeply in the study of sociology. Each chapter includes ideas for lesson plans and in-class activities. Further, the manual culminates with a list of video clips, websites, and articles that can serve as lecture launchers. Our intention is to provide instructors with ideas they may select to include in their teaching toolkit, as it were.

The Enriched Instructor's Manual is organized according to the textbook chapters and includes:

- Introduction
- Learning Outcomes
- Why is this chapter important to sociologists?
- Why should students care?
- What are the common student misconceptions and stumbling blocks?
- What can I do in class?
- How will I know my students achieved the learning outcomes?
- How can I assess my own performance?

Instructors commonly suggest that they want their students to develop critical thinking skills. However, it can be challenging to develop exercises and methods of assessment that address higher levels of learning. The Taxonomy of Educational Objectives (commonly called "Bloom's Taxonomy") proposed by educational psychologist Benjamin Bloom decades ago, is a classification of the different learning objectives that educators set for students. Bloom's Taxonomy divides educational objectives into Affective, Psychomotor, and Cognitive domains, with the latter as the focus for most higher-education classes. The taxonomy is hierarchical (i.e., learning at the higher levels is generally considered to require prerequisite knowledge and skills at lower levels). Considering these levels can be helpful to an instructor when planning classes, tutorials, assignments, and tests.

NETA Assessment. The Test Bank was written by Katherine Brasch, University of Toronto. It includes over 950 multiple-choice questions written according to NETA guidelines for effective construction and development of higher-order questions. Also included are 280 true/false questions, 70 short-answer questions, and 70 essay questions. Test bank files are provided in Word format for easy editing and in PDF format for convenient printing, no matter what system is used.

The Computerized Test Bank by ExamView® includes all the questions from the test bank.

The easy-to-use ExamView® software is compatible with Microsoft® Windows and Mac. Instructors can create tests by selecting questions from the question bank, modifying these questions as desired, and adding new questions they write themselves. Instructors can administer quizzes online and export tests to WebCT®, Blackboard®, and other formats.

NETA Presentation. Microsoft® PowerPoint® lecture slides for every chapter have been created by textbook author Tami Bereska. There is an average of 25 slides per chapter, many featuring key concepts, figures, and tables from *Sociology in Action: A Canadian Perspective*. NETA principles of clear design and engaging content have been incorporated throughout.

Image Library. This resource consists of digital copies of figures, short tables, and photographs used in the book. Instructors may use these jpegs to create their own PowerPoint® presentations.

DayOne. Day One—Prof InClass is a PowerPoint® presentation that instructors can customize to orient their students to the class and their text at the beginning of the course.

CourseMate ⁊ CourseMate
www.nelsonbrain.com

Engaging. Trackable. Affordable. Nelson Education's *Sociology in Action* CourseMate brings course concepts to life with interactive learning and exam preparation tools that integrate with the printed textbook. Students activate their knowledge through quizzes, games, and flashcards, among many other tools.

CourseMate provides immediate feedback that enables students to connect results to the work they have just produced, improving their retention. It encourages contact between students and faculty: Instructors can select to monitor their students' level of engagement with CourseMate, correlating their efforts to their outcomes. Instructors can even use CourseMate's quizzes to practise "Just in Time" teaching by tracking results in the Engagement Tracker and customizing lesson plans to address students' learning needs.

Engagement Tracker. How do instructors assess their students' engagement in the course? How do instructors know their students have read the material or viewed the resources assigned?

Good practice encourages frequent contacts between students and faculty: with CourseMate, instructors can use the included Engagement Tracker to assess student preparation and engagement.

Instructors can use the tracking tools to see progress for the class as a whole or for individual students. This helps instructors identify students at risk early in the course, uncover which concepts are most difficult for the class, monitor time on task, and keep students engaged.

Interactive Teaching and Learning Tools. CourseMate includes interactive teaching and learning tools:

- Quizzes
- Flashcards
- Videos
- Crossword puzzles
- and more.

The variety of tools in CourseMate respect diverse ways of learning and give students ample opportunity to actively engage with the course concepts. Students receive prompt feedback, which helps them to focus their learning efforts on the concepts they have yet to master. Time plus energy equals learning, and CourseMate offers an engaging way for students to increase their time on task.

Interactive eBook. In addition to interactive teaching and learning tools, CourseMate includes an interactive eBook. Instructors can use it as a supplement to the printed text, or as a substitute. Students can take notes, highlight, search, and interact with embedded media specific to their book.

ACKNOWLEDGMENTS

We express our gratitude to the following reviewers who offered candid opinions and suggestions on our early manuscript that helped shape this first edition of *Sociology in Action*:

Angela Conti-Becker, University of Western Ontario

Elizabeth Bishop, Confederation College

Cynthia Booth, Cambrian College

Alan D. Brown, Concordia University

Bede Eke, NorQuest College

Lidia Dorosz, St. Lawrence College

Laurie Milne, Medicine Hat College

Carmen Niessen, Sault College

Alissa Overend, Grant MacEwan University

Síân Reid, Carleton University

Francine Tremblay, Concordia University

Robert Wood, University of Lethbridge

Publishing a textbook is a team effort and we also wish to acknowledge the support, feedback, and assistance provided by everyone we worked with at Nelson Education Ltd.: Maya Castle, Acquisitions Editor; Laura Macleod, Executive Editor; Terry Fedorkiw, Marketing Manager; Christine Gilbert, Content Production Manager; Daniela Glass, Photo and Permissions Researcher; and Karen Rolfe, freelance copyeditor. We would especially like to acknowledge our Developmental Editor, Karina Hope, who had the challenging assignment of keeping two academics on task and within the word limit. It brings to mind the movie *Wonder Boys*, starring Michael Douglas, in which Professor Tripp's manuscript is at 1,000 pages, and the book is still not finished—clearly, he needed a good developmental editor!

A question that is often asked at interviews for academic positions is about the interconnections between research and teaching. It seems that all candidates easily refer to how their research influences their teaching by providing a body of knowledge that they can bring to the classroom. Less common are responses that emphasize how teaching influences their research—how much they, as academics, are able to learn from their students. We have learned more from our students than can be easily expressed. Our students, past and present, are the most important part of the team that has created this book. Our students have inspired us, given us profound ideas at times when our own ideas were in short supply, and shown us how students today *really* learn. The students at Grant MacEwan University, in particular, have shown us the amazing things that can happen when people use their sociological imaginations in their own lives, in their communities, and in the world. Above all, this book is for the students.

About the Authors

DIANE G. SYMBALUK

Probably not unlike the experience of many students, I found sociology quite by accident. While trying to find a course that would fulfill a Canadian content requirement for a Bachelor of Education degree en route to a teaching career, I stumbled across an introduction to sociology course advertised with descriptive words like "people," "society," "families," and "deviance" that appeared interesting. I could never have known then that my tendency to say "don't assume" and "don't take people for granted" underscored the beginnings of the development of my sociological imagination. After completing an introduction to sociology, not only was my interest piqued, but my future career path was set as I switched into the sociology program wherein I earned a Bachelor of Arts degree with honours followed by my Master of Arts and Doctorate degrees. I went on to teach sociology full-time at Grant MacEwan University, where I continue to teach a range of courses including introductory sociology, social psychology, criminology, and social research methods. I love teaching and I appreciate my students even more, which inspires me to write resources that contribute to their success, including numerous study guides, manuals, web-based course tools, and especially this textbook. I am also interested in student ratings of instruction and student assessments of instructor character strengths—the focus of my current research interests. I strive to continuously reevaluate my initial assumptions of people and social situations while maintaining allegiance to the Chinese proverb: He who says it cannot be done should not interrupt the person who is doing it (original author unknown).

TAMI M. BERESKA

I began university as a Psychology major. I had never even heard of sociology. But then I made my discovery. A discipline in which you could study families, teenagers, television shows, popular music, crime, and white supremacists—wow! Who could have ever believed that learning could be so interesting? Sociology grabbed me and has never let me go. Going on to obtain my Master of Arts and my Doctorate in sociology, I've since studied all sorts of interesting topics—adult and adolescent series romance novels (e.g., *Harlequin*, *Sweet Valley High*), what being a "real man" means in young adult novels for boys, and the medicalization of women's lives in magazine advertising. Popular culture, deviance, and youth fascinate me. Along with my love of sociology is a love for teaching undergraduate students. I had my first opportunity to give a university lecture as a teaching assistant while working on my Master's degree. My supervisor had to be away, and asked me to lecture in his Social Organization class, with 180 students. As someone who had always hated giving presentations in class, I was terrified. But 10 minutes into my lecture, I knew that was what I wanted to do with my life. I've since taught courses ranging from deviance to social psychology, with class sizes as small as four and as large as 400. The pleasure I derive from connecting with students has also led me to writing textbooks—first, a book on deviance and social control, and now this book, one that will bring the fascinating world of sociology to those students who, like me, may have never even heard of sociology.

SOCIOLOGY IN ACTION
A CANADIAN PERSPECTIVE

PART 1

Thinking "Sociologically"

Source: Colin Anderson/Getty

Looking and Acting through the Lens of Sociology

LEARNING OBJECTIVES AND OUTCOMES

After completing this chapter, students should be able to do the following:

LO1 Describe the bidirectional nature of the relationship between individual choices and larger social forces.

LO2 Define "sociology" and identify the role of the sociological imagination.

LO3 Elaborate on the similarities and differences between sociology and other related disciplines.

LO4 Describe the role of theory in sociology and be able to contrast positivist, interpretive, and critical approaches.

LO5 Distinguish between "theoretical frameworks" and "theories," and outline the core assumptions of the functionalist, conflict, interactionist, feminist, and postmodern perspectives.

LO6 Identify the role of critical thinking in "doing" sociology, and explain how to engage in critical thinking.

LO7 Describe the four different types of sociology that are emphasized throughout the book.

It can be said that the first wisdom of sociology is this—things are not what they seem.

(Berger, 2008, p. 9)

THINGS ARE NOT WHAT THEY SEEM

"I'll believe it when I see it!" How many times have you heard someone say this, or used this phrase yourself? Although we often come to trust in what we can see for ourselves, sociology asks us to *not* automatically trust what we see. Consider, for example, a television screen like the one in the photo below. If you were asked what you see when you look at that screen, your initial response would likely be, "I see a fish." But if you took a closer look—presuming that there is more than meets the eye—you might see something very different. Walk right up to a television screen and look at it from an inch or two away, and now you'll realize that what first looked like a fish is really rows and columns of pixels, tiny squares of coloured light. If you looked even more closely, you would see that what first appeared to be the colour yellow is really a combination of red, green, and blue pixels. *Things are not what they seem.*

There is more than first meets the eye in this image.

LO1 Now shift your attention to yourself, and to the clothes you wore to class today. Initially, you might say personal choice led you to wear those particular clothes. But if you now look at your classmates, you can see that many of them are wearing clothes that are very similar to yours (e.g., jeans and a T-shirt). That is, you and many other people have made the same personal choice today, suggesting that there is something more than just individual preference operating here. If I were to go on to ask you why you are a university or college student, you might give me a similar answer—personal choice. And indeed, unless someone registered you as a student against your will, physically dragged you to class this morning, and tied you into your chair in the classroom, it most certainly is your choice. But remember, there is more than first meets the eye. If you examine these circumstances more closely, you will start to realize that just as pixels of coloured light underlie the televised image of a fish, an array of social factors and experiences has contributed to your choice to become a university or college student. When you begin to consider the various factors that influenced your personal choices, or the similar decisions reached by others, that is the point at which you are starting to "do" sociology.

When examining your choice to become a university or college student, you might first consider specific people who influenced your decision, such as the family members and friends who supported, encouraged, or demanded that option. You could then go on to look at some of the more personal social and economic resources that enabled you to become a university or college student—a student loan, a Registered Education Saving Plan (RESP), or parents who support you. The people who are a part of your daily life and the personal resources that you have available to you are important factors that underlie your purported choice to go to university or college. Using a sociological perspective requires you to analyze even beyond your own family, friends, and resources. Just as many of your classmates chose to wear similar clothing to you, many others have also elected to attend university or college alongside you. In fact, in the 2008/2009 academic year, there were almost two million students registered in Canadian universities and colleges (Statistics Canada, 2010, 2011). That means that almost two million people—with almost two million different families, sets of friends, and personal resources—all made the same personal choice that year! Explaining this fact requires you to extend your sociological gaze beyond your own life to larger sociocultural and socioeconomic forces affecting many people simultaneously.

For instance, as a result of a worldwide economic recession that limited job opportunities, university undergraduate enrolments increased by 4.1 percent in 2009 and another 3.6 percent in 2010 over the previous year; economic downturns motivate people to improve their educational qualifications and skills (Association of Universities and Colleges of Canada, 2009). That trend is particularly strong for university enrollment, more so than for college, career, or trade school enrollment (Association of Universities and Colleges of Canada, 2011). Conversely, fewer people elect to pursue a university or college education during strong economic times; if you were living in Alberta in 2006 or 2007 when its economy was so strong that workers had to be brought in from across the country and around the world to fill the abundance of lower-skilled, high-paying jobs that were readily available, you might not have made the choice to become a university or college student. The impact of the economy on university and college enrollment is readily apparent. But more subtle influences on the decisions we make come from society's expectations, or **norms**. By virtue of growing up in a specific family in a particular society at a certain time in history, we learn how we are "supposed" to act. Whether or not we actually behave in accordance with those norms, we are still aware of what those expectations are.

In 21st-century Canada, a postsecondary education is **normative** in that it corresponds to social norms about the kind of education people need prior to entering the workforce. In contrast, had you been a young Canadian woman in the 1950s, a university education would *not* have been normative; rather, society's expectations were that you should get married young, have at least three children, and be a full-time homemaker. Sometimes society's norms are so powerful that they influence formalized rules, such as policies and even the law. For example, if you were a Jewish Canadian prior to the end of World War II, or a black Canadian prior to the civil rights movement of the 1950s and 1960s, the doors of many (indeed, most) universities would have been closed to you, regardless of your academic ability and whether or not you wanted to pursue a university education. Similarly, if you were of Aboriginal origin in the late 19th and early 20th centuries, the residential school

Norms: Society's expectations for how we are supposed to act, think, and look.

Normative: Behaviours, appearances, and thoughts that correspond to society's norms.

SOCIOLOGY *IN MY LIFE*

THE IMPACT OF LIFE CHANCES

Think about your own background for a moment—the kind of neighbourhood you lived in, the jobs that your parents had, the sort of lifestyle you grew up with. If the two photos below represent the extreme ends of a continuum, where would you locate your own childhood background—closer to the photo on the left, or the photo on the right? Do individuals who have grown up in these very different types of neighbourhoods have the same freedom to choose to become a university or college student? Is the ability to take advantage of the opportunity equally available to both of them? Think about the kinds of resources that each might have that would facilitate the decision to go to university or college, as well as the sorts

of obstacles that would interfere with the ability to make that decision. Perhaps you had similar resources or encountered similar obstacles in your path. Sociologist Max Weber (1978) referred to these varying opportunities that people face as **life chances**. Social stratification, inequality, race, ethnicity, and gender are just some of the factors that affect one's life chances. You will learn more about all of these factors in later chapters.

Source: karamysh/Shutterstock

Source: Civdis/Shutterstock

Does everyone in Canada have an equal opportunity to pursue a university or college education?

---

that you would have been forced to attend by law would not have given you the education necessary to gain entrance to a university; rather than provide Aboriginal students with an education that was equivalent to that received by non-Aboriginal students, the purpose of residential schooling was to teach Aboriginal children how to act in accordance with Euro-Canadian norms. And while the opportunity for a university education is available to everyone in the 21st century, sociologists point out that the ability to take advantage of that opportunity is not equally available to all (see *Sociology in My Life*).

The essence of sociology is the fundamental connection between individual choices or experiences and larger social forces that exist outside the individual

(see Figure 1.1, page 6). This is also known as the relationship between the **micro level** and the **macro level**. Thus far, we have examined ways that larger social forces (the macro level) influence individual choices and experiences (the micro level). However, the relationship between the micro level and the macro level is bidirectional, in that your personal choices also have an impact on the people around you, your community, and your

> **Life chances:** The opportunities that an individual has in life, based on various factors including stratification, inequality, race, ethnicity, and gender.
>
> **Micro level:** The level of individual experiences and choices.
>
> **Macro level:** The level of broader social forces.

workplace—what sociologists refer to as **agency**. When a sufficient number of people make similar choices or acquire support for particular decisions, the macro level is affected—either the status quo is supported or social change occurs. Social movements can occur, and school practices and policies, workplace culture and policies, social programming, legislation, and larger cultural norms can all be affected.

For instance, when the authors of this book were in elementary school in the mid-1970s, it was rare for children to eat lunch at school; children either had to go home for lunch (regardless of whether there was an adult there to supervise them), or they walked to a nearby care provider's place. If there was an unusual circumstance (e.g., the parent or care giver had to be at an appointment on a certain day), then the parent would write a note to the teacher explaining the nature of this circumstance and request that the child be permitted to eat lunch at school that day in the classroom under the teacher's supervision, or be sent to a classmate's home. Less than a decade later this was no longer a rare occurrence, and the teacher was no longer required to unexpectedly sacrifice her or his lunch hour in order to supervise a student in the classroom. Processes and procedures had been developed around the need for lunch-hour supervision. Why did such a dramatic change occur in such a relatively short period of time? Because economic and social factors changed the lives of parents, and then the changing lives of parents made changes in school practices necessary.

The assumption that mothers were at home to make lunch for their children was based on family patterns that existed in previous decades, and particularly the 1950s, when most middle-class married women were full-time homemakers. This began to change in the 1960s and 1970s. More mothers were entering the workforce, parents were concerned about their children at home alone, and care providers living near the school could not solely be relied upon to meet the needs of families. The changing choices of parents elicited changes in the environment outside the family. But at the same time, larger sociocultural factors were contributing to parental choices. More mothers were entering the workforce because of (a) changes in the Canadian economy that necessitated dual incomes for many families, (b) the influence of the women's movement, which emphasized the

Agency: People's capacity to make choices, which then have an impact on other people and on the society in which they live.

Sociology: The systematic study of society, using the sociological imagination.

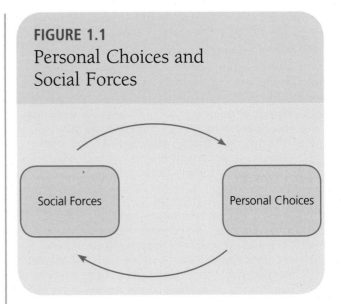

FIGURE 1.1
Personal Choices and
Social Forces

Social Forces

Personal Choices

importance of female equality and the right to personal fulfillment, and (c) the growing acceptance of female employment. The media also played a role in the evolution of a "risk society," created through extensive coverage of missing children cases, which contributed to the growing concerns about children being sent home unsupervised.

Thus, when we look at people's experiences, the micro level and the macro level are intertwined. Recognizing the myriad ways in which they are intertwined requires using something sociologists distinctively call the "sociological imagination."

TIME TO REVIEW

- What do sociologists mean when they say that "things are not what they seem"? In what way is that evident in your choice to become a university or college student?

- What type of relationship exists between the micro level and the macro level? In what way is that relationship evident in the issue of children eating lunch at school?

LO² WHAT IS SOCIOLOGY?

Sociology is the systematic study of society, using the sociological imagination. The connection between the micro level and the macro level is the essence of the sociological perspective. C. Wright Mills (1959/2000) defined the discipline of sociology on the basis of the **sociological imagination**—looking for the "intersections of biography and history" (p. 7), tracing the linkages between individual experiences and larger sociocultural forces. For example, we can use the sociological imagination to explore body modification. If we consider why a particular person gets a tattoo or a piercing, the answer may tell us something specific about that one individual, such as that he or she is a risk-taker. But when we consider the nature of body modification in general among the 51 percent of university undergraduates who have piercings (other than in their earlobes) and the 22 percent who have tattoos (Mayers & Chiffriller, 2008), we learn about larger social relationships and society. For example, we find out about workplace norms, in that many people hide their body art while at work to maintain an image or because workplace policies require it (Newman, Wright, Wrenn & Bernard, 2005; Atkinson, 2003a). We also discover things about family relationships, in that the location, size, and design of body art can be influenced by parental attitudes (Atkinson, 2003a). Similarly, we learn about norms governing gender since women with tattoos continue to be perceived as promiscuous, less attractive, and heavier drinkers (Swami & Furnham, 2007), and those with highly visible tattoos are viewed even more negatively (Hawkes, Senn & Thorn, 2004). We identify allegiances to particular subcultures, such as when we see the tattoo of an aviator-cap-adorned skull, framed by wings, that indicates membership in the Hells Angels Motorcycle Club. We even find out about the ideologies of subcultures, where a "Poison-Free" tattoo on a member of the Straightedge subculture signifies the commitment to a substance-free lifestyle (Atkinson, 2003b).

The sociological imagination lies at the core of sociology, but Mills (1959/2000) did not see the sociological imagination as an intellectual tool to be used solely by sociologists (or even students in sociology classes); he proposed that society as a whole would benefit from, and indeed *needed*, all of its citizens to look for the interconnectedness between the macro and micro levels. He saw the purpose of the sociological imagination as being practical and political, "and its problems of direct relevance to urgent public issues and insistent human troubles" (p. 21). That is, the sociological imagination is not just about *thinking*, it is also about *doing*. That "doing" might be at the level of your everyday life and experiences, where paying attention to the relationship between individual choices and larger social forces will make you a more informed parent, voter, community member,

Snapshots

"I love our lunches out here, but I always get the feeling that we're being watched."

Source: © Love, Jason, jlvn685, CartoonStock.com

social worker, teacher, police officer, office manager, or team member. But it might also be at the level of social action, wherein you might find yourself trying to improve some aspect of your community or even society as a whole.

Within the discipline of sociology, the sociological imagination is used to study just about anything that is related to people. Berger (2008) describes sociologists as professional people watchers who are gripped by curiosity whenever they find themselves "in front of a closed door behind which are human voices" (p. 7). Individual sociologists specialize in different topic areas; for instance, one of the authors of this book specializes in deviance, youth, and popular culture, while the other author specializes in social psychology, criminology, and research methods.

The topics studied within the discipline of sociology translate into a considerable breadth of potential careers for students who graduate with a degree in sociology. Unlike some university programs that train students for specific jobs upon graduation (e.g., teacher, accountant, or dentist), an education in sociology provides its graduates with a knowledge base and a set of skills that constitute a "tool kit" that can then be used in a variety of careers (see Figure 1.2, page 8).

> **Sociological imagination:** The ability to perceive the interconnections between individual experiences and larger sociocultural forces.

FIGURE 1.2
What Can I Do With a Degree in Sociology?

Sociology graduates are frequently employed in the following areas:

- *Community and Social Service Workers:* Community and social service workers administer and implement social assistance programs and community services, and assist clients to deal with personal and social problems. They are employed by social service and government agencies, mental health agencies, group homes, school boards, and correctional facilities. Sample job titles include welfare and compensation officer, addictions worker, youth worker, women's shelter supervisor, and life skills instructor.
- *Health Policy Researchers, Consultants, and Program Officers:* Employees in this area conduct research, produce reports, and administer health policies and programs. They are employed by government departments and agencies, consulting establishments, universities, research institutes, hospitals, community agencies, educational institutions, professional associations, nongovernmental organizations, and international organizations. Sample job titles include health promotion program officer; consultant, drug and alcohol abuse; policy development officer, nursing homes; and research assistant.
- *Probation and Parole Officers and Related Occupations:* People employed in this area monitor the reintegration of criminal offenders into the community, assess offenders and develop rehabilitation programs, and advise/counsel offenders. They are employed by federal and provincial governments, and work in the community and in correctional facilities. Sample job titles include community case manager, probation officer, parole officer, and classification officer.
- *Social Policy Researchers, Consultants, and Program Officers:* Individuals in these types of occupations conduct research, develop policy, and implement or administer programs in areas such as consumer affairs, employment, home economics, immigration, law enforcement, corrections, human rights, housing, labour, family services, foreign aid, and international development. They are employed by government departments and agencies, industry, hospitals, educational institutions, consulting establishments, professional associations, nongovernmental organizations, and international organizations. Sample job titles include Aboriginal issues lobbyist; housing policy analyst; consumer adviser; community policing project consultant; and international aid and development project officer.
- *Government Managers—Health and Social Policy Development and Program Administration:* Government managers in this group plan, organize, direct, control, and evaluate the development and administration of health care policies, social policies, and programs related to the health and social welfare of individuals and communities. These managers are employed by government departments and agencies. Sample job titles include survey research manager; manager, immigration appeals; community planning director; and community rehabilitation manager.

Source: Adapted from Human Resources and Development Canada (2006). National Occupational Classification (NOC) 2006.

LO3 COMPARING SOCIOLOGY AND OTHER DISCIPLINES

As you may have already noticed in some of your classes, similar topics are covered in different disciplines. For example, you may have studied some aspect of families in a psychology, anthropology, or even political science course—and you will also learn about families in your sociology course. In fact, many of the topics studied by sociologists are also analyzed by researchers in other social science disciplines—culture and cultural variations (anthropology, cultural studies), political forces (political science, development studies), occupational and economic forces (economics, political economy), families (family studies, social work), and mass media (psychology, cultural studies, communications, media studies). What are the differences, then, between sociology and other social science disciplines?

Although even ancient philosophers studied various aspects of society, the origins of sociology as a discipline can be traced to a historical period that includes the French Revolution (1789–1799) and the accompanying Enlightenment. This was a time of rapid social, political, and economic change—cities increased in size, there was the transition to a wage economy, absolute monarchies were threatened, the power of religion declined, and the power of science grew. As society changed, intellectuals sought to understand and explain those changes, as well as the consequences of those changes. It was Auguste Comte (1798–1857) who first suggested that science or, more specifically, empirical research and theory, should be used in pursuit of this goal. The sociological perspective developed out of philosophy, economics, history, psychology, and law. And in fact, many of the well-known scholars who are referred to as "sociologists" because their work is central to sociology (and whose work will be presented at various points in this textbook) were, in fact, not "sociologists" by training. For example, Max Weber's training was in economic history, Karl Marx's in philosophy, and Emile Durkheim's in educational thought and philosophy. With that knowledge, they sought to understand social change, and what made "society" possible in the face of change.

Although the sociological perspective emerged in the 18th and 19th centuries, the formation of distinct disciplines is a more recent phenomenon. It was in the 20th century that distinct boundaries began to be constructed around particular bodies of knowledge and the subject matter of specific disciplines (Delanty, 2005, 2007). Thus, while historians studied the past, anthropologists studied premodern societies, political scientists analyzed structures of governance, economists studied the production and consumption of goods and services, psychologists focused on the individual, and social psychologists studied individual thoughts, feelings, and behaviours in social situations. The attention of scholars within each of their corresponding disciplines was focused on a certain part of society. In contrast, sociologists studied *all* of these parts of society, while using a wider range of research methodologies and theories (Delanty, 2005, 2007). Hence, sociology can be thought of as the most *comprehensive* of the social sciences.

However, sociology goes a step further, and proposes that society is greater than the sum of its parts. Society is more than a compilation of history plus government plus the economy (and so on). There is a complex web of interconnectedness among all of its parts—they interact in particular ways and the nature of that interaction contributes to a specific phenomenon of interest, such as tattooing. What governs a sociological approach to a particular subject matter is an analysis of these interactions, and an emphasis on tracing the linkages between individual experiences and larger sociocultural forces.

Distinct disciplines were formed in the early 20th century. However, the 21st century is characterized by what some scholars have called *postdisciplinarity* (e.g., Urry, 2000). This means that while separate disciplines were created a century ago, the differences among those disciplines are less apparent today. For example, traditionally the discipline of anthropology focused on premodern societies; now, anthropologists also study modern societies, which were traditionally in the realm of sociology (Delanty, 2005, 2007).

In addition to the blurring of boundaries between disciplines, the 21st century is also characterized by greater *interdisciplinarity* (Delanty, 2005, 2007), where scholars in a variety of disciplines work together to better understand particular social phenomena. For instance, globalization is not associated with a specific discipline, but rather brings together diverse groups of scholars, including sociologists, economists, and political scientists; you will learn more about globalization in Chapter 14. Interdisciplinarity has created new disciplines as well, such as women's studies, cultural studies, and family studies; university departments that are affiliated with these areas of study will often include faculty members who are sociologists, economists, political scientists, historians, social psychologists, and philosophers.

Thus, sociology is a comprehensive discipline that analyzes the interactions among various parts of society, at both the macro and micro levels, in pursuit of knowledge about a specific aspect of society, such as tattooing. But because of recent trends, the differences among various disciplines are not as apparent today as they were once considered to be. Thus, the body of knowledge presented in this textbook includes the work of people who identify themselves as sociologists, but also the work of those who are embedded within other disciplines, whether a traditional discipline such as psychology or a newer interdisciplinary area such as cultural studies.

Sociology emphasizes the fundamental importance of empirical research and its relationship to theory (as you will learn more about in Chapter 2). Sociological theorizing was central to explaining changes during the French Revolution, and it continues to be crucial to understanding and explaining society. Theory explains the causes of crime, how it is that we come to select one person to marry out of the seven billion people who inhabit the Earth, and the processes by which individuals come to identify themselves as gay, lesbian, or bisexual. In the popular mind, theory is sometimes perceived as being a nonpractical exercise engaged in by academics living in their ivory towers; in reality, by helping us better understand our own lives and the world around us, theory should be considered one of the most practical academic endeavours.

TIME TO REVIEW

- What is sociology, and what is the role of the sociological imagination?
- Who should be using the sociological imagination, and for what purpose?
- How is sociology related to other disciplines?

LO⁴ SOCIOLOGICAL THEORIZING

A **theory** can be defined as a set of propositions intended to explain a fact or a phenomenon. In practice, theorizing can be thought of as "puzzle-building" (Bengston, Acock, Allen, Dilworth-Anderson & Klein, 2005, p. 5), trying to fit the pieces of some social phenomenon together in order to reveal a cohesive picture. Although different types of theorizing can be described in a variety of ways, one of the more common ways categorizes specific theories as either *positivist, interpretive,* or *critical* (White & Klein, 2008).

Positivist theorizing stems from the natural sciences, with an interest in objective *explanation and prediction.* In the social sciences, it is used to examine relationships in an effort to learn more about how society works, enabling subsequent improvements in the social environment (Ashley & Orenstein, 2001). For example, knowledge of factors that contribute to hate crimes can lead to the development of more effective prevention and intervention efforts. In contrast, interpretive and critical theorizing reject the positivist assumption that there are objective "laws" governing the way society works; instead, they emphasize the cultural and historical specificity of all processes.

Interpretive theorizing focuses on *understanding*—the ways that people come to understand themselves, others, and the world around them. It presumes that human beings are "self-interpreting animals" (Taylor, 1985, p. 45), constructed and shaped through culture. Here the goal of sociology is to describe the role that culture plays in creating people and societies, and how people come to think about their positions within that culture and their relations with other people. For instance, interpretive theorizing might explore what being a "real" man means to men who have been convicted of hate crimes.

Critical theorizing explores the role that *power* plays in social processes, the reason that some people's understandings of the world become dominant (such as through being reflected in legislation), and ties that knowledge to *emancipation*—empowering subordinated groups in society. For example, critical theorizing might analyze the ways in which members of certain social groups (e.g., certain religious and/or ethnic groups; gays, lesbians, transsexual, and transgendered persons) are subordinated in society in many ways, including through being victimized by hate crimes—and emphasize the importance of changing society in order to put an end to that subordination.

LO⁵ Positivist, interpretive, and critical approaches to theorizing give rise to a number of theoretical frameworks that have contributed to the sociological knowledge that we have about society. The theoretical *frameworks* (or *perspectives*) outlined herein each provide a systematic set of core assumptions, and a way of approaching the study of society. They may address the micro level, emphasizing individuals as the basic component of society, or the macro level, focusing on social institutions as the basic component of society.

The frameworks or perspectives are characterized by a level of generality that enables other narrower, more specific theories to emerge from them—the frameworks "are like families, with the core . . . providing sufficient richness for the development of offspring" (White & Klein, 2008, p. 30). The remainder of this chapter will provide an overview of each framework or perspective, outlining its core assumptions and ways of looking at society; it is in the rest of the chapters, where detailed theories will be applied to particular topics, problems, and issues that sociological theorizing will become more apparent and meaningful.

The core theoretical frameworks within sociology are the functionalist perspective, the conflict perspective, the interactionist perspective, the feminist perspective, and the postmodern perspective. One easy way to help you consider these perspectives is to think of them as different "lenses" through which one can view the world. Some frameworks are similar to those lenses that become darker or lighter when exposed to different levels of light. By identifying patterns of subordination and inequality in a critical way, society looks somewhat "darker" from these perspectives; however, because these perspectives also provide for the possibility of emancipation, the "brighter" side of society can be seen as well. Other theoretical frameworks are more like "rose-coloured" glasses, where society is viewed in a positive, cohesive manner and the goal is to keep everything running smoothly. You will also encounter perspectives that seem more like regular "clear" glasses, wherein the nature of the viewpoint is dependent on the person who is wearing them. Finally, some lenses are nontraditional, such as

---

Theory: A set of propositions intended to explain a fact or a phenomenon.

Positivist: Theorizing that emphasizes explanation and prediction.

Interpretive: Theorizing that focuses on the ways that people come to understand themselves, others, and the world around them.

Critical: Theorizing that explores the role that power plays in social processes, and emphasizes the importance of knowledge being tied to emancipation.

the lenses created through laser surgery, or the fragmented lens of a kaleidoscope. Although upon first learning about the different frameworks and theories, it may appear that the boundaries between them are impermeable (or rigid), in fact they are not fixed; a growing number of sociologists combine aspects of different theories in order to better understand or explain a specific social phenomenon.

FUNCTIONALIST FRAMEWORK

Functionalism, also known as structural functionalism, has its origins in the early development of sociology. Its overriding concern is how social order or equilibrium is maintained, especially during times of significant societal change. Through this "rosy" lens, everything in society works to restore order and balance. It is a macro-level perspective, in that society is perceived as comprising a number of *structures* (e.g., institutions such as the family, economy, education, government, and religion), each of which fulfills important *functions* that keeps society running smoothly—similar to the manner in which in a pyramidal stack of tin cans, each can plays an important role in maintaining the stability of the pyramid as a whole (Bereska, 2011).

Some of those functions served by each structure are **manifest functions**, those that an institution is intended to fulfill; for instance, the manifest function of postsecondary education is job training. Other functions are **latent functions**, those that are less obvious and unintentional; a latent function of postsecondary education is mate selection. All of society's structures are necessary to maintain social order. Should something go awry with one of the structures (e.g., the family), the entire social order is at risk of collapsing, just as the removal of one of the tin cans in the stack would cause the whole stack to fall apart.

One of the foundational assumptions of the functionalist framework is that consensus and cooperation lie at the core of how social order is maintained. Society is made up of norms and **values** (i.e., criteria by which we determine whether something is right or wrong, such as the *principle of equality*), and those norms and values exist because most people agree that they should exist. But should problems emerge with one or more of the main foundational structures (i.e., should a structure become **dysfunctional**), consensus can be threatened, which then puts society as a whole in peril. Since the focus is on stability and social order, the functionalist perspective assumes that in most cases, other structures will adapt to restore order, just as when the education system started to assume responsibility for the noon-hour supervision of children.

Émile Durkheim (1858–1917), one of the founders of sociology and of the functionalist framework, elaborated on what happens when society changes too rapidly. Rapid social change, such as that seen in Europe following the French Revolution (Durkheim, 1933, 1951) and in Eastern Europe following the fall of the Soviet Union (Walberg et al., cited in McKee, 2002), creates what Durkheim labelled **anomie**, a mass feeling of normlessness, or uncertainty about what the rules are in this unfamiliar situation. The concept of anomie can also be applied to the aftermath of large-scale natural disasters that have an impact on a region's physical or social infrastructure—Japan's earthquake, tsunami, and nuclear crisis in 2011; Haiti's earthquake in 2010; the flooding of the Red River in Manitoba (as well as North Dakota and Minnesota) in 2009; and Canada's deadliest disaster, the Newfoundland hurricane of 1775, which killed more than 4,000 people.

Many of you may recall stories in the media of how these disasters are often followed by acts of violence and looting, and wondered what would cause people who have just gone through such traumatic experiences to act in that way. Following the Haiti earthquake in 2010, why would crowds of looters

Source: pixelfabrik/Shutterstock

According to the functionalist framework, every structure in society plays a necessary role in keeping society together.

Manifest function: An intended function of one of society's structures.

Latent function: An unintended function of one of society's structures.

Values: Collectively shared criteria by which we determine whether something is right or wrong.

Dysfunctional: One of society's structures no longer fulfills its function effectively.

Anomie: A feeling of normlessness.

have set fire to shops and have to be dispersed by riot police using tear gas? Why would groups of people start brawls when aid trucks arrived (Canadian Broadcasting Corporation, 2010)? Durkheim's work provides an answer to that question. He proposed that one of the consequences of anomie is deviant behaviour; when the context of our daily lives rapidly changes and we are no longer certain about which rules do or do not apply, we may act in ways that are dysfunctional for society. As a newspaper article that followed Hurricane Andrew in 1992 put it, people were "popping their corks" in the aftermath of the hurricane (Booth, 1992, para. 13); this article even uses the word "anomie" to describe the atmosphere.

Arising from the core assumptions of the functionalist perspective are several specific theories that will be applied in subsequent chapters. For instance, Talcott Parsons' theorizing about the impact of industrialization on gender roles (e.g., Parsons & Bales, 1955) will be addressed in Chapter 4. Robert Merton's work on the normative structure of science will be presented in Chapter 9, and his theorizing about the causes of deviance in Chapter 10. At the level of practice, the functionalist perspective gives rise to intervention efforts to assist lone parents, programming within inner-city schools to facilitate children's academic and social progress, and more. Although specific functionalist theories and forms of practice may differ from each other considerably, they all have a foundation in what it takes to keep society running smoothly.

CONFLICT FRAMEWORK

Like the functionalist perspective, the conflict perspective also is a macro-level framework that focuses on large-scale institutions. However, while the functionalist framework describes society as based on consensus and cooperation, the conflict perspective (through a darker lens) views society as being characterized by conflict and competition over scarce resources. You might recall playing "king of the castle" as a child, where each child strives to reach the top of the hill (or piece of playground equipment) and then prevent other children from reaching that desired position (see photo). In this game, the child at the top would sing out to the other children, "I'm the king of the castle and you're the dirty rascals!" The king

Bourgeoisie: In Marxist conflict theory, the owners of the means of production.

Proletariat: In Marxist conflict theory, the people who work for the owners of the means of production.

Source: Purestock/Jupiter Royalty Free

Just as in the children's game "King of the Castle," conflict theorists propose that society comprises a small group of powerful people at the top of the social hierarchy and a large group of powerless people at the bottom.

might even use physical force to keep other children from reaching the top by pushing their hands away as they reach for the top of a climbing apparatus, or shoving them back down a slide as they climb it.

Similarly, the conflict perspective views society as comprising a small group of powerful people at the top of society, and a large group of powerless people at the bottom. Those at the top control the resources, and, hence, have a vested interest in creating laws and structuring society in such a way as to keep the large group of powerless people at the bottom; to allow more people to reach the top would mean having to share their own resources with them.

Conflict can be between groups of people or within groups. Karl Marx (1818–1883), who is typically credited as the founder of the conflict perspective, emphasized conflict *between* groups, specifically the owners of the means of production (i.e., the **bourgeoisie**) and those who are employed by those owners (i.e., the **proletariat**) under capitalism. However, various conflict theories identify the basis for conflict between groups differently; *pluralist conflict theory* proposes that there are many types of resources in society, resulting in multiple axes of inequality (economic, educational, religious, gendered, etc.), and that conflict can occur between any of those groups. Because resources can be distributed unequally within a group as well, conflict also occurs *within* groups (Engels, 1884/1972). Within workplaces, some individuals have more power than others to control aspects of the work environment. Even within families, some members may have more power than others by controlling the families' economic or emotional resources.

Throughout the remainder of the book, various specific conflict theories will be applied. For example, conflict theorists highlight how education largely serves to reproduce the existing social order and poses significant disadvantages for particular groups in society (see Chapter 9). And in Chapter 14, *dependency theory* proposes that relationships of exploitation have emerged between developed nations and the underdeveloped nations that have been exploited for their natural resources, such as gold, coffee, and oil.

Conflict theories go further than merely analyzing the nature of social inequality. Just as some lenses may become lighter under certain conditions, conflict theories propose that conditions of inequality can be changed to eliminate that inequality; this draws attention to a "brighter" view of society. In his description of the evolution of world economic systems, Karl Marx described a time in the future when the proletariat would rise up to unite and fight their oppressors. The notion of **praxis**—the responsibility that scholars have to provide subordinated and marginalized groups in society with the knowledge that they need to be able to end their powerlessness—was emphasized in Marx's early work. Thus, the conflict framework is intimately intertwined with practice. Within groups, the fact that conflict is inevitable means that groups must find ways to manage that conflict; for instance, conflict management programs in the workplace teach people skills in conflict resolution and negotiation. Conflict between groups has frequently been the basis for large-scale social movements, such as the civil rights; women's rights; and gay, lesbian, and transgendered rights movements.

Both the conflict and functionalist perspectives emphasize the macro level. Other frameworks focus upon the micro level—that is, the *people* who make up society, rather than the institutions. One of these perspectives is the interactionist perspective.

INTERACTIONIST FRAMEWORK

The interactionist perspective is generally attributed to the pioneering work of George Herbert Mead (1863–1931) and Herbert Blumer (1900–1987). You can think of the interactionist perspective as being a way to look at the world through regular, clear lenses. Within the interactionist framework (also known as the symbolic interactionist perspective), society is depicted as comprising individuals who are engaged in various forms of communication, through words, facial expressions, gestures, and clothing (Mead, 1934; Blumer, 1969). These symbolic forms of communication come to mean particular things to certain people based on common shared understandings that develop between them, much like after many years of marriage, a husband and wife can finish one another's sentences.

Communication can be direct, such as between people who are in the same room, on the telephone, in a chat room, or in an email exchange. It can also be indirect, such as when actors, directors, writers, journalists, news anchors, and musicians communicate to an audience at home. During our lifetimes, as we communicate with others, we come to attribute meaning to our experiences, and thereby develop particular perceptions of, understandings of, and reactions to ourselves, other people, and the world around us. Our understandings grow and change over time and from situation to situation, depending on with whom we are communicating.

Significant others or the specific people who are most important to us, such as parents, partners, children, close friends, or maybe even our favourite professors, play an important role in our socialization, the lifelong process by which we acquire the knowledge and skills necessary for everyday life in society. We can say we have passed through all of the main stages of socialization once we have developed what Mead called a *generalized other*. The **generalized other** is not a specific person in our lives, but rather an overall sense of people's expectations; even if we are not in the physical presence of a specific person who is important to us, we may still care about what "others" think of the way we look or act. This reflects our ability to take into account more than just our individual perspective, or the perspectives of specific people we care about, but also the perspectives of a multitude of nameless, faceless, generic people. For example, when getting ready for a date you might wonder what your best friend would say about your new fragrance (i.e., significant others), or what "people" (none of whom you personally know) will think when you walk into the restaurant in the clothes you are considering wearing (i.e., generalized other).

Within sociology, the interactionist perspective has been applied to an almost endless array of topics—from looking at how we come to develop a particular ethnic or gender identity (Chapters 7 and 8) to how being

Praxis: The responsibility that scholars have to provide subordinated and marginalized groups in society with the knowledge that they need to be able to end their powerlessness.

Significant others: People who are important to us.

Generalized other: An overall sense of people's expectations.

CHAPTER 1 Looking and Acting through the Lens of Sociology **13**

labelled in a negative way can influence our future behaviour (Chapter 10). This array of topics shares an emphasis on how we come to understand our own lives and the lives of others. Consequently, in practice the interactionist framework rears its head in any informal situation or formal program where such an understanding is being encouraged, such as when a teacher tries to get a child to understand what it is like to be on the receiving end of an act of playground aggression.

FEMINIST FRAMEWORK

Feminism is "the system of ideas and political practices based on the principle that women are human beings equal to men" (Lengermann & Niebrugge, 2007a, para. 1). This may be a taken-for-granted assumption for most of you, but as you will see in Chapter 7, it is relatively recent idea in world history, and still not accepted by all. Feminism includes both social and political practice, as well as academic work—empirical and theoretical. Feminism and sociology have had a relationship since the discipline's very beginnings, and that relationship rests upon feminist social and political practice.

FEMINISM AND SOCIOLOGY: THE EARLY YEARS

A history of sociology frequently reads as a history of male scholarship. However, women have played an important role in the development of the discipline. During the "first wave" of feminist sociology (1830–1930), women who were engaged in feminist practice were attracted to this new emerging social scientific field. Their practical efforts at emancipation (e.g., the right to vote) and a discipline that used scientific methods to solve social problems seemed a natural fit (Lengermann & Niebrugge, 2007a, 2007b).

Female sociologists of this time were well-known public figures and were recognized by their male peers in sociology. The scholar who is most commonly recognized as the first female sociologist is Harriet Martineau (1802–1876). In addition to her sociological research and writing, she was an essayist and intellectual critic, and also wrote novels and children's books. She translated August Comte's work into English, and

Feminism: The system of ideas and political practices based on the principle that women are human beings equal to men.

wrote the first major statement of method in sociology. In her career, she wrote eight major books, published more than 200 articles, taught sociology, and was a member of the American Sociological Society. At the time of its writing, her book *Illustrations of Political Economy* (1832–1834) even outsold Charles Dickens. Her scholarly work was intimately intertwined with practice. She was a speaker for social reform, not just for women, but also for trade unions, immigrants, blacks, and the working class (Lengermann & Niebrugge, 2007b).

Source: © Hulton-Deutsch Collection/CORBIS

Harriet Martineau was the first of a long line of influential female sociologists.

A generation later, Martineau was followed by a long list of other female scholars who associated themselves with the discipline of sociology: Beatrice Potter Webb (1858–1943); Anna Julia Cooper (1858–1964); Jane Addams (1860–1935); Charlotte Perkins Gilman (1860–1935); Ida B. Wells-Barnett (1862–1931); Marianne Weber (1870–1954); and more. Like Martineau, in addition to being scholars, they were also socially and politically active.

Feminist sociologists in the early years perceived sociology as "a project of social critique in which research and theory had a morally necessary focus on the description, analysis, and correction of social inequality" (Lengermann & Niebrugge, 2007b, p. 10). But they were also a very diverse group of scholars in terms of the forms of inequality they focused on, the research methodologies they used, and the balance of empirical research and theory in their work. Feminist sociology is equally diverse today (if not more so); this is evident when focusing our attention on feminist theory.

FEMINIST SOCIOLOGY TODAY

Because of the diversity that characterizes feminist theory, the feminist perspective is one of the most difficult to discuss in an overview. Various feminist theories are labelled liberal, radical, multicultural, or postcolonial, and the list goes on (Nelson, 2010). They can differ considerably. Some propose that men and women are inherently similar, with differences emerging only due to socialization; others claim that men and women are inherently different, highlighting female "nurturance" and male "aggression." Some focus exclusively on the experiences of women, while others emphasize the ways that traditional gender roles and **patriarchy** (i.e., legal and/or social power that is vested in males) affect both men and women. In addition, feminist theorizing is done *within* other theoretical perspectives as well. But despite the differences in feminist theorizing, there are some areas of widespread agreement, described below. Like the conflict perspective, feminist perspectives both draw attention to the "darker" side of society (i.e., inequalities based on gender), as well as highlight the "brighter" possibility of social change to reduce these equalities.

First, feminist perspectives contend that academic research has traditionally been **androcentric** (or male-centred), failing to adequately study women's experiences and treating men's experiences as the normative "human" experience. The androcentric bias is also evident in the manner in which the prolific work of female sociologists in the early years was subsequently written out of or erased from the histories of sociology that were developed in the mid-20th century (and which were reproduced in Introductory Sociology textbooks for many decades to come); for the last half century, many feminist sociologists have devoted their attention to the rediscovery of the work of these scholars (Lengermann & Niebrugge, 2007a, 2007b). Second, they assume that society is structured on the basis of gender, and therefore that people's experiences are also structured on the basis of gender. Males and females are often treated differently (e.g., parents buy trucks for their sons and dolls for their daughters), and frequently face differing expectations regarding their behaviour (e.g., women should not get tattoos and if they do, they should not be highly visible). And third, they attest that research and theory must be intertwined with practice—the fundamental objective underlying all critical theories.

Feminist research and theorizing has been done on topics that will be addressed throughout the textbook, including the portrayal of women in the media (Chapter 3), and feminist critiques of science and perspectives on religion (Chapter 9). But even more fundamentally, because gender is one of the bases upon which all societies are structured, gender is addressed throughout the textbook, even if a specific "feminist" theory is not being applied.

Feminist practice ranges from the micro level to the macro level. At the most micro of levels, it can inform the ways that individuals make choices and carry out their everyday activities, as well as the ways in which they interact with their partners or socialize their children. At the community level, feminist practice is the foundation for various programs, such as "women in science" summer camps that encourage girls to pursue further education in science. At a more macro level, it underlies changes in school curriculum, such as the courses that are made available to male and female students, as well as the content of school textbooks. At the most macro of levels, feminism is the foundation for large-scale social movements, such as those that resulted in women being given the right to vote in federal elections (1918) and being legally declared "persons" (1929).

There is a considerable range of work within the feminist framework; in fact, it may be more appropriate to refer to feminist *frameworks* or *perspectives* in the plural, rather than in the singular. Similarly, the last theoretical perspective to be presented—the postmodern framework—also comprises many divergent viewpoints and is even less cohesive than the feminist framework (Downes & Rock, 2003).

POSTMODERN FRAMEWORK

The discipline of sociology emerged from the significant social change that accompanied the French Revolution and the Enlightenment, with the functionalist perspective explaining how social order could be maintained during such times. The postmodern perspective emerged from another time of significant social change, the post–World War II era. Postmodernists point out the ways in which our lives have dramatically changed since World War II. Prior to and during the war, western societies were industrial, based primarily on manufacturing products (e.g., tables, chairs, refrigerators). Since that time, they have largely lost their industrial base, and now primarily produce ideas and images. As we go about our daily lives, we are bombarded by an endless array of ideas and images communicated through movies, music, advertisements, and other forms of media. There are so many messages that it can be difficult to know where to turn our attention! In this regard, it might be easy for you to think of the postmodern perspective as viewing the world through coloured

Patriarchy: Legal and/or social power that is vested in males.

Androcentric: Male centred, failing to account for women's experiences.

contact lenses of your choosing, a technologically modified lens (e.g., via laser surgery), or even the fragmented lens of a kaleidoscope.

Arising from this view of post–World War II society are two forms of postmodernism: skeptical and affirmative (Rosenau, 1992). *Skeptical* postmodernism proposes that the nature of these social changes has created inescapable chaos and meaninglessness; because this form of postmodernism precludes the possibility of any meaning in the world, it has not played a significant role in sociology. In contrast, *affirmative* postmodernism suggests that the manner in which society has changed means that we cannot rely on grand overarching theories of society (such as functionalist and conflict) or broad categories of people (such as the generic labels of "man" or "black"). Instead, affirmative postmodernists focus on the local and specific, deconstructing what is perceived as "knowledge," and asking questions of that knowledge.

In addition to skeptical and affirmative postmodernism, *poststructuralist* theories are sometimes categorized as belonging to the postmodern framework, although this is widely disputed; consequently, at some points in this book you will see postmodern theories being addressed, while at other times the book will explicitly refer to poststructuralist theories. Poststructuralist theories, as exemplified through the work of Michel Foucault (1978, 1980, 1977/1995), emphasize the relationship between knowledge and power. There are many different **discourses** in society, ways of understanding a particular subject or social phenomenon. Which of those discourses comes to be perceived as valid is dependent upon where the competing discourses are located within the structure of power. When a discourse is espoused by people who are in positions of authority, it becomes an *elite discourse*, and becomes widely accepted. For example, consider the role of the "expert" within the media. When significant social issues or news events are presented on a daytime talk show or on the evening news, a sound bite from a token "expert" is frequently included. The role of that "expert" is to explain the phenomenon to us; we have a tendency to accept that explanation as valid knowledge, simply by virtue of the fact that it is an "expert" who has conveyed it. At a broader level, certain types of knowledge are granted more legitimacy by the public than others. In 21st-century Canada, scientific claims to knowledge hold this role; however, in pre-Enlightenment Europe, as well as in some cultures today, religious claims to knowledge were granted the most legitimacy in the eyes of the public (see Chapter 9).

Throughout this book, the postmodern perspective will be represented in diverse forms, such as in relation to the media (Chapter 3) and religion, science, and education (Chapter 9). In practice, poststructuralist and postmodern ideas underlie some forms of social activism (e.g., environmental, antiglobalization), and media literacy efforts. For a review of the key assumptions of the core theoretical frameworks, refer to Figure 1.3.

Discourses: Ways of understanding a particular subject or social phenomenon.

TIME TO REVIEW

- What are the differences among positivist, interpretive, and critical theorizing, and what is the distinction between a "theoretical framework" and a "theory"?
- What are the core assumptions of the functionalist perspective, and what happens when society changes too rapidly?
- What are the core assumptions of the conflict perspective, and what is the role of praxis?
- What are the core assumptions of the interactionist perspective, and how are significant others and the generalized other involved?
- What is the relationship between feminism and sociology, and why may it be more appropriate to refer to feminist theoretical *perspectives* in the plural?
- What are the different forms that postmodernism takes?

This chapter has highlighted the basic assumptions of the five central theoretical frameworks in sociology—functionalist, conflict, interactionist, feminist, and postmodern. Throughout the remainder of the book, more detail regarding some of those assumptions, as well as specific theories that lie within those frameworks, will be presented in more detail as they are applied to particular substantive topics. Those theories, along with the empirical research that has been done on particular topics, will form the basis upon which your sociological imagination can be used to understand those topics. But more than just theoretical and empirical knowledge is needed for the sociological imagination, and there is more than one way of using that imagination.

The Core Theoretical Frameworks of Sociology

Functionalist Framework—Émile Durkheim
- A macro-level perspective that views society as comprising a number of structures, each of which fulfills important functions that keep society operating smoothly.

Conflict Framework—Karl Marx
- A macro-level perspective that describes society as characterized by conflict and competition over resources that are distributed unequally.

Interactionist Framework—George Herbert Mead/Herbert Bloomer
- A micro-level perspective that depicts society as consisting of individuals engaged in various forms of communication that come to have particular meanings.

Feminist Framework—assorted "founders"
- A micro- or macro-level perspective that assumes society is structured on the basis of gender.

Postmodern Framework—assorted "founders"
- Skeptical postmodernism proposes that the nature of social change has created inescapable chaos and meaninglessness, while affirmative postmodernism suggests that we can no longer rely on overarching theories of society or categories of people.

LO⁶ USING THE SOCIOLOGICAL IMAGINATION

As we address a variety of topics and issues in the remainder of the book, a body of sociological knowledge will accumulate. That body of knowledge will provide you with a level of understanding of those topics and issues that goes beyond what you have at the present time. But it is important that you think critically about that knowledge, as well as other bodies of knowledge regarding that topic (such as from the media or your friends), and the issue itself. Thinking "critically" about a source of information or about a particular issue does not mean to *criticize* it, as a parent may have once criticized the music you were listening to. Rather, it means to *critique* that issue or source of information: to recognize valid information, even if you hold a different point of view than the one being postulated; think independently; suspend judgment; and consider implications and consequences. During the course of your academic career, you will have many professors direct you, and expect you, to think critically. But what does critical thinking actually look like? Where do you even begin (see Figure 1.4, The Beginners' Guide to Critical Thinking, on the following page)?

LO⁷ As you begin to (a) critically evaluate the theoretical, empirical, and other forms of knowledge on a topic or issue, (b) in order to analyze the connection between the micro level and the macro level, (c) for the larger purpose of social action (whether your own or someone else's, whether in the short term or the long term), you will be "doing" sociology. In this chapter, you have learned about what sociology is and the core theoretical perspectives that are used to "do" sociology. Chapter 2 provides the rest of the foundation of the sociological approach, by describing the empirical research methods that are used to gather sociological knowledge. Arising from this empirical and theoretical foundation, sociology can take different forms (American Sociological Association, 2004; Nichols, 2007; Clawson et al., 2007), and beginning in Chapter 3 you will see various forms that will have a presence throughout the remainder of this book. *Academic sociology* comprises the theoretical and empirical research conducted by

FIGURE 1.4
The Beginners' Guide to Critical Thinking

Summarize the information
- What is the *topic area* of the information?
- What are the *main ideas*?
- What are the *conclusions*?

Evaluate the information
- Who is the *target audience*? How does the nature of the audience affect the presentation of the material?
- Are the ideas or points that are being made supported by *evidence*?
- Is the argument *balanced* or is it one-sided?
- Are you being *persuaded* to adopt a certain view?
- Does language or tone reveal any *biases*?
- Is the material *well organized* and *well communicated*?

Respond to the information
- What is *your position* on the topic? Upon what is your position based?
- Are there any *other ways of looking at it*?
- Can the main points or conclusions be applied to *other situations/events*? In other words, are there other "places" where you can see this same thing happening?
- What are some of the potential real-world *consequences* of the conclusions?
- What *images of the subject matter* are presented in the argument? What might some of the *consequences* of those types of images be?
- What did this argument *make you think of*? Did it bring to mind something you have experienced? Something else you have read? Something you have learned in another class? Something you have observed?

formally trained researchers; this type of sociology will be apparent throughout the bulk of each chapter, with certain pieces of work highlighted in *Sociology in Theory*. *Policy sociology* refers to the use of the results of theoretical and empirical research for policy development in governments, other public organizations (e.g., public universities), and private organizations (e.g., community agencies); within each of the substantive chapters, policy sociology will be highlighted in boxes titled *Sociology in Practice*. *Public sociology* transmits sociological knowledge to nonacademic audiences; for example, information about same-sex parents may be presented to day care employees as part of their training package, or a sociologist might be interviewed on the evening news about a recent case of bullying. Public sociology will be highlighted in *Sociology in My Community* boxes. Finally, *private sociology* is the application of sociological knowledge to one's own personal life; at various points you will encounter boxes titled *Sociology in My Life*, in which you are asked to consider some aspect of your own experience within the context of the academic material that has been presented.

TIME TO REVIEW

- What is critical thinking?
- What are four of the different forms that sociology can take?

Sociology is the study of society, and the sociological imagination can be used to analyze any aspect of society, including the films, music, websites, and news events that are a part of your daily life. Sociology is everywhere around you—the difficulty you may come to face is learning to occasionally turn off your sociological imagination, so you can simply enjoy a movie or a song without analyzing it!

As you begin looking through the lens of sociology, remember Berger's (2008) message: *Things are not what they seem*.

SOCIOLOGY ONLINE

THE SOCIAL SCIENCE INFORMATION SYSTEM

There is a wealth of online resources available for sociology students. Here is one that you might find useful:

- The Social Science Information System (www.sociosite.net) includes resources on the lives, key ideas, and publications of dozens of sociological theorists. It also provides information on sociological journals, research centres, publishers, and more.

CHAPTER SUMMARY

LO¹ Describe the bidirectional nature of the relationship between individual choices and larger social forces.

Although we think of many of our own actions in terms of personal choice, those choices are embedded within and influenced by larger social forces. At the same time, the choices that we make can have an impact on the people around us and on society itself.

LO² Define "sociology" and identify the role of the sociological imagination.

Sociology is the systematic study of society, using the sociological imagination. The sociological imagination refers to the ability to see the interconnectedness of individual choices and experiences (i.e., the micro level) and larger social forces (i.e., the macro level).

LO³ Elaborate on the similarities and differences between sociology and other related disciplines.

Many disciplines, such as political science, history, and economics, study specific "parts" of society. Sociology is a more comprehensive discipline, in that all of those "parts" of society, and the interactions among them, are studied by sociologists. However, the social sciences and humanities have become increasingly characterized by interdisciplinarity and what some scholars call postdisciplinarity; this means that there are fewer distinctions between various disciplines in the 21st century than there were in the past.

LO⁴ Describe the role of theory in sociology and be able to contrast positivist, interpretive, and critical approaches.

Positivist theorizing has an interest in explanation and prediction, while interpretive theorizing has an interest in understanding ourselves and others, and critical theorizing has an interest in emancipation.

LO⁵ Distinguish between "theoretical frameworks" and "theories," and outline the core assumptions of the functionalist, conflict, interactionist, feminist, and postmodern perspectives.

Theoretical frameworks (or perspectives) are systematic sets of core assumptions, and ways of approaching the study of society. From this general set of assumptions, a multitude of narrower, specific theories emerge. According to the functionalist perspective, society comprises structures that fulfill various functions that are necessary to the smooth running of society. The conflict perspective proposes that society comprises a small group of powerful people at the top of society, and a large group of powerless people at the bottom. The interactionist perspective states that society is made of people who are engaged in continual communication; through these communications, significant others and the generalized other influence our thoughts and behaviours. Feminist perspectives are considerably diverse but have some shared assumptions: academic research has been androcentric; society is structured on the basis of gender; and research and theory must be intertwined with practice. Postmodern perspectives focus on the ways that society has changed in the post–World War II era. In its affirmative form, postmodernism deconstructs what is perceived as "knowledge"; poststructuralist approaches explore the relationship between knowledge and power.

LO⁶ Identify the role of critical thinking in "doing" sociology, and explain how to engage in critical thinking.

Critical thinking is utilized in the construction of sociological knowledge, but it is an important skill for everyone to use in their lives. Critical thinking means to learn to recognize valid information, even if you hold a different point of view from the one being postulated; think independently; suspend judgment; and consider implications and consequences.

LO⁷ Describe the four different types of sociology that are emphasized throughout the book.

Academic sociology is the theoretical and empirical research conducted by formally trained researchers. Policy sociology refers to the use of the results of theoretical and empirical research for policy development. Public sociology transmits sociological knowledge to nonacademic audiences. Private sociology refers to the application of sociological knowledge to one's own personal life.

RECOMMENDED READINGS

1. For an outstanding illustration of how something that seems as personal as tattooing is intertwined with macro-level forces, refer to: Atkinson, M. (2003). *Tattooed: Sociogenesis of a Body Art*. Toronto, ON: University of Toronto Press.
2. To explore the question of whether sociology is sufficiently "radical," see: Porter, M. (1995). You call yourself a sociologist and you've never been arrested. *Canadian Review of Sociology and Anthropology, 32*(4), 415.
3. To see the very first description of what the sociological imagination is all about, see: Mills, C. W. (1959/2000). The promise. In C. W. Mills, *The Sociological Imagination* (40th anniversary ed.) (pp. 3–24). New York: Oxford University Press.

FOR FURTHER REFLECTION

1. Using your sociological imagination, how has your choice of clothing today been influenced by larger social forces? In what ways might your choice of clothing also influence larger social forces?
2. Consider each of the five theoretical frameworks reviewed in this chapter. Do you consider each of those frameworks to be positivist, interpretive, or critical?
3. What current event or issue would you like to explore using the sociological imagination? Why do you think it would be useful to look at that issue through the lens of sociology?

REFERENCES

American Sociological Association. (2004). *An Invitation to Public Sociology*. Washington, DC: American Sociological Association.

Ashley, D., & Orenstein, D. M. (2001). *Sociological Theory: Classical Statements* (5th ed.). Boston, MA: Allyn & Bacon.

Association of Universities and Colleges of Canada. (2009, October 22). Media release: University enrolment up across Canada. Retrieved July 2, 2010, from www.aucc.ca

Association of Universities and Colleges of Canada. (2011). *The Value of a University Degree*. Retrieved March 7, 2011, from www.aucc.ca

Atkinson, M. (2003a). *Tattooed: Sociogenesis of a Body Art*. Toronto, ON: University of Toronto Press.

Atkinson, M. (2003b). The civilizing of resistance: Straightedge tattooing. *Deviant Behavior: An Interdisciplinary Journal, 24*, 197–220.

Bengston, V. L., Acock, A. C., Allen, K. R., Dilworth-Anderson, P., & Klein, D. M. (2005). Family research: Puzzle-building and puzzle solving. In V. L. Bengston, A. C. Acock, K. R. Allen, P. Dilworth-Anderson, and D. M. Klein (Eds.), *Sourcebook of Family Theory and Research*. Thousand Oaks, CA: Sage.

Bereska, T. M. (2011). *Deviance, Conformity, and Social Control in Canada* (3rd ed.). Toronto, ON: Pearson Education Canada.

Berger, P. (2008). Invitation to sociology. In R. Matson (Ed.), *The Spirit of Sociology: A Reader* (2nd ed.) (pp. 5–10). New York: Pearson Education.

Blumer, H. (1969). *Symbolic Interactionism: Perspective and Method*. Englewood Cliffs, NJ: Prentice-Hall.

Booth, W. (1992, September 5). They're "popping their corks" amid Andrew's wreckage; Victims are angry, survivors feel guilty—Miami has gone a bit crazy in the wake of hurricane, counsellors say. *Edmonton Journal*, p. C12.

Canadian Broadcasting Corporation (2010, January 18). *Aid to Haiti increases amid desperation*. Retrieved March 24, 2011, from www.cbc.ca

Clawson, D., et al. (Eds.). (2007). *Public Sociology: Fifteen Eminent Sociologists Debate Politics & the Profession in the Twenty-First Century*. Berkeley, CA: University of California Press.

Delanty, G. (2005). *Social Science: Philosophical and Methodological Foundations* (2nd ed.). Buckingham, UK: Open University Press.

Delanty, G. (2007). Sociology. In G. Ritzer (Ed.), *Blackwell Encyclopedia of Sociology*. Blackwell Publishing. Retrieved March 1, 2011, from www.blackwellreference.com

Downes, D., & Rock, P. (2003). *Understanding Deviance* (4th ed.). New York: Oxford University Press.

Durkheim, E. (1933). *The Division of Labour in Society*. New York: Free Press.

Durkheim, E. (1951). *Suicide*. New York: Free Press.

Engels, F. (1884/1972). *The Origin of the Family, Private Property and the State*. New York: Pathfinder.

Foucault, M. (1995). *Discipline and Punish: The Birth of the Prison* (2nd ed.). (A. Sheridan, Trans.). New York: Vintage Books. (Original work published 1977).

Foucault, M. (1980). *Power/Knowledge: Selected Interviews and Other Writings 1972–1977* (1st American ed.). (C. Gordon, L. Marshall, J. Mepham, & K. Super, Trans.). New York: Pantheon Books.

Foucault, M. (1978). *The History of Sexuality, Volume I: An Introduction*. New York: Vintage Books.

Hawkes, D., Senn, C. Y., & Thorn, C. (2004). Factors that influence attitudes toward women with tattoos. *Sex Roles, 50*(9/10), 593–604.

Lengermann, P., & Niebrugge, G. (2007a). Feminism. In G. Ritzer (Ed.), *Blackwell Encyclopedia of Sociology*. Blackwell Publishing. Retrieved March 4, 2011, from www.blackwellreference.com

Lengermann, P., & Niebrugge, G. (2007b). *Women Founders: Sociology and Social Theory 1830–1930* (2nd ed.). Long Grove, IL: Waveland Press.

Mayers, L. B., & Chiffriller, S. H. (2008). Body art (body piercing and tattooing) among undergraduate university students: "Then and Now." *Journal of Adolescent Health, 42,* 201–203.

McKee, M. (2002). Substance use and social and economic transition: The need for evidence. *International Journal of Drug Policy, 13,* 453–459.

Mead, G. H. (1934). *Mind, Self and Society*. Chicago, IL: University of Chicago Press.

Mills, C. W. (1959/2000). The promise. In C. W. Mills, *The Sociological Imagination* (40th anniversary ed.) (pp. 3–24). New York: Oxford University Press.

Nelson, A. (2010). *Gender in Canada* (4th ed.). Toronto, ON: Pearson Canada.

Newman, A. W., Wright, S. W., Wrenn, K. D., & Bernard, A. (2005). Should physicians have facial piercings? *Journal of General Internal Medicine, 20*(3), 213–218.

Nichols, L. T. (Ed.). (2007). *For Public Sociology: The Contemporary Debate*. New Brunswick, NJ: Transaction Publishers.

Parsons, T., & Bales, R. F. (1955). *Family: Socialization and Interaction Process*. Glencoe, IL: The Free Press.

Rosenau, P. M. (1992). *Postmodernism and the Social Sciences.* Princeton: Princeton University Press.

Statistics Canada. (2010, July 14). University enrolment. *The Daily*. Ottawa, ON: Author. Catalogue No. 11-001-XIE.

Statistics Canada. (2011). College enrolments, by registration status, program level, instructional program, both sexes. CANSIM Table 4770015.

Swami, V., & Furnham, A. (2007). Unattractive, promiscuous and heavy drinkers: Perceptions of women with tattoos. *Body Image, 4,* 343–352.

Taylor, C. (1985). *Human Agency and Language: Philosophical Papers 1*. New York: Cambridge University Press.

Urry, J. (2000). *Science Beyond Societies*. London: Routledge.

Weber, M. (1978). *Economy and Society*. Berkeley, CA: University of California Press.

White, J. M., & Klein, D. M. (2008). *Family Theories* (3rd ed.). Thousand Oaks, CA: Sage.

Sociological Research Methods

LEARNING OBJECTIVES AND OUTCOMES

After completing this chapter, students should be able to do the following:

LO1 Explain why sociological reasoning is important.

LO2 Differentiate between deductive and inductive approaches to reasoning.

LO3 Demonstrate an understanding of the goals of sociological research.

LO4 Identify steps for conducting sociological research.

LO5 Identify the ethical principles that underlie research involving human participants.

LO6 Differentiate between qualitative and quantitative research methods.

LO7 Describe the main use of each of the following research methods: experiments, surveys, interviews and focus groups, secondary analysis of existing data, and ethnographies.

LO[1] WHY SOCIOLOGICAL RESEARCH IS IMPORTANT

In Chapter 1, you learned that things are not always as they seem, and the importance of delving beneath the surface of an issue in order to see the complexities that are not readily apparent. As implied by the opening quotation, in this chapter you will find out how sociological research methods provide a systematic design for learning about real-life issues that are too complex to be left to common-sense assumptions. You will also learn why it is important to follow ethical guidelines when conducting research involving humans and how you can go about studying topics of interest to you.

COMMON SENSE AND SCIENTIFIC REASONING

There are a number of ways that we learn about things: from what our parents and elders teach us as early authority figures in our lives, to what we hear from teachers or the mass media, to what religion may offer us, to what our friends show us and to what we read about or experience for ourselves firsthand. Since the subject matter of sociology is society and we already know a lot about how our world works, sociology is often perceived to be nothing more than a body of common sense and personal opinions. For instance, consider this question: Does money buy happiness? As a student you already know it is difficult to balance all of the demands on your time such as going to class, studying for exams, working on assignments, spending time with family or friends, and, perhaps like many students, on top of that, trying to earn a living. Tens of thousands of dollars would certainly help to ease some of this burden. Using your "common sense," you might be inclined to assume that by virtue of giving *you* greater personal freedom, or making your life more comfortable or less stressful, money probably buys happiness in general. Don't assume! Your own common-sense ideas and observations may serve you well in your immediate experience, but scientific ways of knowing can better help you understand under what circumstances your ideas about everyday life may (or may not) be accurate in the wider context of society. With even a basic understanding of the scientific side of sociology, you will be equipped with skills that will help you to avoid some of the pitfalls of "common sense," and help you to find more accurate answers to life's questions, such as whether money can buy happiness.

SOCIOLOGY AS A SCIENTIFIC METHOD

Is sociology a "real" science, like biology and chemistry? Sociology is considered a social science because as a discipline, it seeks to enhance our knowledge of people and society using **empirical methods**. Sociological research methods are empirical because, through direct observation of the social world, they generate findings that can be verified by other members of the academic community. As with the natural sciences such as biology and chemistry, the social sciences also use *systematic procedures*. This means the steps taken to design and carry out research are organized, methodical, and standardized in such a way that they are recognized by other researchers. Generally, the procedures must be so clear that another researcher could replicate (i.e., exactly duplicate) the study based on how it is described in writing.

SOCIOLOGICAL REASONING

Recall from Chapter 1 that a theory is a set of principles or propositions intended to explain a fact or phenomenon. Empirical research and theory are intertwined, with each informing the other. In fact, it is its interrelationship with empirical research that distinguishes sociological theory from common-sense hunches, since theories are tested repeatedly and verified using scientific methods. The principal components of any theory are concepts. A **concept** is an abstract idea that is expressed as a word or phrase that represents some aspect of the social world, and is often used for categorizing things. For example, the concept "social class" helps us categorize Canadians into levels based on indicators such as income, and may be used in a theory explaining why certain groups are more likely to pursue a university education than others. Concepts used in research take the form of variables. A **variable** is a categorical concept that refers to properties of people or things that can differ and change over time or from situation to situation. An easy way to find a host of variables (as well as a potential partner!) is to visit an online dating site such as Plentyoffish.com. Just about everything contained in a single's ad is a variable (e.g., single, female, outgoing). "Single" refers to a category of the variable "marital status," where the possible categories are single, married, common-law, divorced, or widowed. "Female" refers to a category of the variable "sex," and "outgoing" is a personality trait.

LO² DEDUCTIVE AND INDUCTIVE REASONING

The scientific method entails a cyclical process that is ongoing and can include inductive or deductive forms of reasoning (see Figure 2.1). **Deductive reasoning** starts with theories and follows a "top-down" approach that ends with research findings. For example, based on existing theories, Symbaluk, Heth, Cameron, and Pierce (1997) hypothesized that people would endure the pain of exercise longer if they were first exposed to similar others who could last a long time at the same exercise. The researchers started with existing theories, developed a new hypothesis, and then carried out their own study as follows:

- *Prior Research Lesson 1:* Early research identifies social models (i.e., other people) as an important source of information (Bandura, Ross & Ross, 1963).

Empirical methods: Data collection that produces verifiable findings and is carried out using systematic procedures.

Concept: An abstract idea that is expressed as a word or phrase.

Variable: A categorical concept for properties of people or things that can differ and change.

Deductive reasoning: A theory-driven approach that typically concludes with generalizations based on research findings.

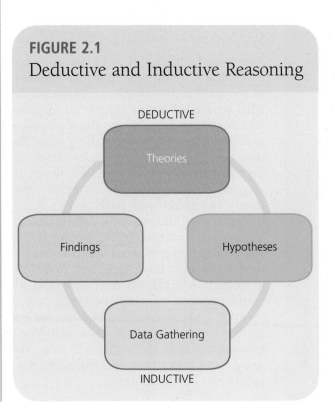

FIGURE 2.1

Deductive and Inductive Reasoning

DEDUCTIVE

Theories

Findings

Hypotheses

Data Gathering

INDUCTIVE

- *Prior Research Lesson 2:* Prior research shows that the ability to endure pain can be influenced. For example, money can motivate people to endure a painful exercise (Cabanac, 1986).
- *New Research Project:* Symbaluk, Heth, Cameron, and Pierce (1997) conducted an experiment to see whether social models could be used to influence pain endurance. The study (described in detail later under "Experiments: What's Causing This") found that watching "pain-*intolerant* models" hindered subsequent exercise performance while prior exposure to "pain-*tolerant* models" enhanced it.

Inductive reasoning, in contrast, is more data driven or "bottom-up," beginning with observations and ending in theory construction. For example, Vivar, Whyte, and McQueen (2010) were interested in learning more about the experiences of cancer survivors who find out their cancer has returned. The researchers began by talking to the cancer patients to see if any common experiences could be identified. Their inductive approach can be summarized as follows:

- *Data Gathering*: In-depth interviews with breast cancer survivors and care providers (i.e., family members and nurses) were used to learn about the experience of subsequent diagnoses of cancer (after initially being cancer-free for a period of time).
- *Findings*: Researchers found that the notion of "again" kept appearing in the participants' statements. "Again" represents both an initial realization that the cancer is back along with an understanding that treatment will be reinstated. They also found that for many of the participants, the shock of reoccurrence was reported to be more crippling than the first diagnosis (Vivar, Whyte & McQueen, 2010). Identifying patterns that appear in the statements from different participants helps to frame the experience in a way that lays the foundation for the development of a theory about the experience of cancer reoccurrence.

Inductive and deductive reasoning may take different paths to finding answers to questions about the social world, but both play a part in reaching the goals of sociological research.

LO³ GOALS OF SOCIOLOGICAL RESEARCH

Sociological research generally rests on one of four purposes: to explore, to describe, to explain, or to critically assess something of interest. The goal of **exploratory research** is to help us understand more about an area that is not well established. You can think of exploratory research as answering the questions: *What is it like to be X?* (where X is a category of people such as cancer survivors) or *What is X like?* (where X is a social phenomenon such as the reoccurrence of cancer). As another example, consider text messaging (i.e., a social phenomenon) or even people who text message (i.e., a category of people). Although text messaging is as common today as are lengthy lineups at Tim Hortons, the first Short Message Service (SMS) was sent only a few decades ago (i.e., in 1992) making this mode of communication ripe for exploratory research. Do you know who sent the very first text message or what it stated?

The goal of **descriptive research** is to note features and characteristics of a group, event, activity, or situation (Adler & Clark, 2003). Descriptive studies on text messaging, for example, can help us identify who (as a group) texts most frequently and can help us learn more about the symbols commonly used to represent the "lingo" of texts messages. **Explanatory research** is designed to clarify aspects

Source: photos.com

The first text message, sent by Neil Papworth in 1992, was the greeting "Merry Christmas" to his friend Richard Jarvis, who was attending a Christmas party at the time (Shannon, 2007).

Inductive reasoning: A data-driven approach that begins with observations and ends in theory construction.

Exploratory research: Explores an area of interest that very little is known about.

Descriptive research: Describes features and characteristics of a group, event, activity, or situation.

Explanatory research: Clarifies aspects of a particular social phenomenon.

Texting while driving increases the risk of motor vehicle accidents.

of a particular social phenomenon so we can better understand what kind of effects it has (or doesn't have). For example, "common-sense" notions that text messaging impairs users' ability to have face-to-face relationships and/or their ability to spell have not been borne out by research. Text messaging does not diminish relationships; rather, it supplements and even helps to maintain them (Bryant, Sanders-Jackson & Smallwood, 2006). Text messaging is also not associated with poor written language outcomes (Plester, Wood & Bell, 2008) or spelling ability (Varnhagen, McFall, Pugh, Routledge, Sumida-MacDonald & Kwong, 2010).

Finally, **critical research** may be conducted in order to help assess outcomes of some aspect of the social world (Adler & Clark, 2003). Few people could anticipate the relationship that is now becoming very apparent between the use of hand-held devices such as cell phones and motor vehicle accidents. The risk of a crash or near crash is 23.2 times greater for text-messaging drivers relative to nondistracted ones (Box, 2009). Critical research is especially important in the establishment of policies. For example, most Canadian provinces have now prohibited the use of hand-held cell phones and/or text messaging while driving (i.e., British Columbia, Alberta, Saskatchewan, Quebec, Ontario, Nova Scotia, Newfoundland/Labrador, P.E.I.) (Hands-Free Information, 2010).

Critical research:
Assesses outcomes of some aspect of the social world.

TIME TO REVIEW

- Why is sociology considered to be a science?
- What is a "concept"?
- How can inductive reasoning be distinguished from deductive reasoning?
- What are the main goals of sociological research?
- Which type of research is best suited to answering the question: *What is it like to be X?*

THE SOCIOLOGICAL RESEARCH PROCESS

If you choose to major in Sociology, at some point you will likely be required to conduct research of your own initiative. This section provides an overview of the steps you need to go through to carry out a research project.

LO⁴ STEPS FOR CONDUCTING SOCIOLOGICAL RESEARCH

1. *Research Question: What interests you?* The best place to start any research project is with a research question or issue you wish to learn more about. As an example, let's return to the question posed at the beginning of the chapter: *Does money buy happiness?*
2. *Literature Review: What is already known about this topic?* Sign into the library to find articles on your

area of interest using Sociology-related databases (e.g., SocINDEX or Sociological Abstracts). Databases help you find research-based articles on your topic when you insert key words such as "money" and "happiness." Research articles inform you about ways that money and happiness are defined, (e.g., yearly employment income and life satisfaction ratings), about studies that have already been conducted (e.g., cross-cultural comparisons and surveys of university students), and about some already known findings (e.g., money is related to happiness but the relationship is complex and depends in part on how happiness is defined).

3. *Narrowed Focus: How can you make your research interest doable?* A research question identifies an area of interest but is often too general or abstract to allow for empirical testing. One way to clarify your research question is by *operationalizing* the main variables. **Operationalization** refers to the process of defining variables in a precise manner that is measureable. Income is often measured as dollars earned but researchers still need to specify whether income refers to gross pay (what a person makes in total) or net pay (what employees end up receiving after taxes and other deductions are taken off). Additionally, is income defined as a weekly, a biweekly, a monthly, or an annual amount? Researchers strive to use measures that are reliable and valid. **Reliability** refers to the consistency of a measure. To show reliability, two different researchers should be able to come up with the exact same value for someone's employment income as stated on that person's pay stub. **Validity** means the measure is a good indicator of the intended concept. Employment income is a fairly valid measure of how much money a person makes but it may not be a good indicator of how much money a person has as someone could inherit money, win a lottery, have savings but no longer work for an income, receive a pension in lieu of an income, or have a very high debt load.

Once you've worked out the measurement issues, you can develop your research question into a hypothesis. A **hypothesis** is a testable research statement that includes at least two variables. For example, a hypothesis for the relationship between money and happiness might be: *People who net a yearly salary of $100,000 or more experience higher life satisfaction than people who take home $25,000 or less per year.* After you've defined your interest in a manner that is amenable to testing, you need to come up with a research design.

4. *Research Design: What is your proposed research design?* A **research design** is a detailed outline of all of the proposed components of a study. At a minimum, it should identify the research interest, whom or what will be studied, and how data collection will take place (i.e., a description of the research method as discussed in the latter part of this chapter). A research design usually contains other relevant details such as how ethical guidelines will be adhered to (more on this shortly) and, in some cases, how a data site will be accessed and left once the study is concluded.

5. *Data Collection: How will you collect your data?* The next stage involves collecting the data (or observations) that form the basis of a study. In a study on money and happiness, you might survey 100 people to obtain their income amounts and reported levels of life satisfaction.

6. *Data Analysis: What can you do with the data?* After you have the observations (or empirical facts), what do you do with them? Data in its raw form can be difficult to understand. **Data analysis** involves the compilation of observations into a format that helps us learn more about the research problem. The exact process depends on the research method used. If interviews are utilized, then data analysis involves carefully recording all of the verbal responses (*transcription*) and then going back over all the responses to identify common themes (a procedure called *indexing* or *coding*). For example, it may turn out that people with higher incomes say similar things about life satisfaction (e.g., they report having happy marriages and liking their jobs). If the data is numerical (as in the case of something such as happiness ratings), analysis is generally conducted using a statistical software package (e.g., SPSS) that provides descriptive information, such as a comparison of the life satisfaction ratings for high-income earners versus low-income earners. There are also software programs such as NVivo for nonnumeric unstructured data that can be

Operationalization: The process whereby variables are defined in a precise manner that is measureable.

Reliability: There is consistency in the measure for a variable of interest.

Validity: A measure is a good indicator of the intended concept.

Hypothesis: A testable research statement that includes at least two variables.

Research design: A detailed outline of all of the proposed components of a study.

Data analysis: Compilation of observations into a format that helps us learn more about the research problem.

used for coding the content of interview responses into categories and themes (Bazeley, 2007).

7. *Draw Conclusions: What does the data tell you?* Once the data is collected and analyzed, researchers *draw conclusions* by revisiting their original research question. Data on money and happiness helps us better appreciate how complex the relationship is. A study using the first Gallup World Poll based on a representative sample of people from 132 countries, for example, tells us that money does buy some degree of happiness since increases in income are associated with increases in life satisfaction; however, there is a declining marginal effect of income on subjective well-being. This means money is far more important to those who don't have it. For example, how unhappy might you be if you were not able to buy a cup of coffee or a piece of pizza, or attend a yoga class or play recreational hockey? Essentially, once all of our basic needs for things such as adequate food, shelter, clothing, living expenses, and even some of the extras like entertainment are met, increasingly greater amounts of income begin to play a lesser role in our overall calculation of happiness compared to nonmonetary things such as respect, autonomy, social support, and having a fulfilling job (Diener, Ng, Harter & Arora, 2010). But this still doesn't negate the link between money and happiness, since on a macro level, the rich tend to be happier than the poor, and those in wealthier countries report greater levels of happiness than those in developing ones. In addition, on a more micro level, people have very different ideas about what constitutes personal happiness. You will learn more about the role of wealth in subsequent chapters, as those who make more money benefit substantially (e.g., they have higher educational attainment, more fulfilling jobs, better social supports, superior health, and longer life expectancies). Sociological research does not always prove something so much as it helps us better *understand* it.

8. *Report Findings: How can you share the findings?* A research process concludes with a *dissemination of findings*. In order to further knowledge in an area of interest, researchers may present their findings at academic conferences or write up articles about their studies for publication in peer-reviewed journals such as the *Canadian Journal of Sociology*. Each subsequent study and article adds another dimension of knowledge to the general area of interest.

A research project may vary slightly from the process described herein depending on the exact

FIGURE 2.2
Steps in a Research Process

1. Research Question
2. Literature Review
3. Narrowed Focus
4. Research Design
5. Data Collection
6. Data Analysis
7. Draw Conclusions
8. Report Findings

nature of the issue, the type of design selected, and the approach followed. For example, qualitative approaches utilize broad research questions and therefore do not operationalize variables or test specific hypotheses. Nonetheless, you can use these eight steps as a starting framework for any project as summarized in Figure 2.2.

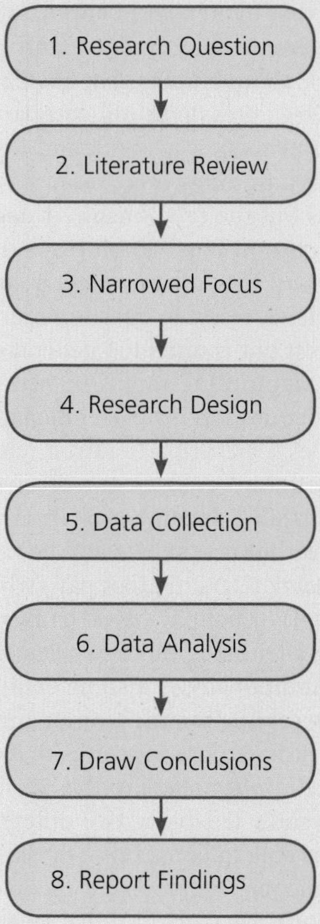

TIME TO REVIEW

- What are the eight main steps in a research process?
- What do sociologists mean when they claim a measure is "reliable"?
- What sorts of information should you include in a research design?

THE IMPORTANCE OF ETHICS IN RESEARCH

HUMAN MISTREATMENT

History is replete with examples of how people have been mistreated in a variety of medical, military, and research contexts. For instance, atrocious medical experiments were conducted in Germany on men, women, and even children who were prisoners of war in the Nazi era (1933–1945). In a well-known case, about 1,500 sets of twin children were taken against their will to a physician named Josef Mengele (also known as the "Angel of Death") in Auschwitz, where they were subjected to abusive procedures and surgeries (e.g., removal of organs, attempts to change eye colour, blood transfusions, injections of germs), often without the aid of an anesthetic and generally resulting in death (Lagnado & Dekel, 1991). Although Mengele fled to South America and managed to evade capture, many other physicians, military officials, and political leaders ended up being tried in Nuremburg for their abusive actions and were eventually sentenced to death or long prison terms. Another outcome of the trials was the development of the Nuremberg Code, the first set of directives for human experimentation that detailed the importance of obtaining prior consent, protecting participants from harm, and acknowledging subjects' right to end participation (National Institutes of Health, 2011).

The unethical treatment of humans extends beyond medical and military contexts to research in the social sciences as evidenced by a series of experiments on obedience to authority conducted by Stanley Milgram in the 1960s. In these experiments, participants believed they were giving harmful electric shocks to another participant, and were told by the researcher that it was essential that they continue. Milgram's (1963) procedures were highly criticized for making participants undergo unnecessary and unreasonable amounts of psychological harm (e.g., see Baumrind, 1964). Similarly, Philip Zimbardo's simulated prison experiment that took place in 1971 also caused harm, in this case to college students, who in their roles as "prisoners," suffered physical and psychological distress for several days. Even those serving as "guards" suffered in the knowledge that they were behaving in sadistic ways toward fellow students (i.e., prisoners). Seeing what was happening, Zimbardo himself finally halted the study. For more information on the Stanford Prison Experiment and to view a slide show, you can visit the home page at www.prisonexp.org.

THE TRI-COUNCIL POLICY STATEMENT

In an effort to reclaim public confidence, promote research with humans, and, at the same time, defend the dignity of those who serve as participants, Canada's three federal research agencies—the Canadian Institutes of Health Research (CIHR), Natural Sciences and Engineering Research Council of Canada (NSERC), and the Social Sciences and Humanities Research Council of Canada (SSHRC)—jointly adopted the Tri-Council Policy Statement: Ethical Conduct for Research Involving Humans (TCPS) in 1998. The TCPS outlines ethical principles and includes a set of guidelines that regulate research carried out by sociologists and researchers from other disciplines. An expanded second edition of the TCPS (referred to as the TCPS 2) was released in 2010 and now serves as the official policy for these agencies.[2] Universities throughout Canada have also implemented the TCPS 2 as the basis for their own policies on research involving human participants.

LO⁵ ETHICAL CONDUCT FOR RESEARCH INVOLVING HUMANS

The underlying value of the TCPS 2 is the need to respect human dignity, and this is outlined as three main principles: respect for persons, concern for welfare, and justice (Canadian Institutes of Health Research, Natural Sciences and Engineering Council of Canada & Social Sciences and Humanities Research Council of Canada, 2010).

1. *Respect for Persons.* Respect for persons is a principle that "recognizes the intrinsic value of human beings and the respect and consideration they are due" (Canadian Institutes of Health Research, Natural Sciences and Engineering Council of Canada & Social Sciences and Humanities Research Council of Canada, 2010, p. 8). This means research participants are granted "autonomy" or the ability to decide whether and how they will be involved in research. Voluntary participation or consent is generally obtained from research participants ahead of time as a means for respecting autonomy. However, in order for consent to be valid, the participant must be capable of freely giving that consent and he or she must be aware that consent is ongoing and can be withdrawn at any time without penalty. Someone who is serving time in jail, for example, may be informed that participation is purely voluntary but that person may believe, instead, that noncompliance will have a negative impact on obtaining early parole. Is that person free to provide informed consent to take part in a study? The onus is on the researcher to protect those who may have limited or impaired autonomy. Voluntary participation is usually secured via a signed consent form that details what the study is about, what participation entails, what the risks and benefits of participation are, and how anonymity and confidentiality are to be maintained. Consent for participation cannot be obtained from minors (akin to parents providing written permission for their children to partake in field trips or have their pictures taken at school). An early study by Laud Humphreys (1975) has been described as somewhat of an ethical nightmare in its failure to obtain informed consent from men who unknowingly became research participants after having sexual relations with other men in public washrooms. The researcher pretended to be part of the action, serving as a voyeur lookout, only to later follow the partakers to their vehicles to obtain their licence plate information. Almost a year later, this information was traced to home addresses wherein the researcher showed up to conduct interviews with the men about their prior sexual behaviours! Usually in a study anonymity and confidentiality are maintained.

   Anonymity exists if a researcher cannot link any individual response to a participant. Participants are anonymous when their names are left off questionnaires (like you are when you complete an instructor evaluation for a course). *Confidentiality* has to do with agreements pertaining to what will be done with the information once it is collected (Sieber, 1992). Confidentiality is upheld when a participant is not identifiable in any way to the public. A researcher may know the identity of an interviewee, for example, but the participant's name would not be included in any of the published findings. Similarly, no information would be released that might allow others to infer the identity of the respondent, such as a job description at a company where there was only one person in a particular role (e.g., the director of sales). In rare cases, participants cannot be informed of all of the essential details at the time of consent. For example, suppose a researcher is interested in whether students would be willing to loan their notes to a fellow student who claimed he missed class due to a work emergency. Disclosing this information ahead of time to obtain consent would render students more likely to help and it would negate the naturalism of the helping behaviour that is the focus of the study. **Debriefing,** or the later disclosure of all relevant details, is mandatory in cases where participants cannot be told all of the information ahead of time. Debriefing should occur as soon as possible and be treated as a "two-way educational process" wherein participants can get further clarification of any aspect of the study (Eyde, 2000, p. 61).

2. *Concern for welfare.* The well-being of research participants is also a foundational ethical principle and researchers need to carefully consider ways to design studies to minimize the potential for harm. This is not always easy to anticipate in advance. While we can appreciate how a physical activity, such as doing push-ups, might lead to possible injury, it isn't always clear how someone might be affected psychologically (e.g., by something he or she disclosed during an interview, by something an experimenter said, or by one's own performance results, etc.). There are also broader social, economic, and cultural issues that may need to be taken into consideration. For example, the deep

Debriefing: The later disclosure of all relevant details in cases where research participants cannot be told all of the information ahead of time.

roots of internal colonialism have had profound effects on Aboriginal cultures. In addition, Aboriginal peoples tend to have a collective or group orientation rather than an individual one. Hence, the well-being of a research participant may extend beyond one person to an entire community.[3]

3. *Justice.* Finally, ethical principles include the prioritization of justice. Justice in this sense means that people will be treated fairly and equitably, and with respect. In some cases, we may wish to conduct research using vulnerable groups such as prison populations (especially if we want to learn more about people who have been labelled as criminals, crime processes, or the criminal justice system), children (e.g., in order to examine specific developmental phases in intelligence or socialization), and certain other social groups (e.g., many Aboriginal cultures are plagued by high levels of school dropout rates, suicide, and/or violence). In such cases, it may be necessary to take additional caution in securing consent, explaining the nature and purpose of the study, and ensuring that safeguards are built into the study to minimize potential harm and uphold dignity.

To familiarize yourself with the guidelines for conducting research with humans, try working your way through the introductory tutorial (TPCS 2 Tutorial) provided at the Government of Canada's Interagency Advisory Panel on Research Ethics site located at www.pre.ethics.gc.ca.

TIME TO REVIEW

- What are the three main principles that form the basis of the need to respect human dignity as outlined by the Tri-Council Policy Statement: Ethical Conduct for Research Involving Humans (2010)?
- What is the difference between anonymity and confidentiality as they relate to the ethical treatment of human research participants?

LO[6] QUALITATIVE AND QUANTITATIVE METHODS

Sociologists distinguish between two main approaches to research depending on the underlying purpose of the research. In the case of *qualitative methods*, the purpose is to better understand or describe the nature (i.e., "quality") of some phenomenon using inductive reasoning, whereas *quantitative methods* are focused on counting things or testing hypotheses in order to

"quantify" or explain something using deductive reasoning. The difference in methods is reflected in the techniques most relevant to the two approaches. For example, quantitative researchers might want to learn more about whether ratings of instruction (i.e., teaching evaluations) should be made public at postsecondary institutions. The researchers could use a survey to test a number of hypotheses including one that predicts students will be in favour of published ratings while faculty will be opposed. Researchers might also ask instructors to rate how they feel about some of the potential disadvantages or have students rate how they feel about certain perceived benefits of published ratings (e.g., see Howell & Symbaluk, 2001). Note that a quantitative researcher already knows what she or he is looking for and uses a technique that specifically addresses the hypothesis that has been developed. A qualitative researcher, on the other hand, might be interested in finding out more about students' perceptions of instructors more generally. With this broader, more inclusive research question in mind, the qualitative researcher might interview students to learn more about what they think of their instructors and the classes they take. Maybe particular themes emerge in the feedback, such as a tendency to comment about instructor knowledge, organization, and appearance. Further in-depth interviews with students might help us better understand the nature of the comments. Is it more important to have an organized instructor or a knowledgeable one? What role does appearance play in how students perceive instructors?

Another difference between qualitative and quantitative methods has to do with how the data is collected and what the data consists of. A qualitative researcher is likely to be the research instrument that collects data (e.g., as an interviewer who gathers opinions in the form of statements) whereas a quantitative researcher is likely to utilize some kind of instrument like a questionnaire (to obtain opinions in the form of ratings such as levels of agreement) or some other measurement device (like a stopwatch to time endurance for an exercise). Quantitative research generates numerical data that is amenable to statistical analysis. Since quantitative approaches are deductive in nature, the research process tends to be linear, with data collection followed by data analysis. Qualitative research, in contrast, follows an inductive approach that involves the gathering of observations in the form of statements or images. The relationship between data collection and data analysis is more circular; while collecting the data, the researcher may make note of an interesting phenomenon (e.g., the interviewee brings up a point that the researcher hadn't thought of), and then the researcher may integrate that point into subsequent interviews with remaining participants. Qualitative approaches sometimes include **triangulation** or the use of multiple data-gathering techniques within the same study (e.g., participant observation, interviews, and focus groups) in order to verify and substantiate the findings (e.g., a participant says something in an interview that is also brought up by members of a focus group and was earlier observed by the researcher).

Although it is common practice to determine in advance whether you are using a more qualitative or quantitative approach, it is generally the goals of the research interest (e.g., an exploration into the experiences of cancer survivors or an account of student and faculty views), the type of reasoning employed (e.g., inductive or deductive), or some other factor (e.g., the availability of existing data or willingness of participants) that are the determinants of the exact method(s) used. In the next section you will learn about the specific research techniques characteristic of quantitative and qualitative methods.

TIME TO REVIEW

- How does the purpose of quantitative methods differ from that of qualitative methods?
- What are some of the other main differences between qualitative and quantitative methods?

LO⁷ SOCIOLOGICAL RESEARCH METHODS

Triangulation: The use of multiple data-gathering techniques within the same study.

Experiment: A deductive research method that is used to test a hypothesis through the use of a carefully controlled environment and random assignment to conditions.

Independent variable: The presumed cause or variable that is manipulated in an experiment.

Control group: Participants in an experiment who are not exposed to the independent variable.

EXPERIMENTS: WHAT IS CAUSING THIS?

Using a quantitative approach, an **experiment** is a deductive research method that is used to test a hypothesis through the use of a carefully controlled environment and random assignment to conditions. Although used only infrequently in sociology, experiments typically take place in a laboratory. The notion of a lab often conjures up images of scientists in white coats and people working with glass beakers and electron microscopes. However, in the social sciences, *any* controlled environment (such as a classroom or an office) can be considered a laboratory. For example, in Symbaluk, Heth, Cameron, and Pierce's (1997) study on pain endurance, the lab was a seminar room at the University of Alberta in which participants completed an isometric quadriceps exercise. This exercise involved sitting against a wall without a seat, legs positioned at a 90 degree angle, which causes lactic acid to build up in the thigh muscles and produces pain. The hallmark of experimental designs is the ability to test cause–effect relationships. This is possible due to the careful control over the environment (which rules out extraneous, or unintended, variables that could affect behaviour, such as distracting noises), and the random assignment to conditions (which eliminates any individual differences that may be present within participants prior to completing the study). For example, some people are naturally more athletic than others. Random assignment spreads a relatively even mix of athletic and nonathletic participants across all of the conditions.

In an experiment at least one variable is manipulated in order to see what kind of effect it produces. An **independent variable** is the presumed cause or the variable that is manipulated in an experiment. In Symbaluk and colleagues' (1997) study, social modelling of pain was one of the independent variables. In this case, social modelling took the form of similar others who demonstrated how to perform an isometric quadriceps exercise. Participants were randomly exposed to a pain-tolerant social model, a pain-intolerant social model, or a control group social model prior to completing the exercise. There were three versions of the same tape, which included general instructions about the study such as how to rate things like pain. The different versions of the videotape constituted the experimental manipulation (i.e., the independent variable). In each version, a person demonstrating the exercise was believed to be a previous participant but the person was actually a social model who either appeared to be pain *intolerant* (i.e., dropped a switch that stopped a timer indicating the first sensation of pain at about 10 seconds into the exercise, displayed signs of pain throughout the exercise such as moaning and rubbing his legs, and ended early), or was pain *tolerant* (indicated feeling the first instance of pain later on and displayed similar signs of pain during the exercise but lasted much longer).

There was also a **control group**, which refers to a condition that includes subjects who are not exposed to the independent variable. Participants in this condition received the same instructions via a videotape except there was no information on the anticipated experience of pain or how long the social model lasted (instead, they saw a freeze-framed social model on the screen in the isometric sitting position and a voiceover simply reiterated how to complete the exercise). The control condition helps establish what would normally happen in the absence of the independent variable (i.e., how long the average person lasts at isometric sitting).

The **dependent variable** is the outcome or variable that is measured in an experiment. In this case, pain endurance was the dependent variable and it was measured in minutes and seconds. As it turned out, participants who were exposed to the tolerant model lasted significantly longer than those in the control and intolerant conditions (Symbaluk, Heth, Cameron & Pierce, 1997). Note that exposure to a tolerant model increased pain endurance and exposure to a pain-intolerant model lessoned the ability to withstand pain. Since the environment was carefully controlled (e.g., there was only one participant in the room at the time, the assistant monitoring the exercise did not know what the research hypothesis was or which condition the participant was assigned to, etc.), the only possible influence on the outcome was exposure to social models (the independent variable).

STRENGTHS AND LIMITATIONS OF EXPERIMENTS

The greatest advantage of an experimental design is that it allows for tests of causality. Robust effects can often be established even with fairly small numbers of participants and the findings are generally definitive. The most serious limitation of this method is artificiality. Rarely can you ever study the precise real-life concepts or processes you wish to learn more about in a highly controlled lab. For example, suppose you are interested in severe acts of violence committed against strangers. It is unethical and impractical to imagine you will be able to control the variable you are most interested in. Instead, you might have to develop a simulated environment such as an opportunity to enact violence against a stranger in a video game. But will this really tell you about your original research interest? Simulated acts of violence are clearly not the same as actual ones; for example, participants may be much more willing to commit acts of simulated violence against fake video game opponents than they would be to ever harm someone in real life. To overcome the artificial nature of a lab, which produces findings that are difficult to generalize the real world, researchers sometimes opt for field experimentation.

Field experiments are experimental designs that are constructed in real-life settings where the variables of interest are more likely to occur naturally. However, the closer to the real world the research setting is, the less able the researcher is to control the environment and factors other than the independent variable can have implications for the findings (e.g., the weather might influence how participants behave or persons other than the participants might enter the field of study).

SURVEYS: WHAT IS YOUR OPINION ON THIS?

Surveys are as common in social science research as they are in everyday life. You have probably completed some kind of survey by filling out a form on customer service in a restaurant, by giving opinions over the phone to someone collecting views on an issue such as the health care system, or by rating instructors and classes you have taken as part of a larger process of faculty evaluation that occurs in most postsecondary institutions. A **survey** is a quantitative research method used to gather opinions or other details about topics of interest from the perspective of respondents using a questionnaire.

A *questionnaire* is an instrument that typically contains a series of close-ended or "forced-choice" questions with prompts participants to choose from a list of answers provided. This is similar to what you encounter on a multiple-choice exam. Answers are later coded and computed into percentages and other group statistics. For example, Roberts, Crutcher, and Verbrugge (2007) examined Canadians' attitudes toward the sentencing of convicted criminals (i.e., sentence severity, the purposes of sentencing, and mandatory sentences of imprisonment). In terms of sentence severity, people were asked if they felt sentences were "too lenient," "about right," "too strict," or "don't know." Consistent with findings from earlier studies, the majority (i.e., 74 percent) of participants claimed that sentence severity was too lenient. This is probably why some politicians, while on the campaign trail, claim they will be tougher on crime if they are elected.

Questionnaires can be administered in a number of ways, including in person or over the telephone, facilitated by a researcher or an assistant. They can also be self-administered as in the case of mail-outs and questionnaires completed

> **Dependent variable:** The outcome or variable that is measured in an experiment.
>
> **Survey:** A method of gathering opinions using a questionnaire.

FIGURE 2.3
An Important Note to Students

A common exam error made by students is to confuse random assignment with random selection. Try to remember that random assignment has to do with how participants are put into the conditions of an experiment whereas random selection refers to how participants are obtained primarily for use in survey research.

online. In a face-to-face or telephone survey, the person administering the survey asks questions of another (the respondent) and records the answers. **Respondents** are persons who consent to provide answers to surveys. A researcher sometimes tries to select a **representative sample** of respondents who comprise a small group that closely resemble the population of interest. For instance, if the population of interest is a university's student body, which consists of 18,000 people, a representative sample might include 100 randomly selected students, most who attend full-time days, some who attend part-time days, and some who take classes on weekends and evenings. *Random selection* means that every person in the population of interest has an equal chance of selection (refer to Figure 2.3). A registrar's office, for example, may contain a listing of all of the students who are currently enrolled in at least one course at a particular university. Using a software program or other suitable method (such as putting every name into a container from which a name is drawn one at a time until 100 are obtained), the researcher could end up with a randomly selected representative sample of students. In some cases, the population of interest is not fully identifiable (as might be the case if you were interested in people who commit certain crimes, since many crimes go unreported and even those that are reported may not result in convictions). When it is not practical or even possible to obtain a representative sample that is randomly selected, researchers may opt for a *sample of convenience*. For example, a researcher interested in the area of sexual offending might administer a questionnaire to a specific group of inmates in a particular maximum security facility who are undergoing treatment for sexual assault.

Respondents: Persons who consent to provide survey answers.

Representative sample: A group that closely approximates the population of interest.

STRENGTHS AND LIMITATIONS OF SURVEY RESEARCH

Survey methods are commonly used and they have fairly high response rates. Survey approaches are great for collecting a lot of rich, detailed information in a relatively short period of time. If each question represents a variable of interest, think about how many relationships can later be examined from answers given on a ten-page questionnaire. Face-to-face and telephone surveys are especially useful in situations where establishing rapport may be helpful in acquiring participants or where questions require further clarification (i.e., lack of understanding may be evident in facial expressions or tone of voice used by a respondent). Self-administered surveys make it easy to utilize a wide range of respondents (e.g., known offenders attending a local program as part of their sentencing might consent to complete a questionnaire or Internet users from all over the world might consent to participate in an online questionnaire). Due to the ease with which anonymity can be accomplished, surveys are also a good method for obtaining information on very sensitive subjects (e.g., crimes or sexual behaviour).

The biggest limitation of surveys is that is difficult to verify the accuracy of the findings, and some respondents might lie or otherwise misrepresent the truth (e.g., exaggerate, forget things, or omit important information). Another potential problem begins with the wording of a survey. With the exception of face-to-face and telephone surveys wherein a researcher may get the opportunity to clarify a question that has been posed, the instructions and wording on a questionnaire (including even the response categories in most cases) are fixed. If respondents cannot properly follow the directions for how to complete the questionnaire, if they cannot understand certain questions, if some questions are poorly worded, or if response categories don't closely approximate the actual experiences and views of respondents, the responses obtained may not be valid measures of the concepts under investigation.

INTERVIEWS: WHAT DO YOU THINK ABOUT THIS?

Qualitative methods frequently include the use of interviews. An **interview** is a verbal question-and-answer technique used to gather rich, detailed, firsthand information about a phenomenon of interest. For example, a researcher interested in video gaming might ask questions about frequency or duration of use, preferred type of games, and game features that a player likes or dislikes. Interviews range in structure from highly standardized to completely unstandardized. A *standardized* or very structured interview follows a set format of predetermined questions with no additional questions or clarification allowed. In this case, the interviewer reads a question, waits for the response, and records it (e.g., "When was the last time you played a video game?" Pause. The person says "last week" and the interviewer goes on to the next question: "What type of game was that?"). A standardized interview is similar to a face-to-face survey technique, except in the case of an interview, the respondent gives whatever answer he or she perceives to be appropriate, rather than responding in a limited-choice fashion imposed by most questionnaires. Hence, the answer to "What type of game was that?" as part of an interview could be "a video game," "a shooting game," a "war game" or "Modern Warfare 2" (and the researcher will later figure out how to code that information), whereas a person completing a survey usually chooses from among a range of responses provided (e.g., "Which of the following best describes the kind of game you last played: An action game, a shooter game, or an adventure game?").

An *unstandardized* interview has no set format so the order or wording of questions can be modified and the interviewer can add, change, or delete items as warranted by the process (Berg, 2009). In this case, an interviewer might begin with something very open-ended and subjective like "Can you tell me about your experience with video gaming?" The nature of the response received, then, will largely determine what sort of question the interviewer will pose next (e.g., a response like "Well, I'm currently addicted to Halo" might be followed

by a question such as "Why do you consider yourself addicted to that particular game?"). Semistandardized interviews fall somewhere between these two versions and allow for some clarification of items and flexibility in the order and wording of questions.

USE OF FOCUS GROUPS: WHAT ARE YOUR VIEWS ON THIS?

Another way to conduct interviews is using *focus groups* of about 8-12 participants. Focus groups are especially useful for gathering information at one time from a small group that shares some trait that is relevant to the topic of interest. For example, a researcher might include students in a focus group designed to learn more about effective study habits, instructors in a focus group on best teaching practices, or recently retired employees to learn more about disengagement from work roles. In focus groups, the interviewer is usually called a *moderator*. A moderator is responsible for introducing the purpose of the focus group (e.g., what the research interest is, what information is being sought, and what is expected of participants), outlining the rules for how the interview session will unfold (e.g., a question might be asked aloud and then participants may be asked to respond in a particular order, one at a time), managing short question-and-answer sessions (e.g., coaching to ensure that each participant gets a chance to speak and that others do not interrupt), and dealing with any unforeseen issues that might arise (e.g., someone might appear upset by something that is said).

STRENGTHS AND LIMITATIONS OF INTERVIEWS

Like surveys, interviews also generate high response rates but they have an added advantage over questionnaires in that answers provided better reflect the respondents' actual views. In addition, confusing questions can be clarified during an interview to further increase the validity of responses. However, interviewing is a two-way process and, as such, responses can be greatly affected by a number of considerations pertaining to both the interviewer and the interviewee. For example, how comfortable is the interviewee with the interviewer? How does the interviewee feel about the subject matter, and how much of her or his time is the interviewee willing to contribute to the research project? Establishing good rapport with a participant is

> **Interview:** A verbal question-and-answer technique used for obtaining information on a topic of interest.

essential and may be accomplished using extra questions that are designed to put the respondent at ease and get him or her talking (e.g., "Have you heard about the new video game that was just released?"). In addition, an interviewer needs to be mindful about how questions are communicated and how information is elicited from the interviewee (e.g., by speaking at a level that is appropriate to the respondent's educational attainment and discussing issues in terms that can be readily understood by the interviewee).

The order of questions is also important. It is best to begin an interview with a few easy-to-answer questions that are less central to the research such as background information (e.g., "Can you please tell me how old you are," "What do you do for a living?" etc.). Sensitive questions should come later in the interview once rapport is established. In some cases, interviewers use probe questions such as "Can you tell me more about that?" or "And then what happened?" to try to obtain additional information. Subsequent questions may develop and change as a result of feedback from the respondent. This is why consent to participate is actually an ongoing social contract and an especially important ethical concern when utilizing interview methods.

Secondary analysis of existing data: A research method used to examine information on a topic of interest that was originally collected by someone other than the researcher for an unrelated purpose.

SECONDARY DATA ANALYSIS: WHAT DOES THIS TELL ME?

Secondary analysis of existing data (also known as *archival analysis*) is a research method used to examine information on a topic of interest that was originally collected by someone other than the researcher for an unrelated purpose. Data sources already exist everywhere: in the information contained in printed materials such as newspaper articles,

Graffiti can be considered a form of artistic expression, a type of vandalism, and even a source of data for sociologists.

Source: Chris Bradshaw/Shutterstock

reports, books, novels, diaries, letters, children's stories, and magazines; in electronic format found on the Internet in databases, on home pages, and on websites; in the graffiti found on urban walls; and in what Webb, Campbell, Schwartz, and Sechrest (2000) call the "physical traces" that people leave behind via their impact on the environment.

Secondary analysis is often conducted using existing statistics from government agencies. Statistics Canada is Canada's national statistical agency, which is legislated to provide statistical information on Canada's population, resources, economy, society, and culture as a whole as well as for each province and territory (Statistics Canada, 2010). Statistics Canada collects information from a representative sample of Canadians every five years using a Census. Statistics Canada also regularly receives information from a number of individual agencies including those found in the criminal justice, health care, and education systems. Information is tabulated in aggregate (grouped) format and presented in reports that contain statistical information, tables, and graphs. In addition to informing Canadians about their country, these reports help the government and other stakeholders to analyze performance, develop policies and programs, and determine how best to allocate resources. Statistics Canada has a wealth of information to share about a range of topics including Aboriginal peoples, business, education and training, crime and justice, families, households, and housing, among others.

Content analysis is a secondary analysis technique used to systematically examine messages contained in text or portrayed in images. For example, researchers looked at newspaper articles to better understand how public health risks of Mad Cow Disease in Alberta in 2003 and E. coli water contamination in Ontario in 2000 were portrayed in the Canadian media following an initial outbreak. Results indicated that how an incident is reported in the first ten days "frames" subsequent media coverage (Boyd, Jardine & Driedger, 2009; Driedger, Jardine, Boyd & Mistry, 2009). Researchers also used content analysis to examine unsafe-driving messages contained in 200 Canadian print and television advertisements. One study revealed that 18 percent of all ads, and especially television ads, include unsafe or aggressive driving practices, which suggests a need for government-imposed regulation (Watson, Lavack, Rudin-Brown, Burns & Mintz, 2010). Content analysis is an especially well-established technique for examining how men and women are portrayed in the media. A recent study by Bemiller and Schneider (2010) examined the sexist nature of 153 Internet jokes and uncovered indicators of *misogyny*, a concept that refers to the hatred of women or girls and is linked to the devaluing of females and the sanctioning of aggression toward them.

STRENGTHS AND LIMITATIONS OF SECONDARY ANALYSES

Existing data is already collected and available so it automatically saves a researcher many long hours and probably dollars that would otherwise be spent collecting firsthand data. In addition to convenience, secondary analysis of existing data is one of the few methods that is nonreactive or unobtrusive, meaning it does not involve gathering information directly from people whose responses may be affected by the very fact that they are taking part in a study (e.g., a respondent might falsely state that she does not smoke in order to be perceived more favourably by the interviewer). The main drawback to this method is that the data was collected for a purpose other than the intended study, so it may be biased or incomplete (i.e., missing variables of interest). This is especially likely when newspaper articles that are written from a particular perspective for a specific audience are later used in content analysis. Because the researcher has no control over how the data was collected in the first place, it is difficult to verify the accuracy of the information and, in the case of existing statistics, determine how variables were originally measured, collected, and coded.

ETHNOGRAPHY: WHAT IS IT LIKE IN THERE/DOING THAT?

Since most qualitative approaches try to get at the nature and meaning of events, it only makes sense that some methods are needed for data gathering in natural settings. **Ethnography** is the broad term for various forms of field work designed to gather data in real-world environments (Willis, 2007). In some cases, field work is carried out in order to assess a social problem and bring about change.

> **Content analysis:** A secondary analysis technique used to systematically examine messages contained in text or portrayed in images.
>
> **Ethnography:** Field work designed to gather data in real-world environments.

ACTION RESEARCH: HOW CAN WE FIX THIS?

Action research is a field method for pursuing change while studying a social system such as a school or a community. An instructor, for example, might wish to address a research question such as "How can I modify my teaching approach to encourage more student participation in class?" The instructor might start by noting the current level of participation, then identify different approaches (e.g., use of debates, student-led discussions, and guest presentations), try them out in different classes, see which one elicited the most student engagement, and then look for ways to utilize this technique more often in future classes. Action research is a systematic process that begins with observations, includes some form of action or intervention, and then entails subsequent evaluation to determine whether the approach was beneficial. Action research in a wider community context tends to be problem focused and typically involves a period of assessment followed by planning and interventions, community participation, and forms of monitoring and evaluation in order to address social problems particular to that system (e.g., high levels of violence or drug and alcohol abuse) (Jackson & Verberg, 2007).

Action research: A field method for pursuing change while studying a social system.

Systematic observation: A naturalistic but nonparticipatory method for collecting data on a social group or process.

Participant observation: A naturalistic method for collecting systematic data while taking part in a social group or process.

SYSTEMATIC AND PARTICIPANT OBSERVATION: WHAT IS HAPPENING?

In a **systematic observation**, a researcher directly observes a social group or process but does not interact with the participants. Observational research is used by both qualitative and quantitative researchers and can take place anywhere a group of interest is located. For example, if a researcher was interested in learning more about the play stage of development, a day care facility or structured play group might be an appropriate place for the observation of children engaged in play. Another way to conduct qualitative research in the field is through the use of participant observation. In **participant observation**, a researcher collects systematic observations while taking part in the activities of the group being observed. Some groups and activities are not particularly amenable to investigation by outsiders. For example, members of an outlaw motorcycle gang are generally unwilling to allow nonmembers access to their business deals or initiation rituals.

Wolfe's study on the Rebels biker group can be considered a case study. A *case study* is an observational study (systematic or participant) that focuses on one particular group, event, or situation as an example of some broader social phenomenon of interest. George and Bennett (2005) argue that a case (e.g., the Rebels) is really a "class of events" (i.e., outlaw biker gangs) that the researcher is interested in and hopes to eventually develop a theory about.

INSIGHT INTO PARTICIPANT OBSERVATION

Daniel R. Wolfe (1991), a researcher who joined the Rebels (a motorcycle gang) in order to study them, best explains participant observation like this:

At the time of beginning my fieldwork I had been riding British-made motorcycles for three years and talked briefly to members of the King's Crew MC in Calgary. But this was not enough to comprehend the outlaw biker community or to study it. My impression of outlaw bikers was narrow and incomplete, and, in that sense, almost as misleading as the stereotype held by most "citizens." I was physically close to the scene but far removed from a balanced understanding; that understanding would only come from "being there." (p.10)

STRENGTHS AND LIMITATION OF FIELD APPROACHES

The greatest advantage of field approaches is that they allow researchers to study areas of interest in natural settings. It doesn't get more realistic than that! Describing what a group is like is best done if a researcher has gained an accurate understanding of the members' own points of view. Participating in a group is one of the most straightforward ways to develop rapport and to ensure a researcher is around when important events and behaviours take place. However, participation poses special challenges for researchers who need to be skilled in observing variables and people of interest while taking accurate field notes. Even if a researcher is only observing a group (i.e., systematic observation), he or she will need to be where the group is in order to code variables of interest.

The biggest drawback to this form of data collection is that the data is compiled by a researcher who may be somewhat biased (e.g., perceptions can sometimes be distorted by prior expectations or experiences). In this case, comparing data from two different observers can provide a check on reliability and help to establish validity. Another difficulty with field studies that poses a special challenge for the researchers is how to access and then later exit a research setting. Gaining permission to join a group, establishing contacts and trust while in the group, and then leaving that group is tricky since the researcher now has social relationships with members of the group. Clearly, field approaches reiterate the importance of developing and following ethical guidelines. Table 2.1 (page 40) summarizes the main research methods discussed in this section including key features, strengths, and limitations.

TIME TO REVIEW

- Which variable is manipulated in an experiment?
- What is the greatest advantage of an experimental design?
- How do field and laboratory experiments compare in terms of their advantages and disadvantages?
- What is a survey used for?

SOCIOLOGY *ONLINE*

RESEARCH RESOURCES

• **The SocioWeb www.socioweb.com**
This site is maintained by Blairworks (Mark R. Blair) and set up in a search engine format akin to Google. Students can search the site for information pertaining to their own topic(s) through the site's search feature, or they can browse the links and resources provided under sections such as articles and essays, sociological associations, sociology topics, giants of sociology, sociological theories, and university departments.

• **Sociology Subject Guide http://ica.library.oregon state.edu/subject-guide/486-Sociology?tab=1331**
This site is maintained by Valery King of The Valley Library, Oregon State University. The Sociology Subject Guide provides a starting point for developing sociological research, including things such as sociology megasites, qualitative and quantitative data sites, policy studies, surveys, timelines, and even a tutorial on Internet information and skills for sociologists.

• **Statistics Canada Website www.statcan.gc.ca**
This is the official site for Statistics Canada, a federal agency that is responsible for generating statistical information on Canada, its provinces, and territories. Here, you can find articles, reports, and data tables that provide information on a wealth of subjects pertaining to Canadians including Aboriginal peoples, agriculture, crime and justice, economic accounts, education, training and learning, environment, population and demography, prices and price indexes, and much more.

TABLE 2.1
Sociological Research Methods

Method	Question	Key Features	Strengths	Limitations
• Experiment • Lab	• What is causing this?	• Control • Random assignment • Manipulation and measurement of variables	• Can test causality • Can isolate variables	• Artificiality and low generalizability
• Survey • Questionnaire	• What is your opinion on this?	• Sample • Series of questions	• High response rate • Rich, detailed information • Relationships among many variables	• Validity • Respondent accuracy
• Interviews • Focus groups	• What do you think about this?	• Series of questions	• Can clarify questions (during interviews) • Participation in the process	• Establishing and maintaining rapport • Group dynamics
• Secondary analysis of existing data • Content analysis	• What does this tell me?	• Statistics, text, or images • Predetermined categories • Indicators	• Convenient • Large data sets • Reliability of measures • Nonreactive measures	• Validity • Incomplete measures
• Ethnography • Action research • Systematic observation • Participant observation • Case studies	• What is it like in there/doing that?	• Action research • Participant observation • Case studies	• Natural settings • Rich, detailed information	• Accessing and exiting research settings • Bias • Reactivity

- What are some of the ways that questionnaires can be administered?
- What is the most serious limitation of surveys?
- What advantage do interviews have over questionnaires?
- What is secondary analysis of existing data used for?
- What is the main drawback of secondary analysis of existing data?
- What is action research used for?
- How does participant observation differ from systematic observation?
- What is the greatest advantage of using field approaches?

CHAPTER SUMMARY

LO¹ Explain why sociological reasoning is important.

Common sense is limited as a result of individual's selective perception, while sociological reasoning uses empirical methods and systematic procedures to study the social world and enhance our understanding of people and society.

LO² Differentiate between deductive and inductive approaches to reasoning.

Deductive reasoning starts with theories and ends with research finding, whereas inductive research begins with observation and ends in theory construction.

LO³ Demonstrate an understanding of the goals of sociological research.

Exploratory research helps us understand an area that is not well established, descriptive research helps denote features and characteristics of a group, explanatory research clarifies aspects of a particular social phenomenon, and critical research helps assess outcomes of some aspect of the social world.

LO⁴ Identify steps for conducting sociological research.

Steps in conducting research include identifying of an area of interest, determining what is already known about the topic, narrowing the research focus, developing a research design, collecting data, analyzing data, drawing conclusions, and disseminating the findings.

LO⁵ Identify the ethical principles that underlie research involving human participants.

Research involving humans should always be carried out in a manner that demonstrates a concern for welfare, respects dignity and the decision to participate in research, and prioritizes justice.

LO⁶ Differentiate between qualitative and quantitative research methods.

Qualitative methods help us better understand or describe the nature of something using inductive reasoning, while quantitative methods are more focused on counting things or testing hypotheses based on deductive reasoning.

LO⁷ Describe the main use of each of the following research methods: experiments, surveys, interviews and focus groups, secondary analysis of existing data, and ethnographies.

An experiment is a deductive method used to test causality as a function of control and random assignment. Surveys are used to gather opinions from respondents using questionnaires. Interviews consist of question-and-answer techniques for obtaining first hand opinions. Sometimes data originally collected for other purposes, such as statistics collected by government agencies, is used for secondary analysis to investigate topics of interest. Field approaches allow researchers to study areas of interest in natural settings.

RECOMMENDED READINGS

1. To better appreciate perspectives on research including distinctions between qualitative and quantitative approaches and an explanation of how to conduct research using the main methods applicable to these approaches, refer to Palys, T., & Atchison, C. (2008). *Research Decisions: Quantitative and Qualitative Approaches* (4th ed.). Toronto, ON: Nelson Education.

2. For a good resource on framing survey research questions and using survey methods, refer to Gray, N. & Guppy, G. (2008). *Successful Surveys: Research Methods and Practice* (4th ed.). Toronto, ON: Nelson Education.

3. To learn more about how to carry out action research and test the validity of this approach, refer to McNiff, J., & Whitehead, J. (2008). *All You Need to Know about Action Research*. Thousand Oaks, CA: Sage Publications.

4. If your research interest warrants the development of grounded theory, you can utilize Charmaz, K. (2007). *Constructing Grounded Theory: A Practical Guide through Qualitative Analysis*. Thousand Oaks, CA: Sage Publications.

FOR FURTHER REFLECTION

1. Suppose you are interested in studying how people adjust after being released from a lengthy prison term. How might you refine this research problem? What kind of ethical issues need to be addressed before you can conduct this sort of research? What research method do you think is best suited to this type of research interest?

2. A health-care provider wishes to survey patients to determine if the facility is meeting the needs of its clients. The health-care provider contracts you to develop a short questionnaire that can be given to patients who come into the lab for blood tests. What kind of questions would you include on the questionnaire? How might you word the questions? Which other issues are important considerations for obtaining useful findings?

3. Try to come up with a research example that would be best investigated using a qualitative approach. Why is a qualitative approach most applicable in this case? Which specific method or methods would you use to study this phenomenon?

4. As a class assignment, you are asked to complete a research assignment on how Canadians spend their money. How might you operationalize the concept of spending? Visit the Statistics Canada website at www.statcan.gc.ca. Using information available at this site, what can we learn about how Canadian households spend money on various goods and services?

REFERENCES

Adler, E. S., & Clark, R. A. (2003). *How It's Done: An Invitation to Social Research* (2nd ed.). Toronto, ON: Thomson Nelson Learning.

Bandura, A., Ross, D., & Ross, S. (1963). Imitation of film-mediated aggressive models. *The Journal of Abnormal and Social Psychology, 66*(1), 3–11.

Baumrind, D. (1964). Some thoughts on ethics of research after reading Milgram's behavioral study of obedience. *American Psychologist, 19,* 421–423.

Bazeley, P. (2007). *Qualitative Data Analysis with NVivo.* Thousand Oaks, CA: Sage Publications.

Bemiller, M. L., & Schneider, R. Z. (2010). It's not just a joke. *Sociological Spectrum, 30*(4), 459–479.

Berg, B. L. (2009). *Qualitative Research Methods for the Social Sciences* (7th ed.). Toronto, ON: Pearson Education.

Box, S. (2009, July 27). *New data from VTTI provides insight into cell phone use and driving distraction.* VirginiaTech Transportation Institute. Retrieved July 9, 2010, from www.vtti.vt.edu/PDF/7-22-09-VTTI-Press_Release_Cell_phones_and_Driver_Distraction.pdf

Boyd, A. D., Jardine, C. G., & Driedger, S. M. (2009). Canadian media representations of mad cow disease. *Journal of Toxicology and Environmental Health: Part A Current Issues, 72* (17–18), 1096–1105.

Bryant, J. A., Sanders-Jackson, A., & Smallwood, A. M. K. (2006). IMing, text messaging, and adolescent social networks. *Journal of Computer-Mediated Communication, 11*(2), (Article 10), 577–592.

Cabanac, M. (1986). Money versus pain: Experimental study of a conflict in humans. *Journal of the Experimental Analysis of Behaviour, 46*(1), 37–44.

Canadian Institutes of Health Research, Natural Sciences and Engineering Council of Canada & Social Sciences and Humanities Research Council of Canada. (2010, December). *Tri-Council Policy Statement: Ethical Conduct for Research Involving Humans.* Retrieved August 9, 2011, from www.pre.ethics.gc.ca

Diener, E., Ng, W., Harter, J., & Arora, R. (2010). Wealth and happiness across the world: Material prosperity predicts life evaluation, whereas psychosocial prosperity predicts positive feeling. *Journal of Personality and Social Psychology, 99*(1), 52–61.

Driedger, S. M., Jardine, C. G., Boyd, A. D., & Mistry, B. (2009). Do the first 10 days equal a year? Comparing two Canadian public health risk events using the national media. *Health Risk & Society, 11*(1), 39–53.

Eyde, L. D. (2000). Other responsibilities to participants. In B. D. Sales & S. Folkman (Eds.), *Ethics in Research with Human Participants* (pp. 61–73). Washington, DC: American Psychological Association.

George, A. L., & Bennett, A. (2005). *Case Studies and Theory Development in the Social Sciences.* Cambridge, MA: MIT Press.

Hands-Free Information. (2010, July 13). *Canadian distracted driving updates.* Retrieved July 15, 2010, from http://handsfreeinfo.com/canadian-cell-phone-law-updates

Howell, A. J. & Symbaluk, D. G. (2001). Published student ratings: Reconciling the views of students and faculty. *Journal of Educational Psychology, 93,* 790–796.

Humphreys, L. (1975). *Tearoom Trade: Impersonal Sex in Public Places.* Chicago: Aldine.

Jackson, W., & Verberg, N. (2007). *Methods: Doing Social Research* (4th ed.). Toronto, ON: Pearson Education Canada.

Lagnado, L. M., & Dekel, S. C. (1991). *Children of the Flames: Dr. Josef Mengle and the Untold Story of the Twins of Auschwitz*. New York: William Morrow and Company.

Milgram, S. (1963). Behavioral study of obedience. *The Journal of Abnormal and Social Psychology, 67*(4), 371–378.

National Institutes of Health. (2011). *Regulations and Ethical Guidelines: Directives for Human Experimentation*. Bethesda, MD: Office of Human Subjects Research. Retrieved August 9, 2011, from http://ohsr.od.nih.gov/guidelines/nuremberg.html

Plester, B., Wood, C., & Bell, V. (2008). Txt msg n school literacy: Does texting and knowledge of text abbreviations adversely affect children's literacy attainment? *Literacy, 42*(3), 137–144.

Roberts, J., Crutcher, N., & Verbrugge, P. (2007, January). Public attitudes to sentencing in Canada: Exploring recent findings. *Canadian Journal of Criminology and Criminal Justice,* 75–107.

Shannon, V. (2007, December 5). Fifteen years of text messages, a "cultural phenomenon." *New York Times.* Retrieved July 9, 2010, from www.nytimes.com

Sieber, J. E. (1992). *Planning Ethically Responsible Research*. Newbury Park, CA: Sage Publications.

Statistics Canada. (2010). *About us*. Ottawa, ON: Author. Retrieved July 15, 2010, from www.statcan.gc.ca/start-debut-eng.html.

Symbaluk, D., Heth, C. D., Cameron, J., & Pierce, W. D. (1997). Social modeling, monetary incentives, and pain endurance: The role of self-efficacy and pain perception. *Personality and Social Psychology Bulletin, 23*(3), 258–269.

Varnhagen, C. K., McFall, G. P., Pugh, N., Routledge, L., Sumida-MacDonald, H., & Kwong, T., E. (2010). Lol: New language and spelling in instant messaging. *Reading and Writing, 23*(6), 719–733.

Vivar, C. G., Whyte, D. A., & McQueen, A. (2010). "Again": The impact of recurrence on survivors of cancer and family members. *Journal of Clinical Nursing, 19*(13–14), 2048–2056.

Watson, L., Lavack, A. M., Rudin-Brown, C., Burns, P., & Mintz, J. H. (2010). Message content in Canadian automotive advertising: A role for regulation? *Canadian Public Policy, 36* (April Sp. Iss), S49–S67.

Webb, E. J., Campbell, D. T., Schwartz, R. D., & Sechrest, L. (2000). *Unobtrusive Measures* (Rev. ed.). Thousand Oaks, CA: Sage.

Willis, J. W. (2007). *Foundations of Qualitative Research: Interpretive and Critical Approaches*. Thousand Oaks, CA: Sage Publications.

Wolfe, D. R. (1991). *The Rebels: A Brotherhood of Outlaw Bikers*. Toronto, ON: University of Toronto Press.

ENDNOTES

[1] Retrieved February 23, 2011, from "Thinkexist.com" (thinkexist.com).

[2] The second edition includes a number of clarifications such as the distinction between research and quality assurance activities, the distinction between withdrawal from participation and withdrawal of data, guidance about balancing confidentiality against legal or professional requirements concerning disclosure of information, guidance concerning the role of an appeal body, clarification about the meaning of community and community engagement within Aboriginal contexts, and a number of other changes.

[3] The TCPS 2 includes an entire chapter dedicated to research involving Aboriginal peoples. Chapter 9 explains how to interpret the ethics framework in Aboriginal contexts, discusses ethical concerns particular to Aboriginal people, delineates how to apply provisions of the policy within Aboriginal contexts, and explains how the research and ethical review processes operate therein.

Mass Media: Living in the Electronic Age

LEARNING OBJECTIVES AND OUTCOMES

After completing this chapter, students should be able to do the following:

LO1 Describe the history of the traditional forms of mass media.

LO2 Describe the role of new media forms, including whether they make traditional ones obsolete.

LO3 Differentiate between media assumptions provided by the core sociological frameworks.

LO4 Evaluate the relevance of media ownership for agenda setting.

LO5 Demonstrate a critical understanding of ways that media shape our perceptions.

LO6 Debate whether violence in the media causes viewers to become violent.

LO7 Illustrate what it means to be "media literate."

> *In a culture like ours, long accustomed to splitting and dividing all things as a means of control, it is sometimes a bit of a shock to be reminded that, in operational and practical fact, the medium is the message.*
>
> (McLuhan, 1964: 7)

MASS MEDIA PREVALENCE AND FORMS

From Facebook updates to iPhone text messaging to the latest episode of our favourite television show captured on personal video recorder (PVR) in high definition (HD), a majority of us spend a considerable portion of our available time plugged into some form of communications technology. Because we are constantly bombarded with information and imagery in news stories, advertisements, and a multitude of entertainment venues such as movies, video games, and music, it is especially important for us to use the sociological imagination to understand our connection with mass media. What forms of media do we use, and how much? Who controls the content of mass media, and why does it matter? What central themes and ideas are represented in the messages and images conveyed by the media? In what ways does mass media content affect our thoughts, feelings, and behaviours? What can we do to become more media literate as consumers? These are all questions of interest to sociologists that you will learn more about in this chapter.

MEDIA CONSUMPTION

Canadians spend more personal time today in front of a computer screen than a television monitor. According to tracking data from an Ipsos Reid poll conducted in 2009, Canadians spent an average of 18.1 hours on the Internet, 16.9 hours in front of a television, 8.9 hours listening to the radio, 2.9 hours reading newspapers, and 1.4 hours reading magazines each week (CBC News, 2010a). Canadians are increasingly substituting the Internet for traditional media forms. While most Canadians use the Internet for leisure in the form of general browsing, a sizeable portion of online users spend time obtaining weather or road conditions (75 percent), viewing news or sports (68 percent), obtaining or saving music (47 percent), listening to the radio (32 percent), downloading or watching television or a movie (31 percent), and making telephone calls (14 percent) (Statistics Canada, 2010). Overall, Canadians use the Internet more than anyone, with an Internet usage rate that is almost double the worldwide average (Akkad, 2011). As consumption patterns continue to evolve, it is likely that Canadians will spend more time multitasking with their Wi-fi-enabled cell phones and less time accessing the Internet from a laptop. While consumption preferences will vary more as new digital applications are developed, overall media consumption continues to reach new heights. Let's begin with a look at early forms of mass media.

Canadians spend more personal time in front of a computer screen than a television monitor.

LO¹ TRADITIONAL FORMS OF MASS MEDIA

Mass media refers to communications that target large audiences in print (e.g., newspapers, magazines, books, and photography) or in electronic format using audio and/or images (e.g., cinema, radio, recordings, television, the Internet, and cell phones). Before global mass communication via the Internet, mass media was concentrated in seven main areas: books, newspapers, magazines, cinema, recordings, radio, and television.

Early forms of pictographic writing and cuneiform words first appeared on clay tablets traced to the Sumerians of Mesopotamia dating back to 3400 and 3000 BC, respectively (Encyclopaedia Britannica, 2011). Nelson Education Ltd., a leader in the Canadian book industry and the publisher of this textbook, has been in the business since 1914 (Nordal, 2010). You are probably familiar with the Harry Potter book series, by British author J.K. Rowling. But are you also familiar with any of the novels or other works by highly acclaimed Canadian authors such as Margaret Atwood or Yann Martel[1]?

Newsprint originated in Canada with John Bushell's sale of the first copy of the *Halifax Gazette* from his print shop on Grafton Street in Halifax, Nova Scotia, in 1752 (Province of Nova Scotia, 2010). As of 2009, there were 96 Canadian daily newspapers with a circulation of 4.1 million copies (Canadian Newspaper Association, 2010).

The first Canadian periodical (magazine) also originated in Nova Scotia. *The Nova Scotia Magazine and Comprehensive Review of Literature, Politics, and News* was published in 1789 (The Canadian Encyclopedia, 2010). Canada's top-selling magazines today are *Chatelaine, Canadian Living, Reader's Digest, Maclean's, Coupe de Pouce, Hello! Canada,* and *Canadian House and Home.* Although these are very successful Canadian magazines, their annual revenues of between $51.4 and $21.1 million pale in comparison to the billions made by American consumer giants such as *People* or *Sports Illustrated* (Maloney, 2010).

Cinema includes the film or movie industry, and it originated in the late 1800s. As with the magazine industry, our neighbours to the south also dominate the movie production and distribution industry; the American film industry is credited with the two highest-grossing movies of all time: *Titanic* and *Avatar,* although James Cameron (the writer and director of both) is Canadian! He was born in Kapuskasing, Ontario (*Filmmakers Magazine,* 2010).

> **Mass media:**
> Communications that target large audiences in print or in electronic format using audio and/or images.

Canadian filmmaking produced the comedies *Trailer Park Boys: Countdown to Liquor Day* and *Trailer Park Boys: The Movie.*

Source: Getty Images

Music is an integral part of Canadian history, from various Aboriginal traditions to the influence of the British and the French. Early sound recording is generally attributed to the invention of Thomas Edison's phonograph in 1877 and Emile Berliner's gramophone in 1878 (Library and Archives Canada, 2010). Vinyl records emerged in 1948 and they were followed by 8-track cartridges (1963) and compact cassettes (1964) in the mid-1960s through the late 1970s (Hubpages, 2011). The Sony Walkman helped to facilitate the demise of the 8-track and increased the popularity of cassettes through the 1980s, wherein compact discs (CDs) came on the scene and had replaced cassettes by the 1990s. Interestingly, while 8-tracks went out of circulation and cassettes became scarce, vinyl records survived; in fact, because of the preference that DJs have for vinyl, and the extensive use of vinyl in hip-hop, their popularity has resurged over the last few years. Vinyl sales doubled in the United States during 2008, prompting Universal Music, the world's largest record company, to continue to release vinyl albums along with CDs (Zuel, 2009).

Nobel Prize winner Guglielmo Marconi is credited with transmitting the first wireless radio signal across the Atlantic Ocean from Poldhu, Cornwall, to St. John's, Newfoundland, in 1901 and with setting up the first licensed wireless telegraphy station at Grace Bay, Nova Scotia, in 1902. The radio operators on the *Titanic* were Marconi employees who sent out distress messages using the early technology while the ship was sinking in 1912 (University of Oxford, 2010). By 1919 the first broadcasting licence was issued to Marconi's company to operate an experimental radio station originally called XWA out of Montreal, Quebec (Hammond Museum of Radio, 2011). By 2007, there were 619 radio stations in Canada (Avery, 2008).

Television was introduced in 1952 and by the end of that decade the majority of Canadian households had one. Virtually every Canadian household today includes a colour TV, and about one-third possess three or more (Statistics Canada, 2009). From cable television to direct broadcast satellites and then to bigger screens, wider screens, and now clearer screens on LCD (liquid crystal display) and LED (light-emitting diode) televisions that are no thicker than picture frames, the industry is continuously utilizing technological advancements in an effort to remain competitive. While the television industry is still a lucrative form of mass media, it is fast losing ground to the Internet. Advertising revenues for television fell in 2009 by 7.4 percent while the telecommunications industry reported an overall increase of 1.8 percent (amounting to $41 billion), largely accounted for by the wireless and Internet sectors. Just about every Canadian home now has broadband (i.e., high-speed) Internet and 96 percent of Canadians with cell phones can access the Internet with them (The Canadian Press, 2010). The Internet has had and continues to have a profound effect on all of the traditional forms of mass media.

THE INTERNET CHANGES EVERYTHING

The seven traditional forms of media are continuously undergoing change as a result of the growing influence of the Internet. Books, newspapers, and magazines can be purchased on the Internet via electronic commerce businesses such as Amazon.ca or Chapters.ca, read using wireless e-readers, or accessed through electronic library resources. We still go to movies (albeit some now in 3D and Real D) and rent or purchase films on digital video discs (DVDs), perhaps in Blu-ray format, but increasingly we pay to download movies from commercial Internet venues such as Netflix Canada, which now enables us to view movies through our game consoles or smart phones. Some people even illegally download movies for free from torrent sites.

Likewise, you don't have to own a radio nowadays to listen to music over a live broadcast. Using a media player on a personal computer or a portable device such as an iPod, more than 5000 radio stations from around the world and more than 600 Canadian stations can be accessed over the Internet via audio streams (e.g., see the online directory at Mike's Radio World, 2010). Many online businesses allow you to purchase or download music (e.g., iTunes) as audio files (e.g., in MP3 and WAV

formats). Recording artists The Black Eyed Peas' 2009 single "Boom Boom Pow" was the largest single-week and debut-download in the history of digital sound sales, holding a number one spot in the United States for 12 consecutive weeks. Another one of their songs later surpassed this record when "I Got a Feeling" claimed the top single for the next 14 weeks; between these two songs, the group held the number-one spot for 26 consecutive weeks (Billboard.com, 2010). Remarkably, for the first time in digital history, both songs each topped $4 million in sales in a single year, as did Lady Gaga's "Poker Face" and Flo Rida's "Right Round" (Evans, 2010). Although considerable money is still being made in this traditional form of mass media, unauthorized file downloading and CD-R burning poses another ongoing and significant Internet-related problem for the media that has yet to be resolved. In addition to revolutionizing traditional forms of media, the Internet itself is considered to be one of the newest forms of mass media.

LO² NEW MEDIA

Modern forms of media technology are often grouped under what is called "new" or "emerging" media. New media encompasses everything on the Internet or more precisely, the entire global system of internet-works, which includes educational resources such as links to library documents, communication services such as email, social networking applications such as Twitter or Facebook, web browsers for surfing the Net, electronic commerce businesses such as eBay Inc. and Dell Canada, audio and video podcasts, Really Simple Syndication (RSS) feeds such as news headlines, and links to a vast array of sites wherein you can do all sorts things including chatting, banking, gaming, reading, and gambling, among others. One of the most popular Internet sites today is YouTube (owned by Google).

YOUTUBE: A MEDIA DISRUPTOR OR A FORCE TO BE RECKONED WITH?

YouTube, founded in 2005, is a leading media source for public expression as evident in its infamous byline: *Broadcast Yourself*. YouTube exists as an online video-sharing platform that is best understood from a media perspective as a "reach business" since it enables exposure through the vast audience it supports in the way of visitors (Burgess & Green, 2009). Those who access the site can find debates on a range of topics from religion to politics, learn how to do things like beat a level in a favourite video game or apply cosmetics, and watch controversial sports and favourite celebrity moments, all uploaded by individuals who have captured events on video. Scenes from just about every major movie, concert, video game, or television series can be located on YouTube, helping to shape public perceptions of YouTube as an acceptable platform for the widespread sharing of illegally reproduced materials.

YouTube's dual purpose as both a distributor of popular culture (e.g., video clips about consumer products and previously broadcasted events) and a source of original creativity (in the form of videos made by amateurs) is the essence of its success and controversy. Burgess and Green (2009) describe YouTube as both a disruptive force to existing media forms as well as an area of media power. It is a disruptive force because it "is variously understood as a distribution platform that can make the products of commercial media widely popular, challenge the promotional reach the mass media is accustomed to monopolizing, while at the same time is a [powerful] platform for user-created content where challenges to commercial popular culture might emerge, be they user-created news services, or generic forms such as vblogging—which might in turn be appropriated and exploited by the traditional mass media" (p. 6). Copyright controversy notwithstanding, YouTube has solidified itself as one of the most popular forms of Internet-based media.

"It's not your traditional report. I've done it in the form of a YouTube video.

CELL PHONES TAKE OVER

In addition to what is found on the Internet, new media also consist of the latest electronic gadgets from games to gaming consoles (i.e., Nintendo Wii, Sony PlayStation 3, Microsoft Xbox 360), digital audio players best known as MP3 players, and, of course, cell phones. Tomi T. Ahonen, one of the world's experts on how money is made in the mobile telecom industry, titled his 2008 book *Mobile as 7th of the Mass Media*. Ahonen combines all types of print (i.e., newspapers, magazines, and books) into one main form of media along with recordings, radio, cinema, television, and the Internet to comprise what he calls the six "old" forms of mass media. Mobile, the seventh form of mass media, then, in his view, refers exclusively to the huge variety of available cell phones. Ahonen demonstrates the increasing prevalence of cell phones through comparisons to the old forms of mass media in a presentation titled "The Next 4 Billion." For example, he claims that "there are 480 million newspapers daily (circulation around the world)—[yet] eight times more people subscribe to a mobile network than buy a daily newspaper" (Ahonen, 2009). He also points out that there are "1.5 billion total television sets on the planet—[but] mobile is two and half times bigger" (Ahonen, 2009). Remarkably, he also contends that "there are 3.9 billion FM radios on the planet"; however, with a reported 4 billion in subscriptions, "mobile is now the most pervasive technology on the planet" (Ahonen, 2009).

Recent increases in Canada's telecommunications revenues are directly attributable to the growth of cell phones (and, to a lesser extent, residential high-speed Internet services). By the end of 2009, 23.8 million Canadians subscribed to wireless and 8.3 million to broadband Internet (Canadian Radio-television and Telecommunications Commission, 2010a).

WEB APPLICATIONS: THE NEXT NEW BEST THING

Uber-company Apple changed the media world with its creation of web-based applications (apps) for its wireless devices (iPhones, iPads, and some iPods). There are now tens of thousands of apps available, not only for Apple devices, but also for other wireless brands (e.g., Research in Motion's Super Apps for BlackBerry smart phones). These apps allow mobile users to do everything from online banking to sending text messages, creating documents, reading newscasts, playing games, researching terms, checking stocks, converting mileage, counting calories, calculating the risk of diseases such as breast cancer, finding out how much

WEB APPS

Scott McKeen's opinion column is a funny illustration of the growing popularity of web apps. The author, a self-proclaimed "appaholic," notes that soon after he purchased his first iPhone and discovered web applications, he downloaded apps "like a madman." McKeen goes on to describe various apps he'd like to create including one called SIMCITY, SOCIAL LIFE that "converts the real world into streaming video … [and] connects directly with nearby smartphones, converting speech to text …, concealing your voice and face so you can remain anonymous … [thereby allowing you to] be just as snotty as you are on web forums, without personal consequence." (McKeen, 2010).

Source: Scott McKeen (2010). An app for everything, and everything in an app. *Edmonton Journal,* August 23, p. A 5. © Postmedia Network.

money can be saved by drinking coffee or eating ice cream at home, and numerous other amusing activities including determining one's age in parrot, turtle, or monkey years. You can now do so many things with apps and spend so much time using them that concerns are raised about how electronically mediated communication might cause people to stop interacting in real life.

If you don't believe there is now an app for everything, then you may wish to consider attending one of Father Tom Eichenberger's Sunday sermons. He recently called his parishioners to their pews by broadcasting the church bell ring tone on his iPhone over the church's sound system (Heneghan, 2010). Yes, even religion has been brought into the new media realm. Smart phones now include applications that contain tools for Christian ministry; scriptures such as the Bible, Book of Mormon, and virtual siddur (a Jewish Prayer book); apps designed to calculate Islamic prayer times and other prayer schedules; as well as many other means for obtaining spiritual guidance.

NEW FORMS OF MEDIA ARE UNIQUE

Newer forms of mass media often improve upon features from previous forms but surprisingly do not make older forms of media obsolete. Recall the chapter's opening quotation which ends with the excerpt: "… the medium is the message." The saying is from Canadian-born Marshall McLuhan (1911–1980) and it first appeared in his book *Understanding Media: The Extensions of Man* (1964). McLuhan claimed that each new modern media form has unique properties that fundamentally change how we now experience things from an audio experience with radio to a more visual one via television and so on. With the advent of big-screen television, we didn't stop going to movies and, although television allowed us to see music videos, it didn't bring an end to the enjoyment we receive from hearing songs played on the radio. This is partly due to the fact that new types of media provide us with a markedly different experience from older ones, which tend to retain their original appeal. Cell phones, for example, contain several features that do not exist elsewhere, such as ring tones. In addition, in spite of their small screen size, cell phones are much more advanced than personal computers, especially when it comes to multiple, simultaneous inputs (e.g., camera, video, and GPS) (Ahonen, 2009). Mobile is also unique in other ways. For example, people who use cell phones are permanently connected to the Internet via their various applications and they can highly personalize their experience with the media as a function of the particular apps they choose to engage with.

"Hold on a minute. I'm downloading an app to monitor my app downloading."

Source: Cable, Carole, ccan239, www.cartoonstock.com

- Prior to the Internet, in which seven areas were the media concentrated?
- Why is YouTube considered to be both a media disruptor and a force to be reckoned with?
- What does Tomi T. Ahonen consider to be the seventh mass media?
- Why don't new forms of mass media make traditional forms obsolete?

 SOCIOLOGY IN THEORY

LO³ FUNCTIONALIST FRAMEWORK

The different sociological frameworks, which you were introduced to in Chapter 1, can be used to help us better understand how the mass media influences us and how we, in turn, influence the mass media. Since the main concern of a macro-level functionalist framework is social order, this perspective helps us see how the media contributes to the maintenance of stability in society. For example, a manifest (or intended) function of the media is to provide us with current, up-to-date communications. By listening to a live news broadcast on a station such as CBC Radio One through a radio or audio-stream on a computer, we can find out about practical issues of local interest such as the weather and traffic conditions as well as global events such as the devastating 2011 earthquake in Japan and its subsequent, tsunami, aftershocks, and ensuing nuclear disaster.

By playing a central role in connecting us to other people and sources of information, the media helps us to become more socially aware—of ourselves, our communities, other people, diverse cultures, current events, and a plethora of issues facing society as a whole. In this sense, we are being taught important skills and values that help us function in relation to one another. **Socialization** is the lifelong process of acquiring skills, internalizing norms, learning values, and discovering particular behaviours and techniques needed to function in society through our interactions with others. In addition to the mass media, major agents of socialization include the family, school, and peer groups. The socializing effects of these agents will be addressed in subsequent chapters. There are many socializing effects of the mass media; some of these effects are less obvious than others, and some may even be harmful, as the conflict framework demonstrates.

Socialization: The lifelong process of acquiring skills, internalizing norms, learning values, and discovering particular behaviours and techniques needed to function in society through our interactions with others.

Monopoly: A company that has exclusive control over a particular product or service.

CONFLICT FRAMEWORK

Similar to the functional framework, the conflict framework also focuses on large-scale institutions such as the mass media, but it views society as being characterized by disparity and power struggles that are linked to an unequal distribution of resources. Because the mass media provides an essential information resource to society, the fact that much of the media is owned by a highly concentrated group means that a relatively small number of individuals and organizations have the power to shape what we are exposed to, and, subsequently, how we come to view certain things the way we do.

MEDIA OWNERSHIP IS CONCENTRATED

Whether we consider newspapers, music, television, or movies, the concentration in ownership is apparent. For example, Quebecor Media alone owns 37.5 percent of Canada's daily newspapers (e.g., *Le Journal de Montréal*, the *Winnipeg Sun*, the *Toronto Sun*, the *Calgary Sun*, the *Ottawa Sun*, and the *London Free Press*, among others). Quebecor Media is second in terms of circulation only to Postmedia Network Inc., which owns fewer newspapers but sells more of them (e.g., the *Montreal Gazette*, the *National Post*, the *Calgary Herald*, the *Edmonton Journal*, and the *Ottawa Citizen*) (Canadian Newspaper Association, 2010). Brunswick News, a private newspaper publishing company owned by James K. Irving, can be considered a **monopoly** since the company has exclusive news print media control over an entire province, owning all three of New Brunswick's English-language daily newspapers (CBC News, 2010b).

The Big Four of Music

Similar patterns are evident in the music industry. As the beginning of any season of *American Idol* demonstrates, there are an infinite number of individuals with varying ranges of musical talent hoping to be discovered. Recording companies are the main agents of power when it comes to determining who gets to produce a song and which songs are played on the radio. Unsolicited music is not accepted for consideration, even from well-known artists. Leading Canadian recording companies are owned by one of four international parent companies (i.e., Sony BMG, Universal Music Group, Warner Music Group, and EMI). These large corporations are known in the recording industry as *the Big Four* because each owns more than one million copyrights (i.e., artists and record labels) and together they control 75 percent of the entire music industry. The Big Four have the power to decide which songs are played on the radio and which artists are promoted through advertisements and, hence, they help to determine who will become the next superstar.

The Big Five of Television

Canadian television operates under six main networks: the Canadian Broadcasting Corporation Radio-Canada (CBC), a publicly owned Crown corporation, along with four private networks (i.e., English-language networks Global and CTV as well as French-language networks TVA and V, which serve mainly Quebec, Ontario, and New Brunswick) and the Aboriginal Peoples Television Network. Canadians actually spend more time watching American networks, where the most popular television series originate (e.g., *True Blood* and *In Treatment* on HBO; *The Apprentice* and *The Biggest Loser* on NBC; *Survivor, Big Brother, NCIS,* and *The Big Bang Theory* on CBS; *Grey's Anatomy, The Bachelorette,* and *Lost* on ABC; *House, American Idol, So You Think You Can Dance,* and *The Simpsons* on FOX). Because Canada is the largest importer of American content, it is pertinent to note who owns and controls these American networks.

American television was historically concentrated under the major networks: the American Broadcasting Company (ABC), Columbia Broadcasting System (CBS), and National Broadcasting Company (NBC). Eventually two other networks emerged (i.e., Home Box Office, Inc. (HBO) and FOX Broadcasting Company (FOX) and together they are linked to five corporations known as *the Big Five of Television*: (1) *Time Warner*, which owns HBO; (2) *Walt Disney*, which owns ABC; (3) *National Amusements Inc.*, the majority shareholder of CBS and Viacom; (4) *News Corp*, which owns Fox Broadcasting Company (FOX); and (5) *NBC Universal*, the owner of NBC (Straubhaar, LaRose, and Davenport, 2010). By subdividing CBS and Viacom into separate entities and reclassifying NBC Universal under General Electric (one of its principal owners), we can now demonstrate how six corporations own and control virtually *all* traditional forms of mass media.

The Big Six of Media

The *Big Six of Media* refers to six large American media-interest corporations: Time Warner, Walt Disney, News Corp, CBS, Viacom, and General Electric. A **conglomerate** is a corporation made up of several different widely diversified companies. The Big Six are conglomerates because they own companies spanning the traditional forms of mass media.

Time Warner, for example, owns HBO, half of the CW Network, and various regional, local, and international television channels. Time Warner also finds its way into film via the Warner Bros. Entertainment Group (e.g., Castle Rock) and publishing, where it controls 150 magazines (e.g., *People, Time,* and *Sports Illustrated*) along with several comic books. Time Warner even has new media interests (e.g., game developer Monolith Productions). Similarly, *Walt Disney* owns major networks (e.g., ABC), cable (e.g., ESPN), international channels and other programming (e.g., World News Now) alongside radio (e.g., ESPN Radio), music (e.g., Hollywood Records), magazines (e.g., *Family Fun*), books (e.g., Disney Press), comic books (i.e., Marvel Comics), film (e.g., Touchstone Pictures), and new media (e.g., Playhouse Disney Preschool Time Online). Likewise, *News Corp* has television (e.g., FOX), print media (e.g., magazines including *Barron's* and *Smart Money*, newspapers such as *The Wall Street Journal*, and books under HarperCollins Publishers), cinema (e.g., Fox Film Entertainment), and Internet holdings (e.g., MySpace .com) (Free Press, 2011).

CBS is most associated with the CBS Television Network's 30 stations, cable, programming, and distribution. However, CBS also has concentration in radio (i.e., 130 radio stations), book publishing (e.g., Simon and Schuster) and the Internet (with CBS-affiliated. com sites). *Viacom* has Music Television (MTV), international channels, and MTV radio. Viacom also owns the Extreme Music Library, Director's Cuts Production Music, and *Nickelodeon* magazine. Viacom's film presence is evident in its Paramount Pictures (e.g., Dreamworks) and its new media includes Internet holdings (e.g., Addictinggames.com), MTV Mobile, and MTV Games (e.g., Rock Band). Lastly, *General Electric* owns television (e.g., three networks including NBC, 26 stations, 14 international channels, and various programming), cinema and film production, print

> **Conglomerate:** A corporation made up of several different widely diversified companies.

SOCIOLOGY *IN PRACTICE*

CANADIAN RADIO-TELEVISION AND TELECOMMUNICATIONS COMMISSION

The Canadian Radio-television and Telecommunications Commission (CRTC) is an independent organization that supervises and regulates Canadian broadcasting. Community channels were introduced in the 1970s to foster Canadian participation in broadcasting and to encourage diversity. However, CRTC audits (i.e., checks on policies and processes) from 2002–2005 revealed that most cable companies fell short of the original intention. In August 2010, the CRTC issued a new policy reflecting the interests of local citizens by making community involvement mandatory in at least half of the programming effective September 1, 2014 (Canadian Radio-television and Telecommunications Commission, 2010b). We'll soon see if this new policy is any better at obtaining compliance.

(e.g., *Sci Fi* magazine) and Internet assets alongside various other major holdings including military production (e.g., F-16 Fighter jets), theme parks (i.e., Universal Studios Theme Parks and Resorts), consumer products (e.g., GE Industrial), and additional sectors (e.g., GE Commercial Finance and GE Healthcare). General Electric is the largest of the Big Six and it also makes the most money—with annual revenues of $157 billion (Free Press, 2011).

Canadian Media Convergence

Media convergence also exists in Canada. For example, Bell Canada Enterprises bought out one of Canada's largest private television networks (CTV Inc.) and rebranded it as Bell Media, which includes the CTV network and its various affiliates (e.g., 27 TV channels, 6 A-Channels, and 30 specialty channels including TSN and Discovery Channel). It also formed an alliance with the Thomson Corporation (one of the world's largest publishing companies originating in Canada), and it controls part of *The Globe and Mail* along with 33 radio stations and various Internet holdings such as Sympatico.ca (CBC News, 2010b).

LO⁴ AGENDA SETTING: THE MEDIA IS NOT NEUTRAL

Business giants such as the Big Four of Music, Big Five of Television, and the Big Six of Media can selectively set the agenda or largely determine what issues we will be exposed to as we read the papers, watch television, or listen to the radio. Will the focus be the economy (e.g., the deficit), the environment, health care, or crime? Things that we are exposed to repeatedly become salient (i.e., relevant) and thereby seem important to us. Hence, the media also tells the public which issues they should be most interested in. There is a link between agenda setting in the media, what the public thinks is important, and the policies that are developed to deal with the issues (Soroka, 2002; Wanta & Ghanem, 2007). As political scientist Bernard Cohen (1963) noted, "the press may not be successful much of the time in telling people what to think, but it is stunningly successful in telling its readers what to think about" (p. 13).

"Let's tweet that there's civil unrest in Torquay and see if it gets reported on the news"

SOCIOLOGY *IN MY COMMUNITY*

FAIRNESS AND ACCURACY IN REPORTING

Fairness and Accuracy in Reporting (FAIR) is a national media watch group that advocates for more diversity and less bias in media reporting.

FAIR identifies marginalizing media practices (i.e., criticizes media bias) and offers the general public alternate viewpoints.

Several theorists in a variety of disciplines highlight the implications of private, centralized ownership of the mass media for agenda setting. For example, in *Manufacturing Consent: The Political Economy of the Mass Media*, Herman and Chomsky (1988) explain how the news media industry is controlled by a concentrated elite group. This group creates propaganda (i.e., biased persuasive communications) about international affairs that then becomes the basis of what the public is repeatedly exposed to as daily news. Herman and Chomsky's ideas became known more widely as *the propaganda model*. In contrast to what the general public perceives to be true about a democratic system (e.g., free and open press), Herman and Chomsky (1988) claim that the mass media serves the interests of those in power by filtering the kind of messages received by the public in a way that generates (i.e., manufactures) consent for particular political and economic agendas. Reflect on how Canada's involvement in international affairs, such as the wars in

Afghanistan or Iraq, is portrayed by the media, or what kinds of messages are emphasized just prior to an election.

Karen Dill (2009), a leading social psychologist in the area of media influence, notes an interesting paradox: We live in a culture that is powerfully influenced by media messages and yet we fail to recognize this because we feel we are invulnerable to such messages. We may accurately perceive that particular shows, messages, and advertisements are fictional, and that they contain paid actors and models who are endorsing specific products for the benefit of corporations. However, we also erroneously believe that the media is transparent—that news programs simply present us with "the facts" and that fictional programming's only function is to entertain us. On one hand, the mass media is an effective medium for conveying news, providing entertainment, sharing views, offering outlets for discussion, disseminating information, and networking. But on the other hand, they are primarily profit-centred businesses and some

SOCIOLOGY *ON SCREEN*

MICKEY MOUSE MONOPOLY

According to a critical documentary titled *Mickey Mouse Monopoly: Disney, Childhood, and Corporate Power,* then chairman and chief executive officer Michael Eisner of Walt Disney once stated in an internal memo, "We have no objective to make history, we have no objective to make art, we have no objective to make a statement, to make money is

our only objective" (Sun and Picker, 2001). In addition to highlighting issues of commercialism and corporate control, this eye-opening documentary encourages viewers to think critically about the stereotyped representations of gender, race, and ethnicity that are portrayed in popular Disney animated films.

become so successful that they come to dominate and thereby control the market as monopolies and conglomerates.

TIME TO REVIEW

- How does a functionalist perspective view the mass media?

- How does a conflict perspective view the mass media?

- What do sociologists mean when they say that mass media ownership is concentrated?

- What are the implications of media ownership concentration for agenda setting?

- What main paradox exists in relation to mass media influence?

LO⁵ HOW THE MEDIA SHAPES OUR PERCEPTIONS

THE INTERACTIONIST FRAMEWORK

The micro-level interactionist theoretical framework helps us appreciate how we are individually and uniquely influenced by people around us, from the significant others who are important to us and central to our well-being (e.g., family members, our intimate partners, and our close friends), to those from whom we take cues or learn particular skills in more temporary or isolated situations (e.g., a manager who trains you to perform the basics of your job, or a professor who teaches you sociology), to the more abstract generalized other that reflects an understanding of group attitudes and norms. In the case of media influence for any given individual, bear in mind that, as consumers, people choose to indulge in certain forms of mass media (e.g., television and social networking), and they select particular versions of those media (e.g., SportsNet and Facebook). People can also opt in or out of forms of mass media, although in some cases they may face social sanctions such as when friends are suddenly unable to reach them through Facebook. Moreover, people may selectively spend a lot of time, a moderate amount of time, or very little time exposed to any or all of the various forms of media. While we will discuss some of the common messages that may result from media socialization shortly, because of individuals' unique experiences with the media, the effects of mass media socialization on any one of us is

quite difficult to establish and continues to generate much debate.

Recall that the symbolic interactionist perspective is interested in communication, interpretation, and meaning. In *Frame Analysis* (1974), Canadian-born sociologist Erving Goffman (1922–1982) explains that *how* an interaction or event is depicted or framed is integral to its perceived meaning. Similarly, sociologist Stuart Hall (b. 1932) used the term *representation* to describe the way in which meanings are attributed to media images. There are multiple interpretations for the media images we see and, hence, the meaning of a particular image emerges from an interaction between the characteristics of the image itself and the nature of individual's own interpretation of that image (Hall, 2009).

Political scientist and public policy analyst Robert Entman (1991) maintains that the most essential determinant of framing is "sizing" since this helps the general public interpret the importance of an event. *Sizing* refers to "the overall salience of the event in the flow of the news" based on "how much material on the event is available" and "how prominently it is displayed" (Entman, 1991, p. 9). Thus, an event that receives a lot of coverage (e.g., it is the leading story in multiple forms of mass media for many days) will be interpreted as most important while other issues will be deemed less relevant mainly because the public is not as aware of them. Clearly, "if it bleeds, it leads," but for how long? Interestingly, while disasters make front-page news, after a few days the media frequently moves on to the next big story, sometimes erroneously leading the public to perceive that the issue has been resolved.

In addition to sizing, Entman (1991) identifies four other properties of news narrative that contribute to frames and help to create meaning by making certain aspects of news media more salient including agency, identification, categorization, and generalization.*

1. *Agency* refers to the inclusion of particular words that suggest where responsibility for an event lies. For example, *Newsweek*'s cover headline "Murder in the Air," and *Time*'s "Shooting to Kill/The Soviets Destroy an Airliner" helped to frame the 1983 downing of Korean Air Lines Flight 007 as an intentional event with a clearly guilty party (Entman, 1991, p. 6).

2. *Identification* includes the use of words that encourage (or discourage) identification with the central characters in a news story. Entman (1991) suggested the inclusion of names of victims or "humanizing" phrases such as "innocent human beings" or "loved ones" encourages identification,

---

*Source: Adapted from Entman, R. (1991). Framing U.S. coverage of international news: Contrasts in narratives of the KAL and Iran air incidents. *Journal of Communication, 41,* (4), 51–58.

while use of neutral terms such as "those who died" or "civilians" discourages identification (p. 17).

3. *Categorization* refers the overall framework used to label an event by the media. The Korean Air Lines incident mentioned earlier was most frequently categorized as an "attack" as opposed to a "tragedy" in the print media (Entman, 1991).

4. Lastly, *generalization* refers to the extent to which a media story is generalized to a larger political system or issue. When Pakistan experienced a catastrophic flood in 2010, financial aid was slow to follow. Because of the country's ongoing state of political instability, media stories frequently speculated that money received for aid might be thwarted by corrupt officials or used to support terrorism.

On television, framing centres on the main characters who deliver messages, such as the lead anchor on the national news or the outspoken judge on a reality series—remember Simon Cowell during his years on *American Idol?* In addition, framing includes the overall objectives of particular shows; the tough guy wins the Ultimate Fighting Championship title and the best-looking young woman becomes America's Next Top Model. Together, the characters and themes perpetuate common but unrealistic cultural notions such as the belief that anyone can achieve success, celebrity status, and popularity.

The same messages are present in product advertisements: Buy this beer and you too will be lounging on a beach surrounded by a bevy of scantily clad beauties! Print advertisements are also laden with techniques such as descriptive words, background colours, and images placed in particular ways to draw our attention, much like pop-up ads on the Internet that grab our focus by claiming we've won something and by encouraging us to click on a tab for more information. The three most prevailing themes portrayed repeatedly in the mass media that raise concerns for academics and viewers centre on (1) consumerism, (2) stereotypes, and (3) violence.

CONSUMERISM: THE MEDIA TEACHES US THAT WE NEED TO BUY PRODUCTS

"It's not fair!" was response from the eight-year-old son of one of the authors who learned he could not have his own credit card nor would he be given access to his mother's Visa. He explained that he needed a credit card to purchase "sand dollars" in the Facebook game *Fish Ville,* which he accessed via his mother's Facebook account. He further protested that the awesome fish and specialty items that he wished to purchase for his virtual tank exceed the number of sand dollars he could ever earn playing the game for free. Not surprisingly, the same child wanted to shop only at a store called West 49, carrying designer-labelled jeans, T-shirts, hoodies, and runners, for his back-to-school clothes. The power of advertising is the second most researched area with respect to media effects on consumers after violence. According to many decades of research on advertising's influence on children, there is a small, but significant, effect of media advertising on children. Repeated exposure to advertising increases brand recognition, which results in positive associations with particular brands, and a desire to select those products (Desmond & Carveth, 2007). The influence on youth is profitable enough from a corporate standpoint to warrant investing billions of dollars targeting children in commercials, prompting the attention of parents, educators, and media critics.

SOCIOLOGY ON SCREEN

CONSUMING KIDS

The Media Education Foundation's best seller *Consuming Kids: The Commercialization of Childhood* is an excellent resource for anyone who wants to learn more about how corporations create a consumer culture through specially designed techniques used to sell children everything from junk foods to vacations. You can find out more about this film and others like it by visiting www.mediaed.org.

FEMINIST FRAMEWORK

In addition to fostering consumerism, the mass media presents us with certain types of messages, repeatedly. One of the negative implications of this practice is that the mass media shows stereotyped depictions of men, visible minorities, people with disabilities, gays, lesbians, the elderly, and especially, women. A **stereotype** is an overgeneralization about a group that is often based on faulty assumptions. Recall that the feminist perspectives point out how differences between men and women are largely the end result of socialization (not biology). Traditional gender roles are emphasized in the mass media in ways that continue to teach females to be nurturing and submissive and males to be aggressive and independent. Part of this occurs through repeated exposure to mass media generalizations about how women and men behave or how they ought to behave in society.

THE MEDIA REINFORCES STEREOTYPED IMAGES OF WOMEN AND MEN

The media teaches us, for example, that popular women are tuned into the latest consumer trends (i.e., they wear brand-name clothing, own many pairs of shoes, and still celebrate the joys of new appliances). The media also emphasizes the importance of women's beauty—especially the ultra-thin, busty Barbie Doll form of beauty. While women's images in the media are changing partly as a result of more women in higher positions of media power such as producers, the overall cultural messages remain. Anderson and Gray (2008) note that "the most common representation of women in the media is as victims, most commonly of sexual violence. Other consistent media images include women as overly feminized or sexualized; women as nurturing and caring, based on their role as mothers; and women as inscrutable and dangerous" (p. 462). Many studies have examined and substantiated the effects of stereotyped portrayal of women in the media. By the time girls reach the age of four or five, they have already internalized the narrow ideal of female beauty we get in media messages. Compared to those who watch less television, girls who are heavy television viewers have more restricted notions of female beauty, share more common perceptions of beauty, and place more emphasis on the importance of beauty (Stern, 2004).

Stereotype: An overgeneralization about a group that is often based on faulty assumptions.

The Bratz Dolls teach young girls about the importance of beauty and fashion.

Males are also portrayed in negative, stereotyped ways by the mass media. In an analysis of how men were depicted in newspapers, magazines, and television shows in the United States, United Kingdom, and Australia, Macnarmara (2006) found that men are consistently portrayed in relation to violence or aggression. In fact, more than 75 percent of media depictions show men as one of four main stereotypes: villains, aggressors, perverts, or philanderers (i.e., womanizers).

VIOLENCE IS THE NORM IN THE MASS MEDIA

Given its prevalence, violence is the most researched topic in the area of mass media. Much of our daily dose of violence comes from television—in sports from hockey to boxing, in the news from local shootings to international warfare, in our favorite prime-time dramas, and even in children's programming—especially in animation, where we've witnessed characters like the Teenage Ninja Mutant Turtles demonstrating their martial arts skills or Pokémon fighting each other to enhance their trainer's skills. Violence is also an integral ingredient of many of the movies we go see in theatres (e.g., *Saw, The Departed, Kill Bill,* and *Inglourious Basterds*). Many of the most popular video games, such as the *Call of Duty, Halo,* and *Grand Theft Auto* series, also contain violent content that is built into the main plots and themes.

Grand Theft Auto, a highly successful series of video games, receives its share of controversy with accusations that the game promotes a subculture of violence and lawlessness among youth by glorifying

VIOLENCE IN RAP MUSIC

Violence is prevalent in the music industry as evident in the lyrics of songs that top the billboard charts. At the time of writing this chapter, Eminem's "Love the Way You Lie" featuring Rihanna was number one on the HOT 100 and it contains the confession "I laid hands on her." Much of Eminem's rap music contains references to violence between males and some songs include references to acts of violence committed by males toward their girlfriends. In the now-notorious suicide song "Stan" by Eminem and featuring Dido, we hear the line "Hey Slim, that's my girlfriend screamin, in the trunk" shortly before Stan drives his car off a bridge. In a study by Burgess, Dill, and Wright (2009), college students reported that the most common representations of women within rap songs they listened to were "ho" or "whore," "bitch," and "slut" and that rappers were most likely to rap about "sex," "drugs," "money," "women," and "violence."

car theft, drug use, random acts of killing, driving under the influence of alcohol, and negative depictions of women. Although both sex and violence can frequently be found in video games, some game developers have taken it to an extreme. For example, in 2006 the game *RapeLay* was released in Japan. In this game, players hold the role of a male character that, based on the players' choices, stalks, sexually assaults, and even gang rapes a mother and her two daughters. As you have already likely guessed, outrage ensued over the release of this game, and it was eventually removed from the market.

Since we are exposed to so much violence and in so many ways, we have to wonder what happens to viewers as a result of all this exposure. Does violence have any real effect on consumers? Should the newest *Call of Duty*, or some other equally violent video game, be banned from distribution or even censored by the government? Most people would say no and, to date, no games have been banned in Canada. This means the more appropriate question is: *Who should be allowed to play them?* Common sense suggests that we should not allow young children to play violent video games rated M (for mature). But what if all of the 8-, 9-, or 10-year-old kids are already playing such games? Is it okay as long as the child has parental consent or knows the content is fictional? Will early exposure to first- and third-person shooter-based war simulation games create violence-prone adults? What does the research tell us? Studies on the links between media violence and aggression are the most prevalent and debated area of research in literature on the effects of the mass media.

LO⁶ SOCIAL LEARNING THEORY

In his now classic studies on observational learning, Canadian-born social psychologist Albert Bandura (b. 1925) and his colleagues conducted a series of

Do video games promote violence?

Source: Getty Images

experiments in the 1960s demonstrating how children learn to imitate aggression displayed by adults. In the first experiment, children who earlier witnessed a social model (i.e., an adult research assistant) act aggressively toward an inflated "Bobo the Clown" doll later imitated the behaviour when engaged in free play (see Bandura, Ross & Ross, 1961). The same process was enacted when children observed the behaviour of aggressive adult on film (see Bandura, Ross & Ross, 1963 and refer to the series of photos shown below). A later study showed that aggressive imitation still takes place but can be eliminated through the introduction of positive incentives and lessoned through the subsequent use of punishment (Bandura, 1965). *Social learning theory* proposes that people learn by observing the behaviour of others (as well as its consequences) (Bandura, 1978), and then go on to imitate that behaviour. Hence, one of the immediate effects of viewing violence is that in the absence of other forms of intervention, it can lead to subsequent acts of aggression.

This theory has been used to explain real-world acts of violence, such as the school shooting that happened in Taber, Alberta, on April 28, 1999, when a 14-year-old boy named Todd Cameron Smith walked into W. R. Myers High and shot two students with his sawed-off .22 rifle; one of the victims was killed, the other seriously injured. This event occurred only eight days after a highly publicized school shooting at Columbine High School in Colorado, where students Eric Harris and Dylan Klebold shot and killed 12 of their fellow students and one teacher, and injured 24 others before committing suicide. The similarity of these two incidents prompted many people to speculate that the Taber shooting had been a "copy cat" crime that was primed by the news exposure and imitated through social learning, much like the children who had beaten up the Bobo doll several decades earlier.

We learn not only about acts of violence in the media, but also how to enact aggression. Lieutenant Colonel Dave Grossman notes that he trains elite military and law enforcement officers and knows of no comparable military skill achievement to that of Michael Carneal, a 14-year-old boy who had previously never fired a real gun but managed to fire eight shots from a .22 pistol into a group of students at Heath High School in West Paducah, Kentucky, hitting eight of them; five with head shots and three with hits to the upper torso. Grossman indicates that Michael Carneal learned these skills playing simulated shooter games at home and in video arcades (Grossman & Degaetano, 1999).

TAKE THAT BOBO. In Bandura's classic experiment, children were shown a movie (top four frames) of a model hitting a Bobo doll. If they saw the model rewarded for this behaviour, they treated the doll similarly (middle and bottom rows).

DESENSITIZATION THEORY

Desensitization theory proposes that repeated exposure to violence lessens its emotional impact. Compare the very strong emotional reaction of a young viewer who sees someone murdered on television for the first time to one who has already seen hundreds of acts of violence in movies, television programs, and video games. Over time, children come to realize that violence is part of television and, like cartoons, it isn't real. The nightmares that children may initially have when they see something scary are real. But over time, the same children will be less emotionally impacted by observing on-screen violence and, in all likelihood, will eventually join the masses who don't think twice about the violence they may be seeing in movies, video games, or even on the evening news.

Professor of communications George Gerbner points out in a video called "Killing Screens: Media & the Culture of Violence," that mass media producers know about desensitization effects and, hence, need to come up with new techniques for gaining attention. Thus, movie sequels tend to have more killings presented in more dramatic, highly sensationalized ways as we move from earlier versions to the more current ones (e.g., the *Saw* and *Scream* series) in order to maintain consumer interest (Dinozzi, 1997). If you don't believe this, try counting the number of murders in the first movie in a violent series compared to one of its sequels. More people will die and/or be killed in much more gruesome ways in the sequels. The effects of violence over time are also accounted for by the cultivation theory.

CULTIVATION THEORY

Unlike desensitization theory, which focuses on diminished emotional reactions, cultivation theory explains how our thinking changes in specific ways as a result of repeated exposure to violence. *Cultivation theory* purports that repeated exposure to television violence results in cumulative effects on viewers. It begins with fear and a sense of vulnerability that one will become a victim of violence, and progresses to the point where people believe that the world is more dangerous than it really is, termed *the mean world syndrome*. This can lead people to seek out more protective measures than are actually warranted, such as greater government intervention (Gerbner, Gross, Morgan, Signorielli & Shanahan, 2002), and explains in part, why some Canadians endorse things such as curfew bylaws to keep adolescents off the streets at night and perhaps why some people feel they need to carry handguns for protection.

SOCIOLOGY *IN PRACTICE*

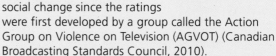

MANAGING CHILDREN'S EXPOSURE TO VIOLENCE

Various efforts have been made to try to manage children's exposure to violence, including the use of V-chips and other program-blocking technology designed to allow parents to customize what their children view at home. All Canadian stations (even if they air an American show) include show ratings and blocking technology embedded into the broadcast signal. Symbols and icons appear on screen to denote program content that includes violence, coarse language, sexuality, and/or mature scenes. This practice has been in effect since 1997 and it demonstrates how collective efforts can promote social change since the ratings were first developed by a group called the Action Group on Violence on Television (AGVOT) (Canadian Broadcasting Standards Council, 2010).

Summing up Lessons Learned about Media Violence

Taken together, research shows us that exposure to media violence teaches people about violence (e.g., how to enact it), can lead to desensitization (where we are less affected by it), and can lead to the eventual acceptance of violence. The propensity to become violent develops over time with media exposure. For example, short-term effects include increased physical and verbal aggression as well as increased aggressive thoughts and emotions. Long-term effects include an increased risk of engaging in physical assaults and even spousal abuse (Anderson, Berkowitz, Donnerstein, Huesmann, Johnson, Linz, Malamuth & Wartella, 2003).

Although a sizable body of research finds short- and long-term negative effects of media violence, other related questions and issues continue to somewhat undermine these results. For instance, are we certain we have a handle on what exactly constitutes an act of aggression in the media? Do we include all psychological and physical forms of aggression—the coworker who starts a nasty rumour about someone in order to get ahead; the wife who playfully slaps her husband on the bottom as he walks by? Is violence in a video game the same as violence found on television? Is the violence in a movie the same as violence on the news? In addition to the issue of how violence should be defined or measured, most of the effects are indirect, they are difficult to establish for any given person, and while most people are exposed to considerable amounts of media violence on a regular basis, relatively few people behave aggressively in the real world. Hence, some academics are still not convinced there is *conclusive* support that exposure to violence creates subsequent violence (e.g., Freedman, 2002; Barker & Petley, 1977). Even if academics were convinced of the negative implications of media violence, it is doubtful that the owners of the media could be persuaded to stop producing what the general public continues to consume in high demand.

In this regard, some researchers have opted for a more holistic approach that moves beyond the arguments that seek to condemn or support views of media violence to consider violence in a broader context such as the social and political factors that encourage it (Trend, 2007). Other approaches consider opposing viewpoints, look at violence as a social problem or consider a range of views on how society should best respond to media violence (e.g., Dudley, 1999). We

Media literacy: The ability to recognize, critically assess, and make informed choices about the messages contained in mass media forms.

won't resolve the media debate here and we'll leave you to consider your own position on this. Perhaps by turning to the postmodern view in closing, you can appreciate more fully why any given perspective will likely be inadequate for explaining the influences of today's ever-changing media.

POSTMODERN FRAMEWORK

The postmodern framework is probably best suited to helping us appreciate the many ways that our lives change with each new media form. Recall that postmodern ideas tend to underlie social action. The popularity of YouTube attests to the ability of consumers to influence the media and each other in ways that reshape cultural trends. Similarly, the ability to communicate quickly and widely via the Internet on the social networking platform Facebook helped students in Egypt successfully mobilize to overthrow the government in a monumental revolution. Postmodern approaches to the media also encourage consumers to be aware of media ownership objectives, to think critically about the messages taken in, and to make informed choices about the kind of messages and mediums they choose to engage with.

LO⁷ Media Literacy: Thinking Critically about the Media

Media literacy refers to the ability to recognize, critically assess, and make informed choices about messages contained in mass media forms. According to the Media Awareness Network (2010), media understanding includes an acceptance of these eight assumptions:*

1. *All media are constructions.* Media content is created to convey a particular message. Media literacy works toward deconstructing (or taking apart) these messages to show how or why they were made.
2. *The media construct reality.* The media is responsible for the majority of the observations and experiences from which we build up our personal understandings of the world and how it works. Recall in Chapter 1 how we noted "things are not what they seem."
3. *Audiences negotiate the meaning in media.* Individuals interpret meanings in a variety of ways depending on their own life experiences, familial and cultural background, age, gender, ethnicity, and so on.
4. *Media have commercial interests.* Media literacy aims to encourage an awareness of how the media is

*Source: Adapted from Media Awareness Network's (2010) Eight Key Concept for Media Literacy. John Pungente, S.J. From Barry Duncan et al. Media Literacy Resource Guide, Ontario Ministry of Education, Toronto, ON, Canada, 1989.

SOCIOLOGY *IN MY COMMUNITY*

MEDIA EDUCATION

Teaching media literacy in schools is a great example of sociology in action. An abundance of free online materials attest to the sharing of information by teachers and educators who wish to incorporate media literacy directly into their lesson plans from elementary school through university. You can learn more about media education in Canada on the Media Awareness Network site, www.media-awareness.ca, where you can view curriculum outcomes for media literacy by province or territory.

influenced by commercial considerations and how these affect content, technique, and distribution. Most media production is a business, and must therefore make a profit. Questions of ownership and control are central. As we noted earlier, the Big Four, Five, and Six own most of the leading recording companies, television networks, newspapers, radio stations, film production companies, and other forms of mass media.

5. *Media contain ideological and value messages.* All media products are advertising, in some sense, since they proclaim values and ways of life. Explicitly or implicitly, the mass media conveys key ideological messages such as the nature of the good life, the virtue of consumerism, the roles of women and men, and the prevalence of violence.

6. *Media have social and political implications.* Media have a great influence on politics and social change. They have the power to set agendas and limit who and what we will be exposed to (e.g., national leaders, health issues, environmental concerns). They give us an intimate sense of national issues and global concerns, so that we

become citizens of what Marshall McLuhan termed a "global village."

7. *Form and content are closely related in the media.* The media as a whole may report the same things, but each medium will have its own grammar and codify reality in its own particular way.

8. *Each medium has a unique aesthetic form.* Just as we notice the pleasing rhythms of certain pieces of poetry or prose, so we ought to be able to enjoy the pleasing forms and effects of the different media.

In order to become media literate, we need to accomplish several things. First, we need to understand the nature of the mass media. (i.e., that the mass media is a profit-centred, highly concentrated industry that uses techniques in order to construct reality for viewers). We also need to appreciate the wider implications of media (e.g., how the media exposes us to large doses of violence, how it portrays stereotypes, and how it promotes consumerism). Finally, we need to develop critical viewing skills. For example, we need to be aware that we are being influenced, we need to consider who is sending the message and we need to think about what that particular message is designed to do.

SOCIOLOGY *IN MY LIFE*

MEDIA LITERACY IN ACTION

Reflect on what you've learned in this chapter. Do you consider yourself to be media literate? What does media literacy mean to you, personally? Here are five ways you can demonstrate media literacy skills through social action.

1. *Check out alternate media sources.* Go to www.adbusters.org for a look at a nonprofit magazine

that is premised on the negative influences of capitalism and consumerism. Visit www.independentmedia.ca to learn more about topics you seldom hear about in the

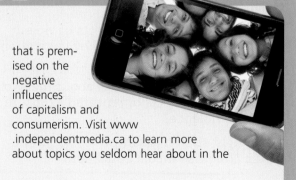

continued

news (e.g., consolidation of corporate power) and locate alternate media sources that are noncorporate independent information suppliers.

2. *Find out what is said about video games that you, your friends, or your children are playing.* There's an excellent site for this called Common Sense Media (www.commonsensemedia.org); it provides ratings of movies, games, mobile apps, websites, television shows, books, and music in terms of their suitability for kids (regardless of their actual rating). The site includes detailed rationale for ratings (e.g., ease of play, educational value, and things to watch out for such as violence, online interaction, language, consumerism, etc.). You can also find recommendation listings by age groups.

3. *Join a media literacy association so you can network with other media literacy advocates.* For example, the Association for Media Literacy is an educational organization that was founded in 1978 and is made up of teachers, professionals, and others (e.g., parents) concerned about the impact of mass media on society.

4. *Sample a variety of media sources instead of just saturating yourself in one main mass media form* (e.g., watch news on television but also find other sources of information on the Internet and read books).

5. *Take a stance on an issue that you feel is being treated inappropriately by the mass media.* For example, if you are fed up with derogatory depictions of women shown on prime-time television and in magazine advertisements, consider boycotting some of the main offenders. Check out cases in point including one from *America's Top Model* which sexualizes a crime scene depicting a murdered woman in the Gallery under Odius Images at www .mediawatch.com. You can also voice your opinion by writing a letter to the editor of your local newspaper or by posting a comment on YouTube that reflects something about the mass media that came to your attention while reading this chapter.

TIME TO REVIEW

- How do individuals' unique experiences influence the kind of socialization provided by the mass media?

- In what ways is media news framed to make messages more apparent?

- How does a feminist perspective shape one's view of the mass media?

- What is the main assumption of social learning theory?

- What does desensitization theory add to our understanding of the effects of media violence?

- What kind of cumulative effects of violent media exposure are predicted by cultivation theory?

- What has research shown us about the short and long-term effects of repeated exposure to media violence?

- What eight shared assumptions about the media comprise media education?

CONCLUSIONS

Much of the research that has been done on the mass media has focused upon the various concerns that have been voiced over aspects of its production and content. But this certainly does not mean that the mass media does nothing but corrupt human kind. New forms of electronically mediated communications such as texting, Tweets, and Facebook updates play a central role in many of our lives, particularly for providing us with real-time information. While the traditional forms of mass media eventually led to the development of new media such as "apps," it is the applications themselves (e.g., Twitter and Facebook), that are changing mass media into media that is truly mediated by the masses as opposed to the corporate elite. Although it is sometimes demonized because of its inherent consumerism, as well as presence of violence and gender stereotypes, the mass media also serves important positive functions. It is only through the media that we can sometimes learn about events affecting our close and more distant friends or relatives (e.g., what issues they support), our communities (e.g., local events happening here), and our world (e.g., the destruction of the Twin Towers on 9/11, the revolution that changed Egypt's political structure, the nuclear disaster in Japan, and the fighting in Libya).

The media can keep us safe, such as by broadcasting a tornado warning or a food alert. Cell phones and texting enable parents to keep closer tabs on their children, and intimate partners to touch base during their busy days. Facebook enables friends and family members who are separated by long distances to have a greater presence in each others' everyday lives. The Internet brings virtual communities together—whether you are a new parent, someone suffering from a debilitating disease, someone too busy to find a potential date any other way, or a GLBT (i.e., gay, lesbian, bisexual, or transgendered) youth, you can find an online group of similar others who provide each other with support and suggestions for life's challenges. And, of course, the media also entertains us (even if this is not its primary purpose), and human beings have been creating means of entertainment for thousands of years. Even the authors of this book have been known to occasionally escape into the violent mass-mediated worlds of *Rambo*, boxing, UFC on pay-per-view, and Mafia Wars on Facebook.

CHAPTER SUMMARY

LO¹ Describe the history of traditional forms of mass media.

Prior to the Internet, the mass media consisted of books, newspapers, magazines, cinema, recordings, radio, and television.

LO² Describe the role of new media forms, including whether they make traditional ones obsolete.

Modern forms of media are referred to as new media and include the Internet, video and computer games, and mobile (cell) phones with downloadable applications. The Internet changed all of the traditional forms of mass media (e.g., books are now available online, radio audio streams can now be accessed over the Internet, etc.) but new forms of media didn't eliminate the traditional ones, which have features we still enjoy for their own unique experience (e.g., watching a movie on a big screen or listening to a radio). However, new forms are also unique and are sometimes better for other reasons, such as multitasking with an iPhone.

LO³ Differentiate between media assumptions provided by the core sociological frameworks.

A functionalist framework points out ways that the media helps us find out about important events and helps us better communicate with each other to become more socially aware and connected with others on an ongoing basis. The conflict framework notes how the mass media is a profit-based business with concentrated ownership, which influences the kind of information we are exposed to. The interactionist framework helps us understand how individuals uniquely interpret media messages.

Feminist frameworks highlight how the mass media portrays stereotyped images of certain groups such as women and emphasizes particular messages such as the importance of beauty. Finally, the postmodern framework helps us better appreciate the many ways our lives have changed with technology and how the media facilitates social action.

LO⁴ Evaluate the relevance of media ownership for agenda setting.

Media ownership is highly concentrated under the Big Four of Music, Big Five of Television, and Big Six of Media. These corporations own most of the ways we receive information and thereby largely determine what issues the public is exposed to and what it comes to think is important.

LO⁵ Demonstrate a critical understanding of ways that media shapes our perceptions.

As a major agent of socialization, the mass media teaches us to hold particular political views, it teaches us to be fixated on consumerism (i.e., the need to buy things), it reinforces stereotypes including beauty standards, and it exposes us to a wealth of violence.

LO⁶ Debate whether violence in the media causes viewers to become violent.

On the one hand, research shows that we become less sensitive to media violence over time such that we require greater amounts for stimulation. Eventually, we suffer cultivated cumulative effects including an increased fear of victimization and the belief that the world is more dangerous than it is in reality. Importantly, increased exposure to violence leads to an increased likelihood of behaving and thinking in subsequent aggressive ways. On the other hand, research also fails to resolve many issues including providing conclusive evidence of a direct link between exposure to violence and subsequent acts of violence and even reaching a consensus about what constitutes an act of violence.

LO⁷ Illustrate what it means to be "media literate."

We can help to diffuse some of the potential negative effects of media viewing by varying our media exposure, by becoming more aware of media influence, and by improving our ability to deconstruct media messages through media literacy education.

RECOMMENDED READINGS

1. To learn more about YouTube's influence as a media power or YouTube's content as a source of popular culture, we recommend: Burgess, J., & Green, J. (2009). *YOUTUBE: Online Video and Participatory Culture*. Digital Media and Society Series. Cambridge, UK: Polity Press.

2. For an exploration of how the mass media portrays men and to find out more about male identity, we recommend: Macnarmara, J. R. (2006). *Media and Male Identity: The Making and Remaking of Men*. New York: Palgrave Macmillan.

3. For more information on the business side of the mass media we recommend: Chouliaraki, L., & Morsing, M. (2010). *Media, Organizations, and Identity*. New York: Palgrave Macmillan.

4. To review some of the main findings on media violence and learn more about how media violence is conceptualized, refer to: Potter, W. J. (1999). *On Media Violence*. Thousand Oaks, CA: Sage Publications.

5. For an elaboration and critical discussion of media saturation, media violence, media representations, agenda setting, and recommendations for improving media habits, we recommend: Dill, K. (2009). *How Fantasy Becomes Reality: Seeing Through Media Influence*. New York, NY: Oxford University Press.

FOR FURTHER REFLECTION

1. Should the Internet be regulated?

2. Who owns the mass media and why is media ownership an important consideration?

3. Select a full-page advertisement from any magazine of your choosing and bring it to class. Record answers to the following questions and be prepared to share them in class:

   a. What product (or service) is the focus of this ad?

   b. Who owns or is responsible for this ad?

   c. What technique(s) are used to attract attention to this ad?

   d. Who is the primary targeted audience for this product?

   e. What is the main message depicted in this ad?

   f. What other representations are evident in this ad?

4. Interview someone in a different generation from you (e.g., your mother, an uncle, a grandparent, or an elderly neighbour) about the media. What was the main media form in his or her youth? What was the primary function of that media form? What was the "leading-edge" media of that time and how was that new form of media expected to change things?

REFERENCES

Ahonen, T. (2009). *Mobile phones: The next 4 billion with Tomi Ahonen*. FORA.tv: The Conference Channel. FORAtvSERIES: PICNIC Festival 2009. Retrieved August 9, 2011, from http://fora.tv/2009/09/24/Mobile_Phones_The_Next_4_Billion_with_Tomi_Ahonen

Ahonen, T. (2008). *Mobile as 7th of the Mass Media*. Futuretext. http://mobile7th.futuretext.com

Akkad, O. E. (2011, March 8). Canadians Internet usage nearly double the worldwide average. In Tech News. *The Globe and Mail*. Retrieved July 25, 2011, from www.theglobeandmail.com/news/technology/tech-news/canadians-Internet-usage-nearly-double-the-worldwide-average/article1934508/

Anderson, C. A., Berkowitz, L., Donnerstein, E., Huesmann, L. R., Johnson, J. D, Linz, D., Malamuth, N. M., & Wartella, E. (2003). The influence of media violence on youth. *Psychological Sciences in the Public Interest, 4*(3), 81–110.

Anderson, R. and Gray, J. (Eds.). (2008). *Battleground: The Media*, Volume 2. Westport, CT: Greenwood Press.

Avery, S. (2008, July 23). Private radio profits up, boosted by ad jumps. *The Globe and Mail*. Retrieved July 25, 2011, from www.theglobeandmail.com/report-on-business/private-radio-profits-up-boosted-by-ad-jumps/article699543/?cmpid=tgc

Bandura, A. (1978). Social learning theory of aggression. *Journal of Communication, 28*(3), 12–29.

Bandura, A. (1965). Influence of model's reinforcement contingencies on the acquisition of imitative responses. *Journal of Personality and Social Psychology, 1,* 589–595.

Bandura, A., Ross, D., & Ross, S. A. (1963). Imitation of film-mediated aggressive models. *Journal of Abnormal and Social Psychology, 66,* 3–11.

Bandura, A., Ross, D., & Ross, S. A. (1961). Transmission of aggression through imitation of aggressive models. *Journal of Abnormal and Social Psychology, 63,* 575–582.

Barker, M., & Petley, J. (Eds.). (1977). *Ill Effects: The Media/ Violence Debate.* New York, NY: Routledge.

Billboard.com. (2010). *Billboard hot 100 chart archives.* Retrieved July 25, 2011, from www.billboard.com/#/ charts/hot-100?chartDate=2009-04-18 and www .billboard.com/#/charts/hot-100?chartDate=2009-10-04

Burgess, M. C. R., Dill, K. E., & Wright, B. A. (2009). You're my bitch: Crude and degrading treatment of women in hardcore rap through the eyes of the predominantly White target audience. In J. H. Urlich and B. T. Cosell (Eds.), *Handbook of Gender Roles: Conflicts, Attitudes and Behaviors.* Hauppauge, NY: NovaScience Publishers.

Burgess, J., & Green, J. (2009). *YOUTUBE: Online Video and Participatory Culture.* Digital Media and Society Series. Cambridge, UK: Polity Press.

Canadian Broadcasting Standards Council. (2010). *Ratings classifications.* Ottawa, ON: Author. Retrieved July 25, 2011, from www.cbsc.ca/english/agvot/ratings.php

(The) Canadian Encyclopedia. (2010). The first periodicals. In *The Canadian Encyclopedia.* Historica-Dominion: Sandra Martin. Retrieved July 25, 2011, from http:// thecanadianencyclopedia.com/index.cfm?PgNm= TCE&Params=A1ARTA0005028#SEC823872

Canadian Newspaper Association. (2010a, April). *Daily Newspapers Circulation Report 2009.* Toronto, ON: Author. Retrieved August 9, 2010 from www.cna-acj.ca/ en/system/files/2009CirculationDataReport_1.pdf

Canadian Newspaper Association. (2010b, July). *About newspapers.* Ownership: Daily Newspapers. Retrieved March 16, 2011, from www.newspaperscanada.ca/about-newspapers/ownership/ownership-daily-newspapers/ ownership-daily-newspapers

Canadian Radio-television and Telecommunications Commission. (2010a). *CRTC issues annual report on the communications industry.* Ottawa, ON: Government of Canada. Retrieved July 25, 2011, from www.crtc.gc.ca/ eng/com100/2010/r100729.htm

Canadian Radio-television and Telecommunications Commission. (2010b, August 26). *CRTC changes community television policy to enhance local participation.* Toronto, ON: CNW News Group. Retrieved July 25, 2011, from www.newswire.ca/en/releases/archive/ August2010/26/c5047.html

CBC News. (2010a, March 22). Canadians prefer PC to TV: survey. In Consumer Life. *CBC News online.* Retrieved July 25, 2011, from www.cbc.ca/consumer/ story/2010/03/22/consumer-tv-online-web-Internet-viewing-habits.html

CBC News. (2010b, April 30). Media convergence, acquisitions and sales in Canada. *CBC News online.* Retrieved July 25, 2011, from www.cbc.ca/news/business/ story/2010/04/29/f-media-ownership-canada.html

Cohen, B. (1963). *The Press and Foreign Policy.* Princeton, NJ: Princeton University Press.

Desmond, R., & Carveth, R. (2007). The effect of advertising on children and adolescents: A meta analysis. In Raymond W. Preiss, Barbara Mae Galue, Nancy Burrell, Mike Allen, and Jennings Bryant (Eds.), *Mass Media Effects Research: Advanced through Meta-Analysis* (pp. 169–179). Mahway, NJ: Lawrence Erlbaum Associates.

Dill, K. (2009). *How Fantasy Becomes Reality: Seeing through Media Influence.* New York, NY: Oxford University Press.

Dinozzi, R. (Producer). (1997). *Killing Screens: Media & The Culture of Violence* [Documentary Film]. Northampton, MA: Media Education Foundation.

Dudley, W. (Ed.). (1999). *Media Violence: Opposing Viewpoints.* San Diego, CA: Greenhaven Press.

Entman, R. M. (1991). Framing U.S. coverage of international news: Contrasts in narratives of the KAL and Iran air incidents. *Journal of Communication, 41*(4), 6–27.

Encyclopaedia Britannica. (2011). *Sumerian writing.* Encyclopaedia Britanica Online. Retrieved July 25, 2011, from www.britannica.com/EBchecked/topic/670291/ Sumerian-writing

Evans, J. (2010, January). US digital sales boom—and vinyl comes for the ride! *9To5Mac: Apple Intelligence.* Retrieved August 15, 2010, from www.9to5mac.com/digital_music_ sales_20291

Filmmakers Magazine. (2010, August). *James Cameron biography.* Retrieved July 25, 2011, from www .filmmakers.com/artists/cameron/biography/index.htm

Freedman, J. L. (2002). *Media Violence and Its Effect on Aggression.* Toronto, ON: University of Toronto Press.

Free Press. (2011). *Who Owns the Media? The "Big Six" Companies.* Washington, DC: The Free Press and the Free Press Action Fund. Retrieved July 25, 2011, from www. freepress.net/resources/ownership

Gerbner, G., Gross, L., Morgan, M., Signorielli, N., & Shanahan, J. (2002). Growing up with television: Cultivation processes. In J. Bryant & D. Zillman (Eds.), *Media Effects: Advances in Theory and Research* (2nd ed.) (pp. 43–67). Mahwah, NJ: Lawrence Erlbaum Associates.

Goffman, E. (1974). *Frame Analysis.* Philadelphia, PA: University of Pennsylvania Press.

Grossman, E., & Degaetano, G. (1999). *Stop Teaching Our Kids to Kill: A Call to Action against TV, Movie, and Video Game Violence.* New York, NY: Crown Publishers.

Hall, S. (2009). The work of representation. In Stuart Hall (Ed.), *Representation: Cultural Representations and Signifying Practices* (pp. 1–11). Thousand Oaks, CA: Sage Publications.

Hammond Museum of Radio. (2011). *Early broadcasting.* Hammond Museum of Radio. Retrieved July 25, 2011, from www.hammondmuseumofradio.org/broadcast.html

Heneghan, T. (2010, August 7). Feel compelled to pray? There's an app for that: Technology brings religious practices into the digital world. *Edmonton Journal*, Reuters Life. Retrieved August 28, 2010, from www.edmontonjournal.com/life/Feel+compelled+pray+There+that/3372200/story.html

Herman, E. S., & Chomsky, N. (1988). *Manufacturing Consent: The Political Economy of the Mass Media.* New York: Pantheon.

Hubpages (2011). A brief history about music media. *Music Media: From 8-Tracks to MP3.* Hubpages.com. Retrieved July 25, 2011, from http://hubpages.com/hub/Music-Media

Library and Archives Canada. (2010). *The virtual gramophone: Canadian historical sound recordings.* Ottawa, ON: Government of Canada. Retrieved July 25, 2011, from www.collectionscanada.gc.ca/gramophone/index-e.html

Macnarmara, J. R. (2006). *Media and Male Identity: The Making and Remaking of Men.* New York, NY: Palgrave Macmillan.

Maloney, V. (2010, November). *Masthead Special Report: The Top 50.* Canadian Magazine Industry News. Retrieved July 25, 2011, from www.mastheadonline.com/news/2010/20100609874.shtml

McKeen, S. (2010, August 23). An app for everything, and everything in an app. *Edmonton Journal*, p. A5.

McLuhan, M. (1964). *Understanding Media: The Extensions of Man* (1st ed.). New York: McGraw Hill; reissued by MIT Press, 1994, with an introduction by Lewis H. Lapham.

Media Awareness Network. (2010). Eight key concepts for media literacy. *Media Literacy.* Retrieved July 25, 2011, from www.media-awareness.ca/english/teachers/media_literacy/key_concept.cfm

Mike's Radio World. (2010). *Canadian web radio: Canada's guide to Internet radio.* Retrieved July 25, 2011, from www.canadianwebradio.com

Nordal, G. (2010). A message from our president. *Nelson's Author Team: Newsletter*, 3 (Summer).

Province of Nova Scotia. (2010). *Halifax Gazette–Canada's first newspaper.* Halifax, NS: Government of Nova Scotia. Retrieved July 25, 2011, from www.gov.ns.ca/nsarm/virtual/gazette/?P=1

Soroka, S. (2002). *Agenda-Setting Dynamics in Canada.* Vancouver, BC: UBC Press.

Statistics Canada. (2010, May 10). Canadian Internet Use Survey. Table 2: Online activities of home Internet users. *The Daily.* Ottawa, ON: Author. Retrieved August 9, 2011, from www.statcan.gc.ca/daily-quotidien/100510/t100510a2-eng.htm

Statistics Canada. (2009). *Selected dwelling characteristics and household equipment.* Ottawa, ON: Author. Retrieved August 8, 2010, from www40.statcan.gc.ca/101/cst01/famil09c-eng.htm?sdi=video

Stern, S. R. (2004). All I really needed to know (about beauty) I learned by kindergarten: A cultivation analysis. In Rebecca Ann Lind (Ed.), *Race/Gender/Media: Considering Diversity across Audiences, Content, and Producers* (pp. 22–29). Boston, MA: Pearson Education.

Straubhaar, J., LaRose, R., & Davenport, L. (2010). *Media Now: Understanding Media, Culture, and Technology* (6th ed.). Boston, MA: Wadsworth.

Sun, C. (Producer, Writer), & Picker, M. (Director, Co-Producer). (2001). *Mickey Mouse Monopoly: Disney, Childhood, and Corporate Power* [Documentary Film]. Northampton, MA: Media Education Foundation.

Trend, D. (2007). *The Myth of Violence: A Critical Introduction.* Malden, MA: Blackwell Publishing.

University of Oxford. (2010). Titanic aftermath. In *Wireless World: Marconi & the Making of Radio.* Wellington Square, Oxford: Author. Retrieved July 25, 2011, from www.mhs.ox.ac.uk/marconi/exhibition/titanicaftermath.htm

Wanta, W., & Ghanem, S. (2007). Effects of agenda setting. In Raymond W. Preiss, Barbara Mae Galue, Nancy Burrell, Mike Allen, and Jennings Bryant (Eds.), *Mass Media Effects Research: Advanced through Meta-Analysis* (pp. 37–51). Mahway, NJ: Lawrence Erlbaum Associates.

Zuel, B. (2009, January 24). Just for the record. *The Sydney Morning Herald.* Retrieved August 16, 2010 from www.smh.com.au/news/entertainment/music/just-for-the-record/2009/01/23/1232471564924.html

ENDNOTE

[1] Margaret Atwood (born in Ottawa, Ontario, in 1939) is a highly acclaimed Canadian author, poet, and feminist. She has written several award-winning novels including *Life Before Man* (1979), *The Handmaid's Tale* (1985), and *Alias Grace* (1996), along with poetry collections, children's books, short fiction, and nonfiction collections. Canadian Yann Martel (born in Salamanca, Spain, in 1963), won the 2002 Man Booker Prize for his well-known fictional work *Life of Pi* (2001).

PART 2

Interconnections between Individuals and Society

Source: © Satori13 | Dreamstime.com

LEARNING OBJECTIVES AND OUTCOMES

After completing this chapter, students should be able to do the following:

LO1 Compare varying definitions of family, and explain why the way family is defined is important.

LO2 Identify the key trends that indicate changes in Canadian families.

LO3 Distinguish between the main assumptions of the family decline and family pluralism perspectives.

LO4 Describe what comprises sociological knowledge about families.

LO5 Describe how colonization affected Aboriginal families, both in the short and long term.

LO6 Explain how each of the following theories contributes to knowledge about families: social exchange, family life course development, functionalist, conflict, feminist, and interactionist.

Other things may change, but we start and end with families.

(Anthony Brandt)[1]

FAMILIES ARE EVERYWHERE

We are surrounded by families, from our own families to other people's families, families in our neighbourhoods and in our workplaces, fictional families on television and in movies, and even families in the news and on the Internet. When you first awaken in the morning, it may be within the home of your own **family of orientation** (the family into which you were born or in which you were raised) or your **family of procreation** (the family that you establish in adulthood). While drinking your morning coffee, you may hear or read about families in the news—a story about a family within which something tragic has occurred, an editorial outlining projected impacts of a new government policy on families, or a lifestyle story describing affordable back-to-school fashions for children. You might look out your window and see parents loading their children into the car to drive them to school (or perhaps you are doing so yourself). Throughout the day you may encounter families in a variety of settings—shopping malls, restaurants, movie theatres, neighbourhoods, and on the pages of your Facebook friends. Families might even more directly affect you throughout your workday. If you are a teacher, you teach children who are growing up in various types of families, and whose family lives influence the classroom; if you are in advertising, you are marketing directly to people whose consumer interests are shaped by their family lives; if you serve in a managerial position in business, your employees are trying to achieve a balance between work and family responsibilities. In the evening, you might return home to your partner and/or children, or to get ready for a date, or perhaps to turn on the television to watch *Family Guy*, *Two and a Half Men*, or *Modern Family*. Families are *everywhere*.

The opening quotation suggests that families are of the utmost importance in determining who we are, creating the frameworks upon which our lives are built. That means that families lie at the core of our socialization experiences throughout our lives. In childhood, our parents and other family members are key socializing agents, providing us with some of the knowledge and life skills we will carry with us during our lifetimes. We undergo further socialization within the context of family life if and when we marry, have children, get divorced, remarry, acquire additional children through remarriage, have our children move out of the family home, and become grandparents. We spend a considerable amount of time and energy both interacting with and thinking about our families. Why can't my family get along or just be more "normal?" How do I find a partner and then create a relationship that will last forever? What should I do to make sure my kids turn out okay? My parents are getting older—how is that going to affect me? Considering the omnipresence of families in society and their centrality to our everyday lives, take a moment to reflect upon the *Sociology in My Life* question on page 70.

Family of orientation:
The family into which you were born or in which you were raised.

Family of procreation:
The family that you establish in adulthood.

What kind of families do you see every day?

Your response to the *Sociology in My Life* question might have addressed diverse characteristics of your family—family structure (i.e., who its members are), patterns of interaction (i.e., conversations, behaviours, activities), emotions that you have toward certain members of your family, the impact of having grown up in your particular family, the degree to which your family does or does not approximate an

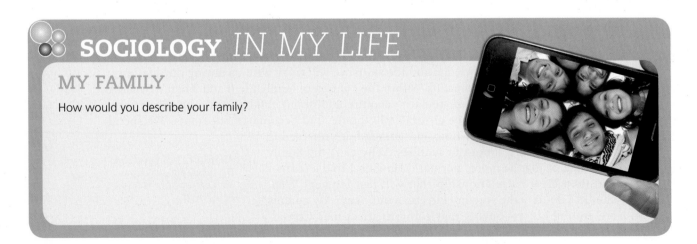

SOCIOLOGY *IN MY LIFE*

MY FAMILY

How would you describe your family?

"ideal" family, or how similar you believe your family is to other families. Personal experience gives us a great deal of knowledge about our own families and that knowledge serves as a foundation for what we "know" about families more generally. But our own family experiences provide us with a mental snapshot of only one small corner of the social world. Using the lens of sociology to better understand families more generally means delving into patterns and variations that exist in families across cultures, over time, and within a given culture at a particular point in time. To accomplish this, we need to explore virtually every aspect of family life, beginning with attempts to define exactly what constitutes a family.

This chapter introduces you to the sociological study of families. The chapter begins with a review of some of the different ways that "family" has been defined, along with a discussion of corresponding macro- and micro-level issues raised by these particular definitions. At the level of our everyday lives, even the specific definition that each of us personally uses frames our attitudes toward changing trends in Canadian families. If one defines family in terms of a legally married heterosexual couple, then couples who are living common law or legally married same-sex couples will not be considered a family, regardless of how long they have been together or whether they have children; the increase in these types of relationships has led some people to think that the "the family" as a social institution is "in crisis" or "declining." In this chapter, the ways that the structure of Canadian families has changed will be explored, as will the debate over family decline. Historical knowledge is included in the chapter to help us learn more about whether families *were* somehow "better" in the past than they are today. Using the example of the impact of colonization on Aboriginal families, historical knowledge also demonstrates the significant ways that macro- and micro-level changes can have a lasting impact on the lives of several generations of families in the long term. Finally, the empirical and theoretical knowledge that informs family sociology will be elaborated upon as well.

WHAT IS A FAMILY?

"Family" is a term that is used so regularly, we often take it for granted. Although we can easily list the individuals whom we consider to be a part of our families, we may not find it as easy to extrapolate from that list to a more general definition of "family." Definitions vary based upon the specific context in question, and the specific needs or interests of groups involved. For instance, the way that family is defined

What is a family?

within a federal benefits policy outlines a precise legal entity, which may differ considerably from the way that you would define family. Various definitions may emphasize structure, process, function, or emotion. But all definitions are both inclusive and exclusive, embracing certain individuals as legitimate family members for the purposes at hand, while barring others. Definitions then have an impact on the macro- and micro-levels of people's lives.

LO[1] STRUCTURAL, FUNCTIONAL, AND EMOTIONAL DEFINITIONS

Much of the information that describes the *demographic* characteristics of Canadian families (i.e., statistical characteristics of families) is drawn from Census data, gathered nationally every five years. The Census uses a very precise definition of "family," clearly outlining whom is to be included (Milan, Vézina & Wells, 2007):

- a married or common-law[2] couple (of the same or opposite sex), with or without children[3] living in the same dwelling, *or*

- a lone parent with one or more children living in the same dwelling, *or*
- a grandparent living with one or more grandchildren[4]

The Census definition has changed a great deal over the years, which means that caution must be exercised when comparing data about families over time. For instance, couples living in common-law relationships were not integrated into the definition until 1981. The 2001 Census family included same-sex couples living in common-law relationships, and as same-sex marriages were being legalized across Canada, the 2006 Census integrated same-sex married couples.

The Census definition is *structural*, defining families on the basis of particular statuses (e.g., parent, child, grandchild) and a specific physical location (i.e., the same dwelling). Its precision, which facilitates social policy and program planning at the community, regional, and national levels, also means that it is restrictive, not including people whom you may have listed in the description of your own family, such as aunts, uncles, cousins, or pets. And, most certainly, many would argue that families are about more than just location and a narrow range of statuses. Other definitions of family do go beyond structure to emphasize the processes, functions, and emotions of families.

Anthropologist George Peter Murdock (1949) provided an early social scientific definition of family that referred not only to its structure, but also to its internal process or functions. He defined a family as "... a social group characterized by common residence, economic cooperation and reproduction. It contains adults of both sexes, at least two of whom maintain a socially approved sexual relationship, and one or more children, own or adopted, of the sexually cohabiting adults" (p. 1). In this definition children are necessary for a "family," as is a heterosexual relationship that is "socially approved" (e.g., legal marriage).

The Vanier Institute of the Family presents a contemporary definition that emphasizes the internal processes and functions of families—the everyday "doing" of family life. The Institute defines a family as follows:

> ...any combination of two or more persons bound together over time by ties of mutual consent, birth, and/or adoption or placement and who, together, assume responsibilities for *variant combinations of some* of the following [emphasis added]:
>
> - physical maintenance and care of group members

- addition of new members through procreation or adoption
- socialization of children
- social control of members
- production, consumption, distribution of goods and services, and
- affective nurturance, otherwise known as "love." (Vanier Institute of the Family, 2009)

This definition provides much looser boundaries around what a family is than does the structural definition of the Census or Murdock's structural/functional definition of the mid-20th century. A family does not require the presence of children, it does not have to be based on a heterosexual relationship, its members do not necessarily live in the same dwelling, and it may engage in a range of functional activities that differs from those engaged in by other families. The Vanier Institute's definition also brings emotions into the picture—"love."

Many of us would consider the emotional dimension of family life to be central to what a family is—or at the very least, what we think a family is *supposed* to be. A large-scale survey in 1989 found that 74 percent of people at that time defined a family as "any group whose members love and care for one another" (Coontz, 1992, p. 21). In cultures throughout the world, individuals who are not related by blood, marriage, or adoption may be brought inside the boundaries of one's family as **fictive kin** (Ahern & Bailey, 1997; Johnson & Barer, 1990), *families of choice*, or what some Aboriginal communities refer to as *"families of the heart"* (Castellano, 2002, p. 23), assuming some of the benefits and/or some of the obligations of family life.

A growing body of research is exploring the manner in which pets are even integrated into this conception of family (Cain, 1985; Grier, 2006; Haraway, 2003; Silva & Smart, 2001). Power's (2008) analysis of dog owners found that more than 95 percent perceived their dogs as family members, referring to them as their children, similar to their children, or as siblings; they also frequently referred to their families as "packs." This use of language serves "to emphasize the intensive nature of the relationship that people experienced with their dogs, and to highlight the love, and ongoing emotional and time commitment engendered by those relations" (p. 541); Power conceptualizes such families as "more-than-human families" (p. 535).

Although defining family on the basis of love offers the most flexibility, its strength is also its weakness. First, while it captures the emotional dimension of family life, it is only the positive emotions—"love" and "care—that are emphasized." This represents somewhat of an idealized version of families, one that characterizes some families very well, but that glosses over the

Fictive kin: Individuals who are not related by blood, marriage, or adoption but assume some of the benefits and/or some of the obligations of family life.

Source: Barbara Peacock/Photographer's Choice/Getty

Many people consider their furry friends to be "family members" rather than "pets."

problems (e.g., family violence) that are experienced by others. Second, by emphasizing only positive emotions, it fails to capture the complexity of emotions within families. Even families that are characterized by positive emotional bonds overall experience many challenges and conflicts, and at times their feelings toward one another can be ambivalent. Popular opinion polls show that although the majority of people surveyed indicate that they look forward to spending time with family during the holidays "a lot" (Ipsos-Reid, 2009), almost one-third of people say that after visiting with family over holidays, they feel "exhausted," and 15 percent look forward to spending the next holiday without family (Ipsos-Reid, 2005). It seems that for many families, the famous 20th century comedian George Burns (1896–1996) was right: "Happiness is having a large, loving, caring, close-knit family *in another city* [emphasis added]."[5]

Whether talking about the structurally defined Census family, the structural/functional family described by Murdock, the functionally defined family of the Vanier Institute, or the emotionally defined family of the average person, certain individuals will be *included* within the family boundaries, while others are necessarily *excluded*. The boundaries placed around families by different groups of people in varying contexts have important real-world implications. Definitions of family determine who is included in social policies, who receives workplace or social benefits, who is accepted as a new immigrant, who can be legally married, and how people are treated in their everyday social interactions. At the micro level, the way that *you* define family underlies the choices that you make for your own life, your judgments about other people's choices, and your attitudes toward changing trends in Canadian families.

TIME TO REVIEW

- How much of a role do families play in our lives?
- What are the similarities and difference between structural, functional, and emotional definitions of family, and why are definitions of family important?

SOCIOLOGY *IN MY LIFE*

DEFINING MY FAMILY

The definitions of family presented above are just a few among the many other specific definitions that exist. However, they do represent the different types of definitions of families that are frequently encountered both inside and outside the academic world.

Which definition best corresponds to your earlier description of your own family?

LO² CHANGING FAMILIES

The past several decades have been characterized by significant changes in family life, reflected in the structure of families. Declining marriage rates, more common-law relationships, increases in lone parenthood, fewer children, and the greater prevalence of same-sex couples are some of the most noteworthy changes, not only in Canada, but throughout much of the Western world (Cliquet, 2003/2004). When taken together, these changes present a very different portrait of families today than that painted by Murdock's definition in 1949. These changes in family structure have led some people to become concerned about the future of family life in Canada.

FEWER MARRIAGES

Fewer people are getting married today than was the case a half century ago. The marriage rate has declined from 8.5 per 1,000 population in 1975 to 4.6 in 2004 (Nault, 1996; Statistics Canada, 2007) (see Figure 4.1). One of the reasons that marriage rates are declining is because people are waiting longer to marry. In 1973, the average age of first marriage was 25.2 for men and 22.8 for women; in 2003 that rose to 30.6 for men and 28.5 for women (Statistics Canada, 2007). Another reason for lower marriage rates is because of more cohabitational (i.e., *common-law*) relationships.

The relationship between declining marriage rates and cohabitation is particularly evident when you see that Quebec, which has the *lowest* proportion of married couples in Canada, also has the *highest* proportion of common-law couples (Milan, Vézina & Wells, 2007).

MORE COMMON-LAW UNIONS

Although fewer people are getting married, more people are living in common-law relationships. When common-law unions were first counted in the 1981 Census, 6 percent of all couples were in common-law relationships. This rose to 14 percent in the 2001 Census, and to 15.5 percent in 2006 (see Figure 4.2). Cohabitational relationships are the most common in Quebec, where 35 percent of all Census couples live in common-law relationships; they are the least common in Ontario (10 percent of all couples). Common-law unions are most common among individuals aged 25 to 29, but such relationships have increased for every age group, including people age 65 and over, indicating the growing acceptability of such relationships in society (Milan, Vézina & Wells, 2007). Some cohabitational relationships may result in marriage, but people cohabit in a variety of circumstances that can range from a permanent alternative to marriage, to a "trial marriage," to a more casual cost-sharing arrangement while dating (Wu, 2000).

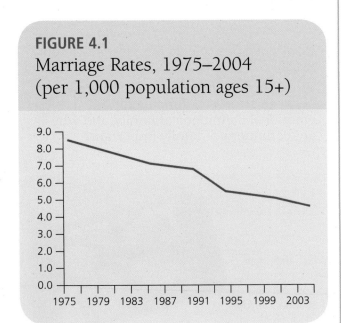

FIGURE 4.1

Marriage Rates, 1975–2004 (per 1,000 population ages 15+)

Source: Adapted from Statistics Canada. CANSIM Table 101-1004, "Crude marriage rates, all marriages, provinces and territories, annual (rates per 1,000 population)" and Nault, F. (1996). Twenty years of marriage. *Health Reports, 8*(2), 39–45. [Table 1: Crude marriage rates, selected countries, 1975, 1980, 1985, 1990, 1994 (p. 42)].

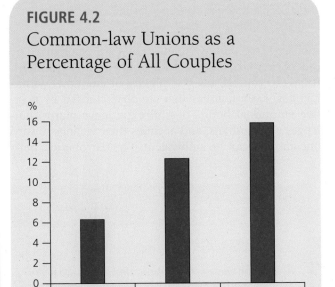

FIGURE 4.2

Common-law Unions as a Percentage of All Couples

Source: Adapted from Milan, A. (2000). One hundred years of families. *Canadian Social Trends, 56* (Spring), 2–12; and Milan, A., Vézina, M., & Wells, C. (2007). *Family Portrait: Continuity and Change in Canadian Families and Households, 2006, 2006 Census* [Table 1: Distribution and growth of Census families, Canada, 2001 and 2006 (p. 8)]. Statistics Canada Catalogue No. 97-553-XIE.

MORE DIVORCES

In the 1950s, fewer than 40 out of every 100,000 people over the age of 15 divorced. In 2005, 220 per 100,000 population divorced (Milan, 2000; Statistics Canada 2008) (see Figure 4.3). This increase does not necessarily mean that significantly more marriages are falling apart. In the past, legislation prevented many couples whose marriages had already "fallen apart" in every meaningful sense from divorcing. Prior to 1968, couples could divorce only if one spouse was able to provide evidence of "fault," such as abuse or adultery; even then, judges had the authority to grant, or not grant, a divorce. The *Divorce Act* changed in 1968, allowing couples to divorce provided they had been separated for a period of at least three years. This legislation also introduced the concept of *no-fault* divorce, so that evidence of abuse or adultery was no longer necessary; couples could divorce for any reason, such as falling out of love. At the same time, property rights were also changing. In the past, married women's rights to property were limited, so that even if a woman could prove abuse or adultery in court, divorce would often mean poverty for herself and her children. With the implementation of new divorce legislation and changing property rights, divorce rates increased, indicating that there were many couples who had already been separated for at least that length of time; now, legislation finally enabled them to legally end their marriages. In 1986, legislation changed again, reducing the required period of separation to one year. Again, divorce rates increased. However, since the late 1980s, divorce rates have been declining. Even with divorce, people still place a value on marriage; the vast majority of people who divorce eventually remarry (Ambert, 2009).

In the media, we often hear casual references to half of marriages ending in divorce, but that is not the case. That number is drawn from the United States, when divorces peaked in the 1980s. In Canada, the risk of divorce by the 30th anniversary is approximately 38 percent. However, this number includes divorces that occur in second (or subsequent) marriages as well, when divorce rates are higher. The risk of divorce in a first marriage is approximately 33 percent (Ambert, 2009).

MORE LONE PARENTS

In 1966, 8.2 percent of all Census families were headed by a lone parent. This had almost doubled by 2006 when 16 percent of all families were headed by a lone parent (see Figure 4.4). This increase is due, in part, to the increase in divorce rates and the dissolution of common-law relationships. Since 2001, the number of lone-parent families headed by fathers has increased more than the number of those headed by mothers, indicating the greater prevalence of joint custody arrangements as well as custody being granted to fathers; however, most lone-parent families remain headed by mothers (Milan, Vézina, & Wells, 2007).

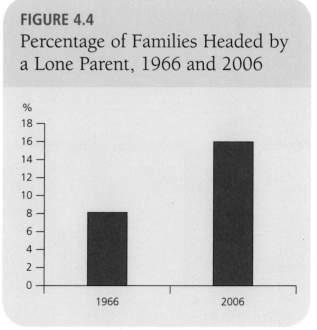

FIGURE 4.3

Divorce Rates, 1960–2005 (per 100,000 population ages 15+)

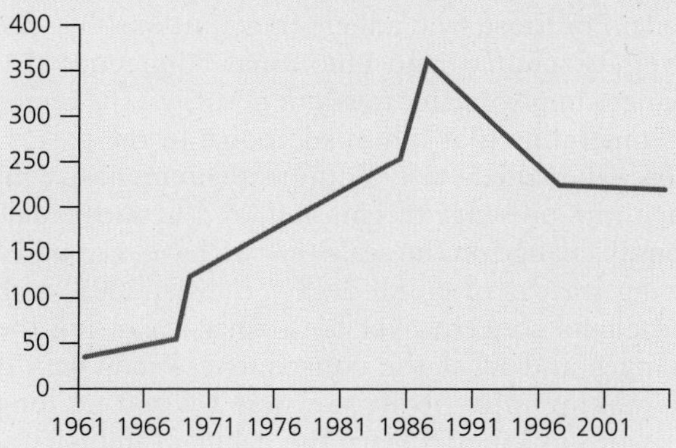

Source: Adapted from Ambert, A. M. (2009). *Divorce: Facts, Causes, and Consequences* (3rd ed.). Ottawa, ON: Vanier Institute of the Family [Table 2, page 7]; and Statistics Canada. CANSIM Table 101-6501. Divorces and crude divorce rates, Canada, provinces and territories, annual.

FIGURE 4.4

Percentage of Families Headed by a Lone Parent, 1966 and 2006

Source: Adapted from Milan, A., Vézina, M., & Wells, C. (2007). *Family Portrait: Continuity and Change in Canadian Families and Households, 2006, 2006 Census.* Statistics Canada Catalogue No. 97-553-XIE.

MORE SAME-SEX COUPLES

Ontario was the first province to legalize same-sex marriage, in June 2003. Two years later, same-sex marriage was legalized throughout Canada. Although the 2006 Census found that less than 1 percent of married or common-law couples were of the same sex, the number of same-sex couples had increased by more than 32 percent since they were first counted in 2001; this is compared to only a 6 percent increase in the number of opposite-sex couples during the same period. Part of this increase may be due to actual increases in the proportion of same-sex couples, but much of this increase is believed to be the result of a greater acceptance of same-sex relationships, which means more people in these relationships may be willing to admit it. Half of all same-sex couples in Canada live in only three cities: Montréal, Toronto, and Vancouver (Milan, Vézina & Wells, 2007).

FEWER CHILDREN

In 1959, the average woman gave birth to 3.9 children. By 2007, this had fallen to 1.6 children (see Figure 4.5). As a result of these lower fertility rates, in combination with an aging population, the 2006 Census revealed that for the first time, the proportion of families comprising couples without children exceeded those with children (Milan, Vézina & Wells, 2007). Lower fertility rates are, in part, the result of people starting

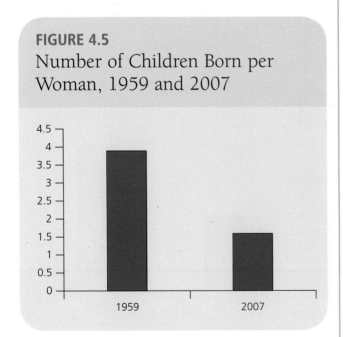

FIGURE 4.5
Number of Children Born per Woman, 1959 and 2007

Source: Adapted from Milan, A. (2000). One hundred years of families. *Canadian Social Trends, 56*(Spring), 2–12; and Statistics Canada (2009). Births 2007. Statistics Canada Catalogue No. 84F0210X.

to have children later in life. Delayed childbearing can have implications for couples, in that with increased age, women are more likely to experience reproductive difficulties. Some may turn to new reproductive technologies such as fertility drugs and in vitro fertilization, but in many cases the decision to delay childbearing for *too* long means having biological children is no longer an option.

The changes that have occurred in Canadian families are considerable. The nature of many of these changes reveals that since the mid-20th century, large numbers of people have been making some very different choices in relation to their family lives. The changing family structures that have resulted have led some people to express concern over the future of the family in Canada. But are there other ways to interpret these trends? What do these statistics actually mean?

> There are three kinds of lies: lies, damned lies, and statistics.
>
> *(Mark Twain)*[6]

The quotation above, popularized by Mark Twain, is not stating that statistics are mere fabrications that lack any meaning. Instead, it is saying that statistics take on meaning only through interpretation; because of this, the same statistics can be used to support very different, and even opposing, arguments. Consequently, political, social, and moral arguments that use statistics as a key source of support must be looked at with a critical eye in order to critique and to ask questions, perhaps the most important of which are whether there are other ways that those statistics could be interpreted, and on what basis a particular interpretation has been made. The way that one defines "family," and the images of family life that are associated with those definitions, serve as the framework within which those interpretations are made. For those who adhere to definitions that stress diversity, choice, and emotional connections, the changes imply greater freedom in society, the removal of constraints that inhibited choice in the past. For those who adhere to definitions that emphasize marriage, the presence of children, and heterosexuality, "family change on the scale that we have seen and are seeing smacks of moral decay" (Lewis, 2003, p. 13) and elicits concern over both what is causing these changes and what the consequences may be: "Are we looking into the abyss where we will no longer care for our kin and learn the habits of industry and respect for others" (p. 52)? Is the family declining? For two decades, the latter is one of the questions at the heart of the sociology of the family (Brooks, 2002; Powell & Branden, 2007).

LO³ IS "THE FAMILY" DECLINING?

Concerns over family decline are not new. In 1893, Charles Henry Pearson argued that the increase in non-arranged marriages, the growth of divorce, and declining parental interest in childcare had weakened the family, forcing the state to take on a greater role in childcare. Public debates over family decline became especially widespread a century later; between 1980 and 1996, Brooks (2002) found a tenfold increase in the proportion of people who cited family decline as the "most important problem" being faced by society. In the 21st century, these concerns have continued unabated.

Debates over family decline arise from two opposing views: the family decline perspective and the family pluralism perspective (Amato, 2005; Coontz, 1992). The *family decline perspective* is voiced both by some religious conservative groups and by some sociologists, the best known of whom is sociologist David Popenoe (1994, 2007). Proponents of this perspective emphasize the disappearance of what they refer to as the "traditional" family—a legally married man and woman, in their first marriage, with children. Increases in divorce, common-law relationships, and same-sex relationships, along with decreases in marriage rates, are considered indicative of the deterioration of marriage. The reduction in birth rates is interpreted as a "loss of childcenteredness" (Popenoe, 2007, p. 21), which further weakens marriage. The presence of two married, biological parents is said to be the "gold standard for childrearing" (Natelson, 2009) and as such, lone parenthood and stepfamilies are equated with ineffective child socialization; the proposed consequences include child poverty, poor school performance, drug use, and criminal behaviour. With the family perceived as the "bedrock" (Lewis, 2003, p. 9) of society, weaker marriages and the decline of the family necessarily mean that the well-being of society as a whole is threatened, destabilizing schools, churches, neighbourhoods, and voluntary organizations (Canada Family Action Coalition, 2006); even democracy itself is endangered (Whitehead, 2006).

While proponents of the family decline perspective underscore the harmful nature of "nontraditional" families, those who support the *family pluralism perspective* applaud the growing family diversity (Coontz, 1992; Amato, 2005). They work toward debunking the decline perspective, arguing that it is based on myths and misunderstandings about family life that draw upon a nostalgic image of some golden age in the past in which families were somehow better off than they are today. Supporters of the pluralism perspective contend that the past was not as "golden" as nostalgic images may suggest. Families in all cultures and at all times have faced difficulties—whether poverty, violence, marital disruption, social disruption, family dissatisfaction, or inequality. The common-law couples, single parents, and remarriages that are lamented within the decline perspective have, in fact, always existed in Canadian society; the difference is that in the past, they were normally not due to choice but rather to circumstances outside the individual's control, such as the death of a spouse or the need to provide care for one's aging parents in an era that lacked public social supports (Milan, 2000). The fact that individuals have greater freedom of choice now than in the past means that they have more opportunity to achieve relationship and life satisfaction (Cliquet, 2003/2004).

However, Coontz (1992) cautions against the extremism evident in both perspectives. She argues

SOCIOLOGY ON SCREEN

THE PERFECT FAMILY DINNER

On YouTube, you can find a ten-minute public service announcement called "1950 Family Date, Dinner in a 1950s Home." It reflects the idealized, nostalgic image of family life that Coontz (1992) suggests underlies the contemporary arguments of proponents of the family decline perspective. This video clip will make some of you laugh, while others may find themselves yelling at the screen. Show your own family this clip the next time you are about to sit down for dinner!

that both the family decline and pluralism perspectives tend to be oversimplified, and are based on idealized images. The decline perspective upholds an idyllic image of a better, stronger family from the past (something akin to an image drawn from 1950s television, like the one presented on page 70). The pluralism perspective often maintains an idealized image of diverse contemporary families freed from the rigid constraints of the past, and offers "soothing words about achieving 'self-actualization'... [and] divorce [as] a 'growth experience'..." (p. 1). The former tends to ignore the family problems and crises of the past, while the latter tends to gloss over those of today.

Because statistical trends require careful interpretation, the lens through which one views those trends is crucial. What do rising divorce rates and declining marriage rates mean? Through one lens, it means that commitment has become unimportant to people; through another lens, it can mean that marriage and commitment are *so* important to people that they are not willing to tolerate the dissatisfying marriages that many people were forced to endure in the past. What about declining birth rates? One lens reveals that people are becoming more selfish and are unwilling to sacrifice their own interests; another lens reveals that people are taking the time to plan for their children (Hareven, 1994).

So how *are* we to interpret the changes in Canadian families? More than 80 percent of Canadians live in some type of Census family (Milan, Vézina, & Wells, 2007), a proportion that has remained relatively stable since 1986. Greater diversity in family life does reflect more freedom and choice, which we value in society. But at the same time, family diversity cannot simply be equated with solely positive outcomes. For example, couples in common-law relationships are more likely to break up (even if those relationships eventually result in marriage) than couples who marry without having lived together previously; child poverty has increased substantially in Canadian society, and divorce is associated with emotional strife and hardships for both adults and children. Any interpretation of the changes in family life carries some level of subjectivity, informed by the definition of family that is being used, and the body of knowledge that one draws upon.

LO**4** Knowledge about families comes from a variety of sources such as media information and portrayals, academic research, and our own experiences. In the academic realm, scientific knowledge about families is produced in a variety of disciplines, including sociology, anthropology, psychology, history, economics, and the interdisciplinary field of family studies. Sociological knowledge about families reveals the intimate connections between the macro and micro levels; it combines historical knowledge, theoretical knowledge, and empirical knowledge.

SOCIOLOGY *ONLINE*

SEEING THE FAMILY DECLINE DEBATE IN ACTION

The Internet has become a valuable tool for organizations that participate in the debate over family decline. Those listed below are some of the best known, and are often referred to in the media, such as when offering their "expert" commentary on the evening news.

Family Decline Perspective

- **The Institute of Marriage and Family Canada (www.imfcanada.org)**
"The IMF exists to present credible, research-based evidence—to governments, media, and all Canadians—that supports mom-and-dad marriage and family life."

- **Canada Family Action (www.familyaction.org)**
"For over ten years, CFAC has defended the family by: ... defending traditional marriage with 1.2 million brochures in five languages, 500,000 postcards, 5,000 lawn signs, billboards, and newspaper ads."

Family Pluralism Perspective

- **Council on Contemporary Families (www.contemporaryfamilies.org)**
"The Council on Contemporary Families was formed in response to the misleading representations of family research that have flooded the media in recent years and influenced the debate over such important issues as welfare reform. ... Our organization is particularly interested in ensuring that families that do not fit within conventional norms are included in the national conversation. We believe that the public will benefit from the actual diversity of ... family life."

Source: Adapted from The Institute of Marriage and Family Canada (www .imfcanada.org); Canada Family Action Coalition (www.familyaction.org); and Council on Contemporary Families (www.contemporaryfamilies.org).

- What are some of the most significant trends in family life over the last several decades, and what do these changes mean?

- What are the arguments used on both sides of the family decline debate, and why does Coontz (1992) warn against extremism?

KNOWLEDGE ABOUT FAMILIES

HISTORICAL KNOWLEDGE

The interconnection between the macro and micro levels of families can be seen when we look at some of the major changes in family lives that have occurred in Canada over the last several decades. The nature of these changes in family structure has elicited debates over family decline. However, a closer look at the history of families in Canada reveals change as a constant feature; it demonstrates that shifting family structures and functions are as old as the nation itself. Exploring family lives in Canadian history illustrates that change has always been present, but it also helps us better understand families of the present day.

> …history is more than just interesting anecdotes. History provides the scaffolding upon which we build our societies, our understandings of ourselves, and our understandings of others.
>
> *(Blackstock, 2006/2007, p. 7)*

Sociologists and family historians have studied the impact of the transition from the preindustrial era through the period of industrialization on Euro-Canadian families, as well as the roles of both slavery and shifting patterns of immigration on the changing face of families in Canada. Perhaps the clearest historical example of how macro-level changes can have a significant and lasting impact on the everyday lives of families is evident in the myriad ways in which colonization changed Aboriginal families, which we will explore in detail in the following section.

LO⁵ ABORIGINAL FAMILIES

Aboriginal cultures have existed in what is now Canada for thousands of years, and oral histories claim "for time immemorial" (Blackstock, 2006/2007). When the first European explorers arrived, the geographically varied land space was already home to several distinct cultural regions among Aboriginal peoples. There were hundreds of tribes, languages, and dialects. Complex relationships existed among tribes, and were characterized by trade, cooperation, and/or conflict.

There were varied family structures and arrangements (Castellano, 2002). In some cultures, the intimate relationships that Europeans labelled "marriages" were **monogamous**, wherein an individual has only one spouse at any given time; in other cultures they were **polygamous** wherein an individual has multiple spouses at any given time.[7] In some cultures, (e.g., the migratory Ojibway), households were **nuclear**, consisting of those within the marital relationship and their children. In others (e.g., the more sedentary Huron), households were **extended**, including additional relatives such as siblings or grandparents.

Monogamous: A marriage that includes two spouses.

Polygamous: A marriage that includes three or more spouses simultaneously.

Nuclear: A family structure comprising parents and their children.

Extended: A family structure that includes parents, their children, and additional relatives.

SOCIOLOGY *IN MY LIFE*

CONTEMPORARY FAMILY STRUCTURES

In Canada today, what type of family do you see more commonly—nuclear or extended? In what contexts do you see extended families playing a role in people's lives? We are all familiar with monogamous marriages, but are polygamous marriages also present in Canadian society?

Among most Aboriginal cultures, the notion of family was (and still is) extensive, and based more on relationships between people rather than static roles within a structure. Families were created and expanded through marriages that joined bloodlines, ceremonial practices, affiliations, adoptions, and the real or symbolic presence of past and future generations (Perrault & Proulx, 2000). Language often reflected the various forms of family ties: Among the Inuit, *qatangutgiit* referred to family relationships based on blood ties, while *ilagiit* referred to an "outer" family of extended relationships, and *tuqlluraniq* referred to the ancestor whose spirit was thought to reside in a particular child and after whom that child was named (Chasonneuve, 2005).

With the beginning of European colonization in the 15th century, every aspect of life within Aboriginal cultures was forced to change, perhaps most evident when looking at families. In the 15th and 16th centuries, the fur trade established patterns of exchange among European traders, Aboriginal male trappers or guides, and Aboriginal women. Because of the skills that the women had in preserving furs, hunting and gathering, languages, and trade, as well as the absence of European women, "customary marriages" emerged between them and the European traders; the women were labelled **les femmes du pays**, or "country wives," and for a period of time, these relationships were encouraged by some trading companies and some missionaries (Razack, 2000). The children who were born from relationships between European men and Aboriginal women were known as *métis*, a French term referring to "mixed blood"; over time, a distinct ethnocultural group emerged, the Métis Nation. The term *Aboriginal* now includes Inuit, First Nations, and Métis.

By the late 18th century, agriculture was becoming the primary economic activity of Euro-Canadians. As the fur trade declined, affiliations with Aboriginal cultures were considered less useful. The presence of Euro-Canadian and Métis women made marriages between Euro-Canadian men and Aboriginal women less acceptable, and as fears of "race mixing" grew, they were outlawed in parts of Canada (Razack, 2000). Differences between Aboriginal and European families were evident from the very start, but recognition of those differences now intensified.

European and Euro-Canadian families were both patriarchal and patrilineal (Gaffield, 1990, 1992). They were *patriarchal* in that power was vested in the male head of the household according to social custom, religious doctrine, and the law. Women did not legally exist as "persons," but rather as the legal property of their husbands. Children were also the property of their fathers, and if marriages dissolved, mothers had no legal rights to their children. Families were also **patrilineal** in that lineage (or ancestry) was traced through the father's side of the family, and particularly its male members; when daughters married, they became part of their husbands' families. In contrast, even though Aboriginal cultures were not **matriarchal** (i.e., with power vested in the female head of the household), women had considerably greater power than their European counterparts. Some Aboriginal cultures were **matrilineal**, with family lineage traced through the female members of the mother's side of the family (Chansonneuve, 2005).

In Euro-Canadian families, due to religious doctrine and social norms, the husband/father bore

Les femmes du pays: The Aboriginal "country wives" of European traders.

Patrilineal: Lineage is traced through the father's side of the family, especially its male members.

Matriarchal: Power is vested in females.

Matrilineal: Lineage is traced through the mother's side of the family, especially its female members.

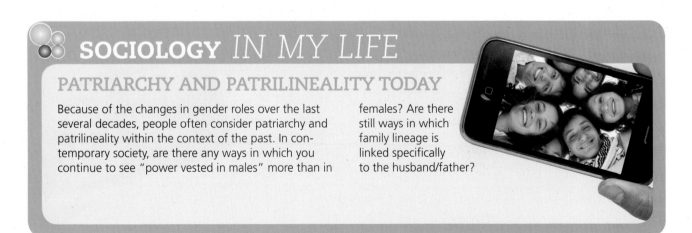

SOCIOLOGY *IN MY LIFE*

PATRIARCHY AND PATRILINEALITY TODAY

Because of the changes in gender roles over the last several decades, people often consider patriarchy and patrilineality within the context of the past. In contemporary society, are there any ways in which you continue to see "power vested in males" more than in females? Are there still ways in which family lineage is linked specifically to the husband/father?

responsibility for his wife and children's salvation; with short life spans and high death rates, *especially* for children and women (see Chapter 11), achieving salvation was considered an urgent matter. Considering this religious interpretation at the time, along with the view of women and children as property rather than "persons," it should come as no surprise that paternal discipline of both wives and children was quite strict, and sometimes even violent. Child abuse and wife abuse would not be criminalized until near the turn of the 20th century, several decades *after* animal abuse was criminalized.

The relative absence of patriarchal authority in many Aboriginal cultures, in conjunction with different spiritual belief systems and intolerance for physical punishment, created very different familial contexts. Children were perceived as gifts from the Creator, gifts not only to the parents but also to the entire community; as such, children were the responsibility of everyone in the community. As "gifts," they were to be treated with kindness and affection. Children were socialized through observation, role modelling, natural consequences for misbehaviour, and counselling by elders, rather than through discipline informed by physical punishment, fear, or humiliation.

Although the government of France had initiated a formal Christian conversion policy as far back as 1632, the pragmatic realities of daily life in the harsh environment and the economic needs surrounding the fur trade meant that cultural differences, and in particular family differences, were tolerated. However, as economic alliances ceased with the decline of the fur trade, more attention was paid to implementing that conversion policy. A series of other policies and pieces of legislation followed, all intended to convert not only the religious beliefs and family lives of Aboriginal people, but also every aspect of Aboriginal cultures. The reserve system, established in 1830, isolated and segregated Aboriginal people, and frequently forced communities to abandon traditional productive activities such as nomadic hunting and gathering. With the *Gradual Civilization Act* (1857) and the *Act for the Gradual Civilization of the Indian* (1869), the goal became full assimilation and the complete eradication of every aspect of those cultures (known as **ethnocide**)—solving what was seen at the time as the "Indian problem." Traditional ceremonies and celebrations were criminalized—even dancing was outlawed in Aboriginal communities for 75 years! Although European explorers and fur traders used alcohol to boost cooperation from Aboriginal communities, it later became illegal to sell alcohol to Aboriginal people until well into the 1950s. The *Indian Act* (1876) made all Aboriginal people wards of the federal government. Women who married non-Aboriginal men lost their Indian status and all related benefits, while non-Aboriginal women who married Aboriginal men gained such status and benefits.

Agents from the Department of Indian Affairs (DIA) held ultimate power over Aboriginal communities, and especially over their family lives. They

> decided what constituted a family unit for the purposes of annuity payments, adjudicating which wives were "valid," and which children were "legitimate."... [They] arranged marriages, approved of some, and refused to recognize the validity of others. They dispensed marriage counselling,... intervened to prevent couples from separating, brought back "runaway" wives, directed the annuities of husbands to deserted wives, and broke up second marriages they regarded as illegitimate. DIA officials decided which widows deserved to inherit from their late husbands—under the *Indian Act,* a wife had to be "of good moral character"... (Carter, 2008, p. 14)

Through the amalgamation of a series of government policies and pieces of legislation, it took less than a century to remove virtually all independence from Aboriginal people. The policy that has had the most devastating effect, and which demonstrates the lasting impact that society's macro level can have on the micro level of families, was that of residential schooling.

RESIDENTIAL SCHOOLING

Changing the way that Aboriginal children were socialized was the key to **assimilation**, whereby a minority group is absorbed into the culture of the dominant group. The government determined that the most effective means of doing this was through schooling. Mission schools, which emphasized learning English so that children could read the Bible and convert to Christianity, existed as far back as the 17th century. But in 1831, the government initiated a formal program to educate and assimilate First Nations and, to a lesser extent, Inuit children. Schools would be funded by the government but operated by various denominations of the Christian church. Initially, these *day schools* were located adjacent to reserves, and children continued to live at home. However, following consultations with American officials, the *Davin Report* (Davin, 1879) concluded that "the influence of the

Ethnocide: The eradication of a culture.

Assimilation: The process by which a minority group is absorbed into the culture of the dominant group.

wigwam is stronger than the influence of the schools," and, as such, the aim of assimilation would be better served by removing children from their homes and placing them in boarding schools. Consequently, although a few day schools continued to exist, *residential* schools came to predominate. By 1896, there were already 45 residential schools in operation, and a total of 130 schools existed over a period of more than 100 years; the last residential school closed in 1996. Approximately 150,000 Aboriginal children attended residential schools; at their peak in 1930, 75 percent of Aboriginal children were in residential schools (Legacy of Hope Foundation, 2009; Chansonneuve, 2005; McGillivray, 1997; Royal Commission on Aboriginal Peoples, 1996).

Because all "Indians" were wards of the government, parents had no choice in whether to send their children away to these boarding schools. By 1884, boarding schools were mandated for all Aboriginal children under the age of 16, and Indian agents from the Department of Indian Affairs had the power to fine, detain, or arrest parents who tried to keep their children at home. In British Columbia, where many Aboriginal children were already voluntary participants in the public school system, children were removed from those schools and placed in residential schools instead (Barman, 2003). Science was able to justify the placement of Aboriginal children in these schools, using the theory of Social Darwinism. Just as Charles Darwin pointed out that life on Earth had evolved from simpler to more complex organisms, Social Darwinists argued that civilizations evolved from "savage" to "civilized." Western European cultures (and their counterparts in Canada and the United States) had reached the "civilized" stage, while Aboriginal people were perceived as still being stuck in the "savage" stage. Thus, the reserve system, legislation that culminated in the *Indian Act*, and most of all education in residential schools, would enable Aboriginal people to evolve to a "civilized" stage more quickly than if they were left to themselves—colonization was "for their own good."

Until 1951, students in residential schools received only a half-day of academic instruction, while the remaining part of the day was spent in manual labour, such as raising crops, shoemaking, cleaning, and sewing. Academic instruction did not only include subjects such as reading, writing, and arithmetic, but also religious and cultural instruction. In practice, that half-day often meant only one or two hours, with the result that even after spending six or seven years in school, most children remained at a grade 1, 2, or 3 level (Barman, 2003); education beyond a grade 8 level was prohibited for Aboriginal youth. Unlike in schools for non-Aboriginal children, most teachers in residential schools had no professional training until well into the 1950s. Instead, they were usually members of the religious order that operated the school; although some were dedicated to providing a quality education to students, others were more interested in religious conversion (Barman, 2003).

The inferior education that children received in the residential school system was just one of its features that created a lasting legacy in Aboriginal families and communities. Psychological, physical, and sexual abuse occurred in far too many of the schools. The first allegations of physical and sexual abuse in a residential school were made in 1880, and of the 150,000 children who attended the schools, 91,000 reported being physically and/or sexually abused. Psychological abuse was even more predominant. Letters were reviewed and censored before being sent home (presuming that their parents could read English, as that was the only language the children were permitted to use). Neglect was even more prevalent than abuse. Funding formulas were such that although the schools were government funded, the government provided only a fraction of the funding per student in residential schools compared to public schools; economic issues were compounded by the fact that many of these schools were operated in pursuit of a profit for their operators. As a result, students were often left hungry, schools were overcrowded, and school buildings were unkempt and unsanitary. In the early 20th century, two government reports documented horrendous living conditions that resulted in student death rates of up to 47 percent in residential schools; the shocking living conditions were documented by the government, yet nothing was done to ameliorate them. But while neglect and abuse were prevalent in many schools, ethnocide occurred in all of them.

All aspects of the students' traditional cultures were forbidden within the schools, and any outward symbols of those cultures were eradicated. When students first arrived at the schools, their hair was cut short, their clothing was burned, and their names were changed (Perrault & Proulx, 2000; McGillivray, 1997). They were to abandon their languages, and speak only English. Some schools used positive reinforcement for the use of English. For instance, students would receive a bag of buttons each week; each time they were caught speaking their first language, a button would be taken away and at the end of the week, the remaining buttons could be exchanged for a prize. But other schools used punishment for language transgressions—having to write lines, having their mouths taped shut, being given the strap, being deprived of food, or even having needles poked through their tongues.

Source: Library and Archives Canada NL-022474

Student Thomas Moore, before and after entering Regina Indian Industrial School, 1897.

When the required period of schooling ended, former students found themselves stranded between cultures. They didn't have any traditional skills, but the inferior education they had received and the discrimination they faced meant they also had difficulty integrating into Euro-Canadian society. Having experienced neglect, abuse, and/or ethnocide, many former students had some degree of psychological damage, what is now referred to as *residential school syndrome*. And multiple generations grew up completely outside any type of family environment. Residential schooling tore families apart; indeed, that was the purpose of the residential

SOCIOLOGY *IN WORDS*

THE VOICES OF RESIDENTIAL SCHOOL STUDENTS

- "I was literally thrown into St. Mary's Residential School at four years of age....My very first memory of my entry into the school is a painful flashback. For whatever reason, I am thrown into a kneeling position. My head is bashed against a wooden cupboard by the boys' supervisor" (Kelly, 2008, p. 14).

- "A nun shaved my head and stripped me bare in front of all the other boys, followed by months of repeated beatings, whippings, sexual abuse and solitary confinement in a dark, locked closet. Why? Because I was bad and deserved it. That's what they said" (Kakfwi, 2008, para. 4).

- "I was hungry from the day I went into the school until they took me to the hospital two and a half years later. Not just me. Every Indian pupil smelled of hunger" (cited in Barman, 2003, p. 222).

- "...the constant message [was] that because you are Native, you are part of a weak and defective race, unworthy of a distinguished place in society....That to me is not training for success, it is training for self-destruction" (cited in Barman, 2003, p. 229).

schooling policy in the first place. Chief Cinderena Williams of the Spallumcheen band (cited in Castellano, 2002, pp. 18–19) explains:

> Later when these children returned home, they were aliens. They did not speak their own language, so they could not communicate with anyone other than their counterparts. Some looked down on their families because of their lack of English, their lifestyle, and some were just plain hostile. They had formed no bonds with their families, and some couldn't survive without the regimentation they had become accustomed to.... Consequently, when these children became parents, and most did at an early age, they had no parenting skills. They did not have the capability to show affection. They sired and bred children but were unable to relate to them on any level.

And then those children were taken to residential schools, facing the very same experience. Domestic violence, substance abuse, and suicide became more prevalent in both rural and urban Aboriginal communities. When the largest **cohort** (i.e., group of people born during the same period of time or who have experienced a significant event at the same time) of residential school students became parents in the mid-20th century, child welfare authorities stepped in, giving rise to the *"sixties scoop."* For instance, in British Columbia in 1955, only 1 percent of all children in foster care were Aboriginal; by 1964 that proportion rose to 34 percent, with virtually all of those children having been placed with non-Aboriginal families in non-Aboriginal communities (Johnston, 1983). Just as taking children away from their families and their communities to be placed in boarding schools had been seen as the solution to the "Indian problem," taking children away from their families and their communities was now perceived as the solution to the difficulties being faced by residential school survivors.

The macro-level process of colonization created lasting changes at the micro level in Aboriginal families, and thereby in communities. Subsequently, the micro-level changes in those families had an impact on the macro level of society. Canadian authorities thought that by changing Aboriginal families, Canadian society as a whole would benefit from full assimilation of Aboriginal peoples; however, the actual consequences of having torn families apart have been far from positive. As you proceed through the remainder of this book, you will learn more about these actual consequences, which continue to the present day in areas such as education and health.

Changes in family lives through Canadian history are not limited to Aboriginal peoples. Over the same period of time that Aboriginal families were compelled to change by various macro-level forces surrounding colonization, non-Aboriginal families were also transforming due to larger economic, political, ideological, and cultural forces. Those broader forces comprised many contributions from Aboriginal cultures—food (e.g., maple syrup); structures of governance (i.e., based on the Iroquois confederacy model); infrastructure (e.g., roads, and later highways, are built along trail routes); and medicine (e.g., quinine; vitamin C for scurvy) (Blackstock, 2006/2007). They also comprised the contributions made by the myriad other groups of people who came to Canada's shores—the French, the English, immigrants from other European and non-European nations, and people brought by force (e.g., slaves). Amid the shift from a preindustrial to an industrial society, *all* families were transformed. Should you take subsequent courses in sociology that focus on families, you will learn more about the ways in which the lives of all Canadian families have been influenced by larger economic, social, ideological, and political changes throughout Canadian history.

The historical knowledge about families that is used by sociologists does more than just demonstrate the connections between the macro and micro levels. When an analysis of the nature of those interrelationships is combined with sociology's theoretical and empirical knowledge, we gain insight into how and why families change, and what the potential impact of these changes are—important knowledge at a time when we have seen, and continue to see, an extraordinary amount of social change not only in Canada, but also throughout the world.

Cohort: A group of people born during the same period of time or who have experienced a significant event at the same time.

TIME TO REVIEW

- What was the structure of Aboriginal families prior to European colonization?
- How did Euro-Canadian/Aboriginal relations change over time?
- In what ways did the positions of women and children in Aboriginal and Euro-Canadian families differ?
- Why it was thought that residential schooling would solve the "Indian problem," and how did the scientific theory of Social Darwinism lend support to this view?
- How did residential schooling affect Aboriginal individuals, families, and communities?

LO6 THEORETICAL KNOWLEDGE: SOCIOLOGY IN THEORY

From its beginning, the study of families has been more empirical rather than theoretical, focusing on analyses of narrow, specific topics (e.g., marital and life satisfaction within arranged marriages; factors influencing the decision to remain childfree, etc.) (Taylor & Bagdi, 2005; Powell & Brandon, 2007; Turner, 2005). Although empirical research normally has some type of theoretical foundation, sometimes that foundation is not explicitly stated. One analysis (Taylor & Bagdi, 2005) reviewed more than 600 empirical articles published in *The Journal of Marriage and the Family* from 1990 through 1999. The researchers found that almost 40 percent contained no explicit references to theory at all; during this same period of time, only 25 nonempirical, theoretical articles were published in the journal. Among those empirical articles that did explicitly refer to a theory, there is little theoretical cohesiveness. The authors found more than 30 different theories being used. The two theories that are the most commonly used—social exchange theory (39 percent of empirical articles that mention theory) and family life course development theory (8 percent of empirical articles)—lie outside the core theoretical frameworks described in Chapter 1.

SOCIAL EXCHANGE THEORY

Social exchange theory is most closely associated with the area of study known as *social psychology*, which studies individual thoughts, feelings, and behaviours in social situations. This area of study straddles the line between sociology and psychology, and is practised by both sociologists and psychologists. This theory begins with the assumption that society is composed of individuals who are motivated by self-interest. Subsequently, in our social interactions, we make choices based on a rational calculation of the costs and benefits of those interactions.

According to Nye (1979), any relationship is an exchange between people that carries with it both benefits and costs; that is, in any relationship we do some "giving" and we do some "getting." The resources that are exchanged can be tangible, such as financial support, or intangible, such as loyalty and affection. Ultimately, individuals wish to pursue or maintain relationships in which a **profit** is derived—the positive benefits outweigh the costs of being in that relationship. However, costs and benefits are relative rather than absolute. First, there is a **comparison level**, wherein we ask ourselves how much we are putting into and getting out of this relationship compared to other people who are in similar types of relationships. Second, there is a **comparison level for alternatives**, wherein we compare our relationship to alternative possibilities for our lives, such as whether we perceive that there are others out there who would make better partners. Furthermore, we also seek some level of **equity** in our relationships, such that the contributions that each party makes are perceived as "fair."

As the most common theory used in the study of families, social exchange theory has been applied to a range of topics, such as dating, sexual behaviour, and level of satisfaction with the household division of labour. One of the topics to which exchange theory is frequently applied is marital cohesiveness, and on its flip side, divorce. The question of what keeps some married couples together while others divorce has been explored using exchange theory since the 1960s (Levinger, 1965).

Previti and Amato (2003) evaluated the tenets of exchange theory in a 17-year longitudinal study of married couples. They found that marital cohesiveness depended more upon the *rewards* associated with the relationship (e.g., love, respect, friendship, good communication), than on perceptions of *alternatives* or on *barriers* to divorce (i.e., the costs associated with divorcing, such as loss of contact with children, financial strain, and religious views). They concluded that barriers to divorce keep unhappy couples together only for a little bit longer. Bodenmann and colleagues (2006) reached similar conclusions in an analysis of divorced couples in three European countries—Switzerland, Germany, and Italy. In their study, participants cited the "loss of love" as the primary attractor to divorce, revealing the high value that people place on this intangible reward. Participants reported that the barriers to divorce that they had given the most consideration were worries about losing contact with children and concerns about financial strain; however, in the end, these couples determined that the loss of love was more important than the potential costs of divorcing.

Profit: The benefits of being in a particular relationship outweigh the costs.

Comparison level: A comparison of the costs and benefits of a particular relationship compared to other people who are in similar types of relationships.

Comparison level for alternatives: A comparison of our relationship to alternative possibilities for our lives.

Equity: The contributions that each party is making in a relationship are perceived as "fair."

FAMILY LIFE COURSE DEVELOPMENT THEORY

This framework has as its core assumption the notion that families transition through a series of qualitatively different "stages" over time. As families transition from one stage to another, family structures, roles, and relationships change. The transition to parenthood is one of the stages of family development that has received the most academic attention. As anyone who has made this transition can likely attest, bringing one's first baby home is accompanied by a considerable amount of stress, caused by everything from the lack of sleep to changes in roles; in fact, research has found that this is one of the most stressful family transitions. The impact of new parenthood particularly takes its toll on the relationship between spouses or partners, causing a significant decline in feelings of "love," as well as increases in conflict and feelings of ambivalence about the relationship. This has been found with both biological and adoptive parents, as well as heterosexual, gay, and lesbian parents (Goldberg, Smith & Kashy, 2010; Mitnick, Heyman & Smith Slep, 2009). However, the magnitude of this impact does vary with the psychological and social resources that the parents bring into their new roles. The decline in relationship quality is greater among parents who are younger, in relationships of shorter duration, from racially or ethnically marginalized groups, who deal with problems in an avoidant (i.e., ignoring) or confrontational (i.e., aggressive) manner, or who did not plan the pregnancy.

Even if one isn't a new parent, having young children creates particular challenges, especially for employed parents. A survey of more than 40,000 IBM employees across 79 countries found that fathers experience *work–family conflict* (i.e., work demands that take time and attention away from family), while mothers experience *family–work spillover* (i.e., emotional strain at work due to family pressures) (Martinengo, Jacob & Hill, 2010).

Thus far, we have seen that sociological knowledge about families is frequently derived from perspectives that lie outside the core theoretical perspectives in sociology. However, although the core theoretical perspectives are not as widely applied, we can see families being addressed within functionalist, conflict, feminist, and interactionist theories.

Becoming a new parent is one of the most stressful family transitions.

Source: John Dolan/Getty

SOCIOLOGY *IN MY COMMUNITY*

HELPING NEW PARENTS

Although the transition to parenthood is associated with declines in relationship quality, people in the midst of this transition are amenable to prevention and intervention efforts intended to improve their intimate relationships. A review of research on couples in this stage of family development finds that those who have attended prenatal classes are less likely to experience significant declines in relationship quality (Mitnick,

Heyman & Smith Slep, 2009). Parenting programs can be found in communities across Canada. For example, the Etobicoke Brighter Futures Coalition offers an array of free programs for parents who are transitioning to parenthood—ranging from prenatal and postnatal nutrition classes to a Parent–Child Mother Goose program, to a Nobody's Perfect Parenting Education program.

FUNCTIONALIST THEORIES

For Émile Durkheim (1858–1917), one of the founders of sociology, issues of family frequently emerged. He questioned how modernization was affecting families and how changes in families were affecting the social order, addressing issues such as the liberalization of divorce, effective socialization of children, and household division of labour (Lamanna, 2002), issues that are also highlighted in contemporary debates about family decline. However, Durkheim himself did not consider the family to be in trouble due to modernization. In response to a colleague who was decrying a decline in parenting and the weakening of the family, Durkheim argued that the family "is not appreciably worse than it was; it is [just] different" (cited in Lamanna, 2002, p. 1).

In addition to seeing the functionalist perspective being applied in current debates about family decline, we also see it in the those definitions addressed earlier in the chapter, which define family in terms of its internal processes and functions, such as the socialization of children and affective nurturance (e.g., Murdock, 1949; Vanier Institute of the Family, 2009). Although functionalist assumptions can be applied to a number of areas within the study of families, there is a sizable body of research on gender role differentiation and the household division of labour (Ingoldsby, Smith & Miller, 2004; White & Klein, 2008).

Talcott Parsons (1902–1979) is best known for addressing families from a functionalist perspective (Parsons, 1954; Parsons & Bales, 1955). He described two key functions of the family—the socialization of children and the stabilization of adult personalities—that are important for the well-being of both individuals and society. He pointed out the macro-level processes of industrialization and urbanization had weakened the bonds among extended family, creating families based on *companionate marriage* rather than broader kin relationships. However, he did not identify this change as negative; instead, he said that in an industrialized and urbanized society, nuclear families based on companionate marriage were still able to fulfill the necessary functions. The functionality of this type of family structure arises from the power of parents over their children and gender-differentiated task orientation.

Males are responsible for *instrumental* tasks, those that connect the family to the outside world (e.g, financial support of the family). In contrast, females are responsible for the *expressive* tasks necessary for the internal world of the family (e.g., nurturing children). The father is the technical expert and executive, while the mother is the expressive charismatic leader. As long as these different types of tasks remained differentiated by gender, families could ensure that everything that needed to get done would get done; should tasks not be differentiated on this basis, time would be wasted in each family member trying to figure out what he or she should be doing, which would impede the actual completion of the tasks. More recently, Don Swenson (2004) has applied functionalist assumptions to child outcomes, suggesting that effective parenting enhances child attachment and improves child outcomes; in contrast, dysfunctional parenting causes insecure attachment in children, which impedes socialization. Of course, in the 21st century, parents increasingly share instrumental and expressive tasks, which has necessitated changes in social policy (see *Sociology in Practice* on page 88).

CONFLICT THEORIES

As with functionalist theories, families were also addressed within early conflict theories. Friedrich Engels (1884), who was one of Karl Marx's colleagues, suggested that the transition from feudalism to

SOCIOLOGY *IN PRACTICE*

PARENTAL LEAVE BENEFITS

As women began entering the workforce en masse in the latter half of the 20th century, social policy had to change in order to accommodate the different day-to-day realities of Canadian families. In 1971, women who met eligibility requirements (in terms of the number of paid work hours they had in the past year) were able to claim up to 15 weeks of maternity leave through Unemployment Insurance (now known as Employment Insurance) upon the birth of a child. In recognition of the greater prevalence of shared parenting in families, as well as to further encourage such sharing, in 1990 the federal Parental Benefits Program included an additional 10 weeks of parental leave that could be utilized by either parent (or shared). In 2000, there were further changes to the Parental Benefits Program. Fifteen weeks of maternity leave are now followed by 35 weeks of parental leave that can be shared between parents (Marshall, 2008).

capitalism resulted in patriarchy. Just as male workers were subordinated by their employers, women and children were subordinated by adult men; children gained power as they grew up (or at least male children did), but women remained subordinated throughout their lives. Engels claimed that female subordination in families would end if women entered paid employment.

Conflict theories propose that resources are distributed unequally within families, and as such, conflict emerges as family members compete over those resources; conflict can range from everyday disagreements to acts of violence. For instance, siblings may have conflicts over valuable resources (e.g., parental attention, the favourite chair in front of the television). Sometimes those conflicts lead to physical violence, ranging from pushing to punching or choking. In fact, sibling violence has been found to be the most common form of family violence. In one study, 70 percent of university undergraduates reported having engaged in at least one form of sibling violence while in their last year of high school; the most common forms of violence were pushing, shoving, or throwing something at the sibling (Hoffman, Kiecolt & Edwards, 2005). This study revealed that acts of sibling violence were frequently related to perceptions of parental favouritism.

Some conflict theories suggest that family conflict is distinctive because of the unique emotional nature of resources that exist within families. But other conflict theories suggest that family conflict is a microcosm of societal conflict, a reflection of broader social inequalities (White & Klein, 2008). In a classic analysis of wife abuse in the United States, Straus (1994) finds some support for this latter view. Straus found that the prevalence of wife assault varied across states, based on both gender inequality (e.g., differences in the average income of men and women) and social disorganization (e.g., high divorce rates, low levels of religious affiliation) within the state. Family violence is one of the topic areas within which conflict theories are most frequently applied. Feminist theories have also addressed family violence, among a range of other topics.

FEMINIST THEORIES

In the midst of tremendous diversity in feminist theorizing, one commonality is the centrality of families. Some feminist theorizing may emphasize the importance of parents socializing their sons and daughters in similar ways, while other theorizing may draw attention to the exploitation of nannies who are brought in from other nations, and yet other more radical theorizing may call for an end to biological reproduction altogether. But in all cases, families are perceived as playing a pivotal role in the gendering of people's experiences at the micro level and the reproduction of the gendered structure of society at the macro level.

Like conflict theories, feminist theories identify families as a site of inequality (or at least *potential* inequality). Even in the 21st century, sons and daughters still tend to be socialized differently, women continue to have greater responsibility for housework and childcare, and men tend to have higher incomes. Feminist scholars point out that where there are family inequalities, there are power differentials, and where there are power differentials, a "dark side" of family life can emerge—such as through physical and/or psychological abuse. Some feminists suggest that because family inequalities are embedded within a patriarchal social structure, women and children are especially vulnerable to abuse. However, other feminist work claims that the influence of a patriarchal social structure on families is such that all family members can be negatively affected. Violence is considered more acceptable for males than for females within a patriarchal society, but that violence may be perpetrated against another male. For example, sibling violence has been found to be most common between brothers, rather than between brothers and sisters, or between sisters (Hoffman, Kiecolt & Edwards, 2005).

Even when feminist theories are not explicitly used, the knowledge that we have about families owes a great debt to feminist scholars and activists. Sociologist Margrit Eichler (1988, 1997) drew attention to the fact that there is no singular, monolithic "family," but rather a plurality of family forms. Feminist scholars were the first to emphasize the importance of analyzing the nature and implications of the gendered division of labour within families; now sociologists of all theoretical orientations explore this area of study. And because feminist scholars pointed to the power of gender in all aspects of our lives, gender is now integrated into virtually every topic area in the study of families, from mate selection, to parenting, to aging families.

INTERACTIONIST THEORIES

Interactionist theories suggest that as the most "significant" of *significant others*, families shape our understandings of the world and our place in it. Similarly, our understandings of the world come into play within our everyday lives as family members. In a classic interactionist analysis of marriage, Jessie Bernard (1972) pointed out that husbands and wives frequently have very different perceptions of their marriage, such that one can refer to "his marriage" and "her marriage." For example, he may indicate that they rarely have disagreements, while she may say that they frequently have disagreements; he may say that he engages in childcare activities on a daily basis, while she states that he does so only a few times a week.

...honestly I just feel like we don't communicate like we used to!

When two people have differing perceptions of the same issue, there can be significant consequences. Research that has been done with divorced mothers and fathers shows that they often have different perceptions of both the fathers' parenting skills and the mothers' willingness to accommodate changes to visitation schedules. When perceptions vary on these issues, parents are less able to establish effective co-parenting styles, and conflicts between them increase—to the detriment of the children involved (Madden-Derdich & Leonard, 2002).

People's subjective perceptions and understandings also play a role in intimate violence. Some victims of dating violence or domestic violence don't identify themselves as having been abused, because they define "abuse" as something more than the slapping and pushing that they may have experienced. Similarly, perpetrators often don't identify themselves as "batterers," because they have hit their partner only a few times, or have perpetrated violence against only one partner throughout their lives (Goodrum, Umberson & Anderson, 2001).

TIME TO REVIEW

- Why has the study of families been described as an empirically driven enterprise?
- What are the two most frequently used theories in empirical research on families? What are their core assumptions, and what family-related topic areas have been studied?
- Which of the core theoretical frameworks in sociology have been recognized as some of the main intellectual traditions in the study of families? In what areas have those theories contributed to our knowledge about families?

As the quotation at the start of the chapter pointed out, "we start and end with families." But precisely which families each of us "starts" and "ends" with can vary—from the specific family structure defined within the Census, to the functional families described by the Vanier Institute, to the relationships established on the basis of love, that are described in emotional definitions of family, to the fictive kin or families of the heart that are a part of many people's lives. Our own family experiences give us valuable knowledge about families more generally. However, the historical, empirical, and theoretical knowledge that comprises the sociology of families provides a broader body of knowledge within which to consider our own family lives, the family lives of the people we interact with during the course of our days, and larger social issues that affect everyone.

CHAPTER SUMMARY

LO¹ Compare varying definitions of family, and explain why the way family is defined is important.

Varying definitions of family include structural, functional, and emotional definitions. Structural definitions emphasize the statuses that make up families, while functional definitions focus on the everyday "doing" of family life, and emotional definitions draw attention to love and affection. The definition used has implications at the macro level and the micro level.

LO² Identify the key trends that indicate changes in Canadian families.

Over the past half century, marriage rates have declined, cohabitation has increased, divorce has increased, same-sex relationships have increased, and people have had fewer children.

LO³ Distinguish between the main assumptions of the family decline and family pluralism perspectives.

The family decline perspective claims that recent changes in families are indicative of the institution of the family being "in crisis." In contrast, the family pluralism perspective suggests that changes in families are indicative of fewer constraints and greater freedom than in the past.

LO⁴ Describe what comprises sociological knowledge about families.

Sociological knowledge about families consists of historical, empirical, and theoretical knowledge.

LO⁵ Describe how colonization affected Aboriginal families, both in the short and long term.

Colonization brought with it the reserve system, changes in legislation that made all Aboriginal people wards of the federal government, and residential schooling, all of which irrevocably changed the way Aboriginal families carried out their daily lives. Several generations of Aboriginal children grew up in residential schools rather than in family environments, and experienced abuse, neglect, and ethnocide. Psychological and social implications continue to the present day.

LO⁶ Explain how each of the following theories contributes to knowledge about families: social exchange, family life course development, functionalist, conflict, feminist, and interactionist.

Social exchange theory claims that all relationships are based on an exchange of resources, and are associated with costs and benefits. Family life course development theory suggests that families progress through a series of qualitatively different stages that are associated with changes in family structures, roles, and interactions. Functionalist theories explore how families are best able to fulfill their functions, such as effective child socialization. Conflict theories state that even within families, there is competition over scarce resources that can be associated with power differentials and family violence. Feminist theories are of a wide range, but the interrelationship between families and gender is central to all of them. Interactionist theories draw attention to the fact that families shape our understandings of the world and ourselves, and that our understandings of the world come into play within our everyday lives as family members.

RECOMMENDED READINGS

1. For a broad introduction to the sociology of families, see: Ward, M., & Belanger, M. (2011). *The Family Dynamic: A Canadian Perspective*. Toronto, ON: Nelson.
2. For more detail on the demographic characteristics of Canadian families revealed by the 2006 Census, refer to: Milan, A., Vézina, M., & Wells, C. (2007). *Family Portrait: Continuity and Change in Canadian Families and Households in 2006, 2006 Census*. Statistics Canada Catalogue No. 97-553-XIE.
3. To learn more about residential schooling, refer to: Chansonneuve, D. (2005). *Reclaiming Connections: Understanding Residential School Trauma among Aboriginal People*. Ottawa, ON: Aboriginal Healing Foundation.

FOR FURTHER REFLECTION

1. Where would you situate yourself in the family decline debate?
2. Consider an issue that you consider to be central in your own family. Which of the theories addressed in this chapter do you think could best address that issue? Which of the theories do you think would be the least useful in exploring that issue?

REFERENCES

(1893/2003). Archives: Charles Henry Pearson on the decline of the family. *Population and Development Review, 29*(2), 299–304.

Ahern, S., & Bailey, K. G. (1997). *Family-by-Choice: Creating Family in a World of Strangers*. Minneapolis, MN: Fairview Press.

Amato, P. R. (2005). Family change: Decline or resilience? In V. L. Bengston, A. C. Acock, K. R. Allen, P. Dilworth-Anderson, and D. M. Klein (Eds.), *Sourcebook of Family Theory and Research* (pp. 112–114). Thousand Oaks, CA: Sage Publications.

Ambert, A. M. (2009). *Divorce: Facts, Causes, and Consequences* (3rd ed.). Ottawa, ON: Vanier Institute of the Family.

Barman, J. (2003). Schooled for inequality: The education of British Columbia Aboriginal Children. In N. Janovicek and J. Parr (Eds.), *Histories of Canadian Children and Youth* (pp. 212–235). Toronto, ON: Oxford University Press.

Bernard, J. (1972). *The Future of Marriage*. New York: Bantam.

Blackstock, C. (2006/2007). Building on the multi-generational strength of First Nations communities. *Transitions, 36*(4), 7–10.

Bodenmann, G., et al. (2006). Attractors and barriers to divorce: A retrospective study of three European countries. *Journal of Divorce and Remarriage, 45*(3/4), 1–24.

Bourgeault, R. G. (1991). Race, class and gender: Colonial domination of Indian women. In J. Vorst et al. (Eds.), *Race, Class, Gender: Bonds and Barriers*. Toronto, ON: Garamond/Society for Socialist Studies.

Brooks, C. (2002). Religious influence and the politics of family decline concern: Trends, sources, and U.S. political behaviour. *American Sociological Review, 67*, 191–211.

Cain, A. O. (1985). Pets as family members. In M. B. Sussman (Ed.), *Pets and the Family* (pp. 5–10). New York: Haworth Press.

Canada Family Action Coalition. (2006). *Canada Family Action Coalition is calling for EVERY Alberta MLA to support Bill 208*. Retrieved September 17, 2009, from www.familyaction.org

Carter, S. (2008). *The Importance of Being Monogamous: Marriage and Nation Building in Western Canada to 1915*. Edmonton/Athabasca, AB: University of Alberta Press/AU Press.

Castellano, M. B. (2002). Aboriginal family trends: Extended families, nuclear families, families of the heart. *Contemporary Family Trends*. (Occasional Paper).

Chansonneuve, D. (2005). *Reclaiming Connections: Understanding Residential School Trauma Among Aboriginal People*. Ottawa, ON: Aboriginal Healing Foundation.

Cliquet, R. (2003/2004). Major trends affecting families in the new millennium—Western Europe and North America. In *Major Trends Affecting Families: A Background Document* (pp. 1–40). United Nations, Division for Social Policy and Development.

Coontz, S. (1992). *The Way We Never Were: American Families and the Nostalgia Trap*. New York: Basic Books.

Davin, N. F. (1879). *Report on Industrial Schools for Indians and Half Breeds*. Retrieved July 7, 2010, from www.canadianshakespeares.ca/multimedia/pdf/davin_report/pdf

Eichler, M. (1988). *Families in Canada Today: Recent Changes and their Policy Consequences* (2nd ed.). Toronto, ON: Gage.

Eichler, M. (1997). *Family Shifts: Families, Policies and Gender Equality*. Toronto, ON: Oxford University Press.

Engels, F. (1884/1972). *The Origin of the Family, Private Property and the State*. New York: Pathfinder.

Gaffield, C. (1992). Canadian families in cultural context: Hypotheses from the mid-19th century. In B. Bradbury (Ed.), *Canadian Family History: Selected Readings* (pp. 135–157). Toronto: Copp Clark.

Gaffield, C. (1990). The social and economic origins of contemporary families. In M. Baker (Ed.), *Families: Changing Trends in Canada* (2nd ed.) (pp. 23–40). Toronto, ON: McGraw-Hill.

Goldberg, A. E., Smith, J. Z., & Kashy, D. A. (2010). Preadoptive factors predicting lesbian, gay, and heterosexual couples' relationship quality across the transition to parenthood. *Journal of Family Psychology, 24*(3), 221–232.

Goodrum, S., Umberson, D., & Anderson, K. L. (2001). The batterer's view of the self and others. *Sociological Inquiry, 71*(2), 221–240.

Grier, K. C. (2006). *Pets in America: A History*. Chapel Hill, NC: University of North Carolina Press.

Haraway, D. (2003). *The Companion Species Manifesto: Dogs, People and Significant Otherness*. Chicago, IL: Prickly Paradigm Press.

Hareven, T. K. (1994). Continuity and change in American family life. In A. S. Skolnick and J. H. Skolnick (Eds.), *Family in Transition* (8th ed.) (pp. 40–47). New York: HarperCollins.

Hoffman, K. I., Kiecolt, K. J., & Edwards, J. N. (2005). Physical violence between siblings: A theoretical and empirical analysis. *Journal of Family Issues, 26*(8), 1103–1130.

Ingoldsby, B., Smith, S.R., & Miller, E. (2004). *Exploring Family Theories*. Los Angeles, CA: Roxbury.

Ipsos-Reid. (2009). Who Knew? *Angus Reid Forum, December*.

Ipsos-Reid. (2005). *One-third of Canadians say they tend to feel exhausted after visiting family for the holidays, 15% look forward to next trip without the family*. Retrieved September 14, 2009, from www.ipsos.ca

Johnson, C. L., & Barer, B. M. (1990). Families and networks among older inner-city Blacks. *Gerontologist, 30*, 726–733.

Johnston, P. (1983). *Native Children and the Child Welfare System*. Toronto, ON: Canadian Council on Social Development and James Lorimer & Company.

Kakfwi, S. (2008, June 12). I accept the Prime Minister's apology. *The Globe and Mail*. Retrieved June 7, 2009, from www.globeandmail.com

Legacy of Hope Foundation. (2009). *Where are the children? Healing the legacy of residential schools*. Retrieved February 18, 2010, from www.wherearethechildren.ca

Kelly, F. (2008). Confession of a born again Pagan. In M. B. Castellano, L. Archibald, and M. DeGagné (Eds.), *From Truth to Reconciliation: Transforming the Legacy of Residential Schools* (pp. 11–42). Ottawa, ON: The Aboriginal Healing Foundation.

Lamanna, M. A. (2002). *Émile Durkheim on the Family*. Thousand Oaks, CA: Sage.

Lewis, J. (2003). *Should We Worry about Family Change? The 2001 Joanne Goodman Lectures*. Toronto, ON: University of Toronto Press.

Levinger, G. (1965). Marital cohesiveness and dissolution: An integrative review. *Journal of Marriage and the Family, 27*, 19–28.

Madden-Derdich, D. A., & Leonard, S. A. (2002). Shared experiences, unique realities: Formerly married mothers' and fathers' perceptions of parenting and custody after divorce. *Family Relations, 51*, 7–45.

Marshall, K. (2008). Fathers' use of paid parental leave. *Perspectives*, (June), 1–10. Ottawa, ON: Statistics Canada. Catalogue No. 75-001-X.

Martinengo, G., Jacob, J. I., & Hill, E. J. (2010). Gender and the work–family interface: Exploring differences across the family life course. *Journal of Family Issues, 31*(10), 1363–1390.

McGillivray, A. (1997). Therapies of freedom. The colonization of Aboriginal children. In A. McGillivray (Ed.), *Governing Childhood* (pp. 135–199). Dartmouth: Aldershot.

Milan, A. (2000). One hundred years of families. *Canadian Social Trends*, (Spring) 2–12. Statistics Canada Catalogue No. 11-008.

Milan, A., Vézina, M., & Wells, C. (2007). *Family Portrait: Continuity and Change in Canadian Families and Households in 2006, 2006 Census*. Statistics Canada Catalogue No. 97-553-XIE.

Mitnick, D. M., Heyman, R. E., & Smith Slep, A. M. (2009). Changes in relationship satisfaction across the transition to parenthood: A meta-analysis. *Journal of Family Psychology, 23*(6), 848–852.

Murdock, G. P. (1949). *Social Structure*. New York: MacMillan.

Natelson, R. (2009). Traditional marriage is better: David Popenoe. *Electric City Weblog, March 19*. Retrieved May 17, 2009, from electriccityweblog.com.

Nault, F. (1996). Twenty years of marriages. *Health Reports, 8*(2), 39–47. Ottawa, ON: Statistics Canada. Catalogue No. 82-003-XIE.

Nye, F. I. (1979). Choice, exchange, and the family. In W. Burr, R. Hill, F. I. Nye, and I. Reiss (Eds.), *Contemporary Theories about the Family* (Vol. 2) (pp. 1–41). New York: The Free Press.

Parsons, T. (1954). *Essays in Sociological Theory*. Glencoe, IL: The Free Press.

Parsons, T., & Bales, R. F. (1955). *Family: Socialization and Interaction Process*. Glencoe, IL: The Free Press.

Perrault, S., & Proulx, J. (2000). Introduction. In J. Proulx and S. Perrault (Eds.), *No Place for Violence: Canadian Aboriginal Alternatives*. Halifax, NS: Ferwood/RESOLVE.

Popenoe, D. (2007). *The State of Our Unions, 2007: The Social Health of Marriage in America*. The National Marriage Project. Piscataway, NJ: Rutgers, The State University of New Jersey.

Popenoe, D. (1994). Housing, suburbia, and family decline: A cross-national perspective. *Research in Community Sociology, 4*, 211–227.

Powell, J., & Branden, K. (2007). Family, sociology of. In G. Ritzer (Ed.), *Blackwell Encyclopedia of Sociology: Blackwell Reference Online*. Retrieved September 14, 2009, from www.blackwellreference.com

Power, E. (2008). Furry families: Making a human-dog family through home. *Social and Cultural Geography, 9*(5), 535–555.

Previti, D., & Amato, P. R. (2003). Why stay married? Rewards, barriers, and marital stability. *Journal of Marriage and Family, 65*, 561–573.

Razack, S. H. (2002). *Race, Space, and the Law: Unmapping a White Settler Society*. Toronto, ON: Between the Lines.

Royal Commission on Aboriginal Peoples. (1996). *Royal Commission on Aboriginal Peoples Final Report*. Ottawa, ON: Government of Canada.

Silva, E. B., & Smart, C. (2001). The 'new' practices and politics of family life. In E. B. Silva and C. Smart (Eds.), *The New Family?* (pp. 1–12). London: Sage Publications.

Statistics Canada. (2007, January 17). Marriages. *The Daily*. Ottawa, ON: Author. Catalogue No. 11-001-XIE.

Statistics Canada. (2008). CANSIM Table 101-6501. Divorces and crude divorce rates, Canada, provinces and territories, annual. Ottawa, ON: Statistics Canada.

Straus, M. A. (1994). State to state differences in social inequality and social bonds in relation to assaults on wives in the United States. *Journal of Comparative Family Studies, 25*, 7–24.

Swenson, D. (2004). *A Neo-Functionalist Synthesis of Theories in Family Sociology*. New York: Mellen Press.

Taylor, A. C., & Bagdi, A. B. (2005). The lack of explicit theory in family research: A case study analysis of the *Journal of Marriage and the Family*, 1990–1999. In V. L. Bengston, A. C. Acock, K. R. Allen, P. Dilworth-Anderson, and D. M. Klein (Eds.), *Sourcebook of Family Theory and Research* (pp. 22–25). Thousand Oaks, CA: Sage Publications.

Turner, J. H. (2005). Is a scientific theory of the family desirable? In V. L. Bengston, A. C. Acock, K. R. Allen, P. Dilworth-Anderson, and D. M. Klein (Eds.), *Sourcebook of Family Theory and Research* (pp. 26–29). Thousand Oaks, CA: Sage Publications.

Vanier Institute of the Family (2009). *Definition of family*. Retrieved September 24, 2009, from www.vifamily.ca/about/definition.html

White, J. M., & Klein, D. M. (2008). *Family Theories* (3rd ed.). Thousand Oaks, CA: Sage Publications.

Whitehead, J. W. (2006). *Without the family, there is no freedom*. Retrieved September 14, 2009, from www.familyaction.org/Articles/issues/family/without-the-family.htm

Wu. Z. (2000). *Cohabitation: An Alternative Form of Family Living*. Toronto, ON: Oxford University Press.

ENDNOTES

1 Retrieved June 30, 2009, from "The Quotations Page" (thequotationspage.com).

2 To be considered a Census family, a common-law couple must have been living together for more than one year.

3 "With children" refers to couples with children age 24 and under. "Without children" refers to couples who have no children in the household, or whose children are age 25 and older.

4 Children and grandchildren who are living with their own spouses, common-law partners, or children are not considered part of the Census family of their parents/grandparents, even if they are living in the same household.

5 Retrieved June 30, 2009, from "The Quotations Page" (thequotationspage.com).

6 Retrieved August 7, 2009, from "The Quotations Page" (thequotationspage.com).

7 Some family historians (e.g., Bourgeault, 1991) suggest that polygamous marriages did not exist in Aboriginal cultures until after colonization, when the intense competition in the fur trade, along with the central role of women in trade relationships, necessitated some men to take on multiple wives for pragmatic, economic reasons.

Culture and Social Structure

LEARNING OBJECTIVES AND OUTCOMES

After reading this chapter, students should be able to do the following:

LO1 Define culture and distinguish between material and nonmaterial forms.

LO2 Explain why language is viewed as a precursor to shared understandings and explain how language confers gender expectations.

LO3 Explain why norms are considered to be regulators of shared behaviours.

LO4 Identify shared values and debate the correspondence between cultural values and norms using functionalist and conflict perspectives.

LO5 Describe features of Canadian culture that make it unique, and discuss critical views of popular culture.

LO6 Outline the basic components of social structure and describe how the symbolic interactionist perspective views social structure.

LO7 Explain how social institutions contribute to social structure and assess the merit of Weber's ideal type of bureaucracy in modern society.

I am Canadian, free to speak without fear, free to worship in my own way, free to stand for what I think right, free to oppose what I believe wrong, or free to choose those who shall govern my country. This heritage of freedom I pledge to uphold for myself and all mankind.

(John Diefenbaker from the Canadian Bill of Rights, July 1, 1960)[1]

TYPES OF CULTURE

LO[1] DEFINING CULTURE

If you were asked to describe what is distinct about "Canadian culture," what would your response include? Would you emphasize similarities or differences among Canadians? Is shovelling snow worth mentioning as a typical expectation for most Canadians? Do you think Canadian culture is distinct because it includes traditions maintained by various groups of Aboriginal peoples? Would you describe the Quebec sovereignty movement? Would your portrayal make reference to well-known Canadian symbols such as the flag, a maple leaf, Molson Canadian beer, hockey games, or the Tim Hortons franchise? Would you locate Canadian culture in music by Leonard Cohen or Justin Bieber or in paintings by Emily Carr or Robert Bateman? Would you reference any of the "cultured" Canadians from the upper classes such as the Irving or Thomson families who maintain a disproportionate share of wealth? Your response could include some, all, or none of these accounts. Indeed, the concept of "culture" is interpreted in so many incompatible ways that it is described as one of the most complicated words in the English language (Williams, 1976, p. 87).

To sociologists, **culture** encompasses the sum total of the social environment in which we are raised and continue to be socialized in throughout our lives. This means culture entails a wide assortment of ideas, customs, behaviours, and practices. Although all societies and even groups within the same culture differ in how they develop and carry out specific practices, they also share common features. For example, all societies find ways to secure food, clothing, and shelter; all societies develop forms of communication and familial structures; all societies implement ways to use tools; and all societies come up with means for self-expression—practices that anthropologist George Murdock (1945) coined as **cultural universals**.

Postmodernists argue against the use of overarching theories and reductionist explanations that tend to view the world in narrow ways. The postmodern framework helps us appreciate diverse Canadian "cultures" that are continuously being created, as opposed to the existence of a single unified Canadian identity (Sumara, Davis & Laidlaw, 2001). For the sake of simplicity, we will continue to use the singular term *culture* in this chapter. However, we recognize cultural differences among divergent groups living within Canada and, hence, are in fact discussing what can be described as multiple simultaneous Canadian *cultures*. Basic elements of culture include the foundations of our expectations that are rooted in geography, climate, language, norms, values, and the existing artifacts of "our" time as well as in the traditions passed onto us from

Culture: The sum total of the social environment in which we are raised and continue to be socialized in throughout our lives.

Cultural universals: Common practices shared by all societies.

SOME PEOPLE THINK CULTURE IS MUSIC... OTHERS THINK IT'S WRITING... WHILE I KNOW IT'S MAKING MONEY

Source: © Foyle, Lindsay, lfon149, Cartoonstock.com

previous generations. In this chapter we discuss basic elements of Canadian culture, try to locate its uniqueness, and examine the broader social structure of patterned arrangements that provide a framework for culture and related social interactions.

MATERIAL AND NONMATERIAL CULTURE

We are where we live! Again we emphasize that, contrary to the popular belief that most of our decisions in life are based on individual choice or free will, many choices are, instead, largely reflections of the culture in which we are raised. It is precisely this culture that informs many (but not all) Canadians about the pleasures of eating steak or a pizza on a Friday night and similarly fails to teach just as many (but not all) Canadians to prefer black pudding (a type of sausage usually made with the coagulated blood of pigs that is popular in the United Kingdom) or *balut* (a hard-boiled egg containing a fertilized duck embryo that is a delicacy in Asia). Similarly, through socialization practices Canadians

Material culture: Tangible or physical items that people have created for use and give meaning to in a given culture.

Nonmaterial culture: Intangibles produced by intellectual or spiritual development and the use of artifacts in a given culture.

Language: An abstract system of word meanings and symbols including spoken, written, and signed forms of verbal and nonverbal communications that are used to encode and decode cultural components.

come to share cultural ideas about what is important (e.g., securing a job) and what the appropriate means are for obtaining desired goals (e.g., going to school to learn skills associated with legitimate forms of employment).

Sociologist William Fielding Ogburn (1922) used the term *social heritage* to describe the common cultural world into which children of a particular group are born. He also noted the importance that people attach to material objects and the central role that the use of material belongings takes on in any given culture. **Material culture** includes all of the tangible or physical items that people have created for use and give meaning to such as pizza and steak, along with works of art, various forms of housing, means of transportation, clothing, tools, and countless electronic gadgets. In contrast, intangibles that are the end product of intellectual and/or spiritual development or ways that people use artifacts are considered aspects of **nonmaterial culture**. Examples of nonmaterial culture include language, knowledge, symbols, customs, morals, beliefs, and practices that help to organize and give meaning to our social world.

TIME TO REVIEW

- How do sociologists define culture?
- Would a practice such as religion be considered part of material or nonmaterial culture?

HOW CULTURE SHAPES OUR IDENTITY

LO[2] LANGUAGE AS A PRECURSOR TO SHARED UNDERSTANDINGS

Language is the primary facilitator of culture because it is the main channel through which people express themselves and pass acquired knowledge on from one generation to the next. Sociologists define **language** as "an abstract system of word meanings and symbols" (e.g., Schaefer, Smith & Grekul, 2009, p. 63) including spoken, written, and signed forms of verbal and nonverbal communications that are used to encode and decode cultural components. Ninety-eight percent of all Canadians can speak English or French and most households have adopted one of these two official languages as the language spoken most frequently at home (Statistics Canada, 2006). English far outweighs French in most provinces and territories with the exception of Quebec, New Brunswick (which is about 30 percent French), and Nunavut (in which more people speak an Inuit language) (Statistics Canada, 2006). This should not be interpreted to mean that Canada comprises a relatively homogeneous group of people.

Canada consists of divergent groups, from Aboriginal peoples to the early colonizers (e.g., the English and the French), along with millions of immigrants (e.g., Chilean, East Indian, Japanese, South Korean, Lebanese, Iranian, Scottish, Irish, German, Chinese, American, Italian, Polish, Ukrainian, Russian, Dutch, Filipino, etc.) as well as their descendants, who in some cases continue to speak languages other than English and French and who continue to engage in a variety of traditional cultural practices. **Mother tongue** refers to the first language learned at home in childhood that is still understood by an individual (Statistics Canada, 2009). One-fifth of the population is considered to be "allophone"—someone whose mother tongue is not English or French. More than 200 languages are reported as mother tongues by Canadians. The third most commonly spoken mother tongue (following English and French and representing about 3 percent of Canadians), is a variety of Chinese (e.g., Mandarin, Cantonese, Hakka, and Taiwanese) (Statistics Canada, 2007).

SOCIOLOGY IN THEORY: THE SAPIR–WHORF HYPOTHESIS

Language serves as a referent such that aspects of material and nonmaterial culture come to take on particular meanings and come to be understood similarly by people who share a culture. Hence, to people living in Canada, the concept of a "dog" clearly represents a four-legged, fur-covered domesticated animal that barks and makes a great pet. But language is even more fundamental than this because it also helps to construct abstract forms of cultural reality. Anthropologist and linguist Edward Sapir (1884–1939) first became intrigued by how language shapes people's world view when he came across Franz Boas's (1911) early study of Hopi Indian language and noted the absence of an objective sense of time. For instance, while we might say "the light flashed," a Hopi Indian would say *Reh-pi* or "flash" without a subject (i.e., the light) and with no reference to time (Carroll, 1956: viii). Because of how language is used and understood, the Hopi likely experience the world quite differently from other groups who use languages with references to time such as past, present, and future verb tenses.

This revelation led Sapir to believe that language helps to establish thinking, a phenomenon we now refer to as the principle of *linguistic determination*.

Benjamin Lee Whorf (1897–1941), Sapir's student, found that how language is used to label and code events and objects is also important for understanding what those things mean in a particular culture. In Whorf's words: "We cut nature up, into concepts, and ascribe significances as we do, largely because we are parties to an agreement to organize it in this way—an agreement that holds throughout our speech community and is codified in the patterns of our language" (Carroll, 1956, p. 213). Whorf notes that in the Hopi language, only some events reflecting a brief duration, such as "lightning," "wave," and "flame," are represented as verbs; while in Nootka (a language native to Vancouver Island), every word is a verb, and hence a "house" (which would be a noun in the English language for a shelter) is stated more in terms of its functional properties as in "it houses" (or provides a shelter) and similarly, a "flame occurs" (Carroll, 1956, pp. 215–216). Whorf's position that language has particular meaning within the given culture in which it occurs is commonly referred to today as *linguistic relativism*. Taken together, the principles of linguistic determination and linguistic relativism form what is called the **Sapir–Whorf hypothesis**. The Sapir–Whorf hypothesis, named after its two proponents, then, is the assertion that language shapes reality.

Language helps us appreciate how vastly different cultures may be from one another; this is especially evident in the language used to describe prevalent aspects of climate, geography, or material culture. This is why Inuit have different words for snow (e.g., to depict crunchy snow, soft snow, old snow); Italians have various types of pasta (e.g., spaghetti, vermicelli, penne); Trobiand Islanders from Papua, New Guinea, have different words for yams; and Arabs use a variety of words to characterize camels and/or camel equipment (Bryson, 1990, pp. 14–15).

The nuances of language and meaning are especially apparent in blunders that occur when products are marketed in foreign countries. As Ricks (1999) notes, "cultural differences are the most significant and troublesome variables encountered by the multinational company" (p. 4). For example, when the Coca-Cola Company began marketing in China, it introduced Chinese characters

Mother tongue: The first language learned at home in childhood that is still understood by an individual.

Sapir–Whorf hypothesis: As a function of linguistic determinism and relativism, language shapes reality.

Should "WIDE VISION" on this sign be taken to mean "SCENIC VIEW"?

that sound similar to the English pronunciation of the product's name (i.e., "ke-ke-ken-la"). However, the literal meaning "bite the wax tadpole" or "a wax-flattened mare" (depending on the dialect) did not resonate well with customers and the characters were soon changed to "ko-kou-ko-le" to fit a more pleasant interpretation of "happiness in the mouth" (Ricks, 1999, p. 38). Likewise, video game software developer Sega Corporation ran into an issue when it began marketing in Italy because "say-ga" as pronounced in English refers to male masturbation in Italian. Hence, to disassociate from any potential misinterpretation, the company goes by "see-ga" in Italy (Texin, 2011).

SOCIOLOGY IN THEORY: GENDERED LANGUAGE

The feminist framework can help us better appreciate how language confers cultural constructions beginning even prior to birth with the names selected for boys versus girls, followed by the qualitatively different adjectives used to describe males versus females later on. For example, a baby boy may be

"strong" and sometimes "cute" but not "pretty" just as an adult female may be described as "beautiful" but never "handsome." Similarly, titles for forms of employment often denote who is expected to hold that position as in "mailman," "fireman," "bellman," "stewardess," and "cleaning lady." Largely attributable to increased female participation in the paid work force, language used to depict occupational titles has shifted to more gender-neutral terms as in "mail carrier," "firefighter" "concierge," "flight attendant," and "house cleaner." Gender "sensitive" language is also evident in the use of "Ms." rather than "Miss" or "Mrs." when addressing a female in reference to her surname (as in Ms. Smith).

LO³ NORMS AS REGULATORS OF SHARED BEHAVIOURS

Language is often used by members of a given culture to communicate expectations about what is or is not considered to be appropriate conduct. How many times did a parent nag you to brush your teeth, wash your hands, or finish your supper before starting your dessert? Did your teachers ever remind

SOCIOLOGY *IN MY COMMUNITY*

GENDER-NEUTRAL LANGUAGE QUIZ

The Language Portal of Canada promotes the development of language skills and showcases Canadian expertise in language through educational resources such as writing tools, quizzes, data bases, glossaries, and dictionaries. Do you use gender-neutral language? Find out by taking the Gender-neutral Language Quiz.

1. Anyone who misses curfew will have _____ privileges revoked.
   a. her or his
   b. their
   c. his (her)
2. Allanah loves to write and dreams of becoming a famous _____.
   a. poetess
   b. poet
   c. female poet
3. Please address this invitation to _____.
   a. Mr. and Mrs. G. Brown
   b. Eleanor and Mr. Brown
   c. Mr. and Mrs. Brown
4. Four _____ and six men sat on the discussion panel.
   a. women   b. ladies   c. girls
5. The geology professor taught the lesson using _____ terms.
   a. layman's   b. lay   c. layperson's
6. Lynette, a _____ manager, always fights for her employees.
   a. petite but fierce
   b. spunky
   c. [nothing]
7. An applicant who wants to study nursing or midwifery must demonstrate that _____ is committed.
   a. he or she
   b. s/he
   c. she

Answers:
1. a. her or his
   Although it is becoming more common to use a plural pronoun (their) as a gender-neutral singular pronoun (anyone) in informal writing, this usage is not fully accepted. Also, most sources agree that parentheses should not enclose one pronoun when both are offered.
2. b. poet
   Avoid using gender-specific occupational titles.
3. c. Mr. and Mrs. Brown
   In correspondence, make sure to use parallel construction.
4. a. women
   Avoid expressions that could be viewed as patronizing. *Girl* should be used only to refer to a minor. *Ladies* is used with gentlemen.
5. b. lay
   Avoid using expressions with the generic term *man*. Although *layperson's terms* is not incorrect, it is cumbersome. *Lay terms* is becoming the acceptable gender-neutral replacement *for layman's terms*.
6. c. [nothing]
   Do not use unnecessary adjectives to describe a person when the detail is irrelevant or the sentence speaks for itself.
7. a. he or she
   We can no longer assume that traditional feminine roles (e.g., nurse, social worker, teacher) apply only to women. In addition, most sources agree that the construction s/he should be avoided.

Source: Government of Canada (2011). Gender-neutral Language Quiz. Language Portal of Canada. Gatineau, QC: Translation Bureau. Retrieved April 16, 2011, from http://www.noslangues-ourlanguages.gc.ca/quiz/jeux-quiz-genre-neutre-gender-neutral-eng.php?c1=1&c2=2&c3=3&c4=1&c5=3&c6=3&c7=2&quiz=Submit&qznm=genre-neutre-gender-neutral-eng&qzlang=eng

you to stay seated, sit quietly, or raise your hand before answering in class? Recall from Chapter 1 that *norms* are expectations for how we are supposed to act, think, and look. To sociologists, **folkways** refer to informal norms that are based in accepted tradition and centre on acts of kindness or politeness that demonstrate respect for the generalized other. For example, unless you have been specifically informed to do otherwise, you likely address your instructor with his or her formal title (e.g., "Doctor" or "Professor"), you wait your turn in a lineup to purchase coffee, and you answer your phone with a greeting such as "hello" or "hey." Failure to comply with folkways generally results in informal sanctions (i.e., punishments) such as expressions of disapproval from others.

Mores, (pronounced mor-ays) on the other hand, refer to more formal norms that embody values

Folkways: Informal norms that are based in accepted tradition.

Mores: Formal norms embedded in laws that are needed to maintain social control.

CHAPTER 5   Culture and Social Structure

and that are needed to maintain social control. Examples of mores in Canadian culture include formal legislation (i.e., laws) stating that no one is allowed to trespass, commit acts of theft, or sell prohibited drugs. **Taboos** are mores that have such strong moral connotations attached to them that the acts are considered wrong in and of themselves (e.g., cannibalism and incest). Transgression of mores and taboos generally results in formal sanctions such as the loss of personal freedom while serving time in prison.

Sociologists also distinguish between prescriptive and proscriptive norms. **Prescriptive norms** are rules depicting behaviours we are expected to do such as covering one's mouth while coughing, respecting the rights of others, and following the appropriate authority structures in the workplace. **Proscriptive norms** are rules outlining behaviours we are expected to refrain from doing as in the case of speaking with a mouth full of food, taking things that belong to others, or drinking and taking drugs that impair one's ability to perform duties while in the workplace.

> **Taboos:** Mores that are considered wrong in and of themselves.
>
> **Prescriptive norms:** Rules concerning behaviours we are expected to do.
>
> **Proscriptive norms:** Rules concerning behaviours we are expected to refrain from doing.

NONVERBAL COMMUNICATION AS A CONVEYER OF CULTURAL MEANING

Source: © Candy Davis. Courtesy of Icon Experience Photography

This gesture is common to Canadians and is used to display pleasure.

Signs of disapproval and other types of informal sanctions are often applied through nonverbal forms of communication. For example, a person who joins a friend at the front of long line-up at Tim Hortons may receive disapproving looks from other patrons. Similarly, when someone cuts in front of you in traffic, you might blow the horn in your vehicle or perhaps even give the other driver a hand gesture such as the well-known middle-finger "salute" to communicate displeasure. Use caution while travelling in a foreign country and attempting to communicate using a gesture from your homeland. There are no universal gestures. Even commonplace Western gestures such as waving hello or showing a peace sign can mean different things in other cultures. Cultures

SOCIOLOGY ON SCREEN

IRON MAN: NO GANG SIGNS

In the Marvel Studios first *Iron Man* (2008) film directed by Jon Favreau, superhero Tony Stark (i.e., Iron Man) played by Robert Downey Jr. jokes about a well-known "gang affiliation" gesture that resembles a peace sign "V" turned sideways:

> Jimmy: Is it cool if I take a picture with you?
> Tony Stark: Yes, it's very cool.
>
> [*Jimmy hands Pratt his camera and poses with a peace sign*]
>
> Tony Stark: I don't want to see this on your MySpace page. Please no gang signs.
>
> [*Jimmy lowers hand*]

Tony Stark: No, throw it up. I'm kidding. Yeah, peace. I love peace. I'd be out of a job for peace.

(The Internet Movie Database, 2010)

While the "no gang signs" exchange is a now famous line credited to *Iron Man,* its relevance in the real world is apparent. Many gangs use unique hand gestures to demonstrate member affiliation, to denote territories, and to communicate to other gang members. Elvis Rodriguez and Richard Figueroa-Santiago were the first to be arrested in Florida for posting gang hand gestures on MySpace.com where a state law criminalizes the use of electronic communication for promoting gang interests (Beardsley, 2009).

do, however, possess similar *categories* of gestures. For example, they have gestures (albeit different ones) for displays of friendship or anger. In addition, some facial expressions are widely recognized across cultures (e.g., happiness, sadness, anger, surprise, disgust, and fear).

Nonverbal gestures with direct verbal equivalents are known as **emblems**. Emblems are typically used in place of words as is case of the traffic salute mentioned earlier or where someone motions by pulling an index finger toward him or her to represent "come here." Gestures are also used for greetings or displays of pleasure. Canadians display what looks like sideways "horns" with the index finger and pinky extended and *pointing sideways* or even down (with the third and fourth finger held against the palm by the thumb) indicate to indicate they are having "fun." A similar gesture with the extended index finger and pinky *pointing up* is often displayed as "devil horns" by fans and band members at heavy metal rock concerts.

LO⁴ VALUES AS SHARED IDEAS

Recall that *cultural values* are collectively shared ideas about what is right and wrong. Interestingly, although references are continuously made to how policies, mission statements, or programs line up with "core Canadian values," there is actually no agreed-upon documented source to which these correspond. Even the prime minister of Canada notes that "we probably need to have some thought about what the shared values really are, and how we strengthen those" (CBC News, 2007). While there may be no obvious consensus concerning core Canadian values, common themes repeatedly emerge. For example, in 1990, the federal government created a task force to gather opinions from Canadians about their views on Canada's future. By the end of the eight-month data-gathering process, 75,069 calls had been received via an idea line, more than 13,000 group discussions had taken place involving 315,000 participants, 7,056 letters had been received, and more than 300,000 elementary and secondary students had participated in various forums (Citizen's Forum on Canada's Future, 1991). Participants identified these seven common unifying Canadian values:*

1. *Belief in Equality and Fairness in a Democratic Society.* The belief in the need for equality and fairness was a principal value identified by the participants as one group from Newfoundland informed the commission: "We believe that most Canadians want a society that . . . protects national interests while remaining responsive and accountable, to individual rights; . . . protects freedom, so that individuals can live in the manner of their choice, so long as they do not infringe on the rights of others; . . . protects the rights of all Canadians to fair and equal treatment: women, ethnic minorities, different linguistic groups, aboriginal peoples, various religions, etc. . . ." (p. 35).

2. *Belief in Consultation and Dialogue.* Canadians regarded themselves as "people who settle their differences peacefully and in a consultative rather than confrontational manner" (p. 37) both at the level of individuals and at the level of government. Participants noted that relations could be vastly improved with more opportunities for educational visitor exchanges, particularly those designed to illuminate issues involving Quebec's place in confederation.

3. *Importance of Accommodation and Tolerance.* "Forum participants recognize the existence of different groups in societies and their need to sustain their own cultures while attaching themselves to the country's society, values, and institutions. As well, they acknowledge the existence of various legitimate competing regional and cultural interests in Canada" (p. 40). Acceptance and support were expressed especially in relation to overall ethnic diversity and the need to accommodate Aboriginal self-government.

4. *Support for Diversity.* Repeatedly, participants noted the importance of retaining and celebrating Canada's rich diversity in terms of differences in language, region, ethnicity, and culture.

5. *Compassion and Generosity.* Canadians recognized the importance of supporting the collective in the form of "universal and extensive social services, our health care system, our pensions, our willingness to welcome refugees, and our commitment to regional economic equalization" (p. 42).

6. *Attachment to Canada's Natural Beauty.* Canada's natural environment was identified as a matter of importance as summarized by one person who said "All Canadians love the land" (p. 42). Widespread concern for the environment was best captured in the words by a group in Nova Scotia who stated "The beauty of our country . . . must be preserved through stricter laws regarding pollution and other environmental hazards" (p. 43).

7. *Our World Image: Commitment to Freedom, Peace, and Nonviolent Change.* Finally, the maintenance of a progressive but free and

> **Emblems:** Gestures with direct verbal equivalents.

---

*Source: Citizen's Forum on Canada's Future—Keith Spicer Commission Report (1991). *Citizen's Forum on Canada's Future: A Report to the People and Government of Canada.* Ottawa, ON: Supply and Services Canada.

peace-keeping country was expressed by forum participants who felt that "Canadians are generally respected throughout the world," . . . that "resorts to violence . . . have no rightful place in Canada" and that "a Canadian is a person, regardless of ethnic origin, who . . . feels free to develop in his or her own, individual way" (p. 44).

CORRESPONDING VALUES AND NORMS

Cultural values and norms are closely related since values reflect group ideas and norms are those ideas translated into expectations about actions. For example, Canadians value freedom and equality including the right to choose marital partners (e.g., based on things such as love and mutual respect) and this translates into laws recognizing same-sex marriages and laws permitting the adoption of children by same-sex couples. Similarly, people agree that diversity is important; the government of Canada officially sanctions diversity, and this is stated within various policies. For example, diversity is specifically recognized in the *Canadian Multicultural Act* as noted in the preamble: ". . . AND WHEREAS the Government of Canada recognizes the diversity of Canadians as regards race, national or ethnic origin, colour and religion as a fundamental characteristic of Canadian society . . ." (Canadian Multicultural Act, 1985, c. 24 [4th Supp.], p. 4).

Social facts: Observable social phenomena external to individuals that exercise power over them.

SOCIOLOGY IN THEORY: FUNCTIONALIST AND CONFLICT PERSPECTIVES

Functionalists contend that shared cultural values are the foundation of what holds society together. According to Émile Durkheim, cultural values and norms are **social facts**—observable social phenomena external to individuals that exercise power over individuals (Durkheim, 1895/1938). For example, Durkheim posits: "When I perform my duties as a brother, husband or citizen and carry out the commitments I have entered into, I fulfil obligations which are defined in law and custom and which are external to myself and my actions. Even when they conform to my own sentiments and when I feel their reality within me, that reality does not cease to be objective, for it is not I who have prescribed these duties; I have received them through education" (p. 50). Durkheim argued that people displayed a *collective conscience*, or recurring pattern by which people respect norms and they follow them largely because they have internalized them through early socialization practices (Durkheim, 1893/1933).

Internalization of norms means that after awhile, people come to accept cultural norms and follow them without even being aware that they are doing so. This is akin to how you habitually come into every sociology class shortly before it begins, you sit facing the front of the room, and you take notes during the lecture. Similarly, Talcott Parsons (1951) claimed that culture is a

SOCIOLOGY *IN PRACTICE*

THE CANADIAN MULTICULTURALISM ACT

The *Canadian Multiculturalism Act,* as a policy of Canada, is to be carried out in ways that reflect core values as illustrated by these excerpts:

"It is hereby declared to be the policy of the Government of Canada to
    (*a*) recognize and promote the understanding that multiculturalism reflects the cultural and racial diversity of Canadian society and acknowledges the freedom of all members of Canadian society to preserve, enhance and share their cultural heritage; . . .
    (*e*) ensure that all individuals receive equal treatment and equal protection under the law, while respecting and valuing their diversity;
    (*f*) encourage and assist the social, cultural, economic and political institutions of Canada to be

both respectful and inclusive of Canada's multicultural character; . . .
    (*i*) preserve and enhance the use of languages other than English and French, while strengthening the status and use of the official languages of Canada; and
    (*j*) advance multiculturalism throughout Canada in harmony with the national commitment to the official languages of Canada.

Source: Canadian Multicultural Act, 1985, c. 24 (4th Supp.), pp. 3–4.

generalized system of internalized symbols and meanings along with role expectations (i.e., norms) and general values held by the collectivity. In this case, norms, values, and beliefs work together at a more general level in the form of social institutions (e.g., the family and school) to keep society running smoothly.

In contrast, the conflict framework points out the lack of correspondence and the apparent contradictions between cultural values and norms. For example, not all groups in Canada are treated similarly, as evident in the case of the many Aboriginal people sent to residential schools. In recognition of injustices associated with residential schooling, the federal government agreed to pay $2 billion in what is referred to as a "Common Experience Payment" (amounting to about $28,000 per person) to an estimated 80,000 former residential-school students (CBC News, 2007). For more information on the Common Experience Payment, visit Service Canada's website at www.servicecanada.gc.ca.

In 2010, Quebec's minister of Justice introduced Bill 94, which bans Canadian women from wearing Muslim faith-based veils or face coverings while providing or receiving government services. Similarly, according to a 2011 ruling from the Quebec national assembly, Sikh Canadians are banned from wearing their faith-required *kirpan* (i.e., a small ceremonial sword) in the legislature (CBC News, 2011). Using these two recent examples, critically assess whether all Canadians are free to worship in their own way as depicted in the chapter's opening quotation by John Diefenbaker who was the prime minister of Canada at that time. Are similar freedoms afforded to all Canadians? Why or why not? Which of the seven core Canadian values are affirmed (or conversely negated) by these rulings?

IDEAL VERSUS REAL CULTURE

In an effort to explain the existence of common values alongside practices that appear to contradict these values, sociologists sometimes distinguish between the notions of "ideal" and "real" culture. **Ideal culture** encompasses the cultural values that the majority of people identify with, while **real culture** refers to the actual practices engaged in. For example, Canadians value equal rights and while men and women are treated similarly under the law, this is not always the case in practice in the workplace, where women are still disadvantaged by inequities in pay (as discussed in more detail in Chapter 7). Similarly, Canadians highly value the natural environment and the need to do things to protect it (ideal culture), and yet they also engage in practices that negate these values as evidenced by the thriving tar sands oil extraction industry in northern

Alberta, which employs thousands of Canadians but also clearly destroys forests, pollutes rivers, and emits dangerous toxins into the environment (real culture).

Note that the discrepancy between cultural values and norms is not uncommon. In fact, Gannon (2008) refers to a GLOBE study of 62 national or societal cultures that found a very interesting paradox: "cultural values, while sometimes positively related to cultural practices, are consistently and negatively associated with cultural practices" (p. 27). In other words, more often than not, cultural values *fail* to correspond with and even go against actual cultural norms. So why does this happen?

TRADITIONAL BELIEFS VERSUS MODERN PRACTICES

In some cases, modern technology or science advocates for practices that may be inconsistent with traditional beliefs that are highly regarded and continue to be part of a group's cultural heritage. For example, despite the well-established health benefits of breastfeeding for both mothers and infants in developing countries, cultural beliefs continue to discourage women from engaging in this practice. Osman, El Zein, and Wick's (2009) study of 353 first-time mothers recruited from 17 hospitals spread over 5 regions of Lebanon, revealed that family members were a primary source of discouragement and that numerous cultural beliefs inhibited breastfeeding altogether or led to its discontinuation within a couple of months. For example, cultural views included a belief that a mother can harm her infant through her breast milk (e.g., the baby could be poisoned by bad milk or abdominal cramps could be transferred from a mother to her child via breast milk) (Osman, El Zein & Wick, 2009). The notion that "a society's customs and ideas should be described objectively and understood in the context of that society's problems and opportunities became known as **cultural relativism**" (Ember, Ember & Peregrine, 2009, p. 219).

Current beliefs may also condone practices that are part of cultural tradition. For example, the United Nations children's agency reports that while 20,000 children were released from the Sudan People's Liberation Army (SPLA) as part of a "demobilization" agreement, at least 900 continue to bear arms and perform hard

Ideal culture: Cultural values a majority of people identify with in a given society.

Real culture: Practices engaged in by the majority of people in a given society.

Cultural relativism: The perspective that a society's customs and ideas should be described objectively and understood within the context of that society's problems and opportunities.

CHAPTER 5 Culture and Social Structure

labour as soldiers (BBC News Africa, 2010). If you consider this practice to be wrong or highly unusual, it is likely because you are viewing it from the perspective of the culture in which you were raised. Sociologists use the term **ethnocentrism** to refer to the tendency to believe that one's cultural beliefs and practices are superior and should be used as the standard to which other cultures are compared.

Although many countries forbid children from serving in the army and the practice is condemned by the United Nations, sociologists uphold *cultural relativism* to learn more about the cultural climate in which such practices occur. For example, reintegration back into Sudanese communities has been exceedingly difficult for the men (and in some cases, boys) who continue to view themselves and be viewed by others as soldiers. In addition, demobilized soldiers face impoverished conditions as many families live off the equivalent of less than a dollar a day, with no access to running water or electricity, and no means to feed additional members (CBC News, 2010). According to the deputy head of the Southern Sudan Demobilization, Disarmament and Reintegration Commission (SSDRC) in Unity State, "Getting food is very difficult. . . . So when a child moves from where he's getting food easily and whatever [in the military], then he goes and he fails [to eat] for something like two days, a day without food, then he has to think of going back" (Baddorf, 2010).

SUBCULTURES AND COUNTERCULTURES

Even within Canada cultural variations exist in beliefs and practices. A **subculture** is a group that can be differentiated from mainstream culture by its divergent traits involving language, norms, beliefs, and/or values. For example, Hutterites choose to live communally as colonies and work on cooperative farms that are owned by the entire group, sharing a traditional and distinct system of beliefs concerning religion, dress codes, and rules for conduct that is unlike that of mainstream society. A **counterculture** is a type of subculture that strongly opposes central aspects of mainstream culture. For example, although the Hells Angels Motorcycle Club may be recognized for charitable contributions to society such as "Toy Runs" involving bike enthusiasts, it is more appropriately classified as a counterculture for its widespread and nonconventional criminal tendencies involving prostitution, drug trafficking, possessing and trafficking illegal weapons, and extortion (Siegel, Brown & Hoffman, 2006). Canadian culture continues to include a blend of diverse groups and traditions coexisting in what sociologists describe as a "cultural mosaic."

Ethnocentrism: The tendency to believe that one's cultural beliefs and practices are superior and should be used as the standard to which other cultures are compared.

Subculture: A group that can be differentiated from mainstream culture by its divergent traits involving language, norms, beliefs, and/or values.

Counterculture: A type of subculture that strongly opposes central aspects of mainstream culture.

Symbol: An object, image, or event used to represent a particular concept.

TIME TO REVIEW

- What two assumptions make up the Sapir–Whorf hypothesis?
- In what ways do folkways differ from mores?
- How can you distinguish between prescriptive and proscriptive norms?
- How is nonverbal communication used to convey meaning?
- What do sociologists mean when they say norms are internalized?
- Do values and norms usually correspond with one another?
- Why is it important to use cultural relativism when viewing cultural practices?
- What is the difference between a subculture and a counterculture?

LO⁵ HOW IS CANADIAN CULTURE UNIQUE?

THE ABUNDANCE OF CANADIAN SYMBOLS

Recall at the beginning of the chapter when you were asked what comes to mind when you think of Canadian culture. In addition to the many divergent groups in Canada, you might have brought to mind aspects of material and nonmaterial culture that are frequently used to "symbolize" Canada. A **symbol** is an object, image, or event that represents a particular concept. For example, a heart is regularly used as a symbol for love. Similarly, a flag is often used to symbolize a country. The Canadian flag, then, serves as an important, uniquely "Canadian" symbol. Similarly, the Royal Canadian Mounted Police (RCMP) is recognized throughout the world as a national symbol of Canada's unique identity.

The maple leaf is also one of Canada's more salient symbols since it, too, is recognized throughout the world. Canadians travelling abroad sometimes wear a maple leaf pin to specifically identify themselves as Canadian or to try to distinguish themselves from Americans. As Ferguson and Ferguson (2001) put it in their playful book *How to Be a Canadian*, "the two central axioms of Canadian identity, the mantra and motto of an entire nation [are]:

a. I. Am. Canadian.
b. I am not American" (p. 159).

Other readily identified cultural symbols in art forms denote Canada's identity as consisting of diverse groups. For example, inukshuks (i.e., stone sculptures built to look like people with their arms outstretched) remind us of Inuit traditions, while totem poles (i.e., sculptures carved from Western Red Cedar) are associated with Aboriginal peoples of the Pacific Northwest. Selection of an inukshuk as the official Vancouver 2010 Olympic logo raised some controversy since totem poles best reflect the culture native to the Vancouver region (National Geographic, 2010).

Even nonmaterial aspects of culture can serve as symbols, such as sports originating in Canada (e.g., hockey, lacrosse, and basketball). Symbols also reflect values, including attachment to the beauty of Canada's distinct natural environment (e.g., the Canadian Rockies) and wildlife (e.g., the loon, Canada goose, beaver, moose, and polar bear). Finally, symbols are especially evident in popular forms of material culture as in Canadian beer, maple syrup, Tim Hortons, and poutine. Note that while many Canadians still associate Molson Canadian breweries with Canada and the slogan "I am Canadian" with Molson beer, all of the

Source: © Sandra Der

A Royal Canadian Mounted Police officer in dress uniform.

Source: 2009fotofriends/Shutterstock

Totem poles in Stanley Park, Vancouver, BC.

largest brewing companies are now owned by foreign companies (e.g., Labatt is owned by a Belgian company called InBev, Molson is owned by the American company Coors, and Sleeman is owned by the Japanese company Sapporo) (White, 2009).

THE PREVALENCE OF HIGH CULTURE AND POPULAR CULTURE

HIGH CULTURE AND THE SOCIAL ELITE

Canada's uniqueness is also evident in the prevalence of high culture and popular culture. To sociologists, **high culture** refers to activities that are shared mainly by the social elite who purportedly possess both the appreciation for and resources needed to be immersed in this culture (e.g., higher education and wealth). High culture consists of the many forms of

> **High culture:** Activities shared by the social elite.

CHAPTER 5 Culture and Social Structure **105**

Source: Canada's Royal Winnipeg Ballet in Moulin Rouge®—The Ballet. Photographer: Bruce Monk

The Royal Winnipeg Ballet.

creative and performing arts (e.g., visual, theatre, and music). Famous Canadian examples in the performance arts industry include the Canadian Opera Company, the Stratford Shakespeare Festival, the Montreal Symphony Orchestra, and the Royal Winnipeg Ballet.

According to French sociologist Pierre Bourdieu (1930–2002), cultural and educational practices lead to the *social reproduction* of classes. Those in the higher classes have more exposure to high culture, having been socialized in their elite families and in higher educational institutions to understand and appreciate various aspects of that culture which they pass on to future generations as a social asset (i.e., a form of cultural capital) that helps them get ahead (Bourdieu, 1973). The higher class can be readily distinguished from lower classes on the basis of status symbols. **Status symbols** are material indicators of wealth and prestige. Examples of status symbols include owning expensive cars (e.g., a Ferrari, Porsche, Mercedes, Rolls-Royce, or Lamborghini), jewellery, clothing, and original works of art.

POPULAR CULTURE AND THE MASSES

High culture is often contrasted with **popular culture**, a term used to describe well-liked, everyday cultural practices and products that are most desired by the masses. Canadian popular culture includes things

Status symbols: Material indicators of wealth and prestige.

Popular culture: Well-liked everyday practices and products.

Ideology: A set of ideas that support the needs and views of a particular group.

such as featured movies and television series, well-utilized Internet sites such as Facebook and YouTube, stylish cell phone applications, and heavily marketed products that may or may not originate in Canada (e.g., iPhones, Webkins, Lego, Barbie, and Affliction or True Religion jeans). Popular culture also includes well-established spots to eat, drink, or shop such as McDonald's, Tim Hortons, Starbucks, and Lululemon. Popular culture, sometimes called "pop culture" in North America, originated with the end of World War II and the subsequent baby boom wherein people had more disposable income to spend on leisure, fashion, and the mass media (e.g., music). Various historical eras are even referred to by the popular culture prevalent at the time (e.g., hippy, disco, punk, hip-hop) and the term "popular culture" is sometimes used interchangeably with the notion of a "youth culture" (Danesi, 2008). Much of pop culture is promoted and even constructed via the mass media (e.g., music idols, television and movie celebrities, and sports icons.).

SOCIOLOGY IN THEORY: CRITICAL VIEWS OF POPULAR CULTURE

Popular cultural theorist John Storey (2009) describes popular culture as an "*empty* conceptual category" that can be filled in a number of potentially conflicting ways. For example, popular culture can be viewed as whatever is left over from the categorization of high culture, as a power struggle involving dominant and subordinate classes, and as a venue for distinguishing various social groups from the dominant one (pp. 1–13). Critical approaches view pop culture from the perspective of ideology. **Ideology** refers to a set of ideas that support the needs and views of a particular group. Conflict theorists generally consider popular culture to be a means for the ruling class to control the masses in the same way the propaganda model was used to explain how the mass media as owned by the elite controls its consumers.

The Frankfurt Institute for Social Research (later known as the Frankfurt school) was founded in 1923 as a research organization made up of critical scholars including pop culture critics Theodor W. Adorno (1903–1969), Erich Fromm (1900–1980), and Max Horkheimer (1895–1973). Proponents of both the Frankfurt school and the propaganda model believe that popular culture serves the dominant class while exploiting the lower class (Danesi, 2008). Adorno points out how the price of commodities forms the basis of most social relations. In his words: "This is the real secret of success . . . what one pays in the market for the product. . . . The consumer is really worshipping the money that he himself has paid for the ticket. . . . But he has not 'made it' by liking the concert, but rather by buying the ticket" (Bernstein, 1991, p. 38). Adorno further explains how the costs of advertising preclude the lower classes from ever getting a chance to make money in the culture industry and although he refers to the culture industry as a form of "mass deception," he does not suggest the consumer is naïve but rather, "the triumph of advertising in the culture industry is that consumers feel compelled to buy and use its products even though they see through them" (Bernstein, 1991, p. 12).

Not everyone views materialism as a form of exploitation. As Goldthorpe, Lockwood, Bechhofer, and Platt (1969) note in their book the *Affluent Worker in the Class Structure*, "it is not to us self-evident why one should regard our respondents' concern for decent, comfortable houses, for labour-saving devices, and even for such leisure goods as television sets and cars, as manifesting the force of 'false' needs; of needs, that is, which are 'superimposed upon the individual by particular social interests in his repression'. It would be equally possible to consider the amenities and possessions for which the couples in our sample were striving as representing something like the minimum material basis on which they and their children may be able to develop a more individuated style of life, with a wider range of choices, than has hitherto been possible for the mass of the manual labour force" (pp. 183–184). Even if consumerism is better viewed as personal "choice," it is important to note that many Canadians' choices are constrained by socioeconomic and other macro-level factors that may be largely beyond their control.

In his work *Understanding Popular Culture*, John Fiske (2010) summarizes these two opposing frameworks and describes a third one that is emerging to help us better appreciate a more balanced, progressive approach to popular culture as it exists in North America today. Situating popular culture within a framework of power relations (as the conflict approach does), emphasizes "so strongly the forces of domination as to make it appear impossible for a genuine popular culture to exist at all." Conversely, situating popular culture outside power relations views popular culture "as a form of ritual management of social differences" (Fiske, 2010, p. 17). The newest perspective "sees popular culture as a site of struggle, but, while accepting the power of the forces of dominance, it focuses rather upon the popular tactics by which these forces are coped with, are evaded, or are resisted" (Fiske, 2010, pp. 17–18).

TIME TO REVIEW

- Of the symbols discussed in this chapter, which one do you think best illustrates Canada's uniqueness?
- What is the difference between high culture and popular culture?
- In what ways does the conflict perspective present a negative view of popular culture?

SOCIOLOGY *IN MY LIFE*

HOW DO YOU VIEW POPULAR CULTURE?

Do you think we live in the materialistic culture depicted by proponents of the Frankfurt school and the propaganda model? As a consumer of popular culture, think about what led you to acquire the many things you possess that are indicative of popular culture. Do you believe you are working to acquire things that will render your life and that of future generations more comfortable or is your paycheque mainly supporting the interests of the dominant class? Would you consider posts on YouTube to be one of the ways that the masses might be viewed as resisting capitalist dominance? Why or why not?

All of the elements of culture discussed thus far help to form the basis of the social structure of a given society. We rely on language, norms, and values to help us make sense of our everyday lives, to guide our behaviour, and to facilitate social interactions with others around us.

LO⁶ THE BASIC COMPONENTS OF SOCIAL STRUCTURE

Social structure is the framework of cultural elements and social patterns in which social interactions take place. Without social structure, you would arrive at your school and have no idea what comes next. There are structural guidelines operating in postsecondary institutions that include norms (e.g., students attend classes, students are expected to take notes, etc.), values (i.e., getting an education is important), and social patterns (e.g., the professor creates a course outline, teaches course content, and evaluates students who, in turn, are expected to attend class, complete assignments, and obtain additional help if needed during scheduled office hours). Like cultural elements, social patterns help us make sense of social situations. Patterned social arrangements exist within three main areas of social structure: statuses and roles, social groups, and social institutions.

STATUSES AND ROLES

Usually when you think of "status" you consider things such as titles (e.g., president or chief) that denote power or people high up in the chain of command or the prestige (i.e., honour) associated with symbols such as expensive houses and fancy cars that are owned by people in the upper classes. These forms of status have to do with social classes, which are discussed in Chapter 6 on social inequality. This chapter is concerned with **status** as it relates to *any* recognized social position held by an individual in society, a position that exists over time regardless of which individual people happen to occupy that position. Examples of statuses include student, professor, caretaker, mother, machinist, prime minister, or brother. A status is a social position because it exists in relation to others (e.g., a person is a mother because she has a son or daughter, a person is a friend because of his or her bond to another individual, etc.), not because it has some kind of prestige or title attached to it.

A **role** is the behavioural component of a given status. For example, a person with the status "professor" also performs the accompanying role with a range of expected behaviours including teaching-related activities (e.g., preparing current notes, giving lectures, and holding regular office hours), research-related expectations (e.g., demonstrated outstanding contributions in a specific discipline such as presentations at conferences and publications in academic journals), and service responsibilities (e.g., being a member of committees and participating in department-sponsored events). Similarly, the status "student" confers various behavioural obligations such as attending class, taking notes, studying for exams, writing papers, and completing assignments. As anthropologist Ralph Linton (1936) put it: "[Whereas] we *occupy* a status, we *play* a role" (as cited in Murray, Linden & Kendall, 2011, p. 118).

We are born with statuses (i.e., you are a son or daughter to someone), we acquire statuses over time (e.g., we might become a sister, aunt, mother, or grandmother later in life), we work to achieve certain statuses (e.g., Bachelor of Arts graduate, sociologist, master electrician, Cisco Certified Network Professional, etc.), we inadvertently end up with some statuses through our actions (e.g., impaired driver, prison inmate serving a life sentence for murder, etc.), we lose statuses (e.g., become widowed or unemployed), and we may give up or exit some of our statuses (e.g., through divorce or retirement). The sum total of all of the statuses that a person holds at any given time is called a **status set**.

ACHIEVED AND ASCRIBED STATUSES

Sociologists make the further distinction between statuses that are ascribed and those that are achieved. **Ascribed statuses** are social positions that people inherit at birth or acquire involuntarily over the life course (e.g., male, son, brother, and widower). **Achieved statuses** are social positions that people obtain through personal actions and effort (e.g., husband, graduate, lawyer, and criminal). Although the term "status" is neutral when it refers to a social position, particular statuses are not neutral in the sense that some are more important than others. Being a devout Mormon, for example, may necessitate behavioural guidelines, such as going on a mission at

Social structure: The framework of cultural elements and social patterns in which social interactions take place.

Status: A recognized social position that exists independently of any given individually who may occupy it.

Role: The behavioural component of a given status.

Status set: The sum total of all of the statuses held by a person at a given time.

Ascribed status: A social position conferred at birth.

Achieved status: A social position obtained through personal effort.

SOCIOLOGY *IN MY LIFE*

WHAT IS YOUR STATUS SET?

Try to write down ten statuses that you currently hold.

1. Think about your relationship relative to people in your family (e.g., Do you have a brother or sister? Are you a niece or nephew?).
2. Think about some of the activities you currently engage in (e.g., Do you attend school full-time? Do you play any sports? Are you employed?).
3. Are there any other people you feel are important to you? (e.g., Do you hold any statuses in relation to the individuals you are considering?)
4. What other defining features make up your identity? (e.g., Do you subscribe to a particular religion? What is your ethnic heritage? What is your gender identity?)

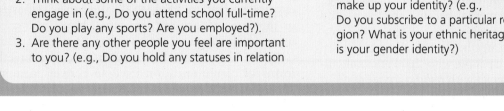

age 19 (if you are a male), that take precedence over other expectations afforded by concurrently held statuses such as those related to friendships, school, or employment.

A **master status** is the most influential one out of all of the statuses in a person's status set. Sociologist Everett Cherrington Hughes (1945) first used the term "master status" to refer to a status that "tends to overpower, in most crucial situations, any other characteristics which may run counter to it" (p. 357). A master status affects both the individual and his or her choices relative to that status, as well as how others accept and interact with that person. As an African-American brought up in the early part of the 20th century, Hughes discussed how membership in the "Negro race" could be considered a master status as could one's professional standing. He noted that when two powerful traits coincide, as in the case of a Negro physician, it posed a real dilemma for Caucasian-Americans who would then have to choose whether to treat "him as a Negro or as a member of his profession" (p. 357). A master status has exceptional importance for a person's identity and even life experiences.

ROLE CONFLICT AND ROLE STRAIN

Sometimes competing demands of different statuses pose challenges for individuals in society. Think about what might happen to Taylor (a fellow student) who has a final exam scheduled at a time when she is supposed to work her regularly scheduled shift at her job. **Role conflict** refers to a situation in which incompatible role demands exist as a result of two (or more) statuses held at the same time. In this case, Taylor is both a student and an employee (i.e., the two statuses);

and the roles of these statuses require her to be in two different places at the same time. Hopefully, Taylor has an extremely understanding professor or she can find a replacement to work her job on short notice. Role conflict is often experienced by students who are also parents (e.g., a child may get sick and require care on the same day as a final exam) and students who are athletes (for whom competitions, playoff games, and matches may require travel away from classes and/or otherwise interfere with study time).

Sometimes conflicts even occur between role requirements of a single status. **Role strain** refers to a situation in which incompatible role demands exist within one status. For example, as a student, you would experience role strain if you were required to write your sociology final exam on the same day and at the same time as your anthropology final exam. Again, it is impossible for you to be in two places at once as necessitated by role requirements; but in this case, the demands result from a single status you occupy as a student. This particular example may work out for you in the end, since it is likely that one of the instructors has erred in communicating the time of the final exam. Final exams are usually centrally scheduled by computer software that ensures no duplication for finals pertaining to classes normally held on different days or at different times. However, you will need to manage your role strain if the anthropology exam is scheduled for the morning

> **Master status:** The most influential status in an individual's status set.
>
> **Role conflict:** A situation in which incompatible role demands exist between two or more commonly held statuses.
>
> **Role strain:** A situation in which incompatible role demands exist within a single status.

and the sociology exam is in the afternoon on the same day. This is generally not considered to be an exceptional case and hence neither instructor is likely to make any kind of special accommodation for you.

SOCIAL GROUPS

In addition to roles and statuses, social groups form an important part of social structure. After all, most of what we are occurs in relation to other people (e.g., one of the authors is a mother because she has a child and stepchild, both of whom result from the relationship she has with her husband). A social group consists of two or more people who share relevant cultural elements and interact with regular frequency. For example, social groups you might belong to include your family of orientation, your family of procreation, friends with whom you participate in a sport, and associates you work alongside. Social groups contribute to the social structure by delineating various statuses and roles as in the case of the authority structure in your place of employment or the various statuses and accompanying norms in your own family.

SOCIOLOGY IN THEORY: THE SOCIAL CONSTRUCTION OF REALITY

People are not just passive recipients of social structure. The symbolic interactionist perspective is a micro-level approach especially suited to explaining how aspects of culture and social structure have particular meanings for individuals. While some meanings are shared by members of a particular culture, as in the case of language, norms, and values, individual interpretations differ. Think about how a husband and wife view a situation differently or how two siblings recall very different realities for mutually shared events from childhood. Meanings also change over time. What you might believe marriage will be like is different from what it becomes once you are in a marital relationship. Similarly, what it means to be a husband in that particular relationship may change depending on various other factors (e.g., the presence of children, a career, and/or other familial obligations).

People not only interpret things in their own ways, but also behave in particular ways to give impressions during face-to-face interactions. Think of how you might act on a first date. Erving Goffman used the term "face-work" to describe how people act to present themselves in the best possible light and to manage their own self-esteem. In some cases, people even avoid encounters that are likely to threaten their self-esteem or they may engage in "corrective" measures such as using an apology to maintain "face" (Goffman, 1967). Goffman also stressed the importance of nonverbal forms of communication used to convey meanings such as acts of deference and demeanour. **Deference** is a way of showing appreciation towards someone else through nonverbal gestures that indicate respect, such as bowing to someone of importance or allowing someone to enter a room before you. **Demeanour** refers to mannerisms and dress that convey particular qualities to others. Goffman (1967) noted that "well-demeaned" individuals in society are those who are able to display modesty, self-control, and poise.

The symbolic interactionist perspective is summarized by Herbert Blumer as resting on these three assumptions:

1. Human beings act toward things [such as other humans or objects] on the basis of the meanings the things have for them.
2. The meaning of things is derived from social interactions.
3. These meanings are handled and modified via an interpretive process.

(Adapted from Blumer, 1969, p. 2)

Ethnomethodology is a research method developed by Harold Garfinkel to examine the ways in which people make sense of social structure in their everyday world. For example, people carry out exchanges based on the assumption that certain meanings are shared. Hence, ethnomethodologists sometimes deliberately pose challenges (e.g., by repeatedly asking *What do you mean?*) during regular conversations. Questioning of "the obvious" generally frustrates the other speaker but also demonstrates, through the frustration, reliance on shared meanings (Sandstrom, Martin & Fine, 2010). Researchers study the "accounts" or verbal exchanges and behaviours of people engaged in regular activities in order to show that "common sense" meanings *do* exist as a function of social structure (Garfinkel, 1967). Ethnomethodologists are also able to demonstrate that people engaged

Social group: Two or more people who share relevant cultural elements and interact with regular frequency.

Deference: Nonverbal shows of appreciation and respect.

Demeanour: Mannerisms and dress that convey particular qualities.

Ethnomethodology: A research method used to examine ways in which people make sense of their everyday world.

in conversations create meanings within exchanges that have implications for subsequent ones.

LO⁷ SOCIAL INSTITUTIONS

Thus far we have mainly discussed patterns of interaction at the micro level. Established social patterns also exist at the macro level of institutions. **Social institutions** are relatively permanent societal structures that govern the behaviour of groups and promote social order. Examples of formative social institutions include the family, religious institutions, school, political system, economy, and mass media. Each institution serves a main purpose in society (i.e., the family provides support and is the primary agent of socialization, religion provides a sense of purpose, education is a mechanism for the transmission of important cultural beliefs, the political system enables groups to have power and authority, the economy helps to sustain society, and the mass media informs people of current events). To accomplish these purposes, social institutions comprise various structures, processes, and rules that exert control over individuals.

A very highly structured social institution is known as a *formal organization* due to the presence of a specific type of organizational structure known as a bureaucracy. A **bureaucracy** is a formal organization model that consists of an explicit chain of authority and a set of procedures and protocols that guide the relationships and processes that exist within it.

Source: © Fran, form 696, www.cartoonstock.com

SOCIOLOGY IN THEORY: MAX WEBER'S IDEAL TYPE OF BUREAUCRACY

Sociologist Max Weber developed an ideal-type model to help illustrate the key features of bureacracy. An **ideal type** refers to an analytical construct that so clearly depicts all of the main features of some social phenomenon it serves as an exemplary tool but is not an entity that can be found in reality (Weber, 1903–1917/1949). Thus, an ideal type is the perfect example from which we can compare real-life cases to see how well they fit (or don't fit) the model. Weber's ideal type of bureaucracy includes a division of labour, a hierarchy of authority, written rules and regulations, impersonality in decision making, and employment based on qualifications (Murray, Linden & Kendall, 2011, pp. 151–152).

A *division of labour* entails people carrying out completely different sorts of tasks. In a university, there are people who work as faculty, staff, or administrators in separate areas such as facilities, finance, or an academic division such as the faculty of arts where a department of sociology is likely to be located. A *hierarchy of authority* refers to a set "chain of command" where positions are arranged according to levels of responsibility and power. In a university, a faculty member is supervised by a department chair who is under the supervision of a dean who is under the authority of a vice president (academic) who is under the authority of the president. All academic institutions include *rules and regulations* that govern the behaviour of staff, faculty, and students as you already know from student codes of conduct, course outlines, and procedures for borrowing resources, paying tuition, registering in courses, and even graduating. Displays of emotion and special considerations are discouraged. *Impersonality* means that all people working within bureaucracies are supposed to perform their duties as a matter of principle (e.g., a student should not receive a break for forgetting the time of his or her final exam and should instead receive a zero as per stated policy in the course outline). Finally, all people employed in a bureaucracy are hired on the basis of

> **Social institutions:** Relatively permanent societal structures that govern the behaviour of groups and promote social order.
>
> **Bureaucracy:** A formal organization model that consists of an explicit chain of authority and a set of procedures and protocols that guide the relationships and processes that exist within it.
>
> **Ideal type:** An analytical construct that so clearly depicts all of the main features of some social phenomenon it serves as an exemplary tool but is not an entity that can be found in reality.

qualifications. Hence, faculty members with the highest or most specialized degrees (e.g., a Ph.D.) are typically hired over those with a Masters degree.

Bureaucracies have many advantages including efficiency, translating into things getting done through various delegated divisions of labour. Hierarchies of authority help to establish where someone goes first to resolve an issue (e.g., a student must first see his or her instructor about a class before going to the department chair). Similarly, clear rules indicate precisely what is or is not allowed (e.g., students may be granted a deferred exam if the exam is scheduled on a day that conflicts with a religious holiday for that individual but the taking of a personal vacation is not considered a valid excuse for missing a final exam). Impersonality and employment based on technical qualifications can result in opportunities for individuals who work hard and continue to upgrade their skills, as opposed to systems that enable people to advance based on connections, as in "who you know."

The bureaucratic model has proven to be a highly successful approach to business and, hence, many of its traits have evolved into other sectors. Ritzer (2011) explains how four main features of bureaucracy are exemplified by McDonald's, the world's most successful franchise. First, self-service increases the *efficiency* or speed with which a consumer can satisfy a craving for a Big Mac, as evidenced by the popularity of drive-thrus. Second, *calculability* "emphasizes the quantitative aspects of products sold (portion, size, cost) and services offered (time it takes to get the product)" (Ritzer, 2011, p. 14). Consumers readily perceive that the "extra-value" meal is a relatively inexpensive way to obtain a sandwich, fries, and drink in only a few minutes. Third, *predictability* refers to the "assurance that products and services will be the same over time and in all locales" (Ritzer, 2011, p. 15). Fourth, part of the success of McDonald's can be attributed to its *control* over customers. As Ritzer (2011) puts it, "lines, limited menus, few options, and uncomfortable seats all lead diners to do what management wishes them to do—eat quickly and leave" (p. 16).

Note that these principles all work in tandem to support each other. For example, the specialized division of labour wherein one person grills hamburgers, someone else puts fries into containers, and another takes the order, renders food service efficient and also contributes to lower prices, since the company does not have to pay higher wages to skilled short-order cooks who multitask. Similarly, predictability ensures that all burgers are sold with the exact same dressings, increasing efficiency while also contributing to high levels of control (Schlosser, 2005).

Ritzer (2011) argues that these four principles now represent values operating in contemporary society more generally as evident in the sheer number of McDonald's restaurants (i.e., as of 2006, there were 767,483 of them in the United States alone), the adoption of these principles by competitor franchises (e.g., Burger King and Wendy's), and extensions of these principles to casual dining (e.g., Red Lobster and Olive Garden). These principles have even been adapted to other businesses (e.g., Walmart, PetSmart, and Curves), have shown successes in international markets (i.e., over 43 percent of McDonald's are now outside the United States), and have led to variants in other nations (e.g., Tim Hortons in Canada). Finally, Ritzer (2011) claims that the best evidence for the dominance of bureaucracy in modern society is found in the resounding success of businesses identified as "exemplary models" of the four principles (e.g., Ikea).*

While bureaucratic principles serve the business sector well, they tend to have shortcomings that are especially apparent to individuals. If you have ever tried to change classes or obtain a tuition refund at a college or university, you can probably relate to "the slowness, the ponderousness, the routine, the complication of procedures and the maladapted responses of the bureaucratic organization to the needs which they should satisfy" (Crozier, 1964, p. 3). Bureaucratic processes take a lot of time and require many steps to completion. Not only that, but in most bureaucracies, the rules, hierarchy of authority, and division of labour are not as clear cut as implied by Weber's ideal type. This is why in academic institutions students are not sure whether they should go to an instructor or the department chair first to handle a class matter, and why some employees such as "instructional assistants" may carry out functions such as providing administrative support to department chairs that bear little or no resemblance to their stated job titles.

TIME TO REVIEW

- What are the three main elements that make up social structure?
- What is the key difference between a status and a role?
- What is the difference between role conflict and role strain?
- Why is the symbolic interactionist perspective especially useful for studying human behaviour?
- What is ethnomethodology used for?
- What is a social institution? Provide an example of one.
- What are some of the advantages and disadvantages of Weber's ideal type of bureaucracy for businesses and individuals?

*Source: Ritzer, G. (2011). *The McDonalization of Society* (6th ed.). Thousand Oakes, CA: Pine Forge Press.

CHAPTER SUMMARY

LO¹ Define culture and distinguish between material and nonmaterial forms.

Culture is the sum total of the social environment in which we are raised and continue to be socialized in throughout our lives. Material culture includes all of the tangible or physical items that people have created for use and give meaning to, while non-material culture includes intangibles produced by intellectual or spiritual development and the use of artifacts in a given culture.

LO² Explain why language is viewed as a precursor to shared understandings and explain how language confers gender expectations.

Language determines how we think and what we think about, thereby shaping the reality experienced by those who share a common language. Cultural constructions are embedded in language as in the case of different words commonly used to describe males versus females.

LO³ Explain why norms are considered to be regulators of shared behaviours.

Norms inform members of a culture about what is considered to be appropriate, and inappropriate forms of conduct and violations of norms result in sanctions.

LO⁴ Identify shared values and debate the correspondence between cultural values and norms using functionalist and conflict perspectives.

Core Canadian values include a widespread belief in equality, consultation, accommodation, support for diversity, compassion, a concern for the environment, and a peaceful world image. A functionalist perspective highlights the existence of shared values such as support for diversity. Functionalists emphasize how shared ideas translate into widely followed practices such as respect for the diversity of languages spoken in Canada. In contrast, a conflict perspective highlights the lack of correspondence between values and norms, as in the case of treatment of Aboriginal people who were not allowed to speak their mother tongues in residential schools.

LO⁵ Describe features of canadian culture that make it unique and discuss critical views of popular culture.

The uniqueness of Canada's culture is evident in the abundance of symbols (e.g., the Canadian flag, the Royal Canadian Mounted Police) and many forms of high culture and popular culture. Popular culture refers to well-liked, everyday cultural practices and products that are widely engaged in by the masses. Critical perspectives view popular culture largely as a means for the ruling class to maintain control over the masses.

LO⁶ Outline the basic components of social structure and describe how the symbolic interactionist perspective views social structure.

Social structure consists of statuses and roles, social groups, and social institutions that provide a framework within which social interactions take place. The symbolic interactionist perspective highlights the importance of subjective interpretations and how meanings are constructed and come to govern face-to-face interactions.

LO⁷ Explain how social institutions contribute to social structure and assess the merit of Weber's ideal type of bureaucracy in modern society.

Social institutions are relatively permanent societal structures that govern the behaviour of groups and promote social order, as in the case of the family as the primary agent of socialization or religion as an institution that provides people with a sense of purpose.

According to Weber, an ideal type of bureaucracy includes a specialized division of labour, a clear hierarchy of authority, written rules and regulations, impersonality in dealings, and employment based on technical qualifications. While a bureaucracy can be highly successful largely attributable to its efficiency, objectivity, and clear directives, a bureaucracy can also result in very time-consuming, inefficient processes that become ends in themselves.

RECOMMENDED READINGS

1. For a critical look at how lack of knowledge about Canadian history contributes to a weak Canadian identity, you might be interested in: Cohen, A. (2007). *The Unfinished Canadian: The People We Are*. Toronto, ON: McClelland & Stewart.

2. To better appreciate ways in which Canada and the United States are becoming increasingly divergent over time, we recommend: Adam, M. (2003). *Fire and Ice: The United States, Canada and the Myth of Converging Values*. Toronto, ON: Pearson Penguin Canada.

3. For a classic symbolic interactionist account of how people act and react in relation to others, refer to: Goffman, E. (1967). *Interaction Ritual: Essays on Face-to-Face Behaviour.* Garden City, NY: Anchor Books.
4. For an excellent discussion of popular culture in capitalist societies, we recommend: Fiske, J. (2010). *Understanding Popular Culture.* (2nd ed.). New York: Routledge.
5. For a critical account of the origins and development of the McDonald's franchise, refer to: Schlosser, E. (2005). *Fast Food Nation: The Dark Side of the All American Meal.* New York: Harper Perennial.

FOR FURTHER REFLECTION

1. Reflect on how language shapes culture. Suppose you or a close friend were raised to only speak English while your parents (or grandparents) still speak another mother tongue. Are any aspects of your parents/grandparents' cultural heritage now lost as a result of having to translate meanings from one language to another?
2. Take a minute to reflect on the seven shared Canadian values identified in this chapter. Is there a value you strongly believe in that is not listed here? Which of the items listed here do you perceive would generate the most agreement among Canadians? Which would receive the least amount of support? Why do you think this is the case? Are there groups of Canadians who might not share these values? Does our government support these values? Why or why not?
3. Can you identify one item that you possess and are especially fond of that would be considered an example of Canadian popular culture? How might your reasons for owning this item be viewed as supporting the interests of capitalists?
4. Would the diagnosis of a terminal illness such as cancer be considered a master status? Explain your answer.
5. Does the university or college you are currently taking this course at fit Weber's notion of an ideal bureaucracy? Why or why not?

REFERENCES

Baddorf, Z. (2010, August 13). Children too hungry to return to civilian life. *Inter Press Service News Agency.* Retrieved July 26, 2011, from www.ipsnews.net/news.asp?idnews=52479

BBC News Africa. (2010, August 31). Army in South Sudan vows to purge itself of child soldiers. *BBC News Africa.* Retrieved July 26, 2011, from www.bbc.co.uk/worldservice/africa/2010/08/100831_sudan_child_soldiers.shtml

Beardsley, S. (2009, July 28). Busted on MySpace: Two men headed to court for gang material on Web sites. *Naples Daily News.* Naples, FL: Scripps Interactive Media Newspapers Groups. Retrieved July 26, 2011, from www.naplesnews.com/news/2009/jul/28/busted-myspace-two-men-headed-court-gang-material-/

Bernstein, J. (Ed.). (1991). *Theodor W. Adorno: The Culture Industry.* Selected Essays on Mass Culture. New York, NY: Routledge.

Boas, F. (1911/1976). *Handbook of American Indian Languages.* St. Clair Shores, MI: Scholarly Press.

Bourdieu, P. (1973). Cultural reproduction and social reproduction. In R. Brown (Ed.), *Knowledge, Education, and Social Change: Papers in the Sociology of Education,* pp. 71–112. Tavistock, UK: Tavistock Publications.

Blumer, H. (1969). *Symbolic Interactionism: Perspective and Method.* Englewood Cliffs, NJ: Prentice-Hall.

Bryson, B. (1990). *The Mother Tongue: English and How It Got That Way.* New York, NY: HarperCollins Publishers.

Canadian Multiculturalism Act. (1985, c. 24 [4th Supp.]). *Canadian Multiculturalism Act.* Ottawa, ON: Department of Justice Canada.

Carroll, J. B. (Ed.). (1956). *Language, Thought, and Reality: Selected Writings of Benjamin Lee Whorf.* Cambridge, MA: The Massachusetts Institute of Technology.

CBC News. (2011, February 10). Kirpan ban blasted by Sikhs. Montreal, QC: *CBC News.* Retrieved July 26, 2011, from www.cbc.ca/news/canada/montreal/story/2011/02/10/qc-kirpan-reaction.html

CBC News. (2010, September 24). The Current. Pt 3: Sudan Soldiers. Toronto, ON: *CBC Radio.* Retrieved July 26, 2011, from www.cbc.ca/thecurrent/episode/2010/09/24/sept-2410---pt-3-sudan-child-soldiers/

CBC News. (2007, September 19). Residential school payout a "symbolic" apology: Fontaine. Toronto, ON: *CBC News.* Retrieved July 26, 2011, from www.cbc.ca/canada/story/2007/09/19/residential-schools.html?ref=rss

Citizen's Forum on Canada's Future—Keith Spicer Commission Report. (1991). *Citizen's Forum on Canada's Future: A Report to the People and Government of Canada.* Ottawa, ON: Supply and Services Canada.

Crozier, M. (1964). *The Bureaucratic Phenomenon.* London, UK: Tavistock Publications.

Danesi, M. (2008). *Popular Culture: Introductory Perspectives.* Lanham, MD: Rowman & Littlefield Publishers.

Durkheim, E. (1895/1938). *The Rules of Sociological Method* (S. A. Solovay and J. H. Mueller, Trans.). Edited with introduction by G. E. G. Catlin. Chicago: University of Chicago Press.

Durkheim, E. (1893/1933). *The Division of Labour in Society* (George Simpson, Trans.). New York: MacMillan.

Ember, C. R., Ember, M., & Peregrine, P. N. (2009). *Human Evolution and Culture: Highlights of Anthropology* (6th ed.). Upper Saddle River, NJ: Pearson Education.

Ferguson, W., & Ferguson, I. (2001). *How to Be a Canadian (Even if You Already Are One)*. Vancouver, BC: Douglas & McIntyre.

Fiske, J. (2010). *Understanding Popular Culture* (2nd ed.). New York: Routledge.

Gannon, M. (2008). *Paradoxes of Culture and Globalization*. Thousand Oaks, CA: Sage Publications.

Garfinkel, H. (1967). *Studies in Ethnomethodology*. Englewood Cliffs, NJ: Prentice-Hall.

Goffman, E. (1967). *Interaction Ritual: Essays on Face-to-Face Behaviour*. Garden City, NY: Anchor Books.

Goldthorpe, J. H., Lockwood, D., Bechhofer, F., & Platt, J. (1969). *The Affluent Worker in the Class Structure*. Cambridge, UK: Cambridge University Press.

Government of Canada. (2011). *Gender-neutral language quiz*. Language Portal of Canada. Gatineau, QC: Translation Bureau. Retrieved July 26, 2011, from www.noslangues-ourlanguages.gc.ca/quiz/jeux-quiz-genre-neutre-gender-neutral-eng.php?c1=1&c2=2&c3=3&c4=1&c5=3&c6=3&c7=2&quiz=Submit&qznm=genre-neutre-gender-neutral-eng&qzlang=eng

Hughes, E. C. (1945). Dilemmas and contradictions of status. *American Journal of Sociology, 50*(5), 353–359.

(The) Internet Movie Database. (2010). *Memorable quotes for Iron Man* (2008). IMDb.com. Retrieved July 26, 2011, from www.imdb.com/title/tt0371746/quotes

Murdock, G. P. (1945). The common denominator of culture. In Ralph Linton (Ed.), *The Science of Man in the World Crisis* (pp. 123–142). New York: Columbia University Press.

Murray, J., Linden, R., & Kendall, D. (2011). *Sociology in Our Times*. (5th ed.). Toronto, ON: Nelson Education.

National Geographic. (2010, February 12). *Vancouver 2010: Olympic logo no "friend" to some*. Daily News. Washington, DC: National Geographic Society. Retrieved July 26, 2011, from http://news.nationalgeographic.com/news/2010/02/photogalleries/100212-vancouver-2010-winter-olympics-logo-ilanaaq/

Ogburn, W. F. (1922). *Social Change with Respect to Culture and Original Nature*. New York: The Viking Press.

Osman, H., El Zein, L., & Wick, L. (2009). Cultural beliefs that may discourage breastfeeding among Lebanese women: A qualitative analysis. *International Breastfeeding Journal* (2009, November 2). Retrieved September 22, 2010, from www.internationalbreastfeedingjournal.com/content/pdf/1746-4358-4-12.pdf

Parsons, T. (1951). *The Social System*. London: Routledge and Kegan Paul.

Ricks, D. A. (1999). *Blunders in International Business*. (3rd ed.). Malden, MA: Blackwell Publishing.

Ritzer, G. (2011). *The McDonaldization of Society* (6th ed.). Thousand Oaks, CA: Pine Forge Press.

Sandstrom, K. L., Martin, D.D., & Fine, G. A. (2010). *Symbols, Selves, and Social Reality: A Symbolic Interactionist Approach to Social Psychology and Sociology*. (3rd ed.). New York: Oxford University Press.

Schaefer, R. T., Smith, E., & Grekul, J. (2009). *Sociology*. (2nd Can ed.). Toronto, ON: McGraw-Hill Ryerson.

Schlosser, E. (2005). *Fast Food Nation: The Dark Side of the All American Meal*. New York: Harper Perennial.

Siegel, L. J., Brown, G. P., & Hoffman, R. (2006). *Criminology: The Core*. Toronto, ON: Nelson Education.

Statistics Canada. (2009). Mother tongue. *2006 Census Dictionary*. Ottawa, ON: Author. Retrieved July 26, 2011, from www12.statcan.ca/census-recensement/2006/ref/dict/pop095-eng.cfm

Statistics Canada. (2007, December 4). 2006 Census: Immigration, citizenship, language, mobility, and migration. *The Daily*. Ottawa, ON: Author. Retrieved July 26, 2011, from www.statcan.gc.ca/daily-quotidien/071204/dq071204a-eng.htm

Statistics Canada. (2006). *Population by mother tongue and age groups, 2006 counts, for Canada, provinces and territories—20 percent sample data*. Ottawa, ON: Author. Retrieved August 9, 2011, from www12.statcan.ca/census-recensement/2006/dp-pd/hlt/97-555/T401-eng.cfm?Lang=E&T=401&GH=4&SC=1&S=99&O=A

Storey, J. (2009). *Cultural Theory and Popular Culture: An Introduction* (5th ed.). Edinburgh Gate, Harlow: Pearson Education.

Sumara, D., Davis, B., & Laidlaw, L. (2001). Canadian identity and curriculum theory: An ecological postmodern perspective. *Canadian Journal of Education, 26*(2), 144–163.

Texin, T. (2011). *Marketing translation mistakes*. Retrieved July 26, 2011, from www.i18nguy.com/translations.html

Weber, M. (1903–1917/1949). Edward Shils and Henry Finch (Eds.), *The Methodology of the Social Sciences*. New York: The Free Press.

White, D. (2009, December 1). *Labatt, Molson, and the Canadian beer industry*. Suite 101.com. Retrieved July 26, 2011, from www.suite101.com/content/labatt-molson-and-the-canadian-beer-industry-a175962

Williams, R. (1976). *Keywords: A Vocabulary of Culture and Society*. New York: Oxford University Press.

ENDNOTE

[1] Retrieved October 5, 2010, from "AllGreatQuotes" (www.allgreatquotes.com/canada_day_quotes9.shtml).

Social Inequality in Canadian Society

LEARNING OBJECTIVES AND OUTCOMES

After completing this chapter, students should be able to do the following:

LO1 Define social inequality and explain how to gauge social inequality using measures of financial wealth.

LO2 Critically assess the low-income cut-off as anestimate of poverty.

LO3 Identify groups most at risk for poverty in Canada and discuss the interrelationship among poverty and education, health, and hardship.

LO4 Discuss social inequality as a stable feature of Canadian society.

LO5 Critically assess Canada's social safety net as a means for reducing poverty.

LO6 Define social stratification and differentiate between caste and class systems.

LO7 Describe Canada's class structure and social mobility.

LO8 Debate why there are social classes and whether stratification is helpful or harmful to Canadian society.

The history of all hitherto existing society is the history of class struggles.

(Karl Marx & Friedrich Engels, 1848, p. 14)

LO¹ SOCIAL INEQUALITY

MEASURING WEALTH

Canada boasts one of the best standards of living in the world as a highly developed nation with an advanced economy, universal access to health care, and publicly funded education. At the same time, Canada is a land of social inequality with a range of very poor, somewhat poor, average, fairly well off, and extremely wealthy citizens. Like culture and social structure, social inequality affects our overall quality of life and it plays an important role in shaping who we are and who we become. If you were born into the Irving or Thomson family, your quality of life would be considerably higher than if you had been born into the average Canadian family. Conversely, if you were born into a low-income family, you likely faced challenges securing basic necessities such as suitable winter clothes and you probably had to forego participation in organized sports or recreational family outings such as going to movies or taking vacations. **Social inequality** refers to an unequal distribution of resources including wealth, prestige, or power that in turn affect personal outcomes such as educational or occupational attainment and health. In this chapter, we examine the extent of social inequality in Canada and consider features and practices of Canadian society that help to sustain it.

FINANCIAL WEALTH

One way to gauge social inequality is through measures of financial wealth.

Financial wealth corresponds to economic assets that are derived from income, real estate, savings, stocks, bonds, income-generating investments, and other sources of revenue or capital. The most common measure of financial wealth is income from employment. Information on the income of Canadians is derived from yearly personal income as stated on Canada Revenue Agency tax returns and from responses provided on surveys about economic assets conducted through Statistics Canada. The median yearly income in Canada for census families including couples with or without children and lone-parent families was $68,860 in 2008 (Statistics Canada, 2010a). *Median* is an indicator of the middlemost value, meaning half of Canadians families have an income above this amount and half have one below it.

Income varies considerably from city to city and from province to province. In 2008, the highest median total family incomes were reported for Calgary ($91,570) and Edmonton ($88,190) in Alberta, followed by Ottawa-Gatineau ($87,160) and Oshawa ($83,220) in Ontario (Statistics Canada, 2010b). High median family incomes are

Social inequality: An unequal distribution of resources.

Financial wealth: Corresponds to economic assets that are derived from income, real estate, savings, stocks, bonds, income-generating investments, and other sources of revenue or capital.

SOCIOLOGY *ONLINE*

THE GROWING GAP PROJECT

The Canadian Centre for Policy Alternatives is an independent, member-based research institute that works on various projects of interest to Canadians (e.g., climate change, economic security, and education). A current focus is *The Growing Gap Project,* which entails an ongoing effort by economists, researchers, and other concerned Canadians to track the disparity between Canada's rich and poor. Here you can find current publications and news releases on social inequality in Canada including things such as disparities in housing and income as well as information on those who suffer the most inequity including the homeless, children and youth, and Aboriginal people. *The Growing Gap Project* can be located at www.policyalternatives.ca

---

somewhat misleading as they tend to be more indicative of social inequality than of a better standard of living for most residents. Alberta, for example, has a high median family income (i.e., $86,080) as well as the most pronounced gap between those who are wealthy and those who are poor, a form of social inequality that has been steadily increasing since 1994 (Pembina Institute for Appropriate Development, 2005). Comparably, there is less social inequality but a much lower median family income in New Brunswick ($59,790), Nova Scotia ($61,980), Prince Edward Island ($61,010), and Newfoundland and Labrador ($59,320) where a greater overall percentage of the population is less wealthy. With the demise of fishing and mining industries over the last several decades, many workers have left the Atlantic region in order to secure gainful employment in other provinces such as Alberta, where high-paying jobs in construction, trades, and energy continue to be plentiful. Refer to Figure 6.1 to see the regional variation in family income in Canada by province and territory for 2008.

Annual earnings also reflect regional differences in employment rates and opportunities as well as the overall **cost of living**, which includes average prices for essential goods and services such as food, housing, transportation, and health care in a given area. In Nunavut, Yukon, and the Northwest Territories, there is a high cost of living "remotely" in an extreme climate where commodities need to be flown into the region, driving up prices for goods and services. In addition, a relatively small population resides in a vast land mass, incurring high costs in relation to communication and transportation infrastructure. To offset the disadvantages and to attract workers to the region, employers sometimes offer wage bonuses or higher than average wages (especially in the mining industry and health sectors of Yukon and the Northwest Territories) and the federal government offers a northern residency and travel benefits deduction (see Canada Revenue Agency, 2011).

Another way to consider financial wealth is through **net worth**, which refers to a dollar value representing remaining financial assets after liabilities are removed. Net worth is calculated by subtracting all existing financial debts (e.g., mortgages, car loans, student loans, and credit line or card balances) from assets (e.g., savings in accounts, bonds, mutual funds, stocks, pension plans, education savings plans, and home equity). Those who earn more have a disproportionately higher net worth because they are more likely to accumulate savings. Moreover, net worth increases as income goes up because a higher proportion of additional earnings can be directed at savings and investments (e.g., the purchase of a home, which usually appreciates to further increase assets over time). For example, in 2005, families who earned between $10,000 and $19,999 after taxes had an average corresponding net worth of $16,000, families between $30,000 and $39,999 had a net worth of $113,020, and those who earned $75,000 or more had a net worth of $505,710 (Statistics Canada, 2010c).

Cost of living: A measure of the average price for essential goods and services in a given area including transportation.

Net worth: Total assets calculated by subtracting all existing financial liabilities from assets.

FIGURE 6.1

Regional Variation in Annual Family Income, Canada 2008

Source: Adapted from Statistics Canada, Regional Variation in Annual Family Income, Canada 2008, http://www40.statcan.ca/l01/cst01/famil108a-eng.htm

The highest income category includes Canadians with high-paying careers, those who have built up equity in a home, those who have contributed to private and employee-sponsored retirement savings plans over many years, and the "ultra" rich who are largely inheritors of family fortunes. The Thomson family best exemplifies this with a reported net worth of $21.99 billion (Canadian Business Online, 2010). Refer to Table 6.1 (page 120) for a list of Canada's 10 richest families by net worth.

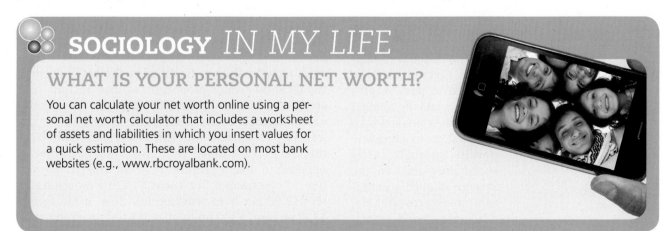

SOCIOLOGY *IN MY LIFE*

WHAT IS YOUR PERSONAL NET WORTH?

You can calculate your net worth online using a personal net worth calculator that includes a worksheet of assets and liabilities in which you insert values for a quick estimation. These are located on most bank websites (e.g., www.rbcroyalbank.com).

TABLE 6.1

Canada's 10 Richest Families by Net Worth (in Billions), 2009

Rank	Name	Net Worth	Residence	Industry	Companies
1	Thomson Family	21.99	Toronto	Media, information distribution	Thomson Reuters, Woodbridge Co. Ltd.
2	James (J. K.), Arthur, John (Jack) Irving	7.28	Saint John	Oil, forestry products, gas stations, media, transportation	Irving Oil Ltd., J. D. Irving Ltd.
3	Weston, Galen	6.47	Toronto	Food, groceries, real estate, retail	George Weston Ltd., Loblaw Cos. Ltd.
4	James (Jimmy) Pattison	5.07	Vancouver	Auto sales, food, media, forestry products, entertainment, export services	Jim Pattison Group
5	Rogers Family (was Ted Rogers)	4.70	Toronto	Cable TV, communications, pro sports	Rogers Communications Inc.
6	Paul Desmarais Sr.	4.28	Montreal	Financial services, energy	Power Corp. of Canada
7	Bernard (Barry) Sherman	3.85	Toronto	Pharmaceuticals	Apotex Group of Cos.
8	David Azrieli	3.73	Montreal	Real estate	Canpro Investments Ltd.
9	Jeff Skoll	3.59	Palo Alto	Internet, media	eBay Inc., Participant Media
10	Fred and Ron Mannix	2.98	Calgary	Mining, energy, real estate	Mancal Group

Source: Adapted from Canadian Business Online (2010): http://list.canadianbusiness.com/rankings/rich100/2009/ranking/Default. aspx?sp2=1&d1=a&sc1=0. Reproduced with permission.

MEASURING POVERTY

Another way to gauge social inequality is to focus on the opposite end of the spectrum by estimating the number of people in society who lack wealth. One of the challenges in determining how many poor there are in Canada begins with how to measure poverty in some consistent way since Canada has no official definition for it. To date, the federal and provincial governments in Canada have not reached a consensus about what it means to "be poor." Poverty as a social issue is contentiously debated since its definition determines those included as poor in official tallies and the number of poor is a precursor to steps taken to eliminate poverty through costly social programs. In the absence of such a definition, most researchers, academics, and social analysts rely on Statistics Canada's *low-income cut-off* as an indicator of poverty marking a threshold below which families assuredly experience financial difficulties.

LO² LOW-INCOME CUT-OFF

The **low-income cut-off** (LICO) refers to an annual family income value in dollars below which a family is considerably worse off relative to the "average" family due to the high proportion of income allocated to food, clothing, and shelter. Families at the LICO spend a significantly greater proportion of their income (i.e., about 63 percent) on these three basic needs relative to the average family who spends about 20 percent less (i.e., 43 percent) (Statistics Canada, 2010d). Note that the LICO is based on a proportion of income as opposed to a set expenditure or an official "poverty line." For example, Joe earns $1920 a month based on $12.00 per hour working full-time. If Joe spends $750 on rent, $300 on food, and $100 on clothing, he

> **Low-income cut-off:**
> An annual family income value in dollars below which a family is worse off than average due to the high proportion of income allocated to food, clothing, and shelter.

would not be below LICO since the basic needs constitute about 60 percent of his regular earnings. However, Joe also has to pay at least 10.77 percent of his income as federal taxes, which reduces his earnings by $207 per month. This means Joe is "poor" (i.e., below LICO) since 71 percent of his "available" income is allocated to the basic necessities. An *after-tax LICO* is commonly used since it provides the most accurate reflection of accessible income. Moreover, the LICO is based on *average family income* and it can be adjusted to allow for greater cost of living in particular cities or provinces.

For 2010, the after-tax LICO for a two-, four-, and six-person Canadian family unit living in a large city in Quebec was $27,601, $41,198, and $52,699 respectively (Citizenship and Immigration Canada, 2010). Based on the after-tax LICO as a gauge of poverty, just over three million people in Canada (or about 9.4 percent) can be classified as "poor" (Statistics Canada, 2010e). Like regional variation in family income, there is disparity in poverty across Canadian cities and provinces, with the largest concentration of families with incomes below the LICO in the larger urban areas of Vancouver (20.9 percent), Toronto (20.6 percent), and the metropolitan community of Montreal (16.0 percent) (Federation of Canadian Municipalities, 2010).

As an estimate of poverty, the LICO is conservative since it fails to take into account much of what Canadians actually pay for as part of their "typical" costs of living. Living expenses include shelter, food, and clothing but they also include other necessary expenditures such as costs associated with operating a household, raising children, paying taxes, obtaining health care, taking care of personal needs, getting an education, acquiring personal insurance, and using transportation. Further to these expenses, most Canadians also regularly spend part of their income on other expenditures such as forms of recreation or tobacco products and alcoholic beverages (Statistics Canada, 2010f).

HOUSEHOLD SPENDING

According to Statistics Canada's annual household spending survey for 2009, an average of $71,120 was spent by households on food, clothing, shelter, personal taxes, personal insurance payments and pension contributions, household operation, household furnishings, transportation, health care, personal care, recreation, reading materials, education, tobacco products and alcoholic beverages, games of chance, gifts of money and contributions, and other miscellaneous expenditures. Food, clothing, and shelter accounted for 34 percent of overall spending (Statistics Canada, 2010f). In contrast, the top one-fifth of Canadian households with the highest incomes spent $147,090 on these items; 27 percent of which went to the three essentials while the bottom one-fifth with the lowest incomes spent only $23,860 but allocated 52 percent of their spending to essentials (Statistics Canada, 2010f). Canadian households spent more on transportation ($9,753) than they did on recreation ($3,843), household operation ($3,428), or clothing ($2,841) (Statistics Canada, 2010f).

Recall our previous example where Joe's after-tax yearly income is $20,556 or $1,713 per month. After covering basic needs, Joe has only $563 each month to divide across all remaining expenses, suggesting he would struggle to pay his bills even at $12.00 per hour. The minimum Canadian hourly wage ranges from $8.00 to $10.25 per hour as shown in Table 6.2 (page 122).

TABLE 6.2

Minimum Wage in Canada by Province for 2010/2011

Province	Minimum Hourly Wage
Alberta	$8.80
British Columbia	$8.00
Manitoba	$9.50
New Brunswick	$9.00
Newfoundland and Labrador	$10.00
Northwest Territories	$9.00
Nova Scotia	$9.65
Nunavut	$10.00
Ontario	$10.25
Prince Edward Island	$8.70
Quebec	$9.50
Saskatchewan	$9.25
Yukon	$8.93

Source: Adapted from Living in Canada (2011). The Canadian Minimum Wage. http://www.livingin-canada.com

LO³ WHO ARE CANADA'S POOR?

Certain groups of people are at greater risk for poverty than others. For example, female lone-parent families, persons 17 years of age and under, unattached individuals, recent immigrants, people with "work-limiting" disabilities, and Aboriginal peoples constitute groups that are at greatest risk for poverty (Hay, 2009; Statistics Canada, 2010g). The same groups (not counting children) are also at greater risk for unemployment and for those with jobs, they are more likely to be employed in "non-standard work arrangements" including temporary, part-time, and self-employed positions with lower pay (Hay, 2009).

Poverty is especially related to sex and age wherein females in many groups (e.g., those 18 to 64, and especially women who are unattached and with children) experience a higher-than-average risk (Statistics Canada, 2010g). Women continue to earn

less than men, and females heading up lone-parent families have the least amount of net worth (Statistics Canada, 2010h). About 606,000 children aged 17 and under live in low-income families with 218,000 of them headed by lone-parent females (Statistics Canada, 2010e). The *feminization of poverty* is most pronounced in Alberta where the greatest proportion of women head lone-parent families, the majority of those in low-earning jobs are females, and females with university degrees earn only 67 percent of what their male counterparts do (Phillips, 2010). Moreover, the government of Alberta allocates the least amount of money toward regulated childcare spaces, there is no provincial child tax benefit for low-income families, and only the bare minimum is obtainable for maternity and parental leave benefits (Phillips, 2010). Finally, it is important to note that the "most vulnerable" Canadian is anyone who falls into more than one "at-risk" group such as Aboriginal female-headed lone-parent families or Aboriginal children wherein 49 percent of those under the age of six reside in a low-income family (Canadian Teacher's Federation, 2009).

LO⁴ NEGATIVE CONSEQUENCES OF SOCIAL INEQUALITY

EDUCATION AND POVERTY

Children who are born into poverty are further disadvantaged once they enter the school system. Although schooling is publicly funded through grade 12, more essential costs are being offloaded onto school boards wherein groups such as parent councils are tasked with raising funds to supplement library resources, classroom resources, computer equipment, field trips, playground equipment, and so on. Parents who are "better off" have more resources to contribute to schools in the form of financial donations, fundraising purchases, and unpaid volunteer efforts. Conversely, families living in poverty are less able to participate in fundraising programs and are less able to utilize "additional fee" enrichment activities such as school field trips, band equipment rentals, organized sports, and hot lunch programs. Those who are impoverished tend to do less well in school, creating a cycle of poverty since those who do poorly in school are more apt to drop out and are more likely to end up being poor as adults.

Educational attainment is a significant determinant of future employment. In 2009, about 85 percent of Canadians who were between the ages of 25 and 44 who had a postsecondary degree were employed, compared to 76 percent with a high school diploma, and 51 percent with less than grade 9 (Statistics Canada, 2010i). Similarly, educational attainment is an important contributor to future earnings. Those who earn a high school diploma or certificate that is less than a Bachelor's earn about $30,116, while those who obtain a university degree (e.g., Bachelor's) make $58,767, and those with an even more advanced university degree (e.g., above the Bachelor level) earn closer to $69,230 (Statistics Canada, 2009).

HEALTH, HARDSHIPS, AND POVERTY

Many Canadians living in poverty live from paycheque to paycheque and must forego certain health-care practices such as regular visits to doctors or dentists because they lack the means to cover plans that pay for necessary prescription medicines, vision care, or supplemental provisions (e.g., chiropractic treatment). The poor also often go hungry and suffer malnutrition since they do not have enough money to regularly purchase groceries, limiting their access to nutritious foods. This also poses long-term health implications including the prevalence of higher rates of diabetes, heart problems, hypertension, and cancer (Phipps, 2003). Refer to Chapter 11 for a detailed discussion of the links between poverty and illness.

Poverty in its most extreme hardship is visible in the prevalence of homeless Canadians. **Homelessness** can be defined as a state in which a person is unable to secure a permanent residence. There is a range of homelessness in Canada, from people living on the street, staying in emergency shelters, or sleeping in vehicles, to those staying "temporarily" with friends and/or relatives. Although homelessness is extremely difficult to measure accurately, the executive director of the advocacy network Canada Without Poverty estimated that as many as 300,000 Canadians are currently without homes (Yarema, 2010). There are even more Canadians (i.e., about 1.5 million) who live in substandard dwellings or homes they cannot afford and, hence, are currently at risk for becoming homeless (Wellesley Institute, 2010).

Risk factors for homelessness can be identified at the micro or individual level as well at the macro or structural level. The two main structural factors that increase risk of homelessness in Canada are inadequate incomes and a lack of affordable housing (Echenberg & Jensen, 2009). Individual-level factors include unemployment, divorce, substance abuse, and mental illness (Canadian Mental Health Association, 2003). Note that the direction of the relationship between mental illness and homelessness is not

More than a million Canadians are at risk for homelessness.

straightforward since mental illness creates problems in securing adequate employment and housing, but homelessness also contributes to mental illness and addiction (Echenberg & Jensen, 2009).

POVERTY AS A FEATURE OF CANADIAN SOCIETY

With the exception of the recent recession (discussed shortly) there has been very little change in the overall rate of poverty over the last several decades, indicating that poverty is a persistent and enduring characteristic of Canadian society (Hay, 2009). The economy is one of the main structural factors that can lead to fluctuations in poverty rates since it represents changes in business cycles that in turn correspond to employment rates, income, and the overall

> **Homelessness:** A state in which a person is unable to secure a permanent residence.

cost of living. A **recession** refers to a general economic decline that persists for two or more three-month periods. A recession is often determined by a drop in a country's Gross Domestic Product. **Gross Domestic Product (GDP)** is an overall indicator of a country's economic productivity based on goods and services as measured by household consumption, government spending, and investments. Canada's GDP dropped 3.3 percent from the fall of 2008 to the summer of 2009 (CBC News, 2010).

Canadians were directly and indirectly impacted by the recession as reflected in the loss of many jobs, increased rent and food costs, bankruptcies, and substantial increases in social assistance programs (e.g., visits to food banks). Existing support measures such as Employment Insurance benefits (EI), welfare programs, housing shelters, and food banks were insufficient relative to the numbers of struggling Canadians. For example, as many as 770,000 Canadians failed to qualify for Employment Insurance benefits, while another 500,000 exhausted their yearly benefits after only a few months (Pasma, 2010). Some of the exacerbating effects are highlighted in Figure 6.2.

Although Canada has made its way out of the recession, the economic plight for many Canadians is ongoing. Record low interest rates make it more attractive to borrow and spend rather than save and this is the main reason many Canadians now carry substantial debt loads they may never be able to repay. Economist Paul Krugman recently noted that Canada has one of the worst debt-to-income ratios compared to other highly developed countries. The average Canadian household *owes* $1.47 on every dollar taken in but only saves about $2.80 on every $100 of household income. Comparably, Canadian savings are currently about half that of Americans; they have not been this low since the 1930s (Yalnizyan, 2010a). Factor existing debt loads in with job losses and the addition of "new" poor Canadians and you can appreciate the lingering effects of the recession on Canadian society. Using Yalnizyan's (2010b) estimate based on the aftermath of previous recessions, it is likely that between 750,000 and 1.8 million *additional* Canadians now live in poverty, with the most significant increases among the class of working poor, bringing the number of impoverished closer to 5 million (or about 1 out of every 6 families).

Recession: A general economic decline that persists for two or more three-month periods.

Gross Domestic Product (GDP): An overall indicator of a country's economic productivity based on goods and services as measured by household consumption, government spending, and investments.

FIGURE 6.2
Implications of the Canadian Recession for Poverty

- The poverty rate likely climbed to 11.7 percent in 2009, an increase of over 900,000 Canadians from three million in 2007.

- The unemployment rate rose from 6.3 percent in October 2008 to 8.6 percent in October 2009.

- 153,600 jobs were lost among parents of small children during the recession.

- The number of regular EI beneficiaries rose to 809,600 in October 2009, compared to 500,340 in October 2008.

- Nearly half of the unemployed did not qualify for EI benefits.

- Social assistance caseloads increased in all ten provinces. Alberta, Ontario, and British Columbia all had increases greater than 20 percent between October 2008 and December 2009.

- Core inflation was 0.3 percent for 2009, but food prices increased by 4.9 percent in 2009.

- Average monthly rent for a two-bedroom apartment increased by 2.3 percent between October 2008 and October 2009, compared to a 0.1 percent inflation rate for this period.

- Consumer bankruptcies increased 36.4 percent between the end of the third quarter of 2008 and the end of the third quarter of 2009.

- Food bank use increased by 18 percent between 2008 and 2009, the highest recorded year-over-year increase.

Source: Pasma, C. (2010). *Bearing the Brunt: How the 2008–2009 Recession Created Poverty for Canadian Families.* Ottawa, Ontario: Citizens for Public Justice.

POVERTY REDUCTION

Government officials have repeatedly made claims concerning the importance of poverty resolution, sometimes even with specific end dates. For example, in 1989, Canadian federal Members of Parliament unanimously pledged to end child poverty in Canada by the year 2000. More than a decade after that date, child poverty remains. Was it impossible to find effective ways to reduce poverty? Federal policies and programs designed to provide income security are highly effective for reducing poverty, as evidenced by the fact that elderly Canadians as a group are not considered at risk for poverty. This is partly because Canadians over the age of 65 years currently have access to ongoing sources of income in the form of Old Age Security implemented in 1951, the Canada Pension Plan initiated in 1964, and/or the Quebec Pension Plan for those living in the province of Quebec. These plans together provide more than $62 billion in benefits annually as a guaranteed income (Human Resources and Skills Development Canada, 2010). For more information on these plans, visit the Government of Canada's Human Resources and Skills Development of Canada page at www.hrsdc.gc.ca. The difficulty is that there are several groups at risk for poverty and one or more costly social programs are needed for each group in order to keep them above the low-income cut-off.

LO5 Poverty-reduction strategies are generally incorporated as part of a society's broader social safety net. A **social safety net** consists of services and programs designed to lessen financial burdens experienced by low-income groups.

Federal and provincial initiatives usually take the form of supplemental financial supports (e.g., income benefits for seniors, child tax benefits for families) along with employment benefits (e.g., employment insurance to cover periods of unemployment). In addition, plans may include programs that specifically address issues related to inadequate income (e.g., housing allowances, food allowances, day care allowances) and other measures (such as fee waivers) that target groups at greatest risk for poverty (e.g., Aboriginal peoples, recent immigrants) (Hay, 2009). While helpful in reducing poverty, all of these initiatives cost money that is not readily available in government budgets and must be derived through cutbacks or increased taxes. Not everyone agrees that such measures are appropriate or even necessary.

Allahar and Côté (1998) depict an ensuing relationship between ideology, inequality, and politics by noting that "because inequalities have the potential of producing conflict and disrupting social order, they need to be politically managed. . . . Canada is a country where White, male, Anglo-Saxon, Protestant, wealthy, middle-aged, and older heterosexuals hold power in the leading institutions (and are generally seen to do so legitimately for historical reasons). Therefore, it is these individuals and the class(es) they represent who often define the 'true' nature of social inequality. These people draft the laws on behalf of the wider society and, as a consequence, they are most responsible for shaping the ways the average citizen perceives her or his society. It stands to reason that such laws, the policies they uphold, and the images they project, will be conservative" (p. 5).

CANADA'S SOCIAL INFRASTRUCTURE

Using a small portion of the money collected through taxes (i.e., about 8 cents from every dollar), municipal governments endeavour to maintain Canada's existing social infrastructure. The *social infrastructure* includes a host of public services such as transit, libraries, parks, and recreation along with various incentives and programs that comprise the social safety net. The president of the Federation of Canadian Municipalities notes that the recent recession along with subsequent federal and provincial support cutbacks has allowed the social safety net to "fray" and this has led to a substantial decrease in quality of life for many Canadians. The 2010 report on the quality of life in Canadian communities highlights some of the negative trends as follows:

- The persistence of poverty despite economic growth from 2001 to 2006;
- The erosion of traditional social-policy tools (e.g., unemployment and family benefits);
- A fraying social safety net (e.g., welfare income does not cover basic living costs);
- Increasing poverty and income inequality (e.g., there is an increased gap between rich and poor and an increased number of working poor) (Federation of Canadian Municipalities, 2010).

Advocates of poverty reduction endorse federal measures that result in a higher guaranteed income to Canadians (e.g., increased minimum wages, higher allowances for child-tax benefits), and/or produce guaranteed affordable housing. The issue then comes back to how to secure the funds to pay for necessary measures. One option would be to increase the taxes paid by corporations wherein, in principle, the rich would be giving to the poor. However, this approach runs contrary to practices designed to stimulate economic growth that generally sanction corporate tax breaks. "Prime Minister Stephen Harper's conservative government further reduced the [corporate] rate from 21 percent in 2007 to 16.5 percent in 2011 with a further

Social safety net: Services and programs designed to lessen financial burdens experienced by low-income groups.

MAKE POVERTY HISTORY CAMPAIGN

In 2005, the *Canadian Make Poverty History* campaign and the larger *Global Call to Action Against Poverty* campaign (of which the Canadian campaign is a part) were launched in an effort to educate and mobilize Canadians on issues related to poverty. One of the main aims is to organize communities to lobby governments to create and enact poverty reduction plans. To sign on or to learn more about the *Make Poverty History Campaign*, visit: www.makepovertyhistory.ca/ At the time of writing this chapter, 263,950 Canadians had already signed on. Check to see how many more have now joined this campaign.

1.5 percentage point reduction legislated for 2012" (Kremmidas, 2011). Even if tax cuts were a viable option, the costs incurred might end up coming out of the very place they are needed as described in an Oxford University Study, which points out that a $1 increase in corporate taxes corresponds to a median wage *reduction* of 92 cents (Kremmidas, 2011). Poverty is not readily resolvable because inequality is built into the very fabric of Canadian society.

TIME TO REVIEW

- What are some of consequences of social inequality in the long run?
- How is financial wealth measured in Canada?
- What do measures of financial wealth tell us about social inequality?
- How is poverty estimated in Canada?
- Who is at greatest risk for poverty in Canada?
- How does poverty relate to other negative consequences?

- In what ways was Canada's social safety net insufficient for warding off the negative effects of the 2008 recession?
- Is poverty decreasing over time?
- What kind of measures help to reduce poverty?

Social stratification: Socially sanctioned patterns (or classes) of social inequality that exist in society and are based on distinguishable attributes such as race, age, gender, income, or occupation.

Caste system: A system of stratification that is based on inherited social standing.

LO⁶ SOCIAL STRATIFICATION

Social stratification refers to socially sanctioned patterns (or classes) of social inequality that exist in society and are based on distinguishable attributes such as race, age, gender, income, or occupation. In essence, social stratification systems are the "built-in" means for hierarchically ranking groups of people. In a *closed system of stratification* there is little or no movement between hierarchical layers. Slavery is an example of the most extreme form of sanctioned inequality since social position is permanent (closed). Individuals who are classified as slaves are owned by others as property and thereby have no "rights" and no means for accumulating wealth, culminating in a minimal subsistence and a relatively short life span. Another commonly used example of a closed system is the caste system or *varna* that characterizes India's vast inequality wherein global economic prosperity exists amid hundreds of millions of people who live in poverty and lack access to health care and education (Luce, 2007).

THE CASTE SYSTEM

A **caste system** is a system of stratification that is based on inherited social standing. People are born into social ranks through ascribed statuses that remain relatively permanent throughout their lives and continue to be reproduced in subsequent generations. The caste system in India has its origins in ancient Hinduism and consists of four hierarchical layers or strata that coincide with historical occupations: The Brahmins (the upper or superior caste consisting of priests), the Ksyatriya (the second caste consisting of warriors and kings), the Vaishyas (the third caste consisting of merchants and traders), and the Shudras (the fourth caste consisting of mainly laborers) (Dirks, 2001). There is a fifth "outcasted" group called Untouchables that is considered to be so far beneath this system that its members are not even recognized in society (Jaffrelot, 2005). Untouchables are a subordinated or oppressed group of individuals, similar to slaves, who lack rights and are predestined to carry out unclean, often unpaid, tasks in society such as cleaning toilets and sweeping debris. As an author from the Ksyatriya caste put it "the [untouchable] sweeper is worse off than a slave, for the slave may change his master and his duties and may even become free, but the sweeper is bound forever, born into a state from which he cannot escape and where he is excluded from social intercourse and the consolations of his religion. Unclean himself, he pollutes others when he touches them" (Anand, 1935, p. 6).

The layers of strata are not entirely closed since it is possible for members born into a lower caste to obtain economic viability through educational attainment and to secure occupations more characteristic of those in the higher castes. However, caste reproduction is inevitable since cultural practices, norms, and beliefs reinforce the existing divisions. For example, marriage tends to be within castes, and the higher castes are generally the only ones with the resources necessary for the educational attainment needed to secure the better-paying jobs that are largely unavailable to the uneducated lower castes. In addition, religious beliefs play an important role in the maintenance of the hierarchical ranking of the caste system, wherein, for example, it is believed that deeds in a past life account for the occupation/caste in the present life. Attempts have been made to facilitate the development of the lowest strata through government-sponsored initiatives (e.g., by allowing a small percentage of those in the lowest groups to attend school). However, given the sheer volume of impoverished people, efforts continue to have negligible outcomes. Moreover, despite the fact that the state no longer recognizes castes (i.e., discrimination on the basis of caste is forbidden), widespread violence in particular regions along caste lines continues to reproduce the subordination and exploitation of the lower castes (Rai, 2009).

"Untouchables" are persons of such of low status that they fall outside of the caste system in India.

Source: William Albert Allard/National Geographic/Getty

EVERY SIXTH INDIAN IS AN UNTOUCHABLE

Every sixth human being in the world today is an Indian, and every sixth Indian is an erstwhile untouchable, a *Dalit*. Today there are 165 million *Dalits* (equal to more than half the population of the United States) and they continue to suffer under India's 3,500-year-old caste system, which remains a stigma on humanity. However, *Dalits* are awakening.

We are struggling against caste discrimination, illiteracy, and poverty; our weapons are education, self-empowerment, and democracy.
(Jadhav, 1993: 1)

Source: Jadhav, N. (1993). *Untouchables: My Family's Triumphant Journey Out of the Caste System in Modern India*. New York, NY: Scribner.

THE CLASS SYSTEM

Most systems of stratification are based on social class distinctions even though the patterns also reflect inequality in other groupings such as race, sex, or age. A **class system** is a system of stratification that is based primarily on economic measures such as annual income or the possession of resources. There can be any number of classes in a society as long as the differences between classes can be quantified in some readily identifiable manner such as using a range of family yearly incomes to denote a low, a middle, and an upper class. Social class as a sanctioned system of stratification means that people come to be recognized as belonging to various strata often on the basis of similar lifestyle patterns including levels of education, types of dwelling, areas of residence, occupational status, and so on.

LO⁷ SOCIAL CLASSES IN CANADA TODAY

How many readily identifiable classes are there in Canadian society? Statistics Canada (2010j) divided the income of economic families of two or more persons who live in the same dwelling and are related by blood, marriage, common law, or adoption into five earning groups (called quintiles) that each contain 20 percent of families. Utilizing family-income quintiles, we can portray how income and wealth is distributed in ranges that denote an existing class structure (see Table 6.3).

Sociologist Dennis Gilbert's (2011) model of class structure (which was originally developed by the late Joseph Kahl) can be adapted to Canada to describe the distinct

economic-based social classes (i.e., income quintiles) and to further differentiate the strata based on educational attainment and the occupation of the primary earner in the household. Note that Gilbert's (2011) model includes six readily identifiable classes: a capitalist class, an upper-middle class, a middle class, a working class, a working-poor class, and an underclass (see Figure 6.3). We can also discuss six classes in relation to Canada, since one of the groups (the capitalist class) is an extremely small outlier consisting of less than one percent of the population that is located at the very end or top of the highest quintile.

The Capitalist Class: At the very end or top of the class structure is a very small *capitalist class* that

> **Class system:** A system of stratification that is based primarily on economic measures such as annual income or the possession of resources.

TABLE 6.3

Family Income Ranges and Share of Total, by Quintile

	Income Ranges	Share of Total Income
Highest quintile	$104,101 and over	47.3 percent
Fourth quintile	$67,401–104,100	23.5 percent
Third quintile	$43,701–67,400	15.4 percent
Second quintile	$24,711–43,700	9.5 percent
Lowest quintile	$0–24,700	4.2 percent

Source: Adapted from Statistics Canada (2010j).

FIGURE 6.3
Gilbert–Kahl Model of Class Structure

Capitalist Class
- $2 million
- Selective education, often postgraduate
- Inherited wealth, top executives

Upper-Middle Class
- $150,000
- College, often post-graduate
- Professionals, business owners

Middle Class
- $70,000
- At least some high school, often some college
- Semi professionals, nonretail sales, craft workers

Working Class
- $40,000
- High school
- Low-skill manual, low-paid craft workers, clerical, retail sales

Working Poor
- $25,000
- At least some high school
- Service workers, low-paid operatives, manual workers

Underclass
- $15,000
- Some high school
- Unemployed, part-time

Source: Gilbert, D. (2011). The American Class Structure in an Age of Growing Inequality. (8th ed.). Thousand Oaks, CA: Sage Publications, Inc.

contains primarily "old money" or the families of long standing inherited wealth that earn income from their assets as well as a very small group of working top executives who have higher "selective" education and an annual income of $2 million (Gilbert, 2011). This class represents only a minute fraction of Canadian families. For example, according to Canada Revenue Agency data, of the 24.5 million tax returns filed in 2009, only 174,000 individuals (or 0.7 percent) reported an income that exceeded $250,000 (Golombek, 2011). The capitalist class in Canada comprises families on Canada's "most rich" list (e.g., the Thomsons, Irvings, and Rogers) and families headed by a chief executive officer of a large corporation or a top-earning physician. Families in the capitalist class are assured social reproduction as their income and net worth rises disproportionate to the rest of Canadians. For example, a Canadian Centre for Policy Alternatives study showed that the

average taxable income for the top 0.1 percent of families rose from $1,270,000 in 1992 to $2,650,000 by 2004 (in 2007 dollars) and to $3,360,000 by 2008 (Dobbin, 2010). The wealthiest 10 percent of families also gained 65 percent in terms of net worth from 1999 to 2005, whereas the accumulated wealth of the bottom 50 percent of Canadians has remained the same since 1984 (Dobbin, 2010).

The Upper-Middle Class: The second-highest class is an *upper-middle class* made up of professionals and managers with at least a college education (but more likely a postgraduate university degree) who earn about $150,000 per year (Gilbert, 2011). As Marger (2011) purports, "if the capitalist class 'owns' society, then those who constitute the upper-middle class 'run' society" (p. 59). Gilbert (2011) refers to this group as the "working rich" since the bulk of their income is derived from a salary. In Canada, the upper-middle class earns $104,101 or more (Statistics Canada, 2010j) and consists of the senior management of large corporations and organizations and professionals with several years of experience and/or higher postsecondary degrees (e.g., lawyers, doctors, engineers, accountants, pharmacists, chiropractors, and some of the tenured professors at universities). Occupations that make up the upper-middle class are regularly rated as high in prestige (Marger, 2011) and they include a high degree of personal freedom (i.e., autonomy) as well as considerable authority or power over others (Hodson & Sullivan, 2008).

The Middle Class: Canadians most commonly perceive themselves to be "middle class." According to Gilbert, the middle class earns about $70,000 on average and includes lower managerial positions, semiprofessionals, and those in nonretail sales (e.g., real estate agents). Recall that the middle-most or median family income in Canada was $68,860. It's unclear how broad the range of family incomes is in American class structure since the middle class as depicted in Gilbert's model starts somewhere above $40,000 and ends somewhere below $150,000. In Canada, the range for the middle class based on quintiles is from $67,401 to 104,101 (Statistics Canada, 2010j). Canada's middle class entails families with semiprofessionals and managers who have at least a four-year university or college degree (e.g., teachers, social workers, graphic designers, computer software engineers, and human resource managers), those in nonretail sales (e.g., insurance representatives), and families headed by people who work in the trades (e.g., welders, pipefitters, machinists).

Perhaps you have read in the papers something about a "shrinking middle class." The *shrinking middle class* refers to the growing inequality in income in Canada (and elsewhere, including the United States) that is most apparent within the middle class due to changes in the occupational structure of society. Gilbert (2011) suggests that it is not so much the middle class that is shrinking, as it is the polarization of incomes toward the upper-middle and the working classes. Specifically, the range of middle-class income earnings is narrowing as a result of the loss of many full-time jobs (especially skilled modest-paying jobs) in areas such as construction and manufacturing, the creation of low-paying jobs in the service industry, and changes in corporate approaches that include "outsourcing" and the creation of alternate "part-time" positions (Kerbo, 2009). This trend is even common in academia where part-time instructors are hired for an hourly wage on a term-by-term basis with little job security and minimal benefits.

The Working Class: The fourth class is what Gilbert (2011) calls the *working class,* a stratification layer characterized by families with occupational heads who have a high school diploma and earn somewhere above $25,000 but below $70,000 with an average family income of $40,000. The working class is concentrated in lower-paid "semiskilled" positions more commonly held by males (known as "blue-collar" jobs), in predominantly female-based clerical areas (traditionally referred to as "pink-collar jobs"), as well as those in retail sales (Gilbert, 2011). In Canada, the working class is located directly below the median family income, earning between $43,701 and $67,400 (Statistics Canada, 2010j). Some of the families in the

working class are on the cusp for low-income cutoffs, particularly those with more than two children. Hence, "new high school graduates can no longer be assured of finding jobs that will enable them to support families" (Gilbert, 2011, p. 248).

The Working Poor. The fifth level down the socioeconomic hierarchy is the *working poor.* The working poor include those who have "some" high school and are employed in the lowest-paying areas, such as unskilled labour, earning an average of $25,000 per year with the range being somewhere higher than $15,000 but lower than $40,000 (Gilbert, 2011). Note that Gilbert's model places only 13 percent of American families as working poor while 20 percent of Canada's families earn between $24,711 and $43,700. Canada's working poor largely depicts families with at least one person working but whose family income falls below LICO. Full-time unskilled labourers as well as the majority of people who earn slightly more than minimum wage (e.g., $11.00–$15.00 per hour) as service providers (e.g., cooks and cashiers) tend to comprise this class. *Unskilled labour* includes physically demanding jobs that require little or no previous experience. There is relatively little or no social mobility among unskilled workers and many of its occupants lack occupational aspirations (Hodson & Sullivan, 2008).

The Underclass: At the very bottom of the stratification system, we find the *underclass,* a group that is poor, relatively uneducated, and often unemployed or employed only part-time. In Gilbert's (2011) model, about 12 percent of American families fall

SOCIOLOGY ON SCREEN

POOR NO MORE

Producer Suzanne Babin and director Bert Deveaux's (2008) *Poor No More ... There is a Way Out,* is an award-winning documentary that depicts the lives of three working-poor Canadians who, contrary to popular belief, cannot simply work their way out of poverty. This film provides a critical look at Canada's corporate elite to help viewers understand the widespread political control and tax benefits accrued by this group. Babin and Deveaux also provide viable alternatives to poverty by demonstrating how taxes are used to fund social welfare practices such as free university and affordable housing in Ireland and Sweden. For more information, visit the *Poor No More* homepage: www.poornomore.ca

into the underclass with an income less than $25,000 and averaging $15,000. Comparably, 20 percent of Canadian families earn $24,700 or less (Statistics Canada, 2010j). While all families in the underclass are clearly poor, most of the working poor also fall below LICO, and even some of those in the working class can be considered impoverished. Hence, it is not just the very bottom class but probably closer to 45 percent of the Canadian population that is not doing particularly well from an economic standpoint relative to what is average or "middle-class."

SOCIAL MOBILITY IN CANADA

Canada's class structure is generally described as an *open system of stratification* because it is characterized by class changes based on achieved statuses such as educational or occupational attainment as well as other life circumstances such as marriage and divorce (which affect women more than men). **Social mobility** is a term used to describe the movement that occurs within and between classes in a stratification system. *Vertical mobility* depicts movement up or down the stratification system, while *horizontal mobility* refers to changes that occur within the same social location (e.g., as in the case of moving from one comparable job to another one without significantly changing overall income).

Intragenerational mobility refers to changes in social class that occur within a person's lifetime. If we consider students taking a sociology class to largely comprise single, unattached Canadians (rather than dependants who are still part of their family of orientation), then most students have incomes that place them in the underclass (i.e., you work for a low wage and probably only part-time, if at all). After obtaining a degree (and possibly even a subsequent postgraduate degree), you will likely secure a full-time position with a modest starting annual salary (e.g., $40,000 to $60,000) that moves you into the working poor or the middle class, thereby demonstrating intragenerational mobility.

Although changes in Canadian occupational status are often upward, these changes most frequently occur *within* existing social classes and they largely pertain to expansions in fairly similar occupations (e.g., moving up within a particular trade as you develop more advanced skills and qualifications such as going from an entry-level welder position to a more senior one). In addition, patterns of social mobility tend to be stable over time from one generation to the next (Wanner, 2004). This is especially evident when comparing the occupational status of fathers and sons. For example, if a father is a welder, it is quite likely that his son will also secure a position in the trades (although it may be of higher rank and pay) and it is just as unlikely that the same son will end up as a physician.

Occupation is often used as a measure of social class since it is closely tied to the other relevant indicators (i.e., income and education). Sociologists use the term **socioeconomic status** to refer to social standing based on a combined measure of education, income, and occupation. Educational attainment is an especially important mediating variable in social mobility and the most influential contributor to socioeconomic status because it is both a prerequisite for many qualification-based occupations and is strongly associated with income. With greater educational attainment, sons and daughters may secure higher-class positions relative to their parents. **Intergenerational mobility** refers to changes in the social class of children relative to their parents. Intergenerational mobility is a good indicator of equality since it demonstrates that social position can be determined by individual merit.

Studies of social stratification tend to examine factors that promote or inhibit social mobility. We have already discussed the importance of educational attainment for intergenerational mobility. Factors that influence mobility are also based on inherited traits. Particular individuals, by virtue of their ascribed traits and family upbringing, have a better or worse chance of succeeding in society. This is not something an individual has control over; rather, it is a feature of biological and cultural preconditions. If you are born into a wealthy family, you will have different opportunities in your social environment throughout your lifetime relative to someone born to a lone mother in a subsidized (government supported) housing project, regardless of your personal intellect or motivation. Similarly, someone who is a Caucasian male has much better "odds" of obtaining wealth than someone who is born an Aboriginal female. Blaming the poor for their respective social standing, then, often reflects a lack of understanding about social stratification and social mobility.

Other factors that contribute to social mobility tend to be structural in nature. For example, changes in the overall division of labour in society may produce changes in

Social mobility: Movement that occurs within and between social classes in a stratification system.

Intragenerational mobility: Changes in social class that occur within a person's lifetime.

Socioeconomic status: Social standing based on a combined measure of education, income, and occupation.

Intergenerational mobility: Changes in the social class of children relative to their parents.

mobility as more highly specialized positions are created, as in the case of developing bureaucracies and expanding sectors of information technology. In addition, changes to the demographics of a society (e.g., age) can contribute to the types and amount of social mobility. Finally, public policies such as those that support education and social programs may reduce or increase financial barriers to education and subsequent employment, thereby impacting social mobility (Organization for Economic Co-operation and Development, 2010).

In summary, let's examine some of the things we've highlighted about social mobility in Canada:

- Canada is characterized by a high level of social mobility.
- Patterns of social mobility are relatively stable over time and mainly include horizontal shifts and modest increases due to changes in occupation.
- Structural effects (e.g., shifts in population demographics) can account for variations in social mobility.
- Educational attainment is the most important factor mediating intergenerational mobility.

Karl Marx (1818–1883).

Source: © Historical image collection by Bildagentur-online/Alamy

LO⁸ SOCIOLOGY IN THEORY: WHY ARE THERE CLASSES IN SOCIETY?

MARX AND WEBER

Most theoretical models used to describe how social classes originate or why they persist have foundations in the conflict perspective since the very notion of classes necessarily implies inequity in terms of resources and power. The opening quotation to this chapter suggests that a class-based system of stratification is inevitable. In his classic work written with Friedrich Engels, *The Communist Manifesto,* Karl Marx observed that people are essentially cooperative by nature when attempting to secure basic needs (i.e., food, shelter, and clothing). However, once basic needs are met and a division of labour emerges in society, class struggles become apparent (Coser, 1977). As production moves away from individuals to factories, workers become exploited by capitalists, referred to as the *bourgeoisie* (i.e., the owners of the means of production), who pay the workers (i.e., the *proletariat*) less than what they deserve for their efforts.

From a Marxist perspective, it is the materialistic nature of *a capitalist society* as rooted in the private ownership of property and the generation of surplus that fosters competition and creates a distinction between owners and nonowners that leads to the emergence of social classes. The economy is the central institution in society, which, like a master status, has a far-reaching impact on all of the other sectors (e.g., religion and politics). Cultural values and practices, then, are more apt to be considered byproducts of capitalist dominance as in the case of religion, which Marx (1843–44) deemed "the sigh of the oppressed creature, the heart of a heartless world and the soul of soulless conditions. It is the opium of the people" (Cowling, Elton, Kedourie, Pocock, Pole, & Ullman, 1970, p. 127; see also Chapter 9). According to Marx, while religion is beneficial in that it provides temporarily relief to the masses who are long sufferers of exploitation, it mainly, largely, serves to maintain the existing social order.

Max Weber's views on capitalism are quite different from Marx's. In the *Protestant Ethic and the Spirit of Capitalism* (1904/1958), Weber emphasizes how the emergence of rationality in the West coincided with the rising "spirit" of capitalism within Protestantism; both promoted ideas that emphasized the importance of economic success, such as "time is money," "be industrious," "be punctual," and "earning money is a legitimate end in itself" (Ritzer, 1992, p. 150). Hence, religion also contributes to the influence of capitalism. Although Weber also focused on economics, he did not view the mode of production to necessarily be the only central influence in society. Instead, things such as religion (or even race) could also be significant contributors to the social inequality between groups. In addition, instead of discussing just two main groups in conflict with one another, Weber recognized a broader range of strata that he discussed as status differences (rather than class differences). This is a very different usage of status than that described in Chapter 5 and in this particular case, status does depict hierarchical ranking.

To Weber, status referred to social standing as based on similarities in upbringing and lifestyle that could be attributed to wealth, power, and/or prestige. *Wealth* in this case refers to economic assets such as income, *power* is the ability to enact one's will, and *prestige* refers to the social advantage conferred by a particular position. The elements of status frequently correspond to one another. For example, as a group, physicians are fairly autonomous and thereby share a high level of prestige while their knowledge and skills translate into high salaries (wealth). In addition, they possess power in terms of the level of control over their own work environment (which also relates to prestige) and they have authority in relation to patients and coworkers such as nurses (which also illustrates power). Whereas Marx emphasized the differences between two classes based on those who owned the means of production and those who worked for the owners, Weber viewed class differences as based in differences of lifestyle and interests afforded by similar social standing.

THE CAPITALIST CLASS

Some conflict theorists have focused exclusively on the capitalist class in an effort to describe who this group is, how they exert influence, and how they maintain their position of power in society; this focus has come to be known as elite theory. *Elite theory* explains power relationships in society as residing in a small group who hold positions of authority in economic and political structures. Weber's contemporaries, sociologists Vilfredo Pareto (1848–1923), Gaetano Mosca (1858–1941), and Robert Michels (1876–1936), for example, wrote extensively about the same small group that possessed wealth and power that they called the "governing elite," the "elite," and/or "ruling class."

Similarly, C. Wright Mills is famous for generating interest in the 1950s in what he called "the power elite," a very cohesive group of top corporate officials from the government, military, and economic structures that share similar backgrounds and play a central role in decision making in the United States (Marger, 2011). In *Who Rules America*, G. William Domhoff (2010) provides a contemporary account of the same power elite.

John Porter (1921–1979), a highly influential sociologist and economist, was the first to demonstrate that Canadian society also consists of hierarchically ranked social classes that are headed by what he termed the "corporate elite." In *The Vertical Mosaic: An Analysis of Social Class and Power in Canada*, Porter (1965) explains how Canada can be divided up into social classes based on measures of inequality (e.g., wealth and power) identified by the early conflict theorists. In addition, we discover that membership in certain ethnic groups confers more or less status. Specifically, those of British origin tend to fall into the highest social classes where power and privilege is concentrated, while Aboriginal peoples tend to be in the lowest classes corresponding to lower education attainment, income, and occupational prestige (Helm-Hayes & Miller, 1998). Finally, Porter (1965) demonstrated the predominance of the corporate elite. The *corporate elite* are highly influential Canadians who head up the economic and political spheres and who both compete and cooperate with one another as central decision makers. While their interests may differ (and hence, create competition), there is also substantial overlap since they are from the higher social class, intermarry, form business partnerships, belong to elite social clubs, and hold similar positions on corporate boards (Helm-Hayes & Miller, 1998). Hence, the elite also tend to support each other when necessary in order to maintain the overall structure. This parallels C. Wright Mill's (1956) and Domhoff's (2010) notions of the American power elite.

IS STRATIFICATION A GOOD OR BAD THING?

Functionalists point out that inequality exists in all societies, suggesting it is inevitable and even necessary. According to Davis and Moore (1945) stratification is beneficial because it leads to **meritocracy**, a condition of advancement

> **Meritocracy:** A condition of advancement based on worth.

based on worth derived from experience, skills, and educational attainment. In this case, social stratification is highly functional because it motivates people to achieve higher education and develop their skills to their potential for success. It also ensures that the most capable people (i.e., those with the highest intellect and the utmost abilities) end up occupying the most important social positions in society (e.g., those that require the greatest amount of skill, the longest period of training, and the highest intellect) (Brym, 2011).

Conflict theorists, in contrast, claim that social stratification is not necessary or even ideal; rather, social stratification is a means for the most powerful to retain their position in the upper echelons of a society. From Karl Marx's perspective, stratification benefits capitalist owners of the means of production and disadvantages those who work for the owners (i.e., the proletariat). Marx used the term **alienation** to refer to the detachment that exists between the worker and his labour as perpetuated under capitalism. To Marx, workers are alienated from productive activity (since they do not work for themselves), from the product (since it belongs to the bourgeoisie), from their fellow workers (especially when forced into competition with one another), and from their own human potential (being reduced to something akin to machines) (Ritzer, 2010). Marx saw the increasing alienation of workers as culminating in a revolution that would eventually overthrow the bourgeoisie and pave the way for communism. *Communism* is a classless economic system in which there is group (or communal) ownership of the means of production.

Other theories fall somewhere between these two approaches. Sociologist Gerhard Lenski's theory of social stratification, for example, is based on the assumption that societal rewards are distributed according to *both* societal needs (the functionalist perspective) and power (the conflict view). According to Lenski (1966), "Men will share the product of their labors to the extent required to ensure survival and continued productivity of those others whose actions are necessary or beneficial to themselves" (p. 44). What is problematic is the existence of surplus and in this case, "power will determine the distribution of nearly all of the surplus possessed by a society" (Lenski, 1966, p. 44). According to Lenski, although there will always be stratification, there should be less inequality in modern industrial societies compared to nonindustrial ones because some of the surplus value will be shared with workers in order to manage the system (i.e., control the working class) and prevent loss of productivity due to things such as strikes (Marger, 2011).

In the absence of widespread sharing of surplus by the corporate elite (or, conversely, an uprising of the poorest classes), the gap between the wealthy and the

Alienation: Refers to the detachment that exists between the worker and his labour as perpetuated under capitalism.

SOCIOLOGY IN PRACTICE

AN ACT TO ELIMINATE POVERTY

On June 16, 2010, Bill C-545 was introduced into the House of Commons for its first reading. Bill C-545, "An Act to Eliminate Poverty in Canada," recognizes poverty as "the condition of human being who does not have the resources, means, choices, and power necessary to acquire and maintain economic self-reliance and to facilitate their integration into and participation in society." Bill C-545 describes poverty within a context of human rights, clearly delineates the negative outcomes of poverty (e.g., on the health of individuals, on the economic and social development of society), and renders the elimination of poverty a federal government obligation (i.e., to develop and implement a strategy that will strengthen the social and economic safety net, promote participation, respect human rights, and reflect the needs of local communities with specified short- and long-term outcomes) (Bill C-545, 2010).

poor continues to persist and widen in Canada. Lessening social inequality requires considerable change and will probably not come about until it is addressed more fully at the federal level of government. The lower classes are the least inclined to vote but would benefit most from representation that specifically targets improved quality of life for all low-income earning groups. While poverty has been conventionally measured in Canada using the low-income cut-off, it is increasingly being viewed within the context of social stratification and as a violation of a basic human right to a reasonable standard of living. The House of Commons is currently considering an anti-poverty bill (i.e., Bill C-545) that may persuade the federal government to design a national antipoverty strategy that more closely links economic and social development.

TIME TO REVIEW

- What is the term for socially sanctioned patterns of social inequality?
- Does slavery exist in Canada? (Explain your answer.)
- How can a caste system be differentiated from a class system of stratification?
- Which two classes make up the majority in Gilbert's (2010) model of class structure?
- What contributes to social mobility in Canada?
- How would a conflict perspective explain the persistence of social classes in Canada?

CHAPTER SUMMARY

LO1 Define social inequality and explain how to gauge social inequality using measures of financial wealth.

Social inequality refers to an unequal distribution of resources including wealth, which is measured by income from employment and net worth. Social inequality is most evident in the widening gap between those with the most versus least amounts of wealth.

LO2 Critically assess the low-income cut-off as a estimate of poverty.

The low-income cut-off is based on the proportion of income spent on only three basic needs (i.e., food, clothing, and shelter). Most Canadians pay other essential costs associated with transportation, childcare, and household operation that are not addressed by the low-income cut-off, suggesting the LICO is too conservative and therefore vastly underestimates the number of poor Canadians.

LO3 Identify groups most at risk for poverty in Canada and discuss the interrelationship among poverty and education, health, and hardship.

Groups most at risk for poverty include children, recent immigrants, lone-parent families (especially those headed by females), people with disabilities, and Aboriginal peoples.

LO4 Discuss social inequality as a stable feature of Canadian society.

There is a persistent gap between Canada's rich and poor and, while poverty has increased in the aftermath of the 2008 recession, it remained relatively consistent for decades prior to this largely because societal institutions continue to support the existing class structure.

LO5 Critically assess Canada's social safety net as a means for reducing poverty.

The existing social safety net is insufficient for keeping at-risk groups at or above low-income cut-offs. This is partly due to the sheer number of low-income Canadians, a lack of affordable housing, and a high cost of living relative to low and minimum wages.

LO6 Define social stratification and differentiate between caste and class systems.

Social stratification refers to sanctioned patterns of social inequality. Castes are closed systems that rank groups based on inherited and relatively permanent social standing. Class systems rank order groups on the basis of economic measures such as income and are more open, providing for horizontal and vertical social mobility.

LO7 Describe Canada's class structure and social mobility.

Based on income, Canada's class structure can be divided into six main groups: the capitalist class, upper-middle class, middle class, working class, working poor, and underclass. Although there is significant social mobility in Canada, much of it occurs within classes and is largely based on educational and occupational attainment.

LO8 Debate why there are social classes and whether stratification is helpful or harmful to Canadian society.

There are distinct social classes in Canada largely because capitalism supports the disparity and the top-earning Canadians tend to benefit most from the existing system in a manner that leads to social reproduction. Conflict theorists highlight the negative consequences of exploitation especially in the form of low wages and differences in power that assist in preventing the lower classes from succeeding while functionalists suggest that social inequality is necessary to ensure that the most capable individuals are sufficiently motivated to undertake the more difficult, challenging, and or more important positions in society.

RECOMMENDED READINGS

1. For illustrations of social stratification, we recommend: Eaton, J. P., & Haas, C. A. (1994). *Titanic: Triumph and Tragedy*. New York, NY: W. W. Norton & Company.
2. For a discussion of the societal benefits of greater income equality, see: Wilkinson, R., & Pickett, K. (2010). *The Spirit Level: Why Equality Is Better for Everyone*. Toronto, ON: Penguin Group Canada.
3. For a critical look at who is most harmed by and who most benefits from social inequality,

we recommend: Dorling, D. (2010). *Injustice: Why Social Inequality Persists*. Bristol, UK: The Polity Press.
4. To find out more about ways that inequality affects the health of Canadians and what you can do about it, we recommend a report by J. Mikkonen and D. Raphael (2010) called *Social Determinants of Health: The Canadian Facts*. It can be downloaded for free at www.thecanadianfacts.org

FOR FURTHER REFLECTION

1. Do you think Canada needs a national poverty reduction strategy? Why or why not? What do you think should be the focal point of a national strategy for ending *world* poverty? How does this differ from measures that address poverty in Canada?
2. Is the middle class shrinking in Canada? Consider why answers to this question rest on how middle class is defined in Canada.

3. Provide examples of occupations in Canadian society that you feel best demonstrate how social stratification leads to meritocracy as predicted by Davis and Moore's functionalist theory. Can you also think of specific examples that can serve as exceptions to this rule (e.g., important positions that are underpaid or occupations that attract salaries that are not warranted by their respective skill levels or value to society)?

REFERENCES

Allahar, A. L., & Côté, J. E. (1998). *Richer and Poorer: The Structure of Inequality in Canada*. Toronto, ON: James Lorimer & Company.

Anand, M. (1935). *Untouchable*. New York: Penguin Putnam.

Bill C-545. (2010, June 16 First Reading). *An Act to Eliminate Poverty in Canada*. House of Commons Canada.

Retrieved July 28, 2011, from the Parliament of Canada website: www2.parl.gc.ca/HousePublications/Publication.aspx?Language=E&File=24&Parl=40&Ses=3&Mode=1&Pub=Bill&Doc=C-545_1

Brym, R. J. (2011). *New Society.* (6th ed.). Toronto, ON: Nelson Education.

Canada Revenue Agency. (2011). *Northern Residents Deductions.* Ottawa, ON: Author. Retrieved July 28, 2011, from www.cra-arc.gc.ca/E/pbg/tf/t2222/README.html

Canadian Business Online. (2010). *Rich 100 2009.* Retrieved October 15, 2010, from http://list.canadianbusiness.com/rankings/rich100/2009/ranking/Default.aspx?sp2=1&d1=a&sc1=0

Canadian Mental Health Association. (2003, April). *Housing and homelessness.* Backgrounder, Citizens for Mental Health, April 2003, p. 1. Retrieved October 15, 2010, from www.cmha.citizens/housingENG.pdf

Canadian Teacher's Federation. (2009). *Supporting education ... Building Canada: Child poverty and schools.* Background Material for Parliamentarians and Staff CTF Hill Day 2009. Retrieved May 2, 2010, from www.ctf-fce.ca/publications/Briefs/FINAL_Hilldayleavebehind_eng.pdf

CBC News. (2010, April 15). *Canada escaped worst of recession: Stats Can.* CBC News.com. Retrieved on July 28, 2011, from www.cbc.ca/money/story/2010/04/15/statscan-mild-recession.html

Citizenship and Immigration Canada. (2010). *Sponsorship of parents, grandparents, adopted children and other relatives—The Sponsor's guide (IMM 5196): Quebec Income Scale, 2010.* Ottawa, ON: Author. Retrieved July 28, 2011, from www.cic.gc.ca/english/information/applications/guides/5196E10.asp

Coser, L. A. (1977). *Masters of Sociological Thought: Ideas in Historical and Social Context* (2nd ed.). Toronto, ON: Harcourt Brace Jovanovich.

Cowling, M., Elton, G. R., Kedourie, E., Pocock, J. G. A., & Ullman, W. (Eds.). (1970). *Cambridge Studies in the History and Theory of Politics: Critique of Hegel's 'Philosophy of Right' by Karl Marx.* (Annette Jolin and Joseph O'Malley, Trans.). Cambridge, UK: Cambridge University Press.

Davis, K., & Moore, W. (1945). Some principles of social stratification. *American Sociological Review, 7* (April), 242–249.

Dirks, N. (2001). *Castes of Mind: Colonialism and the Making of Modern India.* Princeton, NJ: Princeton University Press.

Dobbin, M. (2010). The rich are Canadians, too: But they've stopped acting like it, which is why it's time for tax laws to make them pay their share. *Tyee News.* Vancouver, BC: The Tyee. Retrieved July 28, 2011, from http://thetyee.ca/Opinion/2010/02/22/DobbinRichTaxes/

Domhoff, G. W. (2010). *Who Rules America? Challenges to Corporate and Class Dominance* (6th ed.). New York: McGraw-Hill.

Echenberg, H., & Jensen, H. (2009). *Risk factors for homelessness* [electronic resource]. Publisher: Parliamentary Information and Research Service. Ebrary electronic book. Retrieved October 28, 2010, from http://site.ebrary.com/lib/macewanpubpolicy/Doc?id=10339186&ppg=9

Federation of Canadian Municipalities. (2010). *Mending Canada's frayed social safety net: The role of municipal governments: Quality of life in Canadian communities: Theme report #6.* Ottawa, ON: Author. Retrieved October 12, 2010, from www.fcm.ca//CMFiles/QofL6En_Embargp1KGE-3242010-6436.pdf

Gilbert, D. (2011). *The American Class Structure in an Age of Growing Inequality* (8th ed.). Thousand Oaks, CA: Sage Publications.

Golombek, J. (2011, March 25). How much do Canadians make? *National Post.com.* Retrieved July 28, 2011, from www.nationalpost.com/much+Canadians+make/4497362/story.html

Hay, D. I. (2009). *Poverty Reduction Policies and Programs in Canada* [electronic book]. Canadian Council on Social Development. Accessed via MacEwan's e-library October 28, 2010, from http://site.ebrary.com.ezproxy.macewan.ca/lib/macewanpubpolicy/docDetail.action?docID=10330319

Helm-Hayes, R., & Miller, M. (1998). *The Vertical Mosaic Revisited.* Toronto, ON: University of Toronto Press.

Hodson, R., & Sullivan, T. A. (2008). *The Social Organization of Work* (4th ed.). Belmont, CA: Cengage Learning.

Human Resources and Skills Development Canada. (2010). *Canada Pension Plan and Old Age Security.* Ottawa, ON: Government of Canada. Retrieved July 28, 2011, from www.hrsdc.gc.ca/eng/oas-cpp/index.shtml

Jadhav, N. (1993). *Untouchables: My Family's Triumphant Journey Out of the Caste System in Modern India.* New York, NY: Scribner.

Jaffrelot, C. (2005). *Dr. Ambedkar and Untouchability: Fighting the Indian Caste System.* New York: Columbia University Press/Edmonton, AB: University of Alberta, Office of External Relations.

Kerbo, H. R. (2009). *Social Stratification and Inequality: Class Conflict in Historical, Comparative, and Global Perspective* (7th ed.). New York: McGraw-Hill.

Kremmidas, T. (2011, March 11). Increasing business taxes. *The Canadian Business Journal.* Mississauga, ON: George Media. Retrieved May 3, 2011, from www.canadianbusinessjournal.ca/features/march_11_features/increasing_business_taxes.html

Lenski, G. (1966). *Power and Privilege.* New York, NY: McGraw-Hill.

Living in Canada. (2011). *The Canadian minimum wage.* www.livingin-canada.com

Luce, E. (2007). *In Spite of the Gods: The Rise of Modern India.* New York: Anchor Books.

Marger, M. N. (2011). *Social Inequality: Patterns and Processes* (5th ed.). New York: McGraw-Hill.

Marx, K., & Engels, F. (1848/2010). *Manifesto of the Communist Party.* Charleston, SC: CreateSpace.

Mills, C. W. (1956). *White Collar.* New York: Oxford University Press.

(The) Organization for Economic Co-operation and Development. (2010). *Economic Policy Reforms 2010: Going for Growth.* Chapter 5. A family affair: intergenerational social mobility across OECD countries, pp. 181–198. OECD Publishing. Retrieved October 20, 2010, from www.oecd.org/economics/goingforgrowth

Pasma, C. (2010). *Bearing the Brunt: How the 2008–2009 Recession Created Poverty for Canadian Families* [electronic book]. Saint-Larare, QC: Citizens for Public Justice, 2010. Retrieved October 28, 2010, via Macewan's e-library: http://site.ebrary.com.ezproxy.macewan.ca/lib/macewanpubpolicy/docDetail.action?docID=10406344

Pembina Institute for Appropriate Development. (2005, August). GPI, Indicator #14. INCOME DISTRIBUTION. Retrieved April 27, 2011, from http://pubs.pembina.org/reports/14.Income% 20Distribution.pdf

Phillips, S. (2010, March 8). *Women's equality a long way off in Alberta: Alberta most unequal province in Canada.* Parkland Institute Research: Fact Sheets. Edmonton, AB: Parkland Institute. Retrieved July 28, 2011, from http://parklandinstitute.ca/research/summary/womens_equality_a_long_way_off_in_alberta/

Phipps, S. (2003, June). The impact of poverty on health. *Poverty and Health.* Canadian Population Health Initiative Collected Papers. Ottawa, ON: Canadian Institute for Health Information. Retrieved November 10, 2010, from http://dsp-psd.pwgsc.gc.ca/Collection/H118-11-2003-1E.pdf

Porter, J. (1965). *The Vertical Mosaic: An Analysis of Social Class and Power in Canada.* Toronto, ON: University of Toronto Press.

Rai, M. (2009, March 18). Associate Professor Mridu Rai: Caste system in India. Interview for *The MacMillan Report* hosted by Marilyn Wilkes. New Haven, CT: The Whitney and Betty MacMillan Center for International and Area Studies at Yale. Retrieved July 28, 2011, from www.yale.edu/macmillanreport/ep14-rai-031809.html

Ritzer, G. (2010). *Sociological Theory* (7th ed.). New York: McGraw-Hill.

Ritzer, G. (1992). *Sociological Theory* (3rd ed.). New York: McGraw-Hill.

Statistics Canada. (2010a). *Median total income, by family type, by province and territory.* (All census families). Ottawa, ON: Author. Retrieved July 28, 2011, from www40.statcan.gc.ca/l01/cst01/famil108a-eng.htm?sdi=income

Statistics Canada. (2010b, September 16). Family income and individuals income, related variables: Sub-provincial data. Table 1: Median total income of census families and persons not in census families, by census metropolitan area. *The Daily.* Ottawa, ON: Author.

Statistics Canada. (2010c). *Net worth of family units, by selected family characteristics (by income after-tax group).* Ottawa, ON: Author. Retrieved October 15, 2010, from www40.statcan.gc.ca/l01/cst01/famil112e-eng.htm?sdi=income

Statistics Canada. (2010d). Low income lines, 2008–2009. *Income Research Paper Series.* Ottawa, ON: Income Statistics Division. Retrieved May 5, 2011, from www.statcan.gc.ca/pub/75f0002m/75f0002m2010005-eng.pdf

Statistics Canada. (2010e, June 17). Income of Canadians. *The Daily.* Ottawa, ON: Author. Retrieved July 28, 2011, from www.statcan.gc.ca/daily-quotidien/100617/dq100617c-eng.htm

Statistics Canada. (2010f). *Spending Patterns in Canada 2009.* Catalogue no. 62-202-X. Ottawa, ON: Minister of Industry. Retrieved April 28, 2011, from http://publications.gc.ca/collections/collection_2010/statcan/62-202-X/62-202-x2008000-eng.pdf

Statistics Canada. (2010g). *Persons in low income after tax.* Ottawa, ON: Author. Retrieved July 28, 2011, from www40.statcan.gc.ca/l01/cst01/famil19a-eng.htm

Statistics Canada. (2010h, December 16). Women in Canada: Economic well-being. *The Daily.* Ottawa, ON: Author. Retrieved July 28, 2011, from www.statcan.gc.ca/daily-quotidien/101216/dq101216c-eng.htm

Statistics Canada. (2010i). *People employed, by educational attainment.* Ottawa, ON: Author. Retrieved July 28, 2011, from www40.statcan.gc.ca/l01/cst01/labor62-eng.htm?sdi=educational percent20attainment

Statistics Canada. (2010j). CANSIM Table 2020405. Upper income limit and income share of total income quintiles, by economic family type, 2008 current dollars, annually. Ottawa, ON: Author.

Statistics Canada. (2009). *Average earnings of the population 15 years and over by highest level of schooling, by province and territory (2006 Census).* Ottawa, ON: Author. Retrieved November 1, 2010, from www40.statcan.gc.ca/l01/cst01/labor50a-eng.htm

Wanner, R. A. (2004). Social mobility in Canada: Concepts, patterns, and trends. In J. Curtis, E. Grabb, and N. Guppy (Eds.), *Social Inequality in Canada: Patterns, Problems, and Policies.* (4th ed.). Toronto, ON: Pearson Education Canada.

Weber, M. (1904/1958). *Protestant Ethic and the Spirit of Capitalism* Talcott Parsons, Trans.; with a foreword by R. H. Tawney). New York: Scribner.

Wellesley Institute. (2010, August 16). *Precarious housing in Canada*. Toronto, ON: Wellesley Institute. Retrieved July 28, 2011, from www.wellesleyinstitute.com/news/affordable-housing-news/new-report-precarious-housing-in-canada-2010

Yalnizyan, A. (2010a, August 16). *Canadian households: Among highest debt to income ratios in the world.* Commentary and Fact Sheets. Ottawa, ON: CCPA National Office. Retrieved July 28, 2011, from www.policyalternatives.ca/publications/commentary/canadian-households-among-highest-debt-income-ratios-world

Yalnizyan, A. (2010b, August 17). *The Problem of poverty post-recession.* Ottawa, ON: Canadian Centre for Policy Alternatives National Office. Retrieved August 9, 2011, from www.policyalternatives.ca/publications/reports/problem-poverty-post-recession

Yarema, M. (2010, October 27). *CWP ED Rob Rainer gives speech on our human rights.* Canada Without Poverty. Ottawa, ON: Canada Without Poverty and the CWP Advocacy Network. Retrieved November 1, 2010, from www.cwp-csp.ca/Blog/832

Who We Are and Who Others Say We Are: Gender and Sexuality

LEARNING OBJECTIVES AND OUTCOMES

After completing this chapter, students should be able to do the following:

LO¹ Identify the ways in which master statuses and the perceptions of others affect our individual identities.

LO² Describe the elite discourses that equate sex, gender, and sexuality.

LO³ Explain the ways in which sex, gender, and sexuality are socially constructed.

LO⁴ Discuss the different educational experiences of males and females, both in childhood and in post-secondary studies.

LO⁵ Describe the occupational sex segregation within the labour force.

LO⁶ Discuss the ways that economic experiences are gendered, and what those experiences can be attributed to.

LO⁷ Identify the gendered nature of family life, for both children and adults.

LO⁸ Outline the various sociological theories that address gender.

I know you are, but what am I?

(Paul Reubens)[1]

LO[1] IDENTIFYING OURSELVES AND IDENTIFYING OTHERS

The quotation above was a frequently used phrase by a 1980s children's television and film character, Pee-Wee Herman. He would use it as a child-like retort when another character called him an unpleasant name; it may even be a phrase that brings back schoolyard memories of your own childhood. But the phrase also reveals a more basic aspect of social life—the fact that we are in a constant process both of identifying ourselves and being identified by others. Countless characteristics are integrated into this process, ranging from physical attributes (e.g., blond-haired, blue-eyed) and abilities (e.g., visual-spatial, athletic) to likes/dislikes (e.g., rock versus country music), preferences (e.g., vegetarian), and group affiliations (e.g., full-time student, chess club). When integrated into your own sense of self, those traits fall along a **personal–social identity continuum** (Tajfel & Turner, 1986). The personal–social identity continuum refers to the range of traits you possess that emphasize the manner in which you see yourself as a unique individual on one end and those which underscore your membership in a group on the other end. Precisely which traits stand out the most to you at any given time can vary across contexts. "Lousy dancer" may become more dominant when you are at a wedding, while "father" predominates when you are attending a parent–teacher interview at a school. Identities are always in flux as we change throughout our lives—developing new interests and abandoning some old ones, getting a new job, having children, aging, and accumulating life experience that influences our view of the world and ourselves. Some aspects of identity remain relatively stable, while other aspects are more fluid.

Among the myriad characteristics that contribute to our individual sense of self, some constitute *master statuses*, so fundamental to who we are that they shape almost every aspect of our lives and take precedence over other characteristics. Sex and gender (addressed in this chapter), as well as race and ethnicity (addressed in the next chapter), are some of these characteristics; you may consider them to be essential to your identity, but even if you don't, they are still central to how *others* categorize you and they affect your life in a multitude of ways. And even if the way that others identify you corresponds to the way you identify yourself, there can still be divergent views on the **auxiliary traits** that are presumed to accompany that master status. Auxiliary traits refer to other characteristics that a person associates with a particular master status. For example, you might associate "parenthood" with qualities such as nurturance and patience; in contrast, someone else might associate that same master

Personal–social identity continuum:
The range of traits you possess that emphasize the manner in which you see yourself as a unique individual on one end and those which underscore your membership in a group on the other end.

Auxiliary traits:
Characteristics that are presumed to accompany a specific master status.

status with discipline and authority. Similarly, the interests, skills, and abilities that one person associates with being female might be quite different from those that another person associates with being female.

SOCIOLOGY IN THEORY

Inevitably, children get into disagreements with their peers that sometimes culminate in an exchange of insults such as name calling. When this happens, parents and teachers often tell children that what others think of them shouldn't matter—that "sticks and stones may break my bones, but names will never hurt me." In fact, what others think of you *does* matter, and it can have significant implications. Interactionist theories explain the processes by which the way that others identify and label us affects our self-perception.

An important concept within the interactionist perspective is that of the **looking-glass self**. The looking-glass self refers to the sense of ourselves that we develop based on our perceptions of how others view us. Charles Horton Cooley (1864–1929) proposed that people in our lives serve as a "looking glass" (an historical term for a mirror) (Cooley, 1902). When we interact with them, we "see" ourselves reflected back. There are three core components to the looking-glass self (Yeung & Martin, 2003). First, we imagine how we appear to others. Second, we imagine how they judge that appearance. Third, we incorporate the perceived judgments of others into our own sense of self.

For instance, if we think that our parents consider us to be intelligent, capable, and attractive, we will come to see ourselves in the same way; similarly, if we think they perceive us as incompetent and unattractive, we begin to see ourselves that way as well. Note that it is the perceived judgment of others that is significant. Hence, we may *incorrectly* believe that our parents view us as incompetent and this will still become incorporated into our looking-glass self. In addition, when others identify us on the basis of master statuses such as sex or ethnicity, which they then associate with certain auxiliary traits, our own identities may also be affected by the assumed accompanying auxiliary traits. For example, if parents continuously act in an overly protective manner toward a daughter who is "vulnerable" and "needs protection," that daughter may come to view herself as vulnerable and in need of protection.

"Of course you're big and clumsy but don't forget one thing: you're supposed to be big and clumsy."

Source: Farris, Joseph, jfa1521, Cartoonstock.com

However, the influence of others on our personal and group identity is neither direct nor certain. First, the extent of influence may depend upon how important those others are to us. The perceptions of significant others (e.g., family members) may have more of an impact than those of more distant people in our lives (e.g., coworkers) or than the generalized other (Cooley, 1902; Yeung & Martin, 2003; Gamble & Yu, 2008). Second, there are individual differences in the extent to which the looking-glass self is utilized (Hartner, 1999; Hartner & Whitesell, 2003). That is, some people have more of a *looking-glass self-orientation (LGSO)*, while others have more of a "core" self orientation. A person with more of a LGSO is more dependent on others' perceptions for his or her sense of self. A stronger looking-glass self-orientation is associated with less stability in one's identity, and a greater likelihood of problematic symptoms such as depression or anxiety (Gamble & Yu, 2008). Maruna and colleagues (2004) paint a picture of even more significant potential implications of the looking-glass self, pointing to the subtle (and sometimes not-so-subtle) ways that drug counsellors may communicate a lack of confidence in convicted drug users' ability to really change—which may then affect the likelihood of **recidivism** (i.e., reoffending). Although there may be individual variations in the implications of the looking-glass self, there is no doubt that the way

Looking-glass self:
The sense of ourselves that we develop based on our perceptions of how others view us.

Recidivism: Committing further crimes after having been convicted of a crime.

in which at least *some* other people see you has an impact on how you, in turn, see yourself.

Your own identity, along with the ways that others categorize or label you, has a wide range of implications, extending from the micro level to the macro level—from individual thoughts and feelings, to the nature and content of social interactions, to the structure and functioning of society's institutions. Elite discourses play a significant role in identity and its implications.

LO^2 ELITE DISCOURSES

You may recall the concept of *elite discourses* from Chapter 1. Poststructuralist Michel Foucault (1980) proposed that there are many different ways of understanding any subject or social phenomenon. Those understandings are located in varying positions within the structure of power in society. When a particular understanding is upheld by people and institutions in positions of authority, that understanding of the phenomenon becomes an elite discourse, and becomes widely accepted. Through socialization, elite discourses become so deeply engrained that many people have difficulty even imagining any alternative possibilities. The power of elite discourses is especially evident when we consider sex, gender, and sexuality.

SEX, GENDER, AND SEXUALITY

Being born female or male affects every facet of people's lives. But "female" and "male" do not refer to *gender*, rather they point to *sex*; this distinction is one between social forces and biological forces. **Sex** describes biology, which in the Euro-Canadian culture has traditionally been equated with the **dualism** (i.e., a contrast between two opposing categories) of female/male; we frequently hear references to the notion of the "opposite sex." Sex is determined at the moment of conception, and is then followed by the development of primary and secondary sex characteristics, including internal reproductive organs, external genitalia, and additional physical characteristics.

Gender describes the social world, the "expected and actual thoughts, feelings, and behaviours" (Nelson, 2010, p. 2) that are associated with a particular sex, within a certain culture, at a given point in history. Gender is socially and culturally determined through socialization processes within the context of broader cultural norms. Because sex is based upon a dualism, gender is often presumed to follow; the thoughts, feelings, and behaviours associated with being female are labelled **femininity**, while those associated with being male are labelled **masculinity**.

Masculinity and femininity are often described in terms of certain personality traits or tendencies. Elite discourses of gender in Canadian society equate masculinity with aggression, independence, dominance, athleticism, and self-reliance, and femininity with kindness, shyness, sensitivity, loyalty, and compassion (Bem, 1974). As you

Sex: Biological characteristics that include sex chromosomes, primary sex characteristics, and secondary sex characteristics.

Dualism: A contrast between two opposing categories.

Gender: The expected and actual thoughts, feelings, and behaviours associated with a particular sex, within a certain culture, at a given point in history.

Femininity: The thoughts, feelings, and behaviours associated with being female.

Masculinity: The thoughts, feelings, and behaviours associated with being male.

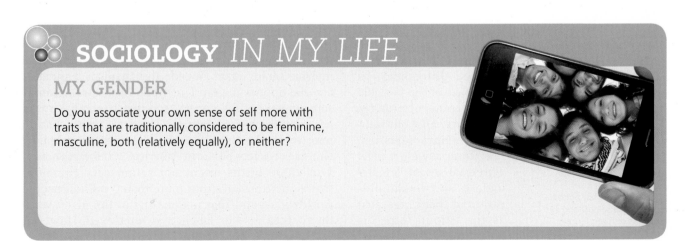

SOCIOLOGY *IN MY LIFE*

MY GENDER

Do you associate your own sense of self more with traits that are traditionally considered to be feminine, masculine, both (relatively equally), or neither?

progress through your education, you will often hear these traits being referred to as "traditional" masculinity and femininity.

The dualisms of sex and gender are also related to yet another dualism, this one in the realm of sexuality. Attraction to members of the "opposite sex" is referred to as **heterosexuality**, while attraction to members of the "same sex" is considered **homosexuality**. Both of these terms are dependent upon the elite discourse of sex that recognizes only two "legitimate" sexes—female and male. The belief that sex can (or should) be equated with gender, and then with sexuality has become an elite discourse, to the extent that it is difficult for many people to even imagine any other way of thinking about the issue or organizing their lives (see Figure 7.1).

TIME TO REVIEW

- What is the *personal–social identity continuum*, and how do master statuses and auxiliary traits fit into it?
- How do other people influence our identities according to interactionist theorists? Do others influence everyone equally?
- What are the dualisms that constitute the elite discourses of sex, gender, and sexuality?

LO³ MOVING OUTSIDE ELITE DISCOURSES

In fact, there are other possible ways of thinking about these concepts. Even a concept that initially appears to be as straightforward as sex is far more complex than we first perceive it to be. Although the elite discourses of sex reflect the dualism of male/female, it is more accurate to speak of a *sex spectrum*, similar to a colour spectrum (Intersex Society of North America, 2008a). Physical sex differences, as well as all of the possible combinations of primary, secondary, and chromosomal characteristics, fall along a wide range. The dualism of female/male is an oversimplification of that range, just as the colour "blue" is an oversimplification of

Heterosexuality: Sexual attraction to members of the "opposite sex."

Homosexuality: Sexual attraction to members of the "same sex."

Intersexed: A person whose physical sex characteristics fall outside the boundaries of the dualism of male/female.

FIGURE 7.1
Elite Discourses of Sex, Gender, and Sexuality

a portion of the colour spectrum. In certain circumstances, such as when we are choosing a paint colour for our walls, we will speak with greater precision—we want a "muted greyish blue" rather than a "tropical turquoise blue." Within the context of sex, there are also instances that draw attention to the nature of the spectrum. For example, an individual may have the external genitalia of a female but the internal reproductive organs of a male, ambiguous external sex organs, or a chromosomal variation of XXY (and the list could go on). When a person's sex characteristics do not neatly fit into the dualism of male/female, that person may be labelled **intersexed**.

How many people do not neatly fit into the dualisms of female/male? Because sex falls along a spectrum, this is a complex question to answer. Some individuals may be labelled as intersexed at birth because of external genitalia. However, other people may not be categorized as such until well into adulthood, such as when they face difficulties in having children. And some people live their entire lives without ever knowing that some aspect of their internal biology falls outside that dualism. Estimates are that approximately 1 in 1,666 births are chromosomally neither XX nor XY, and that 1 in 2,000 births have "ambiguous genitalia" and are immediately referred to the "gender identity teams" in hospitals (Intersex Society of North America, 2008b). Although 1 in 2,000 births might not sound very common, that alone translates into more than 3 million people worldwide—and that is only one of the many ways that people may be labelled as intersexed. However, there is some disagreement among medical doctors

SOCIOLOGY *ONLINE*

ADVOCACY FOR INTERSEXED PERSONS

The Intersex Society of North America (ISNA) was an advocacy group formed in 1993 for individuals with intersex conditions (and their families). The organization's mandate was to "end shame, stigma, and unnecessary genital surgeries" for people considered to be intersexed. Instead, ISNA recommended an ongoing, transparent consultative process among intersexed individuals, families, and health-care professionals, to enable more informed decision making to enhance health and well-being. ISNA ceased operations in 2008 and has placed its support behind a new organization, the Accord Alliance. However, ISNA's website remains active as an important historical document, and it includes a variety of informational resources and videos.

www.isna.org
www.accordalliance.org

about precisely which characteristics should result in that label. Just as the dualism of male/female is a social construction, so is the label of intersexed. As the Intersex Society of North America (2008a) points out, ". . . nature doesn't decide where the category of 'male' ends and the category of 'intersex' begins, or where the category of 'intersex' ends and the category of 'female' begins. Humans decide" (para. 4).

When children are labelled as intersexed, parents face pressure from doctors (among others) to choose whether they want their child to be raised as a male or a female, and then in some cases, surgery is enacted to fit that decision; the elite discourse of the medical community claims that intersexing is a problem that must be fixed, despite the fact that intersexing is frequently not associated with any kind of physical health problem. In fact, there is more evidence to suggest that early genital surgery performed over the last 50 years has resulted in more psychological and sexual problems than it has resolved (Koyama & Weasel, 2003). Thus, although sex is a biological reality, the recognition of two, and only two, "legitimate" sexes is a *social construction*—it emerges from social processes, rather than just biology.

The manner in which gender is socially constructed is even more apparent. There is greater gender variation within sexes than there is between sexes, and the idea that females are "naturally" feminine while males are "naturally" masculine has long been refuted by cross-cultural research. There are cultures where women are aggressive and even violent, where men are the passive nurturers, and where both men and women are expected to embody the same traits. Furthermore, many cultures have recognized multiple sex-gender combinations. Between 100 and 150 Aboriginal cultures in North America have recognized multiple sex-gender combinations in biological males, and 27–75 have recognized multiple combinations in biological females (Nanda, 2000). For example, European explorers used the term *berdache* to refer to (most often) males in Aboriginal cultures who were given the social status of women, and who assumed women's roles; within their communities, these persons were associated with considerable spiritual power, and were perceived as a benefit to the community (Nanda, 2000). The term *berdache* is derived from a French word (*bardache*), which, in a loose translation, refers to male prostitutes; because of the term's derogatory origins, in contemporary academia there is a movement to halt the use of this word and replace it with the term "Two-Spirited" (Roscoe, 1998).

Sociohistorical research points to the socially constructed nature of gender as well. For instance, it was only with industrialization that the female role came to be that of the nurturing parent and homemaker, the creator of a *haven in a heartless world* (Lasch, 1977). A series of pieces of employment legislation removed children and women from workplaces, making the "private" world of families and the "public" world of paid employment increasingly separate in an urban, industrializing society. Men came to be primarily associated with the public sphere, while women and children were primarily associated with the private sphere. Social concerns about the perceived dangers of an industrialized world were growing. Because men spent most of their day in the public sphere, as workers, they were considered to be particularly vulnerable to those perceived dangers. Thus, it was important that when they returned home in the evening they entered an environment that would recharge their physical health, psychological well-being, and moral strength, so they could withstand the temptations of the world once again when they walked out of their homes the next morning. And because women were largely relegated to the home, femininity came to be associated with qualities that would enable the creation of this "haven." Women were to be devoted nurturers who ensured that every aspect of the home—from interactions among family members, to the decor of the rooms, to the types of meals that were prepared—would contribute to such an environment. Mass media and popular culture told them exactly how to achieve this goal; a plethora of cookbooks, housekeeping manuals, guidebooks for women, and popular women's magazines were released, contributing to the emergence of what was known as the *cult of domesticity*. However, this industrialized vision of the ideal female homemaker applied only to the lives of middle-class women; working-class women continued to be primarily workers and income earners for many decades to come. In fact, working-class women were often the ones enabling middle-class women to transform their homes into havens, by working as domestic servants (e.g., maids, nannies, cooks), taking in laundry, and more. Although in contemporary society, we associate having servants with the wealthy, during the period of industrialization, most middle-class families were easily able to afford one or more domestic servants. An image of the cult of domesticity is reflected in Figure 7.2, a document that has made its rounds on the Internet, and can even be found on Wikipedia; the magazine that it refers to does not actually exist,

Hypermasculinity:
Traditional masculinity in an extreme and exaggerated form.

FIGURE 7.2
The Good Wife's Guide

Housekeeping Monthly 13 May 1955

The good wife's guide

- Have dinner ready. Plan ahead, even the night before, to have a delicious meal ready, on time for his return. This is a way of letting him know that you have been thinking about him and are concerned about his needs. Most men are hungry when they come home and the prospect of a good meal (especially his favourite dish) is a part of the warm welcome needed.

- Prepare yourself. Take 15 minutes to rest so you'll be refreshed when he arrives. Touch up your make-up, put a ribbon in your hair and be fresh-looking. He has just been with a lot of work-weary people.

- Be a little gay and a little more interesting for him. His boring day may need a lift and one of your duties is to provide it.

- Clear away the clutter. Make one last trip through the main part of the house just before your husband arrives.

Housekeeping Monthly 13 May 1955

- Gather up schoolbooks, toys, paper etc and then run a dustcloth over the tables.

- Over the cooler months of the year you should prepare and light a fire for him to unwind by. You husband will feel he has reached a haven of rest and order, and it will give you a lift too. After all, catering for his comfort will provide you with immense personal satisfaction.

- Prepare the children. Take a few minutes to wash the children's hands and faces (if they are small), comb their hair and, if necessary, change their clothes. They are little treasures and he would like to see them playing the part. Minimise all noise. At the time of his arrival, eliminate all noise of the washer, dryer or vacuum. Try to encourage the children to be quiet.

- Be happy to see him.

- Greet him with a warm smile and show sincerity in your desire to please him.

- Listen to him. You may have a dozen important things to tell him but the moment of his arrival is not the time. Let him talk first – remember his topics of conversation are more important than yours.

- Make the evening his. Never complain if he comes home late or goes out to dinner, or other places of entertainment without you. Instead, try to understand his world of strain and pressure and his very real need to be at home and relax.

- Your goal: Try to make sure your home is a place of peace, order and tranquillity where your husband can renew himself in body and spirit.

- Don't greet him with complaints and problems.

- Don't complain if he's late home for dinner or even if he stays out all night. Count this as minor compared to what he might have gone through that day.

- Make him comfortable. Have him lean back in a comfortable chair or have him lie down in the bedroom. Have a cool or warm drink ready for him.

- Arrange his pillow and offer to take off his shoes. Speak in a low, soothing and pleasant voice.

- Don't ask him questions about his actions or question his judgment or integrity. Remember, he is the master of the house and as such will always exercise his will with fairness and truthfulness. You have no right to question him.

- A good wife always knows her place.

Source: Image Courtesy of The Advertising Archives

SOCIOLOGY ON SCREEN

HYPERMASCULINITY IN THE MEDIA

The "traditional" masculinity described on the next page is associated with many of the changes that occurred during the process of industrialization. The documentary *Tough Guise* (featuring anti-violence educator Jackson Katz) reveals that during the course of the 20th century, although "alternative" masculinities became more prevalent, at the same time, the "traditional" masculinity became even more extreme—what may be called **hypermasculinity**. Arguing that the media has become "the single greatest pedagogical force of our time," Katz shows us how media images of men have changed. He shows us clips from Hollywood "action" films from the 1950s through the 1990s; during this time, the main characters' guns became much larger, and the characters came to hold those guns in much more aggressive-looking postures. Highlighting the world of children in particular, Katz also analyzes the ways that boys' action figures have

become much more muscular, to the point of being hypermuscular; the clearest demonstration of this is a side-by-side comparison of the Luke Skywalker action figure being sold when the first *Star Wars* film was released in 1977, with the Luke Skywalker figure being sold when the original films were re-released, and a fourth film (*The Phantom Menace*) was released in the 1990s. The film also addresses the implications of such imagery for children and adults, in terms of how its pervasiveness contributes to our perceptions of what a "Real Man" is—and then affects the society we live in (e.g., parenting; violence; self-esteem). This documentary is available through the Media Education Foundation. It may be available through your library (in hard copy or via an online streaming licence); a full-length preview for personal use is also available on the organization's website (www.mediaed.org).

The emphasis on hypermasculinity that has developed over the last few decades is evident when we contrast action figures from the 1970s and the 1990s.

Source: D. Martin Myatt

Source: © Christian Bortz

and its author is unknown. Although it is written in an almost satirical form, former female students who grew up in the 1950s recall similar messages being conveyed in their Home Economics classes at the time. This was also the image reflected in popular television shows in the 1950s (e.g., *Father Knows Best*), an image that serves as a foundation for the *family decline perspective* (Chapter 4).

It was during the same era that the male role came to emphasize the characteristics we consider to represent "traditional" masculinity today (David & Brannon, 1976):

- *The Big Wheel*: Compete for success and achievement (economically and physically).
- *The Sturdy Oak*: Be stable, tough, and in control at all times.
- *Give 'em Hell*: Be dominant and aggressive.
- *No Sissy Stuff*: Avoid anything associated with femininity, such as emotions (other than anger) or sexual attraction to men.

Despite some biological foundations to sexuality, we can also analyze the ways that sexuality is socially constructed. Similar sexual desires and acts may exist throughout the world, but the meaning that is attributed to those desires/acts, and the manner in which they are treated within society, emerge from social processes. Discourses that are based on the heterosexual/homosexual dualism are being replaced by a greater recognition of the spectrum of sexuality, such as the recognition of **bisexuality** (i.e., attraction to both males and females) as well. Thus, the concepts that we use to define and describe sexuality have undergone change over time. If we look across cultures, we see further evidence of this point. For instance, in the language of the Sambian culture (in New Guinea), words that categorize people as heterosexual, homosexual, or bisexual don't even exist; instead, Sambian culture utilizes concepts that refer to different times in the life cycle, when different types of sexual behaviours are considered appropriate or inappropriate (Herdt, 1984).

The socially constructed nature of sexuality also becomes apparent when exploring the distinctions that exist among different aspects of sexuality, such as desires, behaviours, and identities. Simon and Gagnon (1970) were among the first to elaborate upon the distinct components that comprise "sexuality." They pointed out that each of

us has our own **sexual script**—the framework that we use to understand our own sexuality, and that guides us in our sexual lives. Our sexual scripts consist of three distinctive parts, which may or may not correspond with each other (see Figure 7.3). *Intrapsychic scripts* are the private world of our fantasies and desires, not all of which you will necessarily act upon in life. *Interpersonal scripts* emerge from our interactions with others—what we have learned from particular people in our lives (e.g., past partners) about appropriate or inappropriate sexuality. *Cultural scenarios* reflect the larger cultural norms surrounding sexuality. At times, the three components of our sexual scripts may correspond quite nicely. You may have certain sexual desires, have enacted those desires in past relationships with positive results, and know that cultural norms define these desires and activities as acceptable. But in other cases, social norms, what we have learned from our relationships, and/or our personal desires may conflict. In a past relationship you may have learned that a certain desire is better left to the realm of fantasy rather than put into action. Through socialization, you may have learned that cultural norms define that desire as unacceptable. Or even though cultural norms may support that desire, you know that your family members, friends, or intimate partner may disapprove. Alternatively, perhaps you have denied your own desires and instead engaged in certain sexual behaviours so as to avoid being ostracized by your family or dumped by the person you are dating.

Even sexual behaviours and sexual identities don't always correspond. Research consistently finds that a larger proportion of people say they have had a same-sex sexual experience than identify themselves as gay,

Bisexuality: Sexual attraction to both males and females.

Sexual script: The framework that we use to understand our own sexuality and that guides our sexual lives.

FIGURE 7.3
Sexual Scripts

SOCIOLOGY *IN MY COMMUNITY*

THE "IT GETS BETTER" CAMPAIGN

Individuals who fall outside the elite discourses governing sex, gender, and sexuality frequently face significant stigmatization. The situation for lesbian, gay, bisexual, and **transgendered** (LGBT) youth is particularly difficult. LGBT youth hear anti-gay slurs an average of 26 times a day, and 26 percent are forced to leave home. They are often the victims of violent bullying, which can contribute to higher suicide rates; 30 percent of youth suicides are among LGBT youth (PFLAG, 2009). In 2010, there were a number of cases of suicide as a result of such life-long bullying that were highlighted in the media. In response, an online movement ("It Gets Better") began on YouTube,

featuring people who had these types of difficult experiences themselves while growing up, as well as those who did not. Thousands of people—from celebrities such as Neil Patrick Harris to everyday people from all walks of life—contributed their messages to youth, encouraging them to be confident and find the various supports that are out there to help them create the lives that they dream of for themselves. Critics of the campaign have suggested that life is more likely to "get better" for LGBT people who are white and middle class. Visible minorities and economically marginalized individuals frequently face additional challenges that serve as obstacles to life "getting better."

---

lesbian, or bisexual. For instance, although 15 percent of men ages 50–59 have had a sexual experience with another man at some point in their lives, only 8 percent identify themselves as gay or bisexual (Herbenick et al., 2010).

Elite discourses of sex, gender, and sexuality have all traditionally been based on dualisms—male/female; masculine/feminine; heterosexual/homosexual—and those dualisms have been equated with each other, such that to be female is presumed to be both feminine and sexually attracted to men only; similarly, to be male is presumed to be masculine and sexually attracted to women only. In some ways, we might say that these dualisms are not "real." However, they are most certainly real in their consequences. Being identified as male or female affects virtually every aspect of our lives.

TIME TO REVIEW

- In what ways is the recognition of only two sexes a social construction?
- How does knowledge of diverse cultures and of Canadian history demonstrate the socially constructed nature of gender?
- What constitutes femininity, masculinity, and hypermasculinity?
- In what ways does knowledge of Sambian society and of sexual scripts demonstrate the socially constructed nature of sexuality?

Transgendered:
Individuals who identify themselves with another sex, and seek to live their lives on that basis.

SOCIOLOGY *IN MY LIFE*

IMAGINING MY LIFE DIFFERENTLY

Imagine that tomorrow morning you woke up as a member of another sex. How would your life be different? Take five minutes to make a list of the various ways that you think your life would change.

GENDER: THE CONSEQUENCES OF HAVING BEEN BORN FEMALE OR MALE

How would your life be different if you were another sex? This is a question that David and Myra Sadker (Sadker & Sadker, 1994; Sadker, Sadker & Zittleman, 2009) asked thousands of students over several decades of research. It is also a question that one of your textbook authors has asked students in her university classes since the early 1990s. The answers to this question are revealing. They highlight the many ways that our everyday lives are structured upon the basis of biological sex; the answers also underscore the continued presence of the traditional elite discourses that equate sex, gender, and sexuality.

The extent to which children and adolescents are able to recognize the implications of gender might be surprising to some people. Many girls found good things to say about the possibility of being male: getting a better job; earning more money; feeling more secure; being treated with more respect; being less worried about what people thought. But in the end, most girls said that although it might be interesting to be a boy for awhile, they would prefer to be a girl. In contrast, almost all of the boys saw nothing but bad things about the possibility of being female: PMS; having to do all the cooking; having to worry about their hair; being a bad athlete; having less freedom; dieting; being weaker; being smaller; getting no respect; experiencing sexual harassment. One boy says, "I couldn't stand it if people messed with me that way they do with girls" (Sadker, Sadker & Zittleman, 2009, pp. 35/88). And 15 percent of boys went to a seemingly ridiculous extreme, indicating that if they woke up as girls, suicide would be the only answer. Both boys *and* girls had to be prodded to come up with a list of advantages to being a girl: not having to pay for dates; shopping; talking on the phone; and looking gorgeous (Sadker, Sadker & Zittleman, 2009).

The views of the university students in your author's classrooms are more balanced than those of the younger children or adolescents, in that they address both advantages and disadvantages to the possibility of being members of another sex. Based on the most frequent responses given, students perceive women as being at a disadvantage in terms of employment, income, freedom/safety, and respect—largely, the ways that they are treated by other people or located within the social structure. They perceive men as being at a disadvantage in terms of the gendered expectations that are placed upon them—pressures to earn a lot of money, ask someone for a date, "step-up" to pay on the date, and be "tough" all the time.

When the responses of children, adolescents, and young adults are brought together, we can see that even from a young age, people believe that the implications of simply having been born a particular sex extend through all facets of life. Sociological research supports that assumption. Gendered norms result in (1) different educational experiences, (2) different occupational experiences, (3) different economic experiences, and (4) different family experiences.

LO^4 DIFFERENT EDUCATIONAL EXPERIENCES

Children spend much of their time in the classroom. They are at school for approximately seven hours per day, five days per week during the school year—a total of 35 hours per week, equivalent to a full-time job. In fact, they spend more time interacting with teachers and peers at school than they do with parents at home; according to Statistics Canada, parents spend 3.4 hours per day interacting with family members, including children (Turcotte, 2007). Consequently, it is important to explore children's educational experiences, and the gender socialization that is occurring in their classrooms, in some detail.

The different educational experiences of females and males begin within the classrooms of young children. In addition to their interviews with children and adolescents about gender, David and Myra Sadker (along with Karen Zittleman), have spent decades observing classrooms. They have found that although boys and girls are sitting in the same classroom, they are receiving very different educations. Because of the pragmatic demands of the classroom, in combination with gender stereotypes (i.e., overgeneralizations about a group that are often based on faulty assumptions), even the very best teachers may inadvertently treat boys and girls differently. Findings indicate that although blatant examples of biased classroom practices have declined, more subtle differences in the way that male and female students are treated continue (Sadker, Sadker & Zittleman, 2009). Through these understated practices, boys are drawn to the forefront of the classroom (whether they like it or not), while girls slip quietly into the background. Boys are encouraged to figure out how to solve problems on their own, while girls have their problems solved for them (Sadker, Sadker & Zittleman, 2009).

For instance, boys are louder and more active in the classroom, out-talking girls by a three-to-one margin

(Sadker, Sadker & Zittleman, 2009). Thus, maintaining social order in the classroom means controlling the boys—by interacting with them more, speaking to them more, asking them more questions, and disciplining them more often relative to the girls. And while so much attention is being directed to boys, the girls quietly settle in and do their work. When teachers' attention is drawn to the fact that they spend more time interacting with the boys in the classroom (e.g., when teachers watch video footage of the class), their responses emphasize that boys "need" more attention (because they are perceived as being weaker in some subjects) and "demand" more attention (such as by misbehaving and speaking out of turn). But it isn't all boys who receive this attention. It is the boys who exhibit more traditional forms of masculinity—active, loud, and assertive. Those boys who are quieter or who exhibit more traditionally feminine qualities also fade into the background with the girls; they also frequently face harassment from their peers for their nontraditional behaviour.

What type of attention is it that male and female students receive? When teachers are providing feedback on student work, there are four types of possible comments: (a) *praise*, whereby the teacher highlights a specific aspect of the work that has been done well; (b) *remediation*, when the teacher gives direction to a student that enables that student to solve a problem or correct an error; (c) *criticism*, which offers a strong critique about something that has been done wrong;

and (d) *acceptance*, only a brief acknowledgment (e.g., "Okay"). In evaluating more than 100 classrooms, Sadker and Sadker found that boys receive more of every type of response, but especially remediation, which many people would say is the form of feedback that best facilitates learning. When boys are having difficulty with a question on an assignment, teachers are more likely to encourage them to figure it out for themselves (e.g., "Think about what the third step is in solving this type of math problem"); in contrast, when girls are having problems with a question, teachers are more likely to take her pencil from her hand, and *show* her how to solve it. Of the four types of comments, girls most often receive a brief acknowledgement ("Okay"). When teachers are asked why they give girls brief acknowledgements so often, their responses reflect gender stereotypes; they indicate that they don't want to be too "tough" on a girl, or they don't want to hurt her feelings (Sadker, Sadker & Zittleman, 2009).

And yet, despite the greater attention that boys receive in school, it is girls who are more likely to excel. For example, girls achieve higher overall grades and get higher scores on standardized reading tests (Frenette & Zemen, 2007). Boys are more likely to be disciplined; both male and female students say that teachers often "pick on" the boys and punish them unfairly. Although boys are more vocal in the classroom, teachers' perceptions of their behaviour are often inaccurate; teachers perceive boys as being more hyper, aggressive, and inattentive, despite the fact that behavioural scores do not support those perceptions. Not surprisingly, the boys are more likely to be identified by their teachers as possibly having a learning disability, and they are more likely to be diagnosed with learning disabilities. Girls are also more likely to pursue a postsecondary education, and more likely to graduate from postsecondary studies. For instance, in 2007 61 percent of university graduates were female (Statistics Canada, 2010a).

Looking at what goes on in the classroom, it appears that schools are shortchanging girls, yet

Through understated and unintended practices in the classroom, boys are frequently drawn to the forefront of attention, while girls fade quietly into the background.

Source: © Monashee Frantz/Alamy

when considering the gendered differences in student achievement it appears that it may be boys who are being shortchanged. Both concerns have received widespread media attention. Concerns about girls were highlighted throughout the 1990s, while the concerns about boys are currently receiving the most attention in the present day; in October 2010 *The Globe and Mail* included a week-long series on the perceived "crisis" in male education (e.g., Abraham, 2010). Sadker, Sadker, and Zittleman (2009) steer us away from this either/or mentality:

> It is time we understood that gender bias and stereotypes are persistent problems for both males and females. It is not one or the other gender that is the problem; gender bias is the problem. (p. 7)

What is it that boys and girls are ultimately learning in the classroom? Within the official curriculum, both are learning math, science, social studies, and other subjects. When it comes to the mastery of this material, it appears that female students are at an advantage. However, McMullin (2004) highlights the importance of looking beyond sex and gender when analyzing student academic achievement, pointing out that, in fact, the socioeconomic status of a child is a far more significant predictor of academic success than is whether that child is male or female. But in addition to the official curriculum of the school's subjects, students are also exposed to a *hidden curriculum*, whereby they learn what being a male or female means in our society. By being drawn to the forefront of classroom life and encouraged to solve their own problems, boys develop problem-solving skills and independence (traits that are of value outside of the classroom as well), and learn about the assertive competition that is part of the "boys' world." But there is a dark side to these lessons as well, because boys are also learning that no one is going to solve their problems for them, and they are on their own in this world; that they *must* be tough, strong, and independent all the time. Girls are learning passivity, silence, and dependence but at the same time, they also learn that they can rely on others when they are facing difficulties in life.

The gendering of education first appears with young children, but it is not limited to the lives of children and adolescents. Subtle differences in the treatment of male and female students continue in the postsecondary environment as well (Sadker, Sadker & Zittleman, 2009). Furthermore, the gendering of postsecondary studies is also evident in the areas of study that women and men pursue. Why do areas of study matter? At first glance, it might appear that areas of postsecondary study merely reflect people's different interests; thus, some people are more interested in art history while others prefer mathematics. But, remember, individual choices are affected by and embedded within larger social forces. When we dig beneath the surface of these apparent "interests" using our sociological imaginations, we see that these differential interests are gendered. Because gender is socially constructed, that means that so too are these interests. Women are overrepresented in programs in education, humanities, social sciences, and fine arts. Men are overrepresented in programs in mathematics, computer and information sciences, architecture, and engineering (Statistics Canada, 2010a). Although women predominate in college and university programs, men predominate in registered apprenticeship programs, where they comprise 89 percent of the student population (Statistics Canada, 2009). Yet despite these statistical trends, we have only to look at many famous male novelists (e.g., Mordecai Richler) and philosophers (e.g., Plato) to know that men can excel in the humanities. Similarly, we have only to look at women such as Roberta Bondar (a neurologist and the first female Canadian astronaut) and Rachel Zimmerman (a Canadian scientist who designed the Blissymbol Printer, which allows people with severe physical disabilities to communicate verbally) to know that women can excel in science and technology. In recent decades, we have seen some significant shifts in areas of postsecondary study, primarily in terms of women entering areas of study in which men have traditionally predominated (e.g., law, medicine, science). For example, although women were less than half of university graduates in the physical/life sciences and agriculture/conservation/natural resources in 1992, by 2007 they were the majority of graduates in those areas (Statistics Canada, 2010a). Not only are areas of postsecondary study gendered, but also there are important implications of those areas of study. First, certain areas of study are more directly "marketable," such that employment that is directly related to one's area of study may be more certain (e.g., an engineering degree compared to a degree in art history). Second, occupations related to some areas of study are more highly paid than others (Gomme, 2004).

TIME TO REVIEW

- How do children and university students say that their lives would be different if they woke up as members of another sex?

- In what ways are girls and boys treated differently in the classroom? What do they learn from the official curriculum and the hidden curriculum?

- How are postsecondary studies gendered?

LO⁵ DIFFERENT OCCUPATIONAL EXPERIENCES

Arising, in part, from different areas of postsecondary study are divergent occupational experiences. In the mid-20th century, the male breadwinner and female homemaker predominated. However, beginning in the 1960s, women began moving into the labour force on a large scale. Several forces contributed to this social change. Broader economic shifts resulted in inflation rising much more rapidly than people's wages. This meant that it was increasingly difficult for families to survive on only one income. In addition, what was known as the "second wave" of the women's movement emerged and gained strength. The "first wave" of the women's movement in the early 20th century focused on women obtaining the right to vote (which had been restricted to men only), and being legally declared "persons" (rather than as the property of their fathers and husbands). The second wave of the women's movement in the mid-20th century emphasized other aspects of "equality," such as occupational and economic equality. Thus, within this broader context of economic changes and the women's movement, a growing number of women became breadwinners as well. By 2009, 76 percent of Canadian women were participating in the labour force (an increase from only 48 percent of women in 1976); in contrast, 86 percent of men were labour force participants during that same year. Although the majority of women are in the labour force, a greater proportion of women than men are employed part-time (27 percent of women and 12 percent of men), which translates into lower pay and no benefits.

Men and women tend to be segregated into different types of occupations, although sales/service are leading areas of employment for both. Two-thirds of women are employed in the following areas (compared to 30 percent of men): teaching, nursing, clerical, and sales/service. Two-thirds of men are employed in the following areas (compared to 41 percent of women): trades, transport, and construction; management; natural science, engineering, and mathematics; and sales/service (Statistics Canada, 2007). Over the last few decades there has been a decline in occupational sex segregation, with a growing number of people choosing to enter nontraditional occupations. However, most of these shifts have been women entering male-dominated fields, rather than the reverse. In part, this is because occupations in male-dominated fields have tended to be higher paid and feature more independence and authority; thus, women entering those occupations have something to gain, while men entering female-dominated occupations would have something to lose (Furr, 2002).

But in some ways, women also have more freedom to enter nontraditional occupations than men do, in that the boundaries of gendered norms are somewhat more fluid for women than for men (Nelson, 2010). For instance, we would not consider it to be very unusual to see a little girl wearing jeans and climbing a tree, nor to make an appointment with a female doctor or lawyer. In contrast, we are much less likely to see a little boy wearing a dress and playing tea party, or to find a male employee at our children's day care. Men who stray into female-dominated realms often have their sexuality questioned or are even looked upon with suspicion. But although women have more freedom than men to enter nontraditional careers, they are less likely to rise to the top of their fields and hold positions of authority. Women are less likely to serve in management positions than men, and, if they are in management, are less likely to hold senior management positions (Statistics Canada, 2007). The segregation of men and women into diverse types of occupations and the differential likelihood of holding positions of authority, in part, accounts for yet another way in which one's life is affected by virtue of having been born female or male—different economic experiences.

LO⁶ DIFFERENT ECONOMIC EXPERIENCES

When looking at the gendering of economic experiences, what stands out the most is the ratio of female-to-male earnings. Ever since data was first collected on this issue in 1967, women's earnings have been only a fraction of men's earnings. In terms of hourly wages, the earnings differential is 84 percent—that is, for every dollar per hour that men earn, women earn 84 cents. However there are variations based on the type of employment held. For example, among unionized employees, the earnings differential is only 94 percent, compared to 78 percent among nonunionized employees (Statistics Canada, 2010b).

When focusing on annual salaries, the wage gap becomes even more pronounced. In 2008, among full-year, full-time workers, the average male salary was $62,600 compared to the average female salary of $44,700 (see Table 7.1, page 154). Although the earnings differential has declined over time, women are still earning less money than men—regardless of whether we look at full-time, part-time, permanent, temporary, unionized, or nonunionized work.

What accounts for this ongoing wage gap? In part, it emerges from sex segregation in areas of postsecondary study and subsequent career choice.

TABLE 7.1

Average Earnings by Sex and Work Pattern (Full-Time Workers)

Full-Year, Full-Time Workers			
Year	Women	Men	Earnings Ratio
	$ constant 2008		%
1999	38,900	56,900	68.4
2000	40,200	56,900	70.6
2001	40,600	58,100	69.9
2002	40,800	58,200	70.2
2003	40,700	57,900	70.2
2004	42,000	59,900	70.1
2005	41,800	59,400	70.5
2006	43,200	60,000	71.9
2007	44,100	61,700	71.4
2008	44,700	62,600	71.3

Source: Average Earnings by Sex and Work Pattern (Full-Time Workers), 2010, adapted from Statistics Canada Website, Summary Tables, http://www40.statcan.gc.ca/l01/cst01/labor01b-eng.htm

Male-dominated areas tend to be associated with higher wages. A greater proportion of women are employed in jobs that are lower paid and lower status (e.g., clerical, part-time, temporary). They are also less likely to enter supervisory and management positions, and particularly senior-level management positions, which receive greater remuneration. In addition, on average, women work two fewer hours per day in paid employment than men (Lindsay, 2008), and are more likely to have temporary absences from the labour force in response to childbirth and childrearing—mothers earn approximately 12 percent less than women without children (Zhang, 2009). However, educational choices and career patterns have been found to account for less than half of the earnings differential, which means much of the gap is unexplained, and open to alternative explanations (Statistics Canada, 1999; Frenette & Coulombe, 2007). Some explanations emphasize the devaluation of "women's work," whereby historically, the types of work that women were restricted to were less respected and thereby received lower remuneration. Furthermore, it was presumed that women's incomes were "peripheral" to family life; while men's income had to be sufficient to support a family, women's incomes were thought to be only for the little extras. The level of those early wages served as the foundation for subsequent wage increases over the decades, and consequently income differentials between men and women were maintained. Other explanations highlight discrimination within the labour force, where assumptions about the way that family obligations will affect women's job commitment and career patterns influence hiring and promotion practices (Boyd, 2004). And indeed, the different educational, occupational, and economic experiences of both women and men are intertwined with their family experiences.

TIME TO REVIEW

- Why did large numbers of women begin moving into the labour force starting in the 1960s?
- What is the nature of occupational sex segregation in contemporary society?
- What is the earnings differential or wage gap when comparing women and men, and why does it exist?

LO7 DIFFERENT FAMILY EXPERIENCES

The significance of biological sex, and subsequently gender, within families begins before people are even born. The question of whether the child will be a boy or a girl lies at the forefront of people's minds, and at birth, the sex of the child is the very first news that parents receive—in fact, a growing number of expectant parents find the sex of the child to be so important that they request that information while an ultrasound is being performed during pregnancy. Once a child is born, gendered perceptions and treatment begin almost immediately, setting the stage for the gendering that individuals will later experience educationally, occupationally, and economically. Two classic studies illustrate the primacy of gender during infancy. Within 24 hours of birth, parents of newborn girls describe them as "delicate" and "weak," while parents of boys refer to them as "strong" and "alert" (Rubin, Provenzano & Lurra, 1974) while objective measures of these newborns revealed no significant differences in weight, length, muscle tone, reflexes, or heart rate. In another study, infants were shown an unfamiliar toy, while adults observed the infants' reactions. Adults who were told that they were observing a boy described his reaction to the strange toy as "pleasure" or "excitement"; in contrast, those who were told they were observing a girl (although they were, in fact, observing the very same infant) identified her reaction as "fearful" (Condrey & Condrey, 1976).

Gendered perceptions of the characteristics of infants are then translated into behaviour, such that parents subsequently treat their sons and daughters differently. Goldberg and Lewis (1969) found that when mothers brought their six-month-old infants into a child observation lab, mothers of girls kept their infants much closer to them and spoke with them more often than did mothers of boys. When those mothers then brought their children in seven months later, the room was set up in an interesting way. A waist-high barrier divided the room *almost* completely in half; there was a small gap at one end of the barrier that allowed people to move from one side of the room to the other. The toddlers were placed on one side of the barrier, and the mothers on the other side of the barrier; the mothers then waved a toy enthusiastically in order to capture their children's attention. Being separated from both their mothers and the toy resulted in many of the toddlers becoming quite upset. When the little girls started to cry, mothers were likely to pick them up and bring them to the other side. In contrast, the little boys were encouraged to make their way to the gap at the end of the barrier and find their own way to the other side. Thus, just as Sadker, Sadker, and Zittleman (2009) found within the context of teacher behaviours in the classroom, girls were more likely to have their problems solved for them, while boys were encouraged to find the solution to the problem.

Almost 40 years later, research continues to find differential treatment of girls and boys by parents. Clearfield and Nelson (2006) found that mothers of daughters spoke to and interacted with their infants more overall than did mothers of sons. Even while the children were playing independently or exploring the room, mothers of daughters were more likely to talk to them and offer them comfort if they became upset. With three- and four-year-olds, fathers were found to stand closer to their daughters during a risk-taking activity (i.e., transversing a small obstacle course), and both mothers and fathers offered more help to daughters when they reached an especially difficult part of the obstacle course—once again, girls were "rescued," while boys were encouraged to do it themselves. Also similar to what was found in classrooms, more noise, aggression, and assertiveness is tolerated in boys than in girls; however, unlike in classrooms where quiet girls fade into the background, in families parents give boys more attention when they are being loud, and more attention to girls when they are being quiet and polite (Ross & Taylor, 1989).

Within the context of families, children are exposed to gender-stereotyped colours in their clothing and bedroom decor and they are provided with gender-stereotyped toys. The stricter boundaries that surround male gender roles in postsecondary education and occupation are found in families as well, whereby sons are more likely to be punished for gender-inappropriate behaviour, and parents interact with their children using a narrower range of toys with boys relative to girls (Nelson, 2010).

Gendered experiences within families begin with childhood socialization, but continue throughout adulthood as well. There are gendered differences in the household division of labour. Historically, the male breadwinner–female homemaker model meant that tasks associated with paid labour were the realm of men while those associated with unpaid family labour were the realm of women. However, as women moved

Does this room belong to a girl or a boy? You decide.

into the labour force in large numbers beginning in the 1960s, the household division of labour continued. Although women were employed in the labour force, and most often on a full-time basis, they continued to carry the bulk of the responsibility for tasks within the household division of labour. This led Arlie Hochschild (with Machung, 1989) to conceptualize the *second shift*, wherein women would put in a full day in the workplace and then come home and have to put in another "shift" of housework, childcare, and eldercare. In 1986, women were spending an average of 4.8 hours per day on various tasks associated with home and family life—meal preparation and cleanup, laundry, childcare, medical/dental appointments, housework, grocery shopping, etc. In contrast, men were spending 2.1 hours per day in this type of unpaid labour. At the same time, women were spending significantly fewer hours per day in the paid workplace. By 2005, the differences in participation in unpaid labour for women had declined slightly; women had reduced their participation to 4.3 hours per day, while men had increased theirs to 2.5 hours per day (Lindsay, 2008). Men and women now spend approximately equal amounts of time on the combination of paid and unpaid labour; it is just that men spend a greater proportion of that time in paid labour (i.e., two hours more per day), while women spend more of that time in unpaid labour (i.e., two hours more per day) (Lindsay, 2008). When children enter the family, men increase the amount of time they spend each day in both paid and unpaid work—that is, they spend more time at their jobs fulfilling the breadwinner norm, but also more time in housework and childcare. Conversely, with the addition of children, women do not increase their time spent in paid work, but they do increase their level of unpaid work (Marshall, 2006).

Even when men and women do contribute equally to the unpaid labour at home, the nature of their tasks remains gendered. Men are more likely to take care of outdoor tasks while women take on more of the indoor chores. Women are more likely to perform multiple tasks simultaneously (make dinner, do a load of laundry, and help the kids with homework), while men do one task at a time (make dinner *or* do laundry *or* help kids with homework). Men are more likely to be responsible for less regular tasks (e.g., mowing the lawn), women for more regular tasks (e.g., meal preparation). Women do proportionately more housework than childcare, and men more childcare than housework (Hochschild with Machung, 1989).

The gendered nature of family experiences in adulthood interacts with occupational and economic experiences. Because of family responsibilities, women are more likely to choose jobs with fewer hours and/or greater flexibility, both of which typically mean lower earnings (Zhang, 2009). Despite the fact that Canada's parental leave policy enables either parent (or both) to leave the labour force for a period of time following the birth or adoption of a child, women are much more likely to do so than men (and for longer periods of time). These interruptions impede career progress, which also contributes to lower earnings. However, men who do choose to leave the labour force for child-rearing face difficulties as well. They also experience interruptions in career progress that can contribute to lower earnings. In addition, they face other types of negative sanctions—they are looked down upon by their male peers, have their masculinity questioned, are treated as outcasts in organized parent–child activities (e.g., "mommy and me" groups) and are asked why they aren't economically "supporting" their families as they "should" be. Consequently, many men who are primary caregivers of children maintain some type of part-time work in order to maintain a socially acceptable masculine image (Doucet, 2004).

SUMMARY

Simply by virtue of having been born as a particular sex, our lives are affected in myriad ways, from very small and seemingly insignificant differences, such as the side that our shirts button on, to much larger, more profound inequalities such as higher or lower earnings. From the moment we are born (if not prior to that), our parents are likely to perceive and then to treat us in certain ways. When we enter the school system, that pattern continues, despite the best intentions of teachers. We develop, and are reinforced (or punished) for particular interests, and acquire some skills more than others. We are likely to pursue certain postsecondary paths, which then influence the occupations we pursue. If we embark upon heterosexually based families of procreation, having been born male or female contributes to distinctive roles within the family, associated with specific types of responsibilities; this then influences our career trajectories. The occupations that we pursue, in addition to our career trajectories and other "unexplained" phenomena (e.g., devaluation or discrimination), then affect our economic experiences. To some extent, the gendering of educational, occupational, economic, and family experiences has declined in recent years. However, social change is a gradual process: "fundamental societal shifts like these typically take place over an extended period

of time reflecting changes in behaviours of successive cohorts of young people" (McMullen, Gilmore & LePetit, 2010, para. 1). Why do gendered experiences continue to exist?

LO⁸ SOCIOLOGY IN THEORY

The earliest sociological theories—functionalism and conflict theories—addressed the nature of gendered experiences, primarily within the context of families.

In Chapter 4, you learned about Parsons' functionalist theory, which proposed that having women perform *expressive tasks* and men perform *instrumental tasks* helped to maintain cohesion in the family. You also learned about Engels' conflict theory, which claimed that conditions of capitalism maintained patriarchy and the subordination of women within families. Over time, other sociological perspectives came to address gender as well—interactionist, feminist, postmodern, and many others.

INTERACTIONIST THEORIES

Interactionist theories focus upon how we come to *understand* gender, and develop our own gender identities. Through our interactions with significant others, our subsequent development of a sense of the generalized other, and the power of the looking-glass self, we come to know that we are "female" or "male," and precisely what that means in our society. Through our childhood experiences in our families and our classrooms, we come to understand that males and females are supposed to act in certain ways, develop particular interests, enter specific types of occupations, and hold certain roles within families. On the basis of this knowledge, we then "do" gender in our own everyday lives (West & Zimmerman, 1987.

Erving Goffman (1979) has been credited with a classic analysis of gender differentiation from an interactionist perspective. He explored how gender differentiation is reproduced in social interactions through *gender displays*. Gender displays include everything from putting on makeup and selecting the clothes we will wear, to the positions in which we place our bodies, to our facial expressions. It even includes the "appropriate" use of separate public restrooms for men and women—interestingly enough, the restrooms in your authors' university department are private single-person restrooms (as they would be in your home), and yet people will still wait in line to use the "appropriate" restroom (men's or women's) instead of using the one that is currently unoccupied! People engage in *ritualized cultural performances* that are based on agreed-upon *codes* of gender—the rules governing gender displays. These codes of gender both rest upon and reinforce dualisms of sex, gender, and sexuality, as well as assumptions that these dualisms are biological in nature. They also serve to maintain male dominance and independence, and female passivity and subordination. Consequently, Goffman stated that it was important to draw attention to the nature of these hidden codes, so that individuals could make a conscious decision about whether to accept or reject them in their own gender displays.

FEMINIST THEORIES

As you recall from previous chapters, feminist theories are characterized by considerable diversity. However, they all emphasize the manner in which women are subordinated in society; some feminist theories also draw attention to the gender inequalities that are faced by men. Outside of that core shared assumption, there

What do the gender displays in this image tell us about sex, gender, and sexuality?

Source: AFP/Getty Images

are a variety of ways that feminist theories talk about gender (Nelson, 2010). For example, *liberal feminist theories* claim that inequalities that exist within education, occupation, economics, and families are the result of differential opportunities. By reducing forces that restrict opportunities (e.g., stereotyping, discrimination, certain policies, organizational practices), both women and men will be able to pursue life trajectories that fit their interests and skills as *individuals* rather than as *sexes*, and inequalities will be reduced. *Marxist feminists* tie the oppression of women to capitalism; overthrowing capitalism and eliminating private property would end their subordination and the different educational, occupational, economic, and family experiences that women and men currently have. *Cultural feminists* actually support dualistic assumptions about sex and gender, and posit that men and women *are* inherently different; women are peaceful, nurturing, and more in touch with nature, while men are more aggressive and competitive. Those qualities cannot change—what can change is that female abilities and values are given venues for expression, such as through woman-centred activities and organizations. Because cultural feminism reifies male/female difference, it is rarely used in the discipline of sociology. Other types of feminist theories (which are often referred to as *race/ethnicity/imperialism/post-colonial feminist theories*) argue that we can't speak of

SOCIOLOGY ON SCREEN

CODES OF GENDER

In the documentary *Codes of Gender*, writer and director Sut Jhally applies Goffman's work on gender displays to contemporary advertising. The codes of gender that Goffman found in advertising in the 1970s continued to be found in Jhally's analysis of 21st-century advertisements. These codes are not unique to advertising, but rather draw upon the same body of images that already exist in the culture at large. Some of the codes of gender are as follows:

- *The Feminine Touch:* Women trace their fingers along, gently hold, or caress objects (and people). In contrast, men's hands typically grasp, firmly hold, and manipulate.
- *The Ritualization of Subordination:* The position of women's bodies frequently signifies powerlessness. They are shown lying down on the floor or on beds, off-balance (such as while holding a shoe and teetering on one leg), or under the gaze of someone who is watching. Men's bodies are often positioned above women's bodies, and they are usually the watcher rather than the one being watched.
- *Licensed Withdrawal:* Women are portrayed as not paying attention or mentally drifting, or alternatively, displaying out-of-control emotions. In contrast, men are portrayed as being active, aware, and emotionally in control.

- *Infantilization:* Girls and adult women are presented as the same—similar clothes, hair styles, and postures. Women frequently embody a sexualized child-like quality, such as peeking out from behind an object, or holding a finger in their mouths. At the same time, girls are portrayed as mature and somewhat adult-like. In contrast, boyhood and manhood are presented as being distinctly different; men must leave boyhood behind in order to be considered masculine.

Jhally points out that there have been some changes since the time of Goffman's analysis. For example, we are more likely now to see women as assertive or even aggressive characters in films, and as elite athletes. However, even in those cases, traditional codes of gender may be present. Jhally points to the example of Danica Patrick, who is an Indy car racer but who has still been portrayed in numerous magazine spreads as sexualized and defenceless. This documentary is available through the Media Education Foundation. It may be available through your library (in hard copy or via an online streaming licence); a full-length preview for personal use is also available on the organization's website (www.mediaed.org).

"women" as a general category—that the educational, occupational, economic, and family experiences of women of different races, ethnic groups, and classes have very little in common with each other.

"Third-wave" feminist practice is intertwined with these last theories. You may recall that "first-wave" feminism emphasized citizenship and voting rights for women. "Second-wave" feminism drew attention to female equality and the right to personal fulfillment. "Third-wave" feminism is critical of earlier forms of feminism which, in their view, relegated lesbian, bisexual, and transgendered women, women of colour, working-class and poor women, and women of the developing world to the margins of the feminist movement. Third-wave feminism rejects the notion that all women can be grouped together, and instead recognizes the diversity of gendered

experiences based on race, ethnicity, class, sexuality, and various other social characteristics. At times, third-wave feminist practice is also intertwined with postmodern theories.

POSTMODERN THEORIES

Postmodern or poststructural theories question the very notion of gender. In the postmodern world, a gender "identity" is not possible. All that is possible are gender performances that are sometimes contradictory and constantly changing (Butler, 1990). These gender performances emerge from elite discourses that construct only certain forms of gender as possible.

How do we explain the different educational, occupational, economic, and family experiences of women and men? Sociological theorizing shows us that there is no single explanation for either the causes of these differences or their solutions. Functionalist theories emphasize the ways that traditional gender roles may actually be functional for individuals, their families, and society. Conflict theories focus on the forms that power can take, and how the manner in which power is exercised results in the subordination of women. Interactionist theories say that these different experiences emerge from the ways that we come to understand sex and gender, and what is acceptable or not acceptable, through our interactions with others. On the basis of this knowledge, we develop gender identities and "do" gender in our everyday lives. Diverse feminist theories explain these differential experiences in a variety of ways ranging from unequal opportunities, to the devaluation of the female "essence," to drawing attention to the different experiences of diverse groups of women. Postmodern theories deny the possibility of a gender identity, and question whether we can even speak of a cohesive category of "gender."

TIME TO REVIEW

- What do classic and contemporary studies tell us about the ways that parents perceive and treat their sons and daughters differently?

- In what ways do the family experiences of men and women differ in adulthood, in their families of procreation?

- How are family experiences intertwined with gendered educational, occupational, and economic experiences?

- How do functionalist, conflict, interactionist, feminist, and postmodern/poststructuralist theories address gender and gender inequality?

CHAPTER SUMMARY

LO1 Identify the ways in which master statuses and the perceptions of others affect our individual identities.

We are in a constant process of identifying ourselves, being identified by others, and identifying others. Master statuses may be essential to your identity, but even if they aren't they are still central to how others identify you. Through the looking-glass self, we imagine how we appear to others, imagine how they judge that appearance, and then incorporate those perceived judgments into our own sense of self.

LO2 Describe the elite discourses that equate sex, gender, and sexuality.

These elite discourses are based on dualisms: male/female; masculine/feminine; heterosexual/homosexual. These discourses also equate the three, in that to be male is presumed to be both masculine and attracted to women; similarly, to be female is presumed to be both feminine and attracted to men.

LO3 Explain the ways in which sex, gender, and sexuality are socially constructed.

When we question and resist the elite discourses, we see that sex, gender, and sexuality are socially constructed. There is greater variation within groups of men and women then there is between men and women. Cross-cultural research has clearly established that norms governing gender vary across cultures and over time. By exploring sexual scripts, we can see that sexuality is socially constructed as well. Even sex is socially constructed; rather than discrete categories of female/male, it is more accurate to speak of a sex spectrum.

LO4 Discuss the different educational experiences of males and females, both in childhood and in post-secondary studies.

Through subtle, and often unintended, behaviours within the classroom, boys are drawn to the forefront of the classroom and girls (as well as non-traditional boys) fade into the background. Boys learn independence and problem solving, while girls learn passivity and silence. Upon reaching postsecondary studies, areas of study become gender segregated; segregation has decreased to some extent in recent years, but more so for females entering traditionally male areas of study rather than the reverse.

LO⁵ Describe the occupational sex segregation within the labour force.

Educational segregation contributes to occupational segregation. Females tend to be overrepresented in lower-status, lower-paying, part-time, and temporary work.

LO⁶ Discuss the ways that economic experiences are gendered, and what those experiences can be attributed to.

Men continue to earn more money than women, although the magnitude of income differentials varies on the basis of a number of factors. Explanations include the consequences of educational and occupational segregation, a devaluation of women's work that has historical origins, and discrimination based on assumptions about women's family obligations.

LO⁷ Identify the gendered nature of family life, for both children and adults.

Boys and girls continue to be treated very differently in families, in terms of clothing, toys, room decor, and level of supervision. Among adults, although men and women now spend the same number of hours in the combination of paid and unpaid work, women spend more time in unpaid work and men spend more time in paid work. Even when men and women do contribute equally to the household division of labour, the nature of their tasks tends to be gendered.

LO⁸ Outline the various sociological theories that address gender.

Functionalist theories address the functional role of gender differentiated tasks. Conflict theories emphasize the role of power in creating patterns of subordination. Interactionist theories explore the ways in which we come to understand gender via our interactions with others. Diverse feminist theories explain gender differentiation in a variety of ways, ranging from unequal opportunities to an emphasis on the diverse experiences of women in different social groups (e.g., race, ethnicity, social class). Postmodern theories question the very idea of gender.

RECOMMENDED READINGS

1. To see the impact that standards of beauty have on various aspects of women's lives (from eating disorders to employment), see: Wolf, N. (1990). *The Beauty Myth: How Images of Beauty Are Used against Women.* New York: Chatto & Windus.
2. For a complex historical analysis of the interaction of sex, gender, sexuality, politics, popular culture, family, elite discourses, and more, refer to: Valverde, M. (1991). *The Age of Light, Soap, and Water: Moral Reform in English Canada, 1885–1925.* Toronto: University of Toronto Press.
3. For a review of all major topic areas related to gender, including family, work, education, media, and aging, see: Robinson, N. (2010). *Gender in Canada* (4th ed.). Toronto, ON: Pearson Education Canada.

FOR FURTHER REFLECTION

1. What are the implications of different economic experiences and different family experiences in adulthood? For instance, why does it matter if a woman earns less money than her husband? Why does it matter if he is spending two more hours per day in paid employment while she is spending two more hours per day in the unpaid labour associated with family life?

2. In what ways do the different types of theories that were presented either reflect dualisms of sex, gender, and sexuality, or challenge them?

3. Return to the part of the chapter where children and university students talk about how their lives would be different if they woke up as members of another sex. Were they right?

REFERENCES

Abraham, C. (2010, October 15). *Failing boys and the powder keg of sexual politics*. Retrieved October 16, 2010, from www.globeandmail.com

Boyd, M. (2004). Gender inequality: Economic and political aspects. In R. J. Brym (Ed.), *New Society* (pp. 214–243). Toronto: Nelson.

Bem, S. L. (1974). The measurement of psychological androgyny. *Journal of Consulting and Clinical Psychology, 42*, 155–162.

Butler, J. (1990). *Gender Trouble: Feminism and the Subversion of Identity*. New York: Routledge.

Clearfield, M. W., & Nelson, N. M. (2006). Sex differences in mothers' speech and play behavior with 6-, 9-, and 14-month-old infants. *Sex Roles, 54*(1–2), 127–137.

Condrey, J., & Condrey, S. (1976). Sex differences: A study of the eye of the beholder. *Child Development, 47*, 812–819.

Cooley, C. H. (1902). *Human Nature and the Social Order*. New York: Scribner.

David, D. S., & Brannon, R. (1976). *The Forty-nine Percent Majority: The Male Sex Role*. Reading, MA: Addison-Wesley.

Doucet, A. (2004). Fathers and the responsibility for children: A puzzle and a tension. *Atlantis, 28*(2), 103–114.

Foucault, M. (1980). *Power/Knowledge: Selected Interviews and Other Writings 1972–1977* (1st American ed.) (C. Gordon, L. Marshall, J. Mepham, & K. Super, Trans.). New York: Pantheon Books.

Frenette, M., & Coulombe, S. (2007). *Has Higher Education among Young Women Substantially Reduced the Gender Gap in Employment and Earnings?* Catalogue No. 11F0019, No. 301. Ottawa: Statistics Canada.

Frenette, M., & Zeman, K. (2007). *Why Are Most University Students Women? Evidence Based on Academic Performance, Study Habits and Parental Influences*. Analytic Studies Branch Research Paper Series, Catalogue No. 11F0019, No. 303. Ottawa: Statistics Canada.

Furr, S. R. (2002). Men and women in cross-gender careers. In L. Diamant and J. A. Lee (Eds.), *The Psychology of Sex, Gender, and Jobs* (pp. 47–68). Westport, CA: Praeger.

Gamble, W. C., & Yu, J. J. (2008). Adolescent siblings' looking glass self-orientations: Patterns of liabilities and associations with parenting. *Journal of Youth and Adolescence, 37*, 860–874.

Goffman, E. (1979). *Gender Advertisements*. New York: Harper & Row.

Goldberg, S., & Lewis, M. (1969). Play behavior in the year old infant: Early sex differences. *Child Development, 40*, 21–32.

Gomme, I. (2004). Education. In R. J. Brym (Ed.), *New Society* (4th ed.) (pp. 359–381). Scarborough: Nelson.

Hartner, S. (1999). Symbolic interactionism revisited: Potential liabilities for the self constructed in the crucible of interpersonal relationships. *Merrill-Palmer Quarterly, 45*, 677–703.

Hartner, S., & Whitesell, N. R. (2003). Beyond the debate: Why some adolescents report stable self-worth over time and situation, whereas others report changes in self-worth. *Journal of Personality, 71*, 1027–1058.

Herbenick, D., et al. (2010). Sexual behavior in the United States: Results from a national probability sample. *Journal of Sexual Medicine, 7* (supplement 5), 255–265.

Herdt, T. (1984). Ritualized homosexuality in the male cults of Melanesia, 1862–1982: An Introduction. In G. Herdt (Ed.), *Ritualized Homosexuality in Melanesia* (pp. 1–81). Berkeley, CA: University of California Press.

Hochschild, A. R., with Machung, A. (1989). *The Second Shift*. New York: Avon.

Intersex Society of North America. (2008a). *What is intersex?* Retrieved May 2, 2011, from www.isna.org

Intersex Society of North America. (2008b). *Myth #10: Intersex is extremely rare*. Retrieved May 2, 2011, from www.isna.org

Koyama, E., & Weasel, L. (2003). From social construction to social justice: Transforming how we teach about intersexuality. *Teaching Intersex Issues* (2nd ed.) (pp. 2–9). Portland, OR: Intersex Initative Portland.

Lasch, C. (1977). *Haven in a Heartless World*. New York: Basic Books.

Lindsay, C. (2008). Are women spending more time on unpaid domestic work than men in Canada? *Matter of Fact*. Catalogue No. 89630XWE. Ottawa: Statistics Canada.

Marshall, K. (2006). Converging gender roles. *Perspectives on Labour and Income, 18*(3), 7–19. Catalogue No. 75001XPE. Ottawa: Statistics Canada.

Maruna, S., LeBel, T. P., Mitchell, N., & Naples, M. (2004). Pygmalion in the reintegration process: Desistance from crime through the looking glass. *Psychology, Crime, and Law, 10*(3), 271–281.

McMullen, K., Gilmore, J., & LePetit, C. (2010). Women in non-traditional occupations and fields of study. *Education Matters, 7*(1). Ottawa, ON: Statistics Canada. Catalogue No. 81-004-X.

McMullin, J. A. (2004). *Understanding Social Inequality*. Don Mills, ON: Oxford University Press.

Nanda, S. (2000). *Gender Diversity*. Illinois: Waveland Press.

Nelson, A. (2010). *Gender in Canada* (4th ed.). Toronto, ON: Pearson Canada.

PFLAG. (2009). *PFLAG Canada*. Retrieved May 2, 2011, from www.pflagcanada.ca

Roscoe, W. (1998). *Changing Ones: Third and Fourth Genders in Native North America*. New York: St. Martin's Press.

Ross, H., & Taylor, H. (1989). Do boys prefer daddy or his physical style of play? *Sex Roles, 20*(1–2), 23–31.

Rubin, J. Z., Provenzano, F. J., & Lurra, Z. (1974). The eye of the beholder. *American Journal of Orthopsychiatry, 44*, 512–519.

Sadker, D., & Sadker, M. (1994). *Failing at Fairness: How America's Schools Cheat Girls.* New York: Scribner.

Sadker, D., Sadker, M., & Zittleman, K. R. (2009). *Still Failing at Fairness: How Gender Bias Cheats Girls and Boys in School and What We Can Do about It.* New York: Scribner.

Simon, W., & Gagnon, J. H. (1970). Psychosexual development. In J. H. Gagnon and W. Simon (Eds.), *The Sexual Scene* (pp. 23–41). Chicago: Aldine.

Statistics Canada. (1999, December 20). Survey of labour and income dynamics: The wage gap between men and women. *The Daily.* Ottawa, ON: Author.

Statistics Canada. (2007). *Women in Canada: Work Chapter Updates, 2006.* Catalogue No. 89F0133XIE. Ottawa: Author.

Statistics Canada. (2009, October). Fact Sheet. *Education Indicators in Canada: Postsecondary Enrolment and Graduation.* Catalogue No. 81599X, No. 003. Ottawa: Author.

Statistics Canada (2010a, March 8). Social Fact Sheet. *Canadian Social Trends.* Catalogue No. 11008X. Ottawa: Author.

Statistics Canada (2010b). Average Earnings by Sex and Work Pattern (Full-Time Workers). CANSIM table 202-0102. Last modified June 17, 2010. Ottawa: Author.

Tajfel, H., & Turner, J. C. (1986). The social identity theory of intergroup behaviour. In S. Worchel and W. G. Austin (Eds.) *The Psychology of Intergroup Relations* (2nd ed.) (pp. 7–24).

Turcotte, M. (2007). Time spent with family during a typical workday, 1986–2005. *Canadian Social Trends, 83* (Summer). Ottawa, ON: Statistics Canada. Statistics Canada Catalogue No. 11-008-XWE.

West, C., & Zimmerman, D. (1987). Doing gender. *Gender and Society, 1,* 125–151.

Yeung, K., & Martin, J. L. (2003). The looking glass self: An empirical test and elaboration. *Social Forces, 81*(3), 843–879.

Zhang, X. (2009, March). Earnings of women with and without children. *Perspectives.* Catalogue No. 75001X. Ottawa: Statistics Canada.

ENDNOTE

[1] Retrieved September 7, 2010, from bartleby.com.

CHAPTER 8

Race and Ethnicity

LEARNING OBJECTIVES AND OUTCOMES

After completing this chapter, students should be able to do the following:

LO1 Compare and contrast the concepts of ethnicity, race, and visible minority.

LO2 Describe contemporary patterns of ethnicity in Canada.

LO3 List the three objectives of Canada's immigration policy, and describe the types of individuals who enter the country on the basis of each of those objectives.

LO4 Describe contemporary immigration patterns, and explain how and why immigration patterns vary over time.

LO5 Describe the implications of ethnicity for family structures, family

interdependence, and intergenerational relationships.

LO6 Describe how economic experiences vary on the basis of Aboriginal ancestry and immigration status.

LO7 Distinguish between dominant and minority groups, and describe the forms of interaction that can take place between them.

LO8 Outline the three components of prejudice, and describe the different forms that discrimination can take.

LO9 Discuss different theories of the causes of prejudice.

In 1998, actress Catherine Zeta-Jones, star of movies such as *Chicago* (2002) and *Ocean's Twelve* (2004), starred in the movie *The Mask of Zorro*, with Antonio Banderas. Playing the role of a Spanish woman, and with her dark eyes, hair, and complexion, people assumed she was Spanish; in fact, she is Welsh. The quotation above regarding her experience reflects the manner in which we identify ourselves on the basis of ethnicity, but at the same time are identified by others; she identifies herself as Welsh, but other people identified her as Spanish on the basis of her accent in the movie and aspects of her physical appearance. Just as we saw in the previous chapter on gender, at times our self-identity and identifications by others may not coincide. But just as is the case with gender, ethnicity holds a significant place on the personal–social identity continuum.

Actress Catherine Zeta-Jones.

Source: TRISTAR/AMBLIN/THE KOBAL COLLECTION/TORRES, RICO

LO¹ ETHNICITY, RACE, AND VISIBLE MINORITIES

The term **ethnicity** comes from the Greek word *ethnos*, which refers to "people living and acting together in a manner that we might apply to a 'people' or a 'nation': a collectivity with a 'way of life'" (Jenkins, 2007, para. 1). Anthropologists have defined ethnicity in terms of "the social organization of cultural difference" (Barth, cited in Jenkins, 2007, para. 1) or "personal identity collectively defined and publicly expressed" (Geertz, cited in Jenkins, 2007, para. 1). Ethnicity includes cultural characteristics such as language, religion, taste in food, shared descent, cultural traditions, and shared geographical locations. We can speak of **objective ethnicity**, such as where your ancestors are actually from and what language they spoke (or you speak), or **subjective ethnicity**, how you personally identify yourself (Laroche, Annamma, Hui & Chankon, 1992). You may "objectively" be of Lebanese descent, but you might identify yourself as "Lebanese," "Lebanese-Canadian," or "Canadian." Jenkins (2007) emphasizes the importance of both the objective and subjective dimensions. Personally identifying with a particular group is not sufficient for ethnicity; that same group must also be

Ethnicity: Cultural characteristics such as language, religion, taste in food, shared descent, cultural traditions, and shared geographical locations.

Objective ethnicity: The ethnic characteristics of your ancestors.

Subjective ethnicity: How you personally identify your ethnicity.

recognized by others as a distinct group based on language, shared descent, cultural traditions, and so on. If the concept of ethnicity seems somewhat ambiguous to you, that's because it is. The boundaries between ethnic groups are not fixed, but rather are flexible and permeable. Your own ethnic identity may vary to some extent across contexts; when you are travelling outside Canada you may primarily identify yourself as "Canadian," while in your everyday life you normally identify yourself as "Japanese" or "Japanese-Canadian." Furthermore, there are no singular definitions of any particular ethnic group. To be "Polish" do you have to be born in Poland? Do your ancestors have to have come from Poland? Do only some of your ancestors (e.g., grandfather) have to have lived in Poland or is it necessary that all of your ancestors have lived there? Do you have to speak Polish? Do you have to enjoy eating pierogies?

The concept of ethnicity is further complicated by its intersection with **race**. Race is "a system of stratification based on physical differences . . . that are seen as essential and permanent" (Mariel Lemonik Arthur, 2007). Thus, while ethnicity is based on cultural characteristics, race is based on physical characteristics, such as facial features, hair texture, and skin colour. You may think of "races" as including white and black; some of you may also think of Asian (or yellow), or have heard someone referring to her- or himself as brown. Carolus Linneaus (1707–1778) developed the first scientific classification of race. He stated that there are four races: Americanus, Europaeus, Asiaticus, and Afer. Many other racial classification systems followed; some indicating as few as three races, and others as many as 30 races. Although the concept of race is based on "physical characteristics that are seen as essential and permanent," there are varying conceptions of how many "races" there are as well as precisely which physical characteristics are associated with which particular race. Furthermore, due to millions of years of genetic blending, all human beings are far more genetically similar than they are different, sharing more than 75 percent of their genes, with those genes related to "race" constituting only 0.24 percent of any given person's genetic makeup (Ravelli, Webber & Patterson, 2011). That means that race is a category that is socially constructed. In South Africa, under apartheid three races were recognized and defined in law: white, black, and for those who were considered neither white nor black,

"coloured." Historically in the United States, social policies and laws to prevent racial intermarriage resulted in specific definitions of race. Even if only 1/32 of your ancestry was black, you were categorized as being black (despite the fact that as many of 80 percent of "blacks" in the United States possess some white ancestors); this was known as the "one-drop rule." The one-drop rule continued to be applied well into the 20th century, as when, in 1985, "the Louisiana Court of Appeals declared that Susie Guillory Phipps could not have her race on her birth certificate changed from Black (or 'colored') to White because she could not prove that fewer than 1/32 of her ancestors were Black" (Mariel Lemonik Arthur, 2007, para. 6).

Ethnicity and race are intertwined (Jenkins, 2007; Mariel Lemonik Arthur, 2007). Historically, scientific classifications of race sometimes integrated cultural traditions and characteristics in addition to physical characteristics. For instance, one racial classification system referred to four different European races—Nordic (northern European), Alpine (central European), Mediterranean (southern European), and Slavic (eastern European) (Mariel Lemonik Arthur, 2007). In contemporary society, "race" is frequently integrated into conceptions of "ethnicity," just as when people based their evaluations of actress Catherine Zeta-Jones' ethnicity, in part, on her physical appearance. Race is also integrated into the definition of **visible minorities**, such as that used by Statistics Canada. Visible minorities are "persons, other than Aboriginal persons, who are non-Caucasian in race or non-White in colour" (Statistics Canada, 2008a, p. 11).

Canada, as with Australia and the United States, is a nation that exists only because of immigration. That is, prior to European colonization, the land that is now known as North America consisted of numerous distinct Aboriginal groups or nations. With colonization, those nations were denied recognition and instead, through settlement by France and Britain and subsequent immigration from those nations and many others, the nation of "Canada" was eventually created. As a nation founded upon the colonization of Aboriginal cultures and immigration, ethnicity is a concept that is of particular relevance for contemporary discussions of Canadian society.

Race: A system of stratification based on physical differences, such as facial features, skin colour, and hair texture.

Visible minorities: Persons, other than Aboriginal persons, who are non-Caucasian in race or non-White in colour.

TIME TO REVIEW

- What is ethnicity, and how do objective and subjective ethnicity differ?
- In what way is race "socially constructed"?
- Who are visible minorities?

Source: Juriah Mosin/Shutterstock

Source: Roger Jegg · Fotodesign-Jegg.de/Shutterstock

How would you identify each of the individuals in the photos above? On the basis of physical characteristics or on the basis of presumed social characteristics and cultural traditions?

LO^2 CONTEMPORARY ETHNIC PATTERNS

Hundreds of years of immigration have made Canada an ethnically diverse nation, although some regions are more ethnically diverse than others. In 2004 the United Nations Development Programme referred to Toronto as the most ethnically diverse city in the world, ahead of cities such as London, Miami, New York, and Los Angeles. This means that the city's population comprised a wider range of ethnic groups than any other city in the world. Furthermore, Toronto is also the city with the largest proportion of residents who are foreign born. More than 45 percent of its population is foreign born, compared to Miami (36.5 percent), Sydney (31.7 percent), and New York (27.9 percent) (Statistics Canada, 2008b). It may not surprise you that a city as large as Toronto, with a population of more than one million people, is ethnically diverse. But how about Brooks, Alberta, with a population of 13,581? It may surprise you that in this small city, more than 2,000 people speak languages other than English or French and 100 different languages are spoken in total (Broadway, n.d.). The ethnic diversity of this small city is the result of the expansion of one of its businesses, Lakeside Packers, a meat-processing plant. In 1996, its American owners decided to expand the plant, which would require 2,000 more workers. To fulfill this demand, the company began to advertise for employees across the country, and also at immigration and refugee centres in Canada and elsewhere. Since the year 2000 more than 3,500 refugees, primarily from sub-Saharan Africa, have come to Brooks, where they now constitute 25 percent of the population. By 2006, 60 percent of Brooks' labour force were immigrants and refugees (Broadway, n.d.).

Canada's ethnocultural diversity has been analyzed at both the macro and micro-levels. Demographic research done at the macro-level, and the Census in particular, paints us a portrait of the ethnic diversity within Canada. The 2006 Census, which asks questions about *objective ethnicity* (i.e., the ethnic origins of a person's ancestors) revealed more than 200 different ethnic origins being reported,

CHAPTER 8 Race and Ethnicity **167**

ETHNIC DIVERSITY IN BROOKS, ALBERTA

The documentary *24 Days in Brooks*, written and directed by Dana Inkster, follows the first ever strike at Lakeside Packers. The film highlights the plight of these primarily foreign-born workers in their struggle for improved working conditions in an industry that is renowned for its hazardous work environments. The documentary also draws attention to the ethnically diverse nature of the city, and the means by which the employees' ethnic identities have adapted within this new environment—as when Peter Jany Khwai is shown wearing a traditional African shirt along with his cowboy hat. The film can be viewed online, at no cost, on the National Film Board's website (www.nfb.ca).

compared to only 25 different ethnic origins being reported a century earlier, in the 1901 Census. Approximately 5 percent of respondents indicated Aboriginal origins, which refers to North American Indian (e.g., Cree), Inuit, and Métis. Respondents could select more than one origin, so an individual could report *both* Aboriginal and non-Aboriginal origins, such as "Cree" and "Scottish." More than 16 percent of the population are visible minorities, the majority of whom are South Asian, Chinese, or black; 30 percent of visible minorities were born in Canada. Those ethnic groups that have the longest immigration histories in Canada are now those that make up the largest proportion of the population (e.g., English, French, and Scottish). The 10 most frequent ethnic origins reported are listed in Table 8.1. Members of groups that have the longest immigration histories are also more likely to report multiple ethnic origins, as are persons with Aboriginal origins (Statistics Canada, 2008a).

Most of the population (60.5 percent) are *at least* the third generation in Canada, meaning they, their parents, and at least one grandparent were born in Canada (Statistics Canada, 2008a). Almost 20 percent of the population are foreign born, having immigrated from any of a number of different countries. Over the last several decades those countries are increasingly likely to be non-European. From 2006 to 2008, the top ten source countries for immigrants and refugees were (in descending order) China, India, Philippines, United States, United Kingdom, Pakistan, Korea, France, Iran, and Columbia. Immigrants to Canada speak almost 150 different languages as their *mother tongues*. The most commonly reported non-English and non-French mother tongue is Chinese (18.6 percent), followed by Italian (6.6 percent) and Punjabi (5.9 percent). But more than 90 percent of people who immigrated between 2001 and 2006 also speak English and/or French, Canada's two official languages. Recent immigrants are urban dwellers, with more than two-thirds settling in Toronto, Montreal, or Vancouver.

TABLE 8.1

Top 10 Reported Ethnic Origins in Canada, 2006 Census

Ethnic Origin Reported	Proportion of Responses to Ethnic Origins Question
Canadian	32.2%
English	30.9%
French	15.8%
Scottish	15.1%
Irish	13.9%
German	10.2%
Italian	4.6%
Chinese	4.3%
North American Indian (e.g., Cree, Ojibway)	4.0%
Ukrainian	3.9%
Note: Persons can report multiple ethnic origins.	

Source: Adapted from Citizenship and Immigration Canada (2009). Facts and figures: Immigration overview: Permanent and temporary residents 2008. Ottawa, ON.

MY ETHNICITY

How would you describe your ethnicity? Upon what specific characteristics is that identity based: skin colour or other aspects of physical appearance; clothing or hairstyle; place of birth of your ancestors; your own place of birth; languages spoken by your ancestors; languages spoken by you; religious background of your ancestors; your own religious affiliation; cultural traditions or rituals that you participated in during your childhood or continue to participate in currently? To what extent is your description of your ethnicity based on objective and subjective ethnicity?

People immigrating to Canada select their areas of settlement primarily because of support networks of family members and friends who have already immigrated, but also because of climate (Vancouver), language (Montreal), and job prospects (Toronto) (Statistics Canada, 2008b). Historically, immigration patterns have varied considerably over time, and are a reflection of Canada's immigration policies and practices.

LO³ HISTORICAL IMMIGRATION PATTERNS AND POLICIES

The *Immigration and Refugee Protection Act* (implemented in 2002) is based on three objectives: reuniting families; contributing to the nation's economic development, and protecting refugees (Citizenship and Immigration Canada, 2009). Immigrants within the **family class** are those who are sponsored by close relatives living in Canada and include spouses/partners, dependent children, grandparents, and parents. **Economic immigrants** are selected on the basis of their educational backgrounds, occupational skills, and ability to contribute to the Canadian economy. They are selected to fill in gaps in the Canadian labour force, or to meet the economic needs of specific communities. **Refugees** are persons who are forced to flee from persecution. They may meet the criteria of the 1951 Geneva Convention, now institutionalized within international law: "A person must be outside of their country of origin and have a well founded fear of being persecuted for reasons of race, religion, nationality, membership of a particular social group or political opinion" (Canadian Council for Refugees, n.d.). Alternatively, they may be persons who have been displaced or who are otherwise defined by the government of Canada as being in need

of protection. Immigrants and people who have been granted refugee status are known as *permanent residents* until such time as they may apply for and successfully attain Canadian citizenship. Figure 8.1 (page 170) demonstrates the extent to which the number of immigrants and refugees who have been accepted into Canada has varied over the last 150 years.

LO⁴ You will notice that during some periods of time, larger numbers of immigrants and/or refugees were being accepted into Canada. This was the result of "push" factors that motivated individuals and families to leave their countries of origin (e.g., poverty, religious or political persecution, the desire for adventure), as well as "pull" factors, including economic prosperity, the need for workers, and immigration policies that drew people (or at least drew *certain* people) into Canada. Prior to 1906, Canada had no cohesive immigration policy. The Canadian government's goal was to increase the nation's population (or more specifically its Caucasian, English-speaking population), especially once the American government began to express an interest in colonizing the Canadian West. From 1896 to 1905, Minister of the Interior Clifford Sifton widely advertised for agricultural immigrants to settle the West; clearing the land and establishing a homestead within three years of arrival to Canada would entitle these immigrants to that land at no charge. Advertisements were

Family-class immigrants: Immigrants who are sponsored by close relatives living in Canada.

Economic immigrants: Immigrants selected on the basis of their educational backgrounds, occupational skills, and ability to contribute to the Canadian economy.

Refugees: Persons who are forced to flee from persecution.

FIGURE 8.1

Canada—Permanent Residents, 1860 to 2008

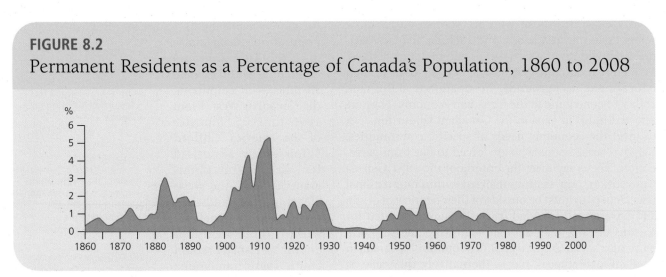

Source: Citizenship and Immigration Canada (2009).

placed in venues in the United States and the United Kingdom, but agricultural immigrants from northern Europe were also considered to be acceptable. Thus, we see immigration increasing in the first years of the 20th century. Canada implemented its first cohesive immigration policy in 1906 (the *Immigration Act*), and immigration reached its peak in 1913, when 400,000 immigrants arrived in Canada (Citizenship and Immigration Canada, 2009). Immigrants who arrived during that year comprised 5.3 percent of Canada's population (see Figure 8.2).

Since that time immigration has waxed and waned, but has never exceeded those numbers from 1913. Immigration tends to decrease during times of

economic decline (e.g., during the Depression of the 1930s), as well as during wartime (e.g., during World War I, 1914–1918, and World War II, 1939–1945). As immigration policies changed over the years, certain groups have been barred from immigration, while others have been accepted as immigrants after many years of being disqualified.

In 1951, the United Nations adopted the *Refugee Convention*, which recognized that refugees are different from immigrants, in that refugees "do not choose to immigrate; they are forced to flee their homes"— and indicated that "protecting refugees is not simply a humanitarian gesture, but a legal requirement" (Canadian Council for Refugees, 2009). Eighteen years later,

FIGURE 8.2

Permanent Residents as a Percentage of Canada's Population, 1860 to 2008

Source: Citizenship and Immigration Canada (2009). Facts and figures: Immigration overview: Permanent and temporary residents 2008. Ottawa, ON: Reproduced with the permission of the Minister of Public Works and Government Services Canada, 2011.

Canada signed the Convention, and implemented its first formal refugee determination system. Since that time, more than 500,000 refugees have been settled in Canada. In 1986, the United Nations High Commission for Refugees recognized Canada for its "major and sustained contribution to the cause of refugees," awarding the people of Canada the Nansen Medal (Canadian Council for Refugees, 2009).

Through these historical and contemporary patterns, Canadian society has become characterized by tremendous ethnic diversity. Individuals "objectively" come from particular ethnic backgrounds, and then "subjectively" incorporate certain ethnicities into their identities. Regardless of whether people identify themselves, or are identified by others, as having a particular ethnicity, there are consequences of that identification.

CONSEQUENCES OF ETHNIC IDENTIFICATION

The implications of ethnicity range from the micro level to the macro level. Two areas where the implications of ethnicity are especially clear are family experiences and economic experiences.

LO⁵ DIVERSE FAMILY EXPERIENCES

Despite the diversity among and within ethnic groups, there are key issues related to family life that are affected by ethnicity and immigration status, such as family structure, family interdependence, and intergenerational relationships.

FAMILY STRUCTURE

The nuclear family predominates in Canada, regardless of ethnic group or immigration status. However, immigrants are four times as likely as nonimmigrants to live in extended families, and members of visible minorities are 20 times as likely as nonvisible minorities to live in extended families. The greater prevalence of extended families among immigrants and visible minorities is the result of a combination of factors—traditional cultural norms, financial reasons, or because the family is perceived as a site of support and protection from what can often be a prejudicial outside world. Aboriginal people are also more likely than non-Aboriginal people to live in extended family households, especially among those who live on reserves. Although the nuclear family–based household is the most common, the *ideal* of the extended family living within a caring community continues to characterize Aboriginal cultures today (Frideres, 2007; Frideres & Gadacz, 2008).

FAMILY INTERDEPENDENCE

Feelings of obligation toward one's family tend to be valued more by individuals from non-European cultures; among those with European backgrounds, interdependence among family members is valued more within Southern European cultures (Vedder, Berry, Sabbatier & Sam, 2008; Georgas, Berry, VandeVijver, Kagitcibasi, & Poortinga, 2006). In these families, youth spend more time with adults, and therefore under adult supervision. Furthermore, youth also see household work as being communal in nature—something that is simply expected of members of the family, rather than something that is financially rewarded through a weekly allowance, or being given money for "helping" with a particular task such cleaning out the garage (Fuligni, Yip & Tseng, 2002; Kagitcibasi, 2007; Vedder, Berry, Sabbatier & Sam, 2008).

Family interdependence is also reflected in the age at which youth move out of the family home. In Canada, home leaving is affected by macro-level

Should this child receive an allowance for his work? Your answer will depend, in part, on your own cultural background.

Source: photos.com

economic conditions (e.g., unemployment rates; the need for a postsecondary education) and demographic forces (e.g., the average age of first marriage). But it is also influenced by factors that vary among and within ethnic groups—family socioeconomic status, family connectedness, ethnocultural norms that govern perceptions of the "appropriate" timing of life events, the degree of segregation of particular ethnic groups in urban centres, and the recency of an ethnic group's immigration to Canada (Mitchell, Wister & Gee, 2004; Boyd, 2000). For example, a comparison of the age of home leaving among Canadian young adults of British, Chinese, Indo, and Southern European origins finds that those of British origin leave home considerably sooner than those from the other ethnic groups (Mitchell, Wister & Gee, 2004). Boyd (2000) finds that ethnicity interacts with gender, with young women remaining at home longer than young men. She also suggests that the age of home leaving may be influenced by the degree to which cultural traditions are integrated into a family's everyday practice, as well as how much hostility members of particular ethnic groups face within society.

INTERGENERATIONAL RELATIONSHIPS

Parenting styles can vary across cultures, such that among some ethnic groups parents may engage in stricter or more lenient parenting practices than parents in other ethnic groups. But the meaning of parenting practices, such as level of supervision and forms of discipline, varies across groups as well, and this means that the impact of parenting practices on child outcomes can differ among ethnic groups (Ho, Bluestein & Jenkins, 2008). For example, very strict parenting styles have been found (on average) to be associated with certain outcomes in children. This type of parenting style is sometimes referred to as **authoritarian parenting**; parents have high expectations, strict rules, they don't explain the rationale for the rules, children are punished for breaking those rules, and communication is largely unidirectional (i.e., parents do the talking and children do the listening) (Baumrind, 1968, 1991). A large body of research finds that this parenting style may be associated with child obedience in the short term, but in the long term is associated with rebellion and resultant negative child outcomes, such as a greater likelihood of aggression, lower grades in school, and substance use. However, more recently researchers have found that this association varies across ethnic and immigrant groups. For instance, Ho, Bluestein, and Jenkins (2008) find that this type of parenting is not associated with negative child outcomes in families from many current immigrant cultures, such as China, India, Pakistan, and Korea.

One aspect of intergenerational relationships that is unique to immigrant families is the potential conflict that can emerge between parents who attained adulthood in their nation of origin, and their children, who may have come to Canada while still quite young or may have been born in Canada. These youth have been described as **bicultural**, being exposed to the characteristics of the family's heritage culture when at home, yet also being a part of the new, national culture when outside the home. Although researchers find that family interdependence is valued more among those from non-European cultures, a generational difference also exists in that a sense of obligation to family is valued more by the parent generation than the youth generation; this can contribute to family conflicts (Vedder, Berry, Sabatier & Sam, 2008). In immigrant families, parents may encourage their children to hang on to the norms, values, and practices of their traditional culture, while children may wish to adopt the norms, values, and practices of the new, national culture. For example, Nazneen (2005) found that Bangladeshi–Muslim parents living in Montreal expressed concern about raising their children in a society with very different standards for youth dating, alcohol consumption, and violence shown in the media. In response to these concerns, some of the parents tried to limit the interactions that their children had with non-Bangladeshi children, instead encouraging them to become friends with other Bangladeshi children (or, if not Bangladeshi, at least other Muslim children). One youth responds to this experience, saying, "We have to re-invent our identity as Muslims in North America. We live in a non-Islamic country, yet we are not allowed to date or socialize with the opposite sex. How are we supposed to find our partners? I don't want my parents to find a bride for me when I am in my late twenties!" (p. 115). Other research has found that South Asian youth frequently act differently inside and outside the home. While in the presence of their families, they conform to traditional cultural norms; when their families are not present, their behaviour is in accordance with dominant Western norms and values (Talbani & Hasanali, 2000). However, doing so can result in stress, depression, and alienation from family members (Shams, 2001).

Bicultural youth may respond to the demands of two cultures in a number of ways. One study looked at the experiences of more than 5,000 immigrant youth from over 30 ethnic backgrounds who were now living in 13 different countries (Berry, Phinney, Sam & Vedder, 2006). They found four different patterns that the youth followed in adapting to the intersection of the two cultures—their heritage cultures and their new national cultures.

The first adaptation pattern is the **integration pattern**, where the youth identify with both their heritage cultures and their new, national cultures. The second pattern is the **ethnic pattern**, with youth identifying primarily with their own heritage cultures. Youth who orient themselves primarily to the new, national culture are following the **national pattern**. Finally, those who are confused about how they should be adapting to their bicultural experiences are following

> **Authoritarian parenting:** A parenting style characterized by high expectations for children, very strict rules, no explanation of the rationale for the rules, strict punishment for rule breaking, and unidirectional communication.
>
> **Bicultural:** Participating in two distinct cultures simultaneously.
>
> **Integration pattern:** Identifying with both one's heritage culture and one's new, national culture.
>
> **Ethnic pattern:** Identifying primarily with one's heritage culture.
>
> **National pattern:** Identifying primarily with one's new, national culture.

FIGURE 8.3

Bicultural Adaptation Patterns

		Identification with Heritage Culture	
		Yes	No
Identification with New Culture	Yes	Integration	National
	No	Ethnic	Diffuse

Source: Adapted from Berry, J. W., Phinney, J. P., Sam, D. L., & Vedder, P. (2006). *Immigrant Youth in Cultural Transition: Acculturation, Identity, and Adaptation Across National Contexts*. Mahwah, NJ: Lawrence Erlbaum Associates.

a **diffuse pattern** (see Figure 8.3). The adaptation pattern that youth follow has implications for both their *psychological adaptation* (i.e., self-esteem, good mental health) and their *sociocultural adaptation* (i.e., few problems in within their community, positive school experiences). Those who follow the integration pattern, identifying with both their heritage cultures and their new, national cultures, have the most positive adaptation experience overall, both psychologically and socioculturally. Youth who orient themselves primarily to their ethnic cultures experience positive psychological adaptation, but negative sociocultural adaptation, and have negative school experiences and problems within the community. Those who follow the national pattern experience negative psychological and sociocultural adaptation, as do youth who follow the diffuse pattern; the negative adaptation experiences of the latter are more significant.

LO⁶ DIVERSE ECONOMIC EXPERIENCES

Economic experiences can vary considerably on the basis of ethnicity. Economic variations become particularly evident when we compare the average incomes of Aboriginal and non-Aboriginal persons, and the average incomes of immigrants and Canadian-born individuals. Economic experiences interact with education as well (see Figures 8.4 and 8.5).

When analyzing the income of Aboriginal and non-Aboriginal persons overall, there are considerable differences, with Aboriginal persons

Diffuse pattern:
Uncertainty about which culture(s) one should or should not identify with.

FIGURE 8.4

Annual Income (2005) for Persons of Aboriginal and Non-Aboriginal Ancestry, 2006 Census, Ages 25–44

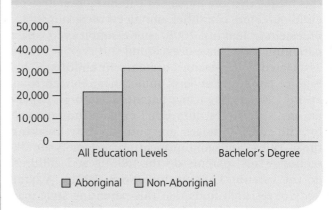

Source: Statistics Canada (2011a).

FIGURE 8.5

Annual Income (2005) for Immigrant and Non–Immigrant Persons, 2006 Census, Ages 25–44

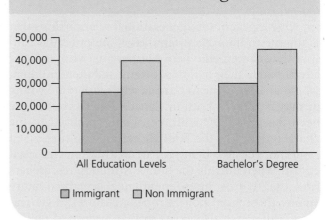

Source: Statistics Canada (2011a).

earning, on average, $10,000 less per year ($21,667 for Aboriginal persons and $31,912 for non-Aboriginal persons). The implications of the lower average income of Aboriginal persons include the fact that they are three times as likely to live in homes needing major repairs (25 percent of the Aboriginal population) and are four times as likely to live in overcrowded housing

(11 percent of the Aboriginal population) (Statistics Canada, 2008c). However, level of education has a significant impact on the degree of income disparity between Aboriginal and non-Aboriginal populations. When comparing only those that have a Bachelor's degree, the income difference virtually disappears; Aboriginal persons earn an average of $40,399, compared to non-Aboriginal persons at $40,650. In fact, Aboriginal women with a Bachelor's degree earn approximately $1,000 *more* than non-Aboriginal women with a Bachelor's degree (Statistics Canada, 2011a).

When analyzing the average incomes of the immigrant and Canadian-born populations, level of education has less of an influence on the magnitude of income disparity. At all education levels, the immigrant population earns approximately $13,000 less than the nonimmigrant population ($26,221 versus $39,931). When comparing those with Bachelor's degrees, immigrants earn almost $15,000 less than those who are Canadian born ($30,127 versus $44,989) (Statistics Canada, 2011b). Income disparity is especially marked among those who have immigrated within the past five years, and has increased over the past several decades. In 1980, recent male immigrants earned 85 percent of comparable Canadian-born males; in 2005, they earned only 65 percent of comparable Canadian-born males. Of particular note is that this growth in the income gap is despite the fact that immigrants in the 21st century have higher levels of education and are more highly skilled than in the past, as *economic immigrants* are selected on the basis of their ability to contribute to our knowledge-based Canadian economy (Picot, Lu & Hou, 2009). The increase in education among recent immigrants is especially evident when looking at the "prime" age group of 25–54. In the early 1980s, only 26 percent of males and 16 percent of females were entering Canada with a university degree; in 2006, 60 percent of recent male immigrants and 51 percent of recent female immigrants had entered Canada with a university degree (Bonikowska, Hou & Picot, 2011). In fact, the immigrant population is more highly educated than the Canadian-born population. Considering those over the age of 15, 31 percent of immigrant males have a university degree, compared to only 18 percent of Canadian-born males. More than 20 percent of immigrant females have a university degree, compared to 17 percent of Canadian-born females (Statistics Canada, 2009).

So if the immigrant population is more educated than ever before, and in fact is more educated than the Canadian-born population, why does the income disparity exist and why has it grown over the past several decades? Several potential contributing factors have been mentioned, arising from the changing source countries for immigrants (from primarily European to primarily Asian and South Asian): degree of proficiency in one of Canada's two official languages; real or perceived differences in educational systems (i.e., the recognition of foreign credentials); cultural differences; and racial discrimination (Picot, Lu & Hou, 2009; Jackson, 2001; Bonikowska, Hou & Picot, 2011; Statistics Canada, 2009).

Ethnicity has implications for various aspects of everyday life, including family structure, family interdependence, intergenerational relationships, and economic experiences. At a more macro level, relationships between groups in society are affected by sociocultural forces related to ethnicity, race, and aspects of immigration.

TIME TO REVIEW

- In what ways are family structure, family interdependence, and intergenerational relationships affected by ethnicity and/or immigration?
- What are the experiences of bicultural youth, what different patterns of adaptation might they use, and what are the implications of those patterns?
- How are economic experiences affected by Aboriginal ancestry and immigration status, and what role is played by level of education?

RELATIONSHIPS BETWEEN GROUPS

LO7 Ethnicity exists only in relative terms. That is, we can speak of ethnic groups only on the basis of persons in one of those groups being distinct from persons in other groups (Jenkins, 2007). In ethnically diverse nations such as Canada, these different groups interact with each other. Based on a nation's history, such as colonization and historical immigration patterns, power differentials emerge, leading to the creation of dominant groups and minority groups. **Dominant groups** are those that have greater power and privilege. For example, when the British defeated the French on the Plains of Abraham in the 18th century, the British became the dominant group and the colony was renamed British North America; similarly, when the British colonized India they became

Dominant group:
A group that has institutionalized power and privilege in society.

the dominant group there as well. **Minority groups** are definable groups that are socially disadvantaged and experience unequal treatment (Wirth, 1945). Minority groups may be based upon skin colour, religion, or other aspects of ethnicity such as nation of origin. It is important to note that "minority" refers to *power*, not to *number*. In other words, a group can be the statistical majority and yet still be a minority group because of lesser power. For example, under apartheid in South Africa, blacks were the statistical majority and yet were subjected to unequal treatment by the white statistical minority in power. Similarly, when the French colonized what is now Canada, they became the dominant group and Aboriginal peoples became a minority group. Interactions between dominant groups and minority groups can take a number of forms: assimilation, pluralism, and segregation and population transfer.

ASSIMILATION

Assimilation occurs when a minority group is "absorbed" into the culture of the dominant group. At times assimilation is sought and/or achieved by force; for example, in the 19th century the Canadian government's policies regarding Aboriginal people were based on the goal of full assimilation (see Chapter 4).

At other times assimilation is voluntary, where over the course of generations people increasingly adopt the norms, values, and practices of the dominant culture; they stop speaking the language of their ancestors, and give up cultural traditions. In the past, it was assumed that assimilation was a linear process characterized by upward mobility, where each successive generation would "have a better life" than the previous generation. However, more recently some scholars have proposed that the linear model of assimilation was based on immigration patterns of the past—Caucasian immigrants from largely European source countries. Source countries for immigration today are such that an increasing proportion of immigrants, and thereby their descendents, are visible minorities. For these groups, physical characteristics may serve as an obstacle to full assimilation; to some extent, they will always be perceived as and will perceive themselves as a distinct "other" (Hiller & Chow, 2005). As one participant in Hiller and Chow's study states, "It is quite confusing sometimes to be Chinese in a Canadian society, *but also difficult to be Canadian with a Chinese look* (emphasis added)" (p. 94). Furthermore, the nature of the immigration experience today means that upward mobility is less common, as was illustrated in the earlier section on earning experiences. Consequently, assimilation is more likely to be "segmented" than "linear"; some groups may become assimilated to a greater extent than other groups (Hiller & Chow, 2005).

PLURALISM

Cultural **pluralism** is characterized by different ethnic groups maintaining traditions of their heritage cultures, and cultural diversity being valued. Switzerland is often considered a model of cultural pluralism, where its French, German, Romanish, and Italian populations maintain their cultures and their languages; all four languages are the "official" languages of the country, and all have similar levels of institutionalized power. Canada is also characterized by cultural pluralism, which is reflected in its multiculturalism policy (see *Sociology in Practice*).

SEGREGATION AND POPULATION TRANSFER

Under **segregation**, minority groups are separated from the dominant group. Until the Civil Rights movement of the 1960s, blacks were segregated from whites in the American South in a variety of ways. They were barred from many public places (e.g., restaurants), had to sit at the back of buses and drink from separate water fountains, their children were required to attend separate schools, and **anti-miscegenation laws** prohibited interracial marriages. Although many Canadians are unaware of it, the segregation of blacks existed here as well. In 1945, Halifax resident Viola Desmond was arrested for sitting in the "white-only" section of a theatre. Although Canadian provinces began to pass legislation banning such segregation in the mid-1940s, the attitudes that underlie segregation remained for some time. In 1954, two black men were refused service in an Ontario restaurant and an undercover story by the *Toronto Telegram* revealed that although segregation no longer existed in law, it was continuing unabated in everyday practice (Black History Canada, n.d.). In

Minority groups: Definable groups that are socially disadvantaged and face unequal treatment.

Pluralism: Cultural differences are maintained and celebrated.

Segregation: Minority groups are separated from the dominant group.

Anti-miscegenation laws: Laws that prohibit interracial marriages.

SOCIOLOGY *IN PRACTICE*

MULTICULTURALISM IN CANADA

Federal multiculturalism has progressed through three phases of development (Dewing, 2009). During the *incipient stage* (pre-1971), Canada's political, social, and economic institutions were based on a British model and, in fact, Canadians were considered to be British subjects until 1947. Large-scale immigration from European countries following World War II, along with the activism of Aboriginal people for greater independence and redress of past wrongs, contributed to the movement away from assimilation. Multiculturalism became an official policy in Canada in 1971, and thus began the *formative period* of development (1971–1981). The objectives of the policy were

- "to assist cultural groups to retain and foster their identity;
- to assist cultural groups to overcome barriers to their full participation in Canadian society; . . .
- to promote creative exchanges among all Canadian cultural groups; and
- to assist immigrants in acquiring at least one of the official languages" (p. 4).

This era of multiculturalism had a folkloric orientation, emphasizing the celebration of the traditional practices often embodied in cultural festivals—food, costume, and dance. In 1982, the third phase of multiculturalism (known as *institutionalization*) began. During the 1980s, multiculturalism policy moved beyond simply promoting multiculturalism to legislating it; with the passage of the *Canadian Multiculturalism Act* in 1988, Canada became the first nation in the world to pass

a national multiculturalism law. "Under the Act, all government agencies, departments, and Crown corporations—not just the ministry responsible for multiculturalism—were expected to provide leadership in advancing Canada's multicultural mix and to take part in the design and implementation of plans, programs, procedures, and decision-making strategies that enhance the full and equal participation of minorities within institutional structures" (p. 6). Ethnic diversity was considered to be of value not only for its own sake, but also because of the number of different languages spoken and people's ties to other nations, which were seen to be of value for the economic betterment of the country. Beginning in the 1990s, attention was drawn to civic participation (the importance of all Canadians shaping our communities) and identity (respecting cultural diversity so that all people feel a sense of belonging to, and identification with, Canada) in multiculturalism policy.

Critics of multiculturalism policy suggest that despite its objectives, it really is nothing more than a superficial celebration of food, costume, and dance at cultural festivals. This emphasis on festivities draws attention away from the more significant issues that prevent the full participation of many people in Canada's institutions. However, surveys find that the majority of Canadians support the principle of multiculturalism, even if they do not necessarily explicitly support the formal act.

SOCIOLOGY *IN WORDS*

THE HELP

The novel *The Help*, by Kathryn Stockett, captures the ways that segregation affected everyday life. Set in the 1960s, the story follows a young white woman, Skeeter Phelan, whose goal is to become a writer. In pursuit of this goal and the desire to change race relations, she starts interviewing several black housekeepers in Jackson, Mississippi, about their experiences. Because of segregation, she and the

housekeepers must sneak around to avoid detection. With the recent deaths of several black men at the hands of white vigilantes, they are literally risking their lives to get their stories told. As of January 2011, *The Help* had been in the top 10 of various Canadian and American bestsellers lists every single week for more than a year and half; the movie was released in August 2011.

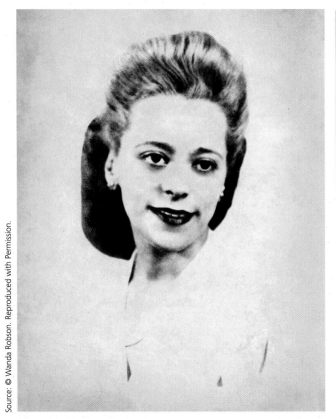

Source: © Wanda Robson. Reproduced with Permission.

Viola Desmond was arrested in a Nova Scotia theatre for sitting in the "white-only" section.

the United Nations Educational, Scientific and Cultural Organization's (UNESCO) archives portal in recognition of the important historical material that it has preserved. Later in Canadian history, Aboriginal people were moved onto reserves created by the Canadian government; these reserves later became a model for the way blacks would be treated in South Africa under apartheid. And during both World Wars, members of those ethnic groups who were defined as "enemy aliens" had their property seized and were relocated into internment campus. During World War I, it was primarily people of Ukrainian descent who were interned; they were used as slave labour, for example, clearing the forest for what would become Kapuskasing, Ontario, and building roads through the Rocky Mountains. During World War II, it was primarily those of Japanese descent who were placed in internment camps.

Segregation and population transfer have their foundations in prejudice and discrimination. Prejudice and discrimination have long histories in Canada and throughout the world, and continue to be problematic in the 21st century.

South Africa, under apartheid those who were legally classified as "black" or "coloured" faced restrictions on where they could live and work.

Population transfer forcibly expels members of certain minority groups from a country, or limits them to a particular location. In Canadian history, this has occurred multiple times. In the mid-18th century, more than 7,000 Acadians (an ethnic group of French descent, living in the Maritimes) were expelled by the British, and all of their farms burned to the ground. They were sent to France, England, and a number of American states. Many eventually settled in Louisiana, and over time "Cajun" culture was born ("Cajun" was a slang for "Acadian"). Thousands of Acadians later returned to Canada and reside today in New Brunswick, Prince Edward Island, and Nova Scotia. Pubnico, Nova Scotia, is the oldest Acadian village in the world still inhabited by Acadians (www.pubnico.ca), and its museum is listed on

Population transfer: Minority groups are forcibly expelled or are limited to a specific location.

At the Castle Mountain Internment Camp in Banff, the plaque on the rock reads as follows: During Canada's first national internment operations in World War One, thousands of immigrants from the Austro-Hungarian Empire, the majority of Ukrainian origin, some citizens of Canada, were imprisoned as "enemy aliens." Internment operations lasted from 1914 to 1920. This plaque is in memory of those held at Castle Mountain camp from 14 July 1915 to 15 July 1917.

Source: Larry MacDougal/TCPI/The Canadian Press

- What are the differences between dominant groups and minority groups?
- What forms of interaction can occur between the dominant group and minority groups in society, and what are some examples?
- How has multiculturalism changed in Canadian history?

LO⁸ PREJUDICE AND DISCRIMINATION

Prejudice is an attitude that is unrelated to reality and is generalized to all members of a certain group. We usually think of prejudice in terms of negative attitudes, but it can also be based on what may be perceived as positive characteristics, such as members of a certain group being hard-working or talented artists. **Racism** is a specific form of prejudice, one based on aspects of physical appearance. Like all attitudes, prejudice has a *cognitive component* and an *affective component*. It is also linked to a third component, the *behavioural component*. These three components correspond to what we *think*, how we *feel*, and how we *act* (Aronson, Wilson, Akert & Fehr, 2010).

THE COGNITIVE COMPONENT

The cognitive component of prejudice reflects *what we think*. Stereotypes are the foundation of the cognitive component of prejudice. Stereotypes are assumptions that members of a particular group are more similar than they actually are; that is, stereotypes reflect our image of the "typical" example of a member of a certain group. Stereotypes can be directed at any type of group—truck drivers, professors, women, ethnic groups, religious groups, and so on. Just as we may overgeneralize by saying that trees are green (when in fact, some trees have red or purple leaves, and the leaves of all deciduous trees change colour in the autumn), we may overgeneralize about the membership of a social group, such as women being poor drivers (when in fact, male drivers have more car accidents).

Stereotypes serve a cognitive function, in that once we hold a specific stereotype, we are more likely to notice, pay attention to, and remember information that is consistent with our stereotype. In one study, participants were presented with photos and labels for people in certain social categories (e.g., a photo of a smiling, grey-haired woman with the label "grandmother"). Then they were given additional information about the person in the photo (e.g., "kind"). At a later point in time, they were asked to recall the information about that person. The researchers found that information was best remembered when it conformed to the stereotype associated with that label; for instance, it was easier to remember descriptions of "kind" and "likes to bake cookies" when shown the photo of the grandmother than it was to recall "likes to race cars" and "aggressive." Furthermore, in trying to recall information about a person in a stereotyped group, we tend to falsely remember information that is consistent with that stereotype; participants in the study would falsely recall "kind" as being part of the description of the grandmother, even if it hadn't been (Brewer, Dull & Lui, 1981).

THE AFFECTIVE COMPONENT

The affective component of prejudice reflects *how we feel*. These are the emotions that we attach to the stereotype. We may feel dislike toward to a particular group that we stereotype as being untrustworthy, or admiration for another group that we stereotype as being hard workers. The fact that prejudicial attitudes are accompanied by strong emotions has repeatedly been demonstrated in research. Sometimes we aren't even aware of the emotions that we may be feeling. One classic study used the Galvanic Skin Response (GSR) to overcome this problem (Porier & Lott, 1967). GSR devices are attached to the skin using wires and sticky patches, and then they are able to measure the electrical conductivity of the skin; electrical conductivity increases when we are in the midst of strong emotions. Participants in this study completed a questionnaire that measured their level of ethnocentrism, the tendency to see things only from the point of view of one's own culture, as the standard for the "normal" way of doing things. They were then attached to the GSR device, and told to wait for a research assistant to come in and assign them a problem-solving task. What the researchers found was that participants who were higher in ethnocentrism showed greater galvanic skin response when in the presence of a black, rather than white, research assistant;

Prejudice: An attitude that is unrelated to reality and is generalized to all members of a certain group.

Racism: A specific form of prejudice based on aspects of physical appearance such as skin colour.

participants who were low in ethnocentrism did not show this pattern. In this study, ethnocentrism resulted in specific reactions to racial differences. Ethnocentrism can also contribute to the many forms of individual, institutional, and systemic discrimination discussed later in the chapter. Furthermore, we can see ethnocentrism when someone judges another culture's food as "weird," or deems that people in England drive on the "wrong" side of the road.

Thus, the cognitive beliefs that make up prejudice are accompanied by emotions, which individuals may not even been aware that they are experiencing. It is this emotional component that makes prejudice so resistant to change. It is much easier to correct someone's inaccurate cognitive beliefs (e.g., by presenting that person with accurate information that dispels their beliefs) than it is to change their emotions (of which they may not even be aware). In addition to what we think and how we feel, prejudice is connected to a behavioural component—how we act.

THE BEHAVIOURAL COMPONENT

Prejudice put into action is **discrimination**—treating someone unfairly because of his or her group membership. Discrimination can occur anywhere from the individual level (e.g., not sitting next to someone on the bus because of the colour of her skin) to the institutional level (e.g., laws that treat certain groups unequally).

Discrimination: Treating someone unfairly because of his or her group membership.

Hate crimes: Criminal offences that are motivated by hate toward an identifiable group.

INDIVIDUAL DISCRIMINATION

Individual discrimination can include avoiding contact with members of certain groups, making offensive jokes, using derogatory names, insulting, verbally abusing, using physical violence, and committing hate crimes. **Hate crimes** are criminal offences that are motivated by hate toward an identifiable group, such as groups based on race/ethnicity, religion, sexual orientation, physical or mental disability, and political beliefs. In the *Criminal Code of Canada,* hate crimes include public incitement of hatred, willful promotion of hatred, advocating genocide, and mischief in relation to religious property; other crimes (e.g., assault) are classified as hate crimes if they have been motivated by hatred against an identifiable group. The significance of hate crimes is that they affect not only the individual who has been victimized, but also indirectly impact members of an entire community; consequently, 30 nations in the world, including Canada, have implemented hate-crime legislation. In 2008, there were 1,036 police-reported hate crimes in Canada, constituting approximately 1 percent of all crimes. However, that number undercounts the true prevalence of hate crimes, in that it is estimated that only 40 percent of hate crimes are ever reported to the police. A victim's decision to report an incident to the police is based on many factors, including the perceived seriousness of the incident, language or cultural barriers, perceived sensitivity of the police, the presence of specialized hate-crimes units, and the accessibility of victim services (Dauvergne, 2010).

The majority of police-reported hate crimes are based on race/ethnicity (55 percent), followed by religion (26 percent) and sexual orientation (16 percent). Hate crimes based on race/ethnicity are primarily directed at blacks (37 percent), followed by

SOCIOLOGY *IN MY LIFE*

HAS RACISM "ALL BUT DISAPPEARED"?

Ten years ago, one of your authors saw a textbook that contained the quotation, "Racism has all but disappeared from Canadian society."

- Do you agree or disagree with that statement?
- Does racism exist at your school?
- Have you ever personally experienced or observed a behaviour, gesture, facial expression, or comment that you consider to be "racist"?

South Asians (12 percent) and Arab and West Asians (7 percent). Hate crimes based on religion are overwhelmingly directed at members of the Jewish faith (64 percent), followed by Catholics (12 percent) and Muslims (10 percent). Most hate crimes overall (60 percent) are property crimes (e.g., mischief). However, most hate crimes based on sexual orientation are violent in nature (75 percent). Hate crimes are most commonly committed by youth and young adults (ages 12–22) (Dauvergne, 2010).

The cognitive and affective components of prejudice do not necessarily correspond with its behavioural component. Individuals may have prejudicial thoughts and feelings, yet not engage in any discriminatory acts; conversely, others may engage in discriminatory acts even though they do not have prejudicial thoughts and feelings. Robert Merton (1949) created a typology that reflects the variety of ways that thoughts/feelings and behaviours may be related; this typology continues to be used today, although the specific labels used can vary (see Figure 8.6).

People who have prejudicial thoughts/feelings and then act upon them are *prejudiced discriminators* (or what Merton called "active bigots"). Those who do not act upon their prejudicial thoughts/feelings are *prejudiced nondiscriminators* (or what Merton called "timid bigots"); as prejudice becomes less acceptable in society, those who have prejudices are less likely engage in overt discrimination. People who do not have prejudicial thoughts/feelings and yet still act in discriminatory ways are *nonprejudiced discriminators* (or what Merton called "fair-weather liberals"). People may engage in discriminatory acts because of group pressure, or without realizing that they are acting in discriminatory ways. Finally, those who do not have prejudicial thoughts/feelings

FIGURE 8.6

Relationships between Prejudice and Discrimination

		Prejudicial Thoughts	
		Yes	No
Discriminatory Actions	Yes	Prejudiced discriminators ("active bigots")	Nonprejudiced discriminators ("fair-weather liberals")
	No	Prejudiced non-discriminators ("timid bigots")	Nonprejudiced non-discriminators ("all-weather liberals")

Source: Merton (1949).

and who do not act in discriminatory ways are *nonprejudiced nondiscriminators* (or what Merton called "all-weather liberals").

INSTITUTIONAL AND SYSTEMIC DISCRIMINATION

Institutional and systemic discrimination is that which is embedded in institutionalized policies and practices. It can occur within organizations, such as with discriminatory hiring practices. Hiring practices may be intentionally discriminatory, where a business will not

SOCIOLOGY ONLINE

THE CANADIAN ANTI-RACISM EDUCATION AND RESEARCH SOCIETY

The Canadian Anti-Racism Education and Research Society (www.stopracism.ca) provides a variety of videos, documents, and volunteer opportunities. With a particular emphasis on the actions of hate groups (e.g., white supremacist groups, such as the Aryan

Nations), it includes information on what racism is and the many forms it can take, how to recognize and respond to racist symbols, and how to report hate-based images and speech found on social networking sites.

hire members of certain ethnic groups. But they may be unintentionally discriminatory as well; for example, for many years, the height restrictions for police officers were indirectly discriminatory against people of Asian descent, who are (on average) slightly shorter than people of British, Western European, or Northern European descent. Subtle forms of discrimination are also evident in some geographic place names. For many years the Chinese community expressed concern over the name of a mountain peak overlooking Canmore, Alberta—"Chinaman's Peak." A series of hearings was held by the Geographic Place Names agency and the Alberta Historical Resources Foundation, and in the late 1990s, the peak was renamed "Ha Ling Peak" (www.kananaskis.com). Similarly, place names using the term "squaw" were also eliminated in Alberta and British Columbia in the 1990s.

Institutional and systemic discrimination can occur at the governmental level as well, as reflected in the policies and legislation that result in segregation and population transfer. Immigration policy itself can be discriminatory; sometimes this is direct and overt, while at other times it is indirect and more hidden. In Canadian history, we can see several examples of discriminatory immigration policies. For instance, until the 1960s the *Immigration Act* allowed for the exclusion of any group of immigrants on the basis of characteristics such as "peculiar customs, habits and modes of life [and] unsuitability with regard to the climate" (Canadian Council for Refugees, n.d.).

Special immigration policies were sometimes directed at particular groups. For example, although Chinese immigration began in Canada in the 1850s, when the Canadian Pacific Railway (CPR) was being built in the 1880s thousands of Chinese men were brought to Canada as labourers. Once the CPR was completed, strong anti-Asian sentiment led the government to restrict further Chinese immigration. A $50 head tax was imposed on Chinese immigrants in 1885, which was later increased to $500 in 1903 (equal to two years' wages for Chinese labourers). A total of $23 million was collected by the federal government through the Chinese head tax, at the same time as the government was *spending* more than $10 million to encourage immigration from Europe. Because the head tax did not sufficiently halt Chinese immigration in the eyes of the government, in 1923 the *Chinese Exclusion Act* was passed, which essentially halted immigration from China until it was repealed in 1947. As a result of the head tax and the *Exclusion Act,* many Chinese immigrants (including those who were brought to Canada to work on the CPR) were later unable to bring their wives and children to Canada, breaking up many families and creating a Chinese "bachelor community" (Canadian Council for Refugees, n.d.; Chinese Canadian National Council, 2003).

At the same time that the federal government was explicitly restricting Chinese immigration, there was also the desire to limit immigration from South Asia (e.g., India). However, like Canada, India was a British colony, and therefore the Canadian government was unable to overtly prohibit immigration from India. Instead, the government implemented a policy that would indirectly halt Indian immigration. The *Continuous Passage Act* (1908) "required all immigrants to arrive on uninterrupted journey on their passage ticket, a 'continuous passage', from their point of origin to Canada" (Citizenship and Immigration Canada, 2008, para. 2). Due to the length of the journey from India to Canada, ships normally had to make a stop in either Japan or Hawaii. Canadian Pacific initially did run a nonstop service from Vancouver to Calcutta, but the government required the company to halt that practice; at that point it was literally impossible for someone to travel from India to Canada on a continuous journey. Like the *Chinese Exclusion Act,* the *Continuous Passage Act* remained in place until 1947.

SOCIOLOGY IN THEORY

LO9 What are the causes of prejudice? Some theories attribute prejudice to characteristics of individuals. Theodor Adorno (1950), a philosopher associated with the Frankfurt school (a group of social theorists affiliated with the Frankfurt Institute for Social Research), suggested that some people have **authoritarian personalities**, which value authority and obedience, are low in tolerance, and are high in stereotypic thinking. People with authoritarian personalities are more likely to have prejudicial thoughts and feelings, and engage in discriminatory behaviour. Other scholars (e.g., Marger, 2003) propose that when experiencing frustration (e.g., through unemployment), some people direct their frustration at a **scapegoat**, someone who they can blame for their difficulties (e.g., blaming immigrants for "taking our jobs").

Authoritarian personality: A personality type that values authority and obedience, is low in tolerance, and is high in insecurity.

Scapegoat: An individual or group that is wrongfully blamed for a personal or social problem.

SOCIOLOGY *IN MY COMMUNITY*

THE INTERNATIONAL DAY FOR THE ELIMINATION OF RACIAL DISCRIMINATION

On March 21, 1960, 69 peaceful demonstrators were killed in South Africa, in a protest against apartheid. The United Nations has since declared March 21 to be the International Day for the Elimination of Racial Discrimination. Canada's first campaign was in 1989, and since that time, most of its campaigns have been targeted at youth. In 1996, the Government of Canada started an annual national video competition associated with the International Day for the Elimination of Racial Discrimination, open to youth ages 10–20. The winning videos are placed on YouTube, and can also be viewed on the website of Citizenship and Immigration Canada (www.cic.gc.ca). Events are held in recognition of this day at universities and colleges across the country as well. What events are being held this year at your institution?

Other theories attribute prejudice to social processes or characteristics of society. For example, one classic study (Sherif et al., 1961) illustrates **realistic conflict theory**, the idea that prejudice emerges from competition over scarce resources. At a boys' summer camp, boys were divided into two groups that were located in separate cabins some distance apart. Each group designed its own flag, and chose a name (i.e., "Rattlers" and "Eagles"). For the first week, the two groups engaged in a variety of activities together. During the second and third weeks, the Rattlers and the Eagles were forced to become competitors in a series of games and activities in which the winning team would receive a variety of valued prizes. It didn't take long for prejudice to appear and to quickly grow in magnitude. Each team started describing the other in derogatory terms (e.g., "bums") and expressed the superiority of their own group. Soon name-calling began, and then physical acts—stealing the property of members of the other team and vandalizing the other team's cabin. In fact, the researchers had to intervene to put a stop to the escalating destruction. Conflict between groups set the stage for the emergence of prejudicial thoughts, feelings, and behaviours.

At a more macro level, Marxist conflict theory proposes that the powerful have a vested interest in maintaining prejudice in society. By doing so, the economically oppressed will be too distracted by fighting with each other over scarce resources to join together to fight against their oppressors (Olzak, 2006). Also based on a conflict perspective,

dual/split labour market theory states that members of the dominant group in society will develop prejudices against minority groups in order to protect their position in the labour market (Bonacich, 1972). The *primary labour market* consists of higher paid, more secure jobs within which upward mobility is possible. The *secondary labour market* comprises jobs that are poorly paid, insecure (e.g., part-time; temporary), and provide little opportunity for advancement—the kind of jobs that people in the primary labour market would consider demeaning. Historically, members of minority groups have been overrepresented in the secondary labour market (Ravelli, Webber & Patterson, 2011).

Interactionist theories attribute prejudice to the processes by which we come to understand the nature of different ethnic groups, and judge them accordingly. As a result of our direct interactions (e.g., with significant others) or indirect interactions (e.g., with media), we may develop understandings of certain groups that are based on stereotypes, and of our own group(s) as being "superior." The labels that we then attach to members of specific groups affects the way that we perceive them, and subsequently treat them—that is, we treat them as the generic label rather than as individuals.

> **Realistic conflict theory:** Prejudice emerges as a result of competition over scarce resources.
>
> **Dual/split labour market theory:** Members of the dominant group in society will develop prejudices against minority groups in order to protect their position in the labour market.

There are other theories that focus less (or not at all) on the causes of prejudice, and more on understanding other aspects of ethnicity. For instance, multicultural feminists propose that there is no unified experience among members of any specific ethnic group, and draw attention to the intersection of race, ethnicity, socioeconomic status, and gender. The multidimensional nature of oppression means that only by listening to and understanding the experiences of specific groups (e.g., working-class Ethiopian women) can a broader understanding of the nature of oppression emerge (Lorber, 1998).

TIME TO REVIEW

- What are the three components of prejudice?
- What is discrimination, and at what levels does it occur?
- Do prejudicial thoughts/feelings and discriminatory behaviours necessarily accompany each other?
- In what ways have Canada's immigration policies been discriminatory?
- What are the causes of prejudice?

CHAPTER SUMMARY

LO¹ Compare and contrast the concepts of ethnicity, race, and visible minority.

Ethnicity refers to classifications of self and others based on cultural characteristics, such as shared ancestry, language, and cultural traditions; we can talk about objective ethnicity and subjective ethnicity. Race refers to a system of stratification based on physical differences, such as skin colour and facial features. According to Statistics Canada, visible minorities are those who are non-Caucasian or non-white in skin colour. Ethnicity, race, and visible-minority status are socially constructed.

LO² Describe contemporary patterns of ethnicity in Canada.

The 2006 Census found more than 200 different ethnic origins being reported by people living in Canada, compared to only 25 reported in 1901. The most frequently reported ethnic origins are those ethnic groups that have the longest immigration histories in Canada, such as English, French, and Scottish. Sixteen percent of people in Canada are visible minorities.

LO³ List the three objectives of Canada's immigration policy, and describe the types of individuals who enter the country on the basis of each of those objectives.

The three objectives of immigration policy are to reunite families; contribute to the nation's economic development, and protect refugees. Immigrants within the *family class* are sponsored by close relatives living in Canada. *Economic immigrants* are selected on the basis of their particular educational backgrounds, occupational skills, and ability to contribute to the Canadian economy. *Refugees* are persons who are forced to flee from persecution.

LO⁴ Describe contemporary immigration patterns, and explain how and why immigration patterns vary over time.

Almost 20 percent of Canada's population today is foreign born, with immigrants increasingly coming from non-European countries and settling in large urban centres. There are almost 150 different mother tongues, but the vast majority of immigrants also speak English and/or French. Immigration patterns are based on a variety of "push" and "pull" factors that have varied considerably over the past century. Immigration to Canada peaked in 1913, when we had a larger number of immigrants come to Canada's shores, and when immigrants made up a larger proportion of the population than at any time since.

LO⁵ Describe the implications of ethnicity for family structures, family interdependence, and intergenerational relationships.

Aboriginal people, immigrants, and visible minorities have a higher likelihood of living within an extended family structure, although most do live in nuclear family–based households. Youth from certain ethnic groups spend more time with adults, perceive household chores as expected rather than to be financially rewarded, and move out of the family home at later ages. Youth who have immigrated, or whose parents were immigrants, are bicultural and must adapt to having both a heritage culture and a new, national culture; this can result in family conflict. Youth may follow integration, ethnic, national, or diffuse patterns, which has implications for both psychological and sociocultural adaptation.

LO6 Describe how economic experiences vary on the basis of Aboriginal ancestry and immigration status.

On average, Aboriginal persons have lower incomes than non-Aboriginal people; however, this income disparity is virtually eliminated among those who have Bachelor's degrees. Those who are immigrants have lower incomes than nonimmigrants regardless of level of education; income disparity has actually increased over the past several decades. This is despite the fact that immigrants have higher levels of education than ever before, and are more likely to have a university degree than the Canadian-born population.

LO7 Distinguish between dominant and minority groups, and describe the forms of interactions that can take place between them.

Dominant groups and minority groups are differentiated on the basis of power. Interactions between dominant and minority groups can take the forms of assimilation, segregation, and population transfer.

LO8 Outline the three components of prejudice, and describe the different forms that discrimination can take.

Prejudice is an attitude that consists of cognitive, affective, and behavioural components. Discrimination can occur at the individual level, with behaviours ranging from offensive jokes to hate crimes. It can also occur at the institutional or systemic levels, such as in immigration policies.

LO9 Discuss different theories of the causes of prejudice.

Some theories attribute prejudice to characteristics of individuals, such as an authoritarian personality or the need to find a scapegoat for one's frustrations. Other theories attribute prejudice to social processes or characteristics of society, such as conflict over scarce resources or the understandings that we develop (through interaction) of the nature of certain ethnic groups. Some sociocultural theories, such as multicultural feminist theory, focus less on the causes of prejudice and more on other aspects of ethnicity or dominant group–minority group relations.

RECOMMENDED READINGS

1. For a thorough exploration of institutionalized racism in Canada, see: Henry, F., & Tator, C. (2010). *The Colour of Democracy: Racism in Canadian Society*. Toronto, ON: Nelson.
2. To see the variety of ways in which being Caucasian affects diverse aspects of everyday life, see: McIntosh, P. (1988). *White Privilege and Male Privilege: A Personal Account of Coming to See Correspondences through Work in Women's Studies*. Wellesley, MA: Wellesley College Center for Research on Women.

FOR FURTHER REFLECTION

1. How can prejudice be reduced? Do you think prejudice can be completely eliminated?
2. What are the pros and cons of assimilation?
3. Many instances of institutional or systemic discrimination have occurred in Canadian history. What are the solutions to redressing these past wrongs?

REFERENCES

Adorno, T. (1950). *The Authoritarian Personality*. New York: Harper.

Aronson, E., Wilson, T. D., Akert, R. M., & Fehr, B. (2010). *Social Psychology* (4th Can ed). Toronto, ON: Pearson Education Canada.

Baumrind, D. (1968). Authoritative vs. authoritarian parental control. *Adolescence, 3*, 255–272.

Baumrind, D. (1991). The influence of parenting style on adolescent competence and substance use. *Journal of Early Adolescence, 11*, 56–95.

Berry, J. W., Phinney, J. P., Sam, D. L., & Vedder, P. (2006). *Immigrant Youth in Cultural Transition: Acculturation, Identity, and Adaptation across National Contexts*. Mahwah, NJ: Lawrence Erlbaum Associates.

Black History Canada. (n.d.). *Timeline*. Retrieved January 17, 2011, from Blackhistorycanada.ca

Bonacich, E. (1972). A theory of ethnic antagonism: The split labor market. *American Sociological Review, 37*, 547–559.

Bonikowska, A., Hou, F., & Picot, G. (2011). Do highly educated immigrants perform differently in the Canadian and U.S. labour markets? *Analytical Studies Branch Research Paper*. Statistics Canada Catalogue No. 11F0019M-No. 329. Ottawa, ON: Statistics Canada.

Boyd, M. (2000). Ethnic variations in young adults living at home. *Canadian Studies in Population, 27*(1), 135–158.

Brewer, M. B., Dull, V., & Lui, L. (1981). Perceptions of the elderly: Stereotypes as prototypes. *Journal of Personality and Social Psychology, 41*, 656–670.

Broadway, M. (n.d.). Meatpacking, refugees and the transformation of Brooks, Alberta. Unpublished manuscript. Retrieved May 6, 2011, from classes.uleth .ca/200601/geog42202/Public_data_reading/Broadway_ meatpacking_brooks.doc

Canadian Council for Refugees. (n.d.). *Talking about Refugees and Immigrants: A Glossary of Terms*. Retrieved January 3, 2011, from www.ccrweb.ca

Canadian Council for Refugees. (2009). *10th Anniversary of Canada Signing the Refugee Convention, 1969–2009: Recognizing Successes. Acting for Change*. Retrieved January 3, 2011, from www.ccrweb.ca

Chinese Canadian National Council. (2003). *Chinese Head Tax and Exclusion Act Redress Backgrounder*. Retrieved November 5, 2010, from www.ccnc.ca

Citizenship and Immigration Canada. (2008). *The 100th Anniversary of the Continuous Passage Act*. Retrieved November 21, 2010, from www.cic.gc.ca

Citizenship and Immigration Canada. (2009). *Facts and Figures: Immigration Overview, Permanent and Temporary Residents 2008*. Ottawa, ON: Author.

Dauvergne, M. (2010). Police-reported hate crime in Canada, 2008. *Juristat, 30*. Ottawa, ON: Statistics Canada. Statistics Canada Catalogue No. 85-002-X.

Dewing, M. (2009). *Canadian Multiculturalism*. Ottawa, ON: Parliamentary Information and Research Service.

Frideres, J. S. (2007). Building bridges: Aboriginal, immigrant, and visible minority families in the 21st century. In C. Cheal (Ed.), *Canadian Families Today: New Perspectives* (pp. 195–212). Don Mills, ON: Oxford University Press.

Frideres, J. S., & Gadacz, R. R. (2008). *Aboriginal peoples in Canada* (8th ed.). Toronto, ON: Pearson Education Canada.

Fuligni, A., Yip, T., & Tseng, V. (2002). Impact of family obligation on daily activities and psychological well-being of Chinese-American adolescents. *Child Development, 73*, 302–314.

Georgas, J., Berry, J. W., VandeVijver, F., Kagitcibasi, C., & Poortinga, Y. (Eds.). (2006). *Families across Cultures: A 30 Nation Psychological Study*. Cambridge: Cambridge University Press.

Hiller, H. H., & Chow, V. (2005). Ethnic identity and assimilation among second-generation Chinese youth. *Sociological Studies of Children and Youth, 10*, 75–99.

Ho, C., Bluestein, D. N., & Jenkins, J. M. (2008). Cultural differences between parenting and children's behaviour. *Developmental Psychology, 44*(2), 507–522.

Jackson, A. (2001). Poverty and racism. *Perception Magazine, 24*(4). Retrieved January 7, 2011, from www.ccsd.ca

Jenkins, R. (2007). Ethnicity. In G. Ritzer (Ed.), *Blackwell Encyclopedia of Sociology*. Retrieved December 3, 2010, from www.blackwellreference.com

Kagitcibasi, C. (2007). *Family, Self, and Human Development across Cultures: Theory and Applications*. Mahwah, NJ: Lawrence Erlbaum Publishers.

Laroche, M., Annamma, J., Hui, M., & Chankon, K. (1992). An examination of ethnicity measures: Convergent validity and cross-cultural equivalence. *Advances in Consumer Research, 18*, 150–157.

Lorber, J. (1998). *Gender Inequality: Feminist Theories and Politics*. Cary, NC: Roxbury.

Marger, M. N. (2003). *Race and Ethnic Relations: American and Global Perspectives* (6th ed.). Belmont, CA: Wadsworth/ Thomson Learning.

Mariel Lemonik Arthur, M. (2007). Race. In G. Ritzer (Ed.), *Blackwell Encyclopedia of Sociology*. Retrieved December 3, 2010, from www.blackwellreference.com

Merton, R. K. (1949). Discrimination and the American creed. In R. M. MacIver (Ed.), *Discrimination and National Welfare* (pp. 77–145). New York: Harper.

Mitchell, B. A., Wister, A. V., & Gee, E. M. (2004). The ethnic and family nexus on homeleaving and returning among Canadian young adults. *Canadian Journal of Sociology, 29*(4), 543–575.

Nazneen, R. (2005). Bangladeshi Muslims in Montreal: A case of divided loyalty. *International Journal of Sociology of the Family, 31*(2), 109–122.

Olzak, S. (2006). *The Global Dynamics of Race and Ethnic Mobilization*. Stanford, CA: Stanford University Press.

Picot, G., Lu, Y., & Hou, F. (2009). Immigrant low-income rates: The role of market income and government transfers. *Perspectives, December*. Statistics Canada Catalogue No. 75-001-X. Ottawa, ON: Statistics Canada.

Poirier, G. W., & Lott, A. J. (1967). Galvanic skin response and prejudice. *Journal of Personality and Social Psychology, 5*(3), 253–259.

Ravelli, B., Webber, M., & Patterson, J. (2011). *Sociology for Everyone*. Toronto, ON: Pearson Education Canada.

Shams, M. (2001). Social support, loneliness and friendship among British Asian and non-Asian adolescents. *Social Behavior and Personality, 29*(4), 399–404.

Sherif, M. O., Harvey, O. J., White, B. J., Hood, W. R., & Sherif, W. (1961). *Intergroup Conflict and Cooperation: The Robbers' Cave Experiment*. Norman, OK: University of Oklahoma Press.

Statistics Canada. (2008a). *Canada's Ethnocultural Mosaic, 2006 Census*. Statistics Canada Catalogue No. 91-209-X. Ottawa, ON: Author.

Statistics Canada. (2008b). Census snapshot—Immigration in Canada: A portrait of the foreign-born population, 2006 Census. *Canadian Social Trends*. Statistics Canada Catalogue No. 11-008-X. Ottawa, ON: Author.

Statistics Canada. (2008c). *Aboriginal Peoples in Canada in 2006: Inuit, Métis and First Nations, 2006 Census*. Statistics Canada Catalogue No. 97-558-XIE. Ottawa, ON: Author.

Statistics Canada. (2009). Earning differences between immigrants and the Canadian-born: The role of literacy skills. *Education Matters, March 2009*. Statistics Canada Catalogue No. 81-004-X. Ottawa, ON: Author.

Statistics Canada. (2011a). Income statistics in constant (2005) dollars, age group, Aboriginal identity, Registered Indian Status and Aboriginal ancestry, highest certificate, diploma, or degree and sex for the population 15 and over with income of Canada, provinces, territories, 2000 and 2005. *2006 Census of Population*. Statistics Canada Catalogue No. 97-563-SCB2006006. Ottawa, ON: Author.

Statistics Canada. (2011b). Income statistics in constant (2005) dollars, age group, immigrant status and period of immigration, highest certificate, diploma, or degree and sex for the population 15 and over with income of Canada, provinces, territories, 2000 and 2005. *2006 Census of Population*. Statistics Canada Catalogue No. 97-563-SCB2006006. Ottawa, ON: Author.

Talbani, A., & Hasalani, P. (2000). Adolescent females between tradition and modernity: Gender role socialization in South Asian immigrant cultures. *Journal of Adolescence, 23*, 615–627.

Wirth, L. (1945). The problem of minority groups. In R. Linton (Ed.), *The Science of Man in the World Crisis*. New York: Columbia University Press.

Vedder, P., Berry, J., Sabatier, C., & Sam, D. (2008). The intergenerational transmission of values in national and immigrant families: The role of Zeitgeist. *Journal of Youth and Adolescence, 38*, 642–653.

ENDNOTE

[1] Retrieved November 27, 2010, from www.brainyquote.com.

Learning What Is "True": Religion, Science, and Education

LEARNING OBJECTIVES AND OUTCOMES

After completing this chapter, students should be able to do the following:

LO1 Explain what belief systems are and identify their components.

LO2 Describe religious patterns in Canada and identify the implications of religiosity for individuals and for society.

LO3 Compare and contrast key sociological theories of religion.

LO4 Identify the different ways that sociologists perceive the nature of scientific "truth," and explain the role of poststructuralist and feminist perspectives in the sociological study of science.

LO5 Compare and contrast theoretical views of the role of education in modern society within contemporary debates about education.

> *Facts are enemies of truth.*
>
> *(Miguel de Cervantes)*[1]

At first glance, the above quotation, from the novel *Don Quixote*, may appear to be a contradiction. After all, aren't "truth" and "fact" one in the same? As the main character in the novel discovers, the two are not necessarily related. In Don Quixote's imagined world, he lives a life of chivalry—to him, the "truth" is that a neighbouring girl is his love, a nearby innkeeper is the lord of a castle with power to grant him knighthood, windmills are evil beasts to be destroyed, and he is the knight in shining armor dedicated to saving the world and winning his true love's heart. Even if not based upon facts, what Don Quixote believes to be true is the foundation for his everyday life, and is the core of his identity. However, eventually "facts" come to light that begin to challenge his beliefs and he discovers that this world was only imaginary; this new "truth," one based on fact, is his demise, sending him into a deep depression from which he never emerges.

How does each of us come to know what the truth of this world is, and what the facts are? Three of society's institutions are central to the processes by which we learn what is true. *Religion* has served as a purveyor of truth for thousands of years; for most of human history, its claims have been granted the greatest legitimacy. Religion continues to play a significant role today. However, following the Enlightenment, *science* became the institution whose claims to truth were perceived as the most legitimate; as the token "expert" on any daytime talk show or in any daily news story illustrates, we frequently believe what a scientist tells us, simply because he or she is a perceived *authority* doing the telling. Finally, the *education* system presents us with various facts and teaches us what is true; throughout its history, it has embodied both religion and science. But "facts" and "truth" are not static—they are dynamic and therefore subject to change. For instance, prior to Copernicus and Galileo, the accepted truth was that the Earth is the centre of the universe. The work of those two astronomers presented new "facts" and eventually changed what was accepted as the truth; however, Galileo was also arrested and convicted as a heretic for proclaiming this truth, and was released from prison only after confessing that he had been lying, and that it was not, in fact, true. The changing nature of facts and truth are not limited to the more distant past. In the early 20th century, for example, scientists claimed that masturbation caused acne, hairy palms, a deformed body, and ultimately resulted in insanity (Hunt, 1998).

LO1 To accept something as true, regardless of whether it is *actually* true or not, is to have a **belief**. When beliefs are interconnected in a systematic fashion and they are shared among groups of people, they are called **belief systems** (Stebbins, 1996). The different religions of the world, disciplines of science, and even ideologies of political parties, are belief systems. Belief systems have three different components (Ben-Yehuda, 1990) (see Figure 9.1, page 190). First, they include *claims about the nature of reality* or what is "real." Thus, Buddhism tells us that reincarnation is real, chemistry tells us that combining hydrogen and oxygen (in specific amounts) creates water, and social conservative political parties tell us that the family is declining.

> **Belief:** Something one accepts as true, regardless of whether it is actually true or not.
>
> **Belief system:** A set of interconnected beliefs that are shared among groups of people.

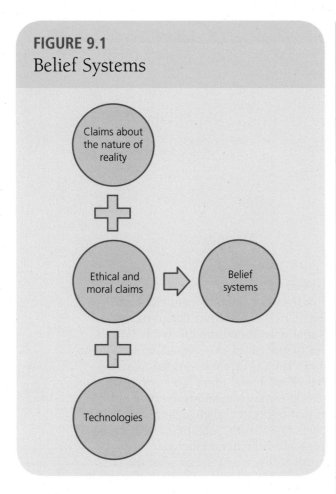

FIGURE 9.1
Belief Systems

- Claims about the nature of reality
- Ethical and moral claims
- Technologies

→ Belief systems

Second, belief systems include *ethical and moral claims* that tell us what is "right." Most of the world's major religions explicitly tell us that the right thing to do is to treat others the way that we would like

them to treat us. The ethical and moral claims in political ideologies are also typically explicit, such as when the Conservative Party's 2006 election platform included a statement condemning the decriminalization of marijuana. In science, ethical and moral claims are less explicit, but still present nonetheless. Such claims are reflected, in part, in what scientists choose to study; for instance, research on cloning contains an implicit claim that cloning is acceptable.

Finally, belief systems include *technologies* (or techniques) that are used to obtain or use the knowledge that is considered to be the truth. Prayer, meditation, and religious rituals are the techniques used in religion; the techniques in science include the scientific method, the specific research methods described in Chapter 2, and methodologies specific to certain scientific disciplines (e.g., astronomers measure radio waves to determine what is happening with stars).

RELIGION

"Religion" is one of those terms that most of us implicitly know what it means, but find it difficult to define. Just as we saw in Chapter 4 that there are varying definitions of "family," similarly there are varying definitions of religion. Definitions of religion typically centre on beliefs about the true meaning of life and they make reference to a supreme being, the sacred cosmos, and/or the supernatural realm. For example, the Ontario Consultants on Religious Tolerance (www.religioustolerance.org) define religion as "any specific system of belief about deity, often involving rituals, a code of ethics, and a philosophy of

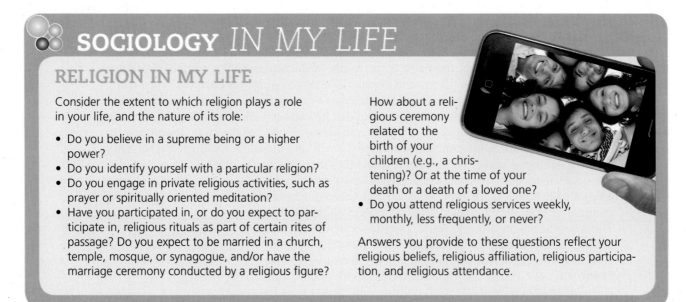

SOCIOLOGY *IN MY LIFE*

RELIGION IN MY LIFE

Consider the extent to which religion plays a role in your life, and the nature of its role:

- Do you believe in a supreme being or a higher power?
- Do you identify yourself with a particular religion?
- Do you engage in private religious activities, such as prayer or spiritually oriented meditation?
- Have you participated in, or do you expect to participate in, religious rituals as part of certain rites of passage? Do you expect to be married in a church, temple, mosque, or synagogue, and/or have the marriage ceremony conducted by a religious figure?

How about a religious ceremony related to the birth of your children (e.g., a christening)? Or at the time of your death or a death of a loved one?

- Do you attend religious services weekly, monthly, less frequently, or never?

Answers you provide to these questions reflect your religious beliefs, religious affiliation, religious participation, and religious attendance.

life." **Religion**, "then, is a social institution involving beliefs and practices based on recognizing the sacred" (Macionis & Gerber, 2008, p. 492).

LO² RELIGIOUS PATTERNS

In the world, there are at least 19 major world religions (e.g., Christianity, Islam, Buddhism), subdivided into more than 270 large religious groups, and even more small religious groups; for instance, there are 34,000 separate and distinct Christian groups in the world (Barrett et al., cited in Ontario Consultants on Religious Tolerance, 2009). The largest religious groups in the world, based on proportion of the population are Christianity (33 percent), Islam (21 percent), and Hinduism (14 percent) (see Figure 9.2) (Adherents.com, 2007). However, projections are that by 2025, Islam will continue to grow to 30 percent, while Christianity is expected to decline to 25 percent (Ontario Consultants on Religious Tolerance, 2009).

In many ways, Canadian society, as well as the rest of the world, is becoming more **secular** (i.e., not governed by religion). However, religion does continue to play a significant role in many people's lives, in that most Canadians still identify with some kind of religious belief system. In Canada, **religious affiliation** (i.e., identifying with a particular religion) declined between 1985 and 2004, from 88 percent to 81 percent (Clark & Schellenberg, 2006). Reflecting Canada's Euro-centric immigration patterns (see Chapter 8), the predominant religious affiliation is Roman Catholicism (43 percent of those with a religious affiliation), followed by various forms of Protestantism. **Religious attendance** (i.e., attendance at organized religious services such as church) has also declined from 78 percent in 1985 to 66 percent in 2005 (Lindsay, 2008). However, although only 66 percent of Canadians attend religious services, 82 percent engage in some form of private religious activity, such as prayer and reading sacred texts (Clark & Schellenberg,

> **Religion:** A social institution involving beliefs and practices based on recognizing the sacred.
>
> **Secular:** The state of not being governed by religion.
>
> **Religious affiliation:** The identification with a particular religion.
>
> **Religious attendance:** Attendance at organized religious services.

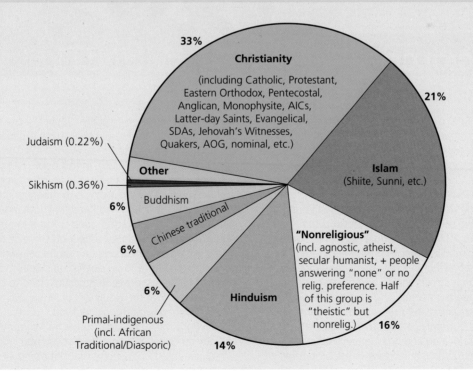

FIGURE 9.2
Major World Religions

Source: Copyright © 2005 Adherents.com. http://www.adherents.com/Religions_By_Adherents.html

2006). Two-thirds of people with a religious affiliation say that religion is of "high" or "moderate" importance to them,

Sociologists combine religious affiliation, religious attendance, participation in private religious activities, and the importance of religion into a single measure, called the **religiosity index**, and people can then score as "low," "moderate," or "high" on this measure (see Figure 9.3). Religiosity tends to be higher among immigrants than among Canadian-born people, especially those from South Asia (e.g., India, Pakistan), South East Asia (e.g., Philippines, Thailand), the Caribbean (e.g., Jamaica, Bahamas), and South America (e.g., Brazil, Argentina). Religiosity also tends to be higher among older age groups than among younger ones (Clark & Schellenberg, 2006).

Among youth, 68 percent of Canadian teenagers express a religious affiliation and 53 percent have attended a religious services in the previous year. However, many youth say that they would be open to greater involvement with religious groups "if I found it to be worthwhile." Furthermore, 84 percent of youth expect to have a religious wedding, and a

Religiosity index:
A combined measure of religious affiliation, attendance, and participation.

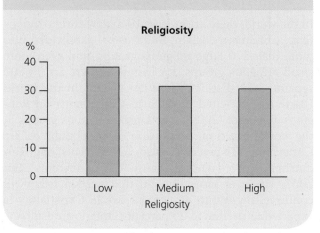

FIGURE 9.3

Religiosity among Canadians (ages 15 and over)

Source: Clark and Schellenberg (2006).

similar proportion expect to call on a religious figure when a funeral is needed (Bibby, 2009).

Religious affiliation, religious attendance, and religiosity in general have declined in Canada over the

SOCIOLOGY *IN MY COMMUNITY*

RELIGION IN THE LIVES OF CANADIANS

Sociologist Reginald Bibby, who has studied religious patterns in Canada over the last few decades, is also a practitioner of public sociology. In 2004, he brought the results of sociological research into the "real world" of Canada's Christian churches in his book *Restless Churches: How Canada's Churches Can Contribute to the Emerging Religious Renaissance*. Directed at an audience involved in ministry, he presents data on religious beliefs, affiliation, attendance, and importance. He critiques media stories that have equated declines in religious affiliation and religious attendance with a decrease in religious *beliefs*, and points out that Canadians are not abandoning religion. Religion is a part of most Canadians' lives, and many Canadians who do not currently participate in religion are in the process of searching and questioning. Although some religions have shown a decrease in the proportion of

Canadians affiliated with them over the last several decades (e.g., Anglican), others have experienced considerable increases (e.g., evangelical Christian, Aboriginal spirituality, Jewish). In this book, Bibby combines sociological research findings with information on what churches can do to remain contemporary and to grow, such as by attracting and keeping youth interest. He states, "What I am attempting to do is to present the key findings with clarity, reflect on some of the major implications, acknowledge a number of significant hurdles that have to be cleared, and spell out some of the tangible responses that groups need to consider. My hope is that the result will be enhanced ministry and enriched living for all involved" (p. ix). Reflecting C. Wright Mill's message from a half-century earlier, Bibby demonstrates that the sociological imagination is not just about *knowing*, it is about *doing* as well.

last few decades. However, despite this decline, regardless of which aspect of religiosity we examine, religion plays a role in the lives of the majority of Canadians. This is an important fact, because religion is about more than just beliefs: it has implications ranging from the micro level to the macro level.

TIME TO REVIEW

- What are *beliefs* and *belief systems*? What are some examples?
- What role do religion, science, and education play in teaching us the "truth"?
- How many religions are there in the world, and which are the largest?
- What are the patterns of religious affiliation, religious attendance, private religious participation, and religiosity in Canada?

IMPLICATIONS OF RELIGION

IMPLICATIONS FOR INDIVIDUALS

At the micro level, religion has an impact on various aspects of people's everyday lives. Among adults, religiosity is associated with better physical health, lower levels of depression and anxiety, and lower levels of substance use (Schieman, 2008). Among adolescents, religiosity (and especially religious attendance) is associated with a wide range of positive outcomes: higher friendship quality; stronger relationships with parents; greater academic orientation; greater feelings of well-being; less permissive attitudes towards risky behaviours (e.g., crime, alcohol use, hard drug use, and marijuana use); less participation in risky behaviours; and lower likelihood of premature sexual activity (Good & Willoughby, 2006). Interestingly, religious attendance was influential for adolescents, regardless of whether they had strong personal religious beliefs or not. That is, even when adolescents attended religious services only because their parents made them, they experienced the same level of positive outcomes as those who attended services *and* had strong personal religious beliefs. Conversely, youth who had personal religious beliefs but did not attend religious services did not have those positive outcomes; instead, their outcomes were similar to youth who had no religious beliefs and did not attend any services. The significance of religious attendance for these positive outcomes among adolescents suggests that the sense of belonging and group membership that comes from regular participation in other types of organized activities (e.g., nonreligious clubs) may be associated with similar benefits (Good & Willoughby, 2006).

Religion provides people with a community and a sense of belonging. Among individuals who attend religious services at least once a month, 22 percent say that it is the people, the community, and the fellowship that is the main thing that religious involvement adds to their lives (Bibby, 2006). Religious involvement provides *social capital* (Putnam, 2000; Bramadat, 2005). **Social capital** refers to resources that we accumulate by virtue of the social networks to which we belong. Just as possessing a screwdriver enables us to assemble the toys that we bought our children, and obtaining a university degree provides us with a higher income, our relationships with other people provide us with resources that we can use in various aspects of our lives—they provide us with knowledge, skills, understandings of the world and ourselves, a network of support, and a source of confidence or self-esteem.

Religion can also provide us with **bridging capital**, where the resources that we accumulate through interactions with our religious group can be used outside the religious realm, just as we saw above that religious attendance is associated with greater academic orientation among adolescents; religious attendance provides youth with intangible resources that enable them to do better in school, and develop higher educational aspirations. It can also provide us with **bonding capital**, that is a sense of community and belonging, and a social identity based on the particular religious group to which we belong (Putnam, 2000). That bonding can have both positive and negative consequences for society, as can other aspects of religious organizations.

IMPLICATIONS FOR SOCIETY

Bramadat (2005) refers to **positive bonding capital** and **negative bonding capital**. The group cohesiveness, solidarity, and social identity that religion can provide can bring benefits to society in some situations, while causing

> **Social capital:** Resources in the form of accumulated social networks.
>
> **Bridging capital:** Resources accumulated within religious groups that can be used outside the religious realm.
>
> **Bonding capital:** Resources in the form of religious community ties and identity.
>
> **Positive bonding capital:** Religious community ties and sources of identity that are of benefit to the wider society.
>
> **Negative bonding capital:** Religious community ties and sources of identity that pose harm to the wider society.

social harms in other circumstances. For example, through its effect on individual and group behaviours, religiosity can "make the world a better place." Canadians with religious affiliations are more philanthropic than those without such affiliations, donating more money to social causes and volunteering more of their time (Berger, 2006). People without religious affiliations donate an average of $105 per year to social causes, or 0.19 percent of their household incomes. In contrast, those with religious affiliations donate between $188 and $687 per year, or 0.32 percent to 1.7 percent of their household incomes. Berger finds that the social identity that religion provides is central to this pattern—the social norms of the group and the personal attitudes of its members. Of particular relevance are feelings of communal responsibility and reciprocity, which were found to be stronger in those with religious affiliations than those without religious affiliations.

Just as religious *individuals* donate their own money or time to social causes, religious *groups* have also taken on social causes, both historically and in the present. During the Victorian era in Canada, the theology of the Social Gospel (which applied Protestant ideals to solving social problems) gave rise to the **child-savers movement,** a movement dedicated to the betterment of social conditions involving children (Platt, 1977; Valverde, 1991; Jordan, 1998). At a time when urbanization was occurring and industrialization progressing, concerns grew over the cities' children. Many children of the working class were employed in unregulated, unhealthy, and exploitive working conditions; few were receiving any formal education; and some were being abused or neglected by their parents. The efforts of the child-savers movement resulted in several new pieces of legislation. Child labour laws restricted the ages at which children could be employed, the industries in which they could work, and the length of their work days. Compulsory schooling legislation required children to attend school for a certain number of days each year, until they reached a particular age. Criminal laws prohibited child abuse and neglect.

In contemporary society, religious groups frequently engage in charitable and humanitarian work. They bring humanitarian aid following natural disasters; offer hot meals to the homeless; operate food bank pickup locations in the basements of churches, temples, mosques, and synagogues; provide education to children in the developing world; and fundraise for various charities. However, not all religious bonding capital serves positive ends. Negative bonding capital can

Child-savers movement: A movement dedicated to the betterment of social conditions involving children.

WE'RE RIGHT

EVERYONE ELSE IS WRONG

WE'RE BETTER THAN YOU

The only Universal Truths that all religions agree upon

contribute to social inequality, religious conflict, acts of violence, and war. When a cohesive group sees itself as "part of a purely embattled minority" (Bramadat, 2005), an "us versus them" mentality is created. Members of such groups perceive their belief system and associated way of living as the only moral path—their ways are "right," and everyone else's ways are "wrong."

As a result, some groups may isolate themselves from the larger society, creating a separate existence based on their own religious ideals and principles. In other cases, members of such groups or the groups as a whole may try to create large-scale change to either spread their belief system or punish those with different belief systems. The consequences can be far-reaching. They include 500 years of war between the Christian and Islamic churches during the Crusades (from the 11th through the 16th centuries); the European "witchcraze," where up to 100,000 people were persecuted as witches from the 14th through the 17th centuries (Anderson & Gordon, 1978; Barstow, 1994; Quaife, 1987; Ben-Yehuda, 1980); the colonization of Indigenous groups worldwide and Canadian residential schooling (see Chapter 4); the murder of doctors who perform abortions by anti-abortion extremists; and suicide bombers (Bramadat, 2005).

TIME TO REVIEW

- What are the implications of religiosity in the everyday lives of adults and adolescents?

- What is *social capital*, and what types of social capital emerge from belonging to a religious group?

- What are some historical and contemporary examples of the positive and the negative ends that can be served by *bonding capital*?

SOCIOLOGY IN THEORY

LO3 When sociologists study religion, they do not try to validate or to disprove particular belief systems. Rather, sociologists analyze "how individuals, social institutions, and cultures construe God or the sacred . . . , how these ideas penetrate public culture and individual lives, and . . . the implications of those interpretations for individual, institutional, and societal processes" (Dillon, 2007, para. 6). *Substantive* approaches focus on the meanings that are contained within specific doctrines, and how those meanings are understood by people in their everyday lives. *Functional* approaches emphasize the social aspects of religion, the functions it serves, and its implications for individuals and for society.

The sociological study of religion is as old as the discipline of sociology itself. Functionalist Émile Durkheim (1915/1965) suggested that religion played an important role in creating and maintaining social solidarity. He stated that in even what he perceived to be as the most "primitive" societies, large numbers of people would gather to participate in religious rituals. Through this process, they would be exposed to the accumulated wisdom of their culture, thereby developing a **collective conscience**. In their group worship of sacred objects and ideals, people would also be caught up in a **collective effervescence**, an enthusiasm or euphoria that enabled them to transcend the challenges of every day. However, Durkheim suggested that with industrialization, over time other institutions would increasingly take over some of the functions that were traditionally fulfilled by religion. Contemporary functionalists continue to focus on the role that religion plays in social integration. They also study the impact of religion on individual behaviours and outcomes, such as those related to physical and mental health, substance use, and philanthropic behaviours (as described earlier). Finally, they analyze some of the *dysfunctions* of religion, such as residential schooling, war, and acts of violence.

Karl Marx (1844/1970) described religion as the *opium of the people* (sometimes referred to as an *opiate of the masses*). The oppressed proletariat escapes from the ugliness of their lives into religion. Although this provides them with temporary relief from life's difficulties, it also prevents them from seeing the structured inequality within which they exist. Consequently, it precludes them from rising up and overthrowing their oppressors. Contemporary conflict theorists continue to look at the ways that religion can serve as an agent of social control, creating, maintaining, and justifying inequality. For example, the conflict perspective gives rise to analyses of inequalities that exist within religion, such as in religions that restrict the participation of women as religious leaders. At a more macro level, the perspective also draws attention to the role of religion in perpetuating societal inequalites, such as the religious justification provided for India's caste system (see Chapter 6), the doctrine that rationalized the colonization of the world's non-Christians (see Chapter 4), and the religious interpretations that are often drawn upon in opposition to same-sex marriage.

Perhaps the most well known sociological analysis of religion comes from Max Weber, who thoroughly explored the relationship between religion and social change, studying Protestantism, Confucianism, Hinduism, Buddhism, and ancient Judaism. His book, *The Protestant Ethic and the Spirit of Capitalism* (1904/1958), has been ranked as the fourth most influential sociology book of the 20th century (Drysdale, 2007). In this book, he analyzes the foundational role that Protestant doctrine played in establishing early capitalism. Unlike Marx, who suggests that changing economic structures create subsequent changes in thought, Weber argued that changes in thought—the way people understand themselves and the world around them—precede structural changes.

Catholicism had emphasized the abandonment of worldly lives; people had to have a vocation in order to survive, but their attention should be focused on their spirituality and faith.

In contrast, Protestant doctrine established that participating in worldly economic activities was a morally worthy vocation. Each of us has been placed on the Earth for a specific purpose, whether it be religious leadership, carpentry, or farming. Working hard at that vocation is fulfilling your life's purpose. Protestant doctrine also emphasized predestination, the belief that what would happen to your soul in the afterlife was already predetermined. Because there was no certain way to know what that future would be, people experienced anxiety. However, achieving economic success in one's vocation was a "reward" from God, and could therefore be taken as a small sign of your soul's predestined path, thereby reducing some of your anxiety. Thus, the accumulation of wealth was a sign of salvation to come, and the accumulation of wealth is the foundation of capitalism. Max Weber's work was the underpinning of the future interactionist perspective. Contemporary interactionists study

> **Collective conscience:**
> The accumulated wisdom of a culture that develops from participation in religious rituals.
>
> **Collective effervescence:** The enthusiasm to transcend the challenges of everyday life, which emerges from religious rituals.

Each of these symbols represents a different world religion.

Source: casejustin/Shutterstock

the ways that the social interactions, rituals, and symbols that comprise religious belief and practice contribute to people's understandings of life and society, and to the development of their identities.

Feminist perspectives focus on various aspects of religion, but with a shared emphasis on the absence or the oppression of women. Feminist research on religion is intimately intertwined with forms of feminist religious and spiritual practice (Stuckey, 1998). *Revisionists* suggest that if the doctrines of the world's major religions are interpreted "correctly," the true message is one of equality. *Reformists* draw attention to the sexist language and rituals that have become a part of some of religions; they emphasize the importance of removing those aspects of religious practice, and integrating more female imagery and symbols. *Revolutionaries* look at how removing some of the traditional boundaries of certain religions, and integrating some images and rituals from outside those traditional boundaries, can serve positive ends for women in society. Finally, *rejectionists* perceive inherent sexism in the world's major religions, and call for abandoning those religions while adopting

Scientism: A world view that uses the insights of natural science to inform people's ways of living, their purpose in life, and the choices they make.

Science: An institution that provides a way to understand the natural makeup of the world by means of rational methods of inquiry.

female-centred spirituality, such as Goddess Worship (Stuckey, 1998).

Postmodern perspectives highlight the plurality of all religions and spiritualities. There is no singular "Hinduism" or "Judaism" that we can speak of, but rather a multiplicity of different forms. For example, the "Islam" of the 9/11 terrorists is not the same "Islam" as that adhered to by most people who consider themselves Muslim (Bramadat, 2005), yet this is arguably the strongest image Westerners have of the Muslim faith. Even within the multiplicity of different forms of particular religions, each individual has his or her own experience and perceptions of that religion and/or spiritual pursuit. In terms of religious practice, postmodern perspectives are associated with individually focused religious and spiritual practice, such as "New Age" spirituality and "spiritual seeking," which may draw upon bits and pieces of a variety of world religions and spiritual pursuits.

TIME TO REVIEW

- What is the difference between substantive and functional approaches to the sociological study of religion?
- How is religion studied within functionalist, conflict, interactionist, feminist, and postmodern perspectives?

LO⁴ THE TRANSITION TO SCIENTIFIC "TRUTH"

Although religion continues to play a role in the "truth" of most people's lives, since the Renaissance and the scientific revolution, **scientism**—"a worldview that uses the insights of natural science to inform people's way of living, their purpose in life, and the choices they make" (Walach & Reich, 2005, p. 425)—has increasingly characterized society. **Science** is an institution that provides "a way to understand the natural makeup of the world by means of rational methods of inquiry" (Walach & Reich, 2005, p. 425). The truths provided by science are often granted the greatest legitimacy in society—if science tells us something, we presume it must be true.

Functionalist Robert Merton (1973) is often credited as the founder of the sociology of science. In the present day, the study of science is highly interdisciplinary, studied by sociologists, historians, feminists, and philosophers. These scholars tend to identify themselves in an interdisciplinary way, rather than associate themselves with any single discipline (Varcoe, 2007). Contemporary social studies of science share the basic assumption that "science is a product in some form of social processes" (Varcoe, 2007, para. 10). Outside of that shared assumption, there are myriad of ways in which science is studied. One way of looking at the diversity in social studies of science is to explore perceptions of scientific truth.

What is the nature of scientific truth? Sociologists do not agree on the answer to that question. One approach proposes that scientific knowledge is a distinct form of knowledge that provides an objective truth. The other approach suggests that scientific truths are no different than any other types of truths. All forms of knowledge are socially constructed, emerging from a complex web of social structures, processes, and interactions. We examine these two approaches in the following sections.

SCIENTIFIC KNOWLEDGE AS OBJECTIVE TRUTH

Sociologists who perceive scientific knowledge as objective and distinct from other forms of knowledge focus their analyses on particular aspects of science. They study "the institutional norms that regulate the activity of the community of scientists; competition; the reward structure of science operating through 'recognition' (citation processes, Nobel prizes, peer review); and similar topics" (Varcoe, 2007, para. 2).

Merton (1973) describes the *normative structure of science*, a set of norms that are embedded within the institution of science itself and which make science a self-governing institution based upon objectivity. The first norm is **communism**, the notion that scientific knowledge is to be freely shared with others. The second norm is **universalism**—scientific knowledge is to be free of any social biases, such as racism. The third norm is **disinterestedness**, whereby scientists do their work for the purposes of discovering truth rather than for any personal gains. The final norm is **organized skepticism**, the idea that scientific claims should be subjected to rigorous scrutiny before they are accepted. It is because of these four norms that scientific knowledge is considered to be a distinct form of knowledge. Merton recognized that the norms of science could be perverted in some societies, such as Nazi Germany, and acknowledged that even in North America, some individual scientists might violate these norms. However, he indicated that when the institution of science was in a fit state, objective truths were uncovered.

SCIENTIFIC KNOWLEDGE AS CONSTRUCTED

Those who perceive scientific knowledge as being no different than other forms of knowledge focus their analyses on how scientific knowledge emerges, is accepted, and is affected by social and political forces. For instance, Thomas Kuhn (1962) placed science within an historical context, and analyzed the processes by which scientific knowledge develops and comes to be accepted as truth. He suggests that the history of science is one of *scientific revolutions* rather than a gradual accumulation of knowledge. Certain **paradigms** (i.e., conceptual frameworks) come to characterize particular sciences; these paradigms govern how reality is understood. Most scientists operate within those paradigms for extended periods of time, building knowledge within it and refining it when necessary. But then once in awhile, a **paradigm shift** occurs—a series of anomalies begin to accumulate, a scientist subsequently proposes a completely different way of understanding the object of study, and changes that scientific discipline forever. However, this shift is frequently resisted. This is what happened when Galileo reiterated Copernicus's claim that the planets in the solar system revolve around the sun, and was subsequently imprisoned. This is also what happened when, in the 20th century, two astronomers claimed that measuring radio waves provided insight into the events that were happening in the solar system and the universe. Although this later became the dominant paradigm within astronomy, initially these astronomers had difficulty finding a journal to publish their paper, and were treated as outcasts within the discipline (Ben-Yehuda, 1986, 1990).

Other analysts of science draw attention to the fact that scientific knowledge is "dependent on the

Norm of communism: The notion that scientific knowledge is to be freely shared with others.

Norm of universalism: The notion that scientific knowledge is free of social biases.

Norm of disinterestedness: The notion whereby scientists do their work solely for the purposes of discovering truth.

Norm of organized skepticism: The notion that scientific claims should be subjected to rigorous scrutiny.

Paradigm: A conceptual framework or model for organizing information.

Paradigm shift: Movement away from a particular conceptual framework.

social frameworks in which it is produced" (Eriksson, 2007, para. 7). Some scholars emphasize the ways that social and political influences shape the topics that scientists study and thereby the scientific truths that are created. For example, in order to appeal to his social conservative supporters, American President George W. Bush halted public funding for stem cell research; existing supplies of stem cells (which can be obtained from embryos) could be utilized, but no funds would be provided for subsequent research. Given the central role of American biomedical research in the world, this political decision had a significant impact on the development of scientific knowledge that could potentially benefit people with spinal cord injuries and Parkinson's disease.

We can also see the manner in which social and political forces can shape scientific knowledge outside the ideologies of specific political parties. The success of the Human Genome Project, which completed a first map of the human genome in the early 21st century, opened up a whole new world of genetic research. However, scientific, social, and ethical concerns have emerged about the potential of that research to violate human rights if used in the wrong way. Consequently, national governments have implemented various forms of legislation to control potential harms, such as by prohibiting human cloning. Various international organizations have also established broader frameworks to guide genetic research (see *Sociology in Practice*).

Sociologists who study the social construction of scientific truths also draw attention to the impact of funding structures, such as those associated with the corporatization of science. Over the last few decades, the proportion of research that is funded by commercial industry and that takes places in commercial research centres has grown tremendously; this is especially the case with biomedical research. This has significant implications for the development of scientific knowledge. First, the contracts between the industry and the scientists frequently give all publication rights to the industry sponsor. The company has the right to decide which research results will or will not be submitted for publication, thereby having a direct impact on the body of scientific knowledge in the area. Second, and even more significantly, research that is sponsored by commercial industry is more likely to have positive findings than research that is publicly funded through research grants. For instance, pharmaceutical research that is conducted by industry-funded scientists is more likely to conclude that a new drug is effective when compared to publicly funded research on the very same drug (Bereska, 2011; Born, 2004; Caulfield, 2004). Thus, the scientific "truths" uncovered within certain funding structures can be very different from those obtained within other types of funding structures.

Analyses of the processes by which scientific knowledge develops, as well as the social, political, and economic forces that can shape it, draw attention to scientific truths being socially constructed rather than revealing an objective reality. At a theoretical level, postmodern/poststructural and feminist approaches play key roles within this perspective.

SOCIOLOGY *IN PRACTICE*

UNIVERSAL DECLARATION ON THE HUMAN GENOME AND HUMAN RIGHTS

The experiences of World War II drew attention to the horrific ways that human beings could be treated in certain situations, as was the case in Nazi concentration camps. Consequently, in 1948 the United Nations developed and adopted the *Universal Declaration of Human Rights*, a document that governs various aspects of international law and serves as the foundation for human rights policies and legislation in countries throughout the world. As genetic research was rapidly progressing in the 1990s, UNESCO (United Nations Educational, Scientific, and Cultural Organization) similarly developed and adopted the *Universal Declaration on the Human Genome and Human Rights*.

This document, as well as similar guidelines developed by other organizations and groups, includes prohibitions against human cloning and principles governing respect for human dignity, genetic equality, the right to genetic privacy, health protection and promotion, and public participation in decision-making processes (Jones, 2001).

SOCIOLOGY IN THEORY

POSTMODERN/POSTSTRUCTURAL THEORIES

Poststructuralist Michel Foucault (1980) explained that "knowledge" is not an independent, objective entity, but rather is intimately intertwined with power. When particular truths are espoused by people who are located within institutions that hold power in society, those truths are accepted by large numbers of people in that society; those claims come to be recognized as legitimate knowledge. Consequently, when Galileo's scientific claims contradicted the claims of the Christian Church, Galileo ended up on the losing end, because the Church had the ultimate institutionalized power in society at the time. It was only as science came to hold more institutionalized power following the Enlightenment that its knowledge became more legitimized. In science today, power continues to be intertwined with knowledge, which we can see in the tangible economic power that governments and commercial industries have in controlling research funds; in this case, power affects not only what is accepted as knowledge, but also what gets *produced* as knowledge in the first place.

FEMINIST THEORIES

Over the past two decades, feminist researchers have devoted a considerable amount of time to analyses of science, lending an explicit social justice dimension to the discussion. Given the diversity of feminist perspectives, there is also substantial diversity in the analyses of science emerging from those perspectives. Broadly, their work has emphasized (1) women in science, (2) tying science to social and political action, and (3) proposing "new" ways of doing science.

The position of women in science, and particularly women's underrepresentation, has been the subject of considerable work (Eriksson, 2007; Kerr, 2003). Feminist scholars address the underrepresentation of women as scientists, and the challenges that female scientists have faced in a male-dominated profession. They also highlight the absence of women from the knowledge that is produced within science. For example, medical research has traditionally studied male research subjects, and then presented the

The institutionalized power of the Christian Church prior to the Enlightenment meant that Galileo was punished for his scientific claims.

findings as applicable to all people—males become the generic "human," and it is presumed that female bodies will work in the same fashion. Consequently, there is a relative lack of knowledge on how various disease processes may vary in men and women (e.g., the most common symptoms of heart attacks) and how pharmaceuticals may affect them differently (e.g., different levels of effectiveness, varying side effects).

In the social sciences, an **androcentric** (or male) **bias** has also traditionally been present. In courses in child development or the sociology of youth, you may learn about Kohlberg's (1958; 1981) theory of moral development, a series of stages through which individuals progress in their development of moral reasoning. That theory was first constructed on the basis of his analysis of males. In response to the absence of the female experience in Kohlberg's theory, one of his students, Carol Gilligan (1984), developed a theory on the development of moral reasoning in females. Similarly, Erikson's (1968) theory of identity formation in youth is based upon the male experience, such that in his book, he has only one chapter on identity formation in females. He has a "theory of identity formation," and then a "theory of *female* identity formation," thus making the male experience the normative experience (and the one that you will most likely learn about in courses on child or youth development).

For these feminist scholars, making science "better" means removing the obstacles that women may face in becoming scientists, as well as the androcentric biases that have pervaded scientific research historically. For other feminist scholars (e.g., Longino, 1990; Nelson, 1990), improving science means tying it to social and political action. Although the traditional model of science dictates that science should be value-free, these scholars point out that knowledge and values are intimately intertwined, that values *should* underlie scientific practice, and that scientists *should* allow their own political affiliations or social movement memberships to guide their research.

Finally, some feminist scholars present a vision of a "new" way of doing science. For instance, Harding (1991) constructed *feminist standpoint theory*, claiming that women occupy a distinctive location in society (i.e., a "standpoint") as a marginalized and oppressed group. Because of their distinctive location, women see and understand the world in a different way than men do—women's unique "standpoint" is not only structural, but also intellectual. Harding claims that science emerging from the standpoint of women (or other oppressed and marginalized groups) would create a superior body of scientific

Androcentric bias: A tendency to favour males.

knowledge. Coming from more of a postmodern or poststructuralist foundation, Donna Haraway (1991) argues that "women" are not a single cohesive group, and do not reflect a unified standpoint. Instead, each has multiple standpoints based on all of the different aspects of her life (e.g., female, Aboriginal, mother, scientist, Catholic); women's perspectives are constantly shifting and may even conflict with each other at times. Constructing "better" scientific knowledge means having as diverse of a group of scientists as possible, who come from as many different standpoints as possible.

TIME TO REVIEW

- What is science?
- What are the two different perspectives on the nature of scientific "truth"?
- What are the components of the normative structure of science, according to Merton?
- According to Kuhn, how does scientific knowledge develop?
- What are some examples of social and political influences on scientific knowledge?
- What impact does the corporatization of science have on scientific knowledge?
- In what ways do poststructuralist and feminist perspectives draw attention to the social construction of scientific knowledge?

LO⁵ RELIGION AND SCIENCE

Religion and science each offer us "truths" about the world around us and about ourselves. Four different types of relationships between religious knowledge and scientific knowledge have been postulated (Barbour, cited in Campbell, 2005). Some scholars suggest that the relationship is one of *independence*; there is no common ground between the two bodies of knowledge, and no realm for conversation between the two. Others claim that the relationship between religious and scientific knowledge is based on *conflict*, wherein accepting one of those bodies of knowledge necessarily means rejecting the other. In contrast, because both religion and science are interested in questions of meaning and existence, some academics suggest that a meaningful *dialogue* is possible. Finally, some scholars take it a step further and address the *integration* that they believe is possible between the two bodies of knowledge. Dialogue and integration are reflected in the academic journal *Zygon: Journal of*

Religion and Science: "Zygon's hypothesis is that, when long-evolved religious wisdom is yoked with significant, recent scientific discoveries about the world and human nature, there results credible expression of basic meaning, values, and moral convictions that provides valid and effective guidance for enhancing human life" (www.zygonjournal.org).

In people's lives, both religion and science play important roles. A survey of more than 400 undergraduate students found that 88 percent think that a person can be both religious and scientific—that one does not necessarily exclude the other. Three-quarters of them say that science influences their own daily lives, while almost half indicate that religion affects their daily lives. However, the power of science in contemporary society is reflected in their views as well; although 84 percent state that science will hold a more important role in future world affairs than at the present time, only 17 percent think that religion will hold a more important role in future world affairs than at the present time (Campbell, 2005).

RELIGION, SCIENCE, AND EDUCATION

The ongoing interplay between religious and scientific belief systems is particularly evident when looking at the education system. At a time when there is a growing array of faith-based educational opportunities for children in separate and private schools, the presence of religious belief systems in publicly funded educational spaces is a matter of considerable debate. In the United States, recently the debate has primarily revolved around the issue of including "intelligent design" in science classes as a balance to the theory of evolution. In some school districts, science teachers have had to present the theory of evolution as "just a theory" that has not been proven beyond doubt, with intelligent design as a theory of equal validity. Court cases have resulted in many states, and in a number of cases, judges have ruled that intelligent design is not a scientific theory, but rather religious ideology which therefore has no place in science classes.

Although the intelligent design–evolution debate does not permeate our educational system in the same way that it does in the United States, discussion and debate about religious belief systems in publicly funded education rears its head in other ways. In December 2010, a parent in Morinville, Alberta, filed a complaint with the school board because she had no choice but to send her daughter to a faith-based school; for historical reasons, the public school system in Morinville is Catholic (it is the only place

Source: © Harris, C., shrn31, Cartoonstock.com

in Alberta where the public schools are faith-based). Although parents are able to exempt their children from religious instruction classes, this parent argued that the religious belief system permeates the entire school day, not just the classes in religious instruction. The provincial government has stated that "now that the issue has been raised, the board has to provide [the parent] with an option that is both feasible and would satisfy the rights of the parents and students involved" (*Edmonton Journal*, 2010, para. 12).

TIME TO REVIEW

- What types of relationships between religious and scientific belief systems have been proposed?
- How do undergraduate students perceive religious knowledge and scientific knowledge, according to Campbell?
- What are some examples of the interplay of religion and science in contemporary schools in the United States and Canada?

THE ROLE OF EDUCATION IN MODERN SOCIETY

Education is a major agent of socialization and a formal institution that systematically instills much of the knowledge that is needed to function as productive adults in society. Sociologists are interested in what is taught, who decides what is taught, how schools teach, what

> **Education:** A formal institution that systematically instills much of the knowledge that is needed to function as productive adults in society.

SOCIOLOGY *IN PRACTICE*

EDUCATION IN CANADA

There is no one unified system of education in Canada. Instead, Canada's *Constitutional Act of 1867* grants educational jurisdiction to each of the provinces and territories to develop and deliver education from the elementary through the postsecondary levels. Each province and territory has one or two educational departments that are most often led by an elected minister. Public education is provided to all Canadians for free, funded by provincial and territorial governments and sometimes by funds raised through local taxes as well (Council of Minister of Education, 2008).

goes on during interactions in the classroom, and what the overall functions are of education for individuals, groups, and society. In addition, sociologists examine the interrelationships between education and other social institutions—family, politics, etc.—and they look at how sociocultural forces such as religious beliefs, scientific views, and cultural values influence educational outcomes and personal development (Kibera and Kimokoti, 2007). In this chapter we explore various theoretical views concerning the functions of schooling that continue to form the foundation of current debates about the educational system including the benefits and drawbacks of public versus private schooling, the costs for obtaining an education, and the ways in which education is socially stratified in Canada.

SOCIOLOGY IN THEORY

The field of education is a complex area of study. Education includes a vast range of processes and functions beyond the basic three R's associated with Reading, Writing, and Arithmetic (i.e., *functional literacy*). It occurs at different stages of people's lives, from the earliest preschool years to postsecondary schooling in adulthood. In October 2010 Francean Campbell-Rich drew widespread attention when she graduated with an honours certificate from a Mohawk College writing program at the age of 90 (Newman, 2010).

Because of the complexity of this area of study, sociologists often specialize in particular areas; some focus on what is taught in schools, others focus on gendered school experiences (Chapter 7), and some focus on differential outcomes for particular groups. As a result, divergent viewpoints emerge with respect to describing the overall functions of education for individuals and society.

FUNCTIONALIST PERSPECTIVES

Functionalist perspectives focus on ways in which educational practices help to promote stability and order in society, by training its members to be respectful of one another, law abiding, and productive as members of the workforce. Durkheim (1956) emphasized the importance of education for instilling cultural values and norms that help to maintain moral order in society.

> Education is the influence exercised by adult generations on those that are not yet ready for social life. Its object is to arouse and to develop in the child a certain number of physical, intellectual, and moral states which are demanded of him by both the political society as a whole and in the special milieu for which he is specifically destined. (cited in Ballentine, 2001: 8)

Similarly, Parsons (1959) explained how schools gradually transition individuals from informal, person-centred roles in their families to more formal roles required by a highly competitive, achievement-oriented work domain (Wotherspoon, 1998). For example, in preschool and kindergarten, a teacher (usually a woman) provides a lot of nurturing and encouragement, similar to that experienced in the home. Children are allotted free time to play with toys and make crafts, and they often sit together in unstructured groups, such as while listening to a story. As children progress through the grades, there is more of an emphasis placed on structure and rules. Students sit in rows at desks, they learn to be on time and to respect the rights of other students and school property, and to follow directions given by a teacher; free time is limited to short periods of recess. Students are increasingly assessed and compared on measures of individual achievement through assignments and exams. Over time, the type of knowledge and skills taught become more specialized. Class time becomes segregated into distinct required subjects such as math and science, and eventually includes optional programs of study, such as Spanish, Aboriginal studies, and drama.

THE MANIFEST AND LATENT FUNCTIONS OF EDUCATION

In Chapter 1, you learned the distinction between the intended *manifest* functions of social institutions, and their unintended or hidden *latent* functions. Functionalists analyze these different functions within the education system (Merton, 1957). Manifest functions are formally documented in provincial school acts, incorporated into assessment practices by teachers, and communicated to parents via student report cards. Four main manifest functions of education are summarized as follows:

1. *Skill and Knowledge Development:* In each grade level, students are taught a standardized curriculum relevant to their age and/or existing level of knowledge and skills. For example, a student in grade 1 would be expected to be able to sort objects or demonstrate an understanding of repeating patterns as part of early math building skills.
2. *Historical and Cultural Transmission*: Schools play a central role in passing on historical knowledge and teaching cultural values and norms. For example, high school graduates in Alberta are expected to be well versed in the history and geography of Canada; understand Canada's political, social, and economic systems; and show respect for Canada's cultural diversity (Alberta Education, 2010a).
3. *Social Development:* The education system helps to socialize members of society so they can get along with each other in a variety of contexts. Teachers provide opportunities for children to play, cooperate, and share with one another, and conversely enact consequences for behaviour that is considered to be unacceptable. As children progress through school, social skills are taught more formally in health and life skill courses. In grade 9, for example, students learn how to refine personal goals relevant to career paths and develop strategies for risk and stress management (Alberta Education, 2010b).
4. *Social Control*: Students learn the importance of respecting authority figures and following rules. This begins in early childhood education and is reflected in various practices such as raising your hand before speaking, waiting in a line to exit and enter the classroom, sitting quietly at a workstation for a given periods of time, keeping a workspace organized, and completing projects in the time allotted.

The expectation is that most students will acquire particular normative learning outcomes as well as some more specialized forms of knowledge that will enable them to best contribute to society as citizens and employees. For example, after a basic education to the end of grade 12, students in Alberta are able to read, write and speak clearly, use math, understand the scientific method, and describe the history and geography of Canada. In addition, they can work independently, manage time, and are able to demonstrate important social characteristics such as fairness and respect for others (Alberta Education, 2010a).

In addition to its manifest functions, the education system serves latent functions as well. For example, because of changing patterns of parental employment, schools have come to serve primary day care functions, such as lunch-hour supervision (Chapter 4) and after-school care. Schools also serve a latent match-making

Social control is one of the main functions of education.

Source: © PhotoAlto/Alamy

SOCIOLOGY *IN MY COMMUNITY*

SUPPLEMENTAL SCHOOL FEES

Think back to your earliest school days. Were there any items or events for which you or your parents had to raise money to try and cover the costs? Consider the following example of supplemental school fees. Shortly before school commenced, one of your authors purchased $130 worth of required school supplies, spent $70 on other necessary items such as gym shoes, and doled out $350 on new back-to-school clothes for one child entering grade 3. During the first week of classes, there was a $100 regular school fee along with a special fee of $95 for lunch supervision. This was followed by $80 for the school's discount book fundraiser, $80 for milk coupons for use at lunch time throughout the year, and $59.95 for grade-level readers from affiliated school Book Clubs. The second week of classes brought the purchase of the first set of hot lunches to be provided by the school (for $73.75) a few times a week via a catering company, and fees for her child to join the school's chess club ($130.75).

Hot lunches, book club offerings, and fundraisers continued to crop up. In October, $40 went to a book fair that was a major fundraiser for library resources, $60 was spent on magazine subscriptions in what was dubbed the "school's most important fundraiser of the year," and another $44 went to school pictures. The second month of school was not even over, and access to a free education had already resulted in $1313.46 in costs. Over the course of a typical year, hidden costs for the child used in this example amounted to an average of $250 a month. How might these costs differentially affect Canadian families who have several children and can barely budget for regular fees? How do you think certain students feel or are treated when they have to opt out of the milk and lunch programs, when they fail to sell magazine subscriptions and discount books to their parents and relatives as major fundraisers (especially when the results of fundraising efforts are displayed in the school newsletter—right down to the average number of books sold per child!), and/or they are unable to attend the book fair or join in any of the extracurricular activities?

function. Although schools have the intended purpose of facilitating social development, schools go further than this as students often develop their first serious crush on a classmate or begin to date fellow students. In addition to match-making for romantic relationships, schools facilitate the development of important friendships and social networks that in turn can provide future benefits, such as eventual business contacts.

CRITICAL PERSPECTIVES

While functionalist views emphasize the many benefits of education for producing skilled employees, conflict and feminist views highlight how the education system reproduces the existing social order and poses disadvantages for particular groups.

THE SOCIAL REPRODUCTION OF CLASS

The example of hidden school costs shows that the school experience can be quite different for children of varying social classes. But according to conflict perspectives, the education system does more than just treat the social classes differently; it actually maintains and reproduces class differences and social inequality (Gintis and Bowles, 1980). As noted in Chapter 7, although women now constitute the majority of postsecondary students, jobs in which women are

"No response. We'll use the corporate logo flashcards again."

overrepresented tend to be lower paying and of lower status. Similarly, more Aboriginal people are obtaining high school and postsecondary educations than in the past, but non-Aboriginal people are still more likely to graduate from high school and pursue a postsecondary education. Members of the lower classes are also underrepresented among high-school and postsecondary graduates. These inequalities are often discussed by critical theorists as resulting from educational-based practices known as the hidden curriculum, streaming, and credentialism.

Hidden Curriculum: Conflict perspectives are concerned not only with whose values and norms are transmitted but also the ways in which learning takes place and the environment in which it takes place, something that Philip W. Jackson (1968) originally termed the *hidden curriculum* in his book, *Life in the Classroom.* The **hidden curriculum** refers to the process by which a subtle agenda of norms, values, and expectations that fall outside the formal curriculum are learned inadvertently through participation in the school system. Much of the knowledge learned via the hidden curriculum resembles indicators of social control, such as raising your hand before answering a question and sitting quietly at a desk for long periods of time. However, the hidden curriculum also includes more subtle lessons and messages learned during the educational process as a function of the teaching methods and the interactions among and between teachers and students. You may recall from Chapter 7 that the hidden curriculum conveys important messages about gender that have lasting impacts on people's lives.

Streaming: In addition to the hidden curriculum, school systems also aid in social reproduction through an educational policy called **streaming** in Canada (or *tracking* in the United States), which places students into specific programs and levels of curriculum based on perceived individual levels of achievement. In elementary school, streaming is generally used to identify children with learning disabilities or behavioural problems who may require specialized assistance (Curtis, Livingstone & Smaller, 1992). In high school, this practice is largely used to sort students into an advanced upper tier bound for university and a lower tier geared more toward vocational training (Davis & Guppy, 2006; Taylor & Krahn, 2009). Your own high school may have required students to select a "matriculation" or "nonmatriculation" route for core classes based on some combination of previous grades, teacher assessments, advice of counsellors, and/or parental input.

Streaming may also be influenced in part, by processes and practices that inadvertently include components of what Bourdieu called *cultural capital* (Chapter 5), a mechanism by which higher classes exclude the lower classes. Bourdieu and Passeron (1964; 1970) explained how initial differences in cultural capital are legitimized in the school system in a way that contributes to social reproduction (Izquierdo & Mínguez, 2003). Because the school is viewed as a neutral forum, students in the lower classes come to accept status symbols associated with high culture (e.g., theatre, ballet) even though these are not cultural elements they are likely to experience for themselves (Feinberg & Soltis, 2009).

Students from lower classes are also socialized within their families to communicate in ways that may further differentiate them from those in the higher classes. For example, Bernstein (1973) notes how working-class mothers tend to use a "restricted code" of communication emphasizing specific behaviours when reprimanding children, rather than the "elaborate code" based on general

> **Hidden curriculum:** The process by which a subtle agenda of norms, values, and expectations that fall outside the formal curriculum are learned inadvertently through participation in the school system.
>
> **Streaming:** A process whereby students are placed into specific programs and levels of curriculum based on perceived levels of achievement.

EDUCATION AS CONTROL

Hey, teachers! Leave those kids alone!
These lyrics are from Pink Floyd's classic song "Another Brick in the Wall," written by Roger Waters from the album *Another Brick in the Wall (Part II)* released by EMI in 1979. The anti-authoritarian song is a form of protest against the strict regime of the British educational system, particularly in boarding schools. The South African Government banned the song in 1980 because it became the anthem for a national strike involving students protesting the social stratification of education based on race (Seivert, 2010).

Source: Lyrics from Pink Floyd's classic song "Another Brick in the Wall" written by Roger Waters from the album *Another Brick in the Wall (Part II)* released by EMI in 1979.

IQ AS OPPRESSION

As Kamin (1974) purports:

> . . . the IQ test has served as an instrument of oppression against the poor-dressed in the trappings of science, rather than politics. The message of science is heard respectfully, particularly when the tidings it carries are soothing to the public conscience. There are few more soothing messages than those historically delivered by IQ testers. The poor, foreign-born, and racial minorities were shown to be stupid. They were shown to have been born that way. The under-privileged are today demonstrated to be uneducable, a message as soothing to the public purse as to the public conscience (pp. 15–16) (as cited in Gillborn & Youdell, 2001: 79–80).

behavioural principles that is used by the higher classes and the school system (Barakett & Cleghorn, 2000). Furthermore, written and spoken assessments as well as intelligence (IQ) tests that are used in school to gauge ability use language that is more familiar to children from the upper classes, providing them with a distinct advantage.

From a critical perspective, streaming promotes social reproduction since those in the middle and upper classes are more likely to end up in the upper tracks en route to university, while the lower classes are disproportionately streamed into lower educational tiers (Oakes, 2005). Contemporary debates centre around whether the practice of streaming diverts lower-class students from the university track and into lower-status and lower-paying jobs, or whether it helps them develop the necessary skills to render them productive in the workforce. Shavit and Müller's (2000) comparative research on tracking found that vocational secondary education in a number of countries served as both a diversion and a safety net. That is, tracking into vocational routes helped to produce more skilled rather than unskilled workers, yet also led to jobs of lower status compared to students with academic-based educations. Hence, tracking aids lower-class students to obtain jobs, albeit the less desirable ones.

Private versus publicly funded schools also serve to illustrate how students are streamed, in this case by familial resources. A **private school** is one that accepts

"MY FATHER SAYS, THESE INTELLIGENCE TESTS ARE BIASED TOWARD THE INTELLIGENT."

Source: © Edgar Argo, ear0868, www.cartoonstock.com

Private schools: Schools that are operated by private individuals or corporations, for which parents pay an annual tuition.

Public schools: Schools that are funded through provincial and local governments.

Credentialism: The reliance on increasingly higher educational qualifications as necessary minimal requirements for employment.

fees, usually in the form of an annual tuition, and is run by private individuals or corporations. Private schools are most likely to be attended by individuals from the upper strata of society. There are about 1,700 private schools in Canada, attended by approximately 6 percent of school children. Private schools vary considerably depending on the location, size, student-to-teacher ratio, and costs that can range from as low as $5,000 to as much as $40,000 for boarding schools (*The Globe and Mail*, 2009). In contrast, **public schools** are provided by and funded through provincial and local governments, and most of the student population attends these schools.

Credentialism: Lastly, social stratification is also fostered in the educational system through a process called **credentialism**. Credentialism refers to the reliance on increasingly higher educational qualifications as the minimal requirements for employment. For example, a Ph.D. is now usually required for full-time, permanent employment as a university or college professor, wherein four decades ago a master's degree was sufficient. Functionalists argue that higher educational attainment is necessary due to technological advancements in society and to ensure that specialized occupations are filled by the most qualified people (Chapter 6). Conflict theorists refute this claim, pointing out that skills can often be learned on the job and that those with higher levels of education are not always more productive (Collins, 1977). Critical views also point out how increased education in industrial societies has moved well beyond the technical needs of the workforce, such that there is a surplus of overeducated unemployed individuals (e.g., see Feinberg & Soltis, 2009 or Livingstone, 1998). There are even many forms of employment that yield incomes that may be considered questionable in terms of their comparable worth or value to society for their relative importance and length of training. Is a hockey player who earns several million dollars in a season more valuable to society than a day care worker who earns only about $12 an hour? Which position is more vital?

Conflict theorists claim that credentialism serves to reproduce inequality since it is linked to social class privilege and, hence, it is an explanation in itself for why people with higher education attainment end up with better paying jobs (Bills, 2004). In other words, as educational requirements increase in relation to specific occupations, so do the odds that those positions will be disproportionately filled by members of society who came from privileged families who could most afford to send them to the best schools and universities. Combine credentialism with government cutbacks and increases to tuition and you can begin to appreciate how those in the upper echelons of society have a tremendous advantage over those in the lower classes when it comes to completing a postsecondary education.

INTERACTIONIST VIEWS

To understand how educational practices influence individuals, it is necessary to understand how teachers perceive their students, how teachers act and react in relation to the meanings they ascribe to the actions and words of pupils, and, in turn, how students interpret their instructors, the curriculum, and the behaviour of fellow students. Power differentials between students and teachers can play an important role in how meanings are constructed in classroom settings. The teacher is the authority figure who can make and enforce rules, while a student is in a position of deference to the teacher, who, at any given time, may label a student's behaviour as appropriate or inappropriate.

Because of the generalized other and the looking-glass self (Chapter 1, Chapter 7), how one is labelled by others has important implications for future behaviours and one's self-esteem. One of the potential outcomes of labelling in the educational system is the development of a self-fulfilling prophecy. A **self-fulfilling prophecy** is an originally false belief that becomes true simply because it is perceived as such. For example, suppose a student frequently disrupts others and fails to finish his assignments. The teacher, believing he has an attention-deficit disorder, moves the student to a table separated from the rest of the class designated for extra help. Because the boy has now been moved into the "special" section, other students become more tolerant and accepting of infractions—because he probably "can't help himself." The student continues to fidget and not work on his assignments largely because he now realizes that the teacher will eventually help him finish his work since he is perceived as not capable of finishing it himself—a self-fulfilling prophecy come true. Are students always streamed appropriately based on their true abilities and according to objective, fair, and equitable criteria? Webb and colleagues (2005) suggest that many children (especially boys) who are actually gifted with high IQs are misdiagnosed as having attention-deficit hyperactivity disorder (ADHD). Because they are not being intellectually challenged in school and subsequently become restless, teachers (and later, parents and physicians) *incorrectly* label their misbehaviour in the classroom as indicative of an inability to maintain focus.

A classic study by Rosenthal and Jacobson (1968) also illustrates the role of the self-fulfilling prophecy in classrooms. In this study, teachers were informed that a special intelligence test would not only measure intelligence quotient (IQ), but also identify which students would make the most significant progress over the academic year; these children were labelled "academic bloomers." The test really did nothing more than measure IQ, and the "academic bloomers" were actually selected at random. However, a second intelligence test given at the end of the year revealed that those students who had been randomly identified as "academic bloomers" showed an increase in IQ of approximately 12 points. Once the students were falsely labelled as "academic bloomers," the teachers began to perceive and treat them as children who would make significant progress. Subsequently, these students began to perceive themselves in that way, and their academic behaviours changed to enable them to meet those expectations.

POSTMODERN PERSPECTIVES

Postmodern perspectives discount traditional theories of education that make general assumptions

> **Self-fulfilling prophecy:** An originally false belief that becomes true simply because it is perceived as such.

about educational practices and processes and, instead, try to locate educational issues within the contexts and tensions in which they occur. For example, in *Postmodernism and Education*, Usher and Edwards (1994) note how the experiential learning practices that emerged in the 1980s can be seen in many different ways: as opportunities for trying out innovative practices (e.g., learning contracts); as spaces for understanding the values and struggles of marginalized groups; or as new middle-class movements that served to break down some of the barriers of social and cultural reproduction. Similarly, while various theorists might argue for or against a particular form of testing, postmodern approaches advocate for the use of a variety of methods to assess student achievement and the selection of methods that work for best for individual outcomes (Ballentine, 2001).

TIME TO REVIEW

- What does a functionalist perspective on education focus on?
- What are the four main manifest functions of education?
- What does a critical perspective on education highlight?
- In what ways is social reproduction fostered by the hidden curriculum, streaming, and credentialism?
- What is a self-fulfilling prophecy and how might a teacher create one?
- What view of education is held by postmodernists?

CHAPTER SUMMARY

LO1 Explain what belief systems are and identify their components.

Belief systems are sets of interconnected beliefs that are shared among groups of people. They consist of claims about the nature of reality, ethical/moral claims, and technologies.

LO2 Describe religious patterns in Canada and identify the implications of religiosity for individuals and for society.

There are more than 270 large religious groups in the world. Currently, the largest religious group in the world is Christianity, followed by Islam; however, it is projected that by 2025 Islam will be the largest religious group. In Canada, although religious affiliation and religious attendance have declined over the past several decades, religion continues to play a role in the majority of Canadians' lives. Religiosity has positive implications for individuals, in terms of physical and mental health, social capital, performance in school, and more. At a societal level, religiosity is associated with both positive outcomes (e.g., philanthropic and charitable work) and negative outcomes (e.g., isolation, conflict, war).

LO3 Compare and contrast key sociological theories of religion.

Substantive approaches focus on the meanings that are contained within specific doctrines, and how those meanings are understood by people in their everyday lives. *Functional* approaches emphasize the social aspects of religion, the functions it serves, and its implications for individuals and for society. Sociological theorizing about religion is as old as the discipline of sociology itself. Durkheim addressed the role of religion in maintaining social solidarity, Marx spoke of religion as an obstacle to proletarian revolution, and Weber explored the role of Protestantism in establishing early capitalism. Diverse feminist perspectives share a foundation in analyzing the oppression of women in religion, and postmodern perspectives draw attention to the multiplicity of individual religious experiences.

LO4 Identify the different ways that sociologists perceive the nature of scientific "truth," and explain the role of poststructuralist and feminist perspectives in the sociological study of science.

Some sociologists perceive scientific knowledge as a distinct form of knowledge based on objective truth; for instance, Merton described the normative structure of science. Other sociologists perceive scientific knowledge as being socially constructed, as are all other forms of knowledge. Thus, Kuhn analyzed the scientific revolutions, and other scholars explore social and political influences on what is studied within science (and therefore what knowledge is produced), as well as the influence of funding structures. Poststructuralist Foucault proposed that claims made by groups with institutionalized power come to be accepted as "legitimate" knowledge; that is the position of science today. Feminist perspectives analyze the position of women in science, the need to tie science with social and political action, and "new" ways of doing science.

LO⁵ Compare and contrast theoretical views of the role of education in modern society within contemporary debates about education.

Functionalist views identify ways in which schools teach members of society to become law-abiding, productive members of the workforce. Critical perspectives point out ways in which educational practices and processes serve to perpetuate inequality and reproduce the existing social order through the hidden curriculum, streaming, and credentialism. Interactionists are interested in how educational practices such as labelling influence individuals based on teacher expectations. Postmodernists emphasize the need to locate educational practices and processes within the modern contexts and conflicts within which they occur.

RECOMMENDED READINGS

1. For an overview of the religious patterns of Canadians, as well as what those patterns may mean, see: Bibby, R. (2011). *Beyond the Gods and Back*.

2. Robert Merton is often credited as being the founder of the sociology of science. His groundbreaking book (1973) is: Merton, R. K. (1973). *The Sociology of Science*. Chicago: University of Chicago Press.

3. For a better understanding of how teachers implicate self-development, particularly in the area of aspirations and how schools help to reproduce inequality, we recommend the following: MacLeod, J. (1987). *Ain't No Making It: Leveled Aspirations in a Low-Income Neighborhood*. Boulder, CO: Westview Press.

FOR FURTHER REFLECTION

1. Some scientists may engage in scientific misconduct, such as forging data. How might this practice be connected to the corporatization of science?

2. Do you think a person can be both religious and scientific? In what ways might such a person reconcile those two belief systems?

3. Do you have any siblings? In what ways do you think the educational experience of a younger sibling is affected by that child having older brother or sister?

REFERENCES

Adherents.com. (2007). *Major religions of the world by number of adherents*. Retrieved November 20, 2010, from adherents.com

Alberta Education. (2010a). *Guide to Education: ECS to Grade 12*. (The) Crown in Right of Alberta, as represented by the Minister of Education. Alberta, CA: Alberta Education, Policy Research and Development. Retrieved August 10, 2011, from http://education.alberta.ca/media/832568/guidetoed.pdf

Alberta Education. (2010b). *Grade 9 at a Glance*. (The) Crown in Right of Alberta, as represented by the Minister of Education. Alberta, CA: Alberta Education, Policy Research and Development. Retrieved August 10, 2011, from http://education.alberta.ca/media/446175/9bro.pdf

Anderson, A., & Gordon, R. (1978). Witchcraft and the status of women—the case of England. *British Journal of Sociology*, 29, 171–184.

Ballentine, J. H. (2001). *The Sociology of Education: A Systematic Analysis* (5th ed.). Englewood Cliffs, NJ: Prentice Hall.

Barakaett, J. & Cleghorn, A. (2000). *Sociology of Education: An Introduction View from Canada*. Scarborough, ON: Prentice-Hall Canada.

Barstow, A. L. (1994). *Witchcraze*. San Francisco: Pandora.

Ben-Yehuda, N. (1980). The European witch craze of the 14th to 17th centuries: A sociologist's perspective. *American Journal of Sociology*, 86(1), 1–31.

Ben-Yehuda, N. (1986). Deviance in science. *British Journal of Criminology*, 26(1), 1–27.

Ben-Yehuda, N. (1990). *The Politics and Morality of Deviance: Moral Panics, Drug Abuse, Deviant Science, and Reversed Stigmatization*. Albany, NY: State University of New York Press.

Bereska, T. M. (2011). *Deviance, Conformity, and Social Control in Canada*. Toronto, ON: Pearson Education Canada.

Berger, I. E. (2006). The influence of religion on philanthropy in Canada. *Voluntas*, 17, 115–132.

Bernstein, B. B. (1973). *Class, Codes and Control, vol. 1: Theoretical Studies Toward a Sociology of Language*. London: Routledge & Kegan Paul.

Bibby, R. W. (2004). *Restless Churches: How Canadian Churches Can Contribute to the Emerging Religious Renaissance*. Toronto, ON: Novalis.

Bibby, R. W. (2006). "Why bother with organized religion? The views of insiders, marginals, and outsiders." Paper presented at the Annual Meeting of the Pacific Sociological Association, Hollywood CA, April 2006.

Bibby, R. W. (2009). "Restless gods and restless youth: An update on the religious situation in Canada." Paper presented at the Annual Meeting of the Canadian Sociological Association, Ottawa, May 2009.

Born, L. (2004). Fast-tracking the plague: Drugging America to death. *International Socialist Review, 33*. Retrieved May 19, 2006, from www.isreview.org

Bills, D. B. (2004). *The Sociology of Education and Work*. Malden, MA: Blackwell Publishing.

Bourdieu, P., & Passeron, J. C. (1964). *Les Héritiers*. Paris, FR: Les Éditions de Minuit.

Bourdieu, P., & Passeron, J. C. (1970). *La Reproduction: Éléments pour une théorie du système d'enseignement*. Paris, FR: Les Editions de Minuit.

Bramadat, P. A. (2005). Religion, social capital, and "the day that changed the world." *Journal of International Migration and Integration, 6*(2), 201–217.

Campbell, R. A. (2005). Students' views on the relationship between religion and science: Analysis of results from a comparative survey. *Canadian Review of Sociology and Anthropology, 42*(3), 249–265.

Caulfield, T. (2004). The commercialisation of medical and scientific reporting. *PLoS Medicine, 1*(3), 178–179.

Clark, W., & Schellenberg, G. (2006). Who's religious? *Canadian Social Trends, Summer,* 2–9. Ottawa, ON: Statistics Canada. Statistics Canada Catalogue No. 11-008.

Collins, R. (1977). Some comparative principles of educational stratification. *Harvard Educational Review, 47*(1): 1–27.

Council of Minister of Education, Canada. (2008, July). *Education in Canada*. Toronto, ON: Author. Retrieved November 28, 2010, from www.cmec.ca/Publications/Lists/Publications/Attachments/64/EducationCanada.en.pdf

Curtis, B., Livingstone, D.W., & Smaller, H. (1992). Stacking the deck: The streaming of working-class kids in Ontario schools. Montréal, QC: La maîtresse d'école.

Davis, S., & Guppy, N. (2006). *The Schooled Society*. Don Mills, ON: Oxford University Press.

Dillon, M. (2007). Religion, sociology of. In G. Ritzer (Ed.), *Blackwell Encyclopedia of Sociology*. Blackwell Publishing. Retrieved December 5, 2010, from www.blackwellreference.com

Drysdale, D. (2007). Weber, Max (1864–1920). In G. Ritzer (Ed.), *Blackwell Encyclopedia of Sociology*. Blackwell Publishing. Retrieved December 23, 2010, from www.blackwellreference.com

Durkheim, E. (1915/1965). *Elementary Forms of Religious Life*. Trans. J. W. Swain. New York: Free Press.

Durkheim, E. (1956). *Education and sociology* (S. Fox, Trans.). New York: The Free Press.

Edmonton Journal. (2010, December 20). Morinville mother asks for school without religion. Retrieved January 1, 2011, from Canada.com

Erikson, E. H. (1968). *Identity: Youth and Crisis*. New York: Norton.

Eriksson, L. (2007). Science, social construction of. In G. Ritzer (Ed.) *Blackwell Encyclopedia of Sociology*. Retrieved December 1, 2010, from www.blackwellreference.com

Feinberg, W., & Soltis, J. F. (2009). *School and Society* (5th ed.). New York: Teachers College Press.

Foucault, M. (1980). *Power/Knowledge: Selected Interviews and Other Writings 1972–1977* (1st American ed.). Trans. C. Gordon, L. Marshall, J. Mepham, & K. Super. New York: Pantheon Books.

Gillborn, D., & Youdell, D. (2001). The new IQism: Intelligence, "ability" and the rationing of education. In J. Demaine (Ed.), *Sociology of Education Today*. New York: Palgrave Publishers, 65–99.

Gilligan, C. (1984). *In a Different Voice*. Cambridge, MA: Harvard University Press.

Gintis, H., & Bowles, S. (1980). Contradiction and reproduction in educational theory. In Len Barton, Roland Meighan, and Stephen Walker (Eds), *Schooling, Ideology and the Curriculum* (pp. 51–65). London: Falmer Press.

Good, M., & Willoughby, T. (2006). The role of spirituality versus religiosity in adolescent psychosocial adjustment. *Journal of Youth and Adolescence, 35*(1), 41–55.

Haraway, D. (1991). Situated knowledges: The science question in feminism and the privilege of partial perspectives. In *Simians, Cyborgs and Women*. New York: Routledge.

Harding, S. (1991). *Whose Science? Whose Knowledge? Thinking from Women's Lives*. Ithaca, NY: Cornell University Press.

Hunt, A. (1998). The great masturbation panic and the discourses of moral regulation in nineteenth- and early twentieth-century Britain. *Journal of the History of Sexuality, 8*(4), 575–615.

Izquierdo, H. M., & Mínguez, A. M. (2003). Sociological theory of education in the dialectical perspective. In C. A. Torres and A. Antikainen's (Eds.), *The International Handbook on the Sociology of Education* (pp. 21–41). Lanham, MD: Rowman & Littlefield Publishers.

Jackson, P. W. (1968). *Life in Classrooms*. New York, NY: Holt, Rinehart, & Winston.

Jones, D. J. (2001). *Selected Legal Issues in Genetic Testing: Guidance from Human Rights*. Ottawa: Health Canada.

Jordan, T. E. (1998). Victorian child savers and their culture: A thematic evaluation. *Mellon Studies in Sociology,* Vol. 19. Lewiston, NY: Edwin Mellon Press.

Kerr, C. (2003). Phony research earns 1-year suspension. *Canadian Medical Association Journal, 168*(8), 1032.

Kibera, L. W., & Kimokoti, A. (2007). *Fundamentals of Sociology of Education: With Reference to Africa*. Nairobi, Kenya: University of Nairobi Press.

Kohlberg, L. (1958). *The development of modes of moral thinking and choice in the years 10 to 16*. Unpublished doctoral dissertation. University of Chicago.

Kohlberg, L. (1981). *Essays on Moral Development. Vol. 1: The Philosophy of Moral Development*. New York: Holt, Rinehart and Winston.

Kuhn, T. (1962). *The Structure of Scientific Revolutions*. Chicago: University of Chicago Press.

Lindsay, C. (2008). Canadians attend weekly religious services less than 20 years ago. *Matter of Fact, No. 3*. Statistics Canada Catalogue No. 89-630-X. Ottawa, ON: Author.

Livingstone, D. W. (1998). *The Education-Jobs Gap: Underemployment or Economic Democracy*. Boulder, CO: Westview Press.

Longino, H. (1990). *Science as Social Knowledge*. Princeton: Princeton University Press.

Macionis, J. J., & Gerber, L. M. (2008). *Sociology* (6th Can ed.). Toronto, ON: Pearson Education Canada.

Marx, K. (1844/1970). *Introduction to a Contribution to the Critique of Hegel's Philosophy of Right*. Cambridge: Cambridge University Press.

Merton, R.K. (1957). *Social Theory and Social Structure*. Gencoe, IL: The Free Press.

Merton, R. K. (1973). *The Sociology of Science: Theoretical and Empirical Investigations*. Chicago, IL: University of Chicago Press.

Nelson, H. L. (1990). *Who Knows: From Quine to a Feminist Empiricism*. Philadelphia: Temple University Press.

Newman, M. (2010, November 11). At 90, Francean plans to keep on writing: Oldest Mohawk College grad. *Mountain News*. Retrieved July 29, 2011, from www.hamiltonmountainnews.com/news/article/223711

Oakes, J. (2005). *Keeping Track: How Schools Structure Inequality*. New Haven, CT: Yale University Press.

Ontario Consultants on Religious Tolerance. (2009). *Religions of the world*. Retrieved November 20, 2010, from www.religioustolerance.org

Parsons, Talcott. (1959). The school class as a social system: Some of its functions in American society. *Harvard Educational Review, 29*(4), 297–318.

Platt, A. M. (1977). *The Child Savers: The Invention of Delinquency*. Chicago, IL: University of Chicago Press.

Putnam, R. (2000). *Bowling Alone: The Collapse and Revival of American Community*. New York: Simon & Schuster.

Quaife, G. R. (1987). *Godly Zeal and Furious Rage: The Witch Craze in Early Modern Europe*. New York: St. Martin's Press.

Rosenthal, R., & Jackson, L. (1968). *Pygmalion in the Classroom*. New York: Holt, Rinehart & Winston.

Schieman, S. (2008). The education-contingent association between religiosity and health: The differential effects of self-esteem and the sense of mastery. *Journal for the Scientific Study of Religion, 47*(4), 710–724.

Shavit, Y., & Müller, W. (2000). Vocational secondary education, tracking, and social stratification,. In Maureen T. Hallinan (Ed.), *Handbook of the Sociology of Education* (pp. 437–474). New York: Kluwer Academic/Plenum Publishers.

Sievert, W. (2010, January 14). Another Brick in the Wall. *Mises Daily*. Retrieved November 16, 2010, from http://mises.org/daily/4017. (Originally published as "Song that's driving teachers up the wall" in *Libertarian Review* 9(9) (September 1980): 42–43).

Stebbins, R. A. (1996). *Tolerable Differences: Living with Deviance*. Toronto, ON: McGraw-Hill Ryerson.

Stuckey, J. H. (1998). *Feminist Spirituality: An Introduction to Feminist Theology in Judaism, Christianity, Islam and Feminist Goddess Worship*. York, ON: CFR.

Taylor, A., & Krahn, H. (2009). Streaming in/for the new economy. In C. Levine-Rasky (Ed.), *Canadian Perspectives on the Sociology of Education* (pp. 103–124). Don Mills, ON: Oxford University Press.

The Globe and Mail. (2009; April 03). A private school primer. *Globe and Mail Update*. Toronto, ON: CTVglobemedia Publishing. Retrieved July 29, 2011, from www.theglobeandmail.com/globecampus/article789704.ece

Usher, R., & Edwards, R. (1994). *Postmodernism and Education: Different Voices, Different Worlds*. New York, NY: Routledge.

Valverde, M. (1991). *The Age of Light, Soap, and Water: Moral Reform in English Canada, 1885–1925*. Toronto, ON: McClelland & Stewart.

Varcoe, I. (2007). Science. In G. Ritzer (Ed.), *Blackwell Encyclopedia of Sociology*. Retrieved November 10, 2010, from www.blackwellreference.com

Walach, H., & Reich, K. H. (2005). Reconnecting science and spirituality: Toward overcoming a taboo. *Zygon, 40*(2), 423–441.

Webb, J.T., Amend, E.R., Webb, N.E., Goerss, J., Beljan, P., & Olenchak, F. R. (2005). *Misdiagnosis and Dual Diagnosis of Gifted Children and Adults: ADHD, Bipolar, OCD, Asperger's, Depression, and Other Disorders*. Scottsdale, AZ: Great Potential Press.

Weber, M. (1904/1958). *Protestant Ethic and the Spirit of Capitalism* (Talcott Parsons, Trans.; with a foreword by R. H. Tawney). New York: Scribner.

Wotherspoon, T. (1998). *The Sociology of Education in Canada: Critical Perspectives*. Toronto, ON: Oxford University Press.

ENDNOTE

[1] Retrieved November 16, 2010, from "Quoteland.com" (www.quoteland.com).

The World of Deviance and Crime

LEARNING OBJECTIVES AND OUTCOMES

After completing this chapter, students should be able to do the following:

LO1 Compare and contrast different ways of defining deviance, and explain how exploring deviance historically and cross-culturally illustrates its socially constructed nature.

LO2 Distinguish between high-consensus and low-consensus deviance.

LO3 Differentiate among varying types of social control.

LO4 Explain how deviance and crime, as well as deviance specialists and criminologists, are related.

LO5 Demonstrate an understanding of the legal meaning of a crime and differentiate among crime classifications.

LO6 Describe the criminal justice system and the rationale for punishment as the primary means for controlling crime.

LO7 Explain how restorative justice differs from retributive forms of punishment such as imprisonment.

LO8 Identify and describe the theories used by more objective versus more subjective deviance specialists.

The essence of deviance is to be found not in the behavior defined as deviance, but in the social processes that define deviance.

(Sacco and Kennedy as cited in Winterdyk, 2006, p. 11)

DEVIANCE

SOCIOLOGY *IN MY LIFE*

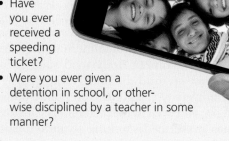

ARE YOU DEVIANT?

Consider the following questions:

- Has an image in a magazine ever made you feel "too fat" or "too skinny"?
- Have you ever received a negative or derogatory look from someone as a result of something you did such as playing a certain type of music or hanging out with a given group of people?
- Did your parents ever make you go back to your room and change your clothes before going out?

- Have you ever received a speeding ticket?
- Were you ever given a detention in school, or otherwise disciplined by a teacher in some manner?

If you answered "Yes" to *any* of the questions in the *Sociology in My Life* box, then you have been identified by somebody, at some point in time, as being "deviant." We often think of deviance as being a characteristic of *particular others* (e.g., criminals), what Liazos (1972) calls "nuts, sluts [and] preverts [sic]" (p. 103). But in reality, deviance is a socially constructed part of our lives that occurs on a daily basis. Whenever someone labels us because of a certain behaviour or characteristic and then treats us in a specific way because of that label (or when we do that to others), we are involved in the social typing of deviance. Thus, if you have ever commented that another person is too skinny, if you have ever ostracized a classmate for being too "weird," or you have avoided someone based on how he or she was dressed, you were socially typing that person as deviant.

LO1 You will frequently find "deviance" defined on the basis of normative violations. For instance, the Encarta Dictionary embedded within Microsoft Word defines deviance as "behaviour that is sharply different from a customary, traditional, or generally accepted standard." However, from a sociological perspective, deviance is far more complex than this definition suggests. For instance, whose "standard" are we referring to and how do we recognize a "customary" or "traditional" standard when we encounter one? Even within academic literature deviance is defined in various ways. Some definitions identify deviance as an objective phenomenon, in one of the following ways: a behaviour or characteristic that is statistically rare (e.g., smoking); that causes (or at least potentially causes) harm (e.g., running a red light); that is considered to be wrong by society's masses (e.g., murder);

and/or that violates societal norms (e.g., stealing) (Deutschmann, 2002; Sacco, 1992; Bereska, 2011). But even "objective" criteria can be called into question because there are times when a person engages in a behaviour that would be considered deviant based on one of these definitions (i.e., statistically rare) and yet he or she is not socially typed as deviant (e.g., sport prodigies such as Wayne Gretzky). Or, conversely, there are times when a person engages in a common behaviour but he or she is still socially typed as deviant. For example, alcohol consumption is statistically *common* among junior high school students but considered deviant since this behaviour is prohibited by law.

Thus, as most contemporary deviance specialists point out, we cannot objectively identify deviance on the basis of particular characteristics. Instead, the concept of deviance is best understood as one that emerges from complex social processes that teach us how to label behaviours and characteristics as good/bad, right/wrong, and normal/abnormal. Contemporary sociological views of deviance tend to emphasize the subjective manner in which deviance is socially constructed, and can vary cross-culturally and historically. For instance, educational programs in schools, public service announcements on television, and graphic images on cigarette packages are designed to reduce smoking, and no-smoking bylaws prohibit it in most places. But in the 1950s prominent Hollywood stars advertised cigarettes, and up until the mid-1980s, people could smoke in university classrooms, on public transportation systems, and even in hospital rooms. Doctors even sometimes prescribed smoking to individuals who wished to lose weight or who were experiencing stress or anxiety! Similarly, although alcohol consumption is considered acceptable now (among adults) and is sold in liquor stores in most neighbourhoods, the sale of alcohol was considered criminal during a period of national prohibition from 1918 to 1919.

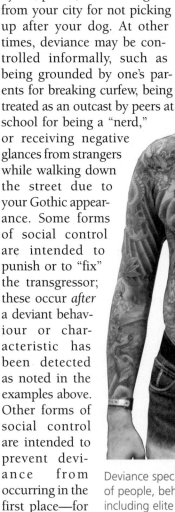

LO2 Cross-culturally, we can see even greater variations in the construction of deviance; for example, there are a number of countries in the world where homosexuality is a crime that carries the death penalty (e.g., Iran, Yemen, Saudi Arabia) (Mackay, 2000). Subjective perspectives on deviance are more likely to state that "there is nothing inherent in a

behaviour or characteristic that makes it deviant; a particular behaviour or characteristic is deviant only if the dominant moral codes of a specific society at a certain time in history say that the behaviour is deviant" (Bereska, 2011, p. 18)—in other words, a behaviour or characteristic is "deviant" if enough important people say so. In some cases, there will be considerable agreement in society that a specific behaviour or characteristic is deviant; this is what Thio (1983) calls **high-consensus deviance** (e.g., breaking into someone's home and stealing items). In other cases there will be less agreement over whether a certain behaviour or characteristic is deviant, or what Thio refers to as **low-consensus deviance** (e.g., body modification, such as facial piercings).

LO3 Once a behaviour or characteristic has been socially typed as deviant, measures of **social control** are applied. Sometimes deviance is controlled formally, through an "official" mechanism that carries some institutionalized authority—such as receiving a detention from the school principal, being arrested and charged by the police, or receiving a fine from your city for not picking up after your dog. At other times, deviance may be controlled informally, such as being grounded by one's parents for breaking curfew, being treated as an outcast by peers at school for being a "nerd," or receiving negative glances from strangers while walking down the street due to your Gothic appearance. Some forms of social control are intended to punish or to "fix" the transgressor; these occur *after* a deviant behaviour or characteristic has been detected as noted in the examples above. Other forms of social control are intended to prevent deviance from occurring in the first place—for

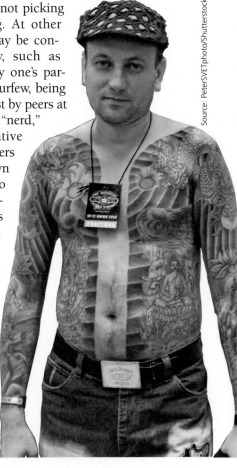

Deviance specialists study a wide range of people, behaviours, and characteristics, including elite tattoo collectors.

High-consensus deviance: Behaviours or characteristics that are widely accepted as being deviant and in need of social control.

Low-consensus deviance: Behaviours and characteristics about which there is considerable disagreement over whether they are deviant or not.

Social control: Actions that are intended to punish, "fix," or prevent deviant behaviour.

example, educational programs in elementary schools that teach children about the dangers of smoking or using illicit drugs (to prevent substance use), community programs that provide leisure activities for inner-city youth (to prevent criminal activity), or parents providing their children with a healthy diet and a wide range of physical activities (to prevent obesity) (Edwards, 1988; Bereska, 2011; Becker, 1963; Newman, 2008).

LO⁴ Deviance specialists study a wide range of behaviours ranging from tattooing (Atkinson, 2003) to customers in adult novelty stores (Hefley, 2007). Some focus their analyses on noncriminal forms of deviance that are socially controlled in everyday life, what is typically referred to as "social" deviance. Other deviance specialists conduct their research on criminal behaviour in particular; they are known as **criminologists**. Because there has always been widespread concern over crime in society, regardless of the period in history, **criminology** has become a significant area of study within the sociology of deviance.

TIME TO REVIEW

- On what basis do some sociologists "objectively" define and identify deviance?

- On what grounds do sociologists argue for subjective definitions of deviance and what are some examples of cross-cultural and historical variations in behaviours considered deviant?

- How do deviance specialists who emphasize the socially constructed nature of deviance define it?

- What is the difference between high-consensus deviance and low-consensus deviance?

- In what ways can deviance be socially controlled?

CRIME

What exactly is "criminal" behaviour? Like deviance, criminal behaviour embodies the violation of norms and more specifically, mores—the formal rules related to social control that were discussed in Chapter 5. Although some crimes go undetected, in order for someone to be found guilty of a criminal act, that act must first be formally stated as an offence. Crimes and their corresponding penalties are listed in the *Criminal Code of Canada*.

A criminal offence has officially occurred when a criminal act has taken place and there was corresponding *intent* to commit the act (Verdun-Jones, 2011). Intent means "blameworthy" in the sense that a reasonable person would understand the outcome of his or her actions. For instance, an adult may deliberately take and keep someone's unattended purse, including the money and credit cards that it contains. However, there would not be intent if the person took the purse in order to return it to the owner. Finally, criminal laws apply equally to everyone, irrespective of ascribed or achieved characteristics such as ethnicity or social status. Hence, anyone who has the capacity to commit an act of theft with intent would be subject to an arrest and, if convicted, would end up with a similar consequence for this violation against society.

LO⁵ LEGAL DEFINITIONS OF CRIME

In a formal sense, **crime** refers to a violation of *criminal law*. While this may seem like a straightforward definition, there are a number of considerations that need to be explained in order for you to fully appreciate the notion of crime from a legal perspective. First, as one of England's former colonies, Canada's legal system originates with early English law in a system called "common law." The common law system was developed by judges in Great Britain and it centres on published decisions from individual cases which set a "precedent" such that future similar cases are to be treated in a similar fashion. Common law continuously evolves, since new and/or slightly different circumstances require modifications to the existing legal code (Siegel & McCormick, 2010). In Canada, there are two main types of law: private law and public law. *Private law* concerns relationships between individuals, often in the form of contracts and agreements (e.g., marriage, property, wills, and trusts), whereas *public law* concerns matters that affect society more generally (e.g., constitutional law, criminal law, and taxation law).

When there is an issue in the case of private law, it involves a misgiving

---

Criminologists: Researchers who specialize in the study of crime, which is a specific form of deviant behaviour.

Criminology: The academic discipline that focuses on the study of crime and those labelled as criminals, and is considered to be either a subdiscipline within sociology or a discipline related to sociology.

Crime: A specific form of deviance that involves the violation of criminal law.

where one party ends up being blamed for some wrongdoing and thereby pays for damages or otherwise compensates for the wrongdoing (Vago & Nelson, 2008). For example, traffic laws pertaining to speed limits are developed at the provincial and municipal levels under private law wherein offenders pay fines, receive demerit points, and/or pay compensation to victims. In contrast, issues under public law are considered wrongs against the state. For example, a drug dealer is committing a crime of "trafficking" an illegal substance against society rather than in relation to the person who purchases the drugs.

Located within the realm of public law, criminal law encompasses all of the codified statutes in the *Criminal Code of Canada, Youth Criminal Justice Act*, and *Controlled Substances Act*. These outline actions which are deemed to be wrongs committed against the state along with their corresponding penalties. For example, Section 265.(1) of the *Criminal Code* (R.S., 1985 c. C-46) precisely defines what constitutes a general "assault": "A person commits an assault when (a) without the consent of another person, he [sic] applies force intentionally to that other person, directly, or indirectly; . . ." Section 266 outlines the penalty for this crime: "Everyone who commits an assault is guilty of (a) an indictable offence and is liable to imprisonment for a term not exceeding five years" (Department of Justice, 2010). Criminal law relates mainly to acts that pose a threat to the perceived social order and, hence, formal criminal sanctions are relied upon for protection. These are the acts of central interest to criminologists who study crime statistics and factors associated with the tendency to commit crimes in order to try to better understand and explain criminal behaviour (see Figure 10.1).

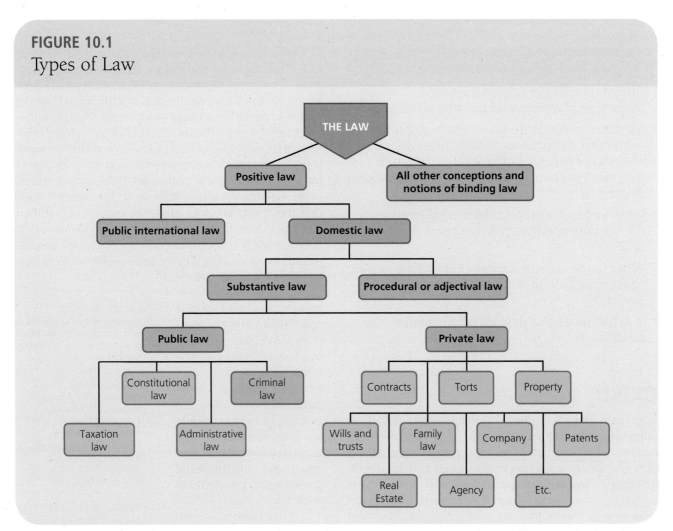

FIGURE 10.1

Types of Law

Source: Figure 2.7 "The Law" from The *Canadian Legal System*, Fifth Edition, by Gerald L. Gall (2004 edition 0-459-24128-1 (HC); 0-459-24153-2 (PB)), Chapter 2 The Divisions of Law, p. 29. Reprinted by permission of Carswell, a division of Thomson Reuters Canada Limited.

CRIME CLASSIFICATIONS AND STATISTICS

Crimes are often categorized on the basis of their *perceived seriousness* into summary, indictable, or hybrid conviction offences. This helps to establish the most appropriate form of punishment and in cases where an offender commits multiple crimes, that person is usually charged with only the most serious offence. **Summary conviction offences** are the least serious in terms of their resulting harm, and they correspond to a maximum punishment of two years in prison, a $2,000 fine, or both (Department of Justice Canada, 2010). Examples of summary conviction offences are possession of marijuana, theft of $5,000 or less, possession of stolen property under $5,000, and taking a motor vehicle without consent (Jourard, 2010). **Indictable conviction offences** are the most serious forms of crime (e.g., trafficking in cocaine or heroin, robbery, sexual assault with a weapon, homicide) and they correspond to much greater penalties such as a lengthy prison term (Jourard, 2010). *Hybrid offences* are moderately serious and can be prosecuted as summary or indictable convictions. Examples of hybrid offences are theft or forgery of a credit card, unauthorized possession of a firearm, impaired driving, dangerous driving, fleeing the police, failing to stop at the scene of an accident, and possession of cocaine or heroin (Jourard, 2010).

Crimes are also treated somewhat differently within the legal system depending on the object or *intended victim of harm*. **Violent crimes** are offences committed against a person and they include things such as first-degree murder (i.e., an unlawful killing that is planned in advance), manslaughter (i.e., unlawful "passionate" killing or killing that results from sudden provocation), and sexual assault (i.e., any unwanted form of sexual contact that occurs without consent). In the case of violent crimes, every instance is treated as a separate event. Hence, if an offender harms three different people during a single shooting episode, three separate crimes have taken place.[1] **Property crimes** are offences committed against property, such as theft of someone's property or break and enter (Siegal, Brown & Hoffman,

2006). Property crimes are counted as one crime per episode even if multiple crimes takes place during that episode. That means that if a perpetrator breaks into someone's home and steals a multitude of items, he or she does not receive separate charges for every single item stolen.

Standard definitions of crime help facilitate processes whereby crime can be counted or measured. Information on the nature and number of violent crimes and property crimes originates with individual police agencies that collect information using a standardized procedure called *uniform crime reporting (UCR)*. UCR surveys are forwarded to Statistics Canada annually, where data is compiled into statistics that give us information about crimes that can be compared across cities and provinces and over time. For example, despite media attention on violence, we learn that 80 percent of the 2.2 million crimes reported in 2009 were property crimes rather than violent crimes, and that since 1991, the crime rate has actually been declining (Statistics Canada, 2010a). Violent crime rates and property crime rates are highest in the territories, followed by Manitoba and Saskatchewan as shown in Figure 10.2 (page 218) (Dauvergne & Turner, 2010).

The main limitation of official statistics is that they contain information only on crimes that came to the attention of the police and resulted in convictions. This means some crimes will be underestimated (e.g., especially those involving victims who are reluctant to contact the police), some will be more accurately reflected (e.g., motor vehicle thefts), and others may even be overrepresented (e.g., crimes deemed a priority by communities or individual policing agencies). To help gain a broader perspective on crime, official statistics are sometimes supplemented by data obtained from victimization surveys. The *General Social Survey*, which is conducted regularly in Canada, includes questions on whether respondents have been victimized by a criminal act in the past 12 months, and whether they reported the incident to the police. Results of the 2009 *General Social Survey* indicated that 27 percent of Canadians

Summary conviction offences: Less serious criminal offences that are punishable by a maximum of two years in prison and/or a $2,000 fine.

Indictable conviction offences: More serious criminal offences punishable by more than two years in prison.

Violent crimes: Criminal offences that involve physical harm to another person.

Property crimes: Criminal offences that are directed at someone's property, rather than at someone's physical person.

FIGURE 10.2

Police-Reported Crime Rates by Province and Territory, per 100,000 Population, 2009

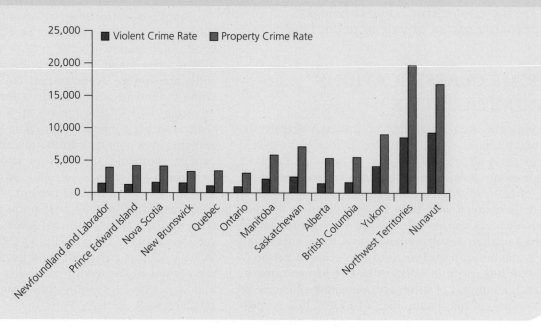

Source: Dauvergne, M., & Turner, J. (2010). Police-reported crime statistics in Canada, 2009 (Table 5, p. 30). *Juristat*, *30*(2), 1–37. Ottawa, ON: Statistics Canada. Statistics Canada Catalogue No. 85-002-X.

aged 15 and over claimed they had been a victim of a criminal incident with the last year, although just under one-third of these incidents were ever reported to the police (Statistics Canada, 2010b).

Some crimes are classified as "victimless" in nature. **Victimless crimes** refer to offences involving agreed-upon or consensual relations in the exchange of illegal goods or services, such as drug use, prostitution, and Internet gambling. These are also sometimes referred to as "crimes involving morality" or "crimes against public order" (Winterdyk, 2006). Calls for the decriminalization of prostitution that claim it is a victimless crime may not draw a lot of support considering the circumstances of individuals who are coerced into prostitution, many of whom lack resources and/or suffer abuse in their families of origin, at the hands of their customers, or by "pimps" who live off their earnings. However, some feminist organizations support the decriminalization of prostitution-related offences to help improve conditions for sex trade workers, the group most likely to get arrested.

> **Victimless crimes:**
> Criminal offences that involve consensual relations in the exchange of illegal goods or services.

Prostitution is often referred to as a "victimless" crime.

Source: Robin Beckham @ Beepstock/Alamy

SOCIOLOGY *IN PRACTICE*

CHANGING VIEWS OF PROSTITUTION

In Canada, the act of prostitution (i.e., exchanging money for some type of sexual behaviour) is not illegal. However, it is difficult to engage in prostitution without violating a criminal law related to prostitution; it is illegal to communicate in public in order to obtain prostitution service, to operate a bawdy house (i.e., a place where prostitution occurs), and to live off the avails of prostitution (i.e., this is what a pimp does). On September 28, 2010, a Superior Court of Justice judge in Ontario struck down those three laws in response to a constitutional challenge raised by three prostitutes who claimed these prohibitions force them to leave their homes (where they are safer) to work in the streets where they are subject to violence. Essentially, Justice Susan Himel agreed that the current laws posed an unnecessary risk of violence to sex trade workers and noted that Parliament would have to "fashion corrective action" (CBC News, 2010). The federal government filed an appeal, which was heard in the Court of Appeal for Ontario in June 2011. At the time of writing, a decision still had not been reached.

What are some pros and cons of the decision made by Himel?

Finally, categorizations of crime by sociologists are sometimes based on *societal views of crime* that help to distinguish between conventional and non-conventional forms. *Conventional crime* describes the most common form of crime or "those traditional, illegal behaviours that most people think of as crime" (Koenig & Linden, 2009, p. 429). Examples of conventional crimes include well-known violent and property offences that we regularly hear about in the news such as break and enters, motor vehicle thefts, and assaults.

Another benefit of categorizing crimes is that it allows social scientists to examine relationships between crimes and associated variables such as characteristics of the "typical" offender or patterns related to how certain crimes take place (e.g., the method for carrying out the crime, type of location for the crime, etc.). For example, standard categories of crime give us a picture of youth crime, which stands in contrast to dramatic media portrayals of youth out of control. Youth are overrepresented as offenders, given the proportion of

SOCIOLOGY *IN MY COMMUNITY*

CRIMINALIZATION OVER BROTHELS

Tania Fiolleau is a former prostitute and madam (i.e., person who runs a brothel) from Vancouver, BC, who gives interviews as an advocate for raising the awareness of the problems associated with prostitution and for trying to help people exit the sex trade industry. In an interview "Trafficked" with Dottie Laster available on Fiolleau's website (www.savethewomen.ca), Ms. Fiolleau argues that prostitution should be criminalized and that the penalties need to be greater for the customers and for individuals involved in the recruitment of prostitutes. She claims that removing provisions, such as allowing brothels to operate, does not make prostitution safer since those working in brothels are usually controlled by pimps, traffickers, or criminal organizations (Fiolleau, 2011).

FIGURE 10.3

Youth Accused of Police-Reported Crime, 2009, Rates per 100,000 Youth

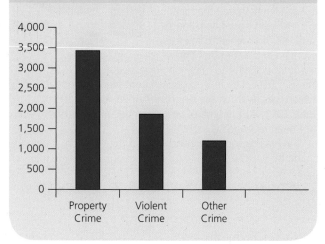

Source: Dauvergne, M., & Turner, J. (2010). Police-reported crime statistics in Canada, 2009. Table 7b (p. 33). *Juristat, 30*(2), 1–37. Ottawa, ON: Statistics Canada. Statistics Canada Catalogue No. 85-002-X.

false advertising and failure to comply with health or safety standards for products). Canadian police define **organized crime** as "two or more persons consorting together on a continual basis to participate in illegal activities, either directly or indirectly, for gain" (*The Canadian Encyclopedia*, 2011). In Canada, organized crime generally pertains to the activities of Mafia-related groups or motorcycle gangs. Although it was traditionally believed that crime was largely a lower-class phenomenon, official statistics and results from offender surveys suggest that people of all classes commit crimes. However, those arrested for white-collar and corporate crimes are more likely to be individuals from higher social classes who have access to financial resources while those arrested for property and violent offences are most likely to come from lower classes.

The most contemporary area of crime that is continuously evolving into new forms is **Internet crimes**, which involve illegal activities that take place online. Internet crimes encompass all of the types of crimes discussed above in new and unique ways. For example, the Internet constitutes a new medium for facilitating the exploitation of children (e.g., child pornography sites), for acting in aggressive ways (e.g., cyber bullying and stalking), and for posing contact risks (e.g., exposure to age-inappropriate sexual materials, communication with pedophiles, contact with hate groups, and networking with criminal organizations) (Schmalleger & Pittaro, 2009). It also provides opportunities for illegal drug trafficking (e.g., online pharmaceutical sales involving prescription drugs), Internet gambling, and various sales scams (Schmalleger & Pittaro, 2009). Finally, the Internet has increasingly produced white-collar crimes involving deception such as identity theft and email fraud scams that often begin with "phishing" (Schmalleger & Pittaro, 2009). *Phishing* is a method used by identity thieves to obtain personal information such as a credit card number or a bank account PIN. This is often done through email requests that supposedly come from the recipient's affiliated bank.

the population that they comprise. Age-specific crime rates are highest for persons ages 15 to 22, peaking at the age of 17 (Dauvergne & Turner, 2010). However, youth ages 12 to 17 constitute only one-third of all those accused of *Criminal Code* offences, and adults are the primary offenders for every category of crime (Taylor-Butts, 2010). As is the case with overall patterns of crime, most criminal offences among youth are property crimes (see Figure 10.3).

Nonconventional crime takes the form of white-collar, corporate, or organized crime. **White-collar** crime pertains to offences involving misappropriated financial resources such as stock manipulations, identity theft, and various forms of fraud. **Corporate crimes** are offences carried out by organizations or by knowledgeable employees in the course of their employment (e.g.,

White-collar crime:
Criminal offences involving the misappropriation of financial resources.

Corporate crime:
Criminal offences carried out by organizations or by knowledgeable employees in the course of their employment.

Organized crime:
Two or more persons consorting together on a continual basis to participate in illegal activities, either directly or indirectly, for gain.

Internet crime:
Criminal offences that take place online.

TIME TO REVIEW

- In what ways is it helpful to classify crimes into types?
- What are the three main types of crime by offence seriousness?
- Why are certain crimes considered to be victimless in nature, and why do some people dispute the notion that some of these crimes are "victimless"?

LO⁶ THE CRIMINAL JUSTICE SYSTEM

In Canada, those individuals who have engaged in deviant behaviours that have been criminalized are labelled as "criminal" and are then subjected to social control measures that emerge from the criminal justice system. The **criminal justice system** is made up of the police, courts, and prisons, which are responsible for the apprehension, prosecution, and punishment of those deemed offenders. The entire process begins with the commission of an act, that if reported to the police and subsequently investigated, may result in an arrest. Law enforcement in Canada operates at various levels from the Royal Canadian Mounted Police, which is a national police service, to provincial police forces (e.g., Ontario Provincial Police, la Sûreté du Québec), and those that operate in municipalities (e.g., city police in many urban areas such as the Edmonton City Police).

After initial contact with the police who investigate and perhaps lay charges (through a Crown attorney), people who are accused of crimes then come into contact with the courts, which hear the case and treat the individuals based on principles of fairness and justice. The court system comprises various courts (e.g., provincial courts, federal court) that operate at different levels with specified authority. Most cases involve summary conviction offences and they are dealt with in the provincial and territorial courts located at the lowest level of the court system. After being convicted, offenders may end up in the final stage of the criminal justice

Criminal justice system: The social institution responsible for the apprehension, prosecution, and punishment of criminal offenders.

system known as "corrections" where they serve time in a provincial or federal prison. In most cases, convicted offenders end up under the responsibility of provincial correctional organizations, such as the Corrections Division of Manitoba Justice or the Ministry of Community Safety and Correctional Services for Ontario. Only those who are sentenced to two or more years in prison become a federal responsibility under the Correctional Service of Canada.

CRIME CONTROL THROUGH PUNISHMENT

One of the main means for controlling behaviour is through the use of punishment. Although punishment in the form of penalties such as paying a fine or spending time in prison is sometimes viewed as a form of **retribution** (i.e., a morally justified consequence as in an "eye for an eye"), from the perspective of criminal law and functionalists among others, the main purpose of punishment is to deter people from committing crimes.

CRIMINAL DETERRENCE

Deterrence theory rests on the assumption that punishment can be used to prevent crime. Deterrence can operate on a specific and general level such that an offender is deterred from repeating the act in the future as a result of receiving the punishment (i.e., *specific deterrence*) while others in society also come to avoid the act by witnessing the consequences for the offender (*general deterrence*). Deterrence theory originates with the *classical school of criminology*, a perspective from the late 18th and early 19th century attributed to key theorists Jeremy Bentham (1748–1832) and Cesare Beccaria (1738–1794). This school of thought rests on the premise that people are rational, and that crime, therefore, is the end result of a decision-making process wherein the individual decides that the benefits of committing the act outweigh the perceived costs. Social order can be achieved through deterrence if rules (i.e., laws) with appropriate punishments are put into writing and enforced by the state (Tierney, 2009). According to Beccaria (1963), in order for punishment to be effective in preventing crime, it must be prompt, severe, and certain (as cited in Martin, Mutchnick & Austin, 1990).

> **Retribution:** A morally justified consequence.

1. Promptness: The punishment should occur very close in time to when the actual event happened in order to establish an association between the act and its consequence.

2. Severity: The punishment must be severe enough to outweigh the benefits but not be so severe that it constitutes torture.

3. Certainty: There must a high probability that an offender will be caught and that the punishment will be enacted.

One difficulty faced by the criminal justice system today is that punishment often does not meet the three criteria simultaneously, and hence, punishment cannot effectively deter future crime. However, critiques of deterrence theory call into question the very notion of deterrence itself. These critiques suggest that offenders' actions are frequently not the result of rational decision making, and point out that countries with very harsh penalties such as the death sentence or high rates of incarceration have not managed to reduce crime rates.

PROTECTING SOCIETY AND REHABILITATING OFFENDERS

In addition to deterrence, punishment that involves incarceration, particularly a lengthy jail sentence, generally serves as a means for *protecting society* from an offender who could otherwise continue to do harm. Incarceration also constitutes an opportunity for *rehabilitating an offender*, which involves helping the offender to become law abiding, such as through providing resources to help the offender overcome addictions or develop anger management skills. According to the *Corrections and Conditional Release Act* (S.C. 1992, c. 20), the purpose of Correctional

Kingston Penitentiary, a maximum security prison in Kingston, Ontario, that opened in 1835, is one of Canada's oldest prisons.

SOCIOLOGY *IN PRACTICE*

HARPER'S "GET TOUGH ON CRIME" APPROACH

Prime Minister Stephen Harper is well known for making public statements that suggest crime is increasing and for identifying a need to get tough on crime. This position is part of the Conservative government platform and it represents a belief in the need for better societal protection via incarceration. Hence, proposed plans for dealing with crime revolve around keeping criminals in prison longer, by implementing more mandatory minimum prison sentences, eliminating statutory release from prison with supervision, and no longer requiring judges to use prison as a last resort. You can view the plans beginning in the Conservative Party of Canada's Policy Declaration available on the Conservative Party of Canada's website: www.conservative.ca/party/key_documents

For a critique of this plan and a summary of literature that calls into question the merit of policy based on statistical data, we recommend you read the article, *The Fear Factor: Stephen Harper's "Tough on Crime" Agenda* by Paula Mallea. It is available for download from the *Canadian Centre for Policy Alternatives*: www.policyalternatives.ca

---

Services Canada is to "contribute to the maintenance of a just, peaceful and safe society by

(a) carrying out sentences imposed by courts through the safe and humane custody and supervision of offenders; and

(b) assisting in the rehabilitation of offenders and their reintegration into the community as law-abiding citizens through the provision of programs in penitentiaries and in the community" (Department of Justice Canada, 2011, p. 4).

TIME TO REVIEW

• Which social institutions comprise the criminal justice system?

• What is the main purpose behind the punishment of known offenders?

• What three components of punishment need to be present in order for it to be effective in deterring crime?

ALTERNATIVES TO PRISON

LO7 Most societies, including Canada, have relied largely on punishment (or *retribution*) as a means for dealing with offenders and to protect society from further harm. Sociologists question whether the extensive use of punishment is effective for rehabilitating offenders or deterring future crime, and whether it is the best overall use of societal resources. Some have even joined **abolitionism**, a movement calling for a complete overhaul or dismantling of the criminal justice system.

Abolitionists claim that imprisonment

• is a punitive response that deflects attention away from the social circumstances and experiences that lead to offending in the first place;

• is the culmination of social control and judicial processes that discriminate on the bases of class and "race." The criminal justice system concentrates on the crimes of the powerless rather than the crimes of the powerful;

• does not provide an appropriate setting for rehabilitation, or as abolitionists put it, dispute settlement and the integration of the offender into society. On the contrary, imprisonment exacerbates social exclusion and reduces the likelihood of successful reintegration back into society. This is reflected in high rates of recidivism;

• may remove an individual from society and thus the opportunity to offend, but only in terms of the "outside world." A great deal of offending, for example, violence and illicit drug use, occurs in prisons;

• places the offender into a brutal and brutalizing enclosed society, one where there are countless opportunities to learn new criminal skills and join new criminal networks;

> **Abolitionism:** A movement calling for the dismantling of the criminal justice system.

- increases, rather than reduces, feelings of anger, resentment, humiliation, frustration and alienation (Tierney, [2009], pp. 2–3).*

In recognition of the limitations of a criminal justice system focused mainly on retribution, critical and feminist criminologists have developed alternative frameworks to the "war on crime." For example, *peacemaking criminology* is a nonviolent movement and approach to crime that centres on transforming individuals and society in order to reduce the suffering and social injustices that result from structural inequalities based on class, race, and gender (e.g., refer to Braswell, Fuller, Lozoff, 2001 or Pepinskey & Quinney, 2001).

In addition, many criminologists now advocate for **restorative justice**, an approach based on informal justice processes that emphasizes healing and the reparation of harm caused by offenders to victims. In this case, an offender is obliged to assume responsibility for his or her actions and to attempt to make some kind of restitution to the victim (such as a formal apology). In addition, restorative justice emphasizes the need to involve all of the stakeholders in the process of justice (e.g., victims, offenders, and other members of the community). Finally, restorative justice rests on the premise of rebuilding relationships (Zehr, 2002). Restorative justice practices take a

> **Restorative justice:**
> An approach to justice emphasizing healing and reparation of harm.

*Source: Tierney (2009) pp. 2–3. Tierney, J. (2009). *Key Perspectives in Criminology.* Berkshire, ENG: Open University Press McGraw-Hill Education.

Okimaw Ohci Healing Lodge—Maple Creek, Saskatchewan.

number of forms including victim–offender reconciliation programs, victim–offender mediation, community justice circles, and reparative probation programs (Winterdyk, 2006). Prior to colonization, Aboriginal peoples in Canada regularly practised restorative justice and more recently attempts have been made to reimplement restorative justice programs in various communities. For example, the Tsuu T'ina Peacemaker Court in Alberta (established in 2000), the Cree-speaking and Dene-speaking courts in Saskatchewan

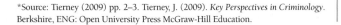

SOCIOLOGY ON SCREEN

RESTORATIVE JUSTICE: HOLLOW WATER

Hollow Water is a candid documentary depicting an Ojibway village on the shores of Lake Winnipeg in Northern Manitoba where about 450 people live in a community plagued by various forms of deviance and crime including incest, alcoholism, and psychological abuse. The community is a case study in restorative justice that utilizes sentencing circles in an effort to promote healing and change. Viewers learn about the limitations of prison, the need to bring together offenders and victims, and the benefits of involving community members in a process of justice. This film, produced by J. MacDonald and directed by B. Dickie, is available from the National Film Board of Canada.

(introduced in 2001 and 2006 respectively), the Gladue Court in Ontario (which commenced in 2001 and was expanded to three courts in 2007), and the First Nations Court in British Columbia (which opened in 2006) utilize sanctioned traditional forms of dispute resolution (Whonnock, 2008).

TIME TO REVIEW

- On what bases do abolitionists call for the overhauling of the criminal justice system?
- What are the main premises on which restorative justice rests?

SOCIOLOGY IN THEORY

LO8 A variety of theories have been used in the analyses of crime, and of deviance more generally. Some are embedded within broader sociological theories, such as Durkheim's theory of anomie (see Chapter 1), while others are specific to deviance and crime (e.g., Merton's strain theory). The manner in which deviance is initially defined has implications for the theories that are used to study it (Bereska, 2011). Deviance specialists and criminologists who suggest that deviance can be defined objectively (through rarity, the violation of norms, harm, or a negative societal reaction) subsequently are interested in studying *why* an individual might engage in deviance—the focus is on the deviant individual. If you know that stealing a car is against the law, or that you will be treated as an outsider at school because of a Gothic appearance, then why would you do it in the first place? In contrast, those deviance specialists and criminologists who draw attention to the socially constructed nature of deviance—the notion that there is nothing inherently deviant in a specific behaviour or characteristic, but rather that what is considered deviant emerges from culturally and historically specific social processes—are less interested in explaining the deviant behaviour. They are more interested in analyzing the social processes that contribute to our perceptions of certain behaviours/characteristics as deviant in the first place, and they are also interested in societal reactions to those labelled as deviant. These two different approaches to deviance and crime are shaped by theories that deal with either the causes of deviant behaviour or the processes that result in the social construction of deviance as discussed in the following sections.

THEORIZING ABOUT THE CAUSES OF DEVIANT BEHAVIOURS AND CHARACTERISTICS

There are three different categories of theories that help deviance specialists and criminologists understand the causes of deviant behaviour: functionalist theories, learning theories, and social control theories (Bereska, 2011). Within these broader categories of theories are numerous specific theories. The following sections review the basic assumptions that underlie each of these main categories and provide just a few examples of the specific theories within each.

FUNCTIONALIST THEORIES OF DEVIANCE

Functionalist theories of deviance link deviance to characteristics of the social structure; that is, there is something about the social structure that contributes to deviance. For example, Durkheim indicates that deviance emerges out of *anomie* (see Chapter 1). When society changes too rapidly (such as during the process of industrialization, or when a large-scale natural disaster occurs), people become unsure of precisely what is expected of them, and a feeling of *normlessness* emerges. Within a context of normlessness, people will begin to engage in excessive levels of deviant behaviour including the commission of crimes, or even acts of suicide (the focus of Durkheim's analysis). However, Durkheim suggests that only *excessive* levels of deviance are harmful to society, disrupting the smooth running of the social order. Less-than-excessive levels of deviance can actually contribute to the maintenance of the social order. For instance, seeing someone being punished for a transgression reminds the rest of us what the rules are, and what is expected of us; this resembles the concept of general deterrence, discussed earlier in the chapter.

In the previous chapter, you learned about Robert Merton as the founder of the "sociology of science." However, what Merton (1938, 1968) is perhaps most well known for is his theory of deviance, known as *classic strain theory*. This theory dominated the sociological study of deviance for several decades, and is recognized by some as one of the most significant sociological theories of all time, in terms of the impact that it had on the discipline (Featherstone & Deflam, 2003; Pfohl, 1994).

Like Durkheim, Merton connected deviance to characteristics of the social structure. He explains that an individual's location within the larger social structure, such as in terms of socioeconomic status, can contribute to deviance. That is, people who are located in some parts of the social structure face more constraints than those located in other parts of the social structure. The constraints that are of direct relevance to deviance are related to what Merton labelled institutionalized goals and legitimate means. The **institutionalized goals** of our contemporary society are wealth, power, and prestige. From the time that we are young children, we are socialized to aspire to earn a lot of money, be a leader rather than a follower, and be respected. We are taught that the **legitimate means** for attaining those goals include getting a good education, working hard, investing your money wisely, and so on. However, Merton pointed out that society is structured in a way that some people, such as children growing up in an inner-city neighbourhood, have less access to those legitimate means. Regardless of the lack of available legitimate means, most people will still dream of achieving institutionalized goals, hence, a "gap" exists between the goals and the means for obtaining them, which creates a sense of "strain." People may respond to this "gap" in different ways; that is, they engage in different *modes of adaptation.*

Most people continue to aspire to conventional goals and do their best to pursue the legitimate means of achieving them; Merton labelled this mode of adaptation *conformity.* For example, a former student of one of the authors grew up in the "killing fields" of Cambodia. He spent virtually his entire childhood running from one refugee camp to another with his mother, trying to evade capture and death at the hands of the Khmer Rouge. At the age of 18, he finally made it to Canada, not speaking a word of English and having never learned to read, write, or do arithmetic. He and his mother lived in poverty, and many members of his community who were in a similar situation became involved in crime. However, this particular young man did not—he continued to pursue institutionalized goals through only legitimate means and by the time he was 25 years old, he had not only earned a high school diploma but also had graduated from university and was about to embark on a career with an international aid agency.

Others respond to the gap between goals and means by accepting the goals of wealth, power, and prestige, but rejecting or giving up on the legitimate means for obtaining them. Using *innovation,* some people find alternative means of attaining the goals; for instance, obtaining wealth through selling drugs, becoming powerful through gang membership, or gaining prestige through using performance-enhancing drugs to become a star baseball player. Some individuals engage in *ritualism,* whereby they give up on the institutionalized goals but continue to engage in the means, such as by reliably working at their low-paid jobs until retirement even though they will never earn enough money to purchase a new car or obtain a mortgage for a home. Others may adapt to the discrepancy between means and goals by rejecting *both* the institutionalized goals and the legitimate means, perhaps escaping into drug or alcohol abuse or not even bothering to look for work anymore; a mode of adaptation called *retreatism.* Finally, some people engage in *rebellion,* rejecting the current goals and means, but living according to an alternative set of goals and means. For instance, in the 1960s some Hippies created alternative lifestyles for themselves in communes, pursuing peace, love, and sharing of material goods.

In Merton's description of the structural constraints that lead some people into deviance, and Durkheim's suggestion that excessive levels of deviance emerge within contexts of anomie, we see the foundational assumptions of functionalism at work. That is, there is something about the *social*

Institutionalized goals: The goals that we are *supposed* to aspire to in contemporary society.

Legitimate means: The socially accepted ways of attaining wealth, power, and prestige.

During the countercultural era of the 1960s, some Hippies utilized the mode of adaptation that Merton labelled "rebellion."

Source: Michael Ochs Archives/Stringer/Getty Images

structure rather than the individual that causes deviance. There are numerous additional functionalist theories of deviance as well that are based on this foundational assumption. For example, *differential opportunity theory* (Cloward & Ohlin, 1960) points out that not only does a person's location in the social structure determine his or her access to legitimate means of attaining goals, it also determines his or her level of access to *illegitimate* means of attaining goals (such as access to gangs or the illegal drug industry). Functionalist theories of deviance all have in common an emphasis on characteristics of the social structure as the impetus for deviance. In contrast, learning theories shift their attention to a different cause of deviance.

LEARNING THEORIES

Learning theories propose that deviant behaviours emerge through processes of learning—that is, some people "learn" to act in deviant ways while others do not (Bereska, 2011). Thus, *social learning theory* states that deviant behaviours occur when individuals are rewarded for those acts; are not punished for those acts; or, through processes of imitation and modelling, see others being rewarded for similar acts. Edwin Sutherland's (1947) *differential association theory*, one of the most influential theories in the study of deviance, claims that we learn deviant behaviour through the very same processes by which we learn conforming behaviour. Via interactions within small, intimate groups that are important to us (e.g., friends; family), we learn both **techniques** (i.e., skills) and **motives** (i.e., reasons) to engage in particular behaviours. If we learn more "deviant" techniques and motives (e.g., how to smoke, roll a joint, or hotwire a car and why we might enjoy smoking, doing drugs, or stealing a car) than "conforming" techniques and motives (e.g., how to do well in school and why it is important to do well in school), then we are more likely to engage in deviant behaviour than if we had, conversely, learned more conforming techniques and motives.

One of the learning theories of deviance that is frequently used today is Sykes and Matza's (1957) *neutralization theory*. This theory proposes that we learn **techniques of neutralization** or rationalizations that allow us to justify our behaviour to others and to ourselves and, hence, facilitate or promote future deviant behaviours. With the *denial of injury*, we can claim that we really aren't hurting anyone, as in the case of perpetrators of supposed "victimless crimes" or exotic dancers who claim that what they do doesn't cause any harm (Thompson, Harred & Burks, 2003).

Denial of the victim involves the claim that the person on the receiving end of our behaviour deserved what he or she got. For instance, someone who shoplifts may claim that stores jack up their prices anyway, or someone who downloads pirated music off the Internet may state that the music industry makes tons of money anyway (Ingram & Hinduja, 2008).

With *denial of responsibility*, the transgressor argues that he or she isn't *really* responsible for what happened. Any of us who have ever watched an episode of the TV show *Cops* has seen this occur when the officers find drugs in a person's car, and that person claims that he or she didn't know they were there—or even in the individual's pants and he or she exclaims, "But these aren't my pants!" *Condemning the condemners* involves the transgressor (i.e., the person who committed the act) arguing that the person or group that is condemning him or her is guilty of even worse behaviours. For example, exotic dancers talk about the way that some police officers will sit and watch their performances for hours before writing tickets for lewd dancing (Thompson, Harred & Burks, 2003). Finally, in an *appeal to higher loyalties*, transgressors claim that they engaged in that deviant behaviour for a good reason. For instance, environmental activists who are arrested for vandalizing company property in the oil sands may claim that their actions were necessary in order to draw attention to the way that oil companies are destroying the environment.

Functionalist theories of deviance and crime focus on the social structure, while learning theories emphasize the processes by which deviance is learned. *Social control theories* take a very different approach to their analyses.

SOCIAL CONTROL THEORIES

Unlike the other categories of theories that attempt to explain why some people engage in deviance, social control theories analyze why we *all* don't engage in deviance—what it is that restrains people from deviant acts (Bereska, 2011). Travis Hirschi's (1969) early social control theory rests on the premise that *social bonds* prevent most people from engaging in deviance. Social bonds are connections that people have to conventional society; they

> **Techniques:** The skills needed to engage in either deviant or conforming behaviour.
>
> **Motives:** The reasons for engaging in either deviant or conforming behaviour.
>
> **Techniques of neutralization:** Rationalizations that allow us to justify our behaviour to others and to ourselves.

take the form of attachment, commitment, involvement, and beliefs. Emotional *attachment* to others holds us back from deviant behaviour. *Commitment* to conventional values (e.g., getting good grades) constitutes an "investment"—people who have strong commitments simply have too much to lose by engaging in deviance. People who are high in *involvement* are so busy carrying out conventional activities there isn't enough time in the day to engage in deviance as well; think of yourself, where you may be taking a full course load, working part time (or even close to full time), taking care of family responsibilities, working out at the gym three times a week, and volunteering for a community organization (whew!). Finally, *belief* in the norms and values of the conforming world (e.g., such as respect for the law) restrains people from deviance—since behaving is the right thing to do. Via these four types of bonds, social control theory states that most people are prevented from engaging in deviant behaviour. For example, several studies have found that youth who have these social bonds are less likely to be sexually active or to use substances, including cigarettes (Lauritsen, 1994; Hawdon, 1996).

More recently, Hirschi has proposed a new control theory—what was initially called the *general theory of crime*, and is now referred to more generally as *self-control theory* (Gottfredson & Hirschi, 1990; Grasmick, Tittle, Bursik & Arneklev, 1993). Self-control theory rests on the assumption that self-control, which develops in early childhood through socialization by one's parent, is what restrains most of us from committing deviant acts. Hence, it is the failure to develop adequate self-control that causes deviance. Low levels of self-control have been found to be associated with criminal behaviour (both for street crime and white-collar crime), truancy, risky behaviours (related to driving, sexuality, and substance use), and binging/purging (Kubrin, Stucky & Krohn, 2009; Hope & Chapple, 2005; Stylianou, 2002; Jones & Quisenberry, 2004).

Functionalist, learning, and social control theories each have distinct areas of emphasis. However, what they have in common is that they are all theories that are of greatest use to deviance specialists and criminologists who consider deviance to have certain "objective," easily recognizable characteristics, and who are thereby most interested in the causes of deviant behaviour. In contrast, those scholars who emphasize the manner in which deviance is socially constructed find other types of theories to be most useful (Bereska, 2011).

Primary deviance:
The little acts of deviance that many of us engage in occasionally.

TIME TO REVIEW

- Why do deviance specialists and criminologists who use more objective definitions of deviance utilize different theories than those who use more subjective definitions of deviance?
- What are the basic assumptions of functionalist, learning, and social control theories of deviance?
- How is deviance explained by Durkheim, and within classic strain theory?
- How is deviance explained by differential association theory and neutralization theory?
- How is deviance explained by social control theory and self-control theory?

THEORIZING ABOUT THE SOCIAL CONSTRUCTION OF DEVIANCE

With an emphasis on the social construction of deviance, interest does not lie in explaining deviant acts, but rather in explaining the processes that are involved in creating our perceptions of and reactions to those acts. Consequently, interpretive and critical theories (see Chapter 1) are of the greatest value.

INTERPRETIVE THEORIES

Interpretive theories have a foundation in the interactionist perspective. From this perspective, through our interactions with *significant others* and the *generalized other*, as well as the influence of the *looking-glass self*, we develop understandings of what is "deviant" and what is "normal"; we also come to understand ourselves within this context, and choose our appearances and our actions on that basis. Although some of those understandings will be shared with other people, our interactions are not identical to anybody else's and as such, different understandings may develop as well; thus, you might understand facial piercing to be deviant, while someone else does not.

Edwin Lemert's (1951) *labelling theory* emerges from this interactionist foundation. Lemert states that all of us engage in some deviant acts, little acts of **primary deviance**—they are usually minor acts that are done rarely or infrequently (e.g., drinking alcohol to excess). Because infrequent deviant transgressions are likely to go undetected, people are able to maintain a nondeviant self-image. However, with more frequent acts of deviance, the chances of detection are greater. Lemert argues that getting *caught* at deviance (especially at a formal level) is the impetus for a whole chain of events that changes how people are treated, and how they come to understand and identify themselves. For example, getting caught drinking alcohol at work may lead an employer to attach the label "problem drinker" or "alcoholic" to the employee. Because of that label, people start to treat the deviant differently; a person who is labelled as a problem drinker at work may be reprimanded by his or her boss, avoided by fellow workers, and/or required to take a leave of absence to seek treatment. The legitimate world starts to reject the deviant and only similar others in the deviant world, such as one's fellow patrons of the familiar bar, continue to accept him or her. The deviant also comes to view him- or herself differently as a result of the label, increasingly accepts the label, and builds a lifestyle and an identity around it—this is known as **secondary deviance**. A person who has been labelled a "problem drinker" may drink even more to cope with deteriorating relationships at work and/or at home, because he or she has internalized that label and is acting in accordance with its role.

Canadian sociologist Erving Goffman (1963) spoke of a similar process, whereby people who engage in certain acts or who have particular characteristics face **stigmatization** in society; that is, they become treated as "outsiders" once they are labelled as such. Those individuals may respond to stigmatization in a number of ways, ranging from trying to hide that stigmatized characteristic to developing a lifestyle around it and publicly embracing it. Thus, the person who frequently drinks to excess may try to prevent detection by using mouthwash or drinking vodka out of a water bottle, or alternatively may be known to friends as throwing the best parties because of his or her well-stocked bar.

Interpretive theories involving processes such as labelling and stigmatization, then, explain how we come to understand certain behaviours, characteristics, and people (including ourselves) as deviant, and how we learn to respond accordingly. Critical theories explain why some people's understandings of deviance have more of an influence in society overall, are accepted by larger numbers of people, and end up reflected in society's institutions (e.g., the criminal justice system, the education system, the mass media) (Bereska, 2011).

CRITICAL THEORIES

Conflict theories propose that structures of power determine which behaviours or characteristics are defined and treated as being deviant. Although different conflict theories describe that structure of power in distinct ways (see Chapter 1), they agree that holding power enables groups to define their own behaviours as "normal" while defining the behaviours of others as "deviant" and in need of social control. The powerful then also have the means to enforce those measures of social control, whether that be in the creation of laws or the development of standards of what being a "good" mother means (Beaman, 2000; Bereska, 2011).

Poststructuralist Michel Foucault (1995) analyzed the social control aspect of deviance. He focused on means by which we frequently don't have to be controlled by others, but actually control our own behaviours through **self-surveillance**. We live in a society where we are constantly monitored, or at least feel that we are being monitored, through

> **Secondary deviance:**
> Chronic deviance as a lifestyle.
>
> **Stigmatization:**
> The process by which individuals are excluded because of particular behaviours/characteristics.
>
> **Self-surveillance:**
> Monitoring our own behaviours in order to prevent being considered deviant.

SOCIOLOGY *IN MY LIFE*

AVOIDING DEVIANT LABELS

Think about the various activities that make up your own lifestyle. Are there any practices you engage in that run the risk of stigmatization? Do you monitor or modify any of these behaviours in certain environments or around certain people in order to decrease the odds of detection?

CHAPTER 10 The World of Deviance and Crime **229**

Source: Celeborn/Shutterstock

Foucault proposes that we don't always need other people to monitor us for transgressions, since we frequently monitor ourselves.

surveillance cameras, photo radar, bureaucratic mechanisms that influence everything from who is/is not allowed to drive to how you are/are not allowed to sell your home, and strangers judging our physical appearance when we walk down the street. Because of the perception of ongoing monitoring, we eventually monitor our own behaviours—we weigh ourselves once a week, renew our driver's licences simply because we received a letter in the mail telling us that it is time to do so, or we slow down when we see what the speed limit is on a given street.

Feminist theories draw attention to facets of deviance such as the differential standards that women and men face in determining what is considered deviant, and the varying experiences they have of being socially typed as deviant and subjected to measures of social control. For instance, they point out that what is considered acceptable behaviour/characteristics in society is gendered (see Chapter 7). A male who wishes to be a day care worker is more likely to be considered deviant than a woman with that same wish, while a women who wants to work on an oil rig is more likely to be socially typed as deviant than a male in that position (Bereska, 2011). Feminist criminologists explore the manner in which the experiences of women who commit crimes are influenced by gender. For example, some scholars have explored female prostitution as an extension of women's oppression in society overall, while others address the unique issues surrounding mothers in prison (Larsen, 2000; Downes & Rock, 2003). As with other critical theories, feminist perspectives on deviance emphasize the broader social processes that result in certain perceptions of and reactions to deviance carrying more weight in society as a whole.

TIME TO REVIEW

- What is the role of interpretive and critical theories in those approaches to deviance that emphasize its socially constructed nature?
- What are the basic interactionist assumptions regarding deviance, and how are those reflected in Lemert's labelling theory and Goffman's notion of stigmatization?
- What aspects of deviance do conflict theories, Foucault's work, and feminist theories focus on?

CHAPTER SUMMARY

LO1 Compare and contrast different ways of defining deviance, and explain how exploring deviance historically and cross-culturally illustrates its socially constructed nature.

In academia there is no consensus about how deviance should be defined. Some theorists prefer definitions that emphasize "objective" characteristics such as rarity, harm, normative violation, or a negative reaction by members of society. Others prefer to view

deviance as socially constructed wherein some behaviours are considered deviant in one culture but not another, or at one historical moment but not another.

LO2 Distinguish between high-consensus deviance and low-consensus deviance.

High-consensus deviance and low-consensus deviance refer to the level of agreement pertaining to the labelling of particular behaviours/characteristics as deviant by members of society.

LO3 Differentiate among varying types of social control.

Deviant behaviour may be controlled through organizations and institutions (formally), or via the actions of individuals in everyday interactions (informally). Some forms of social control punish or attempt to "fix" deviance that has already occurred, while other forms attempt to prevent deviance from occurring in the first place. Some forms of social control are directed at others, while other forms are those that we direct at ourselves.

LO4 Explain how deviance and crime, as well as deviance specialists and criminologists, are related.

Deviance consists of any behaviours/characteristics that are socially typed as deviant and subjected to various measures of social control; crime is a specific form of deviance, which consists of behaviours that are socially typed, formally stated as laws, and are dealt with via the criminal justice system. Deviance specialists are scholars who study deviance, while criminologists focus their analyses on criminalized forms of deviance in particular.

LO5 Demonstrate an understanding of the legal meaning of a crime and differentiate among crime classifications.

Crime refers to violations of criminal law. Crimes are treated somewhat differently by the criminal justice system depending on how they are categorized (e.g., property crimes are counted differently than violent crimes, summary conviction offences correspond to more lenient forms of punishment than indictable conviction offences, etc.).

LO6 Describe the criminal justice system and the rationale for punishment as the primary means for controlling crime.

The criminal justice system consists of police, courts, and prisons, which attempt to control criminal behaviour through the use of punishment that is designed to prevent (or deter) criminal activity, rehabilitate offenders, and protect society.

LO7 Explain how restorative justice differs from retributive forms of punishment such as imprisonment.

Restorative justice seeks to heal and repair harm caused by an offender. This approach requires that an offender take responsibility for the resolution process that includes relationships among victims, offenders, and the wider community.

LO8 Identify and describe the theories used by more objective versus more subjective deviance specialists.

Scholars who emphasize objective characteristics of deviance are interested in why deviant acts emerge, while those who focus on the social construction of deviance are interested in the processes involved in our perceptions of and reactions to particular behaviour/characteristics. Functionalist, learning, and social control theories are most useful to the former, while interpretive and critical theories are most useful to the latter. Functionalist theories include Durkheim's theory of anomie, classical strain theory, and differential opportunity theory. Learning theories include social learning theory, differential association theory, and neutralization theory. Social control theories include social bond theory and self-control theory. Interpretive theories include Lemert's labelling theory and Goffman's notion of stigmatization. Critical theories include conflict theories, poststructuralist theories, and feminist theories.

RECOMMENDED READINGS

1. To gain a better understanding of the origins of the sociological study of deviance, we recommend: Becker, H. (Ed.). (1964). *The Other Side: Perspectives on Deviance*. New York, NY: The Free Press.
2. For an in-depth look at the sociology of deviance, which explores deviance in relation to sexuality, youth, physical appearance, mental disorders, religion, and science, see: Bereska, T. M. (2011). *Deviance, Conformity, and Social Control in Canada* (3rd ed.). Toronto, ON: Pearson Education Canada.
3. For a critical focus on youth crime in relation to issues of power and justice in Canada, refer to: Minaker, J., & Hogeveen, B. (2009). *Youth, Crime, and Society: Issues of Power and Justice*. Toronto, ON: Pearson Education Canada.
4. If you want to learn more about cyber crimes, we recommend: Schmalleger, F., & Pittaro, M. (2009). *Crimes of the Internet*. Upper Saddle River, NJ: Pearson Education.

FOR FURTHER REFLECTION

1. At what times in your life have *you* been socially typed as deviant and subjected to forms of social control? Were the measures of social control intended to punish you, "fix" you, and/or prevent you from breaking the rules in the first place?

2. Based on your understanding of how crime and deviance is defined in this chapter, how is prostitution (i.e., the exchange of sex for money) best classified? Defend your answer.

REFERENCES

Atkinson, M. (2003). *Tattooed: Sociogenesis of a Body Art.* Toronto, ON: University of Toronto Press.

Beaman, L. G. (2000). *New Perspectives on Deviance: The Construction of Deviance in Everyday Life.* Scarborough, ON: Prentice Hall.

Becker, H. (1963). *Outsiders: Studies in the Sociology of Deviance.* New York: Free Press.

Bereska, T. M. (2011). *Deviance, Conformity, and Social Control in Canada* (3rd ed.). Toronto, ON: Pearson Education Canada.

Braswell, M., Fuller J., & Lozoff, B. (2001). *Corrections, Peacemaking, and Restorative Justice: Transforming Individuals and Institutions.* Cincinnati, OH: Anderson Publishing Co.

(The) Canadian Encyclopedia. (2011). Organized Crime. In *The Canadian Encyclopedia.* Historica-Dominion: William I. Macadam, James R. Dubro, and Pierre De Champlain. Retrieved August 2, 2011, from www .thecanadianencyclopedia.com/index.cfm?PgNm=TCE& Params=A1ARTA0005979

CBC News. (2010, September 28). *Prostitution laws struck down by Ontario court.* CBC News Online. Retrieved December 15, 2010, from www.cbc.ca/canada/ story/2010/09/28/prostitution-law028.html

Cloward, R. A., & Ohlin, L. E. (1960). *Delinquency and Opportunity: A Theory of Delinquent Gangs.* New York: Free Press.

Dauvergne, M., & Turner, J. (2010). Police-reported crime statistics in Canada, 2009. *Juristat, 30*(2), 1–37. Ottawa, ON: Statistics Canada. Statistics Canada Catalogue No. 85-002-X.

Department of Justice Canada. (2011). *Corrections and Conditional Release Act (S.C. 1992, c. 20).* Purpose of correctional system. Retrieved August 2, 2011, from http://laws-lois.justice.gc.ca/eng/acts/C-44.6/page-2 .html#h-4

Department of Justice Canada. (2010). *Criminal Code (R.S., 1985, c. C-46).* Retrieved December 5, 2010, from http:// laws.justice.gc.ca/eng/C-46/20101206/page-6.html?rp2= HOME&rp3=SI&rp1=assault&rp4=all&rp9=cs&rp10= L&rp13=50

Deutschmann, L. B. (2002). *Deviance and Social Control* (3rd ed.). Scarborough, ON: Nelson Thomson Learning.

Downes, D., & Rock, P. (2003). *Understanding Deviance* (4th ed.). New York: Oxford University Press.

Edwards, A. R. (1988). *Regulation and Repression: The Study of Social Control.* Sydney: Allen & Unwin.

Featherstone, R., & Deflam, M. (2003). Anomie and strain: Context and consequences of Merton's two theories. *Sociological Inquiry, 73*(4), 471–489.

Fiolleau, T. (2011). *Personal interview for Trafficked with Dottie Laster.* Retrieved May 16, 2011, from http:// herewomentalkradio.com/home/archives_details/709

Foucault, M. (1995). *Discipline and Punish: The Birth of the Prison* (2nd ed.). Trans. A. Sheridan. New York: Vintage Books.

Goffman, E. (1963). *Stigma: Notes on the Management of Spoiled Identity.* Englewood Cliffs, NJ: Prentice Hall.

Gottfredson, M. R., & Hirschi, T. (1990). *A General Theory of Crime.* Stanford, CT: Stanford University Press.

Grasmick, H. G., Tittle, C. R., Bursik, R. J., & Arneklev, B. J. (1993). Testing the core empirical implications of Gottfredson and Hirschi's general theory of crime. *Journal of Research in Crime and Delinquency, 30*(1), 47–54.

Hawdon, J. E. (1996). Deviant lifestyles: The social control of daily routines. *Youth & Society, 28*(2), 162–188.

Hefley, K. (2007). Stigma management of male and female customers to a non-urban adult novelty store. *Deviant Behavior, 28*(1), 79–109.

Hirschi, T. C. (1969). *Causes of Delinquency.* Berkeley, CA: University of California Press.

Hope, T. L., & Chapple, C. L. (2005). Maternal characteristics, parenting, and adolescent sexual behavior: The role of self-control. *Deviant Behavior, 26*, 25–45.

Ingram, J. R., & Hinduja, S. (2008). Neutralizing musical piracy: An empirical examination. *Deviant Behavior, 29*, 334–366.

Jones, S., & Quisenberry, N. (2004). The general theory of crime: How general is it? *Deviant Behavior, 25*, 401–426.

Jourard, R. (2010). *Criminal offence penalty charts.* Toronto, ON: Website of Ron Jourard, criminal lawyer, specializing in defence of driving-related charges including impaired and dangerous. Retrieved December 6, 2010, from www .defencelaw.com/chart-contents.html

Koenig, D. J., & Linden, R. (2009). Convention or "Street" Crime. In Rick Linden (Ed.), *Criminology: A Canadian Perspective.* (6th ed.). (pp. 429–462). Toronto, ON: Nelson Education.

Kubrin, C. E., Stuckey, T. D., & Krohn, M. D. (2009). *Researching Theories of Crime and Deviance.* New York: Oxford University Press.

Larsen, N. (2000). Prostitution: Deviant activity or legitimate occupation? In L. G. Beaman (Ed.), *New Perspectives on Deviance: The Social Construction of Deviance in Everyday Life* (pp. 50–66). Scarborough, ON: Prentice Hall.

Lauritsen, J. L. (1994). Explaining race and gender differences in adolescent sexual behavior. *Social Forces, 72*(3), 859–884.

Lemert, E. M. (1951). *Social Pathology: A Systematic Approach to the Study of Sociopathic Behavior*. New York: McGraw-Hill.

Liazos, A. (1972). The poverty of the sociology of deviance: Nuts, sluts, and perverts. *Social Problems, 20,* 102–120.

Mackay, J. (2000). Global sex: Sexuality and sexual practices around the world. Paper presented at the 5th Congress of the European Federation of Sexology, June 29–July 2, 2000, Berlin.

Martin, R., Mutchnick, R. J., & Austin, W. T. (1990). *Criminological Thought: Pioneers Past and Present.* New York, NY: Macmillan Publishing Company.

Merton, R. K. (1938). Social structure and anomie. *American Sociological Review, 3,* 672–682.

Merton, R. K. (1968). *Social Theory and Social Structure.* New York: Free Press.

Newman, G. (2008). *Comparative Deviance: Perception and Law in Six Cultures.* New Brunswick, NJ: Transaction Publishers.

Pepinsky, H. & Quinney, R. (Eds.). (2001). *Criminology as Peacemaking.* Bloomington: Indiana University Press.

Pfohl, S. (1994). *Images of Deviance and Social Control: A Sociological History.* New York: McGraw-Hill.

Sacco, V. F. (1992). *Deviance, Conformity and Control in Canadian Society.* Scarborough, ON: Prentice Hall.

Schmalleger, F., & Pittaro, M. (2009). *Crimes of the Internet.* Upper Saddle River, NJ: Pearson Education.

Siegel, L. J., & McCormick, C. (2010). *Criminology in Canada: Theories, Patterns, and Typologies.* Toronto, ON: Nelson Education.

Siegel, L. J., Brown, G. P., & Hoffman, R. (2006). *Criminology: The Core.* Toronto, ON: Nelson Education.

Statistics Canada. (2010a, July 20). Police-reported crime statistics. *The Daily.* Ottawa, ON: Author. Retrieved August 2, 2011, from www.statcan.gc.ca/daily-quotidien/100720/dq100720a-eng.htm

Statistics Canada. (2010b, September 28). General Social Survey: Victimization. *The Daily.* Ottawa, ON: Author. Retrieved August 2, 2011, from www.statcan.gc.ca/daily-quotidien/100928/dq100928a-eng.htm

Stylianou, S. (2002). Control attitudes toward drug use as a function of paternalistic and moral principles. *Journal of Drug Use, 32*(1), 119–152.

Sutherland, E. H. (1947). *Principles of Criminology.* Philadelphia, PA: J. B. Lippincott.

Sykes, G., & Matza, D. (1957). Techniques of neutralization: A theory of delinquency. *American Sociological Review, 22,* 664–670.

Taylor-Butts, A. (2010). Where and when youth commit police-reported crimes, 2008. *Juristat, 30*(2), 1–23. Statistics Canada Catalogue No. 85-002-X. Ottawa, ON: Author.

Thio, A. (1983). *Deviant Behavior* (2nd ed.). Boston: Houghton Mifflin.

Thompson, W. E., Harred, J. L., & Burks, B. E. (2003). Managing the stigma of topless dancing: A decade later. *Deviant Behavior, 24,* 551–570.

Tierney, J. (2009). *Key Perspectives in Criminology.* Berkshire, U: Open University Press McGraw-Hill Education.

Vago, S., & Nelson, A. (2008). *Law and Society.* (2nd Can ed.). Toronto, ON: Pearson Education Canada.

Verdun-Jones, S. (2011). *Criminal Law in Canada: Cases, Questions, and the Code.* (5th ed.). Toronto, ON: Nelson Education.

Whonnock, K. (2008). *Aboriginal Courts in Canada: Fact Sheet.* The Scow Institute. Retrieved August 2, 2011, from www.scowinstitute.ca/library/documents/Aboriginal_Courts_Fact_Sheet.pdf

Winterdyk, A. (2006). *Canadian Criminology.* (2nd ed.). Toronto, ON: Pearson Education Canada.

Zher, H. (2002). *The Little Book of Restorative Justice.* Intercourse, PA: Good Books.

ENDNOTE

[1] The exception to this rule is robbery, which is defined as theft of property but is considered a violent crime since it is carried out using force or a threat of force. Hence, there is one robbery counted per victim.

Health and Illness

LEARNING OBJECTIVES AND OUTCOMES

After completing this chapter, students should be able to do the following:

LO1 Outline the development of the field of medical sociology and describe its focus.

LO2 Describe how patterns of morbidity and mortality have changed through human history.

LO3 Identify the top causes of death in Canada today, and explain what the "actual" causes of death are.

LO4 Describe the roles that tobacco use, alcohol misuse, diet, physical inactivity, and obesity play in morbidity and mortality on a global level.

LO5 Describe patterns of tobacco use, alcohol use, diet, physical activity, and obesity in Canada.

LO6 Outline the social determinants of health, and describe the link between socioeconomic status and health and illness.

LO7 Describe the link between ethnicity and health and illness.

LO8 Describe the evolution and objectives of the Canadian health-care system, and identify the challenges it faces in contemporary society.

LO9 Explore how functionalists, interactionists, conflict theorists, feminist theorists, and postmodern/poststructuralists address health and illness.

Every human being is the author of his [or her] own health or disease.

(Prince Guatama Siddharta, 563–483 BCE, founder of Buddhism)[1]

Precisely what constitutes "health" can be a matter of discussion and debate, but the World Health Organization (1948) defines health as "a state of complete physical, mental and social well-being and not merely the absence of disease or infirmity" (p. 100). The chapter-opening quotation suggests that health and illness are the result of characteristics at the micro level. We might think of the extent to which an individual engages in health-promoting behaviours, such as eating right, getting enough exercise, and not smoking. However, the sociology of health and illness (also known as medical sociology) draws our attention to the macro level, the social context within which each "author" lives, since this also has a significant influence on health and illness.

LO[1] Medical sociologists are one of the largest groups of sociologists in the world. They are found inside academia (e.g., sociology departments, medical schools, nursing schools, schools of public health), and outside academia in government agencies and research organizations. The sociology of health and illness emerged in the post–World War II era, as "funding agencies and policymakers . . . viewed it as an applied field that could produce knowledge for use in medical practice, public health campaigns, and health policy formulation" (Cockerham, 2007, para. 5). Weeks (2008) points to four important changes in medicine in the 1950s and 1960s that contributed to the rapid development of medical sociology. First, as degenerative diseases such as heart disease replaced infectious diseases as the primary causes of death, the role of social patterns and lifestyles became more obvious. Second, preventive medicine and public health efforts drew attention to significant factors such as poverty and malnutrition. Third, modern psychiatry emphasized the role of the social environment in psychological healing. Finally, medicine became more bureaucratic and administrative, in terms of the "settings in which care is delivered, in the ownership of medical facilities, [and] in the bureaucracies that were created to regulate and finance medical care" (p. 3). Research funds were made widely available to study the "social causes and consequences of health and illness" (Cockerham, 2007, para. 1), and the sociology of health and illness developed rapidly. Because of the field's close ties to health practice and policy, it was largely nontheoretical at first. However, as we will see at a later point in the chapter, theory now holds a significant place in this field of study.

In this chapter, we will explore the following topics: how patterns of health and illness have changed over time; the effects of tobacco use, alcohol consumption, diet, physical activity, and obesity on global patterns of health and illness; the social determinants of health and illness; the larger health-care system within which our patterns of health and illness exist in Canada today; and the forms of sociological theorizing that have dominated this field of study.

PATTERNS OF HEALTH AND ILLNESS

Patterns of health and illness have changed considerably over time. Until very recently in the course of human history, **morbidity** (i.e., the prevalence and patterns of disease in a population) and **mortality** (i.e., the incidence and patterns of death in a population) were concentrated in the young, and were primarily the result of infectious diseases. It was only in the latter half of the 20th century that morbidity and mortality became concentrated in the older population, and primarily due to degenerative diseases (Weeks, 2008).

LO² HISTORICAL PATTERNS

For most of human history, life expectancy was between 20 and 30 years of age. In the premodern world, one-third of infants did not survive to their first birthday and 50 percent of deaths occurred in children under the age of 5. Only one-third to one-half of people lived to the age of 25, and a mere 8 percent to 17 percent to the age of 65 (Weeks, 2008). By the Middle Ages, infectious diseases were the primary cause of death. For example, up to one-third of the European population died of bubonic plague, due to a bacteria spread by fleas carried on rats, in a period of just four years during the 14th century.

By the early 1800s, life expectancy had increased to approximately the age of 40. More than 25 percent of deaths were still in children under the age of 5, but two-thirds of people were now surviving to the age of 25, and 29 percent to the age of 65 (Weeks, 2008). Infectious diseases remained the primary cause of death. During the 19th century, housing, nutrition, and sanitation gradually improved, enhanced by the scientific discovery of germs and subsequent knowledge about how to prevent the spread of germs. However, infectious disease remained the leading cause of death into the 20th century. People died of smallpox, measles, mumps, whooping cough, and more—in 1918, an influenza pandemic killed more than 500,000 people in Canada and the United States, and more than 20 million people worldwide (Crosby, cited in Weeks, 2008).

During the latter half of the 20th century, significant advances in medical care improved the treatment of disease.

Morbidity: The prevalence and patterns of disease in a population.

Mortality: The incidence and patterns of death in a population.

Knowledge about disease prevention improved as well:

> . . . improved nutrition . . . ; clean water to prevent the spread of water-borne disease and to encourage good personal hygiene; piped sewers to eliminate contact with human waste; adequate clothing and shoes to prevent parasites from invading the body; adequate shelter to keep people dry and warm; eradication of or at least protection against disease-carrying rodents and insects; vaccinations against childhood diseases; use of disinfectants to clean living and eating areas, sterilization of dishes, bed linen and clothes of sick people; and the use of gloves and masks to prevent the spread of disease from one person to another. (Weeks, 2008, pp. 154–155)

Subsequently, life expectancy increased rapidly. In the 21st century, life expectancy in Canada exceeds 80, 99 percent of people live to the age of 25, and 91 percent to the age of 65. Most deaths (90 percent) are now in people over the age of 65. Less than 1 percent of deaths are in children under the age of 5, in part due to childhood vaccinations that reduce the prevalence of many childhood infectious diseases, and virtually eliminate others. However, in the 1990s, one scientist made a claim linking childhood vaccinations with autism. Although that claim was later discovered to be fraudulent, in part because of falsified data, his research received widespread media attention at the time. This led to a reduction in the proportion of parents who were vaccinating their children (Picard, 2011a, 2010b) and, as a result, these infectious diseases are now making a comeback. For instance, recently more than 100 children in Ireland were hospitalized for measles, and three died. In 2010, California faced its worst outbreak of whooping cough in more than 60 years, with more than 9,000 cases and 10 deaths, leading the state to legislate mandatory whooping cough vaccinations for children (Johnson, 2011).

LO³ CONTEMPORARY PATTERNS

Unlike most of human history, when infectious diseases were the primary causes of death, in contemporary society degenerative diseases predominate. Seven of the top 10 causes of death in 2007 were degenerative diseases (see Figure 11.1). However, there are some variations in the leading causes of death based on both sex and age (Statistics Canada, 2010a).

FIGURE 11.1
Top 10 Causes of Death in Canada (2007)

1. • Malignant neoplasms (cancer)
2. • Diseases of the heart (heart disease)
3. • Cerebrovascular disease (stroke)
4. • Chronic lower respiratory diseases
5. • Accidents (unintentional injuries)
6. • Diabetes mellitus
7. • Alzheimer's disease
8. • Influenza and pneumonia
9. • Nephritis, nephrotic syndrome, and nephrosis (kidney disease)
10. • Intentional self-harm (suicide)

Source: Adapted from Statistics Canada (2010). Leading Causes of Death in Canada, 2007. Statistics Canada Catalogue No. 84-215-X. Ottawa, ON.

The leading causes of death among 15- to 34-year-olds—accidents and suicide—are, to a large extent, preventable through individual behaviours. But so are the degenerative causes of death among those in older age groups. The leading causes of death are listed, in official records, using standardized terms from the World Health Organization's *International Classification of Diseases (ICD)*, such as "malignant neoplasms (cancer)" and "cerebrovascular diseases (stroke)" (Weeks, 2008). But what are the *actual* causes of death? What is causing strokes, accidents, or heart disease? Research into this question has found that the top three *actual* causes of death are (in rank order) tobacco use, diet and activity patterns, and alcohol misuse (McGinnis & Foege, cited in Weeks, 2008). Tobacco use, alcohol use, a lack of physical activity, and a poor diet are each associated with a greater risk of heart disease, stroke, cancer, and other diseases (e.g., diabetes). Thus, it appears that Prince Guatama Siddharta, quoted at the beginning of this chapter, may have been right—to some extent, we are the authors of our own health and disease. We choose whether or not to smoke, how much to drink (if at all), and whether to step away from the computer for some exercise or not. However, a sociological perspective shows us those behaviours that may initially appear to be a matter of individual choice are, in fact, embedded within and affected by larger social forces.

Men and women share 6 of the top 10 leading causes of death, but there are some differences in the rankings of those causes. The top three causes of death in women are cancer, heart disease, and stroke; in men they are cancer, heart disease, and accidents. Men are three times as likely to die as a result of suicide, and twice as likely due to liver diseases.

Degenerative diseases are less common in younger age groups than in older age groups. Among those ages 15 to 34, accidents and suicide are the top two causes of death. In fact, accidents remain the leading cause of death in men up to the age of 44. When we look at the variations in the leading causes of death for people of different ages, and for women and men, we begin to make note of the social contexts of morbidity and mortality.

Accidents are the leading cause of death in women up to the age of 34, and in men up to the age of 44.

Source: Jack Dagley Photography/Shutterstock.com

- What is the sociology of health and illness, and what are its origins?
- How have patterns of morbidity and mortality changed since the premodern era, and why did those changes occur?
- What are the leading causes of death in Canada?
- What are the top three "actual" causes of death, and what does this tell us about the role of individual health behaviours?

LO⁴ PERSONAL DETERMINANTS OF HEALTH

LO⁵ TOBACCO USE

Tobacco use is the leading cause of preventable death in the world, killing up to half of its users and resulting in more than five million deaths per year—one person every six seconds. Tobacco caused 100 million deaths in the 20th century, and if smoking trends continue, one billion people will die of tobacco-related illnesses in the 21st century (World Health Organization, 2010a).

Tobacco use is increasing globally, but this is primarily due to smoking patterns in low- and middle-income countries, where 80 percent of the world's smokers live (World Health Organization, 2010a). Tobacco use has been declining in many upper middle- and high-income countries, including Canada. Approximately 20 percent of the Canadian population smokes daily or occasionally. However, the prevalence of smoking has declined considerably since the early 1970s, and has declined by more than 5 percent since 2001.

Most people who smoke begin as teenagers; if someone hasn't smoked by the age of 20, it is unlikely that he or she ever will. Thus, the best predictor of future smoking patterns in society is the current smoking patterns of youth (see Figure 11.2). Among 18- and 19-year-olds in Canada, 27 percent of males and 15 percent of females smoke, and the numbers are even lower for younger teens (Statistics Canada, 2010b). Should the trends among those younger teens persist, then tobacco use will continue the decline it has shown since 2001, and tobacco-related illnesses and death will decline as well. However, should the trend among 18- and 19-year-olds continue, we will see more adult males smoking than we do today, which will have implications for morbidity and mortality.

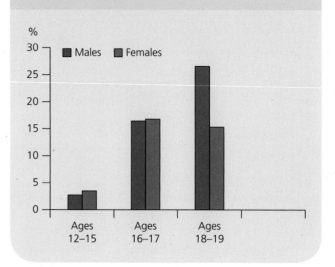

FIGURE 11.2

Youth Smokers, by Age and Sex (2009)

Source: Adapted from Statistics Canada (2010). Fact Sheet: Smoking, 2009. Statistics Canada Catalogue No. 82-625-X. Ottawa, ON.

Why do youth begin to smoke, setting the stage for potentially becoming lifelong tobacco users? There are a number of macro-level factors that contribute to smoking among youth—cultural norms, the availability of tobacco products, tobacco control policies and strategies, and the promotion of cigarettes by tobacco companies. Advertising and marketing are of specific significance because they have their greatest impact on youth (World Health Organization, n.d.). In 2000, tobacco companies spent just under $20 million on advertising in Canada (Physicians for a Smoke-Free Canada, 2003). Advertising expenditures vary across countries, in part, based on policies and legislation governing tobacco advertising. For instance, in the United States more than $12 billion was spent on tobacco advertising and promotion in 2006 (Federal Trade Commission, 2009). As smoking rates decline in some nations as a result of social policies (e.g., workplace smoking bans) and public health efforts (e.g., educating children), tobacco companies devote greater attention to countries that are lacking similar policies and public health efforts.

ALCOHOL USE AND MISUSE

Alcohol is directly related to more than 2.5 million deaths worldwide per year, including more than 350,000 deaths among those ages 15 to 29. In

2004, it was responsible for 4 percent of all deaths, and almost 5 percent of the global burden of disease (World Health Organization, 2010b). There is a causal relationship between alcohol and more than 60 types of diseases and injury, ranging from heart disease and liver cancer, to accidents and sexually transmitted infections. Alcohol consumption is greater in high-income countries, but causes more harm in lower-income nations: ". . . there is a clear discrepancy between the increasing availability and affordability of alcohol beverages in many developing and low- and middle-income countries and those countries' capability and capacity to meet the public health burden that follows" (World Health, 2010b, p. 6). This means that the burden of disease caused by alcohol varies across nations, with those countries formerly in the Soviet Union (e.g., Russia, Ukraine) facing the greatest burden of disease due to alcohol misuse (World Health Organization 2011).

Worldwide, only 54 percent of men and 27 percent of women have ever consumed alcohol, with abstaining primarily due to religion and culture (World Health Organization, 2011). In Canada, the situation is very different. The *Canadian Alcohol and Drug Use Monitoring Survey* (CADUMS) surveyed more than 13,000 Canadians over the age of 15. In 2009, CADUMS revealed that 89 percent have consumed alcohol at some point in their lives, and 77 percent in the last year. More than half have consumed alcohol within the past 30 days and more than one-third within the past week (Health Canada, 2009).

There are significant variations in alcohol use based upon both sex and age. Men are more likely than women to drink (see Figure 11.3). They are more likely to have engaged in lifetime use, use within the past 12 months, and use within the past 30 days. Male and female drinking patterns vary as well, in that men are more likely to consume alcohol at least once per week (46 percent of men versus 28 percent of women).

There are also age variations in patterns of alcohol use, when comparing youth (ages 15 to 24) with adults over the age of 25. Adults over the age of 25 are more likely to have consumed alcohol in their lifetimes, within the past 12 months, and within the past 30 days. However, youth ages 15 to 24 are more likely to drink "heavily," wherein they consume five or more drinks on any single occasion (22 percent of youth ages 15 to 24, compared to 6 percent of adults over the age of 25) (Health Canada, 2009).

Because heavy drinking is more prevalent among youth ages 15 to 24, so are many of the harms caused by alcohol use. CADUMS collects data on eight different areas of harm caused by substance use—physical

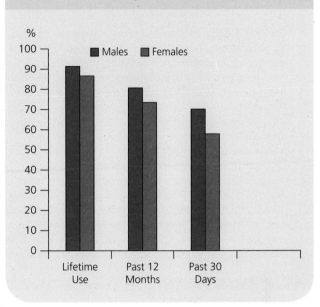

FIGURE 11.3

Alcohol Use by Sex (2009)

Source: Adapted from Health Canada (2009). *Canadian Alcohol and Drug Use Monitoring Survey 2009*. Ottawa, ON.

health, friendships and social life, home life or marriage, work/studies/employment opportunities, financial position, legal problems, housing, and difficulties learning. Youth are more likely to have experienced one or more of these harms in their lifetimes (21 percent of youth versus 15 percent of adults ages 25+), and in the past 12 months (15 percent of youth versus 5 percent of adults ages 25+). Although alcohol misuse can result in a variety of types of harms, alcohol dependence is of particular concern because of its long-term impact on diseases such as heart disease and cancer. The 2002 *Canadian Community Health Survey* found that of those Canadians who have drunk "heavily" at least once per month over the past 12 months, 3 percent meet the criteria for alcohol dependence, ranging from a low of 2 percent in Quebec to a high of 4 percent in Saskatchewan (Tjepkema, 2004).

Despite the significant role that alcohol misuse plays in morbidity and mortality on a global level, the World Health Organization (2010b) finds that governments are less willing to develop reduction strategies for alcohol than for tobacco use. Governments derive some economic benefits from both tobacco and alcohol sales and production. However, alcohol also holds a central place in the economies of many nations, and has for centuries. Even in the early 1800s in Canada, the taxation of alcohol

SOCIOLOGY *IN MY LIFE*

HOW DOES ALCOHOL AFFECT YOUR LIFE?

To what extent, and in what ways, is your life affected by your alcohol consumption? The website for the Centre for Addiction and Mental Health (www.camh .net) includes an Online Drinking Survey (via its Alcohol Help Center; select 'Alcohol' on the 'Top Searched Topics' menu). This survey asks questions about your frequency of drinking, amount of alcohol consumed, and consequences you may have experienced. Your results are placed within the context of your sex and age group as a whole, and provide you with a wide range of information. It indicates how much money you have spent on alcohol in the past year, how many extra calories you are consuming per day from alcohol, your chances of experiencing negative consequences in your life from your drinking patterns, how long it takes your liver to process one drink, and an AUDIT score that represents the extent to which your drinking could be considered problematic. You can complete the survey and have your results sent to you via email, or if you are interested in monitoring and/or reducing your alcohol consumption, you can sign up for a free program that enables you to identify your personal triggers, track your consumption, set goals, create a reward program, plan ahead for high-risk situations, participate in an expert-moderated support group, receive motivational emails or text messages, and create your own blog or upload your own motivational video.

producers constituted more than half of all government funds in some regions. By the 1890s, the federal government was receiving $7 million per year from the taxation of alcohol, and provincial governments more than $1 million per year. At that time, distillers and brewers were paying out more than $1 million per year in wages, and alcohol retailers more than $10 million per year (Heron, 2003). The economic power of the alcohol industry has only increased since that time. In 2009, provincial and territorial governments received more than $5 billion in alcohol-related revenues, including "sin taxes" on consumers, and revenues from liquor licences and permits (Statistics Canada, 2010c). Its role as an economic powerhouse is also evident by looking at alcohol sales in retail outlets. During the fiscal year ending March 2009, retail sales of alcohol in Canada totalled more than $19 billion, almost $700 per person. The physical amount of alcohol sold, as measured in "litres of absolute alcohol," is staggering. "Litres of absolute alcohol" is a calculation that standardizes the amount of pure alcohol sold, which enables one litre of any type of alcohol (beer, wine, or spirits) to be equated with one litre of any other type of alcohol. In that same fiscal year, more than 200 million litres of absolute alcohol were sold in Canada (Statistics Canada, 2010b). Governments must attempt to strike a balance between developing health strategies to benefit the population in the long term and economic development in the shorter term (World Health Organization, 2010b).

DIET AND PHYSICAL ACTIVITY

Some people use tobacco or consume alcohol, while others do not. However, everybody eats and engages in some level of physical activity. Precisely *what* you eat and *how much* physical activity you engage in has a significant impact on health and illness. Several interrelated factors play a role in morbidity and mortality—poor eating habits, a lack of physical activity, and being overweight or obese. These factors are most commonly associated with lifestyles in high-income countries, but are increasingly present in low- and middle-income countries as well. Globally, low consumption of fruits and vegetables is associated with almost one-third of cases of heart disease; increasing consumption could potentially save almost three million lives per year (World Health Organization, 2005). Approximately 6 percent of all deaths are caused by a lack of physical activity, as are between one-quarter and one-third of cases of breast and colon cancer, diabetes, and heart disease. And 65 percent of the world's population lives in a country where being overweight kills more people than does malnutrition. One billion adults are overweight, as are 42 million children under the age of 5 (World Health Organization, 2010c, 2010d). Clearly, eating habits, physical activity, and the prevalence of overweight and obesity creates a significant burden of disease in the world. And when we narrow our focus to Canada, we see the magnitude of these problems.

EATING HABITS

The 2004 *Canadian Community Health Survey* was the first national survey of Canadians' eating habits conducted since the 1970s. More than 35,000 participants were asked about their eating habits, and their responses were compared to the guidelines in the Canada Food Guide (Garriguet, 2007). Half of adults were not eating enough fruits and vegetables, nor were 60 to 70 percent of children ages 4 to 13. The majority of Canadians over the age of 10 were not consuming the minimum recommended amounts of dairy products, and the same was true for one-third of young children. More than 25 percent of young children were not eating enough grains, and that proportion increased with age. Adults and male children were consuming enough meat and alternatives, but female children were not. One food group that all Canadians were consuming more than enough of was the "other" group—soft drinks, salad dressings, sugars/syrups/preserves, beer, and fats (in that rank order). In fact, these "other" low-nutrient, high-calorie foods comprise approximately one-quarter of all calories consumed. Canadians consume more of their daily calories in snack foods than in breakfast, and one-quarter have eaten fast food in the past day.

PHYSICAL ACTIVITY

If the eating habits of Canadians leave something to be desired, levels of physical activity are even worse. The World Health Organization and Health Canada provide the following guidelines for physical activity: adults should engage in 150 minutes of moderate activity or 75 minutes of vigorous activity weekly, while children ages 5 to 17 should engage in 60 minutes of moderate to vigorous activity daily. In the past, people were asked how much physical activity they engaged in during the previous week. However, the *Canadian Health Measures Survey* had people wear accelerometers for a week, which measured exactly how much movement they engaged in. Perhaps not surprisingly, it turns out that people aren't getting as much exercise as they say they are getting. Only 15 percent of adults and 7 percent of children engage in the recommended level of activity. In fact, almost half of adults aren't even engaging in 30 minutes of physical activity *per week*.

Children are more active than adults, with 29 percent of boys and 21 percent of girls physically active for 30 minutes each day. But even children are sedentary for 62 percent of their waking hours, while adults are sedentary for 69 percent of their waking hours (Statistics Canada, 2011).

OVERWEIGHT AND OBESE

For some people a lack of physical activity can be associated with weight problems, although diet and exercise have implications for morbidity and mortality in people without weight problems as well. Adult weights are classified on the basis of the Body Mass Index (BMI), which is calculated by dividing one's weight in kilograms by the square of one's height in metres. A BMI of 25 is classified as "overweight," and a BMI of 30 as "obese." However, "there is evidence that the risk of chronic diseases in populations increase progressively from a BMI of 21" (World Health Organization, 2006, para. 4).

In 2009, almost 60 percent of men and 44 percent of women in Canada were overweight or obese, and were therefore at a greater risk of various health problems, Of those proportions, 19 percent of men and 17 percent of women were obese, based on self-reports (Statistics Canada, 2010e). However, just as people tend to be inaccurate in self-reports of physical activity, they also inaccurately report their weight and/

For most adults, the body mass index (BMI) is one of the indicators of the risk for disease.

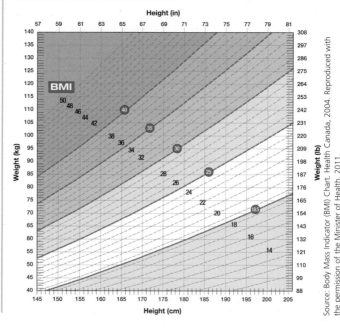

Source: Body Mass Indicator (BMI) Chart. Health Canada, 2004. Reproduced with the permission of the Minister of Health, 2011.

or height. Previous research has found that women tend to underestimate their weight, while men overestimate their height (Shields, Gorber & Tremblay, 2008). When we take this into consideration, we see that obesity is more than 7 percentage points higher than reported and overweight almost 2 percentage points higher than reported; this would mean that approximately one-quarter of Canadians are actually obese.

SUMMARY

The top three "actual" causes of death are tobacco use, poor diet and inactivity, and alcohol use. Globally, these patterns of behaviour are having an increasing impact on patterns of morbidity and mortality. Because of this, the World Health Organization and its member states (of which Canada is one) have developed global strategies to reduce these problematic behaviours and their impact (see *Sociology in Practice* below).

Behaviours related to smoking, drinking, diet, and physical activity are significant for individuals and their own health as well as for national and global patterns of morbidity and mortality. Initially, these behaviours may first appear to be matters of individual choice. However, our choices are made within a social context, and various social factors can facilitate or constrain our choices.

TIME TO REVIEW

- What are the patterns of tobacco use, globally and in Canada?
- Why do youth start smoking, and what role does advertising play?
- What are the patterns of alcohol use, and how prevalent are various types of harms that are caused by alcohol use?
- Why may governments be more reluctant to implement alcohol reduction strategies than other types of health promotion strategies?
- To what extent do people in Canada and globally eat well, engage in physical activity, and maintain a healthy weight?

SOCIOLOGY *IN PRACTICE*

WHO FRAMEWORK CONVENTION ON TOBACCO CONTROL

The World Health Organization has developed global strategies governing tobacco use, poor diet and inactivity, and alcohol misuse. For example, the WHO Framework Convention on Tobacco Control (FCTC) "is the pre-eminent global tobacco control instrument, which contains legally binding obligations for its Parties, sets the baseline for reducing both demand for and supply of tobacco, and provides a comprehensive direction for tobacco control policy at all levels" (World Health Organization, 2009, p. 12). The strategies for reducing the supply of tobacco products focus efforts on

- Illicit trade in tobacco products;
- Sales to and by minors;
- Provision of support for economically viable alternative activities.

The strategies for reducing the demand for tobacco products focus efforts on

- Price and tax measures;
- Protection from exposure to second-hand smoke;
- Regulation of content of tobacco products;
- Regulation of tobacco product disclosures;
- Packaging and labelling of tobacco products;
- Education, communication, training, and public awareness;
- Tobacco advertising, promotion, and sponsorship;
- Reduction measures concerning tobacco dependence and cessation.

You can download a copy of the FCTC from the website of the World Health Organization at www.who.int

Source: Adapted from WHO Framework Convention on Tobacco Control, www.who.int/fctc/text_download/en/index.html. p. 12.

LO⁶ SOCIAL DETERMINANTS OF HEALTH

Individual behaviours related to smoking, alcohol use, diet, and activity are often referred to as *personal determinants* of health. But those personal determinants are embedded within and influenced by *social determinants* of health. In fact, social determinants have an impact on health and illness even after controlling for alcohol use, smoking, diet, and exercise (Canadian Institute for Health Information, 2008). Social determinants include environmental, economic, and various social factors. Environmental factors are based on characteristics of where we live and where we work—the nature of our housing and neighbourhoods; air, land, and water quality; and potentially dangerous work environments. Economic factors include our socioeconomic status, which comprises income, education, and occupational status. Social factors can include the nature of social supports that we have (or do not have) in our lives, family structure, and the quality of our work.

Research finds that the single most important determinant of health globally is socioeconomic status. In any nation, a higher position in the social structure is associated with better health (Canadian Institute for Health Information, 2008, 2010a; Clarke, 2008; Cockerham, 2007). For instance, Canadians who live in the least affluent neighbourhoods have a 37 percent higher risk of heart attack than those living in the most affluent neighbourhoods (Canadian Institute for Health Information, 2010a).When we compare people who are in the lowest and highest socioeconomic quintiles, we see numerous health differences. In Canada, people in the highest quintile live an average of three years longer than those in the lowest quintile, have lower mortality, lower infant mortality, and a greater likelihood of living to the age of 75. People in the lowest quintile are more likely to have asthma, be obese, and/or have a mental illness. Furthermore, as we look at progressively higher incomes, diseases related to individual behaviours (smoking, drinking, diet, and physical activity) decline (Canadian Institute for Health Information, 2008; Statistics Canada, 2010f).

SOCIOECONOMIC STATUS

Socioeconomic status is associated with access to material resources, such as adequate housing, safe neighbourhoods, food, clean water, clean air, and health care.

The physiological changes caused by stress are useful if one is trying to escape from an axe murderer, but not so beneficial if they become chronic.

A lack of some material resources (e.g., clean water) can have a direct impact on health and illness. A lack of material resources can also have a more indirect impact on health and illness, such as through chronic stress. Stress causes physiological changes in the body, such as an increase in heart rate and blood pressure, and the release of the hormone cortisol. These physiological changes are functional when facing a short-term threat; when characters in a "slasher" film are being chased by an axe murderer, these changes enable them to run more quickly (until they trip on the inevitable fallen tree branch). However, when stress is long term, such as because of job insecurity or chronic worry over being able to pay the bills, these physiological changes slowly chip away at health and contribute to high blood pressure, heart disease, and digestive diseases (Clarke, 2008).

SOCIOECONOMIC STATUS AND MENTAL HEALTH

Most Canadians are affected by mental illness. One-fifth of the population will experience a mental disorder, and 80 percent of Canadians personally know someone who has a mental disorder (Health Canada, 2002). When analyzing the relationship between patterns of morbidity and socioeconomic status, we see that mental disorders (especially anxiety and depression) are more common among people with lower socioeconomic status, not just in Canada, but globally (World Health Organization, 2001; Doherwend et al., 1992; Miech et al., 1999).

CANADIAN MENTAL HEALTH ASSOCIATION

The Canadian Mental Health Association provides information and education about mental illness, as well as resources to promote resilience and recovery. Its information and resources address issues such as achieving work–life balance, dealing with financial difficulties, how employers can create work environments that facilitate mental resilience, and reducing the stigmatization that people with mental disorders often face in society. The association provides newsletters, brochures, full research reports, and video clips. Its website is located at www.cmha.ca

The **social selection hypothesis** suggests that if people's mental disorders are not effectively treated, they may experience functional difficulties in school or work that subsequently create economic difficulties, which then cause them to "drift" into a lower socioeconomic status, or prevent them from rising into a higher status position. But the **social causation hypothesis** claims that a lack of material resources creates stress among people with lower socioeconomic status, which then contributes to the development of mental disorders. In sorting out these contradictory hypotheses, research lends greater support to the social causation hypothesis. However, other research emphasizes variations across different types of mental disorders. The social selection hypothesis may apply to people with disorders such as schizophrenia and attention deficit disorder, while the social causation hypothesis may apply to the "common mental disorders" (CMDs) of depression and anxiety (Eaton, 2001; Turner, Wheaton & Lloyd, 1995; Kessler et al., 1994; Doherwend et al., 1992).

In addition to the relationship between socioeconomic status and mental illness, socioeconomic status also has an impact on tobacco use, alcohol consumption, diet, and physical activity. Tobacco use is more common among people who have a lower socioeconomic status, presumably because of the role nicotine can play in easing the stress created by a lack of material resources (Clarke, 2008). Individuals who are lower in socioeconomic status are also less likely to engage in physical activity (Clarke, 2008). Using the sociological imagination, we can consider why that might be. Low socioeconomic status means that people probably cannot afford gym memberships. That leaves the option of exercising at home. However, going for a 30-minute walk around the neighbourhood may not be possible if that neighbourhood is unsafe, and even working out inside one's home may be difficult if living in small or overcrowded conditions. Low socioeconomic status may also mean working at more than one job—a full-time job during the day and a part-time job at night, or a series of part-time jobs, leaving little leisure time for physical activity.

Eating an adequately nutritious diet is also more challenging for low-income individuals. Processed, high-calorie, low-nutrient foods are frequently much cheaper than healthy fare. For example, in a local supermarket flier a generic box of macaroni and cheese is on sale for 34 cents while a whole, fresh chicken is close to $14; each of these items would serve a family of four. In addition, access to healthy foods can be limited as well. Large supermarkets provide a wider range of nutritious foods, and at lower prices, than do convenience stores; having access to supermarkets is associated with better eating habits (Larsen, Story & Nelson, 2009). However, people living in lower-income neighbourhoods are less likely to have a supermarket within a reasonable distance for walking or easy public transit (Larsen, Story & Nelson, 2009), and low-income individuals are less likely to own vehicles (Ghirardelli, Quinn & Foerster, 2010). This trend has become emphasized in recent years as the ownership of retail food outlets has become more concentrated. Five supermarket chains

Social selection hypothesis: The suggestion that people with mental disorders may drift into lower levels of socioeconomic status, or be prevented from rising out of lower levels of status.

Social causation hypothesis: The suggestion that the stresses associated with having a lower socioeconomic status contribute to the development of mental disorders.

control 82 percent of the Canadian market, and Loblaws alone constitutes 40 percent of the market. Over the last two decades, these chains have closed many of their smaller urban locations in favour of larger superstores in increasingly suburban areas, where large parcels of open land are available for construction. In 1990, there were approximately 33,000 supermarkets in Canada, but by 2003, the number had declined to only 23,000 (Peters & McCreary, 2008). But regardless of the geographical location of supermarkets, one thing is for certain—a healthy diet is frequently more expensive than a poor diet. Williams and colleagues (cited in Clarke, 2008) looked at the cost of a nutritious diet in 43 grocery stores across Nova Scotia, and found that people who were earning minimum wage would simply not be able to afford an adequately nutritious diet.

Socioeconomic status has an impact on the extent to which people are able to engage in physical activity and/or eat a nutritious diet.

> High educational achievement is key to gaining rewarding jobs with considerable control and autonomy over work and better income, and hence to gaining a better position in the social hierarchy. These factors increase individuals' sense of control over their lives and provide motivation to live a healthy lifestyle. . . . (Bolaria & Bolaria, 2009, p. 509)

However, socioeconomic status continues to have an effect on morbidity and mortality even when individual factors such as physical activity, diet, smoking, and alcohol use are controlled for. Socioeconomic inequality is also frequently interconnected with ethnic inequality.

LO7 ETHNIC INEQUALITY AND HEALTH

Aboriginal populations in Canada have greater morbidity and mortality. Compared to non-Aboriginals, Aboriginal people are more likely to experience degenerative diseases such as diabetes, arthritis, asthma, ulcers, heart problems, cancer, stroke, and emphysema (Garner, Carriere & Sanmartin, 2010). They are also more likely to die from accidents, and their life expectancies are approximately five years less for men, and seven years less for women (Clarke, 2008). The legacy of colonization has contributed to, on average, lower levels of education, more unemployment, higher levels of poverty, and lower quality housing. Resource extraction (e.g., the Alberta oil sands industry) and hydroelectric development have resulted in environmental destruction of the land surrounding some Aboriginal communities, raising concerns about the possibility of toxins contributing to health problems. Those living on reserves have limited control over the location and the quality of housing, as these arise from complex negotiations with the federal government (Clarke, 2008) (see *Sociology in the News*, page 246).

Although Aboriginal persons, on average, have higher rates of morbidity and mortality, there are variations among different groups. Degenerative diseases are more common among First Nations and Métis people than among the non-Aboriginal population, but this is not the case for Inuit persons (Garner, Carrier & Sanmartin, 2010). Furthermore, the patterns of morbidity and mortality among Aboriginal people are not only the result of socioeconomic status, nor behaviours such as tobacco use or physical activity. When controlling for income, education, and various health behaviours, the disparities between Aboriginal and non-Aboriginal health are reduced, but not eliminated. Why might these health differences remain? That question requires further research, but it may be that the chronic stress caused by loss of culture and identity, racism, and social exclusion plays a role (Garner, Carrier, & Sanmartin, 2010).

Socioeconomic status alone does not entirely explain patterns of morbidity and mortality for other ethnic populations either. For instance, despite the fact that recent immigrants face financial challenges and lower occupational status, they are actually *healthier* than people who are Canadian-born; this is known as the **healthy immigrant effect**. Canadian immigration policy favours immigrants who have higher levels of occupational skills and education, which means that immigrants tend to be located at higher levels of the social structure in their countries of origin and therefore experience the health benefits of those social positions. Furthermore, the immigration process is an intensive one. Many of us know how physically and emotionally taxing it can be to simply plan and execute a move from one part of the city to other—imagine the extent to which that is amplified when having to plan and execute a move from one country to another! This suggests that individuals who do immigrate are likely those who have higher levels of physical and mental well-being to start with. However, the longer that immigrants have been in Canada, the more their health patterns come to more closely approximate that of people who are Canadian-born, whereby socioeconomic status comes to play an increasing role (Clarke, 2008).

Healthy immigrant effect: Recent immigrants tend to have better health than people who are Canadian-born.

FROM THE DAVIS INLET TO NATUASHISH

Until 1967, the Innu lived nomadic lives in Labrador. In 1967, the federal government relocated the Innu to a permanent settlement in order to better provide services for them. Told that they would be given comfortable homes with indoor plumbing, schools, and access to health care, they were relocated to a distant island off the coast of Labrador, where their way of life completely changed, and the government's promises were left unfulfilled. "Crammed living spaces. No running water. Buckets for toilets. No reliable heating" (Canadian Broadcasting Corporation, 2005, para. 1). Alcoholism became rampant, the community's youth began sniffing gasoline, family violence increased, and the suicide rate was 13 times higher than anywhere else in Canada (Clarke, 2008). The situation came to a head in 1993, when a videotape surfaced of three teenagers sniffing gasoline and screaming to a tribal police officer that they wanted to die. As a result of the efforts of the community's chief and others across the country who were appalled at the footage they saw on the evening news, the federal government agreed to relocate the Innu back onto the mainland. This finally occurred in 2002, when the community of Natuashish was formed. The Labrador Innu Healing Strategy was also created to help resolve the community's social problems. However, critics point out that due to financial mismanagement and program misdirection on the part of the government, many social problems are still pervasive. There is no safe house for the 80 percent of women who report being victimized by physical violence at home; instead, the two social workers in the community frequently bring those women into their own homes for protection. "Treatment programs are run in a tent in the woods. There's no detox facility, not even a place to hold alcohol treatment sessions" (Canadian Broadcasting Corporation, 2005, para. 19). In this community with a strong recent history of addiction and limited resources to treat it, bootleggers make their way into the community, selling alcohol for $300 a bottle (Canadian Broadcasting Corporation, 2005; Clarke, 2008). Community leaders and individuals who are working with them say that the healing strategy needs considerable revision if the community's problems are to be effectively resolved.

TIME TO REVIEW

- What are the social determinants of health, and what is the single most important determinant of health?
- What is the link between socioeconomic status and mental health?
- Why are people of lower socioeconomic status less likely to engage in physical activity or eat an adequately nutritious diet?
- How does the health of Aboriginal and non-Aboriginal populations in Canada compare, and why do these disparities exist?
- How do patterns of health and illness for immigrants to Canada change over time?

LO⁸ HEALTH-CARE SYSTEMS

The prevention and treatment of illness and injury exists within the broader context of health-care *systems*. The first systems of health care and medicine were those of Aboriginal cultures, each of which had its own definition of what constituted health and illness, and its own medical treatments (Clarke, 2008). Depending upon the specific culture in question, medical care may have been provided by shamans, medicine men, or other members of the community, such as the *midewiwin* of the Ojibway. Many of the plants that were used to treat illness have since been found, by modern science, to have treatment properties. For instance, the Iroquois introduced early European explorers to the bark of the white cedar (now known to be high in vitamin C) to prevent scurvy, which was one of the greatest health dangers explorers faced during long periods of time at sea (Historica Foundation, 2011).

Early settlers in New France received medical treatment at the hands of apothecaries who acted as general practitioners, and barber-surgeons—barbers who were also trained in some forms of surgery, most commonly the amputation of limbs. By the early 19th century, Euro-Canadians received treatment from a wide variety of different types of practitioners—lay healers who had no formalized training, homeopaths, midwives, and, for the wealthy, physicians trained in the United States or Great Britain—as well as through traditional folk remedies and products sold by travelling salespeople (Clarke, 2008).

Canada's first formal medical school was established in 1832, and following the implementation of the *Ontario Medical Act* in 1869, a number of privately owned medical schools opened that would later become affiliated with various universities. However, although medical schools flourished in the late 19th century, it wasn't until 1912 (with the *Canada Medical Act*) that licensing procedures and criteria were standardized in Canada.

Until the 1950s, Canadians had to pay for physicians' services and medical treatments. Calls for universal medical insurance were made as early as 1919, by Mackenzie King and various organized labour groups. Despite these early calls, and various failed provincial attempts at providing medical insurance, the first publicly funded medical insurance came in 1957, with the Hospital Insurance and Diagnostic Services Act. Receiving half of the funding from the federal government and half from the provincial governments, this act provided for medically necessary care and services within hospital settings only. In 1961, the Royal Commission on Health Services was formed. This led to the 1968 *Medical Care Act*, implemented in 1972, which created Canada's system of universal medical insurance, more commonly known as "medicare." It was based on four objectives: (a) *universality*, with equal access to medical care for all residents of Canada, regardless of income, age, social group memberships, or previous health conditions; (b) *portability* across provinces; (c) *comprehensive coverage* of all necessary medical services; and (d) *administration* that would be nonprofit. In 1984, a fifth objective was added, that of *accessibility*; medicare would involve 50/50 cost sharing between the federal and provincial governments, as well as the redistribution of income across richer and poorer provinces.

Medicare emerged as a result of a variety of forces. One of the most significant was the "trend in Western industrialized nations towards rationalization and bureaucratization within the context of monopoly capitalism" (Clarke, 2008, p. 277). That is, as bureaucracy evolved in society in general, such as in the world of business, it evolved in health care as well. Another important force was "the spread of similar policies in the Western industrialized world" (Clarke, 2008, p. 279). Social welfare policies, including medical insurance, were established in Germany and Western Europe as far back as the 1880s. In the early 20th century, Great Britain and New Zealand followed suit.

THE HEALTH-CARE SYSTEM TODAY

As a result of medicare, Canadians do have more access to medical services. However, there are some questions about the extent to which the objectives of medicare have been achieved. For example, Canada has lower physician-to-population ratios than most other member countries of the Organization for Economic Co-operation and Development (OECD). In 2002, we had 2.1 physicians per 1,000 population, compared to the nations with the highest ratios—Greece (4.5 physicians per 1,000 population), Italy (at 4.4), and Belgium (at 3.9). The only nations with lower physician-to-population ratios were New Zealand, the United Kingdom, Japan, Korea, and Turkey (Clarke, 2008). Thus, although Canadians across all social and

In New France, some medical care was provided by barbers, who were also trained as surgeons.

Source: © Christie's Images/CORBIS

economic groups have more access to medical services than was the case prior to medicare, there are limitations to the extent of medical services that actually are available. The shortage of family and general practitioners in particular has resulted in widespread concern and media coverage of the "doctor shortage," with a growing proportion of the population having to use walk-in medical clinics characterized by high turnover in medical staff. In addition to the limits on access to medical services, "some medical services require out-of-pocket expenditures that are not affordable to every Canadian. In a system that relies so heavily on drugs yet does not insure the out-of-hospital cost of drugs, it is impossible to claim universality" (Clarke, 2008, pp. 281–282).

The health-care system today is in a state of transition. At a time when concerns are being expressed about out-of-pocket medical expenditures, a shortage of physicians, and long wait times in the nation's emergency rooms, parallel concerns about the rapidly rising costs of health care are being expressed at the government level. Not only in Canada, but also throughout much of the world, health-care spending is growing "at an uncomfortable pace" (Statistics Canada & Canadian Institute for Health Information, 2010, p. 2). In trying to "strike a balance between the demand for care and other competing priorities while at the same time controlling costs" (p. 15), alternative health structures, funding models, and policies are being explored.

THE RISING COSTS OF HEALTH CARE

In 2008, out of 26 OECD countries with comparable accounting systems, the nation that spent the most per person on health care was the United States, at US$7,538. Canada was in the top 20 percent of nations in per capita health care spending (US$4,079), similar to other nations with publicly funded health-care systems, such as the Netherlands, Austria, Germany, and France. Turkey (US$767) and Mexico (US$852) had the lowest per capita health-care spending (Canadian Institute for Health Information, 2010b).

Total health-care expenditures in Canada in 2008 were $171.8 billion, or 10.7 percent of the Gross Domestic Product (GDP). Since the late 1990s, 70 percent of health-care expenditures have been publicly funded by federal and provincial governments; this equalled approximately $121.1 billion in 2008. The largest component of health-care spending is hospitals, almost 30 percent of total health-care expenditures. This is followed by drugs (16 percent of spending) and physicians' services (14 percent of spending) (Canadian Institute for Health Information, 2010b).

The Aging Population

One explanation offered for the rising costs of health care is the aging of the population. As more people within the population are in older age groups, health-care utilization increases. Canada's population has been aging for most of the 20th century. The exception to this was the **baby boom**, a time when the birth rate increased substantially (Statistics Canada, 2007). In Canada, the baby boom occurred between 1946 and 1965; most Western nations experienced a post–World War II baby boom, but the precise dates of the boom vary across nations. The baby boom emerged as a result of several forces. First, the economic Depression of the 1930s led many women to postpone childbearing; with considerable economic improvement during and after World War II, these women finally began having the children they normally would have had earlier in their lives. Second, during this era the marriage rate increased, and those who married tended to have more children. Third, people were getting married at younger ages than in previous decades, and having their children within the first few years of marriage. Consequently, during the baby boom, 18 percent (or 1.5 million) more births occurred than would have normally happened. Beginning in the late 1960s, the boom was over; women were getting married at later ages (in part, due to their entry into the labour force), and were postponing parenthood until they were older (in part, due to the availability of more reliable methods of birth control).

In 1966, the people who had been born during the baby boom comprised 40 percent of the population. At that time, people ages 65 and older were less than 8 percent of the population; in 2006, they were almost 14 percent of the population. The **median age** (i.e., the age that divides the population in half) in 1956 was 27.2 years. Since that time, the population has become increasingly older. By 2006, the median age was 39.5 years. It is projected that as the baby boomers age, by 2031 the median age in Canada will be more than 44 years. You can see the age-by-sex structure of the population by looking at a **population pyramid**,

Baby boom: The period from 1946 to 1965 during which several demographic forces coalesced, resulting in a larger number of births than would normally be the case.

Median age: The age that divides the population in half.

Population pyramid: A horizontal bar chart that shows how many people are in the various age groups, divided by sex.

FIGURE 11.4

Different Cohorts among the Age Pyramid of the Canadian Population, 2006

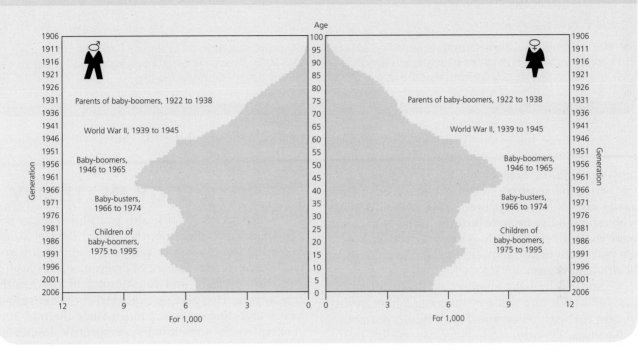

Source: Statistics Canada (2007). Portrait of the Canadian Population in 2006, by Age and Sex, 2006 Census. Ottawa, ON: Author. Statistics Canada Catalogue No. 97-551-XIE.

a horizontal bar chart that shows how many people in a population are members of particular age groups, divided by sex. You can see the population pyramid for 2006 in Figure 11.4, an enhanced population pyramid that also indicates the years during which different generations were born. Members of the baby boom are indicated by a large "bulge" in the pyramid (ages 41–60 in 2006) (Statistics Canada, 2007).

Implications of the Aging Population

As people age, they are more likely to develop chronic health conditions that require health-care services and that can interfere with functioning and quality of life (Canadian Institute for Health Information, 2011; Ramage-Morin & Shields, 2010). People ages 65 and over are four times as likely as 18- to 24-year-olds to have a chronic health condition. The two most common chronic conditions are high blood pressure (which 47 percent of seniors have) and arthritis (which 27 percent of seniors have). However, it is not age itself that determines health-care utilization,

but rather the presence of multiple chronic conditions. The Canadian Institute for Health Information (2011) finds that controlling for chronic health conditions, older seniors (those ages 85 and over) do *not* use more health care services than younger seniors (those ages 65 to 84) do. Those seniors with three or more chronic health conditions made three times as many visits to health professionals as did those with only one or two conditions. In fact, although this group is only 24 percent of the senior population, they constitute 40 percent of health-care use among seniors.

However, chronic health conditions are not an inevitable part of aging. As discussed earlier in the chapter, degenerative diseases are closely tied to health behaviours. Ramage-Morin and Shields (2010) analyzed the presence of eight different health behaviours among people ages 45 to 64, and 65 and over—smoking, body mass index, physical activity, diet, sleep, oral health, stress, and social participation. Each of these health-promoting behaviours was individually associated with health, and the more

health-promoting behaviours that were engaged in, the better the resulting health. Although advancing age is associated with poorer health overall, seniors who reported five or more positive health behaviours were more likely to be in good health than 45- to 64-years-olds who reported two or fewer positive health behaviours.

Thus, as the baby boomers age, controlling the costs of health care while maintaining a high quality of care is closely intertwined with health-promoting behaviours. Unfortunately, as we saw earlier in the chapter, Canadians' participation in some health-promoting behaviours (e.g., diet, physical activity) leaves much to be desired, and in some cases is getting worse rather than better. Furthermore, those behaviours are embedded within and affected by social determinants of health, such as socioeconomic status. This means that people's experiences of health and illness, the nation's larger patterns of morbidity and mortality, and the functioning of the health-care system, are dependent upon both promoting healthy lifestyles *and* addressing the macro-level factors that affect health (e.g., poverty).

TIME TO REVIEW

- How has the health-care system changed in Canadian history?
- What are the five objectives of medicare?
- What challenges are being faced within the health-care system today?
- In what ways does Canada's aging population affect larger patterns of health and illness, and patterns of health-care utilization?

SOCIOLOGY IN THEORY

LO⁹ The sociology of health and illness began primarily as an applied, nontheoretical field of study, exploring issues such as patterns of morbidity and mortality, personal and social determinants of health, and the structure and functioning of the health-care system. However, sociological theorizing about health and illness has expanded since the mid-20th century. As the functionalist perspective dominated the discipline of sociology in the mid-20th century, the first theorizing about health and illness was also functionalist.

FUNCTIONALIST PERSPECTIVES: THE SICK ROLE

In the mid-20th century, Talcott Parsons was perhaps the pre-eminent sociologist of the time. Consequently, when he theorized about the *sick role*, he added considerable legitimacy to the new field of medical sociology (Parsons, 1951). Parsons described sickness as being dysfunctional for society. When people are sick, they are unable to fulfill their roles as students, employees, or parents; this threatens the well-being of society as a whole. Instead, they adopt the sick role, a temporary role associated with certain rights and responsibilities. There are four components of the sick role. First, the sick person is granted a temporary exemption from his or her normal social roles. It is considered acceptable to miss an exam or a day of work, although some official documentation may be required to legitimize the absence. Second, the sick person is not considered to be responsible for his or her condition. The sick person is not blamed, but rather is given sympathy. Third, it is the sick person's responsibility to try to get well; failure to do so results in the sick role no longer being considered legitimate. Finally, it is the sick person's responsibility to seek competent technical help and to cooperate with the physician's directions.

Subsequent research finds that the components of the sick role do not always apply. For instance, the extent to which someone is exempted from normal social roles varies with the nature and severity of the illness (De Maio, 2010). In your workplace, a cold may not be considered a legitimate excuse for missing a day of work, while a chronic health problem (e.g., diabetes) may result in an ongoing level of exemption. Similarly, although Parsons indicated that individuals are not blamed for their illnesses, this is not always the case (De Maio, 2010; Clarke, 2008). A smoker who develops lung cancer is likely to receive less sympathy than a nonsmoker with that same illness. Similarly, a coworker who is overweight, eats fast food for lunch every day, and drinks to excess may receive more "blame" for a heart attack than would an athlete training for a triathlon.

Beginning in the 1960s, functionalist perspectives began to lose their dominance in the discipline of sociology as a whole, as well as in the field of medical sociology in particular. Interactionist, conflict, feminist, and postmodern or poststructuralist perspectives emerged, offering explanations of the various topics addressed throughout this chapter— patterns of health and illness, personal and social determinants of health and illness, and the health-care system.

INTERACTIONIST PERSPECTIVES: THE CULTURAL MEANINGS OF HEALTH AND ILLNESS

While demographers analyze *patterns* of health and illness, sociologists who use interactionist theories instead focus their attention on the *experience and meanings* of that health or illness. Schneider and Conrad (1983) make an important distinction between *sickness* and *illness*. Sickness is the pathology of the body, while illness is the meaning that is attached to that physical experience. The field of medicine studies sickness, while the discipline of sociology studies illness.

Schneider and Conrad interviewed people who had been diagnosed with epilepsy. They found that

something as seemingly straightforward as following physicians' instructions is actually embedded within a complex system of meaning and understanding. The use of medication is not merely a matter of following physician's instructions, but rather emerges from the interaction between physicians' instructions and one's own relationships, beliefs, and experiences. Thus, the manner in which people with epilepsy use their medication is based on factors such as the meaning that seizures have for the individual, perceptions of the side effects of the medication, the desire to prevent others from becoming aware of the epilepsy, the need to prevent protect oneself from seizures in some social situations more than others, and more.

These authors find that upon being diagnosed with epilepsy, *uncertainty* plays a key role in people's understandings and experiences of illness— uncertainty about whether a certain physical feeling is a "normal" feeling or instead is a new "symptom," uncertainty about one's physical future, uncertainty about how one's relationships will change, and uncertainty in the realm of identity and one's sense of self. In an analysis of people diagnosed with cancer, Fife (1994) also finds that self-meanings lie at the core of their experiences. Interviews reveal a loss of personal control (e.g., "You just have to put your trust in the doctors"), changes in self-esteem and self-worth (e.g., "I'm not the same person that I used to be"), and changes in body image (e.g., "If I take off my hat, I'll look like someone who has cancer").

Research with interactionist foundations explores not only the understandings of people with particular illnesses, but those of other people as well. For example, Straus (cited in Clarke, 2008) conducts interviews with the caregivers of people with Alzheimer's disease, and Payne-Jackson (1999) analyzes the divergent understandings that people with diabetes and their medical practitioners have.

CONFLICT PERSPECTIVES: THE CONSEQUENCES OF POWER AND INEQUALITY

While the interactionist perspective emphasizes the subjective meanings of health and illness at the micro level, conflict theories focus their attention on the macro level. They analyze topics such as the social determinants of health and problems with the health-care system. Because of social inequality and relations of power, groups of people have differing levels of access to both health-promoting resources and sickness-causing factors. We saw this earlier in the chapter within the context of patterns of morbidity and mortality among people of low versus high socioeconomic status, recent and longer-term immigrants, and the relocated Innu people. Engels (1845/1985) was the first conflict theorist to address the social determinants of health and illness. He pointed out that as a result of capitalism, large numbers of people left rural agricultural life for wage labour in the urban areas. But the bourgeois owners of the means of production were guided by their own profit motives. In order to make the largest profit possible, their workers were underpaid and had no choice but to live and work in unhealthy conditions that set the stage for the emergence and rapid transmission of infectious diseases.

Navarro (1976) indicates that there is an inherent contradiction between the profit motive of capitalism and the health needs of people. The corporate need for profit that resulted in people having to live or work in unhealthy conditions is not limited to the late-19th-century Europe that Engels studied; it continued into the 20th century as well. In fact, we still see this pattern in the 21st century. In order to enhance profit, multinational corporations move their production facilities into low-income countries that often have lower occupational health and safety standards, and where they can pay employees a fraction of what they would pay employees in a high-income nation (Clarke, 2008). It is also because of the profit motive that when smoking rates began to decline in countries such as Canada and the United States, tobacco companies shifted much of their marketing focus to lower-income countries, where 80 percent of the world's smokers now live (World Health Organization, 2010a; Clarke, 2008).

In addition to analyzing the social determinants of health and illness, conflict theorists also critique the health-care system itself, such as the state's power to legitimize some forms of health care (e.g., a visit to a physician) over others (e.g., a visit to an acupuncturist), and the power of the corporate elite in the health-care system's structure. In a capitalist system, health becomes a commodity (Navarro, 1976), and the pursuit of health occurs via gym memberships, athletic shoes and apparel that help you get fitter just by wearing them, vitamins and supplements, meditation classes, audio recordings to help you quit smoking, and various other consumer products and

According to conflict theorists, the capitalist profit motive is even integrated into fundraising efforts, such as for breast cancer research.

services. Health is about convincing people to engage in health-promoting behaviours (using the right products), rather than about changing the structural conditions that contribute to health and illness in the first place. The capitalist motive is even evident in fundraising efforts, in what is called "cause marketing" or "social marketing" (King, 2006). Purchasing a particular product during a certain period of time—a shade of lipstick, specially marked case of beer, cup of Tim Hortons' coffee, McDonald's Big Mac, or even a certain model of car—means that *a portion* of the proceeds will go to support a particular cause, such as breast cancer or autism. This practice "blurs the boundaries between the responsibility of governments for caring for their citizens and the profit needs of corporations" (Clarke, 2008, p. 15).

FEMINIST PERSPECTIVES: WOMEN'S HEALTH AND ILLNESS

Feminist analyses of health and illness are diverse, and can address topics ranging from the micro level to the macro level. For example, at the micro level Werner and Malterud (2003) analyze the "credibility work" that women with chronic pain engage in when trying to manage their interactions in the health-care system and be taken seriously by medical professionals. Historically, women's physical symptoms were often dismissed as being the result of stress or anxiety rather than a physical illness. Werner and Malterud suggest that this tendency continues into the 21st century. The women they interviewed spoke of the various techniques they use in order to be perceived as credible by doctors. For instance, they tried to strike a careful balance with the way they styled their hair and makeup prior to a visit to a physician—if they looked too put together, doctors would explicitly tell them, "Well, you don't look sick," but if they looked too unkempt then the doctors would quickly attribute their symptoms to stress.

At a more macro level, some feminist analyses of health and illness have focused attention on the processes by which certain characteristics and conditions come to be perceived as indicative of health or illness in the first place. In this regard, they have analyzed the medicalization of women's lives. **Medicalization** refers to the ways that certain characteristics or conditions are "defined in medical language, understood through the adoption of a medical framework, or 'treated' with medical intervention" (Conrad, 2007, p. 5). For example, pneumonia, heart disease, and cancer have all been medicalized (and most of us would agree with their medicalization). However, there are other conditions whose medicalization has been subjected to critique, such as attention-deficit hyperactivity disorder, erectile dysfunction, and sexual addiction. That is, the real concerns are not with medicalization itself, but rather with *overmedicalization* (Conrad, 2007).

Beginning during the second wave of the women's movement in the 1960s, feminist researchers and activists pointed to the ways that women's lives had been inappropriately medicalized. During the course of the 20th century, women's bodies and lives were increasingly appropriated by the medical profession. For most of human history, issues related to pregnancy and childbirth were handled by other women, such as midwives. But in the more recent medicalized environment, both became conditions that required a physician's care—childbirth now occurred in sterile hospital rooms. Even the normal functioning of the female body (e.g., menstruation, PMS, menopause) became conditions to be monitored and treated by medical professionals (Findlay & Miller, 2002).

POSTMODERN AND POSTSTRUCTURAL PERSPECTIVES: KNOWLEDGE, POWER, AND DISCOURSE

Postmodern and poststructural approaches also address the (over)medicalization of society, and its connection to the relationship between knowledge and power. As discussed earlier in the textbook, Michel Foucault described the connection between knowledge and power—those claims to truth that are made by people in institutionalized positions of power become legitimized and accepted as "truth." Thus, as the power of the Christian Church declined in Europe during the Renaissance and the power of science grew, so did the power of their claims to knowledge. Similarly, as physicians became increasingly intertwined with rational-bureaucratic health-care systems in the 20th century, their claims about health and illness gained supremacy over those of other types of health practitioners. As Foucault (1965, 1966) points out, as medical discourses became increasingly legitimized and institutionalized in society, more aspects of people's lives become subjected to the medical gaze, and are monitored by the medical profession. And because medical discourses are elite discourses, we perceive them as the only possible means of understanding the world.

More recently, Fox (1993) applies Foucauldian assumptions to an analysis of communications between physicians and patients during post-surgical ward rounds. He notes that the way that surgeons structure postoperative communications ensures that their status as "healers" and medical discourses more generally, remain privileged. Physicians begin these communications while the patients are still recovering from sedation, or are under the

> **Medicalization:** Certain characteristics or conditions are defined in medical language, understood through the adoption of a medical framework, or "treated" with medical intervention.

influence of high doses of pain medication, which immediately places limitations upon the extent to which patients can participate in the communication. The structure of postsurgical discourses involves a transition from communicating about the patient's physiology, to the conditions of the wound (where healing of the wound is presented as a sign of "successful" surgery), to aspects of recovery/discharge. When patients try to disrupt this linear transition (e.g., they ask about when they might be discharged while the physician is still addressing the condition of the wound), physicians quickly use medical discourses to bring the communication back on track. Thus, the nature of communication between doctor and patient at the micro level helps to reinforce the power of medical discourses in society at the macro level.

TIME TO REVIEW

- In what way did Talcott Parsons first theorize health and illness?

- What are some of ways that interactionists have explored the experience of health and illness?

- What aspects of health and illness are emphasized by conflict theorists, and what are some examples?

- What are some of the ways that feminist perspectives inform research about health and illness at the micro and macro levels?

- What do postmodern analyses of medical communications tell us?

CHAPTER SUMMARY

LO¹ Outline the development of the field of medical sociology and describe its focus.

The sociology of health and illness (also known as medical sociology) emerged in the post–World War II era. This field of study, found both inside and outside academia, analyzes the social causes and consequences of health and illness.

LO² Describe how patterns of morbidity and mortality have changed through human history.

For most of human history, mortality has been primarily the result of infectious diseases. Infant and child mortality rates were extremely high, and few people reached the age of 65. The discovery of germs, improvements in living conditions, and the development of the field of medicine in the 19th and 20th centuries resulted in significant changes to morbidity and mortality. Beginning in the 20th century, degenerative diseases replaced infectious diseases as the primary causes of death. Most people now live to the age of 65.

LO³ Identify the top causes of death in Canada today, and explain what the "actual" causes of death are.

The top three causes of death for women in Canada are cancer, heart disease, and stroke; for men they are cancer, heart disease, and accidents. The top causes of death vary to some extent not only for women and men, but also for people of different ages. However, the *actual* causes of death (i.e., the behaviours that contribute to cancer, heart disease, stroke, accidents, and so on) are tobacco use, diet and inactivity, and alcohol misuse.

LO⁴ Describe the roles that tobacco use, alcohol misuse, diet, physical inactivity, and obesity play in morbidity and mortality on a global level.

Tobacco use killed more than 100 million people in the 20th century, and now causes approximately five million deaths per year globally. Alcohol misuse contributes to 2.5 million deaths per year, and constitutes 5 percent of the global burden of disease. Improving diet through greater consumption of fruits and vegetables could save three million lives per year. Inactivity causes 6 percent of deaths, and 65 percent of the world's population lives in nations where more people die as a result of being overweight than underweight.

LO5 Describe patterns of tobacco use, alcohol use, diet, physical activity, and obesity in Canada.

In many high-income countries, tobacco use has declined over the past several decades. In Canada, approximately 20 percent of the population smokes. The vast majority of Canadians consume alcohol; more than half in the past month, and more than one-third in the past week. Patterns of alcohol use, as well as resultant harms, vary on the basis of sex and age. Most Canadians do not consume enough of any food group except for "other" (i.e., soft drinks, sugars, fats). Only 15 percent of adults and 7 percent of children engage in the minimum amount of recommended physical activity. More than 60 percent of men and 44 percent of women are overweight or obese.

LO6 Outline the social determinants of health, and describe the link between socioeconomic status and health and illness.

Social determinants of health include environmental, economic, and various social factors. The single most important determinant of health globally is socioeconomic status. Morbidity and mortality are higher in groups of lower socioeconomic status. People in these groups have less access to material resources, face greater stressors, and are less likely to engage in health-promoting behaviours such as physical activity and a healthy diet.

LO7 Describe the link between ethnicity and health and illness.

Ethnicity can overlap with socioeconomic status. For example, Aboriginal people in Canada, on average, have lower levels of education and income than non-Aboriginals, and also have shorter life spans and more degenerative diseases. However, even when controlling for socioeconomic status and individual health behaviours, differences in the morbidity and mortality of Aboriginals and non-Aboriginals remain, pointing

to the potential health impacts of loss of culture, racism, and social exclusion. The relationship between socioeconomic status and health is not straightforward among immigrants either. New immigrants are healthier than people who are Canadian-born, but the longer they are in Canada, the more their health comes to approximate that of the Canadian-born.

LO8 Describe the evolution and objectives of the Canadian health-care system, and identify the challenges it faces in contemporary society.

Health-care systems have changed over time, from the systems of health care that existed in Aboriginal cultures; to the barber-surgeons and travelling medical salespeople of the 17th, 18th, and 19th centuries; to the rational-bureaucratic system of the 20th century and beyond. Medicare was implemented in 1972, and has five objectives—universality, portability, nonprofit administration, comprehensive coverage, and accessibility. In the 21st century, governments face the challenge of controlling the rapidly rising costs of health care, while maintaining a high quality of care.

LO9 Explore how functionalists, interactionists, conflict theorists, feminist theorists, and postmodern/poststructuralists address health and illness.

Functionalist Talcott Parsons was the first to theorize about health and illness, in terms of the sick role. Interactionist perspectives emphasize not the patterns of health and illness, but rather the experiences of health and illness, such as changing conceptions of self. Conflict theorists devote much of their attention to the inequalities that underlie social determinants of health (such as socioeconomic status) as well as the inherent contradiction between the profit motive and providing for the health of the population in capitalist societies. Feminist theorizing about health and illness is diverse, ranging from the micro to the macro levels—from analyzing the credibility work that women with chronic pain must engage in to be taken seriously by health professionals, to the (over)medicalization of women's lives. Postmodern/poststructuralist theories, informed by Foucauldian notions of knowledge, power, surveillance, and discourse, also address medicalization.

RECOMMENDED READINGS

1. For a thorough overview of the theorizing that has been done in the sociology of health and illness, as well as its intimate interconnections with empirical research, see: De Maio, F. (2010). *Health & Social Theory*. Themes in Social Theory (Series Editor: R. Stones). London/New York: Palgrave Macmillan.

2. The pre-eminent scholar in the area of medicalization explores the overmedicalization of society with topics such as male baldness, erective dysfunction, adult ADHD, and biomedical enhancement in the following: Conrad, P. (2007). *The Medicalization of Society: On the Transformation of Human Conditions into Treatable Disorders*. Baltimore: The Johns Hopkins University Press.

FOR FURTHER REFLECTION

1. How has your own experience of health and illness been affected by your individual behaviours, social determinants of health (environmental factors, socioeconomic status, ethnicity), and the structure and functioning of the health-care system? What changes would be necessary at each one of these levels for your health to improve?

2. In your opinion, what is the single most important health issue of our time? How would that issue be explored within each of the theoretical perspectives presented in this chapter? How might that health issue be resolved?

REFERENCES

Bolaria, B. S., & Bolaria, R. (2009). Personal and structural determinants of health and illness: Lifestyles and life chances. In B. S. Bolaria and H. D. Dickinson (Eds.), *Health, Illness, and Health Care in Canada* (4th ed.) (pp. 506–519). Toronto: Nelson.

Canadian Broadcasting Corporation. (2005, February 14). The Innu of Labrador: From Davis Inlet to Natuashish. *In-Depth: Aboriginal Canadians*. Retrieved August 2, 2011, from www.cbc.ca/news/background/aboriginals/natuashish.html

Canadian Institute for Health Information. (2008). *Reducing Gaps in Health: A Focus on Socio-Economic Status in Urban Canada*. Ottawa, ON: Author.

Canadian Institute for Health Information. (2010a). *Data Brief: Exploring Urban Environments and Inequalities in Health*. Ottawa, ON: Author.

Canadian Institute for Health Information. (2010b). *National Health Expenditure Trends, 1975–2010*. Ottawa, ON: Author.

Canadian Institute for Health Information. (2011). *Seniors and the Health Care System: What is the Impact of Multiple Chronic Conditions?* Ottawa, ON: Author.

Clarke, J. N. (2008). *Health, Illness, and Medicine in Canada* (5th ed.). Don Mills, ON: Oxford University Press.

Cockerham, W. C. (2007). Medical sociology. In G. Ritzer (Ed.), *Encyclopedia of Sociology*. Retrieved January 20, 2011, from www.blackwellreferenceonline.com

Conrad, P. (2007). *The Medicalization of Society: On the Transformation of Human Conditions into Treatable Disorders*. Baltimore, MD: The Johns Hopkins University Press.

De Maio, F. (2010). *Health and Social Theory*. New York: Palgrave MacMillan.

Dohrenwend, B. P., Levav, I., Shrout, P. E., & Schwartz, S. (1992). Socioeconomic status and psychiatric disorders: The causation selection issue. *Science, 255*, 946–952.

Eaton, W. W. (2001). *The Sociology of Mental Disorders*. Westport, CT: Praeger Publishing.

Engels, F. (1845/1985). *The Condition of the Working Class in England*. Stanford, CA: Stanford University Press.

Federal Trade Commission. (2009). *Federal Trade Commission Cigarette Report for 2006*. Washington, DC: Author.

Fife, B. (1994). The conceptualization of meaning in illness. *Social Science and Medicine, 38*(2), 309–316.

Findlay, D. A., & Miller, L. J. (2002). Through medical eyes: The medicalization of women's bodies and women's lives. In B. S. Bolaria and H. D. Dickinson (Eds.), *Health, Illness, and Health Care in Canada* (3rd ed.) (pp. 185–210). Toronto: Nelson.

Foucault, M. (1965). *Madness and Civilization*. New York: Random House.

Foucault, M. (1966). *Birth of the Clinic*. New York: Vintage.

Fox, N. J. (1993). Discourse, organisation and the surgical ward round. *Sociology of Health and Illness, 15*(1), 16–42.

Garner, R., Carriere, G., & Sanmartin, C. (2010). *The Health of First Nations Living Off-Reserve, Inuit, and Métis Adults in Canada: The Impact of Socio-economic Status on Inequalities in Health.* Statistics Canada Catalogue No. 82-622-X, No. 004. Ottawa, ON: Statistics Canada.

Garriguet, D. (2007). Canadians' eating habits. *Health Reports, 18*(2), 17–32. Statistics Canada Catalogue No. 82-003. Ottawa, ON: Statistics Canada.

Ghirardelli, A., Quinn, V., & Foerster, S. B. (2010). Using geographic information systems and local food store data in California's low-income neighborhoods to inform community initiatives and resources. *American Journal of Public Health, 100*(11), 2156–2162.

Health Canada. (2002). *A Report on Mental Illness in Canada.* Ottawa, ON: Author.

Health Canada. (2009). *Canadian Alcohol and Drug Use Monitoring Survey (CADUMS) 2009.* Ottawa, ON: Author.

Heron, C. (2003). *Booze: A Distilled History.* Downsview, ON: Between the Lines.

Historica Foundation. (2011). Plants, native uses. *The Canadian Encyclopedia.* Retrieved February 17, 2011, from www.thecanadianencyclopedia.com

Johnson, L. (2011, June 30). California teenagers to get whooping cough vaccinations. Retrieved August 18, 2011, from www.reuters.com

Miech, R. A., Caspit, A., Moffitt, T. E., Wright, B. R. E., & Silva, P. A. (1999). Low socioeconomic status and mental disorders: A longitudinal study of selection and causation during young adulthood. *American Journal of Sociology, 104*(4), 112–147.

Kessler, R. C., McGonagle, K. A., Zhao, S., Nelson, C. B., Hughes, M., Eshelman, S., et al. (1994). Lifetime and 12-month prevalence of DSM-III-R psychiatric disorders in the United States. *Archives of General Psychiatry, 51*, 8–19.

King, S. (2006). *Pink Ribbons, Inc.: Breast Cancer and the Politics of Philanthropy.* Minneapolis: University of Minnesota Press.

Larsen, N. I., Story, M. T., & Nelson, M. C. (2009). Neighborhood environments: Disparities in access to health foods in the U.S. *American Journal of Preventative Medicine, 36*(1), 74–81.

Navarro, B. (1976). Social class, political power and the state and their implications for medicine. *Social Science and Medicine, 10*, 437–457.

Peters, E. J., & McCreary, T. A. (2008). Poor neighbourhoods and the changing geography of food retailing in Saskatoon, Saskatchewan, 1984–2004. *Canadian Journal of Urban Research, 17*(1), 78–106.

Parsons, T. (1951). *The Social System.* Glencoe, IL: Free Press.

Payne-Jackson, A. (1999). Biomedical and folk medical concepts of adult onset diabetes in Jamaica: Implications for Treatment. *Health, 3*(1), 5–46.

Physicians for a Smoke-Free Canada. (2003). *Tobacco Industry Advertising Expenditures in Canada, 1987–2000.* Ottawa, ON: Author.

Ramage-Morin, P. L., & Shields, M. (2010). Health-promoting factors and good health among Canadians in mid- to late life. *Health Reports, 21*(3). Statistics Canada Catalogue No. 82-003-X. Ottawa, ON: Statistics Canada.

Schneider, J., & Conrad, P. (1983). *Having Epilepsy: The Experience and Control of Illness.* Philadelphia: Temple University Press.

Shields, M., Gorber, S. C., & Tremblay, M. S. (2008). Effects of measurement on obesity and morbidity. *Health Reports, 19*(2), 77–84. Statistics Canada Catalogue No. 82-003. Ottawa, ON: Statistics Canada.

Statistics Canada. (2007). *Portrait of the Canadian Population in 2006, by Age and Sex, 2006 Census.* Statistics Canada Catalogue No. 97-551-XIE. Ottawa, ON: Author.

Statistics Canada. (2010a). *Leading Causes of Death in Canada, 2007.* Statistics Canada Catalogue No. 84-215-X. Ottawa, ON: Author.

Statistics Canada. (2010b). Smoking, 2009. *Health Fact Sheets.* Statistics Canada Catalogue No. 82-625-X. Ottawa, ON: Author.

Statistics Canada. (2010c, April 20). Control and sale of alcoholic beverages. *The Daily.* Ottawa, ON: Author. Catalogue No. 11-001-X.

Statistics Canada. (2010e). Overweight and obese adults, 2009. *Health Fact Sheets.* Statistics Canada Catalogue No. 82-625-X. Ottawa, ON: Author.

Statistics Canada. (2010f). *Health People, Healthy Places.* Statistics Canada Catalogue No. 82-229-XWE. Ottawa, ON: Author.

Statistics Canada. (2011, January 19). Canadian health measures survey: Physical activity of youth and adults. *The Daily.* Ottawa, ON: Author. Catalogue No. 11-001-X.

Statistics Canada & Canadian Institute for Health Information. (2010). *Health Care in Canada 2010.* Ottawa, ON: Authors.

Tjepkema, M. (2004). Alcohol and illicit drug dependence. *Supplement to Health Reports, 15*, 9–20.

Turner, R. J., Wheaton, B., & Lloyd, D. A. (1995). The epidemiology of social stress. *American Sociological Review, 60*(1), 104–127.

Weeks, J. R. (2008). *Population: An Introduction to Concepts and Issues.* Belmont, CA: Thomson Wadsworth.

Werner, A., & Malterud, K. (2003). It is hard work behaving as a credible patient: Encounters between women with chronic pain and their doctors. *Social Science and Medicine, 57*, 1409–1419.

World Health Organization. (n.d.). *Tobacco*. Retrieved February 10, 2011, from www.who.int

World Health Organization. (n.d.). (1948). *Preamble to the Constitution of the World Health Organization as adopted by the International Health Conference, New York, 19 June–22 July 1946; signed on 22 July 1946 by the representatives of 61 states (Official Records of the World Health Organization, no. 2, p. 100) and entered into force on 7 April 1948.* Geneva: Author.

World Health Organization. (n.d.). (2001). *Costs of Mental Illness: Fact Sheet No. 218.* Geneva: Author.

World Health Organization. (n.d.). (2005). *Fruit and Vegetables for Health.* Geneva: Author.

World Health Organization. (n.d.). (2006). *Obesity and Overweight: Fact Sheet No. 311.* Geneva: Author.

World Health Organization. (n.d.). (2009). *WHO Report on the Global Tobacco Epidemic, 2009: Implementing Smoke-Free Environments.* Geneva: Author.

World Health Organization. (n.d.). (2010a). *WHO Report on the Global Tobacco Epidemic, 2009: Implementing Smoke-Free Environments.* Geneva: Author.

World Health Organization. (n.d.). (2010b). *Global Strategy to Reduce the Harmful Use of Alcohol.* Geneva: Author.

World Health Organization. (n.d.). (2010c). *Global Strategy on Diet, Physical Activity and Health.* Geneva: Author.

World Health Organization. (n.d.). (2010d). *Fact File: 10 Facts on Obesity.* Geneva: Author.

World Health Organization. (n.d.). (2011). *Alcohol (Fact Sheet).* Geneva: Author.

ENDNOTE

[1] Retrieved January 31, 2011, from www.thinkexist.com.

PART 3

Our Changing World

Social Change: Collective Behaviour and Social Movements

LEARNING OBJECTIVES AND OUTCOMES

After completing this chapter, students should be able to do the following:

LO1 Define collective behaviour, identify its central features, and differentiate it from conventional behaviour.

LO2 Identify the different types of crowds and explain which ones contribute to collective behaviour.

LO3 Explain how sociological theories (i.e., social contagion, convergence, and emergent norm) contribute to our understanding of collective behaviour.

LO4 Describe fads, rumours, urban legends, moral panic, and disasters

as dispersed forms of collective behaviour.

LO5 Explain how social movements are both similar to and different from collective behaviour and discuss the relevance of claims making for movement organizations.

LO6 Differentiate between alternative, redemptive, reform, and revolutionary social movements.

LO7 Compare and contrast theoretical views on the development of social movements.

> *Never doubt that a small group of thoughtful, committed citizens can change the world. Indeed, it is the only thing that ever has.*
>
> (Margaret Mead)[1]

SOCIAL CHANGE AND SOCIAL PROGRESS

From what you've learned thus far, it may be difficult to believe that Canada is "The True North strong and free!"— given at least 200 years of history involving the exploitation of particular social groups (e.g., the treatment of Aboriginal peoples and reliance on child labour). It wasn't until the late 1800s, when the Social Gospel (a part of Protestant theology that applies Christian principles to the solving of social problems) was increasingly adopted by the middle classes, that groups including the Victorian child-savers movement started rallying for change (Valverde, 1991). By the 20th century, various groups were making strides in their efforts toward the legal protection of their own rights and the rights of vulnerable others (e.g., human rights, Aboriginal people's rights, workers' rights, women's rights, minority rights, gay and lesbian rights, animal rights, political rights, religious rights, and environmental rights). The pursuit of these goals has entailed attempts to change people's views and value systems through educational efforts (e.g., awareness campaigns), widespread action (e.g., organized protests, the formation of unions and the establishment of movements), and even acts of violence (e.g., terrorism).

Just as we witnessed in the end of autocratic rule in Egypt in 2011, social change often results from some form of precipitating behaviour by a group of ordinary people, as suggested by cultural anthropologist Margaret Mead (1901–1978) in the opening quotation. Similarly, Robert E. Park (1864–1944), an American sociologist who founded the area of study called *collective behaviour*, believed that the actions of crowds were essential for instigating social change. In this chapter we examine how various forms of collective behaviour and social movements develop and promote change. Figure 12.1 (page 262) summarizes some important events in Canadian history that have origins in collective behaviour and social movements.

LO¹ DEFINING COLLECTIVE BEHAVIOUR

Collective behaviour is not synonymous with all group behaviour. **Collective behaviour** refers to group behaviour that is relatively spontaneous, unstructured, and unconventional in nature (Goode, 1992). It is spontaneous and unstructured in the sense that it is unplanned and does not take a specific form. It is unconventional because it generally lies outside what is considered normative. For example, people rioting in the street following a popular sporting event such as the Stanley Cup playoffs could be yelling, drinking, smashing windows of nearby businesses, climbing light posts, or even lighting cars on fire. That is not to say that all collective behaviour is entirely random and destructive, just that compared to conventional behaviour, it is *less* predictable and *less* institutionalized. Let's begin with a look at the behaviour of crowds.

> **Collective behaviour:**
> Group behaviour that is relatively spontaneous, unstructured, and unconventional in nature.

FIGURE 12.1
Historical Events with Origins in Collective Behaviour

Women gain the right to vote in Canada in 1917.

Canada supports the *Universal Declaration of Human Rights* (1947/1948).

Non-enfranchised Aboriginal peoples (i.e., with Indian status) are given the right to vote in 1960.

The Canadian Civil Liberties Association is formed in 1964.

The *Canadian Charter of Rights and Freedoms* is enacted in 1982.

Canada adopts the United Nations Convention on the Rights of the Child in 1989.

Same-sex marriage is legalized via the *Civil Marriage Act* in 2005.

COLLECTIVE BEHAVIOUR IN LOCALIZED CROWDS

LO² CASUAL, CONVENTIONAL, EXPRESSIVE, AND ACTING CROWDS

A **crowd** is a temporary gathering of people who are in the same place at the same time (McPhail, 1991). Herbert Blumer (1969) distinguished among four main types of crowds: casual, conventional, expressive, and acting. A **casual crowd** is a gathering of people who by proximity alone happen to be in the same location at the same time. For example, several individual families might be in the same park or picnic ground on the same day at the same time; some might be having lunch, others might be playing games, and others may be taking a walk. Since casual crowds do not originate for any intended larger purpose or shared interest, they do not comprise a focal point for collective behaviour. That is, people who are part of a casual crowd are most likely to engage in rule-abiding individual (and even parallel) forms of conventional behaviour.

A **conventional crowd** is a group of people who have gathered in the same place at the same time because of a common shared interest or objective. For example, as a conventional crowd you and your classmates are currently attending a scheduled Sociology lecture. Similarly, people in a movie theatre constitute a conventional crowd with a specific shared objective. A conventional crowd's behaviour tends to be planned, structured, predictable, and also controlled by social norms. For example, people sit quietly in a theatre in seats, facing forward, in order to watch the show. They also turn off their cell phones and sometimes eat and drink but only products purchased at the theatre concession. Like casual crowds, conventional crowds generally do not lead to collective behaviour.

An **expressive crowd** is a gathering of people who share a common interest and are gathered at the same event at the same time with an explicit participatory purpose. Whereas the conventional crowd is attending a movie in order to watch the show, the expressive crowd has gathered because as a group it can be responsive or emotionally reactive in particular ways (e.g., by shouting or cheering to indicate encouragement). Fans at a hockey game engage in a variety

Crowd: A temporary gathering of people who are in the same place at the same time.

Causal crowd: A gathering of people who by proximity alone happen to be in the same location at the same time.

Conventional crowd: A group of people who have gathered in the same place at the same time because of a common shared interest or objective.

Expressive crowd: A gathering of people who share a common interest and are gathered at the same event at the same time with an explicit participatory purpose.

Saskatchewan Roughrider fans wear melonheads to support their team.

of collective behaviours: They wear jerseys to denote their favourite players/teams, they paint their faces, and they also participate in spontaneous "waves." A small group starts "the wave" by standing up and reaching their arms in the air, prompting people directly next to them to do the same at which point the originators stop doing the wave (i.e., they sit back down), and it continues in this fashion all the way around the stadium.

Finally, an **acting crowd** consists of people gathered at the same place at the same time who engage in overt collective behaviour in pursuit of a common goal. For example, in 1990, a highly publicized protest took place to put a stop to plans by the neighbouring village of Oka, Quebec, to expand a private golf course into what is considered a sacred Mohawk burial ground by the Mohawk communities of Kahnawake, Kanehsatake, and Akwesasne. During what is referred to as the "Oka Crisis," Mohawk supporters marched through Oka protesting the golf course expansion and publicly declaring Mohawk land ownership. In the ensuing 78-day dispute, the group set up barricades that restricted access to roadways, confronted Quebec's provincial police and national police forces, and stood off against members of the Royal Canadian Mounted Police and later the Canadian armed forces before finally negotiating an agreement to stand down (Alfred, 1995; Ciaccia, 2000; Swain, 2010). In an earlier failed attempt to mitigate the crisis, then Quebec's Native Affairs Minister John Ciaccia wrote a letter to the mayor and the councillors noting the stakes involved and requesting a suspension to the golf course plans. Ciaccia (2000) argued that historic land claims, cultural context, and community relations went well "beyond the strict legality of the situation as interpreted by our tribunals, which base themselves on laws put into place by our society, laws which do not necessarily answer to the claims of Native people" (p. 59). The Oka Crisis underscored the importance of recognizing Mohawk claims to land and their fight to retain traditions that had been going on since 1770.

If you would like to learn more about the Oka Crisis, Canadian filmmaker Alanis Obomsawin spent the full 78 days on site capturing the event in its entirety in the multiple award-winning 1993 National Film Board documentary called *Kaneshatake: 270 Years of Resistance.*

> **Acting crowd:** A group of people gathered at the same place at the same time and who engage in overt collective behaviour in pursuit of a common goal.

SOCIOLOGY *IN MY LIFE*

CROWDS AND ENTERTAINMENT

Think about the last time you were part of a crowd attending some kind of entertainment event (e.g., a sporting event or a concert). What sorts of behaviours were fans or attendees engaged in? Can you recall any unconventional behaviour displays? Would you classify these behaviours as forms of collective behaviour? Why or why not?

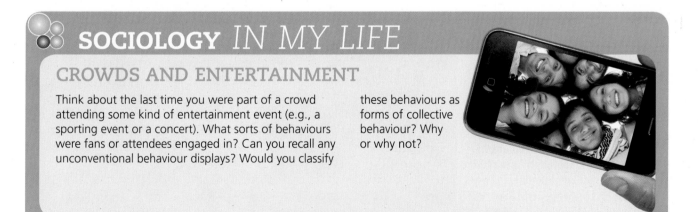

CHAPTER 12   Social Change: Collective Behaviour and Social Movements

- In what ways has collective behaviour led to social progress in Canadian society?
- What is the main difference between a casual and a conventional crowd?
- In which two types of crowds is collective behaviour most likely to occur?
- What is the main difference between an expressive and an acting crowd?

 # SOCIOLOGY IN THEORY

EXPLAINING COLLECTIVE BEHAVIOUR IN CROWDS

LO³ CONTAGION THEORY

One of the earliest explanations for crowd behaviour can be traced to French social psychologist Gustave Le Bon (1841–1931) who wrote extensively about characteristics that increased the likelihood of group displays of expression and social action. In his most influential work, *The Crowd* (1895/2006), Le Bon describes how people lose their individuality in crowds as they are transformed into a "collective mind" that leads them to think and behave in ways quite unlike how they would otherwise behave as individuals. According to Le Bon (1895/2006), the transformation into a collective mind occurs as a function of *anonymity*, *contagion*, and *suggestibility*. Because people in crowds cannot be readily singled out for individual actions (i.e., they are anonymous), they are free from social constraints, and thereby are more likely to act on desires that might otherwise be held in check. This kind of anonymity was later described by Festinger, Pepitone, and Newcomb (1952) as "deindividuation" or the loss of self-awareness that occurs in groups. Le Bon noted that members of crowds are easily swayed into action by others (i.e., they are subject to suggestibility) as a result of a type of "automaton"

that is akin to the notion of mass hypnosis (i.e., contagion).

Herbert Blumer (1900–1987) elaborated on Le Bon's early ideas by clarifying how the collective transformation to social action takes place. According to Blumer (1939, 1969), crowds engage in collective behaviour when individual forms of "restlessness" get communicated to one another, creating a general state of social unrest that is likely to result in one of three forms of collective behaviour. First, it can lead to "*milling*," wherein "individuals move around amongst one another in aimless and random fashion." While harmless, milling increases emotions (excitability), and makes the members of the crowd "more sensitive and responsive to one another" and less responsive to "objects and events that would ordinarily concern them" (Blumer, 1969, p. 75). In addition, crowds may engage in "*collective excitement*," or "a more intense form of milling" that is accompanied by an emotional enthusiasm that is obvious to others. You see this in crowds that linger after a football or hockey game to extend a winning celebration in honour of their favourite team by shouting victory cheers at strangers. In this state, people are "more likely to be carried away by impulses and feelings . . ." prompting behaviours "which previously they would not likely have thought of, much less dared to undertake" (Blumer, 1969, p. 76). Finally, crowds may partake in "*social contagion*," the "rapid, unwitting, and nonrational dissemination of a mood, impulse, or form of conduct" (p. 76). Riots following sports games are a prime example of this.

Contagion theory helps explain the impulsive behaviour displayed by crowds.

Source: THE CANADIAN PRESS/Geoff Howe

CONVERGENCE THEORY

While contagion theory suggests that anyone who happens to be in a crowd is likely to get caught up in the action, *convergence theory* states that people in crowds specifically come together in a particular location in order to behave in accordance with their *prior predispositions*. In other words, like-minded individuals "converge" on a place where in collective behaviour ensues. In this sense, crowd behaviour is not irrational as suggested by contagion theorists but rather a natural outcome of existing psychological impulses. Hence, we can make the inference that "*certain kinds of people* have the propensity to engage in *certain kinds of behaviour*" (Goode, 1992: 59, emphasis in original). This view suggests that blame lies within individual actors and it resonates with preconceived ideas about groups that are well known for engaging in violent collective acts (e.g., Islamic extremist terrorist organizations such as al Qaeda and extreme right wing supremacist groups promoting neo-Nazi ideologies). However, this perspective fails to account for group influences in the same way that contagion theory cannot account for individual differences. A more middle-of-the-road approach is offered by emergent norm theory.

EMERGENT NORM THEORY

Ralph H. Turner and Lewis M. Killian (1987) claim that collective behaviour is both normal (as opposed to irrational) and diverse with various courses of action available to members of a group. A particular course of action generally results from new norms being established as meaning is constructed by a group within a particular situation. *Emergent norm theory* states that collective behaviour in crowds is the end result of developing norms that redefine "right" and "wrong" in response to unique situational events (Turner & Killian, 1987).

For example, imagine you head for your class tomorrow as per your usual schedule. Normally, your instructor is already in the classroom setting up her laptop for a PowerPoint-facilitated lecture when students arrive. However, this time when you reach your class, the door is locked and students are gathered in the hallway. Due to the uncertainty of the present situation (e.g., your instructor appears to be absent and the door is locked), the student crowd is likely to start offering up ideas about what is taking place (maybe the instructor is ill or has gone to find security to open the locked door). People who have never spoken to each other in or out of class might now converse, as they attempt to figure out what is going

on, and ultimately what should happen next (Should everyone wait or leave? How long should everyone wait?). As suggestibility increases, new norms may be established. The crowd may determine that it is appropriate to wait ten more minutes and then leave. In this type of ambiguous situation, the crowd also comes up with *justifications* for emergent norms established. Some students may say that they think there is an existing rule that says you have to wait for only a maximum of ten minutes while others might suggest that the instructor wouldn't want them to waste their time standing in the hallway for an entire period.

Justifications are the end stage of the process, which is a redefinition of the situation that ultimately resolves the original uncertainty—the instructor is not going to make it to class today. The collective behaviour may not be uniform, as some students may leave early while others may choose to wait a little longer, or a few may act in some other fashion during the established ten-minute wait period (e.g., go check the instructor's office or ask a department administrative assistant if anyone knows why the instructor is not at class). Emergent norm theory, then, entails a process whereby collective behaviour results from the sharing of information in groups, which helps to establish situation-appropriate forms of social action.

TIME TO REVIEW

- According to contagion theory, what promotes the development of a collective mind?
- What does convergence theory point to as the main contributor to collective behaviour?
- According to emergent norm theory, how is situational ambiguity resolved?

LO⁴ DISPERSED FORMS OF COLLECTIVE BEHAVIOUR

Recall that crowds are considered to be localized when people are gathered in one place at the same time. Fairly large numbers of people can also be engaged in similar behaviours or be invoked by similar causes *while not in the general proximity of one another*. For example, people dispersed across Canada who have never been in contact with one another may share interests in the latest fads and fashion.

FADS AND FASHION

Fads refer to temporary but highly popular social patterns such as activities, events, music genres, hobbies, or types of collectables that make up a current trend. **Fashion** also includes popular social patterns but they are much longer lived, are more apt to adhere to existing norms, and tend to be more closely associated with identity. For example, people wear a particular brand of perfume or cologne as their personal scent for decades. Fashion also typically involves clothing lines (e.g., casual wear, sportswear, and swimwear) and accessories (e.g., sunglasses, shoes, and purses) that represent an entire fashion industry of designers and brand labels. In contrast, fads generally pertain to particular products (e.g., Build-A-Bear, Silly Bandz, or Webkinz) or activities (e.g., planking and owling).

Fads and fashion are forms of collective behaviour because they impact a large scattering of people who end up buying similar products (e.g., the latest iPhone or Kindle), wearing similar styles (e.g., skinny jeans and hoodies), and acting in similar ways such as trying out the latest diet or regularly posting profiles on Facebook. *CWGMagazine* playfully classifies "Emo" (a genre that is somewhat of a cross between punk and rock), reality television, Twitter, and Guitar Hero among the top "worst fads" of the decade (Madenski, 2010).

> **Fads:** Temporary but highly popular social patterns such as activities, events, music genres, or hobbies.
>
> **Fashion:** Long-lasting popular social patterns that typically involve clothing and clothing accessories.
>
> **Rumours:** Unsubstantiated stories about people or events.

The "Emo" look.

RUMOURS, GOSSIP, AND URBAN LEGENDS

In 2010, a rumour circulated that Canadian folk music artist Gordon Lightfoot had died. The rumour spread worldwide, beginning with a posting on Twitter by "someone in Ottawa." It was eventually proven to be false (wherein it stopped being a rumour) but not before one of Lightfoot's close friends heard about it and passed the message onto his wife who emailed the news to other friends in the music industry (Nurwisah, 2010). Luckily, Lightfoot was able to reach the media and his five children to quickly dispel the rumour. He displayed a sense of humour about the whole episode even after hearing about his own supposed death on the radio while driving to his Toronto office following a dental appointment. He notes that while he was "shocked of course," it was also "the best day for airplay that we've had in weeks" (CTV News, 2010).

Rumours are unsubstantiated stories about people or events. Rumours often accompany ambiguous situations as people try to determine what is going on and how they should proceed. *Why are all the tenants gathered outside my apartment building—is there a fire in the building? Do I need to find somewhere else to stay until this gets sorted out?* Rumours are common in advance of major events and they generally involve categories of people. For example, the mass media may circulate rumours about hockey or football teams that may be involved upcoming trades or sales. Similarly the mass media sometimes informs us that certain groups such as teachers or nurses are rumoured to go on strike possibly due to failed contract negotiations. Goode (1992) indicates that rumours are universal since they exist in all societies and they are good examples of collective behaviour since they result from social interaction (i.e., group processes), they "fill in the gaps" with spontaneous bits of information, and the content and even the process can be somewhat unconventional in nature.

The spread of rumours generally follows a predictable pattern wherein information tends to get modified and lost over time and from person to person as the story is retold. Rumours are highly inaccurate since as much as 70 percent of the original details are lost by the time a rumour has been retold five or six times (Allport & Postman, 1947). Allport and Postman (1947) note that information loss and distortion occurs largely as a result of three common practices. First, information during rumour transmission gets *levelled.* That is, a lot of the original details get omitted or lost. In addition, information becomes *sharpened* to the viewpoint of the particular teller. In this case, details that are more interesting or more

SOCIOLOGY *IN MY COMMUNITY*

THE RUMOUR PROCESS

To demonstrate how this process works, one of the authors told a fictitious story in class with 20 details concerning a traffic accident (e.g., where the female motorist was going, the vehicle she was driving, how the accident happened, who was involved, what sort of injuries and damage resulted, etc.).[2] Five student volunteers waited outside the classroom while one remained in the class to hear the original version of the story. The student in the room then repeated the story to one of the students who was brought in from the hallway. A list of the actual details was shown out of view of the rumouring students so the class could follow along and note exactly what was being lost and changed during the process. Each person waiting outside was individually brought in to hear the story for the first time and then asked to retell it to the next person. Results for the exercise described above revealed *levelling* (the story ended up with about five main points rather than 20). In addition, storytellers sharpened details (i.e., they tended to focus on injuries and the people involved rather than where or how the accident took place) and they assimilated the information (e.g., they created additional details about the people who caused the accident, making them younger in age, and they added to the injuries from the accident).

---

salient to that particular storyteller are most likely to be retained. Finally, a type of *assimilation* also occurs wherein the storyteller concentrates on a particular theme or part of the rumour and may even embellish upon it by adding details so that the story better fits the story teller's personal viewpoint.

Gossip pertains to unsubstantiated or substantiated stories about specific individuals. Although it was dubbed as a rumour by the mass media, the alleged death of Gordon Lightfoot is more accurately classified as gossip since it pertains to a specific person rather than a group such as a story about musicians in general. Sales for gossip-based magazines and tabloids such as *People, Star, Celebrity News, Hello!, Us Weekly,* or the *National Enquirer* can attest to the vast popularity of this form of collective behaviour. Clearly, gossip is unconventional (i.e., it's generally not considered nice or appropriate to tell often hurtful, private, and personal stories about other people); it is spontaneous (e.g., a celebrity can be engaged in any multitude of behaviours at the moment when a photographer catches a glimpse of the person on camera); and it may or may not be verifiable (i.e., true with any degree of certainty). We may never find out whether Canadian celebrity Ryan Reynolds had a crush on his *Proposal* costar Sandra Bullock, but we can substantiate that Sandra Bullock and Jesse James's divorce was finalized (Fleeman, 2010).

Urban legends (also sometimes called contemporary legends or urban myths) refer to unsubstantiated stories that persist over time and contain an underlying message or moral. Jan Harold Brunvand (b. 1933) refers to urban legends as "believed oral narratives" that are passed on from person to person, similar to folklore (Brunvand, 2003). Although urban legends are purportedly about specific people and events, references to them tend to be general or abstract (e.g., a hitchhiker, a babysitter, a motorist, and a fast-food restaurant) and the details change from place to place and over time akin to the rumour process. In addition, urban legends contain a moral, such as "Keep a close watch on your children" or "Do not trust strangers." Urban legends span a variety of topics from stories about contaminated food, to cruelty toward animals, to natural disasters, and especially horror (e.g., they are often about death, murders, accidents, and ghosts) (Brunvand, 2001). How the legend originally gets picked up is unknown but legends tend to circulate among "relatively sophisticated, educated, urbanized modern people" (Brunvand, 2011). This may be in part because the source of an urban legend is believed to be an actual credible person who is a FOAF or a "friend of a friend," an "unnamed, elusive, but somehow readily trusted anonymous individual" (Brunvand, 2003, p. 51).

> **Gossip:** Unsubstantiated or substantiated stories about specific individuals.
>
> **Urban legends:** Abstract unsubstantiated stories containing an underlying message or moral that persist over time.

SOCIOLOGY *IN MY LIFE*

DEBUNKING URBAN LEGENDS

Did you ever hear a story or receive an email warning that bears a resemblance to an urban legend? Did you believe it? Students of ours frequently mention an urban legend about gang members who, as part of a "gang initiation" requirement purposely drive around at night in a vehicle with the headlights turned off. Then, when an oncoming motorist flashes his or her headlights (to indicate the gang member is driving with the lights off), instead of accepting the courtesy gesture, the gang members go after and kill the motorist who has unknowingly self-selected him-or herself as a target! For a comprehensive Internet resource dedicated to urban legends including the one described above, we recommend Barbara and David Mikkelson's site called Snopes.com. Here you can examine more than 40 categories of urban legends (e.g., those dealing with computers, horror, music, sports, weddings, etc.) and find out whether some of the stories you know of have been proven credible or not.

WIDESPREAD PANIC AND MORAL PANIC

A shared fear underlying an impending threat such as that posed by terrorist attacks or a pandemic can sometimes produce collective action in the form of a **widespread panic** wherein a large number of people may try to flee an area, believing they have little time left before meeting some horrible fate. A famous historical example of a large-scale panic originated with a radio broadcast on October 30, 1938. At a time when radio was known for its factual content, listeners heard what came across as news reports of a Martian invasion with references to actual buildings, streets, and towns. The broadcast was in fact a theatre adaptation of H. G. Wells's short story "War of the Worlds" in which Martians invade New England but many listeners failed to catch the qualifying station break announcement (Miller, 2000). Although the print media likely exaggerated claims concerning public reactions (e.g., noting widespread stampedes and high numbers of personal injuries), a significant portion of listeners, *did,* nonetheless, believe the broadcast and subsequently acted upon that belief (e.g., by trying to contact police, hospitals, family members and so on) (Miller, 2000). Few people today worry about the impending threat of Martian attacks; however, many are concerned about health and safety issues associated with possible influenza pandemics. For more information on emergency planning and responses, refer to the Canadian Pandemic Influenza Plan for the Health Sector located on the Public Health Agency of Canada's website at www .phac-aspc.gc.ca.

Stanley Cohen (1972) used the term **moral panic** to describe the irrational but widespread worry that certain *groups* represent an enormous threat to the social order of society. A moral panic "is a scare about a threat or supposed threat from deviants or 'folk devils,' a category of people who, presumably, engage in evil practices and are blamed for menacing a society's culture, way of life, and central values" (Goode & Ben-Yehuda, 2009, p. 2). Three sources contribute to the development of moral panics (Zajdow, 2008). First, there is the particular group whose behaviour is causing the moral panic (i.e., the folk devils). Cohen (2002) notes that youth are a reoccurring target of blame for society's moral decay as are those associated with the taking or selling of banned drugs. For example, shortly after three young Canadians died from taking the drug ecstasy, a moral panic spread in the Toronto area regarding the risks associated with "rave communities" and "rave dance parties" (Hier, 2002).

In addition to the actors, there are people known as **moral entrepreneurs** who deem it important to bring the morally damaging behaviour to the attention of others. Moral entrepreneurs can include concerned

Widespread panic: A generalized belief regarding impending danger that can lead a large number of people to flee an area or engage in other protective measures.

Moral panic: Irrational but widespread worry that certain groups present an enormous threat to the social order of society.

Moral entrepreneur: Person who brings perceived morally damaging behaviour to the attention of others.

SOCIOLOGY *IN MY COMMUNITY*

CHIROPRACTIC FOLK DEVILS

Chiropractors are health-care professionals who treat disorders related to the neuromusculoskeletal system (Canadian Chiropractic Association, 2011). On September 12, 1996, an Ontario woman named Lana Dale Lewis died of a stroke at the age of 45. Her family and various moral entrepreneurs were convinced that the cause originated in a chiropractic manipulation she had received for migraines. The ensuing moral panic surrounding use of chiropractic services lasted from 1996 to 2005 and was fuelled by media coverage, which occurred daily throughout the 22-month-long

investigation into her death (Villanueva-Russell, 2009). The inquest into the death of Lewis by a coroner's jury eventually rendered a verdict of "death by means of an accident" (Laeeque & Boon, 2004). Nonetheless, the media was successful in creating a moral panic and antichiropractic messages began appearing in magazines and on websites (e.g., Chirowatch.com). The end result was a widespread but largely unfounded fear relative to statistical realities, which damaged the reputation of the chiropractic profession (Villanueva-Russell, 2009).

parents, citizens, or others who try to advocate for measures that help alleviate what they perceive to be a social problem. Moral entrepreneurs, for example, write letters to politicians or editors of newspapers to detail their views and attempt to elicit support. Moral entrepreneurs in this case tried to get raves banned from city-owned property (Hier, 2002).

The third agent is the mass media, which facilitates the spread of panic by making a particular version of the story widely available. Hier (2002) reported that

there were 192 stories in Toronto newspapers on raves over a four-month period. A final distinguishing feature of a moral panic is that the "scare" is disproportionate to the real threat of the event occurring. In this case, there was a supposition that youth who attended raves constituted a group most likely to use designer drugs and that raves constituted a particular type of social setting which intensified the risks associated with taking drugs such as ecstasy; neither of these assumptions turned out to be supported by verifiable empirical data.

SOCIOLOGY *IN PRACTICE*

CHIROPRACTIC DELISTING

Interestingly, the latter stage of the moral panic coincided with reforms to Canadian health insurance systems. After 30 years of coverage, in 2004, chiropractic services were "delisted" from the Ontario Health Insurance Plan with the other provinces following suit. This meant that from then on, people who utilize chiropractic services have to pay for the treatment themselves (amounting to about 1.2 million people in Ontario alone) (Deloitte, 2004). An initial visit to a chiropractor located in Toronto is about $75.00 and subsequent treatments range from $39.50 to $59.50 (Emkiro Health Services, 2011). Some private

workplace insurance plans still cover part of the costs with a maximum per visit (e.g., $20 or $25) and an annual limit (e.g., $200 or $300). The delisting of chiropractors likely resulted in a decrease in the health and well-being of Canadians as well as an adverse effect on the health system (i.e., some people will stop going to chiropractors and leave conditions untreated, others will go less often, and patient care in general may get off-loaded back to higher-priced physician services) (Deloitte, 2004).

DISASTERS

Disasters constitute a socially disruptive and often very harmful setting from which collective behaviour emerges. In most cases, a **disaster** consists of "a relatively sudden, unscheduled, one-time event that causes a great deal of property or ecological damage, or large-scale loss of life, and substantial disruption or stress among residence in the stricken area" (Goode, 1992, 219). As recent events around the globe have taught us, naturally occurring climate-based disasters including earthquakes, floods, tsunamis, cyclones, and heat waves have resulted in large numbers of death and even more cases of injury. In 2010 alone, an earthquake struck Haiti killing more than 230,000 people while floods in Pakistan killed more than 1700 and affected 17.2 million others (CBC News, 2010a). Canada also has in its history a legacy of natural hazards including hurricanes, earthquakes, floods, volcanic eruptions, storm surges, landslides, forest fires, and even tsunamis (Natural Resources Canada, 2009). The worst hurricane in Atlantic history struck the coast of Newfoundland in 1775 and killed more than 4000 people (Stokes Sullivan, 2010).

Gulf of Mexico oil spill, 2010.

Source: Getty Images

Disasters also occur in the wake of human inventions (e.g., plane crashes, train derailments, sinking ships), power relations (e.g., acts of war, terrorism, and the creation of weapons of mass destruction), and technological advancement (e.g., industrial explosions, oil spills, mining accidents, or engineering failures). Two of the most notorious industrial disasters occurred in the 1980s—one in Bhopal, India, in 1984 involving a poisonous leak from the Union Carbide pesticide factory that resulted in as many as 4000 fatalities and 50 000 injuries and one at Chernobyl, Ukraine, in 1986 involving a nuclear power explosion that killed 56 people and contributed to 4000 subsequent cancer cases (Lepisto, 2009). Canada also had a few of its own disasters with casualties in the 1980s including the capsizing of an oil-drilling rig known as the Ocean Ranger off the coast of Newfoundland in 1982 (CBC News, 2002), the crash of an Air Canada DC-9 plane en route from Dallas to Toronto in 1983 (Noland, 2011), and a collision in 1986 involving a CN freight and Via Rail passenger train east of Hinton in Alberta (Landry, 2011). One of Canada's more recent disasters was a spill of more than 28 000 barrels of oil in Northern Alberta. Eaves (2011) notes that "when it comes to oil spills, the question is never if but when and how bad" and reminds us that at least 4.5 million litres of spilled oil have already negatively impacted the Peace River watershed.

The interest for sociologists lies not so much in distinguishing among types of disasters or noting how a natural or a human-made disaster occurs, but in identifying commonalities that underlie all forms of disaster such as social, political, and economic factors which predispose certain groups to disproportionately higher disaster risks and affect how resources are deployed throughout and in the aftermath of such crises. Sociologist Kai Erikson (1976, 1994) has examined disasters for several decades and he draws attention to the fundamental importance of the relationship people have with their environment and the wider community for understanding collective behaviour including the seemingly irrational behaviour of people who fail to leave a disaster site, even when remaining continues to pose additional hardships (such as living in close proximity to a contaminated water supply or a location at a high risk of a repeat event such as a flood). Erikson (1994) draws an analogy between the trauma experienced by disaster survivors and the long-term suffering experienced by people who live in poverty, both of whom lack important ties to the existing social structure.

Disaster: A relatively sudden, unscheduled, one-time event that causes a great deal of property or ecological damage, or large-scale loss of life, and substantial disruption or stress among residents in the stricken area.

- Are fads considered to be forms of collective behaviour? Why or why not?
- In what ways does information get lost and distorted during the rumour process?
- How do urban legends differ from rumours?
- What does widespread panic entail?
- What three sources contribute to moral panic?
- Why might certain groups be at greater risk for disasters?

LO⁵ SOCIAL MOVEMENTS

Recall at the start of the chapter that we discussed the importance of collective behaviour and social movements for helping to facilitate social change. **Social movements** are "organized efforts by a substantial number of people to change or to resist change, in some major aspect or aspects of society" (Goode, 1992, p. 28). For example, early Canadian social movements advocated for civil liberties (e.g., freedom of speech and the right to own property) and human rights (e.g., workers' rights and women's rights). American sociologist Charles Tilly (1929–2008) and others consider social movements to be a kind of "contentious politics"—"contentious in the sense that social movements involve the collective making of claims that, if realized, would conflict with someone else's interests, political in the sense that governments of one sort or another figure somehow in the claims making, whether as claimants, objects of claims, allies of the objects, or monitors of the contention" (Tilly, 2004, p. 3 as cited in Staggenborg, 2008, p. 5).

Social movements share some of the characteristics of earlier-mentioned forms of collective behaviour including their *unconventional nature*, which tends to go against established cultural values and practices. Social movements also share with collective behaviour a reliance on social action stemming from group efforts (e.g., a fad necessarily must have followers). Social movements, however, are not considered a form of collective behaviour because they also possess a number of disqualifying features. Specifically, while collective behaviour is relatively spontaneous and unstructured, social movements involve prior *organization* and *planning*. Social movements also often have identifiable leaders (e.g., the late Martin Luther King, Jr. is considered to be a main leader of the American Civil Rights Movement) and they include public campaigns or efforts to recruit participants who act on behalf of the movement to further its goals. In addition, while collective behaviour tends to be fairly short lived as in

TABLE 12.1

Differentiating between Collective Behaviour and Social Movements

Collective Behaviour & Social Movements	Collective Behaviour	Social Movements
Involves the behaviour of a fairly large number of individuals	Spontaneous	Prior organization
Unconventional in nature	Unstructured	Prior planning
	Short-lived	Enduring

the case of a riot following a hockey game that plays itself out after a number of hours, gossip about your professor that may last only a few days, or a fad that runs its course over a season, social movements can endure for many years. For example, the environmental movement has been especially active since the 1960s and continues to develop momentum today (see Chapter 13). A summary of the main similarities and differences is provided in Table 12.1 above.

CLAIMS AND CLAIMS MAKING

The concepts of "claims making" and "change" are central for understanding the purpose of social movements and differentiating between them. Every social movement rests on some kind of claim. In this context, a **claim** is a statement about the nature of some phenomenon that is constructed as a social problem. Social movements engage in **claims making**, a process wherein a social movement declares that a particular condition is unjust

Social movements: Organized efforts by a substantial number of people to change or to resist change in some major aspect or aspects of society.

Claim: A statement about the nature of some phenomenon that is constructed as a social problem.

Claims making: A process wherein a social movement declares that a particular condition is unjust and identifies measures needed to resolve the unfairness.

and identifies measures needed to resolve the unfairness. For example, the lesbian, gay, bisexual, and transgender (LGBT) social movement claimed that LGBT couples were treated unjustly in Canada since they lacked rights that married couples have (e.g., property and parenting rights). Organizations such as Canadians for Equal Marriage and Egale Canada then advocated for legalized same-sex marriages as a solution, which subsequently occurred Canada-wide in 2005.

DIMENSIONS OF SOCIAL CHANGE

Social movements are largely distinguished by their underlying claim and by dimensions related to the social change proposed as part of their claims making, including the type of change sought, the degree of change sought, the intended recipient of the change sought, and the means utilized to obtain change. First, in terms of the *type of change* sought, social movements generally seek to either promote or prevent change from occurring. More progressive movements challenge existing norms and values by presenting new ideas and claims advocating change while more conservative movements challenge new ideas to prevent change from occurring in an effort to maintain the status quo. This dichotomy is especially evident in social movements for and against abortion (i.e., pro-choice versus pro-life).

In addition, social movements are distinguished by the *degree of change*, which ranges from movements seeking limited change, such as an adjustment to an existing policy, to those wishing to effect large-scale change such as converting a political system from communism to democracy. Similarly, social movements may seek to direct their efforts at *particular recipients* (e.g., Aboriginal youth, working Canadians, impaired drivers, or seniors) or they may seek to change the views of all Canadians (e.g., to promote green living or healthy lifestyles). Finally, social movements differ greatly with respect to the *means utilized* in the pursuit of change (e.g., confrontational versus nonconfrontational or peaceful versus violent).

In addition to the four dimensions related to social change, social movements also vary in terms of size

SOCIOLOGY IN MY COMMUNITY

G20 SUMMIT PROTESTS

The fourth annual meeting of the G20 Summit was held in Toronto, Ontario, on June 26–27, 2010. The G20 is a forum for informal discussions about economic and financial matters including the development of recommendations for strategies that might help ease the world recession. The G20 consists of heads of government representing 19 countries and the European Union along with representatives from the International Monetary Fund and the World Bank. G20 member countries include Argentina, Australia, Brazil, Canada, China, France, Germany, India, Indonesia, Italy, Japan, Mexico, Russia, Saudi Arabia, South Africa, Korea, Turkey, the United Kingdom, the United States, and the European Union (University of Toronto, 2011). Prior to the G20 Summit meetings, social movement organizations put out calls for collective action to protest the G20 on various grounds.

For example, the Our World Is Not for Sale (OWINFS) network of organizations and social movements claims the G20 comprises a capitalist class that prioritizes financial growth over global priorities such as mitigating the impact of climate change. Similarly, organizations in the 172 countries that are not included in the discussions perceive the annual event to be one that perpetuates inequality between rich and poor countries and works against collective efforts to eliminate world poverty (Social Watch, 2010). More than a billion dollars was spent on G20 security as Toronto became the epicentre for massive protests in the form of peaceful demonstrations as well as violent confrontations with police, rioting, widespread vandalism, and other forms of destruction culminating in more than 400 arrests (CBC News, 2010b).

(e.g., number of supporters) and according to their geographical scope from small, grassroots local movements in a particular city or province, to country-wide, and even large-scale, international-based social movements. Women's movement of various sizes emerged in 32 different countries over a 100-year period, beginning in the mid-1800s (Staggenborg, 1998). The actual "work" of social movements is typically carried out by social movement organizations. A **social movement organization (SMO)** is "a complex or formal organization which identifies its goals with the preferences of a social movement or a countermovement and attempts to implement those goals" (McCarthy & Zald, 1977, p. 1218; as cited in Staggenborg, 2008, p. 6).

LO⁶ TYPES OF SOCIAL MOVEMENTS

Based on the degree of change sought and the intended recipient of the change, four main types of social movements can be identified: alternative, redemptive, reformative, and revolutionary[3] as shown in Figure 12.2.

Alternative social movements are social movements that seek limited societal change for a specific group or narrow segment of society. For example, there are social movements that promote alternate sources of information (e.g., the Canadian Alternative News Media) to engage with citizens who want to learn more about perspectives other than those depicted on mainstream radio or television stations controlled by the Canadian Broadcasting Corporation or the main American networks such as ABC or NBC. Similarly, there are alternative religious movements (e.g., Scientology and Integral Yoga), alternative educational movements (e.g., Canadian homeschooling), alternative dispute resolution movements (e.g., negotiation, mediation, and arbitration), and alternative political movements (e.g., the Marijuana Party of Canada and the Canadian Action Party).

Social movements that seek large-scale change for a specific group in society are known as **redemptive social movements**. In this case, the goal of a social movement might be to change the entire way of life for a particular group as in the case of Alcoholics Anonymous wherein the goal is to help people with drinking problems develop a completely new life without ever drinking alcohol again. An animal rights movement such as the Animal Liberation Front seeks to obtain considerations for animals that are closer to those afforded for humans (e.g., prohibiting the consumption of animals, the use of leather or fur for clothing, and the use of animals in experimentation). Slow Food Canada is a redemptive food movement that recognizes the connection between pleasure and eating and encourages people to strike a balance between food enjoyment and agricultural biodiversity while discouraging consumption in the fast-food industry.

Reformative social movements are social movements that seek limited societal change but the recipient of the change is everyone. This type of movement seeks to get everyone in society to adopt a new viewpoint or a particular position on an issue. The People's Health Movement, for example, is a progressive global network of organizations that seeks to get each person in society to recognize health (and therefore access to health care) as a human right. Other examples of very important influential historical reformative social movements include the

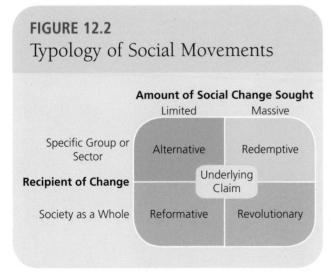

FIGURE 12.2

Typology of Social Movements

	Amount of Social Change Sought	
	Limited	Massive
Specific Group or Sector	Alternative	Redemptive
Recipient of Change	*Underlying Claim*	
Society as a Whole	Reformative	Revolutionary

Source: Based on Aberk (1966).

Social movement organization (SMO): A complex or formal organization that identifies its goals with the preferences of a social movement or a countermovement and attempts to implement those goals.

Alternative social movements: Social movements that seek limited societal change for a specific group or narrow segment of society.

Redemptive social movements: Social movements that seek large-scale change for a specific group.

Reformative social movements: Social movements that seek limited societal change for everyone in society.

civil rights movement, the women's movement, and the LGBT movement.

Finally, social movements that seek large-scale societal change that affects everyone in society are known as **revolutionary social movements**. Wars that lead to the overthrow of an existing political system in order to pave the way for a new political system based on a different ideology are generally rooted in revolutionary social movements. The Russian Revolution of 1917, for example, which included various forms of collective behaviour including riots, strikes, mass demonstrations, and attacks, centred on two pivotal events: The February Revolution, which removed then Tsar Nicholas II from power, and the October Revolution, which established the Soviet Union in place of the temporary government. The fascist revolutions in Italy and Germany also provide us with historical examples. Islamic revolutionary movements (e.g., the Salafi jihadist movement and the Al Qaeda network, which are based on an Islamic fundamentalist ideology) provide more current illustrations of enduring movements seeking large-scale changes to existing belief systems. The 2011 Egyptian revolution provides a recent example of how quickly a civil movement can organize to achieve its goals especially when communication is facilitated by the social media (e.g., Twitter, Facebook, and the Internet).

Revolutionary social movements: Social movements that seek large-scale change that affects everyone in society.

TIME TO REVIEW

- How are social movements different from other forms of collective behaviour?
- What does claims making entail?
- What are the four dimensions of change that help differentiate among social movements?
- Which type of social movement seeks massive change for a narrow segment of society?

More than a million protesters gathered in Tahrir Square, Cairo, on February 8, 2011.

Source: 2011 AFP/Getty

LO⁷ SOCIOLOGY IN THEORY

VALUE-ADDED THEORY

In explaining social movements, it is important to consider historical conditions and events since social movements often arise in response to existing social conditions, particularly those that cause sources of strain. In his *value-added theory*, Neil Smelser (1962, pp. 15–18) discussed six interrelated factors that facilitate social action:

1. *Structural conduciveness*—the broad social conditions that are necessary for collective behaviour to take place (e.g., economic pressure).
2. *Structural strain*—the underlying factors that represent problems that have resulted from or that have not been adequately dealt with within the current system (e.g., gender inequality, racism, pay inequities, environmental degradation, etc.).
3. *Growth and spread of a generalized belief*—the widespread awareness that a particular issue is a social problem and that steps should and can be taken to change it.
4. *Precipitating factors*—events or behaviours that serve as "triggers" or breaking points by making an issue even more salient (i.e., when the police officers who were seen on national television beating Rodney King were later found not guilty, the announcement of the verdict set off a riot in Los Angeles).
5. *Mobilization of participation for action*—the gathering of potential participants often requires the inspiration of leaders who help spread the message and encourage others to get directly involved in the solution.
6. *The operation of social control*—in the absence of strong forms of direct control by police or military organizations, people are no longer restrained from carrying out collective efforts (as was the recent case in Egypt).

According to Smelser (1962), each factor in its corresponding order must be present to promote the next step or stage in the development of collective behaviour (i.e., if one or more of these precipitating factors is absent, collective action is unlikely to occur).

Critiques of value-added theories (e.g., see McAdam, 1982) point out how they fail to address the larger political context within which many social movements arise and therefore "collective behaviour is more likely to be perceived as deviant behaviour than political action" (Buechler, 2010, p. 51). In addition, by focusing on strain, such theories imply that those who participate versus those who do not participate in collective action will largely be determined by whether people constitute a deprived category (i.e., those who are most disadvantaged are the ones who always rise up against the existing system). A value-added approach, then, fails to explain how a movement gathers a diverse range of individual supporters who come to collectively believe in a cause (McAdam, 1982).

RESOURCE MOBILIZATION THEORY

Proponents of resource mobilization approaches suggest that structural strains including relative deprivation in certain sectors are present in most societies and, hence, what weighs more heavily in the development of social movements is resource mobilization (e.g., McCarthy & Zald, 1973). The main assumption underlying resource mobilization theory is that social movements develop as a function of how resources are brought together and utilized by leaders. According to Edwards and McCarthy (2004), this includes how leaders organize *moral resources* (i.e., the legitimacy of the claim), *cultural resources* (e.g., the channelling of sophistication in terms of knowing what to do strategically), *social–organizational resources* (e.g., the development of networks), *human resources* (e.g., experienced activists and people with skills needed to further organizational goals), and various *material resources* (e.g., finances and office space) (as cited in Staggenborg, 2008). Whether or not social movements develop in particular places at particular times, then, is largely a function of how well leaders manage to facilitate the development and channelling of various needed resources.

Social movements are far more organized, institutionalized, and enduring relative to other forms of collective behaviour. This is an important shift since it also implies that members of social movement organizations are "rational actors" who come together as a result of collective interests (Buechler, 2010) rather than people who get out of hand when they become part of a group as would be implied by contagion theory, for example. Building on the more rational and organized approaches, *political process theory* developed to emphasize the importance of *cycles of contention* (wherein there is large-scale unrest) and *political opportunities* for paving the way for protest movements (e.g., Tarrow, 1998; Tilly & Tarrow, 2006). In his 1998 book, *Power in Movement*, Tarrow explained that political opportunities are situational features that enable movement development through access (e.g., elections), shifting alignments (e.g., changes in what a particular political party supports or does not support), divided elites, influential allies, and repression or facilitation by the state (pp. 77–80).

More recent approaches combine the assumptions of early resource mobilization theory and political process theory into a resource mobilization/political process model of "political entities aiming to create social change" (Staggenborg, 2008, p. 18). Within this combined approach, theorists (e.g., Benford and Snow, 2000) have emphasized the injustice that was the foundation of early strain/value-added approaches in the form of *collection action frames*. Collection action frames are similar to our earlier depiction of claims and claims making, wherein a social movement (often with the aid of leaders and a social movement organization), develops an interpretation of a particular issue as a form of social injustice that becomes the focal point for subsequent action (Staggenborg, 2008).

NEW SOCIAL MOVEMENT THEORY

A final approach known as the *new social movement theory* focuses exclusively on social movements that have arisen in postindustrial/advanced societies largely from the 1960s onward. The underlying claim of new social movement theorists is that postindustrial movements differ in their emphasis on human rights (e.g., women's rights or gay, lesbian, bisexual, and transsexual rights) and global issues (e.g., global warming, poverty, peace) as opposed to the economic emphasis of earlier labour/worker movements.

One of the most important contributions of the new social movement theory is the notion of a **collective identity**. A collective identity is a shared sense of belonging or "we-ness" that binds individuals in a social movement and serves as the "animating spirit" that propels them to take action on behalf of that social movement (Snow, 2001). The construction of a social identity is paramount to both the existence and endurance of a social movement (Gamson, 1991). Hunt and Benford (2010) summarize the distinction between old and new social movements by noting that "class consciousness" has, for all intents and purposes, been replaced by "collective identity" "as the factor that accounts for mobilization and individual attachments to new social movements" (p. 437). Current research is now aimed at developing our understanding of how collective identities develop, how tensions develop between multiple identities, and how collective identities translate into various forms of action (della Porta & Diani, 2008). The environmental movement, which is the focus of the next chapter, is an exemplary new social movement that includes a growing collective identity in the form of environmental awareness that is working toward a global call to action.

> **Collective identity:** A shared sense of belonging that binds individuals in a social movement and propels them to take action on behalf of that social movement.

CHAPTER SUMMARY

LO1 **Define collective behaviour, identify its central features, and differentiate it from conventional behaviour.**

Collective behaviour refers to group behaviour that is relatively spontaneous, unstructured, and unconventional relative to conventional behaviour, which is planned, structured, and normative in nature.

LO2 **Identify the different types of crowds and explain which ones contribute to collective behaviour.**

A crowd is a temporary gathering of people who are in the same place at the same time (i.e., a crowd is localized whereas other groups are more dispersed). Casual crowds share only proximity, conventional crowds share an interest, expressive crowds share an interest and are participatory, and acting crowds engage in the pursuit of a common goal. Both expressive and acting crowds facilitate collective behaviour.

LO3 **Explain how sociological theories (i.e., social contagion, convergence, and emergent norm) contribute to our understanding of collective behaviour.**

Contagion theory suggests that people are transformed in a group much like hypnosis, which causes them to behave in irrational ways; convergence theory claims that like-minded people come together to behave in accord with predisposition; and emergent norm theory suggests that crowds are more likely to consist of rational people who develop new rules in order to manage ambiguous situations.

LO⁴ Describe fads, rumours, urban legends, moral panic, and disasters as dispersed forms of collective behaviour.

Dispersed crowds engage in similar behaviours while not in the same general proximity. Fads are popular social patterns, rumours are unsubstantiated stories about people and events, gossip pertains to unsubstantiated and substantiated stories about specific individuals, and urban legends are unsubstantiated stories that persist over time. Widespread panic refers to shared fear, while moral panic describes irrational but widespread worry that certain groups pose a threat to the social order of society. Disasters are relatively sudden events that cause damage and disruption but often bring together collective relief efforts.

LO⁵ Explain how social movements are both similar to and different from collective behaviour and explain the relevance of claims making for movement organizations.

Social movements and collective behaviour both include unconventional forms of group-based action. However, collective behaviour is spontaneous and unstructured whereas social movements involve prior organization and planning. Social movements rest on the premise of claims making, which identifies a perceived social problem that the movement wishes to remedy usually through varying dimensions of social change (e.g., by changing norms or resisting new ones, by seeking limited or massive changes, via changes that affect only a small group versus the entire society, and through various means used to obtain the change).

LO⁶ Differentiate between alternative, redemptive, reform, and revolutionary social movements.

Alternative social movements seek limited societal change for a specific group while redemptive ones seek massive (or large-scale) changes for a specific group. Reformative social movements seek limited societal change but the recipient of the change is everyone in society, while revolutionary ones seek massive changes that affect everyone.

LO⁷ Compare and contrast theoretical views on the development of social movements.

In identifying factors that promote social action, value-added theory identifies the importance of structural conduciveness, structural strain, generalized beliefs, precipitating factors, mobilization for action, and a lack of social control; resource mobilization theory emphasizes resources over other structural factors; and new social movement theory emphasizes the formation of a collective identity.

RECOMMENDED READINGS

1. For an introduction to collective behaviour, we recommend: Goode, E. (1992). *Collective Behavior*. Orlando, FL: Harcourt Brace Jovanovich.
2. As an overview of the history and development of Canadian social movements, see: Staggenborg, S. (2008). *Social Movements*. Toronto, ON: Oxford University Press.
3. For an in-depth look at the emergence of human rights and civil liberties associations in Canada, we refer you to Clément, D. (2008). *Canada's Rights Revolution: Social Movements and Social Change, 1937–1982*. Vancouver, BC: UBC Press.
4. To better appreciate the development of the gay and lesbian movement in Canada, we recommend: Adam, B. (1995). *The Rise of a Gay and Lesbian Movement*. New York: Twayne Publishers.
5. For a detailed overview of revolutionary movements (particularly of the 20th and 21st centuries), we recommend: Defronzo, J. (2011). *Revolutions and Revolutionary Movements* (4th ed.). Boulder, CO: Westview Press.

FOR FURTHER REFLECTION

1. List five current fads. How are these fads similar to and different from ones that you participated in when you were younger? What are some of the main factors that contribute to the end of a fad's popularity?
2. Think about the last time you heard a rumour or participated in spreading one. In what ways might a rumour be considered a functional form of collective behaviour?
3. Choose a recent example of a large-scale social uprising. Can you identify any existing social conditions that you think may have promoted social action? Did a collective identity contribute to the collective behaviour that came about?

REFERENCES

Aberle, D. F. (1966). *The Peyote Religion among the Navaho.* Chicago, IL: Aldine.

Alfred, G. R. (1995). *Heeding the Voices of Our Ancestors: Kahnawake Mohawk Politics and the Rise of Native Nationalism.* Toronto, ON: Oxford University Press.

Allport, G. W., & Postman, L. (1947). *The Psychology of Rumor.* New York: Henry Holt.

Benford, R. D., & Snow, D. A. (2000). Framing processes and social movements: An overview and assessment. *Annual Review of Sociology, 26,* 611–639.

Blumer, H. (1969). Collective behavior. In Alfred McClung Lee (Ed.), *Principles of Sociology* (3rd ed.). New York: Barnes & Noble, pp. 67–120.

Blumer, H. (1939). Collective Behavior. In Robert E. Park (Ed.), *Outline of the Principles of Sociology.* New York, NY: Barnes & Noble, pp. 221–279.

Brunvand, J. H. (2011). Dr. Jan Harold Brunvand: Frequently asked questions. *Dr. Jan Harold Brunvand Homepage.* Retrieved February 10, 2011, from www.janbrunvand.com/faq.html

Brunvand, J. H. (2003). *The Choking Doberman: And Other Urban Legends.* New York: W. W. Norton & Company.

Brunvand, J. H. (2001). *Encyclopedia of Urban Legends.* New York: W. W. Norton & Company.

Buechler, S. M. (2010). The strange career of strain and breakdown theories of collective action. In D. A. Snow, S. A. Soule, & H. Kriesi. (Eds.), *The Blackwell Companion to Social Movements.* Malden, MA: Blackwell Publishing, pp. 47–66.

Canadian Chiropractic Association. (2011). *Facts and FAQs. What conditions do chiropractors treat?* Toronto, ON: Canadian Chiropractic Association. Retrieved February 17, 2011, from: www.chiropracticcanada.ca/en-us/Home.aspx

CBC News. (2010a, August 30). The world's worst natural disasters: Calamities of the 20th and 21st centuries. In *World: CBC News Online.* Retrieved February 14, 2011, from www.cbc.ca/world/story/2008/05/08/f-natural-disasters-history.html

CBC News. (2010b, June 27). G20 protest violence prompts over 400 arrests. In *Canada: CBC news online.* Retrieved August 11, 2011, from www.cbc.ca/news/canada/story/2010/06/26/g20-saturday-protests.html

CBC News. (2002, February 25). The Ocean Ranger disaster. *Extreme Weather: CBC Digital Archives.* Retrieved August 3, 2011, from www.archives.cbc.ca/environment/extreme_weather/topics/349

Ciaccia, J. (2000). *The Oka Crisis: A Mirror of the Soul.* Dorval, QC: Maren Publications.

Cohen, S. (1972). *Folk Devils and Moral Panics.* London: MacGibbon & Kee.

Cohen, S. (2002). *Folk Devils and Moral Panics: The Creation of the Mods and Rockers* (3rd ed.). New York: Routledge.

CTV News. (2010, February 18). Lightfoot very much alive, despite reports of death. In Entertainment. CTV News: BellMedia. Retrieved August 3, 2011, from www.ctv.ca/CTVNews/Entertainment/20100218/gordon_lightfoot_100218

della Porta, D., & Diani, M. (2008). *Social Movements: An Introduction* (2nd ed.). Malden, MA: Blackwell Publishing.

Deloitte. (2004, September). *Impact of Delisting Chiropractic Services: Final Report Ontario Chiropractic Association.* Retrieved August 3, 2011, from www.chiropractic.on.ca/ecms.ashx/9bcc593e-6d4e-40a5-9277-92a6cf8c6a38/ResearchandReportsDocument/Deloitte_Report.pdf

Eaves, S. (2011, May 4). Alberta's biggest oil spill in 30 years is a call to action for Canadians. Blogs. *Notes from the Panther Lounge.* Vancouver, BC: David Suzuki Foundation. Retrieved August 3, 2011, from www.davidsuzuki.org/blogs/panther-lounge/2011/05/albertas-biggest-oil-spill-in-30-years-is-a-call-to-action-for-canadians

Edwards, B., & McCarthy, J. D. (2004). Resources and social movement mobilization. In D. A. Snow, S. A. Soule, & H. Kriesi (Eds.), *The Blackwell Companion to Social Movements.* Maden, MA: Blackwell Publishing, pp. 116–152.

Emkiro Health Services. (2011). Chiropractic health care. Retrieved February 16, 2011, from www.emkiro.ca/torontochiropractic.html

Erikson, K. (1994). *A New Species of Trouble: The Human Experience of Modern Disasters.* New York: W. W. Norton & Company.

Erikson, K. (1976). *Everything in Its Path: Destruction of Community in the Buffalo Creek Flood.* New York: Simon & Schuster Paperbacks.

Festinger, L., Pepitone, A., & Newcomb, T. (1952). Some consequences of deindividuation in a group. *Journal of Abnormal and Social Psychology, 47,* 382–389.

Fleeman, M. (2010, June 28). Sandra Bullock and Jesse James finalize divorce. People.com News: *People.* Retrieved August 3, 2011, from www.people.com/people/package/article/0,20364464_20397673,00.html

Gamson, W. (1991). Commitment and agency in social movements. *Sociological Forum, 6,* 27–50.

Goode, E. & Ben-Yehuda, N. (2009). *Moral Panics: The Social Construction of Deviance* (2nd ed.). West Sussex, UK: Wiley-Blackwell.

Goode, E., (1992). *Collective Behavior.* Orlando, FL: Harcourt Brace Jovanovich.

Hier, S. P. (2002). Raves, risks and the ecstasy panic: A case study in the subversive nature of moral regulation. *Canadian Journal of Sociology, 27(1),* 33–57.

Hunt, S. A., & Benford, R. D. (2010). In D. A. Snow, S. A. Soule, & H. Kriesi (Eds.), *The Blackwell Companion to Social Movements.* Malden, MA: Blackwell Publishing, pp. 433–457.

Laeeque, H., & Boon, H., (2004). Print media coverage on the Lana Dale Lewis inquest verdict: Exaggerated claims or accurate reporting? *Health Law Review,* 13(1): 7–26.

Landry, F. (2011, February 7). Hero survivor recalls brutal Hinton train crash that killed 23. In *News: Alberta. Edmontonsun.com.* Retrieved August 3, 2011, from www.edmontonsun.com/news/alberta/2011/02/07/17184211.html

Le Bon, G. (1895/2006). *The Crowd: A Study of the Popular Mind.* New York: Cosimo Classics.

Lepisto, C. (2009, October 21). 8 worst man-made environmental disasters of all time. In *Travel and Nature: Treehugger.* Retrieved August 3, 2011, from www.treehugger.com/files/2009/10/8-worst-man-made-environmental-disasters.php#

Madenski, H. (2010, January 12). CWG's 10 worst fads of the decade. CWGMAGAZINE.COM. Retrieved August 3, 2011, from www.cwgmagazine.com/features/2010/01/cwgs-10-worst-fads-of-the-decade

McAdam, D. (1982). *The Political Process and the Development of Black Insurgency.* Chicago, IL: University of Chicago Press.

McCarthy, J. D., & Zald, M. N. (1973). *The Trend of Social Movements in America: Professionalism and Resource Mobilization.* Morristown, NJ: General Learning.

McPhail, C. (1991). *The Myth of the Madding Crowd.* New York: Aldine de Gruyter.

Miller, D. L. (2000). *Introduction to Collective Behavior and Collective Action* (2nd ed.). Prospect Heights, IL: Waveland Publishing.

Natural Resources Canada. (2009). The Atlas of Canada: Natural Hazards. *Government of Canada.* Ottawa, ON: Natural Resources Canada. Retrieved August 3, 2011, from www.atlas.nrcan.gc.ca/auth/english/maps/environment/naturalhazards/#naturalhazards1999

Noland, D. (2011). 10 plane crashes that changed aviation. *Popular Mechanics.* Retrieved August 3, 2011, from www.popularmechanics.com/technology/aviation/crashes/4221138

Nurwisah, R. (2010, February 18). Gordon Lightfoot death rumours sparked by internet hoax. *National Post.*

Retrieved August 3, 2011, from www.network.nationalpost.com/np/blogs/theampersand/archive/2010/02/18/singer-gordon-lightfoot-alive-despite-internet-hoax.aspx

Smelser, N. J. (1962). *Theory of Collective Behavior.* New York: The Free Press.

Snow, D. A., (2001). Collective identity and expressive forms. In N. J. Smelser & P. B. Baltes (Eds.), *International Encyclopedia of the Social and Behavioral Sciences* (pp. 196–254). London, UK: Elsevier Science.

Social Watch. (2010, October 21). A call to social movements around the world to protest the G20 Summit in Seoul. Retrieved August 3, 2011, from www.socialwatch.org/node/12269

Staggenborg, S. (2008). *Social Movements.* Toronto, ON: Oxford University Press.

Staggenborg, S. (1998). *Gender, family, and social movements.* Thousand Oaks, CA: Pine Forge Press.

Stokes Sullivan, D. (2010, October 2). The forgotten storm. *The Telegram.* Retrieved August 3, 2011, from www.thetelegram.com/News/Local/2010-10-02/article-1815597/The-forgotten-storm/2

Swain, H. (2010). *Oka.* Vancouver, BC: Douglas & McIntyre.

Tarrow, S. (1998). *Power in Movement: Social Movements and Contentious Politics* (2nd ed.). Cambridge, UK: Cambridge University Press.

Tilly, C., & Tarrow, S. (2006). *Contentious Politics.* Boulder, CO: Paradigm Publishers.

Turner, R. H., & Killian, L. M. (1987). *Collective Behavior* (3rd ed.). Englewood Cliffs, NJ: Prentice-Hall.

University of Toronto. (2011). G20 Information Centre. University of Toronto: University of Toronto Library and the G20 Research Group at the University of Toronto. Retrieved August 11, 2011, from www.g20.utoronto.ca

Valverde, M. (1991). *The Age of Light, Soap, and Water: Moral Reform in English Canada, 1885–1925.* Toronto, ON: McClelland & Stewart.

Villanueva-Russell, Y. (2009). Chiropractors as folk devils: Published and unpublished news coverage of a moral panic. *Deviant Behavior, 30,* 175–200.

Zajdow, G. (2008). Moral panics: The old and the new. *Deviant Behavior, 29,* 640–664.

ENDNOTES

1. Opening quotation retrieved August 2, 2011, from www.quotationspage.com/quote/33522.html.
2. This is described in detail as Exercise 20.3: The Rumour Process in Action in the *Guide to Classroom Engagement* to accompany Jane Lothian Murray, Rick Linden, and Diana Kendall's (2011) *Sociology in Our Times,* (5th Canadian Edition), prepared by Diane G. Symbaluk.
3. In Aberle's (1966) original classification of social movements, revolutionary movements were called "transformative" movements, degree of change was discussed as "amount of change," and the intended recipient was referred to as the "locus of change" wherein the recipient could be an individual or "supra-individual," including a social institution such as the economy or political order as well as society as a whole.

"Going Green": Environmental Sociology

LEARNING OBJECTIVES AND OUTCOMES

After completing this chapter, students should be able to do the following:

LO1 Explain how social factors pose environmental challenges.

LO2 Provide an overview of the growing awareness of environmental issues.

LO3 Explain how human exemptionalism, the new ecological paradigm, functionalist, and critical approaches further our understanding of environmental issues.

LO4 Demonstrate an understanding of strategies for making better environmental choices.

> *When we tug at a single thing in nature, we find it attached to the rest of the world.*
>
> *(John Muir)*[1]

When you think of economic prosperity, what comes to mind? Are you able to readily conjure up items you could buy or activities you could do while "living the good life", such as purchasing a nice home complete with a multitude of electronic devices and a few new vehicles or travelling to exotic places for holidays? Indeed, very few of us think of the downside of economic prosperity in terms of fossil fuel consumption, the excessive use of water, the creation of pollution, or waste disposal. Until fairly recently, sociologists largely viewed economic prosperity and technological advancement as societal development toward improved standards of living, better health, higher educational attainment, more global business opportunities, and greater social mobility as opposed to a progression with negative lasting implications for the environment in the form of resource depletion, degradation, and eventual climate change. However, early environmentalists (i.e., naturalists) such as John Muir, who is responsible for the opening quotation, understood our connectedness with nature and advocated for environmental protection long before the formalization of environmental sociology.

Today, *environmental sociologists* study the interrelationships between societal issues and environmental concerns including the impact of the behaviour of individuals, groups, and organizations on the environment as contributors to problems in the form of environmental waste and destruction as well as enablers of solutions such as sustainable development. In this chapter, we explore some of the social factors that pose environmental challenges, examine global environmental issues, look at the social construction of environmental issues, and discuss strategies for making better environmental choices.

LO¹ SOCIAL FACTORS POSING ENVIRONMENTAL CHALLENGES

HUMAN OVERPOPULATION

Social factors begin with people. According to United Nations demographers, more than 9 billion are expected to inhabit Earth by 2045 (Kunzig, 2011). These figures beg a central question that scientists, theorists, and sociologists who study changes that affect human populations (i.e., **demographers**) are now trying to answer: *Exactly how many people can Earth sustain?* The notion of an ecological footprint was developed as one measure for gauging human impact on Earth's ability to regenerate. An **ecological footprint** "estimates how much land and water area a human population requires to produce the resources it consumes and to absorb its wastes, using prevailing technology" (Global Footprint Network, 2011).

Demography: The study of human populations.

Ecological footprint: An estimate for gauging how much land and water area a human population requires to produce the resources it consumes and to absorb its wastes, using prevailing technology.

ENVIRONMENT CANADA

Environment Canada was established in 1971 as a federal government department dedicated to environmental enhancement, preservation, conservation, and protection. Much of Environment Canada's budget is allocated to science and technology (e.g., research institutes, climate monitoring networks, weather offices, water survey offices) in an effort to improve our understanding of ecosystems (e.g., wetland, forests, the Arctic) and various forms of risk assessment (e.g., changes in air quality, weather hazards). You can learn more about Environment Canada's mandate and the services it offers by visiting the home page www.ec.gc.ca

---

According to the Global Footprint Network (2011), the ecological footprint for humanity is 1.5 planets. That is, it takes Earth a year and half to regenerate for each year of human use. Consumption and waste are greatest in the United States (although Canadian consumption is likewise not "eco-friendly"). If all people on Earth lived similarly to those in the United States, we would need five planets to support them (Global Footprint Network, 2011); under these conditions, Earth could sustain a maximum of two billion people (Robbins, Hintz & Moore, 2010). Earth's ability to provide resources is finite and therefore the need to stabilize Earth's population and change how people use its resources is a global call to action.

Early demographer and political economist Thomas Robert Malthus (1766–1834) wrote about factors that limit population overgrowth (e.g., widespread diseases and famines due to drought) in *An Essay on the Principles of Population*. Malthus (1798/1998) predicted that in the absence of certain "population checks," exponential population growth would soon exceed Earth's capacity to sustain it in terms of the available food supply. **Population checks** refer to factors that help to limit population growth such as events that lead to deaths including war or disease as well as factors that prevent births such as the postponement of child-bearing or birth control.

The world's population, however, did not grow beyond its **human carrying capacity** (i.e., the number of people that can be supported in a given area indefinitely) in Malthus's lifetime or even in more modern times, largely as a result of technological advancements applied to agriculture that led to increased food production. Hence, while global populations continued to increase exponentially, food supplies also increased and they did so at a rate that far exceeded early Malthusian arithmetic calculations; for example, wheat production in India tripled between 1965 and 1980 (Robbins, Hintz & Moore, 2010). Nonetheless, academics and scientists today continue to be deeply concerned about sustained population growth and its effect on the environment, particularly in countries that have the greatest proportion of the world's inhabitants (e.g., China, India, and the United States) and those with higher growth rates relative to the rest of the world (i.e., Africa and Asia).

FACTORS THAT CONTRIBUTE TO POPULATION GROWTH

Fertility, mortality, and *migration* are the three main factors that largely account for a country's population growth. **Fertility** refers to the actual level of childbearing for an individual or a population (Murray, Linden & Kendall, 2011, p. 526). Fertility is most affected by the number of females of childbearing age (i.e., 15–45) and it is generally measured by a country's *total fertility rate, crude birth rate*, or *infant mortality rate*. The **total fertility rate** is an estimate of the number of live births a female can be expected to have in her lifetime based on current age-specific rates (Statistics Canada, 2009). Canada's total fertility rate for 2007 was 1.7 (Statistics Canada, 2009) and was estimated at 1.6 for 2010

Population checks: Factors that limit population growth.

Human carrying capacity: The number of people that can be supported in a given area indefinitely.

Fertility: The actual level of childbearing for an individual or a population.

Total fertility rate: The number of live births a female can be expected to have in her lifetime.

(*CIA World Factbook*, 2011a). This is quite low and it indicates that women of childbearing ages today are having few children. The **crude birth rate** is the actual number of live births in a given year per 1,000 people. Canada's crude birth rate was 11.2 in 2007 (Statistics Canada, 2009) and estimated to be 10.3 for 2010 (*CIA World Factbook*, 2011a). The crude birth rate reflects the proportion of women in childbearing years relative to the rest of the population. In Canada there are fewer women in their childbearing years relative to older age groups (i.e., Canada has an aging population as discussed in Chapter 11). Comparatively, the estimated crude birth rate for South Africa was almost double, at 19.61. In South Africa roughly one-third of the population is 14 years of age and under (compared to only 16 percent in Canada) and life expectancy is a mere 50 years (relative to 81 in Canada) (*CIA World Factbook*, 2011b).

Mortality is the incidence of death in a given population and it is influenced by factors that promote longevity (e.g., access to clean water, proper nutrition, and health care) as well as factors that can reduce life expectancy (e.g., diseases such as AIDS or widespread unrest as in the case of civil war). Mortality is measured by the **crude death rate**, indicating the number of deaths in a given year per 1,000 people, or by the **infant mortality rate**, which is specific to the number of deaths of infants under one year of age. The infant mortality rate best illustrates a country's level of economic and social development in inverse relation to factors such as health care, education, and proper sanitation; countries that have high infant mortality rates have correspondingly low economic and social development. Canada's estimated crude death and infant mortality rates for 2010 were low at 7.87 and 4.99 (*CIA World Factbook*, 2011a) compared to 16.99 and 43.78 for South Africa (*CIA World Factbook*, 2011b).

In addition to fertility and mortality, population growth can be greatly affected by **migration** or the movement of people into or out of a country via immigration or emigration, respectively. Historically, migration was a useful means for locating and inhabiting new environmental resources. Although there are no remaining or few potentially habitable new places left on Earth, immigration policies and practices continue to impact population growth as people move between existing countries (e.g., one of the largest concentrations of movement is from Mexico into the United States). Canada is known for actively encouraging legal immigration as a means for stimulating the economy in order to offset the potential negative implications of *low population growth rate*.

Specifically, immigrants from the *economic category* (i.e., those best able to contribute to the economy based on their high level of existing financial resources, or existing educational and occupational qualifications/skills) are given preference and priority in an effort to sustain economic productivity (as explained in Chapter 8). Canada needs individuals in the workforce in order to pay for social programs developed largely for those outside the workforce including the aging group drawing from pension plans. This is one of the main reasons Canada currently has an excess of persons entering the country relative to those leaving as measured by the estimated **net migration rate** of 5.64 for 2010 (*CIA World Factbook*, 2011a).

INDUSTRIALIZATION

Early demographers (e.g., Notestein, 1945; Landry, 1934) introduced the notion of a demographic transition that later became known as **demographic transition theory** (or the demographic transition model of development). Demographic transition theory explains changes in populations as countries progress from premodern societies with high birth and death rates to modern ones characterized by low birth and death rates (Kirk, 1996) as shown in Figure 13.1 (page 284).

Largely due to the Industrial Revolution (which began in Europe in the late 1700s, subsequently spread to North America in the 1800s, and is still evolving throughout the world today), countries experienced tremendous economic growth and innovation in various sectors (e.g., textile manufacturing, iron production, steam power). These innovations eventually led to other massive societal changes (e.g., the growth of cities, the development of an industrial workforce,

Crude birth rate: The number of live births in a given year per 1,000 people.

Crude death rate: The number of deaths in a given year per 1,000 people.

Infant mortality rate: The incidence of deaths among infants under one year of age per 1,000 live births in a given population.

Migration: The movement of people into or out of a country.

Net migration rate: The difference between the number of persons entering and leaving a country during a specified year per 1,000 people.

Demographic transition theory: As a result of modernization, societies eventually progress from being characterized by high fertility and mortality rates to being characterized by low fertility and mortality rates.

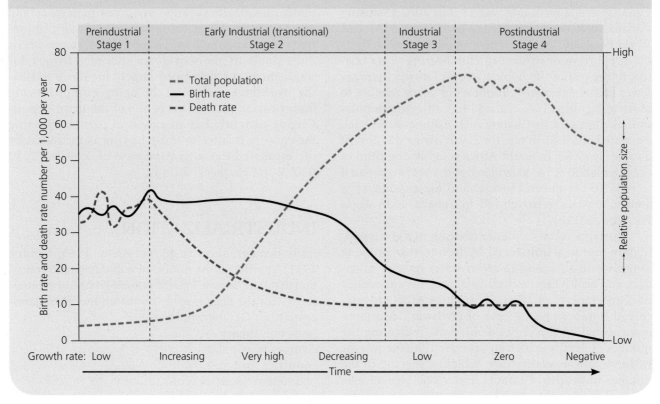

FIGURE 13.1

The Demographic Transition Model of Development

Source: From DRAPER/REED. *Our Environment*, 4E. © 2009 Nelson Education Ltd. Reproduced by permission. www.cengage.com/permissions

the reliance on child labour, and the accumulation of capital), which furthered economic development cycles (e.g., the introduction of new industries such as steel and petroleum) and spawned subsequent changes in cultural values and practices (e.g., health care, family planning). Although specific examples of economic growth and social development vary considerably from country to country, fertility and mortality trends and patterns are strikingly similar as described by demographic transition theory.

That is, in Stage 1 of demographic transition, we can locate *preindustrial societies* (i.e., those with entirely agricultural-based economies) where fertility rates are high in order to offset correspondingly high infant mortality rates. High birth rates also reflect a lack of family planning (e.g., the absence of contraception) in conjunction with a need to supply labour for agricultural subsistence, a need to repopulate given low life expectancy, and a need to care for the elderly in the absence of social safety nets. Mortality is high

due to various factors such as inadequate health care, lack of sanitation, deficient education, and the occurrence of famine, drought, or disease. Stage 1, then, is characterized by high and highly fluctuating birth and death rates, resulting in very little overall population growth. All countries in existence today have progressed past this stage; however, there are still agriculture-based villages that exist within countries (e.g., Peru, Brazil). In addition, some preindustrial societies (e.g., early Polynesian societies settled on remote islands in the Pacific) collapsed altogether before reaching the second stage after a period of population growth that too quickly depleted the natural environment (Diamond, 2000), akin to a small-scale version of the fate described by Malthus.

Stage 2 includes societies characterized by *early industrialization*. Here, we can locate the onset of industrialization in the form of early technological advancements that improved the ability to cultivate crops (such as irrigation and water storage systems) and led to improved education and health care. Population growth continues with the introduction of more machines and the greater use of human-made innovations (e.g., fertilizers, pesticides) alongside the widespread extraction of resources (e.g., fossil fuels). Early industrialization is the essence of transition since it is the stage wherein the most population growth occurs as a result of high birth rates alongside corresponding *lowered* death rates. Developing countries in Stage 2 can be found today in parts of East and Southeast Asia (e.g., Afghanistan, Bangladesh, Cambodia), and especially in Africa, which includes some of the countries with the highest overall growth rates in the world (e.g., Niger, Uganda, Burundi, Ethiopia, Zimbabwe, Rwanda, and Somalia). A few countries now have advanced economies (e.g., Mexico, Brazil, India, and Turkey) with modest birth rates that straddle the line between Stage 2 and Stage 3.

Stage 3 refers to *advanced (or mature) industrialization* and it corresponds to a *declining* birth rate coupled with the already lowered death rate, which produces only a slight increase in population growth (i.e., one that is substantially lower than in Stage 2). The birth rate declines as a result of people having fewer children, since most children now survive to adulthood and they are no longer considered economic assets (e.g., farm hands) as much of the industrial sector now consists of exported manufactured products as opposed to farming and the extraction of raw resources. With increased emphasis on higher education (e.g., credentialism) and economic productivity, family size becomes a planning consideration and it is influenced by new technologies (e.g., birth control in the form of oral contraceptives or voluntary sterilization). The birth rate may also decline as a function of other social changes including higher rates of female participation in the workplace, later age at first marriage, and later age at first childbirth. The death rate continues to decline in this stage largely due to various improvements in the standard of living and health care. A society in this advanced stage includes both industry and service-oriented work as a main means of subsistence (e.g., people are employed in areas such as information technology, manufacturing, and education). Some examples of Stage 3 countries include Canada, the United Kingdom, the United States, and Iceland.

Finally, Stage 4 refers to *a postindustrial economy* in which birth rates continue to decline in conjunction with stable low death rates largely attributed to higher socioeconomic status or wealth, health, education, and gender equality. This results in *near to zero* or even a declining population growth. Postindustrial societies tend to be more service based with much of the working population employed in areas such as finance, health care, or sales, as opposed to industry. Examples of countries that have completed a demographic transition through to Stage 4 include Italy, Germany, Greenland, Belgium, and Sweden.

URBAN SPRAWL

URBANIZATION

One of the logical progressions of population growth and economic development is urbanization. Human development in the form of *urbanization* requires the extensive use of land and other nonrenewable natural resources (e.g., energy sources) representing the principal human-made contributor to environmental issues in the form of resource depletion and pollution. As Grimm et al. (2008) put it: "beyond climate, land use—and its manifestation as land-cover change and pollution loading—is the major factor altering the structure, function, and dynamics of Earth's terrestrial and aquatic ecosystems" (p. 264).

More than 80 percent of Canada's population currently lives in an urban centre (Statistics Canada, 2010), with more than half of the entire population concentrated in one of four main urban regions encompassing Montreal, Quebec; British Columbia's Lower Mainland (i.e., Vancouver); an Edmonton/Calgary corridor in Alberta; and the Greater Golden Horseshoe in Southern Ontario (NRTEE, 2003). The Golden Horseshoe is the fastest growing urban area in Canada, comprising a group of cities in Southern Ontario that form a horseshoe shape around Toronto and house more than 7.5 million Canadians (Ontario Ministry of Infrastructure, 2006) (see Figure 13.2, page 286). Rapid growth of urban centres leads to the absorption of land and coastal ecosystems in a process known as **urban sprawl** wherein natural land is converted for human-made uses (i.e., residential, commercial, transportation). Urban centres and the area surrounding them becomes the primary hub for activities that contribute to global pollution from transportation, to industry, to waste disposal and power generation (Wali, Evrendilek & Fennessy, 2010).

Urban sprawl:
A process by which rapid urban growth necessitates the conversion of natural land for human-made uses.

FIGURE 13.2
Map of the Golden Horseshoe

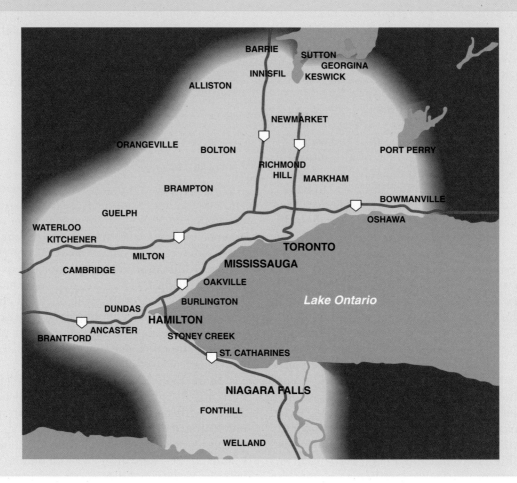

OVERCONSUMPTION OF RESOURCES

Consumption: The general use of natural resources.

Overconsumption: Use of resources at a rate that exceeds sustainability.

Sustainability: Use of natural resources at a rate on par with natural replenishment.

For countries that have reached advanced stages of industrial development, much of the population is concentrated in and around large urban centres wherein inhabitants exhibit excessively high levels of consumption, a phenomenon known as *overconsumption*. While **consumption** refers the general use of natural resources as people go about their daily lives, **overconsumption** refers to the use of resources at a rate that exceeds **sustainability** (i.e., the use of natural resources at a rate on par with natural replenishment). There are vast differences in rates of consumption between developed and developing countries. For example, the average North American consumes the equivalent of about 90 kilograms of resources per day eating, drinking, driving, and in relation to housing relative to the average African who consumes only about 10 kilograms per day (Sustainable Europe Research Institute, Austria and GLOBAL 2000 & Friends of Earth Europe, 2009). This means that North Americans correspondingly contribute considerably more to the emissions that produce air pollution and global climate change.

SOCIOLOGY *IN MY LIFE*

HOW BIG IS YOUR CARBON FOOTPRINT?

The notion of a **carbon footprint** was developed largely as a method for identifying and keeping track of behaviours that negatively impact the environment through greenhouse gas production. You can calculate your own carbon footprint using one of the calculators provided at various sites online (e.g., refer to www.carbonfootprint.com).

DISPOSABLE SOCIETIES

When was the last time you ordered "take-out" food? Did you purchase your last new cell phone because you lost the old one or it no longer worked, or did you simply decide one day to "upgrade" in order to keep up with the latest trend? Advanced industrial societies are distinguished by an overabundance of material culture particularly in the form of technologies (e.g., televisions, computers, cell phones) that are used for only a short period of time and then thrown away, contributing to the creation of what is best described as **disposable societies**. From electronics to food containers, plastic packaging, bags, and storage wrap alongside household cleaning and dusting products, hygiene products, razor blades, and baby products (e.g., diapers, bottle liners, food, and wipes), Canadians purchase items they use for only a short period of time and then throw them away. Try to imagine what you throw away in the garbage daily, weekly, monthly, or even on a yearly basis. The average amount of waste is 2.2 kilograms per day per person (EcoKids, 2011). Households account for 39 percent of the total solid waste with the remainder coming from industrial, commercial, and institutional sectors (Statistics Canada, 2005). On a yearly basis, Canada's solid waste adds up to about 34 million tonnes, most of which (76 percent) ends up as disposed garbage picked up by collection services and sent on to landfill sites (Statistics Canada, 2008).

GREENWASHING

Marketers have tried to mitigate the growing awareness of the need to reduce consumption via claims that products are "*environmentally friendly*" or "*organic*"—so you are enticed to continue to consume at your usual rate, guilt-free, by purchasing particular "green" brands. Environmentally friendly is generally taken to mean that a product or service was developed with minimal harm incurred by the environment, while organic usually means the item was produced without

> **Carbon footprint:** A method for identifying and keeping track of behaviours that negatively impact the environment through greenhouse gas production.
>
> **Disposable societies:** Societies characterized by an excess of manufactured products that are used for only a short period of time and then disposed of.

Landfill sites are heavily relied on for waste disposal.

Source: Huguette Roe/Shutterstock

TABLE 13.1
A Sample of Eco-Label Names

General Information Process			Certification or Labelling			
Eco-Label Name and Website	Year Founded	Product Categories	Lifecycle-based*	Third-Party Certified	Publicly Available Standard	Transparent Standard Development Process
Design for Environment (DfE) www.epa.gov/dfe	1992	Cleaning Products, Office Products	√			
EcoCert www.ecocert.com	2000	Organic Ingredients	Single-issue (organic certification)	√	√	√
EcoLogo www.ecologo.org	1988	Health and Beauty Products, Cleaning Products, Home Products, Office Products, Electronics, Building/Construction Products	√	√	√	√
Energy Star www.energystar.gov	1992	Home Products, Building and Construction Products, Electronics	Single-issue (energy efficiency)		√	√
EPEAT www.epeat.net	2005	Electronics	√		√	√
Forest Stewardship Council (FSC) www.fsc.org	1993	Wood and Paper Products	Single-issue (forest management)	√	√	√
Green Seal www.greenseal.org	1989	Cleaning Products, Office Products, Building/Construction Products	√	√	√	√
Greenguard www.greenguard.org	2001	Building/Construction Products, Home Products, Cleaning Products, Office Products	Single-issue (indoor air quality)	√	√	√
Sustainable Forestry Initiative (SFI) www.sfiprogram.org	1995	Wood and Paper products	Single-issue (forest management)	√	√	√
USDA Organic www.ams.usda.gov	2002	Organic Ingredients	Single-issue (organic certification)	√	√	√
WaterSense www.epa.gov/WaterSense	2006	Home Products, Building/Construction Products	Single-issue (saving water)	√	√	√

*Lifecycle-based eco-labels consider the environmental impacts from all phases of a product's life including the raw materials, the manufacturing process, the product itself, its distribution and use, and its ultimate disposal (or recycling/reuse).

Source: TerraChoice (2009). The Seven Sins of Greenwashing: Environmental Claims in Consumer Markets. Summary Report: North America April 2009. Ottawa, ON: TerraChoice Environmental Marketing Inc.

the aid of chemicals such as pesticides or hormones. An Ottawa-based environmental marketing firm found that while the number of "green" products in Canada and the United States nearly doubled from 2007 to 2008, the vast majority of products examined (i.e., 98 percent of the 2,739 items) failed to live up to their green claims, committing at least one of the "seven sins of greenwashing" (CBC News, 2010). **Greenwashing** refers to the "misleading of consumers regarding the environmental practices of a company or the environmental benefits of a product or service" (TerraChoice, 2009, p. 1).

The "seven sins of greenwashing" include the following:

1. **Sin of the Hidden Tradeoff**, committed by suggesting a product is "green" based on an unreasonably narrow set of attributes without attention to other important environmental issues. Paper, for example, is not necessarily environmentally preferable just because it comes from a sustainably harvested forest. Other important environmental issues in the paper-making process, including energy, greenhouse gas emissions, and water and air pollution, may be equally or more significant.

2. **Sin of No Proof**, committed by an environmental claim that cannot be substantiated by easily accessible supporting information or by a reliable third-party certification. Common examples are facial or toilet tissue products that claim various percentages of postconsumer recycled content without providing any evidence.

3. **Sin of Vagueness**, committed by every claim that is so poorly defined or broad that its real meaning is likely to be misunderstood by the consumer. "All-natural" is an example. Arsenic, uranium, mercury, and formaldehyde are all naturally occurring, and poisonous. "All natural" isn't necessarily "green."

4. **Sin of Irrelevance**, committed by making an environmental claim that may be truthful but is unimportant or unhelpful for consumers seeking environmentally preferable products. "CFC-free" is a common example, since it is a frequent claim despite the fact that CFCs are banned by law.

5. **Sin of Lesser of Two Evils**, committed by claims that may be true within the product category, but that risk distracting the consumer from the greater environmental impacts of the category as a whole. Organic cigarettes are an example of this category, as are fuel-efficient sport-utility vehicles.

6. **Sin of Fibbing**, the least frequent Sin, is committed by making environmental claims that are simply false. The most common examples were products falsely claiming to be Energy Star certified or registered.

7. **Sin of Worshipping False Labels** is committed by a product that, through either words or images, gives the impression of third-party endorsement where no such endorsement actually exists. *(TerraChoice, 2010, p. 10)**

The same firm conducted follow-up studies on products in 24 stores in North America in 2009 and 2010, and found that while green offerings substantially increased by 73 percent (to 4,744 products), misrepresentation of environmentally friendly practices had declined only slightly (i.e., 95 percent of the products still included some form of greenwashing), indicating a persistent use of greenwashing techniques. Interestingly, Rona, Canada's largest hardware distributor and retailer, was identified as a leader in legitimate green retailing (TerraChoice, 2010). To familiarize yourself with eco-labels that refer to good environmental products and practices, refer to Table 13.1.

TIME TO REVIEW

- What are the four main social contributors to environmental problems?
- What factors contribute most to population growth?
- How is mortality measured?
- What does the net migration rate refer to?
- Why is early industrialization considered to be the essence of transition?
- How does urban sprawl pose implications for the natural environment?
- What distinguishes overconsumption from regular consumption?
- What are some of the common forms that greenwashing takes?

LO² GROWING AWARENESS OF ENVIRONMENTAL ISSUES

Sociological interest in the environment can be largely traced to the 1960s and 1970s wherein it was starting to become evident that social and economic factors posed challenges for the natural environment. During this era, the focus of scientists, conservationists, and early environmental sociologists

Greenwashing: The misleading of consumers regarding the environmental practices of a company or the environmental benefits of a product or service.

---

*© The Sins of Greenwashing and Family Edition 2010: A Report on Environmental Claims Made in the North American Consumer Market. Ottawa, ON: TerraChoice Environmental Marketing Inc.

SOCIOLOGY *IN MY COMMUNITY*

WORLD WILDLIFE FUND CANADA

World Wildlife Fund Canada (WWF-Canada) is a conservationist organization working to protect wildlife and to promote the sustainable use of resources along with the reduction of waste. A founding *Conservation First Principle* is that "there should be no new or expanded large-scale industrial development in Canada until a network of protected areas is reserved which adequately represents the natural region(s) affected by that development" (WWF-Canada, 2011). In accordance with this principle, WWF-Canada assisted Aboriginal groups with proposals that eventually led to the suspension of some of the industrial activity in the Mackenzie River Basin area, enabling

local groups to come up with more permanent plans for establishing protected areas (WWF-Canada, 2011). The Mackenzie River Basin extends all the way from the Mackenzie and Rocky Mountains in the West to the Canadian Shield in the East and includes boreal forest, alpine, and arctic tundra. The Basin covers about 1.8 million square kilometres, comprising 20 percent of Canada's landmass, and it also includes 9 lakes of over 1,000 square kilometres (e.g., Great Bear Lake, NWT; Great Slave Lake, NWT; and Lake Athabasca, SK). (Mackenzie River Basin State of the Aquatic Ecosystem Report, 2003).

was largely on air and water pollution, waste management, improving urban spaces, and wildlife conservation (Dunlap, Michelson & Stalkers, 2002). The *Sierra Club* (a grassroots environmental organization founded by American conservationist John Muir) became active in Canada in 1963, an environmental group called *World Wildlife Fund Canada* was founded in 1967, and the first "*Earth Day*" was held on April 22, 1970 (in the United States but this event is now celebrated annually in more than 175 countries including Canada). *Greenpeace,* an international organization dedicated to increasing awareness of environmental issues through direct action and government lobbying, took its first anti-nuclear voyage from Vancouver in 1971 and the rise of modern environmentalism

continued with the establishment of the Canadian government's *Department of the Environment* and the *United Nations Environment Programme* in 1972.

THE FIRST WAVE OF ENVIRONMENTALISM

The first wave of environmentalism in the 1960s and 1970s highlighted negative implications of industrialization and population growth by bringing people's awareness and attention to various forms of pollution, resource depletion, and environmental disasters in the form of oil spills and energy shortages. Pesticides, for example, were originally developed to control organisms that interfere with agricultural pursuits. While some of the early forms were biodegradable (i.e., they contained compounds that would eventually break down), most of the more effective "second-generation" pesticides were nonbiodegradable and contained damaging toxic substances. Dichloro-diphenyl-trichloroethane (DDT) was one such chemical; it was originally constructed as a "miracle-compound: highly toxic to insects, virtually insoluble in water, and of low toxicity to mammals," but after many years of use wherein the adverse environmental and human risks became more readily apparent, it was reframed as one of the "dirty dozen" of "persistent organic pollutants." This refers to chemicals that stay "intact in the environment for long periods, become widely distributed geographically, accumulate in the fatty tissue of

The Mackenzie River Basin area.

living organisms, and are toxic to humans and wild-life" (Wali, Evrendilek & Fennessy, 2010, p. 245).

Parallel lessons were learned via the use of many highly convenient but ozone-depleting substances such as chlorofluorocarbons (CFCs), which are commonly associated with aerosol sprays (e.g., cooking spray, hair sprays, and cleaning products), but are also part of blowing agents for plastic foam packaging, and are most often used as cooling agents in refrigerators and air conditioners. Consider how many refrigerators there are in Canada alone! When CFCs are released into the air, as is the case when products containing them are disposed of, they can persist long enough to be broken down in a chemical reaction that contributes to ozone depletion (Draper, 1998).

Many of the early efforts directed at managing environmental issues (particularly air pollutants) were "band-aid solutions," focused mainly on technological innovations in the industry sector such as the creation of pumps rather than aerosol sprays or the addition of specialized filters on power plants and automobile engine modifications to reduce harmful chemical emissions. These supposed solutions actually created other environmental problems (e.g., the need to dispose of hazardous waste) or they failed to address the bigger issue of energy reform (i.e., the need to discontinue the use of CFC as a coolant, to construct fewer power plants, and to use fewer automobiles, particularly in urban areas). As a result, in more cases than not, increased production continues to override the benefits of emission-efficiency measures (Cheremisinoff, 1992).

THE SECOND WAVE OF ENVIRONMENTALISM

In the 1980s it became clear that human consumption and development (e.g., industries such as forestry, mining, fisheries, and transportation) contribute to new and potentially greater environmental threats in the form of ozone depletion, acid rain, and global warming. In 1985, an ozone "hole" was discovered in the Antarctic and representatives from various countries met at the Vienna *Convention for the Protection of the Ozone Layer* to collectively discuss research on ozone depletion as a worldwide environmental issue. Note that it wasn't a hole in the literal sense, but it was socially constructed as such when ozone depletion above the Antarctic turned out to be substantially greater than what was predicted by scientists. An international agreement was reached in 1987 called *The Montreal Protocol on Substances that Deplete the Ozone Layer,* which outlined the eventual phasing out of production of most of the known ozone-depleting compounds (e.g.,

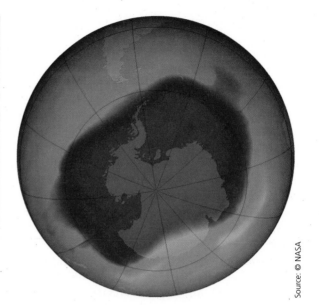

Source: © NASA

Image of the ozone hole in the Antarctic.

CFCs, halons, and methyl chloroform). The agreement was signed by 24 countries responsible for more than 80 percent of the world's consumption (Hernan, 2010; United Nations Environment Programme, 2000).

In addition to ozone concerns, scientists and environmentalists were also teaching the public about acid rain as a major contributor to air, land, and water pollution. **Acid rain** refers to the dilute sulphuric and nitric acids that, many believe, are created when fossil fuels (such as coal and oil) are burned in power stations, smelters, and motor vehicles, and which fall over areas long distances downwind of possible sources of pollutants (Park, 1992, p. 1). It was originally believed that pollutants would reach Earth's surface only if the acids mixed with water and hence, the term acid "rain"; however, they were later discovered in hail, snow, and even in dry forms such as dust. Increased acidity is damaging to aquatic systems (e.g., it is highly toxic to fish and other forms of biological life found in lakes); it affects soil, which, in turn, affects plant life; and it is deemed contributory to the degradation or death of forests. Acid rain also contributes to air pollution and accompanying health problems associated with the inhalation of acid aerosols and it reduces air quality more generally (The Acid Rain Report, 1989; Environment Canada, 1998; Houle, 2004; Kahan, 1986; Kahaner, 1988; Leaf, 1990; Raloff, 1988; Schindler, 1988).

Global warming (or climate change) refers to Earth's atmospheric heating and is often explained using

> **Acid rain:** The dilute sulphuric and nitric acids created when fossil fuels are burned.
>
> **Global warming:** An increase in the temperature of Earth's atmosphere.

an analogy to how warming occurs in a greenhouse. Similar to how a greenhouse traps warmer air inside it, air pollutants made up of airborne toxic chemicals such as carbon dioxide form a covering around Earth's surface, wherein heat becomes trapped. This is intensified by ozone depletion since solar energy (i.e., in the form of ultraviolet rays) now enters the atmosphere in even higher concentrations but is less readily transmitted back out (i.e., it is trapped by the pollution-based gases in the lower portion of the stratosphere). The end result is an increase in Earth's temperature and changes to long-term weather patterns.

It is important to note that climate change is not just a human-induced problem. Climate change is also a natural process that results from variations in global temperatures that would occur regardless of the actions of humans (e.g., as in the case of pollution caused by volcanic eruptions). Air pollution as caused by people in developed nations has actually been on the *decline* since 1970. Given the unpredictability, climate change could even conceivably amount to less than a 2.5-centimetre rise in sea level each century—akin to what has already been occurring as a function of Earth's "inherently chaotic" nature for centuries (Foss, 2009).

From the 1990s onward, it became apparent that dealing with environmental issues is paramount to the survival of all life forms as we became more knowledgeable about the scarcity of resources such as nonpolluted freshwater, the lasting effects of deforestation, overcultivation, soil degradation, and the loss of habitat. For example, although there are substantial water reserves on Earth, much of that water

SO... IS THE SEA RISING OR IS THE ICE MELTING?

Source: © Foyle, Lindsay, lfon264, Cartoonstock.com

is salt water from oceans, while less than 3 percent by volume is actually freshwater (Wali, Evrendilek & Fennessy, 2010). Not only is the availability of water for agricultural pursuits an impending threat, but also access to safe drinking water will be an even greater issue for at least two-thirds of the population by 2025 given the current trends in population growth, urbanization, and consumption (United Nations, 2009).

In addition, the endless search for energy sources and the accompanying extraction and processing of minerals has led to competition and even war within and between countries for nonrenewable resources. Not only are there implications for the environment in terms of depletion and degradation, but also these

SOCIOLOGY *IN PRACTICE*

INTERGOVERNMENTAL PANEL ON CLIMATE CHANGE

The Intergovernmental Panel on Climate Change (IPCC) was established by the United Nations Environment Programme and the World Meteorological Organization as a collective and consensus-reaching scientific body for assessing human-induced climate change. The IPCC (2007) concludes that "warming of the climate is unequivocal, as is now evident from observations of increases in global average air and ocean temperatures, widespread melting of snow and ice and rising global average sea level." Increases in carbon dioxide concentrations are largely attributed to fossil fuel use and land use change, while methane and nitrous oxide buildup is primarily the result of agriculture. The IPCC (2007) notes that global warming is most apparent over the last 50 years, it has negatively impacted ecological systems, and in the absence of mitigating factors it will continue to do so. Some of the especially salient negative implications include an increased risk of extinction among certain plant and animal species, and an increased vulnerability of many regions to extreme weather conditions such as heat waves and floods.

practices are especially problematic for their waste production (i.e., atmospheric pollution and toxic waste) (Wali, Evrendilek, & Fennessy, 2010). The shortage of crude oil, for example, has led to the search for alternate energy sources. One leading alternate form of oil today comes from Alberta, in the form of a substance called *bituminous sands,* more often referred to as "tar sands" due to the resemblance in appearance to tar-covered sand or dirty oil containing substances such as sand, clay, and water. While extraction of bituminous sands help to replete a scarce energy form, the process needed to extract the oil is much more energy damaging in the form of greenhouse gas emission than conventional oil extraction.

Even greater dangers have resulted from oil spills, leaks, and the disposal of the ensuing hazardous wastes in water ecosystems, creating the need to study what theorists call "risk societies" and the potential for "mega-hazards"—in the form of disasters that are the end result of human actions. The term **environmental refugee** (sometimes called *climate refugee*) is now widely used to describe the forced migration and environmental displacement that results from life-endangering natural and human-made environmental change (Boano, Zetter, & Morris, 2008). The label applies as readily to survivors of Hurricane Katrina as to those affected by exposure to industrial disasters including the Bhopal pesticide leak in India in 1984 or the Chernobyl nuclear explosion in Ukraine in 1986.

TIME TO REVIEW

- What issues were focal concerns of the first wave of environmentalists?
- What issues and concerns distinguish the second wave of environmentalism from the first?

 ## LO³ SOCIOLOGY IN THEORY

ENVIRONMENTAL SOCIOLOGY

Unlike other areas of sociological inquiry, environmental sociology as a subdiscipline of sociology tends to be more empirical than theory driven. This is in part because environmental sociology originated as an approach to the study of environmental issues, rather than one focused on the interrelationships between society and the natural environment (Dunlap & Catton, 1979). Hence, classical origins centre on topics such as population growth, urbanization, and

capitalist expansion. For example, Karl Marx emphasized the economy as a driving force for productivity, Herbert Spencer spoke of consumption in terms of survival of the fittest, and human ecology perspectives (e.g., Park and Burgess) depicted the growth of cities (Buttel & Humphrey, 2002).

HUMAN EXEMPTIONALISM AND THE NEW ECOLOGICAL PARADIGM

Early environmental sociologists pointed out how theoretical debate is lacking because the physical environment is largely viewed as separate and distinct from that of human society. In some cases, the impact of society on the natural environment is taken to be "inconsequential" (Petty et al., 2007). Furthermore, as William R. Catton and Riley Dunlap (1978) claimed, most early sociological theories tend to be human centred, or based in **anthropocentrism**— a view of the world that places humans above all other forms of life in terms of overall value or importance. This framing notion is best captured by what Catton and Dunlap (1978) coined the *Human Exceptionalism Paradigm* or what is now more commonly called the **Human Exemptionalism Paradigm (HEP)**, which refers

> **Environmental refugee:** A person who is forced to flee his or her country as a result of environmental displacement resulting from life-endangering natural and human-made environmental change.
>
> **Anthropocentrism:** A world view that considers humans to be the most important form of life.
>
> **Human Exemptionalism Paradigm (HEP):** The view of human as unique from other organisms in the natural world because of their capacity to reason and develop culture.

"THERE'S NINETY-NINE ZILLION OF US, AND THEY THINK THEY'RE RUNNING THINGS."

Source: © Harris, S, shr0002, Cartoonstock

to the tendency to consider humans as unique from other organisms in the natural world because of their capacity to reason and develop culture.

In relation to environmental issues, HEP assumes that humans readily have the ability to overcome problems through technological innovation. Unfortunately, this kind of thinking perpetuates the propensity to believe that humans are somewhat beyond or exempt from environmental constraints. Even if we reject the assertion that we are independent from the natural environment, Williams (2007) argues that we persist in believing that we have features such as the ability to reason that make us "exceptional." In this case we still end up "taking the world for granted," assuming that we can always come up with technological solutions and that people will readily follow through on the necessary solutions; in reality, however, both assumptions probably amount to little more than wishful thinking. After all, you can appreciate various ways in which you are making a negative impact on the environment, but how willing are you to change and how much are you willing to forego indefinitely in order to preserve the environment for future generations?

Catton and Dunlap also identified a competing environmental paradigm that formed as a critique to the HEP and its early failure to study human–environmental interrelations, called the New Ecological Paradigm (Buttel & Humphrey, 2002). The **New Ecological Paradigm (NEP)** highlights the superior capacity of humans to reason and adapt to social/cultural conditions while also recognizing the interdependence between humans and the natural environment. This paradigm does not assume that technology can solve all problems, since it recognizes there is a feedback loop with nature wherein human actions can have unintended consequences and that the natural environment consists of limited resources (Catton & Dunlap, 1980).

Overall, the HEP paradigm is especially useful for identifying why environmental concerns were lacking in sociology (i.e., the focus was on humans as separate and distinct from the environment) while the NEP paradigm was instrumental in pointing out that the environment was left out by the classical theorists and that it was important to consider the interrelationships between society and the "finite" natural environment.

FUNCTIONALIST PERSPECTIVES: ECOLOGICAL MODERNIZATION

Functionalist approaches to the study of the environment emerged in the 1980s based on an assumption that industry, humans, and the environment can coexist

New Ecological Paradigm (NEP): The view of humans as possessing a superior capacity to reason and adapt to social/cultural conditions while also recognizing the interdependence between humans and the natural environment.

SOCIOLOGY *IN MY COMMUNITY*

DISCUSSING ENVIRONMENTAL ISSUES

Once a month, the Blue Mountain Trust Foundation and Elephant Thoughts host a documentary-based film series discussion event in Collingwood, Ontario, that enables community members to learn more about environmental and social justice issues (e.g., overfishing, overreliance on oil, and sustainability). Some of the recent documentaries shown are outstanding resources for environmental issues including the following:

- *Fuel* (2008) discusses implications of American overdependence on oil and potential solutions involving renewable forms of energy.

  Refer to: www.thefuelfilm.com

- *At the End of the Line* (2009) deals with the devastating effects of overfishing.

  Refer to: www.endoftheline.com

- *2012 Time for Change* (2010) focuses on how postindustrial society can be restructured away from materialism based on ecological principles.

  Refer to: www.2012timeforchange.com

- *Dirt! The Movie* (2010) teaches us about soil including its function in the regulation of Earth's climate.

  Refer to: www.dirtthemovie.org

provided everyone (e.g., politicians, industry management, environmentalists) works together to protect the environment for the collective good of society. This movement is collectively known as *ecological modernization* and it entails many of the global efforts toward greening practices including energy reforms, energy-efficiency regulations, sustainability efforts, the phasing out of hazardous chemicals, improved methods for dealing with waste, and new forms of environmental governance. For example, functionalists advocate for alternative and more efficient fuel sources such as the widespread use of solar and wind energy in developed countries and the use of bioenergy (burning plants and agricultural waste) in developing countries in order to help reduce oil and coal consumption.

CRITICAL PERSPECTIVES: THE TREADMILL OF PRODUCTION

While functionalists focus on the interconnectedness between people and the environment, and the need for everyone to work toward energy-efficient alternatives, critical theorists point out important ways in which societal and environmental dynamics differ. For example, American sociologist Schnaiberg (1980) notes, "whereas the ecosystem reaches a steady-state by permitting the growth of just enough species and populations to offset the surplus [energy], societies tend to use the surplus to *accumulate* still more surplus in future periods" (emphasis in original, p. 19). Schnaiberg describes the incessant need to increase production and profit as a **treadmill of production**. In accordance with a Marxist paradigm, the treadmill of production places the economy at the heart of decision making. However, Schnaiberg's (1980) model also identifies two environmental concerns that became apparent in the last half of the 20th century with the growth of modern factories. Specifically:

1. *High extraction of natural resources.* Modern factories required substantial capital that was invested in machinery which largely replaced workers and necessitated the use of greater and greater amounts of raw materials such as land (i.e., *resource depletion*).
2. *High accumulation of waste.* Modern factories utilize "energy/chemical intensive technologies to transform raw materials into finished products" en masse, contributing to the creation of more and *more pollution and waste* (Schnaiberg, Pellow & Weinberg, 2002, p. 2).

In addition to highlighting the ways in which productivity extracts from the natural environment and contributes to its demise, Gould, Pellow, and Schnaiberg (2008) identify five shared pillars of modern industry: economic expansion; increased consumption; a propensity to solve social and ecological problems by speeding up the treadmill; economic expansion via large firms; and alliances among capital, labour, and governments. The pillars help us better understand the changing relationship between capitalists, workers, and the state and, in part, explain why environmental issues get constructed as "proeconomic" measures that are readily condoned by capitalists, individuals, and the state. For example, in addition to the benefits incurred by capitalists, workers perceive that economic expansion will benefit them through enhanced employment opportunities that could even help to reduce poverty, while governments perceive they will gain tax revenues that will exceed investment expenditures and can be redistributed into education or housing.

Foster, Clark, and York (2010) point out how "ironically, most analyses of the environmental problem today are concerned less with saving the planet or life or humanity than saving capitalism" (p. 7). Consequently, conflict theories now emphasize a treadmill of *accumulation* over one of production and view any inference of "sustainable capitalism" as a form of "ecological denial" since capitalism necessitates greater and greater economic expansion, which corresponds to ever-increasing amounts of worker exploitation and environmental degradation irrespective of efforts to manage this (Foster, Clark & York, 2010). Given the speed at which irreversible climate changes are occurring, modern conflict theorists suggest that the only remaining solution is an ecological revolution, wherein capitalism is replaced with socialism (Foster, Clark & York, 2010; Foster, 2009).

Environmental issues are not equally created, experienced, or dealt with. It is becoming overwhelmingly apparent that those who have the least amount of resources (e.g., the poor, minority groups) are most likely to suffer the greatest negative environmental impacts (i.e., exposure to environmental hazards). *Ecofeminism* is a social movement based in the common linkage of women and nature (i.e., oppression against women and the domination of nature). Patriarchal society from this perspective is viewed as resting on four main pillars of injustice: racism, sexism, class exploitation, and environmental destruction (Davis, 1988; Harris, 2011; Plant, 1989). *Environmental justice* is a movement aimed at environmental security or the equitable treatment of all people in relation to environmental impacts. This is

Treadmill of production model: A theoretical model that explains environmental issues as resulting from an incessant need to increase production and profit.

SOCIOLOGY *ON SCREEN*

TIPPING POINT: THE AGE OF THE OIL SANDS

Tipping Point: The Age of the Oil Sands (2011), directed by Tom Radford and Niobe Thompson of Clearwater Media in association with CBC-TV, aired on CBC News Network in January 2011. The film describes the early health and environmental concerns of residents of Fort Chipewyan regarding high rates of rare forms of cancer and suspected pollution in the Athabasca River. The documentary highlights the struggle for environmental justice as government and industry officials maintain that the oil sands do not contribute to pollution. The "tipping point" is a culmination of media attention involving James Cameron, who recently visited the tar sands and met with the Premier of Alberta to express his concerns alongside of new research confirming the presence of toxic pollution. The sponsor-paid congratulatory message to James Cameron shown in the ad below was used to further awareness of the environmental issues posed by the tar sands.

primarily an effort on behalf of activists to expose environmental issues as abuses disproportionately incurred by the disadvantaged and to advocate for better environmental policies and regulations that include representation by those most affected.

In Canada, environmental justice spans a range of current issues involving land claims, health risks, and environmental politics (e.g., Agyeman et al., 2009). A recent study by University of Alberta biologists and ecologists concluded that "contrary to claims made by industry and government in the popular press" the oil sands project is responsible for 13 toxic elements currently polluting the Athabasca River, all of which are deemed "priority pollutants" that warrant federal government follow-up (Dearing, 2010). The Athabasca River provides a primary food source to many Aboriginal peoples (e.g., those living in Fort McKay and Fort Chipewyan). The Canadian Indigenous Tar Sands Campaign (CITSC) is an emerging movement that seeks to halt further tar sands expansion (Indigenous Environmental Network, 2011).

Source: Corporate Ethics International

TIME TO REVIEW

- Why were environmental concerns largely ignored by early sociologists?
- What is the main assumption of the human exemptionalism paradigm?
- How does the new ecological paradigm differ from the human exemptionalism paradigm?
- Why might a functionalist perspective believe that sustainable development is a foreseeable possibility in advanced societies?
- What two postindustrial changes are emphasized by the treadmill of production model?
- What does ecofeminism consider to be the pillars of patriarchal society?
- What does environmental justice refer to?

LO⁴ STRATEGIES FOR BETTER ENVIRONMENTAL CHOICES

LIVING GREEN: CHANGING THE BEHAVIOUR OF INDIVIDUALS

While we are not advocating that you take extreme measures such as attaching yourself to a tree in order to save the forest, we hope you will consider modifying a few of your daily activities in order to reduce waste and pollution. The first step to living green is acknowledging behaviours that represent consumption (e.g., driving to school, purchasing coffee in a Styrofoam cup, buying snacks from a vending machine) and then enacting measures to change some of the unnecessary or particularly wasteful habits. Here are five suggestions for becoming "greener" at home:

1. *Conserve energy and water.* Turn off lights, computers, and the television when you leave a room. Don't stand in front of the fridge looking in with the door open! Take more showers than baths and consciously use less water by getting out of the shower sooner.

2. *Recycle and donate.* You can divert the majority of your garbage from reaching a landfill by sorting and recycling your trash into organics (i.e., compostable food items), recyclable materials (plastics, Styrofoam, glass), and waste. Pass on your clothes, furniture, and electronics. (There are numerous organizations and charities that will even come to your door to pick up various household items and used articles of clothing).

3. *Reduce the number of toxins found in your home*—but don't throw them out as they need to be disposed of as hazardous waste. Household cleaners (e.g., toilet bowl cleaners, oven cleaners, glass cleaners, and laundry detergents) can all be replaced with greener alternatives (i.e., products that are nontoxic and biodegradable).

4. *Reduce the number of paper and plastic products you use.* Send e-cards instead of Christmas cards, use reusable cloth rags instead of paper towels, use cloth bags when you purchase groceries, put food in reuseable containers, and don't print your essay until it is in its final form.

5. *Keep electronics longer or find ways to pass on electronics for reuse.* Resist the urge to upgrade your LCD TV to a plasma 3D. As O'Sullivan (2008) notes, very little electronic waste is recycled and disposal is problematic as television and computer monitors contain lead.

To help the environment farmer Mick converted his tractor to gas

SUSTAINABLE DEVELOPMENT: CHANGING PRACTICES IN GROUPS AND ORGANIZATIONS

The term **sustainable development** has been used for some time now, and is generally taken to mean development "which meets the needs and aspirations of the present generation without compromising the ability of future generations to meet their own needs" (World Commission on Environment and Development, 1987, p. 5). While this seems straightforward, if we consider more closely what "needs of the present" might entail and whose needs should take priority, competing interests render actual sustainability difficult to achieve. For example, economic objectives might centre on the need to produce efficient food supplies, social concerns might centre on the humane treatment of animals and reduced health risks to humans, and environmental concerns might centre on mitigating climate change. What this generally boils down to in the way of developing effective environmental policies and action plans is a determination of how much consideration should be given to current economic priorities versus various social and environmental concerns.

In addition, sustainable development can be achieved only once other factors and conditions are in put in place in the economy, in society, and in the environment. For example, a healthy economy has multiple buyers and sellers and the absence of corruption, and a healthy society has a base level of subsistence, protection, and participation alongside strong systems of health care and education, and a large middle class (i.e., little disparity between those with and those without resources). A healthy environment has

> **Sustainable development:** Development that meets the needs of the present without compromising the ability of future generations to meet their own needs.

a generous supply of contained fossil fuels, minerals, and other resources (i.e., not ones that are extracted and used to deplete Earth in greater and greater concentrations) (Hitchcock & Willard, 2009).

Assuming the necessary factors are in place to begin with or could feasibly be put into place, society as a whole needs to adopt sustainable practices everywhere—in homes, in schools, in government, and in business. In *The Business Guide to Sustainability*, Hitchcock and Willard (2009, pp. 21–22) show us what a sustainable pizza operation might entail:

- **Materials:** All your produce, pizza boxes, cleaning products, etc. came from sustainable/green/socially responsible sources. (You could buy organic tomatoes from farmers who provide good working conditions and wages for their migrant workers. Your pizza boxes could be made from 100 percent recycled paper or pulp from certified forests. Cleaning products would be environmentally benign.)
- **Energy:** All your energy for cooking, transportation and space heat came from renewable resources. (You could buy "green power'" from your utility and your delivery vehicles could run on biodiesel.)
- **Process:** Your cooking and other processes are as efficient as possible. (You could even use non-disposable tableware and capture the waste heat from your ovens.)
- **Product Design:** Your main product is biodegradable, even edible, so it is quite benign. (Do the ingredients come from local and sustainable or organic sources? You could vary the menu to take advantage of seasonal availability. What about the packaging? Could you invent a reusable pizza box?)
- **Waste:** All your waste products can either be reused, recycled, or composted. (You could choose biodegradable serving items, eliminating plastic drink covers or polystyrene cups.)
- **Industry influence:** You apply your leadership and buying power to drive the rest of the industry toward sustainability. (To have an adequate and affordable supply of organic produce, you might help set up a cooperative.)
- **Community contribution:** You have a program to help solve a pressing social problem that relates in some way to your business. You might work on migrant labour issues and/or hunger, for example. If you serve beer, then drunk driving might [be] an issue to address.*

---

*Copyright: © Hitchcock & Willard (2009). *The Business Guide to Sustainability: Practical Strategies and Tools for Organizations.* Sterling, VA: AXIS Performance Advisors, Inc. pp. 21–22.

Finally, sustainable development encompasses more than a consideration of what is important now along with a consideration of how green practices can be implemented in the future (e.g., use of biodegradable products and recycling). It also entails a look at how practices can be modified to correct for problems that have already occurred (e.g., waste cleanup) and necessitates a look *toward the future*. Increasingly, governments have developed regulatory controls for dealing with yesterday's waste and managing today's emissions but corporate and government initiatives that deal with future greening tend to be lacking (Hart, 1999). An example of this is evident in Canada in relation to the federal government's recent mandate to reduce energy by banning standard incandescent bulbs in favour of spiral-shaped ones by 2012. While the new bulbs are widely available, there is no plan or standard in place for future disposal of the energy-efficient but highly toxic (mercury-containing) bulbs, which cannot be thrown into the trash (CBC News, 2011).

A GLOBAL CALL TO ACTION: BRINGING EVERYONE ON BOARD

One Planet Living is a global campaign developed by the international organization World Wide Fund for Nature (WWF) (originally called the World Wildlife Fund and still recognized as such in Canada and the United Sates). The WWF's mission is to stop environmental degradation and help achieve sustainable growth through a commitment to the ten principles of One Planet Living including zero carbon, zero waste, sustainable transport, local and sustainable materials, local and sustainable food, sustainable water, the protection of natural habitats and wildlife, the protection of local cultural heritage, the promotion of equity and free trade, and the pursuit of increased health and happiness (WWF, 2011). Refer to Table 13.2 to see how global challenges align with One Planet Living principles, goals, and strategies.

Many communities, schools, and businesses have already taken the lead in pursuing global challenges. Toyota Motor Corporation, for example, achieved zero waste across all of its European manufacturing plants back in 2006 (Hitchcock & Willard, 2009). Carbon footprint–neutral programs exist in all of the offices that are part of the David Suzuki Foundation. Canadian zoologist David Suzuki is well known for his advocacy of nature and his willingness to challenge government and industry representatives about practices they support that pose environmental issues. Suzuki concludes "only by confronting the enormity and unsustainability of our impact on the biosphere will we take the search for alternative ways to live as seriously as we must" (2010, p. 3).

- What are some individual-level strategies that reflect better environmental choices?
- Why is sustainable development so difficult to achieve?

- What are global challenges and what sort of principles and strategies do they correspond to?

TABLE 13.2

Global Challenges Aligned with **One Planet Living** Principles, Goals, and Strategies

Global Challenge	OPL Principle	OPL Goal and Strategy
Climate change due to human-induced buildup of carbon dioxide (CO_2) in the atmosphere	Zero Carbon	*Achieve net CO_2 emissions of zero* Implement energy efficiency in buildings and infrastructure; supply energy from on-site renewable sources, topped up by new off-site renewable supply where necessary.
Waste from discarded products and packaging create a huge disposal challenge while squandering valuable resources	Zero Waste	*Eliminate waste flows to landfill and for incineration* Reduce waste generation through improved design; encourage reuse, recycling, and composting; generate energy from waste cleanly; eliminate the concept of waste as part of a resource-efficient society.
Travel by car and airplane can cause climate change, air and noise pollution, and congestion	Sustainable Transport	*Reduce reliance on private vehicles and achieve major reductions of CO_2 emissions from transport* Invest in transport systems and infrastructure that reduce dependence on fossil fuel use, e.g., by cars and airplanes. Neutralize carbon emissions from unavoidable air travel and car travel.
Destructive patterns of resource exploitation and use of non-local materials in construction and manufacturing increase environmental harm and reduce gains to the local economy	Local and Sustainable Materials	*Transform materials supply to the point where it has a net positive impact on the environment and local economy* Where possible, use local, reclaimed, renewable, and recycled materials in construction and products, which minimizes transport emissions, spurs investment in local natural resource stocks, and boosts the local economy.
Industrial agriculture produces food of uncertain quality and harms local ecosystems, while consumption of non-local food imposes high transport impacts	Local and Sustainable Food	*Transform food supply to the point where it has a net positive impact on the environment, local economy, and people's well-being* Support local and low-impact food production that provides healthy, quality food while boosting the local economy in an environmentally beneficial manner; promotes low-impact packaging, processing, and disposal; and benefits a low-impact diet.
Local supplies of freshwater are often insufficient to meet human needs due to pollution, disruption of hydrological cycles, and depletion of existing stocks	Sustainable Water	*Achieve a positive impact on local water resources and supply* Implement water-use efficiency measures, reuse, and recycling; minimize water extraction and pollution; foster sustainable water and sewage management in the landscape; restore natural water cycles.

(continued)

TABLE 13.2 *Continued*

Global Challenge	OPL Principle	OPL Goal and Strategy
Loss of biodiversity and habitats due to development in natural areas and overexploitation of natural resources	Natural Habitats and Wildlife	*Regenerate degraded environments and halt biodiversity loss* Protect or regenerate existing natural environments and the habitats they provide to fauna and flora; create new habitats.
Local cultural heritage is being lost throughout the world due to globalization, resulting in a loss of local identity and wisdom	Culture and Heritage	*Protect and build on local cultural heritage and diversity* Celebrate and revive cultural heritage and the sense of local and regional identity; choose structures and systems that build on this heritage; foster a new culture of sustainability.
Some in the industrialized world live in relative poverty, while many in the developing world cannot meet their basic needs from what they produce or sell	Equity and Fair Trade	*Ensure that a community's impact on other communities is positive* Promote equity and fair trading relationships to ensure a community has a beneficial impact on other communities both locally and globally, notably disadvantaged communities.
Rising wealth and greater health and happiness increasingly diverge, raising questions about the true basis of well-being and contentment	Health and Happiness	*Increase health and quality of life of community members and others* Promote healthy lifestyles and physical, mental, and spiritual well-being through well-designed structures and community engagement measures, as well as by delivering on social and environmental targets.

Source: World Wide Fund for Nature (WWF) (2011). The ten principles of one-planet living. http://wwf.panda.org/what_we_do/how_we_work/conservation/one_planet_living/about_opl/principles/

CHAPTER SUMMARY

LO1 Explain how social factors pose environmental challenges.

Human overpopulation, industrialization, urban sprawl, and overconsumption all result in practices (i.e., extraction of minerals, agricultural production, pollution) that deplete and degrade the natural environment (e.g., soil, air, water, wildlife, and fossil fuels).

LO2 Provide an overview of the growing awareness of environmental issues.

Since the early 1960s, scientists, naturalists, and sociologists have helped us better understand the interconnectedness of human actions and environmental concerns. The first wave of environmentalism highlighted the negative implications of industrialization (e.g., forms of pollution and the use of pesticides) while the second wave taught us more about ozone depletion, acid rain, and climate change. With increased competition and the extraction of scarce resources, we can continue to expect environmental degradation and the threat of even greater dangers associated with hazardous waste and accidents such as oil spills.

LO3 Explain how human exemptionalism, the new ecological paradigm, functionalist, and critical approaches further our understanding of environmental issues.

The human exemptionalism paradigm identifies the anthropocentrism of early sociology while the new ecological paradigm helps us realize the interdependence between humans and the natural environment. Functionalist approaches assume that pro-environmental changes will result from similar views regarding the need to make the world a better place while critical approaches maintain that divergent societal and environmental interests in the capitalist pursuit of profit will continue to pose ever-greater environmental threats.

LO⁴ Demonstrate an understanding of strategies for making better environmental choices.

Strategies for making better environmental choices at the level of individuals include practices that reflect greener living (e.g., conservation of energy and water), while strategies at a more macro level include efforts to achieve sustainable development and meet global challenges (e.g., to mitigate climate change, reduce waste, and preserve natural habitats and wildlife).

RECOMMENDED READINGS

1. For an in-depth look at disasters and the environmental lessons learned from them, we recommend: Nash, G. (2010). *This Borrowed Earth: Lessons from the Fifteen Worst Environmental Disasters Around the World.* New York, NY: Palgrave and Macmillan.
2. To learn more about the historical determinants of fertility and mortality and the historical underpinnings of demographic transition theory, we recommend: Kirk, D. (1996). Demographic transition theory. *Population Studies, 50,* 361–387.
3. For more information on the treadmill of production and how environmental costs are disproportionately borne by the poor refer to:

Gould, K., Pellow, D. N., & Schnaiberg, A. (2008). *The Treadmill of Production: Injustice and Unsustainability in the Global Economy.* Boulder, CO: Paradigm Publishers.
4. For information on population growth, we recommend this year-long special series: National Geographic Society. (2011). Chris Johns (Editor-in-Chief). *National Geographic Magazine.* Washington, DC: National Geographic Society.
5. As a practical guide to green practices for individuals, we recommend: Rogers, E., & Kostigen, T. M. (2007). *The Green Book: The Everyday Guide to Saving the Planet One Simple Step at a Time.* New York, NY: Three Rivers Press.

FOR FURTHER REFLECTION

1. Which is more important: Protecting the environment or feeding everyone who currently exists on Earth? Defend your answer.
2. Are environmental problems mainly the end result of population overgrowth or structural inequality? Explain your answer.

3. Is sustainable development achievable in postindustrial societies? Why or why not?

REFERENCES

(The) Acid Rain Report. (1989). *Congressional Digest, 68* (2), February, pp. 38–39.

Agyeman, J., Cole, P., Haluza-DeLay, R., & O-Riely, P. (Eds.). (2009). *Speaking for Ourselves: Environmental Justice in Canada.* Vancouver, BC: University of Columbia Press.

Boano, C., Zetter, R., & Morris, T. (2008). Environmentally displaced people: Understanding the linkages between environmental change, livelihoods and forced migration. *Forced Migration Policy Briefing.* Oxford, UK: Refugee Studies Centre.

Buttel, F. H., & Humphrey, C. R. (2002). Sociological theory and the natural environment. In R. E. Dunlap and W. Michelson (Eds.), *Handbook of Environmental Sociology.* Westport, CT: Greenwood Press, pp. 33–69.

Catton, Jr., W. R., & Dunlap, R. E. (1978). Environmental sociology: A new paradigm. *The American Sociologist, 13,* 41–49.

Catton, Jr., W. R. & Dunlap, R. E. (1980). A new ecological paradigm for post-exuberant sociology. *American Behavioral Scientist, 24,* 15–47.

CBC News. (2010, April 19). Charlene Chandler. Greenwashing meets disposable society. CBC News. Retrieved August 3, 2011, from www.cbc.ca/consumer/story/2010/04/17/f-earth-day.html

CBC News. (2011, February 3). Energy-saving regulations: How do you dispose of your old light bulbs? CBC News. Retrieved August 3, 2011, from www.cbc.ca/news/pointofview/2011/02/energy-saving-regulations-how-do-you-dispose-of-your-old-light-bulbs.html

Cheremisinoff, P. N. (1992). Emissions Control Options for Power Plants. In D. G. Marowski (Ed.), *Environmental Viewpoints: Selected Essays and Excerpts on Issues in Environmental Protection,* (pp. 43–49). Detroit, MI: Gale Research.

CIA World Fact Book. (2011a, January 12). North America: Canada. Central Intelligence Agency: The World Factbook. Washington, DC: Office of Public Affairs. Retrieved January 20, 2011, from https://www.cia.gov/library/publications/the-world-factbook/geos/ca.html

CIA World Fact Book. (2011b, January 12). Africa: South Africa. Central Intelligence Agency: The World Factbook. Washington, DC: Office of Public Affairs. Retrieved January 20, 2011, from https://www.cia.gov/library/publications/the-world-factbook/geos/sf.html

Davies, K. (1988). What is ecofeminism? *Women and Environments, 10* (Spring), pp. 4–6.

Dearing, S. (2010, August 31). Study finds Alberta's Athabasca River polluted by oil sands. In the Media. *Digital Journal.* Retrieved August 3, 2011, from www.digitaljournal.com/article/296829

Diamond, J. (2000). Ecological collapses of pre-industrial societies. The Tanner Lectures on Human Values. Lecture delivered at Stanford University, May 22–24, 2000. Downloaded on January 20, from www.tannerlectures.utah.edu/lectures/documents/Diamond_01.pdf

Draper, D. (1998). *Our Environment: A Canadian Perspective.* Scarborough, ON: ITP Nelson.

Dunlap, R. E., Michelson, W., & Stalkers, G. (2002). Environmental sociology: An introduction. In R. E. Dunlap and W. Michelson (Eds.), *Handbook of Environmental Sociology.* (pp. 1–32) Westport, CT: Greenwood Press.

Dunlap, R. E., & Catton, Jr., W. R. (1979). Environmental sociology. *Annual Review of Sociology, 5,* 243–273.

EcoKids. (2011). *About waste: How much do we produce?* Toronto: ON: Earth Day Canada. Retrieved August 3, 2011, from www.ecokids.ca/pub/eco_info/topics/waste/itsnotwaste/aboutwaste/how_much.cfm

Environment Canada. (1998). *1997 Canadian Acid Rain Assessment.* Vol. 4. The Effects on Canada's Forests. Prepared for the Canadian Council of Ministers of the Environment (CCME). Environment Canada: Atmospheric Environment Service.

Foss, J. E. (2009). *Beyond Environmentalism: A Philosophy of Nature.* Hoboken, NJ: John Wiley & Sons.

Foster, J. B. (2009). *The Ecological Revolution.* New York: Monthly Review Press.

Foster, J. B., Clark, B., & York, R. (2010). *The Ecological Rift: Capitalism's War on the Earth.* New York: Monthly Review Press.

Global Footprint Network. (2011). Footprint Basics—Overview. Oakland, CA: Global Footprint Network. Retrieved August 3, 2011, from www.footprintnetwork.org/en/index.php/GFN/page/footprint_basics_overview

Gould, K., Pellow, D. N., & Schnaiberg, A. (2008). *The Treadmill of Production: Injustice and Unsustainability in the Global Economy.* Boulder, CO: Paradigm Publishers.

Grimm, N. B., Foster, D., Groffman, P., Grove, J. M., Hopkinson, C. S., Nadelhoffer, K. J., Pataki, D. E., & Peters, D. P. C. (2008). The changing landscape: Ecosystem responses to urbanization and pollution across climatic and societal gradients. *Frontiers in Ecology and the Environment, 6*(5), 264–272.

Harris, A. (2011). "Ecofeminism." *The Green Fuse.* Retrieved August 14, 2011, from www.thegreenfuse.org/ecofem.htm

Hart, S. L. (1999). Business decision making about the environment: The Challenge of sustainability. In *Better Environmental Decisions: Strategies for Governments, Businesses, and Communities.* Washington, DC: Island Press, pp. 77–90.

Hernan, R. E. (2010). *This Borrowed Earth: Lessons from the Fifteen Worst Environmental Disasters around the World.* New York, NY: Palgrave Macmillan.

Hitchcock, D., & Willard, M. (2009). *The Business Guide to Sustainability: Practical Strategies and Tools for Organizations.* Sterling, VA: AXIS Performance Advisors.

Houle, D. (2004). Effects on forests and soils. In *2004 Canadian Acid Deposition Science Assessment,* (pp. 163–202). Downsview, ON: Environment Canada.

Indigenous Environmental Network. (2011). *Canadian Indigenous Tar Sands Campaign.* Bermidji, MN: Indigenous Environmental Office. Retrieved February 2, 2011, from www.ienearth.org/tarsands.html

Intergovernmental Panel on Climate Change (IPCC). (2007). *Climate Change 2007: Synthesis Report. Contribution of Working Groups I, II and III to the Fourth Assessment Report of the Intergovernmental Panel on Climate Change* Core Writing Team R. K. Pachauri and A. Reisinger (Eds.). Geneva, Switzerland: IPCC.

Kahan, A. M. (1986). *Acid Rain: Reign of Controversy.* Golden, CO: Fulcrum.

Kahaner, L. (1988). Something in the air: 'Creeping degradation' joins the list of threats to the nation's parks and forests. *Wilderness, 52* (183), pp 18–27.

Kirk, D. (1996). Demographic transition theory. *Population Studies, 50,* 361–387.

Kunzig, R. (2011, January). Population 7 billion. *National Geographic, January 2011.* Special Series: 7 Billion. Washington, DC: National Geographic Society. Retrieved August 3, 2011, from www.ngm.nationalgeographic.com/2011/01/seven-billion/kunzig-text.

Landry, A. (1934). *La Révolution Démographique.* Paris: Sirey.

Leaf, D. A. (1990). Acid rain and the clean air act. *Chemical Engineering Progress, 86* (5), 25–29.

Mackenzie River Basin State of the Ecosystem Report (2003). *Mackenzie River Basin State of the Ecosystem Report.* Ft. Smith, NT: Mackenzie River Basin Board. Retrieved February 2, 2011, from www.mrbb.ca/information/34/index.html

Malthus, T. (1798/1998). *An Essay on the Principles of Population.* London, UK: Printed for J. Johnson, in St. Paul's Church-Yard. Retrieved February 1, 2011, from www.esp.org/books/malthus/population/malthus.pdf

Murray, J. L., Linden, R., & Kendall, D. (2011). *Sociology in Our Times.* (5th Can ed). Toronto, ON: Nelson Education.

Notestein, F. (1945). Population: The long view. In Theodore W. Schultz (Ed.), *Food for the World,* (pp. 36–57). Chicago: University of Chicago Press.

NRTEE. (2003). *Environmental Quality in Canadian Cities: The Federal Role.* Ottawa, ON: National Round Table on the Environment and Economy.

Ontario Ministry of Infrastructure. (2006). *Places to Grow: A Guide to the Growth Plan for the Greater Golden Horseshoe, 2006.* Ottawa, ON: Queen's Printer for Ontario.

O'Sullivan, L. (2008, November 24). Environmental hazards of electronic waste: The negative environmental impact of E-waste disposal. *Waste Reduction.* Vancouver, BC: Suite 101.com Media Inc. Retrieved August 3, 2011, from www.suite101.com/content/environmental-hazards-of-electronic-waste-a80267

Park, C. C. (1992). The Acid Rain Debate. In D. G. Marowski (Ed.), *Environmental Viewpoints: Selected Essays and Excerpts on Issues in Environmental Protection* (pp. 1–4). Detroit, MI: Gale Research.

Plant, J. (1989). *Healing the Wounds: The Promise of Ecofeminism.* Philadelphia, PA: New Society.

Petty, J., Ball, A. S., Benton, T., Guivant, J. S., Lee., D. R., Orr, D., Pfeffer, M. J., & Ward, H. (2007). Introduction to environment and society. In J. Petty, A. S., Ball, T. Benton, J. S. Guivant, D. R. Lee, D. Orr, M. J. Pfeffer, and H. Ward (Eds.), *The Sage Handbook of Environment and Society.* (pp. 1–32). Thousand Oaks, CA: Sage Publication.

Raloff, J. (1988). New acid rain threat identified. *Science News, 133* (18), p. 275.

Robbins, P., Hintz, J., & Moore, S. A. (2010). *Environment and Society: A Critical Introduction.* West Sussex, UK: John Wiley & Sons.

Schindler, D. W. (1988). Effects of acid rain on freshwater ecosystems. *Science, 239* (4836), 149–157.

Schnaiberg, A., Pellow, D. N., & Weinberg, A. S. (2002). The treadmill of production and the environmental state. In A. P. J. Mol and F. H. Buttel (Eds.), The Environmental State Under Pressure, pp. 15–32. Amsterdam: Elsevier Science.

Schnaiberg, A. (1980). *The Environment: From Surplus to Scarcity.* New York: Oxford University Press.

Statistics Canada. (2010). Fast facts—Population. Ottawa, ON: Author. Retrieved August 3, 2011, from www.statcan.gc.ca/edu/edu02_0018-eng.htm

Statistics Canada. (2009). Crude birth rate, age-specific and total fertility rates, by geography. Ottawa, ON: Author. Retrieved January 20, 2010 from www.statcan.gc.ca/pub/84f0210x/2007000/t005-eng.htm

Statistics Canada. (2008). Waste management industry: Business and government sectors. *The Daily.* Ottawa, ON: Author. Retrieved August 3, 2011, from www.statcan.gc.ca/daily-quotidien/101222/dq101222b-eng.htm

Statistics Canada. (2005, December 2). Human activity and the environment: Solid waste. *The Daily.* Ottawa, ON: Author. Retrieved August 3, 2011, from www.statcan.gc.ca/daily-quotidien/051202/dq051202b-eng.htm

Sustainable Europe Research Institute (SERI), Austria and GLOBAL 2000 (Friends of the Earth Austria), and Friends of the Earth Europe. (2009, September). Overconsumption? Our Use of the World's Natural Resources. Retrieved August 3, 2011, from www.foeeurope.org/publications/2009/Overconsumption_Sep09.pdf

Suzuki, D. (2010). *The Legacy: An Elder's Vision for Our Sustainable Future.* Vancouver, BC: Greystone Books.

TerraChoice. (2010). *The Sins of Greenwashing Home and Family Edition 2010: A Report on Environmental Claims Made in the North American Consumer Market.* Ottawa, ON: TerraChoice Environmental Marketing.

TerraChoice. (2009, April). *The Seven Sins of Greenwashing: Environmental Claims in Consumer Markets.* Summary Report: North America. Ottawa, ON: TerraChoice Environmental Marketing.

United Nations. (2009, February 5). Majority of world population face water shortages unless action taken, warns Migiro. *United Nations News Centre.* New York: Secretary of the Publications Board. Retrieved August 3, 2011, from www.un.org/apps/news/story.asp?NewsID=29796&Cr=water&Cr1=agriculture

United Nations Environment Programme. (2000). *Montreal Protocol on Substances that Deplete the Ozone Layer as adjusted and/or amended in London 1990, Copenhagen 1992, Vienna 1995, Montreal 1997, and Beijing, 1999.* Nairobi, KE: Ozone Secretariat.

Wali, M. K., Evrendilek, F., & Fennessy, M. S. (2010). *The Environment: Science, Issues, and Solutions.* Boca Raton, FL: CRC Press.

Williams, J. (2007). Thinking as natural: Another look at human exemptionalism. *Human Ecology Review, 14* (2): 130–139.

World Commission on Environment and Development. (1987, June 8). Presentation of the Report of the World Commission on Environment and Development to UNEP's 14th Governing Council Session. Nairobi, KE: G. H. Brundtland.

World Wide Fund for Nature (WWF). (2011). The ten principles of one-planet living. Retrieved August 3, 2011, from www.wwf.panda.org/what_we_do/how_we_work/conservation/one_planet_living/about_opl/principles

World Wide Fund for Nature—Canada (WWF-Canada). (2011). Conservation First Principle. In Conservation. Retrieved August 3, 2011, from www.wwf.ca/about_us/advocacy/conservation_first.cfm

ENDNOTE

[1] Opening quote retrieved August 3, 2011, from www.goodreads.com/author/quotes/5297.John_Muir.

CHAPTER 14

Globalization

LEARNING OBJECTIVES AND OUTCOMES

After completing this chapter, students should be able to do the following:

LO1 Define "globalization" and differentiate it from "globality."

LO2 Describe historical precursors to globalization.

LO3 Explain how changes after World War II precipitated modern globalization.

LO4 Describe the technological, economic, political, cultural, and social characteristics of globalization.

LO5 Outline the vision of globalization including its proposed world benefits.

LO6 Describe the dark side of globalization highlighted by various social organizations.

LO7 Describe global justice movements including their affiliated activities.

LO8 Explain how modernization theory, dependency theory, and world systems theory contribute to our understanding of global inequality.

> *The speed of light does not merely transform the world. It becomes the world. Globalization is the speed of light.*
>
> *(French writer Paul Virilio, [b. 1932])*[1]

In the 21st century, the term "globalization" has become common parlance. We read about it in the news, hear it mentioned on television, and listen to our employers or coworkers discussing it in our places of business. We are also participants in globalization every single day and it affects virtually every aspect of our lives. Indeed, globalization has become the world.

DEFINING GLOBALIZATION

LO1 **Globalization** is defined in a variety of ways ranging from formal to informal expressions. Formal definitions typically resemble the following: Globalization is "a set of [uneven] social processes that appear to transform our present social condition of weakening nationality into one of globality" (Stegar, 2009, p. 7). In constrast, **globality** is "a social condition characterized by tight global economic, political, cultural and environmental interconnections and flows that make most of the current borders and boundaries irrelevant" (Stegar, 2009, p. 8). That is, globalization is a *process* while globality is a *condition*. Others define globalization more informally, as simply "the greater interconnectedness of the world's people" (Eitzen & Zinn, 2009, p. 1).

A better understanding of what globalization entails comes from an exploration and analysis of when and why it emerged, its essential characteristics, what it has achieved, and what critics say about the problems that it has wrought. All of these issues will be addressed in this chapter. As you progress through the chapter, you will see that globalization is intimately intertwined with the topics that have been discussed throughout this book. Globalization affects and is affected by mass media, culture, social structure, stratification and social inequality, families, gender, ethnicity, crime, religion, science, education, health and illness, social movements, and the environment.

> **Globalization:** A set of [uneven] social processes that appear to transform our present social condition of weakening nationality into one of globality.
>
> **Globality:** A social condition characterized by tight global economic, political, cultural, and environmental interconnections and flows that make most of the current borders and boundaries irrelevant.

GLOBALIZATION MEANS WHEN YOUR EMAIL ACCOUNT IS FULL WITH SPAM FROM COUNTRIES YOU'VE NEVER HEARD OF...

THE EMERGENCE OF GLOBALIZATION

LO2 Globalization is based on "the exchange of goods, the development of trade routes, the migration of peoples, and the spread of information . . ." (Hebron & Stack, 2011, p. 2). This is a dynamic that has existed for thousands of years, from the migration of ancient peoples, to the explorations of Marco Polo (1254–1324) that resulted in trade relationships between Europe and the Far East (see Figure 14.1), to the international trade of today.

Technological developments in the latter half of the 19th century were central to creating the foundation for modern globalization (Hebron & Stack, 2009; Stegar, 2009). The invention of the steamship increased the speed and decreased the costs of transporting both goods and people. It also enabled the first transatlantic telegraph cable to be laid on the floor of the Atlantic Ocean, increasing the speed of international communication.

LO3 Although there are historical foundations, the interconnectedness of people separated by geography and politics became emphasized during and after World War II. First, colonial empires were dismantled, a process known as **decolonization**. European colonial governments, such as the English, French, and Dutch, granted independence to their colonies throughout the world. This resulted in 88 new countries that had their own governments, and control over their own economic activities. Second, a variety of transnational political and financial institutions were created to address the consequences of World War II, and the underlying social, economic, and political forces that had facilitated the emergence of worldwide conflict. For example, the United Nations was formed to address issues of human rights, international peace and security, and international economic and political cooperation. It has a number of subsidiary organizations as well, including the World Health Organization (WHO); the United Nations Educational, Scientific, and Cultural Organization (UNESCO); and the International Court of Justice, which is an international court that deals with cases of war crimes and crimes against humanity.

The transnational financial institutions that were formed near the end of World War II are the institutions that most commonly come to mind when speaking of globalization—the International Monetary Fund (IMF), the World Bank, and the General Agreement on Tariffs and Trade (GATT), which later became the World Trade Organization (WTO) (see Figure 14.2). These institutions were formed, in part, to facilitate the reconstruction of Europe and Japan after World War II. They were also formed to assist in the post-war economic recovery of countries throughout the world. A hard economic lesson was learned following World War I. At that time, countries sought economic recovery by tightening their economic borders, engaging in competitive currency devaluation to gain export advantages, and imposing large **tariffs**,

> **Decolonization:** The process whereby colonial empires are dismantled and former colonies are granted political and economic independence.
>
> **Tariffs:** Fees imposed by a government on imported goods.

FIGURE 14.1
Early Trade Routes

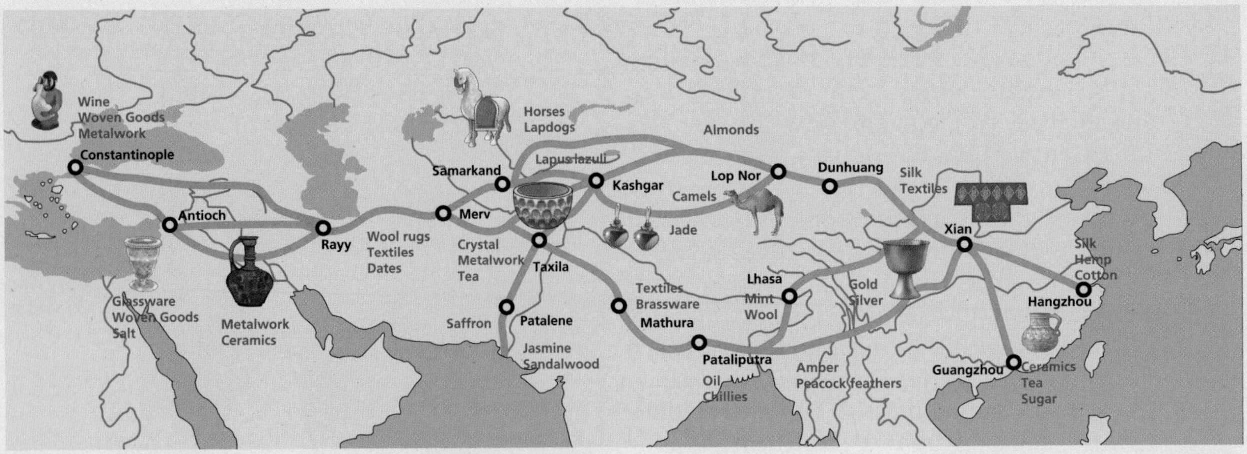

Source: Courtesy of the Penn Museum

fees that are levied by a government on imported goods. Each nation focused on its own market, with devastating results. In the long term, this practice contributed to the stock market crash of October 1929, which resulted in the Great Depression of the 1930s. It was thought that the means for avoiding a similar outcome following World War II could be found in the economic philosophy of **neoliberalism**. This philosophy emphasizes the benefits of allowing the freedom of market forces unimpeded by government. It proposes that through privatization, deregulation, and free trade, both prosperity and democracy will flourish.

Post–World War II changes such as decolonization and the creation of transnational political and financial institutions mark the beginnings of modern globalization. But globalization matured with the fall of the Soviet Union in 1989. This resulted in the creation of 18 new, independent countries, with control over their own economies. Even more importantly, the fall of the Soviet Union was indicative of one of the last major boundaries in the world—the boundary between East and West,

The destruction of the Berlin Wall in 1989 marked both the fall of the Soviet Union and maturation of the concept of globalization.

between capitalism and communism. It suddenly became much easier to imagine a world without borders, with free-flowing goods, information, and

Neoliberalism: An economic philosophy claiming that when market forces are unimpeded by government, prosperity and democracy will flourish.

FIGURE 14.2

The International Monetary Fund, World Bank, and World Trade Organization

In the 21st century, the most significant transnational economic institutions are the International Monetary Fund, the World Bank, and the World Trade Organization.

International Monetary Fund (IMF)
The IMF provides short-term lending to governments, and collects data on the world economy. It comprises 186 member states, and has a 24-member board of executive directors. Voting power is based on the size of each member state's economy. The United States, with the world's largest economy, has the most voting power on the Board—in fact, it has veto power. The IMF provides three categories of loans. Standby loans are for short-term financial crises, extended loans are for longer-term financial problems, and concessional loans are part of a poverty-reduction strategy available to the poorest countries of the world. Being granted a loan from the IMF is a necessary precursor to being considered for a loan from the World Bank (Lee, 2007a).

World Bank
The World Bank is an international bank that provides low-interest or interest-free loans, as well as technical assistance for development projects (infrastructure, agriculture, private enterprise development, and social programs) in low- and middle-income countries. As with the IMF, voting power

is based on the size of a member state's economy, with the United States having the most influence. The World Bank has two components. The International Bank for Reconstruction and Development (IBRD) offers loans of 15 to 20 years to credit-worthy developing nations. In fiscal year 2008, it granted $13.5 billion in loans for 99 projects in 34 countries. Its second component, the International Development Association (IDA), provides interest-free loans of 35 to 40 years to the poorest countries. Almost 80 nations qualify for IDA loans, based on their per capita income. In 2008, the IDA granted $11.2 billion in loans for 199 projects in 72 countries (Lee, 2007b).

World Trade Organization (WTO)
The World Trade Organization, with its 150 member states, "regulates world trade and provides a forum for negotiations to reduce trade barriers" (Lee, 2007c, para. 1). In part, its member states agree to extend their best tariff rates to other member states, treat foreign goods equally with domestic goods, and engage in trade fairly. Negotiations take place through rounds of talks involving the 150 member states as a whole. In order to give smaller, less powerful nations equal participation, decisions are made through consensus rather than a majority vote. Because of the consensus model, negotiations can frequently extend over a period of years (Lee, 2007c).

people, a world characterized by globality (Ray, 2007; Eitzen & Zinn, 2009).

TIME TO REVIEW

- What is globalization, and how is it related to globality?
- What are the historical foundations of globalization?
- Why did globalization become emphasized during and after World War II?
- What are the IMF, World Bank, and WTO?
- Why did the fall of the Soviet Union cause globalization to enter its mature form?

LO⁴ CHARACTERISTICS OF GLOBALIZATION

In the 21st century, globalization is characterized by "the Internet, instantaneous 24-hour news stations, interconnected financial markets, the spread of communications and transportation systems, unprecedented integration of economic activities, and the rise of increasingly important nonstate, transnational actors . . ." (Hebron & Stack, 2011, p. 2). It has a range of technological, economic, political, and cultural dimensions.

TECHNOLOGICAL DIMENSION

Technology facilitates all other dimensions of globalization: ". . . robotics, fiber optics, container ships, computers, communications satellites, and the Internet—have transformed information storage and retrieval, communication, production, and transportation" (Eitzen & Zinn, 2009, p. 4). The economic, political, and cultural dimensions of globalization are enabled by modern technology, and yet also influence technological development. Each of these dimensions is associated with various problems, which will be addressed at a later point in the chapter.

ECONOMIC DIMENSION

Informed by neoliberalism, the economic dimension of globalization is reflected in the transnational financial institutions already described, as well as expanded markets, flexible production and assembly, and the concentration of economic power (Ray, 2007; Eitzen &

Zinn, 2009, Stegar, 2009). In Canadian history, we saw the early expansion of markets in the transition to industrialization. At that time, Canadians who were involved in farming and lumber were encouraged to expand their economic activities. First, they started to produce slightly more agricultural products and lumber than was needed for their own families' survival, in order to provide those types of products to the growing urban population. As the United States and Western Europe were already much more urbanized at that time, there was an even greater need for those products. Consequently, the agricultural and lumbering industries were expanded even further, with the surplus being sold internationally. Under globalization, markets have expanded more than anyone would have ever imagined at the turn of the 20th century.

For example, Toronto-based Harlequin Enterprises (most well-known as the publisher of series romance novel lines such as *Harlequin Presents* and *Silhouette Desire*) has taken advantage of new market opportunities that have arisen, such as those following the fall of the Soviet Union in 1989 and the increased trade opportunities with China in the mid-1990s. The company now publishes 110 titles each month in 32 languages, in 115 international markets, on six continents. Ninety-five percent of its books are sold outside Canada, and half overseas. The list of countries within which Harlequin has principal offices is a reflection of the concept of globalization: Toronto, New York, London, Tokyo, Milan, Sydney, Paris, Madrid, Stockholm, Amsterdam, Hamburg, Athens, Budapest, Granges-Paccot, Warsaw, Rio de Janeiro, Mumbai, and Istanbul. In addition, it has licensing agreements in 14 other countries. Since the company's inception in the mid-20th century, it has sold more than 6 billion books (Harlequin Enterprises, 2011). Harlequin is one of the most successful publishing houses in the industry, with $585 million in sales in 2003, $124 million in profit, and a 21 percent profit margin (Wyatt, 2004).

As markets expand globally, so does production. Flexible production makes use of various nations' physical and human resources. The "global assembly line" (Eitzen & Zinn, 2009, p. 3) manufactures a finished product using the resources of a variety of nations. A sweatshirt from Gap involves cotton being harvested by workers in Uzbekistan, which is then spun and processed into textiles by workers in South Korea, and then sewn into sweatshirts by seamstresses in Russia (Gordon & Knickerbocker Designs, 2009). The nature of the global assembly line is such that manufacturing jobs are typically moved into low-wage countries. A growing number of service jobs

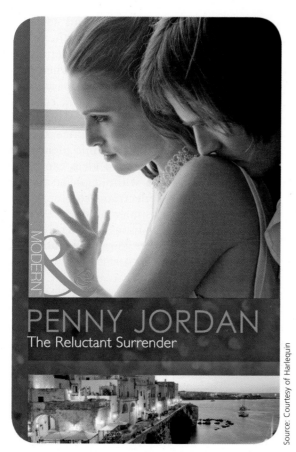

Romance goes global: Canadian-based Harlequin romance novels are sold in 115 international markets.

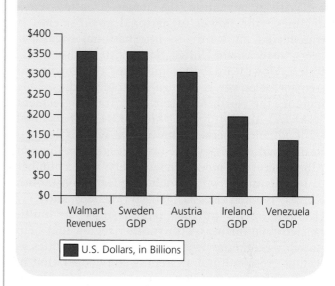

FIGURE 14.3

Walmart's Revenues versus Nation-States' Gross Domestic Products

U.S. Dollars, in Billions

Source: Stegar (2009).

are being outsourced to different parts of the world as well. For instance, if someone in the world who has purchased a new printer phones the help line, that person may be connected to a call centre in Edmonton, Houston, Mexico City, Mumbai, or any of a number of other cities around the world. Cities, regions, and nations offer competitive advantages to try to attract these exported or outsourced jobs, advantages to corporations that can be detrimental to workers and communities, as will be addressed later in the chapter.

In addition to expanding markets and flexible production, the economic dimension of globalization also involves a concentration in economic power. Beginning in the 1980s, widespread corporate restructuring and merging occurred, creating larger, economically powerful corporations, such as the media giants described in Chapter 3 and the supermarket superstore corporations discussed in Chapter 11. Even Harlequin Enterprises has been part of this corporate restructuring, having been acquired by Torstar in 1981, the largest newspaper publisher in Canada.

In 2006, the 2,000 largest global corporations represented 55 countries, employed 68 million people, and had $24 trillion in revenues, $88 trillion in assets, and $1.7 trillion in profits (Eitzen & Zinn, 2009). Transnational corporations have greater wealth than do many nations. In 2005, 42 of the top 100 economies in the world were corporations rather than countries. In 2007, Walmart had revenues of more than $351 billion, compared to the gross domestic products of Sweden ($354 billion), Austria ($304 billion), Ireland ($196 billion), and Venezuela ($138 billion) (Stegar, 2009) (see Figure 14.3). The economic power of transnational corporate giants has led some people to describe globalization as "corporate globalization" (Stegar, 2009, p. 50).

POLITICAL DIMENSION

The economic dimension of globalization is intertwined with its political dimension. For instance, the International Development Association (IDA) of the World Bank has its origins in the Cold War, the conflict between the Soviet Union and the United States, which were the world's two greatest superpowers during the latter half of the 20th century. During the Cold War, the United States feared that the world's poorest nations would approach (or be approached by) the Soviet Union, and thereby contribute to its expanding power. Consequently, the United States provided 42 percent of the IDA's initial funding to assist in the development of these nations and prevent them from becoming part of the Soviet empire (Lee, 2007b).

With globalization, the power of nation-states declines. The power of national governments is transferred "upward" to international organizations, such as the United Nations. It is also transferred "downward." In some cases the downward transfer of power is to regional trade bodies. This includes the North American Free Trade Agreement (NAFTA), the European Union (EU), and regional trade alliances between individual regions located in different countries. For example, the province of Alberta has *sister province relationships* with a number of regions in the world, including Gangwon (South Korea), Tyumen (Russia), Jalisco (Mexico), and Lviv (Ukraine). **Sister province relationships** "are multifaceted relationships with another region that help promote economic development–related activities as well as cross-cultural awareness and cooperation in areas such as culture, education, sports, agriculture, technology, governance, and tourism" (Government of Alberta, 2011).

In other cases, power is transferred downward to *global cities*, those cities that play a central role in the global economic system, independent of their nation-states. Cities such as New York, Tokyo, London, and Toronto have a strong influence on world affairs, and house many of the head offices of transnational corporations, as well as stock market indices. Because of the shared characteristics, experiences, and interests of global cities, they frequently form economic, political, and cultural alliances (Ray, 2007). The power of nation-states has also been transferred downward to global civil society (Stegar, 2009). Citizens who form and participate in groups such as Amnesty International and Human Rights Watch monitor and report on the actions of governments, thereby serving as indirect regulators of nation-states.

Sister province relationships: Multifaceted relationships with another region that help promote economic development–related activities as well as cross-cultural awareness and cooperation in areas such as culture, education, sports, agriculture, technology, governance, and tourism.

CULTURAL DIMENSION

The cultural dimension of globalization involves areas as diverse as tourism, media, communication, global consumption culture, transnational migration, and identities. People may migrate to other nations either temporarily as students or foreign workers, or permanently as residents. As discussed in Chapter 8, when people immigrate to another country, they adopt aspects of that country's culture, and at the same time contribute aspects of the cultures of their countries of origin. And the longer ago that an individual or one's ancestors migrated to a country, the more ethnic identity may change. But cultural products and ideas can be conveyed transnationally even without physical migration, through the Internet, electronic communication, and the marketing of consumer products. Whether you live in Canada or in countless other countries in the world, on any given day you may be able to eat poutine, chicken vindaloo, or sushi. You can purchase blue jeans, a sari, or maybe even a Montreal Canadiens jersey. You can watch the news on CBC, CNN, BBC, or Al Jazeera. For entertainment, you can watch a Justin Bieber music video, a Bollywood movie, or an episode of *American Idol*. For a vacation, Vancouver's great restaurants, the pyramids of Egypt, or an eco-tour in Costa Rica are all just a plane ride away. After forming a friendship with someone you met on a holiday, you can quickly and easily keep in touch by picking up your cell phone, sending an email, or posting a message on your friend's Facebook wall. And when an important event happens in the world, you can learn about it almost instantaneously through media and communications technologies.

The technological, economic, political, and cultural dimensions of globalization have irrevocably

The International Indian Film Awards (the Bollywood equivalent of the Oscars) were held outside India for the first time in 2011, in Toronto.

SOCIOLOGY *IN MY LIFE*

WHAT ROLE DO YOU PLAY IN GLOBALIZATION?

Consider how various dimensions of globalization have permeated the products and activities that make up your day. Think about the food you buy in the grocery store (e.g., bananas) or the restaurants that you frequent (e.g., McDonalds', Indian, and/or Japanese). Where do you shop (e.g., Zellers or Walmart)? Look at the tags on your clothing, television, laptop, and cell phone to see where they were manufactured. Make note of the Internet sites that you visit, or the movies, television shows, and YouTube videos that you watch. What are the means by which you learn about world events? You can even go online and try to trace the goods that you consume, such as the ownership structure of the companies, and who is involved in the production of those goods, and under what type of conditions. In all likelihood, a consideration of your daily life will reflect the global assembly line, expanding markets, the concentration of economic power in transnational corporations, and the centrality of technology. Who do you think benefits from the particular way that globalization permeates your life, and in what way? Who might be harmed?

changed the way that the people of the world live their daily lives. Whether those changes are for the better or the worse is a matter of discussion and debate.

TIME TO REVIEW

- What is the role of technology in globalization?
- What is the nature of expanding markets, the global assembly line, and the concentration of corporate power?
- How does globalization transfer power away from nation-states?
- What are some examples of the cultural dimension of globalization?

THE VISION OF GLOBALIZATION AND ITS REALITY: THE GOOD, THE BAD, AND THE UGLY

LO⁵ THE GOOD

The vision of the neoliberal forces underlying globalization is that it will improve the conditions of the people of the world in a number of ways (Hebron & Stack, 2011). Better living conditions will emerge from the globalization of production and the global assembly line that brings employment to the developing world and contributes to the development of those nations' economies.

Communication technologies, such as the Internet, increase people's knowledge of the world, and of their own society. Consequently, people become aware of the different possible ways of living and being in the world, and they hold their politicians to greater accountability. Proponents of globalization might point to the central role that communication technologies played in the myriad revolutions that took place in the Middle East in early 2011, when the people of various nations demanded an end to their dictator-run governments and the implementation of democratic rule. Beginning in Tunisia, and then spreading to Egypt, Libya, Yemen, and elsewhere, cell phones, Facebook, and the Internet were used to instantaneously coordinate protesters' activities, and send photos, videos, and information to each other and to the rest of the world. Their photos, videos, and audio served two functions. First, the rest of the world was made aware of the activities of the protesters and the responses of the government in real time, as they were happening. Various organizations and governments in the rest of the world were able to respond as well. When protesters in Libya sent out images of government forces shooting and killing peaceful protesters, the United Nations held an emergency meeting of its members that resulted in an arms embargo, a travel ban for the Libyan leader and his relatives, and the freezing of his family's international bank accounts. The images and audio served a second function as well. As the government of Tunisia fell, and then Egypt's, these forms of communication demonstrated to citizens in surrounding nations that change is actually possible—that the demands of ordinary people can change the country they live in. Finally, the greater level of knowledge that develops through globalization also increases understanding and tolerance of others—other people, and other cultures. With knowledge, understanding, and tolerance, conflicts between groups should decline.

Many people acknowledge that transnational institutions such as the International Monetary Fund have, to some extent, helped maintain financial stability and have supported development (Qureshi, 2004). Legrain (2002) draws attention to the successes of globalization during the latter half of the 20th century. Between 1950 and 2000, per capita income increased by four times. In the 1970s and 1980s, those developing nations that opened themselves up to trade had their economies expand by 4.5 percent per year. In contrast, the economies of those developing countries that did not open up to international trade grew by less than 1 percent per year. Finally, each percentage point increase in a nation's gross domestic product is associated with a similar increase in the standard of living. " . . . The process of economic cooperation and integration has helped a number of countries benefit from high rates of economic growth and employment creation, to absorb many of the rural poor into the modern urban economy, to advance their developmental goals, and to foster innovation in product development and the circulation of ideas" (International Labour Organization, 2009, p. 5).

But the experiences of globalization are diverse. Some people benefit, while others are harmed (Eitzen & Zinn, 2009), and measures are necessary to ensure that the benefits of globalization are equally shared by all (UNESCO, 2004). The most important question to ask is *who benefits* from globalization and who does not.

LO6 THE BAD AND THE UGLY

> Globalization, as defined by rich people like us, is a very nice thing... you are talking about the Internet, you are talking about cell phones, you are talking about computers. This doesn't affect two-thirds of the world's people.... If you're totally illiterate and living on one dollar a day, the benefits of globalization never come to you.
>
> *(Jimmy Carter, former American president and recipient of the 2002 Nobel Peace Prize)*[2]

SOCIAL INEQUALITY

Social inequality determines the nature of the effects of globalization. As Jimmy Carter points out in the previous quotation, those who live in extreme poverty do not benefit from globalization in the same way as those who live in wealth. Although we might not normally consider ourselves as part of the phrase "rich people like us," in comparison to people living in much of the world, we are living in relative wealth. In 2005, 37 percent of the developing world's population lived below the international "extreme" poverty line of US$1.25 per day. Most of these are the working poor, those who are employed but whose wages are less than that amount (United Nations, 2010). The average income of those living below the international poverty line is US$0.88 per day. Following the worldwide economic crisis of 2007/2008, which was precipitated by the collapse of the housing market in the United States, 50 million more people were below the international poverty line in 2009, and 64 million more in 2010 than would have otherwise been the case had the economic crisis not occurred. More than 800 million adults are illiterate, and more than 100 million children are not receiving even a basic primary school education. More than 800 million people are undernourished, and one-third of child deaths are

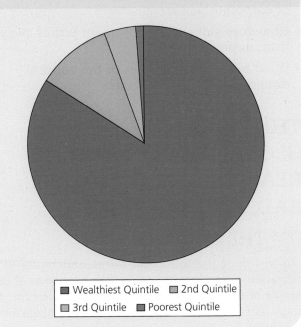

FIGURE 14.4

Proportion of the World's Wealth Owned by Each Quintile

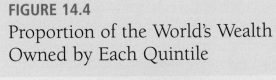

■ Wealthiest Quintile ■ 2nd Quintile
■ 3rd Quintile ■ Poorest Quintile

Source: Akyuz et al., cited in Ray (2007).

Source: Institute for Global Labour and Human Rights

Workers at this electronics factory must live in the company's dorm, under crowded conditions where they hang sheets in front of their narrow metal bunk beds for privacy.

caused by undernourishment. In the developing world, 43 percent of child deaths are due to four conditions: pneumonia, diarrhea, malaria, and AIDS. More than one billion people have no access to clean drinking water, and 40 percent of the world's population has no access to basic sanitation (UNESCO, 2004).

Although the vision of globalization includes better living conditions, the gap between the wealthy and the poor, and between rich nations and poor nations, has increased. In the last decade of the 20th century, world income increased by an average of 2.5 percent per year. Yet, over that same period of time, the number of people living in extreme poverty grew by millions (Ramos, 2004). The wealthiest 20 percent of the world's population owns 80 percent of the world's wealth, while the poorest 20 percent own less than 1 percent of the wealth (see Figure 14.4) (Akyuz et al., cited in Ray, 2007).

ECONOMIC CONSEQUENCES

Exploitation and Working Conditions in the Developing World

Globalization has also been criticized for the harms that its economic dimensions have caused for many people in the world. Critics suggest that globalization is fundamentally based on wealthy corporations and nations exploiting the people of the developing world. Flexible production exports jobs to countries where the wages are lower and there are fewer regulations governing working conditions. Corporations are able to pay employees low wages, and make them work long hours in poor conditions, all of which contribute to (1) the corporations' profits, and (2) lower prices for consumers living in the developed world.

The exploitation of workers in developing nations is illustrated in an analysis of female workers in electronics manufacturing (Ferus-Comelo, 2009). Electronics manufacturing is characterized by a preponderance of female workers on the assembly line. Gendered stereotypes about women's manual dexterity and attention to detail provide the rationale for female employment in this industry. However, the reality is that women are paid less than men, and in the developing world, there are many nations where it is legal to do so. Because companies desire flexible production that can expand or contract based on market forces, electronics manufacturing is increasingly done by contract labour provided by recruitment agencies rather than by full-time employees. For example, at one IBM plant in Mexico, 6,500 out of 7,000 employees are contract labourers provided by labour agencies. In many nations, most contract labour is female; for instance, at a Nokia plant in Brazil, 80 percent of the contract workers are women (Ferus-Comelo, 2009).

The industry is frequently characterized by mandatory overtime, often with no extra pay. An analysis of 20 companies in Malaysia found that 60 percent of the employees had to work mandatory overtime, and 50 percent did at least five hours of overtime per day. Similarly, a study of several plants in China found that employees were working seven days a week, and 100 to 120 hours of overtime every month (Ferus-Comelo, 2009).

In addition to contract labour and mandatory overtime, in some countries the industry is characterized by a preference for young, single female employees due to better physical health, better eyesight, and quicker reflexes. In countries where there is no shortage of labour, high employee turnover is not considered problematic. It may even be encouraged as worker productivity declines over time due to occupational health hazards and injuries. Furthermore, as women marry and have children, the company's costs can increase, whether through health-care costs, maternity leave, or more absences from work. At one company in Bangalore (India's equivalent to Silicon Valley), when women marry they are forced to work more overtime, in the hope that family members will encourage them to quit their jobs in order to better fulfill their responsibilities as wives. When they get pregnant, they are moved to more physically demanding and uncomfortable tasks, lifting and carrying heavy objects, and standing all day long in an overheated room with no fan and no breaks provided. At plants located in some countries, companies require female employees to undergo routine pregnancy tests; if they become pregnant, they are fired. In order to keep their jobs, some women undergo medically unsafe abortions (Ferus-Comelo, 2009).

SOCIOLOGY *IN PRACTICE*

THE ILO DECLARATION ON SOCIAL JUSTICE FOR A FAIR GLOBALIZATION

The International Labour Organization (ILO) is a tripartite agency of the United Nations that gives equal voice to workers, employers, and governments in shaping policies and programs related to labour standards. ILO's "vision is based on the premise that lasting peace can only be established if it is based on social justice" (www.ilo.org). Its objectives are to (1) promote rights at work, (2) enhance social protection, (3) encourage decent employment opportunities, and (4) strengthen dialogue on work-related issues.

In June 2008, the 182 member states of the United Nations adopted the *ILO Declaration on Social Justice for a Fair Globalization*, a set of objectives and processes to ensure that globalization has a fair outcome for all. Member states are legally obligated to adhere to the declaration's four objectives. The first objective is to promote employment by creating a sustainable institutional and economic environment, which includes an environment in which workers have the opportunity to develop the competencies and skills that they need for full economic participation. The second objective is to develop and enhance measures of social security and labour protection—a basic income, healthy working conditions, and policies that govern working hours, wages, and conditions. The third objective is to promote social dialogue in order to translate economic progress into social progress (and vice versa), achieve consensus on policies, and make labour laws effective. The fourth objective is to respect and promote fundamental rights at work, such as the right of association and collective bargaining. The declaration also outlines the means by which the ILO can and will assist member states in meeting these objectives. You can find a copy of the declaration, as well as material related to the implementation plan, on the ILO's website (www.ilo.org).

Although working conditions in electronics manufacturing are frequently based on exploitative working conditions, the female employees need their incomes. And they report deriving other benefits from employment, such as a sense of independence in cultures that remain strongly gendered. Femus-Comelo (2009) notes that in a number of countries, female workers are organizing, and even attempting to form unions in order to improve their wages and working conditions.

WISCONSIN BUDGET REPAIR BILL

As a result of the recent worldwide recession, the state of Wisconsin faced a $137 million deficit, and a projected $3.6 billion shortfall in the 2011–2013 budget. Consequently, Governor Scott Walker proposed measures to improve the state's economy. One of these measures was to remove most collective bargaining rights for all public employees, which include school teachers, police officers, and government employees. In particular, although some collective bargaining rights would be maintained in the area of wages, unions would no longer have the ability to bargain in other areas, such as working conditions.

Tens of thousands of citizens participated in protests across the state in response to this perceived attack on workers' rights. In early March 2011, the State Senate passed the bill into law. However, a few weeks later Judge Maryann Sumi ruled that the meeting at which the vote took place violated the state's laws governing public meetings and, as such, the bill had not become law; any public officials who tried to enforce the bill would face legal sanctions. Her ruling was subsequently overturned, and the bill went on to be the subject of ongoing legal battles for some time (Johnson, 2011; Treleven, 2011).

The ways in which globalization negatively affects wages and working conditions are not limited to the developing world. A *race to the bottom* results in lower wages, declining working conditions, and job insecurity in both the developing and developed worlds (Eitzen & Zinn, 2009; Hebron & Stack, 2011). For example, although the United States is one of the member states of the United Nations, the right to collectively bargain, as stated in the *ILO Declaration on Social Justice for a Fair Globalization*, is being removed from some American workers (see *Sociology in the News*).

The Race to the Bottom

The globalization of production, combined with the economic power of transnational corporate giants, means that a corporation's threat to move operations to another country wields considerable influence. This creates job insecurity for workers who are employed with a specific company or in a particular industry; they must live in constant fear of losing their jobs.

The world market becomes a place for corporations to shop for the best deal. Different nations compete to become the location for a company's operations, trying to undercut each other in terms of employee wages and benefits, tax breaks, and costs associated with social and environmental regulations. For example, following the implementation of the North American Free Trade Agreement (NAFTA) in

1994, companies began exporting jobs from Canada and the United States "to maquilador factories along the [Mexican] border, where the Mexican government assures a docile labor force and virtually no environmental restrictions" (Faux, 2009, p. 64). Critics suggest that it is only the wealthy in Mexico who have truly benefited. In the ten years following the implementation of NAFTA, real wages in the manufacturing industry in Mexico actually declined. Pressure to limit increases in the minimum wage in Mexico meant that in 2004, a minimum wage could purchase less than half of the tortillas than the minimum wage could purchase in 1994 (Faux, 2009). And just as countries such as Canada and the United States have lost manufacturing jobs when cheaper production environments became available, nations like Mexico are now experiencing the same thing. Corporations that moved production to Mexico in the past are now moving that production from Mexico to countries where production will be even cheaper, such as China (Stegar, 2009).

However, corporate decisions to move production facilities are made within a broader context. Both consumers and the growing number of big-box retailers such as Rona and Walmart are demanding lower-priced products (Moberg, 2009). There are two ways to reduce the prices of products—reduce either production costs or the company's profit. A decline in a company's profit has larger implications for the company, so the path to reducing prices is typically controlling production costs. For example, closing down a Maytag plant in Illinois and moving it to Mexico meant that the retail price of Maytag refrigerators declined by $50 to $350 (Moberg, 2009).

Production facilities that are closed down in one country are not always moved to another. Transnational corporate giants have money vested in a range of goods or services throughout the world. Sometimes a business operation is shut down as part of a corporation's larger business plan. For example, in 2006 the Canadian government approved the purchase of Canadian mining company Inco by Vale, a Brazilian company and the second largest mining company in the world. One of Inco's assets was a nickel smelter and refiner located in Thompson, Manitoba. In 2010, Export Development Canada granted Vale a $1 billion loan for its proposal to increase employment. Demonstrating that job insecurity exists even within a context of economic success, only six weeks later Vale announced that it would be closing the Thompson mine by 2015, despite the company's record-setting profits of $17.3 billion in 2010 and its intention to invest $10 billion in activities in other parts of the country. Almost 600 jobs would be lost, devastating Thompson's economy. "Vale's chief executive Roger

"Sorry lads. I'm closing this workshop down, and relocating in the far east."

Source: © Kes, ksmn81, Cartoonstock.com

Agnelli said in the company statement that Vale is living through its best days. 'However, given the size and quality of our pipeline of growth projects amid a scenario of sustained global demand growth for our products, I strongly believe that even better days are ahead of us . . .'" (Galloway, 2011, para. 11).

People are differentially advantaged, or disadvantaged, by globalization as a result of the exploitation and subsequent working conditions of people in the developing world, as well as the race to the bottom that affects both the developing and developed worlds. Economic harms have also caused more to some people than to others because of aspects of transnational financial and trade organizations themselves.

Institutional Concerns

Although the International Monetary Fund and the World Bank are intended to facilitate development and ease financial crisis, critics argue that, in practice, developing countries are not always helped. One of the primary criticisms of these organizations is that they are not held accountable to the people that they are supposed to be helping. Instead, their accountability is to the wealthy, powerful nations that steer their activities—especially the United States, where their offices are located. The poorest nations have no input into the composition of the 24-member board of executive directors of the IMF, and therefore no direct influence on the IMF's policies and programs. The United States, Japan, Germany, France, the United Kingdom, China, Russia, and Saudi Arabia each appoint one director

Washington Consensus: The structural adjustment programs supported by the IMF, the World Bank, and the United States Treasury Department.

to the board. The remaining directors are voted upon, and because voting power is based on the size of each member state's economy, the United States controls 17 percent of the vote, and European nations as a whole control another one-third of the vote. The European Union gets to appoint the IMF's managing director, and the United States gets to appoint the first deputy managing director. A similar process is involved with the board of executive directors of the World Bank, except that it is the United States that appoints the president of the World Bank (who is also the head of the board). Because the poorest nations have no input into the board of either organization, they have no institutional influence on the policies, programs, or reforms that are adopted (Lee, 2007a, 2007b; UNESCO, 2004; Ramos, 2004; Stegar, 2009).

Another criticism of the IMF and World Bank is of the structural adjustment programs that they implemented in the 1980s. These programs are collectively known as the **Washington Consensus** because they were supported by the IMF, the World Bank, and the United States Treasury Department, all of which are located in Washington, DC. Structural adjustment programs were developed as a result of the worsening debt crisis in the 1980s. Loans would be granted to developing nations only if they reduced government spending and liberalized their trade policies. Government expenditures were to be controlled by reducing spending on social programs. That is, in nations that frequently have limited social programs in the first place, governments were supposed to spend even *less* on health, education, and housing than before (Lee, 2007a, 2007b; UNESCO, 2004; Stegar, 2009; Hebron & Stack, 2011). The most vulnerable groups in society have been the most negatively affected by structural adjustment programs. "Feeding programs and medical clinics closed, food subsidies and housing assistance ended, and the cost of living climbed precipitously. Many developing nations perceived a new colonialism, with poor nations suffering for the sake of profits and bank balance sheets in rich nations" (Lee, 2007b, para. 12).

Developing nations that receive funding are not to subsidize agriculture. However, countries such as Canada and the United States continue to offer extensive subsidies to their farmers. Developed nations spend, in total, $350 billion each year in agricultural subsidies, almost $1 billion per day. Because of these subsidies, agricultural commodities from these nations can be sold at lower prices. This drives agricultural prices down worldwide. The unsubsidized farmers in developing nations aren't able to compete, and as a result the livelihoods of the two-thirds of the world's population who are dependent upon agriculture are threatened or destroyed (Hebron & Stack, 2011; Stegar, 2009; Ray, 2007). One consequence is that people are forced to migrate to urban areas to find work, frequently in other countries. Women from developing nations leave their own children in the care of others, while they migrate to Canada, the United States, France, and the United Kingdom to work as nannies and housekeepers for others (Ehrenreich & Hochschild, 2002). Similarly, during Alberta's economic boom (roughly 2004 to 2007), thousands of men were recruited as temporary foreign workers primarily (but not exclusively) for the oil and construction industries, leaving their families behind in their countries of origin.

For some people, globalization has negative economic consequences, which are transformed into social consequences such as unemployment and separated families. But for people in many countries, the cultural dimension of globalization has made even more of an impact than its economic dimension.

CULTURAL CONSEQUENCES

Just as the cultural dimensions of globalization are diverse, so are their consequences. UNESCO sees the trend toward homogenization and uniformity of culture as alarming (UNESCO, 2004). Concerns about the loss of local cultures are prevalent. Small local enterprises that may reflect aspects of culture—its food, clothing, or folk art—are unable to compete with multinational corporations and go out of business. Instead, a growing proportion of people buy blue jeans at Walmart and eat lunch at McDonald's. The homogenization of culture is even reflected in the loss of languages. In the 1500s, there were more than 14,000 distinct languages being spoken in the world, but by the late 20th century, there were fewer than 7,000. It is estimated that by the end of the 21st century, between 50 percent and 90 percent of the languages that currently exist will be extinct (Stegar, 2009). English has become more dominant in the world. It is the first language of 350 million people, and a second language of another 400 million. Communications technologies, such as the Internet, are central to globalization; more than 80 percent of content on the Internet is English (Stegar, 2009).

Concerns about cultural homogenization abound. But some people argue that it isn't just *homogenization* that is occurring, it is *Americanization*. Just as the United States exerts considerable control over the global economy, it also is central to global culture. America is home to 52 of the top 100 brand names in the world. And although Bollywood releases more movies each year, Hollywood movies are the only ones to have penetrated every market in the world. The biggest-grossing films, and the top-rated TV shows in every country are American (Hebron & Stack, 2011).

However, Robertson (1992) argues that global culture does not necessarily mean the destruction of local culture or cultural diversity. He draws attention to the emergence of **glocalization**, the blending of the global and the local. The newest restaurant cuisine is "fusion" cuisine, combining the tastes of two cultures—Cuban–Chinese, Asian–Italian, and more. When Walt Disney expanded outside

> **Glocalization:** The blending of the global and the local.

McDonald's is McDonald's? At this McDonald's in Japan, menu items include Juicy Chicken Akatougarashi, Teriyaki Mac Burger, and Shrimp Filet-O.

Source: REUTERS/Susumu Toshiyuki

the United States, the company first went to France and established Euro-Disney. It was almost a colossal failure, in part because Disney did not take the local culture into consideration; for example, its alcohol-free policy was problematic for people living in a culture where the moderate consumption of wine is integrated into daily life. Learning from its mistakes, when the company expanded into Hong Kong, it integrated Chinese food and music (Hebron & Stack, 2011).

Although the economic and cultural consequences of globalization that disadvantage some people in the world are the most emphasized, there are myriad other potentially negative consequences of globalization as well. These include increased conflict, terrorism, organized crime networks, environmental destruction (as described in Chapter 13) and even epidemics and pandemics (Eitzen & Zinn, 2009; Stegar, 2009; Hebron & Stack, 2011).

Proponents of globalization suggest that the knowledge it brings to people promotes understanding and tolerance, and thereby reduces conflict between different cultures and different groups. However, others argue that conflict actually becomes more pronounced with globalization. Historically, European colonial empires brought together disparate groups of people in borders that were constructed by the colonizers. This created politically cohesive colonial states, but there was no pre-existing cultural cohesiveness. Thus, in postcolonial societies, people are more likely to define themselves in terms of their religion and ethnicity, rather than their nation. This actually serves to increase hostility between different ethnic and religious groups that were forcibly brought together into the borders of a nation-state (Hebron & Stack, 2011). With the progress of globalization, people must "reflexively respond to the common predicament of living in one world" (Ray, 2007, para. 5). Religion can "provide an ultimate justification of one's view of the world" (para. 5). This sets the stage for conflicts that have some degree of religious foundation, such as conflicts between Sunni and Shia Muslims in some countries in the Middle East (Ray, 2007; Stegar, 2009; Hubrin & Stack, 2011).

Other scholars argue that terrorism has been enhanced by globalization as well (Eitzen & Zinn, 2009). Ramos (2004) suggests that the "democratization of technology . . . equip[s] terrorists with a frightening array of skills and weapons unimaginable a decade ago," and that this has "scattered power away from governments and enabled fanatical individuals and groups of conspirators to play powerful roles in world politics" (p. 53). Technology is used as an ideological tool as well. That is, it is through modern communications technologies that Al Qaeda leader Osama bin Laden was able to communicate messages to his followers, and to the rest of the world, via video from caves somewhere in Afghanistan or Pakistan (Stegar, 2009).

Organized crime networks also benefit from the technologies and process of globalization. Just as the ease of transportation of goods and people facilitates legitimate business, it also facilitates illegitimate business—the flow of drugs, weapons, money, victims of human trafficking, and criminal actors. Communications technologies are sites for organized crime as well. As people, companies, and governments carry out increasingly more of their business in electronic environments, they can be criminally victimized within those environments (Sheptycki, 2007).

Globalization even affects people's health—not just through environmental destruction or unhealthy working conditions, but also from human movement across regions of the world. Pandemics have always been a byproduct of the transportation of people. As trade routes between Europe and the Far East were established hundreds of years ago, it wasn't only silk and spices that began to flow across borders. It was through these trade routes that the bubonic plague was introduced to Europe (Hebron & Stack, 2011), killing up to one-third of the European population in a period of just four years during the 14th century (Weeks, 2008).

A few hundred years later, European colonization introduced various diseases to indigenous people in the Americas (e.g., smallpox, influenza). It is estimated that up to 100 million indigenous people in the Americas died as a result of epidemics, over a period of approximately 100 years; this has been referred to as "the great dying" (Clarke, 2008, p. 151). And the influenza pandemic of 1918 (see Chapter 11) was the result of soldiers returning home from the battlefields of Europe at the end of World War I (Hebron & Stack, 2011).

In contemporary society, the ease and speed of human migration has contributed to a number of different health scares. In 2003, the World Health Organization declared a pandemic of severe acute respiratory syndrome (SARS). It began in China in 2002, and in February 2003 Chinese health officials notified WHO that they had an outbreak of this new disease, with 305 cases. When a Chinese professor travelled to Hong Kong, the global spread of SARS began. By the end of March, it had spread to many other countries in the world, including Canada. Hospitals were shut down to visitors, schools were closed, and thousands of people quarantined. Before the pandemic ended, more than 8,000 cases of SARS had been confirmed, with more than 700 deaths worldwide (including 43 in Canada) (CBC, 2003; WHO, 2003). As the response of governments and health organizations was evaluated after the pandemic,

SOCIOLOGY *IN MY COMMUNITY*

A 12-YEAR-OLD BOY CHANGES THE WORLD

In 1995, 12-year-old Craig Kielburger was reading the *Toronto Star* when he came across a story about a boy in South Asia, Iqbal Masih, who had spent most of his childhood chained to a loom in a carpet factory. After gaining his freedom, he began speaking out about child labour—and was murdered for it. Craig Kielburger gathered together 11 of his classmates from his Thornhill, Ontario, school and formed the organization Free the Children to fight against child exploitation and poverty. Since that time, Free the Children has become the largest network of "children helping children." It now includes more than one million child activists in 45 countries, including 3,500 "Youth in Action" groups in Canada and the United States. It has also partnered with a variety of other global justice organizations and corporate groups. Since its inception, Free the Children has been responsible for building 650 schools (with 55,000 students); shipping $15 million in medical supplies; providing one million children with access to clean water, health care, and sanitation; helping 30,000 women in the developing

world to become self-sufficient through micro-loans and alternative income programs; and rescuing thousands of children from child labour. In an interview with Craig when he was just 12 years old, he was asked about his motivation for forming the organization. His response was, "We're just doing what adults should have been doing all along."

The website for Free the Children (www .freethechildren.com) includes resources for youth, families, and educators. Based on the fundamental assumption that education is necessary for effective social action, youth are able to access educational resources on hunger, child labour and children's rights, education, health, poverty, and sustainable development. The website also provides teachers with detailed lesson plans for both elementary and secondary school students on all of these topics. The pragmatic tools for social action are included as well—campaigns that people can get involved in, toolkits for making documentaries and planning events, and opportunities to volunteer overseas.

policies and practices were reformed and changed. These changes facilitated a more effective response to the world's next pandemic, the H1N1 virus in 2009.

Globalization has benefited people in the world in many ways. And yet, its impacts are not uniform. Various aspects of globalization contribute to negative consequences for large numbers of people. In response, global justice movements have emerged.

LO⁷ GLOBAL JUSTICE MOVEMENTS

Global justice movements are those social movements whose unifying feature is a resistance to neoliberalism and its effects. However, global justice movements consist of a diverse range of individual groups—labour groups, leftist activists, agricultural workers, religious groups, feminist groups, environmental organizations, anarchist groups, and more. Although global justice movements have existed for several decades, they came to widespread public awareness during the World Trade Organization summit in Seattle in 1999 (Stegar, 2009; Della Porta & Tarrow, 2005; Tarrow,

2005). Between 40,000 and 50,000 activists descended upon Seattle and, as skirmishes between activists and the police gained in magnitude, the event came to be known as the Battle of Seattle. These types of groups were initially labelled the "antiglobalization movement." However, they are not opposed to globalization in its entirety, but only certain aspects of globalization. Furthermore, they are actually participants in globalization as well. They organize transnational networks, and use the communication technologies of globalization to organize activities that occur simultaneously in countries around the world. Consequently, they are now more accurately described as "global justice movements" rather than "antiglobalization movements."

Global justice movements participate in different types of activities: they organize protests at meetings of the World Bank, IMF, and WTO; they operate their own summits to counter the meetings of the transnational institutions; they develop campaigns related to specific issues, such as the Alberta oil sands, debt relief for developing nations, and working conditions (see *Sociology in My Community*); and they create infrastructures, such as the World Social Forum and the Independent Media Center (Indymedia).

The World Social Forum is an annual meeting, first held in 2001, that acts as a counter-summit to the World Economic Forum. The World Social Forum, attended by more than 100,000 people each year, "is an open meeting place where social movements, networks, NGOs and other civil society organizations opposed to neo-liberalism and a world dominated by capital or by any form of imperialism come together to pursue their thinking, to debate ideas democratically, for formulate proposals [sic], share their experiences freely and network for effective action" (World Social Forum, 2002). Regional social forums have emerged in a number of countries in the world as well. Indymedia is a collective of independent, alternative media organizations and journalists that provide noncorporate news coverage of events occurring throughout the world. Anyone can upload photos, videos, or audio to the site (www.indymedia.org).

TIME TO REVIEW

- In what ways do communication technologies enhance people's knowledge?

- How has globalization improved the economies of some developing nations?

- In what way does social inequality determine the effects of globalization?

- How does the economic dimension of globalization contribute to the exploitation of workers in the developing world, and to the race to the bottom in both the developing and developed worlds?

- Why have the IMF and the World Bank been criticized for their structures and some of their programs?

- What is the nature of the debate over the homogenization of cultures versus glocalization?

- How does globalization contribute to conflicts, terrorism, pandemics, and crime?

- What are global justice movements?

 # SOCIOLOGY IN THEORY

LO8 Because globalization is connected to a wide range of topics—social inequality, families, gender, ethnicity, media, religion, education, science, crime, environment, social movements, and health—the theories that can be applied to globalization are just as wide ranging. Thus, many of the theories that have been presented throughout the chapters in this book are applicable to those particular aspects of globalization as well. In addition to those particular theories, there are an almost countless number of what one might call "mini-theories" related to several of the specific topics addressed in this chapter, such as cultural homogenization, glocalization, Americanization, transnational capitalism, the transfer of nation-state power "upward" and "downward" (and the list could go on) (Ritzer, 2008). In fact, the lines between empirical and theoretical research can become quite blurred, in that some authors refer to many of the ideas presented in this chapter as "theories" rather than "concepts" (e.g., glocalization). But when trying to explain the global inequality that has emerged over time, and in some cases been enhanced with globalization, three theories are of particular relevance: modernization theory, dependency theory, and world systems theory.

The origins of *modernization theory* go back more than 200 years, when it was first argued that economic growth and technological innovation would yield moral and social progress. In the post–World War II era, modernization theory created a foundation for globalization. During the Cold War, the United States and the Soviet Union each argued that developing nations would be best served on their path to modernization by adopting the superpower's ideology (capitalism or communism) (Inglehart & Welzel, 2007).

Drawing upon functionalist assumptions, the post–World War II era version of modernization placed the responsibility for underdevelopment on the underdeveloped nations themselves. They lacked the capital to invest in modern industrial and agricultural practices. They also remained too tied to traditional, irrational values, and therefore lacked the rational values necessary to create a drive toward achievement, investment, and education (Lerner, 1958; Inkeles & Smith, 1976). By providing these nations with capital (e.g., through foreign aid and loans from transnational financial institutions) and instilling them with Western values, wealthy "modernized" nations could assist underdeveloped countries on a path to modernization; this was the solution to global inequality. Critics of modernization quickly emerged, and pointed out that underdevelopment is actually created by developed nations (Frank, 1966). This critique was embedded within dependency theory, and more recently world systems theory, both of which draw upon, in part, conflict theory—particularly Marxism.

Dependency theory proposes that the nations that were first to industrialize exploited other countries for their natural resources, such as oil, gold, and coffee. Although rich in natural resources, relationships of exploitation turned the latter countries into the mines or plantations of the developed world. Whichever resource was the most valued by colonizers and by the industrialized world as a whole was increasingly emphasized in the nation's economic production. As a result of domination and exploitation, these nations did not have the opportunity to develop their own independent economies (Frank, 1966; Furtado, 1984). Following decolonization, countries may have gained political independence but, because of the pattern of economic exploitation, have remained economically dependent on the developed world (Eitzen & Zinn, 2009).

Related to dependency theory, *world systems theory* (Wallerstein, 2000) also describes hierarchical relationships between nations that interact in the world system. *Core nations* are those that first industrialized; in many cases, they are also the countries that headed colonial empires. Core nations are wealthy and powerful within the world system. *Semiperipheral nations* are those that became economically dependent on the core nations, because of trade relationships. Next are the *peripheral* Eastern European nations whose economies are even less developed. Finally, there is the *external area* that historically has had limited or nonexistent economic relationships with the core nations; however, this has changed with globalization, and these are the countries that are most vulnerable to exploitation. For both dependency theory and world systems theory, globalization is problematic. But there are varying points of view on what the solution is. Some adherents of these views suggest that countries within the semiperiphery, periphery, and external areas would benefit from separating from the global economy and developing their own cooperative economic relationships with each other. Other adherents of these views argue that the solution to exploitative relations and global inequality lie in creating new transnational financial and political institutions, or reforming the existing ones (Chase-Dunn, 2007)

TIME TO REVIEW

- In what way does modernization theory blame underdeveloped nations for their own lack of development?
- According to dependency theory, why do developing nations remain dependent upon the developed world, even after being decolonized?
- According to world systems theory, what are the relationships between core, semiperipheral, peripheral, and external nations?

As proposed by Paul Virilio, quoted at the beginning of this chapter, globalization has not just transformed the world, but also has become the world. Through its technological, economic, political, and cultural dimensions, it affects the lives of virtually every person on the planet. We see its presence in media, culture, social structure, stratification and social inequality, families, gender, ethnicity, crime, religion, science, education, health and illness, the environment, and social movements. The importance of the sociological imagination is perhaps most evident when considering the nature and implications of globalization. Who benefits from globalization? Who is harmed by it, and in what ways? And how do we maximize the benefits while minimizing the harms for people who are living in both the developed and developing nations of the world? These are questions that can be answered only by using the sociological imagination, tracing the complex interconnections between the micro level of individual choices and experiences, and the macro level of larger sociocultural and global forces.

CHAPTER SUMMARY

LO¹ Define "globalization" and differentiate it from "globality."

"Globalization" is the process by which "globality"—the tight global economic, political, cultural, and environmental interconnections and flows that make most of the current borders and boundaries irrelevant—is achieved. More informally, globalization is sometimes referred to as the greater interconnectedness of the world's people.

LO² Describe historical precursors to globalization.

The dynamic that underlies globalization is thousands of years old, involving the migration of people, the exchange of goods, the creation of trade routes, and the sharing of information. In the late 19th century, the invention of the steamship and the laying of the first transatlantic telegraph line lowered the cost and increased the speed of transportation and communication.

LO³ Explain how changes after World War II precipitated modern globalization.

Several changes following World War II heralded modern globalization: the dissolution of colonial empires; the formation of transnational political and financial institutions such as the United Nations, the International Monetary Fund, the World Bank, and the World Trade Organization; and the fall of the Soviet Union.

LO⁴ Describe the technological, economic, political, cultural, and social characteristics of globalization.

Technology facilitates all other dimensions of globalization. Information storage and retrieval, transportation, communication, and production have been transformed. The economic dimension includes expanding markets, flexible production and the global assembly line, and corporate restructuring that resulted in a concentration of economic power. The political dimension of globalization involves the declining power of nation-states, shifting their power "upward" to transnational bodies and "downward" to regional trade bodies, global cities, and global civil society.

LO⁵ Outline the vision of globalization including its proposed world benefits.

Proponents of globalization suggest that its technological, economic, political, and cultural dimensions have the potential to (1) improve living conditions through the globalization of production, (2) spread democracy, and (3) increase knowledge and understanding, thereby decreasing conflict.

LO⁶ Describe the dark side of globalization highlighted by various social organizations.

Global social inequality not only continues to be a problem, but also in many ways has increased.

Workers in developing nations are frequently exploited and subjected to poor working conditions. The "race to the bottom" lowers wages and increases job insecurity in both developing and developed nations. Transnational organizations such as the IMF and the World Bank are criticized for being governed by the interests of wealthy, powerful nations, and for their structural adjustment programs that require spending on social programs to be reduced. A trend toward homogenization and uniformity of culture occurs, at the expense of local cultures. Concerns about the Americanization of global culture are paramount, although others argue that global and local cultures are frequently combined.

LO⁷ Describe global justice movements including their affiliated activities.

Global justice movements are social justice movements with a unifying interest in resisting neoliberalism and its effects. They are opposed to certain aspects of globalization, yet are also participants in it. Their activities include organizing protests at meetings of transnational financial institutions; hosting counter-summits; developing campaigns about specific issues, such as child labour; and developing infrastructures such as the World Social Forum and Indymedia.

LO⁸ Explain how modernization theory, dependency theory, and world systems theory contribute to our understanding of global inequality.

Modernization theory attributes underdevelopment to characteristics of the underdeveloped nations themselves. Consequently, developed nations are in a position to "help" other countries on the path to modernization. Dependency theory suggests that the countries first to industrialize exploited the resources of other nations, turning them into their own personal mines or plantations. World systems theory describes a hierarchical relationship between core, semiperipheral, peripheral, and external countries, where the latter three are all economically dependent on the core.

RECOMMENDED READINGS

1. For a detailed look at the way that globalization has affected women in the developing world, see: Ehrenreich, B., & Hochschild, A. R. (2002). *Global Women: Nannies, Maids, and Sex Workers in the New Economy*. New York: Henry Holt and Reinhart.

2. George Ritzer uses the fast-food restaurant as a metaphor for the way that rationality, efficiency, and uniformity have come to characterize the globalizing world, in the following book: Ritzer, G. (2010). *The McDonaldization of Society* (6th ed.). Thousand Oaks, CA: Sage.

3. To further explore the argument that Canadian popular culture has not become homogenized, but rather is distinct from the popular culture of other nations, see: Beaty, B., Briton, D., Filax, G., & Sullivan, R. (Eds.) (2010). *How Canadians Communicate III: Contexts of Popular Culture.* Edmonton, AB: Athabasca University Press.

FOR FURTHER REFLECTION

1. In your opinion, in what ways has Canadian culture been "Americanized," and in what ways is it characterized by glocalization?
2. What image of global justice movements is portrayed in the media? What impact might these portrayals have on the efforts of global justice groups?
3. What are the solutions to reducing global inequality? What changes are needed economically, politically, and culturally?

REFERENCES

Canadian Broadcasting Corporation. (2003). *CBC News: Indepth: SARS Timeline.* Retrieved January 7, 2011, from www.cbc.ca/news/background/sars/timeline.html

Chase-Dunn, C. (2007). Dependency and world systems theories. In G. Ritzer (Ed.), *Encyclopedia of Sociology.* Retrieved February 19, 2011, from www.blackwellreferenceonline.com

Clarke, J. N. (2008). *Health, Illness, and Medicine in Canada* (5th ed.). Don Mills, ON: Oxford University Press.

Della Porta, D., & Tarrow, S. (2005). *Transnational Protest and Global Activism.* Lanham, MD: Rowman and Littlefield.

Eitzen, D. S., & Zinn, M. B. (2009). Globalization: An introduction. In D. S. Eitzen and M. B. Zinn (Eds.), *Globalization: The Transformation of Social Worlds* (pp. 1–9). Belmont, CA: Wadworth Cengage Learning.

Ehrenreich, B., & Hochschild, A. R. (2009). Global women: Nannies, maids, and sex workers in the New Economy. In D. S. Eitzen and M. B. Zinn (Eds.), *Globalization: The Transformation of Social Worlds* (pp. 165–174). Belmont, CA: Wadworth Cengage Learning.

Faux, J. (2009). NAFTA at 10: Where do we go from here? In D. S. Eitzen and M. B. Zinn (Eds.), *Globalization: The Transformation of Social Worlds* (pp. 64–67). Belmont, CA: Wadworth Cengage Learning.

Ferus-Comelo, A. (2009). Double jeopardy: Gender and migration in electronics manufacturing. In D. S. Eitzen and M. B. Zinn (Eds.), *Globalization: The Transformation of Social Worlds* (pp. 87–98). Belmont, CA: Wadworth Cengage Learning.

Frank, A. G. (1966). The development of underdevelopment. *Monthly Review, 18*(4), 17–31.

Furtado, C. (1984). *Recession and Unemployment: An Examination of the Brazilian Economic Crisis.* London, UK: TW Foundation.

Galloway, G. (2011, February 25). Michael Moore adds star power to Manitoba mining battle. *The Globe and Mail.* Retrieved February 25, 2011, from www.globeandmail.com

Gordon, J., & Knickerbocker Designs. (2009). The sweat behind the shirt: The labor history of a Gap sweatshirt. In D. S. Eitzen and M. B. Zinn (Eds.), *Globalization: The Transformation of Social Worlds* (p. 86). Belmont, CA: Wadworth Cengage Learning.

Government of Alberta. (2011). *Asia Pacific.* Retrieved February 25, 2011, from www.international.alberta.ca

Harlequin Enterprises (2011). *Harlequin: About Us.* Retrieved February 23, 2011, from www.eharlequin.com

Hebron, L., & Stack, J. F. (2011). *Globalization* (2nd ed.). New York: Longman.

Inglehart, R., & Welzel, C. (2007). Modernization. In G. Ritzer (Ed.). *Encyclopedia of Sociology.* Retrieved February 19, 2011, from www.blackwellreferenceonline.com

Inkeles, A., & Smith, D. H. (1976). *Becoming Modern: Individual Change in Six Developing Countries.* Cambridge, MA: Harvard University Press.

International Labour Organization. (2008). *ILO Declaration on Social Justice for a Fair Globalization.* Geneva: Author.

Johnson, D. (2011). Unions file suit to halt collective bargaining legislation. *JSOnline, June 15.* Retrieved August 18, 2011, from www.jsonline.com

Lee, S. H. (2007a). International Monetary Fund. In G. Ritzer (Ed.), *Encyclopedia of Sociology.* Retrieved February 19, 2011, from www.blackwellreferenceonline.com

Lee, S. H. (2007b). World Bank. In G. Ritzer (Ed.), *Encyclopedia of Sociology.* Retrieved February 19, 2011, from www.blackwellreferenceonline.com

Lee, S. H. (2007c). World Trade Organization. In G. Ritzer (Ed.), *Encyclopedia of Sociology.* Retrieved February 19, 2011, from www.blackwellreferenceonline.com

Legrain, P. (2002). *Open World: The Truth About Globalization.* London: Abacus.

Lerner, D. (1958). *The Passing of Tradition Society: Modernity in the Middle East.* Glencoe, IL: Free Press.

Moberg, D. (2009). Maytag moves to Mexico. In D. S. Eitzen and M. B. Zinn (Eds.), *Globalization: The Transformation of Social Worlds* (pp. 81–85). Belmont, CA: Wadworth Cengage Learning.

Qureshi, M. (2004). Globalization: Friend or foe in the developing world. In UNESCO (Ed.), *Globalization with a Human Face: Benefitting All* (pp. 58–62). Paris: UNESCO.

Ramos, F. (2004). Caring, sharing, and daring: Making globalization work for all. In UNESCO (Ed.), *Globalization with a Human Face: Benefitting All* (pp. 48–57). Paris: UNESCO.

Ray, L. (2007). Globalization. In G. Ritzer (Ed.), *Encyclopedia of Sociology*. Retrieved February 19, 2011, from www .blackwellreferenceonline.com

Ritzer, G. (2008). *Modern Sociological Theory* (7th ed.). Whitby, ON: McGraw Hill Ryerson.

Robertson, R. (1992). *Globalization: Social Theory and Global Culture*. Belmont, CA: Sage.

Sheptycki, J. (2007). Transnational crime and transnational policing. *Sociology Compass, 1*(2), 485–498.

Stegar, M. B. (2009). *Globalization: A Very Short Introduction*. New York: Oxford University Press.

Tarrow, S. (2005). *The New Transnational Activism*. Cambridge, MA: Cambridge University Press.

Treleven, E. (2011, March 18). Judge orders temporary halt to collective bargaining; state will appeal. *Wisconsin State Journal*. Retrieved April 23, 2011, from http://host. madison.com/wsj.

United Nations. (2010). *The Millenium Development Goals Report 2010*. New York: Author.

UNESCO. (2004). *Globalization with a Human Face: Benefitting All*. Paris: Author.

Wallerstein, I. M. (2000). *The Essential Wallerstein*. New York: The New York Press.

Weeks, J. R. (2008). *Population: An Introduction to Concepts and Issues*. Belmont, CA: Thomson Wadsworth.

World Health Organization. (2003). *The World Health Report 2003: Shaping the Future*. Geneva: Author.

World Social Forum. (2002). What the World Social Forum is. Retrieved February 1, 2011, from www .forumsocialmundial.org.br/main.php?id_menu=19&cd_ language=2.

Wyatt, E. (2004, August 17). "Sorry, Harlequin," she sighed tenderly, "I'm reading something else." The *New York Times*. Retrieved February 23, 2011, from www.nytimes.com

ENDNOTES

[1] Retrieved February 17, 2011, from www.brainyquote.com

[2] Retrieved February 17, 2011, from www.brainyquote.com

Glossary

A

Abolitionism: A movement calling for the dismantling of the criminal justice system. p. 223

Achieved status: A social position obtained through personal effort. p. 108

Acid rain: The dilute sulphuric and nitric acids created when fossil fuels are burned. p. 291

Acting crowd: A group of people gathered at the same place at the same time and who engage in overt collective behaviour in pursuit of a common goal. p. 263

Action research: A field method for pursuing change while studying a social system. p. 38

Agency: People's capacity to make choices, which then have an impact on other people and on the society in which they live. p. 6

Alienation: Refers to the detachment that exists between the worker and his labour as perpetuated under capitalism. p. 134

Alternative social movements: Social movements that seek limited societal change for a specific group or narrow segment of society. p. 273

Androcentric: Male-centred, failing to account for women's experiences. p. 15

Androcentric bias: A tendency to favour males. p. 200

Anomie: A feeling of normlessness. p. 11

Anthropocentrism: A world view that considers humans to be the most important form of life. p. 293

Anti-miscegenation laws: Laws that prohibit interracial marriages. p. 176

Ascribed status: A social position conferred at birth. p. 108

Assimilation: The process by which a minority group is absorbed into the culture of the dominant group. p. 81

Authoritarian parenting: A parenting style characterized by high expectations for children, very strict rules, no explanation of the rationale for the rules, strict punishment for rule breaking, and unidirectional communication. p. 173

Authoritarian personality: A personality type that values authority and obedience, is low in tolerance, and is high in insecurity. p. 182

Auxiliary traits: Characteristics that are presumed to accompany a specific master status. p. 141

B

Baby boom: The period from 1946 to 1965 during which several demographic forces coalesced, resulting in a larger number of births than would normally be the case. p. 248

Belief: Something one accepts as true, regardless of whether it is actually true or not. p. 189

Belief system: A set of interconnected beliefs that are shared among groups of people. p. 189

Bicultural: Participating in two distinct cultures simultaneously. p. 173

Bisexuality: Sexual attraction to both males and females. p. 148

Bonding capital: Resources in the form of religious community ties and identity. p. 193

Bourgeoisie: In Marxist conflict theory, the owners of the means of production. p. 12

Bridging capital: Resources accumulated within religious groups that can be used outside the religious realm. p. 193

Bureaucracy: A formal organization model that consists of an explicit chain of authority and a set of procedures and protocols that guide the relationships and processes that exist within it. p. 111

C

Carbon footprint: A method for identifying and keeping track of behaviours that negatively impact the environment through greenhouse gas production. p. 287

Caste system: A system of stratification based on inherited social standing. p. 126

Causal crowd: A gathering of people who by proximity alone happen to be in the same location at the same time. p. 262

Child-savers movement: A movement dedicated to the betterment of social conditions involving children. p. 194

Claim: A statement about the nature of some phenomenon that is constructed as a social problem. p. 271

Claims making: A process wherein a social movement declares that a particular condition is unjust and identifies measures needed to resolve the unfairness. p. 271

Class system: A system of stratification based primarily on economic measures such as annual income or the possession of resources. p. 128

Cohort: A group of people born during the same period of time or who have experienced a significant event at the same time. p. 84

Collective behaviour: Group behaviour that is relatively spontaneous, unstructured, and unconventional in nature. p. 261

Collective conscience: The accumulated wisdom of a culture that develops from participation in religious rituals. p. 195

Collective effervescence: The enthusiasm to transcend the challenges of everyday life, which emerges from religious rituals. p. 195

Collective identity: A shared sense of belonging that binds individuals in a social movement and propels them to take action on behalf of that social movement. p. 276

Comparison level: A comparison of the costs and benefits of a particular relationship compared to other people who are in similar types of relationships. p. 85

Comparison level for alternatives: A comparison of our relationship to alternative possibilities for our lives. p. 85

Concept: An abstract idea that is expressed as a word or phrase. p. 24

Conglomerate: A corporation made up of several different widely diversified companies. p. 51

Consumption: The general use of natural resources. p. 286

Content analysis: A secondary analysis technique used to systematically examine messages contained in text or portrayed in images. p. 37

Control group: Participants in an experiment who are not exposed to the independent variable. p. 32

Conventional crowd: A group of people who have gathered in the same place at the same time because of a common shared interest or objective. p. 262

Corporate crime: Criminal offences carried out by organizations or by knowledgeable employees in the course of their employment. p. 220

Cost of living: A measure of the average price for essential goods and services in a given area including transportation. p. 118

Counterculture: A type of subculture that strongly opposes central aspects of mainstream culture. p. 104

Credentialism: The reliance on increasingly higher educational qualifications as necessary minimal requirements for employment. p. 206

Crime: A specific form of deviance that involves the violation of criminal law. p. 215

Criminal justice system: The social institution responsible for the apprehension, prosecution, and punishment of criminal offenders. p. 221

Criminologists: Researchers who specialize in the study of crime, which is a specific form of deviant behaviour. p. 215

Criminology: The academic discipline that focuses on the study of crime and those labelled as criminals, and is considered to be either a subdiscipline within sociology or a discipline related to sociology. p. 215

Critical: Theorizing that explores the role that power plays in social processes, and emphasizes the importance of knowledge being tied to emancipation. p. 10

Critical research: Assesses outcomes of some aspect of the social world. p. 26

Crowd: A temporary gathering of people who are in the same place at the same time. p. 262

Crude birth rate: The number of live births in a given year per 1,000 people. p. 283

Crude death rate: The number of deaths in a given year per 1,000 people. p. 283

Cultural relativism: The perspective that a society's customs and ideas should be described objectively and understood within the context of that society's problems and opportunities. p. 103

Cultural universals: Common practices shared by all societies. p. 95

Culture: The sum total of the social environment in which we are raised and continue to be socialized throughout our lives. p. 95

D

Data analysis: Compilation of observations into a format that helps us learn more about the research problem. p. 27

Debriefing: The later disclosure of all relevant details in cases where research participants cannot be told all of the information ahead of time. p. 30

Decolonization: The process whereby colonial empires are dismantled and former colonies are granted political and economic independence. p. 306

Deductive reasoning: A theory-driven approach that typically concludes with generalizations based on research findings. p. 24

Deference: Nonverbal shows of appreciation and respect. p. 110

Demeanour: Mannerisms and dress that convey particular qualities. p. 110

Demographic transition theory: As a result of modernization, societies eventually progress from being characterized by high fertility and mortality rates to being characterized by low fertility and mortality rates. p. 283

Demography: The study of human populations. p. 281

Dependent variable: The outcome or variable that is measured in an experiment. p. 33

Descriptive research: Describes features and characteristics of a group, event, activity, or situation. p. 25

Diffuse pattern: Uncertainty about which culture(s) one should or should not identify with. p. 174

Disaster: A relatively sudden, unscheduled, one-time event that causes a great deal of property or ecological damage, or large-scale loss of life, and substantial disruption or stress among residents in the stricken area. p. 270

Discourses: Ways of understanding a particular subject or social phenomenon. p. 16

Discrimination: Treating someone unfairly because of his or her group membership. p. 180

Disposable societies: Societies characterized by an excess of manufactured products that are used for only a short period of time and then disposed of. p. 287

Dominant group: A group that has institutionalized power and privilege in society. p. 175

Dual/split labour market theory: Members of the dominant group in society will develop prejudices against minority groups in order to protect their position in the labour market. p. 183

Dualism: A contrast between two opposing categories. p. 143

Dysfunctional: One of society's structures no longer fulfills its function effectively. p. 11

E

Ecological footprint: An estimate for gauging how much land and water area a human population requires to produce the resources it consumes and to absorb its wastes, using prevailing technology. p. 281

Economic immigrants: Immigrants selected on the basis of their educational backgrounds, occupational skills, and ability to contribute to the Canadian economy. p. 169

Education: A formal institution that systematically instills much of the knowledge that is needed to function as productive adults in society. p. 201

Emblems: Gestures with direct verbal equivalents. p. 101

Empirical methods: Data collection that produces verifiable findings and is carried out using systematic procedures. p. 24

Environmental refugee: A person who is forced to flee his or her country as a result of environmental displacement resulting from life-endangering natural and human-made environmental change. p. 293

Equity: The contributions that each party is making in a relationship are perceived as "fair." p. 85

Ethnic pattern: Identifying primarily with one's heritage culture. p. 173

Ethnicity: Cultural characteristics such as language, religion, taste in food, shared descent, cultural traditions, and shared geographical locations. p. 165

Ethnocentrism: The tendency to believe that one's cultural beliefs and practices are superior and should be used as the standard to which other cultures are compared. p. 104

Ethnocide: The eradication of a culture. p. 81

Ethnography: Field work designed to gather data in real-world environments. p. 37

Ethnomethodology: A research method used to examine ways in which people make sense of their everyday world. p. 110

Experiment: A deductive research method that is used to test a hypothesis through the use of a carefully controlled environment and random assignment to conditions. p. 32

Explanatory research: Clarifies aspects of a particular social phenomenon. p. 25

Exploratory research: Explores an area of interest about which very little is known. p. 25

Expressive crowd: A gathering of people who share a common interest and are gathered at the same event at the same time with an explicit participatory purpose. p. 262

Extended: A family structure that includes parents, their children, and additional relatives. p. 79

F

Fads: Temporary but highly popular social patterns such as activities, events, music genres, or hobbies. p. 266

Family of orientation: The family into which you were born or in which you were raised. p. 69

Family of procreation: The family that you establish in adulthood. p. 69

Family-class immigrants: Immigrants who are sponsored by close relatives living in Canada. p. 169

Fashion: Long-lasting popular social patterns that typically involve clothing and clothing accessories. p. 266

Femininity: The thoughts, feelings, and behaviours associated with being female. p. 143

Feminism: The system of ideas and political practices based on the principle that women are human beings equal to men. p. 14

Fertility: The actual level of childbearing for an individual or a population. p. 282

Fictive kin: Individuals who are not related by blood, marriage, or adoption but assume some of the benefits and/ or some of the obligations of family life. p. 72

Financial wealth: Corresponds to economic assets that are derived from income, real estate, savings, stocks, bonds, income-generating investments, and other sources of revenue or capital. p. 117

Folkways: Informal norms that are based in accepted tradition. p. 99

G

Gender: The expected and actual thoughts, feelings, and behaviours associated with a particular sex, within a certain culture, at a given point in history. p. 143

Generalized other: An overall sense of people's expectations. p. 13

Global warming: An increase in the temperature of Earth's atmosphere. p. 291

Globality: A social condition characterized by tight global economic, political, cultural and environmental interconnections and flows that make most of the current borders and boundaries irrelevant. p. 305

Globalization: A set of [uneven] social processes that appear to transform our present social condition of weakening nationality into one of globality. p. 305

Glocalization: The blending of the global and the local. p. 317

Gossip: Unsubstantiated or substantiated stories about specific individuals. p. 267

Greenwashing: The misleading of consumers regarding the environmental practices of a company or the environmental benefits of a product or service. p. 289

Gross Domestic Product (GDP): An overall indicator of a country's economic productivity based on goods and services as measured by household consumption, government spending, and investments. p. 124

H

Hate crimes: Criminal offences that are motivated by hate toward an identifiable group. p. 180

Healthy immigrant effect: Recent immigrants tend to have better health than people who are Canadian-born. p. 245

Heterosexuality: Sexual attraction to members of the "opposite sex." p. 144

Hidden curriculum: The process by which a subtle agenda of norms, values, and expectations that fall outside the formal curriculum are learned inadvertently through participation in the school system. p. 205

High culture: Activities shared by the social elite. p. 105

High-consensus deviance: Behaviours or characteristics that are widely accepted as being deviant and in need of social control. p. 214

Homelessness: A state in which a person is unable to secure a permanent residence. p. 123

Homosexuality: Sexual attraction to members of the "same sex." p. 144

Human carrying capacity: The number of people that can be supported in a given area indefinitely. p. 282

Human Exemptionalism Paradigm (HEP): The view of human as unique from other organisms in the natural world because of their capacity to reason and develop culture. p. 293

Hypermasculinity: Traditional masculinity in an extreme and exaggerated form. p. 146

Hypothesis: A testable research statement that includes at least two variables. p. 27

I

Ideal culture: Cultural values a majority of people identify with in a given society. p. 103

Ideal type: An analytical construct that so clearly depicts all of the main features of some social phenomenon it serves as an exemplary tool but is not an entity that can be found in reality. p. 111

Ideology: A set of ideas that support the needs and views of a particular group. p. 106

Independent variable: The presumed cause or variable that is manipulated in an experiment. p. 32

Indictable conviction offences: More serious criminal offences punishable by more than two years in prison. p. 217

Inductive reasoning: A data-driven approach that begins with observations and ends in theory construction. p. 25

Infant mortality rate: The incidence of deaths among infants under one year of age per 1,000 live births in a given population. p. 283

Institutionalized goals: The goals that we are *supposed* to aspire to in contemporary society. p. 226

Integration pattern: Identifying with both one's heritage culture and one's new, national culture. p. 173

Intergenerational mobility: Changes in the social class of children relative to their parents. p. 131

Internet crime: Criminal offences that take place online. p. 220

Interpretive: Theorizing that focuses on the ways that people come to understand themselves, others, and the world around them. p. 10

Intersexed: A person whose physical sex characteristics fall outside the boundaries of the dualism of male/female. p. 144

Interview: A verbal question-and-answer technique used for obtaining information on a topic of interest. p. 35

Intragenerational mobility: Changes in social class that occur within a person's lifetime. p. 131

L

Language: An abstract system of word meanings and symbols including spoken, written, and signed forms of verbal and nonverbal communications that are used to encode and decode cultural components. p. 96

Latent function: An unintended function of one of society's structures. p. 11

Legitimate means: The socially accepted ways of attaining wealth, power, and prestige. p. 226

Les femmes du pays: The Aboriginal "country wives" of European traders. p. 80

Life chances: The opportunities that an individual has in life, based on various factors including stratification, inequality, race, ethnicity, and gender. p. 5

Looking-glass self: The sense of ourselves that we develop based on our perceptions of how others view us. p. 142

Low-consensus deviance: Behaviours and characteristics about which there is considerable disagreement over whether they are deviant or not. p. 214

Low-income cut-off: An annual family income value in dollars below which a family is worse off than average due to the high proportion of income allocated to food, clothing, and shelter. p. 120

M

Macro level: The level of broader social forces. p. 5

Manifest function: An intended function of one of society's structures. p. 11

Masculinity: The thoughts, feelings, and behaviours associated with being male. p. 143

Mass media: Communications that target large audiences in print or in electronic format using audio and/or images. p. 46

Master status: The most influential status in an individual's status set. p. 109

Material culture: Tangible or physical items that people have created for use and give meaning to in a given culture. p. 96

Matriarchal: Power is vested in females. p. 80

Matrilineal: Lineage is traced through the mother's side of the family, especially its female members. p. 80

Media literacy: The ability to recognize, critically assess, and make informed choices about the messages contained in mass media forms. p. 60

Median age: The age that divides the population in half. p. 248

Medicalization: Certain characteristics or conditions are defined in medical language, understood through the adoption of a medical framework, or "treated" with medical intervention. p. 253

Meritocracy: A condition of advancement based on worth. p. 133

Micro level: The level of individual experiences and choices. p. 5

Migration: The movement of people into or out of a country. p. 283

Minority groups: Definable groups that are socially disadvantaged and face unequal treatment. p. 176

Monogamous: A marriage that includes two spouses. p. 79

Monopoly: A company that has exclusive control over a particular product or service. p. 50

Moral entrepreneur: Person who brings perceived morally damaging behaviour to the attention of others. p. 268

Moral panic: Irrational but widespread worry that certain groups present an enormous threat to the social order of society. p. 268

Morbidity: The prevalence and patterns of disease in a population. p. 236

Mores: Formal norms embedded in laws that are needed to maintain social control. p. 99

Mortality: The incidence and patterns of death in a population. p. 236

Mother tongue: The first language learned at home in childhood that is still understood by an individual. p. 97

Motives: The reasons for engaging in either deviant or conforming behaviour. p. 227

N

National pattern: Identifying primarily with one's new, national culture. p. 173

Negative bonding capital: Religious community ties and sources of identity that pose harm to the wider society. p. 193

Neoliberalism: An economic philosophy that claims that when market forces are unimpeded by government, prosperity and democracy will flourish. p. 307

Net migration rate: The difference between the number of persons entering and leaving a country during a specified year per 1,000 people. p. 283

Net worth: Total assets calculated by subtracting all existing financial liabilities from assets. p. 118

New Ecological Paradigm (NEP): The view of humans as possessing a superior capacity to reason and adapt to social/cultural conditions while also recognizing the interdependence between humans and the natural environment. p. 294

Nonmaterial culture: Intangibles produced by intellectual or spiritual development and the use of artifacts in a given culture. p. 96

Norm of communism: The notion that scientific knowledge is to be freely shared with others. p. 197

Norm of disinterestedness: The notion that scientists do their work solely for the purposes of discovering truth. p. 197

Norm of organized skepticism: The notion that scientific claims should be subjected to rigorous scrutiny. p. 197

Norm of universalism: The notion that scientific knowledge is free of social biases. p. 197

Normative: Behaviours, appearances, and thoughts that correspond to society's norms. p. 4

Norms: Society's expectations for how we are supposed to act, think, and look. p. 4

Nuclear: A family structure comprising parents and their children. p. 79

O

Objective ethnicity: The ethnic characteristics of your ancestors. p. 165

Operationalization: The process whereby variables are defined in a precise manner that is measureable. p. 27

Organized crime: Two or more persons consorting together on a continual basis to participate in illegal activities, either directly or indirectly, for gain. p. 220

Overconsumption: Use of resources at a rate that exceeds sustainability. p. 286

P

Paradigm: A conceptual framework or model for organizing information. p. 197

Paradigm shift: Movement away from a particular conceptual framework. p. 197

Participant observation: A naturalistic method for collecting systematic data while taking part in a social group or process. p. 38

Patriarchy: Legal and/or social power that is vested in males. p. 15

Patrilineal: Lineage is traced through the father's side of the family, especially its male members. p. 80

Personal–social identity continuum: The range of traits you possess that emphasize the manner in which you see yourself as a unique individual on one end and those which underscore your membership in a group on the other end. p. 141

Pluralism: Cultural differences are maintained and celebrated. p. 176

Polygamous: A marriage that includes three or more spouses simultaneously. p. 79

Popular culture: Well-liked everyday practices and products. p. 106

Population checks: Factors that limit population growth. p. 282

Population pyramid: A horizontal bar chart that shows how many people are in the various age groups, divided by sex. p. 248

Population transfer: A process whereby minority groups are forcibly expelled or are limited to a specific location. p. 178

Positive bonding capital: Religious community ties and sources of identity that are of benefit to the wider society. p. 193

Positivist: Theorizing that emphasizes explanation and prediction. p. 10

Praxis: The responsibility that scholars have to provide subordinated and marginalized groups in society with the knowledge that they need to be able to end their powerlessness. p. 13

Prejudice: An attitude that is unrelated to reality and is generalized to all members of a certain group. p. 179

Prescriptive norms: Rules concerning behaviours we are expected to do. p. 100

Primary deviance: The little acts of deviance that many of us engage in occasionally. p. 228

Private schools: Schools that are operated by private individuals or corporations, for which parents pay an annual tuition. p. 206

Profit: The benefits of being in a particular relationship outweigh the costs. p. 85

Proletariat: In Marxist conflict theory, the people who work for the owners of the means of production. p. 12

Property crimes: Criminal offences that are directed at someone's property, rather than at someone's physical person. p. 217

Proscriptive norms: Rules concerning behaviours we are expected to refrain from doing. p. 100

Public schools: Schools that are funded through provincial and local governments. p. 206

R

Race: A system of stratification based on physical differences, such as facial features, skin colour, and hair texture. p. 166

Racism: A specific form of prejudice based on aspects of physical appearance such as skin colour. p. 179

Real culture: Practices engaged in by the majority of people in a given society. p. 103

Realistic conflict theory: Prejudice emerges as a result of competition over scarce resources. p. 183

Recession: A general economic decline that persists for two or more three-month periods. p. 124

Recidivism: Committing further crimes after having been convicted of a crime. p. 142

Redemptive social movements: Social movements that seek large-scale change for a specific group. p. 273

Reformative social movements: Social movements that seek limited societal change for everyone in society. p. 273

Refugees: Persons who are forced to flee from persecution. p. 169

Reliability: There is consistency in the measure for a variable of interest. p. 27

Religion: A social institution involving beliefs and practices based on recognizing the sacred. p. 191

Religiosity index: A combined measure of religious affiliation, attendance, and participation. p. 192

Religious affiliation: The identification with a particular religion. p. 191

Religious attendance: Attendance at organized religious services. p. 191

Representative sample: A group that closely approximates the population of interest. p. 34

Research design: A detailed outline of all of the proposed components of a study. p. 27

Respondents: Persons who consent to provide survey answers. p. 34

Restorative justice: An approach to justice emphasizing healing and reparation of harm. p. 224

Retribution: A morally justified consequence. p. 222

Revolutionary social movements: Social movements that seek large-scale change that affects everyone in society. p. 274

Role conflict: A situation in which incompatible role demands exist between two or more commonly held statuses. p. 109

Role strain: A situation in which incompatible role demands exist within a single status. p. 109

Role: The behavioural component of a given status. p. 108

Rumours: Unsubstantiated stories about people or events. p. 266

S

Sapir-Whorf hypothesis: As a function of linguistic determinism and relativism, language shapes reality. p. 97

Scapegoat: An individual or group that is wrongfully blamed for a personal or social problem. p. 182

Science: An institution that provides a way to understand the natural makeup of the world by means of rational methods of inquiry. p. 196

Scientism: A world view that uses the insights of natural science to inform people's ways of living, their purpose in life, and the choices they make. p. 196

Secondary analysis of existing data: A research method used to examine information on a topic of interest that was originally collected by someone other than the researcher for an unrelated purpose. p. 36

Secondary deviance: Chronic deviance as a lifestyle. p. 229

Secular: The state of not being governed by religion. p. 191

Segregation: Minority groups are separated from the dominant group. p. 176

Self-fulfilling prophecy: An originally false belief that becomes true simply because it is perceived as such. p. 207

Self-surveillance: Monitoring our own behaviours in order to prevent being considered deviant. p. 229

Sex: Biological characteristics that include sex chromosomes, primary sex characteristics, and secondary sex characteristics. p. 143

Sexual scripts: The framework that we use to understand our own sexuality and that guides our sexual lives. p. 148

Significant others: People who are important to us. p. 13

Sister province relationships: Multifaceted relationships with another region that help promote economic development–related activities as well as cross-cultural awareness and cooperation in areas such as culture, education, sports, agriculture, technology, governance, and tourism. p. 310

Social capital: Resources in the form of accumulated social networks. p. 193

Social causation hypothesis: The suggestion that the stresses associated with having a lower socioeconomic status contribute to the development of mental disorders. p. 244

Social control: Actions that are intended to punish, "fix," or prevent deviant behaviour. p. 214

Social facts: Observable social phenomenon external to individuals that exercise power over them. p. 102

Social group: Two or more people who share relevant cultural elements and interact with regular frequency. p. 110

Social inequality: An unequal distribution of resources. p. 117

Social institutions: Relatively permanent societal structures that govern the behaviour of groups and promote social order. p. 111

Social mobility: Movement that occurs within and between social classes in a stratification system. p. 131

Social movement organization (SMO): A complex or formal organization that identifies its goals with the preferences of a social movement or a countermovement and attempts to implement those goals. p. 273

Social movements: Organized efforts by a substantial number of people to change or to resist change, in some major aspect or aspects of society. p. 271

Social safety net: Services and programs designed to lessen financial burdens experienced by low-income groups. p. 125

Social selection hypothesis: The suggestion that people with mental disorders may drift into lower levels of socioeconomic status, or be prevented from rising out of lower levels of status. p. 244

Social stratification: Socially sanctioned patterns (or classes) of social inequality that exist in society and are based on distinguishable attributes such as race, age, gender, income, or occupation. p. 126

Social structure: The framework of cultural elements and social patterns in which social interactions take place. p. 108

Socialization: The lifelong process of acquiring skills, internalizing norms, learning values, and discovering particular behaviours and techniques needed to function in society through our interactions with others. p. 50

Socioeconomic status: Social standing based on a combined measure of education, income, and occupation. p. 131

Sociological imagination: The ability to perceive the interconnections between individual experiences and larger sociocultural forces. p. 7

Sociology: The systematic study of society, using the sociological imagination. p. 6

Status: a recognized social position that exists independently of any given individual who may occupy it. p. 108

Status set: The sum total of all of the statuses held by a person at a given time. p. 108

Status symbols: Material indicators of wealth and prestige. p. 106

Stereotype: An overgeneralization about a group that is often based on faulty assumptions. p. 56

Stigmatization: The process by which individuals are excluded because of particular behaviours/characteristics. p. 229

Streaming: A process whereby students are placed into specific programs and levels of curriculum based on perceived levels of achievement. p. 205

Subculture: A group that can be differentiated from mainstream culture by its divergent traits involving language, norms, beliefs, and/or values. p. 104

Subjective ethnicity: An individual's own self-definition of ethnicity. p. 165

Summary conviction offences: Less serious criminal offences that are punishable by a maximum of two years in prison and/or a $2,000 fine. p. 217

Survey: A method for gathering opinions using a questionnaire. p. 33

Sustainability: Use of natural resources at a rate on par with natural replenishment. p. 286

Sustainable development: Development that meets the needs of the present without compromising the ability of future generations to meet their own needs. p. 297

Symbol: An object, image, or event used to represent a particular concept. p. 104

Systematic observation: A naturalistic but nonparticipatory method for collecting data on a social group or process. p. 38

T

Taboos: Mores that are considered wrong in and of themselves. p. 100

Tariffs: Fees imposed by a government on imported goods. p. 306

Techniques of neutralization: Rationalizations that allow us to justify our behaviour to others and to ourselves. p. 227

Techniques: The skills needed to engage in either deviant or conforming behaviour. p. 227

Theory: A set of propositions intended to explain a fact or a phenomenon. p. 10

Total fertility rate: The number of live births a female can be expected to have in her lifetime. p. 282

Transgendered: Individuals who identify themselves with another sex, and seek to live their lives on that basis. p. 149

Treadmill of production model: A theoretical model that explains environmental issues as resulting from an incessant need to increase production and profit. p. 295

Triangulation: The use of multiple data-gathering techniques within the same study. p. 32

U

Urban legends: Abstract unsubstantiated stories containing an underlying message or moral that persist over time. p. 267

Urban sprawl: A process by which rapid urban growth necessitates the conversion of natural land for human-made uses. p. 285

V

Validity: A measure is a good indicator of the intended concept. p. 27

Values: Collectively shared criteria by which we determine whether something is right or wrong. p. 11

Variable: A categorical concept for properties of people or things that can differ and change. p. 24

Victimless crimes: Criminal offences that involve consensual relations in the exchange of illegal goods or services. p. 218

Violent crimes: Criminal offences that involve physical harm to another person. p. 217

Visible minorities: Persons, other than Aboriginal persons, who are non-Caucasian in race or non-White in colour. p. 166

W

Washington Consensus: The structural adjustment programs supported by the IMF, the World Bank, and the United States Treasury Department. p. 316

White-collar crime: Criminal offences involving the misappropriation of financial resources. p. 220

Widespread panic: A generalized belief regarding impending danger that can lead a large number of people to flee an area or engage in other protective measures. p. 268

Index

Note: Entries and page numbers in bold refer to key terms and the pages in the text on which they are defined. Page numbers followed by an *f* refer to figures; page numbers followed by an *i* refer to illustrations or photographs; page numbers followed by a *t* refer to tables.